GW00649865

# THE
# ECONOMY OF THE COVENANTS

### BETWEEN

## GOD AND MAN,

#### COMPREHENDING

## *A COMPLETE BODY OF DIVINITY.*

#### IN TWO VOLUMES.

### BY HERMAN WITSIUS, D. D.

PROFESSOR OF DIVINITY IN THE UNIVERSITIES OF FRANEKER,
UTRECHT, AND LEYDEN;

AND ALSO

REGENT OF THE DIVINITY COLLEGE OF THE STATES OF HOLLAND
AND WEST-FRIESLAND.

FAITHFULLY TRANSLATED FROM THE LATIN, AND
CAREFULLY REVISED,

### BY WILLIAM CROOKSHANK, D. D.

TO WHICH IS PREFIXED,

## *THE LIFE OF THE AUTHOR.*

### VOL. II.

### EDINBURGH:

*PRINTED BY JOHN TURNBULL;*

AND SOLD BY MANY OF THE PRINCIPAL BOOKSELLERS
IN GREAT BRITAIN.

1803.

# CONTENTS

## OF

## VOLUME SECOND.

—o꞉O꞉o—

### BOOK THIRD.

### BOOK FOURTH.

CHAP.

# CONTENTS.

# THE
# ECONOMY
### OF THE
## *DIVINE COVENANTS.*

### BOOK III. CHAP. II.

#### *Of Sanctification.*

I. THE apostle Peter, 1 Pet. ii. 9. has, in very high terms, declared, that the chosen, the regenerate, and the accepted sons of God, are a HOLY NATION. And this holiness being really the most excellent ornament of the house of God, Psal. xciii. 5. is a subject which ought not to be passed over in silence, especially as it is none of the least of the promises in the covenant of grace, that God will be the sanctifier of his people Israel.

II. In order profitably to explain the nature of sanctification, we must consider, not so much the etymology and import of the Latin word, as of the Hebrew קדשׁ and Greek ἁγιότης, ἁγιωσύνη, ἁγιασμός, and ἁγιωσύνη, with words of the like original, as most frequently made use of by the sacred penmen. It will be proper therefore to enquire more distinctly first, what is meant by holiness, and then, what by sanctification.

III. The word *holy* in scripture is asserted *first* of whatever is separated from a promiscuous and civil, but especially from a profane use : In this sense even the elect are called *holy*, as being separated from the profane world, Lev. xx. 26. "And ye shall be holy unto me, because I have severed you from other people, that ye should be mine." 2 Cor. vi. 17. "Wherefore come out from among them, and be ye separate, saith the Lord, and touch not the unclean thing, and I will receive you." It is no less true of the mystical, than of the literal Israel, that they are a peculiar people, *whose laws are divers from all people*, Eph. ii. 8.

IV. Balaam has beautifully prophefied of them, Num. xxiii. 9. "Lo! the people fhall dwell alone, and fhall not be reckoned among the nations." Ifrael is called *the people*: 1ft, On account of their prodigious numbers, ver. 10. "Who can count the duft of Jacob, and the number of the fourth part of Ifrael;" 2. On account of thofe facred ties, by which this vaft congregation was united together. They were not a promifcuous affembly but a multitude, under a proper polity, or form of government, united together by covenant, governed by falutary laws, with rights and an inheritance, and having God himfelf for their head. Thus the apoftle, 1 Pet. ii. 10. *οἱ ποτε ὁ λαος, νῦν δὲ λαὸς Θεῦ, which in time paft were not a people, but are now the people of God.* This is the meaning of עם. λαος, the *people*, when ufed in its emphatical fenfe, and diftinguifhed from גוים, *Gentiles*. And עם לא, *not a people*, Deut. xxxii. 21. is a multitude that has no fuch privileges. Balaam teftifies of the former that they dwell *alone*, or are *feparate*, *not reckoned among the nations*: they are fevered and diftinguifhed from the reft of the world, by peculiar laws, cuftoms, and inftitutions. Tacitus in his hiftory, book 5. fays, "Mofes, the better to attach the people afterwards to himfelf, appointed them new rites, contrary to thofe of the reft of the world. There all things are accounted profane, which we look upon as facred; and thofe things are allowed by them which we hold to be inceftuous."

V. This feparation of the Jewifh people, in as far as it was the effect of ceremonial inftitutions, conftituted a ceremonial holinefs; but if we confider it as the effect of the excellency of thofe laws, which prefcribed moral duties, in that refpect, they much furpaffed other nations, yet that conftituted a holinefs common to the godly in all ages. Hence the church of the New Teftament is called, "the flock of thine heritage, which dwell folitarily." Micah vii. 14. And Chrift fays of his people; "they are in the world, but not of the world; for he has chofen them out of the world," John xv. 19. "Delivering them from this prefent evil world, according to the will of God, and our Father," Gal. i. 4. To this purpofe is the admonition of Paul, Rom. xii. 2. *Μη συσχηματίζεσθε τω αιωνι τουτω*, "Be not conformed to this world."

VI. And this is that fingularity of piety fo recommended by fome, which does not confift in external niceties of an over-ftrained will-worfhip, and an aufterity of difcipline, as was generally the practice of the Pharifees among the Jews, and of the Afcetics formerly among the ancient Chriftians; concerning whom Cafaubon may be feen in his Efere, ad Baron. Exerc. 1. No. 9. A manner of life fignificantly called by Epiphanius,

Epiphanius, ἀκρωτηριωτατα δικαιωσυνη, the utmost pitch of self-righteousness: but in ſhunning the vices of the age, pride, drunkenneſs, luſt, and vanities of every kind. 1 Pet. iv. 3, " For the time paſt of our life may ſuffice us, to have wrought the will of the Gentiles, when we walked in laſciviouſneſs, luſts, exceſs of wine, revellings, banquetings, and abominable idolatries." Eph. v. 7, " Be not ye therefore partakers with them;" and v. 11. " and have no fellowſhip with the unfruitful works of darkneſs." Tertullian, in his *Apologetica*, adviſes us, that *in what we ſay, ſee and hear, we correſpond in nothing with the madneſs of the circus, the lewdneſs of the theatre, the ſhocking cruelty of the amphitheatre, and the vanity of the Xyſtus: we are not to attend in ſuch ſhows and repreſentations as theſe.* 2. That in opinions and ſentiments we keep at a diſtance from thoſe of the vulgar: that is what Paul hints in what follows: " but be ye transformed by the renewing of your mind, that ye may prove what is the will of God." By the *vulgar* I mean, not only the loweſt claſs of people, of whom Tacitus ſays, *they have neither judgment nor truth*; but even ſuch as ſeem to themſelves and others extremely wiſe in this world; from whom God generally conceals thoſe myſteries of his, which he reveals to babes, Mat. xi. 25. 3. In will and affections, 1 Pet. i. 14. " Not faſhioning yourſelves according to the former luſts in your ignorance." 4. In the exerciſe of ſuch a generous and noble virtue, or holineſs, as is infinitely beyond the reach of other people, Phil. ii. 15. " That ye may be blameleſs and harmleſs, the ſons of God, without rebuke, in the midſt of a crooked and perverſe nation, among whom ye ſhine as lights in the world."

VII. *Secondly*, the word *holy*, denotes whatever is dedicated to, or ſet apart for God and his ſervice. Thus the altar, and what belonged to it, are called *moſt holy*, Exod. xxx. 29: alſo, Aaron with his ſons, 1 Chron. xxiii. 13. So in like manner the truly godly are " a peculiar treaſure to God above all people," Exod. xix. 5. In the Hebrew it runs : סגלה לי והייתם. To Segullah the laſt of theſe, the Latin word *ſigillum* has an affinity : ſo that סגלה SEGULLAH denotes a thing, which a perſon declares to be his own property, by impreſſing it with his ſeal ; nay indeed, it denotes ſuch a thing, on account of which, perſons and kings themſelves are accounted rich, and by which they diſplay their grandeur, Ecclef. ii. 8. " I gathered me alſo ſilver and gold וסגלת מלכים, and the SEGULLAH peculiar treaſure of Kings." Thus " God hath choſen Iſrael לסגלתו for his Segullah, or peculiar treaſure," Pſ. cxxxv. 4. Concerning this word; fee *Waferus de nummis*, lib. 1. c. 1. The Septuagint exprefs it by κιρικοιαςμον ιουτω, Deut. vii. 6. סגלה עם, " a fpecial people;" which Paul, in imitation of the LXX. calls Λαοςπεριουσιος, " a peculiar people;" Tit. ii. 14. And Jerome affirms, he could not learn the meaning of that Greek word from any one, that was converfant in profane literature; but gathered it from the above place in Deuteronomy, and the like. Yet I think Grotius has not improperly obferved, that περιουσιος is derived from περιειναι, which fignifies, to *excel;* and hence περιουσιος denotes the fame as εξδιφιλος, *excellent* : and περιουσια *fuper-abundance* : in which fenfe *Clemens Alexandrius* ufes it in *Admoss. ad Gentes* p. 5. μιςτοι ημιν τας μαθησιας, ικπεριουσιας, βασιλιαν ουρανων ιπαγγελλεται : *promifes to us, fuperabundantly, or over and above, the kingdom of heaven, as the reward of our doctrine.* And again, p. 69. Φερι υμιν, εκ περιουσιας, ιην περι τε λογε παραβησομαι πειθω; *I fhall abundatly bring a convincing proof concerning the word.* In the fame manner, as Demofthenes fays, ετος, εκ περιουσιας, μοι κατηγορει, *he fuperabundantly accufes me:* Polybius, book 4. c. 38, oppofes περιουσια to the αι αναγκαιαι τε βιε χρειαι, the necefaries of life. The godly therefore are God's excellent poffeffion, which he claims and preferves, and in which he boafts, as his *crown of glory and royal diadem,* Ifa. lxii. 3. Which he efteems as his riches, and fuffers not to become the property of another : and in this fenfe alfo may holinefs be afcribed to them : ιθνος αγιον, λαος ις περιποιησιν, *a holy nation, a peculiar people,* are joined together, 1 Pet. ii. 9.

VIII. God alfo truly feals his fervants, as his property, which he would keep from being loft, and in this fenfe, he likewife accounts fuch facred or inviolable. Rev. vii. 2, 3. John faw an angel *afcending from the eaft,* diftinct from the four miniftring angels, and giving orders unto them : now Chrift himfelf is ανατολη εξ ινψος, *the day fpring from on high,* Luke i. 78. and the Gofpel was publifhed chiefly from Jerufalem to the weft, namely to *the ifles of the fea,* or to Europe. This angel *had the feal of the living God,* viz. the Spirit of God, who is alfo *the fpirit of the Son,* Gal. iv. 6. and by whom the elect are feal-ed, Eph. i. 13. becaufe he imprints upon them the character of holinefs declared in the Gofpel, whereby they are known to be the property of God. This angel gave his orders to the others not to hurt any one, *till,* fays he, *we have fealed the fervants of our God in their foreheads;* from which words we are not to imagine, that God has any fellow labourers in this fealing-work, but Chrift fays this concerning himfelf and his Spirit; who may well call God the Father, their God, as both are fent from him, Ifa. xlviii. 16. *The Lord God hath fent me and his fpirit;*

from

as thus the Hebrew may very properly be rendered. Moreover, this seal was *in the foreheads* of God's servants; because, as the forehead is the most conspicuous part of man, so the truth of the Gospel and the efficacy of true piety, which is impressed upon their hearts by the Holy Spirit, discover themselves in the public profession, and open practice of holiness, which strike the eyes and ears of all. Nor is it improbable, there is here an allusion to a received custom in the East, by which the names of masters were stamped on the foreheads of their servants, as Grotius has observed from Hesychius and Aristophanes. The godly then are God's peculiar property; for they bear his name on their foreheads, Rev. xiv. 1. They also profess themselves to be set apart for his service.

IX. And as God sets his seal upon them, so in like manner they *subscribe with their hand* to be only the Lords, Isa. xliv. 5. The Roman soldiers of old according to *Vegetius de re Milit.* Lib. 2. c. 5. being marked with indelible characters in the skin, were wont to be sworn when they were enlisted: and hence in the law of Mauritius, *Signati in manu,* they who are marked in the hand is a circumlocution for soldiers: for, στιγμαδα τι των στρατευομενων ιν ταις χιρσιν, *the marks of soldiers are in their hands,* says Ælian. This is what Chrysostom on Rom. iv. 11. calls σφραγιδα τυ στρατιωτυ, *the seal of the soldier:* see Grotius on Revelations xiii. 16. In much the same manner, believers being sealed by God with the efficacy of the * flaming spirit, and a truly indelible and never fading character, do, at the same time, bind themselves by an oath, to be faithful to God, as soldiers to their general. For, while they profess themselves to be God's, they also give themselves up to his service alone, Acts xxvii. 23. *Whose I am, and whom I serve.* In a word, the chosen and called are all saints, because separated from the rest of the world, they are declared to be God's on several accounts. But we have not yet mentioned the principal thing.

X. Thirdly, Holiness denotes that purity of a man, in his nature, inclinations and actions, which consists in an imitation and expression of the divine purity or holiness. God is the great pattern of his rational creatures. His will is expressed in the law, which was the pattern shewn to Moses in the mount, according to which the sanctuary of our soul ought to be framed. But his divine virtues or perfections are a pattern, which we are

---

* I suppose the author here alludes, by this designation, to the descent of the Holy Ghost on the Apostles, when there appeared unto them cloven tongues like as of fire, and sat upon each of them, Acts ii. 3. and he is called the spirit of burning. Isa. iv. 4. and John the Baptist declared, that Christ should baptise with the Holy Ghost and with fire. Mat. iii. 11.

are to contemplate with so much diligence, attention and devotion, as to be ourselves transformed according to that, 1 Pet. i. 15, 16. " But as he which hath called you is holy, so be ye holy in all manner of conversation: because it is written, Be ye holy, for I am holy." Virtue or holiness may be considered in different respects. As it agrees with the prescription of the law, it is called *righteousness*; but as it is a conformity to God, and an expression of his purity, it is termed *holiness*. And it is chiefly in this sense, that we shall now speak concerning holiness.

XI. Having thus previously explained these things, it will not be hard to infer, what we mean by SANCTIFICATION; namely that *real work of God, by which they, who are chosen, regenerated and justified, are continually more and more transformed from the turpitude of sin, to the purity of the divine image.*

XII. We distinguish this work of God from the first regeneration, and first effectual calling to Christ. For, the immediate term, or effect of regeneration, is a principle of spiritual life, which, in a moment, is put into the soul, by the immediate energy of the Holy Spirit. The term, or effect of effectual calling is the mystical union, and communion with Christ. But the term or effect of SANCTIFICATION are the habits of spiritual virtues or graces, and their lively exercise: and thus sanctification follows upon regeneration and effectual calling, at least in the order of nature, and supposes those actions of God as going before it.

XIII. There is still a further difference between sanctification and justification; for justification is a judicial act, terminating in a relative change of state; namely, a freedom from punishment and a right to life: sanctification a real work, which is performed by a supernatural influence, and which terminates in a change of state as to the quality both of habits and actions.

XIV. Yet we are to take notice, that the term sanctification is not always taken by divines in this strict sense; sometimes they comprehend under it regeneration and the first infusion of a new life, and take sanctification, renovation of the spirit, regeneration, the new creature, the first resurrection, for synonymous terms; as the Leyden professors, Synops. Disput. 33. §. 2. Sometimes also they include justification under the same term. " It is well known," says the abridger of Chamierus, p. 860, " that the terms justification and sanctification are put one for the other." Gomarus in like manner, on 1 Pet. 1. 2. " Sanctification, taken in a general sense, comprises regeneration and justification." Nay sometimes the word sanctification is taken so largely, as to include the whole

whole of man's salvation. Polanus in Syntagm. lib. 6. c. 37. sometimes both appellations, viz. " regeneration and sanctification, are taken in a larger sense, for the whole of our salvation, or beatification, if I may so speak, as Heb. x. 10. But yet the accuracy of those is more commendable, who distinguish those terms in the manner I have explained: especially as the Scripture often distinctly mentions those benefits, and describes sanctification, as a continued work of God, leading the elect gradually on to perfection, and as I do not remember to have observed it speak so of regeneration.

IV. Nor are we to omit, that sanctification is sometimes laid forth as a blessing from God to man, 1 Thess. v. 23. " And the very God of peace sanctify you wholly ;" sometimes as man's duty towards God, 1 Thess. iv. 3. " For this is the will of God, even your sanctification." The former God powerfully works in us, according to the purpose of his gracious decree; the latter he justly requires of us, by the will of his holy command.    When sanctification denotes the first implantation of spiritual habits, it is a mere blessing from God, in procuring what we do not co-operate with him, but receive it from him.    As it signifies the activity, or lively exercise of infused habits, and their corroboration and progress, so far we are active; but then it is as we are acted upon under God, and dependently on him : for these things can never be separated.

XVI. *The term from which*, in sanctification, is the pollution of sin.    Adam in departing from the prescribed rule, forfeited the ornament of the image of God, in which he was formed, for himself and and all his posterity.    And whilst he wickedly affected a forbidden equality with God, came most to resemble the devil, and, like that evil spirit, deformed himself by his own crime; than which we can imagine nothing more hideous or base.    The soul of the sinner is a horrid monster, misshapen, huge and devoid of light; mere darkness, mere confusion, every thing disjointed and out of order there; nothing properly placed; the things we should despise are esteemed, and what we should value most are neglected.    Was any to take a clear view of his inward disposition in a faithful mirror, he would certainly, with the utmost horror fly from himself as from a most terrible spectacle.    And indeed, if holiness is the most beautiful ornament of the divine perfections, that thing must needs be the most deformed, which is not only the most unlike, but diametrically opposite to that ornamental beauty. This is that ' περισσεία και υπερβολη κακιας mentioned Jam. i. 21. *Filthiness and superfluity of naughtiness*, to this it is owing, that

man

man is become abominable in the fight of God, who cannot
but turn away the radiant eyes of his unfpotted holinefs, Hab.
i. 13.

XVII. Moreover, Adam propogated this vile refemblance of
the devil to his pofterity, not excepting thofe whom grace has
fanctified.  For he alfo *begat Seth in his own likenefs, after his
image*, Gen. v. 3.  I do not chiefly apply this to the likenefs of
the human nature, much lefs to the likenefs of that holinefs
which God gracioufly reftored to Adam, as Chryfoftom, Lyranus and Clarius contend for.  For, 1ft. Holinefs and righteoufnefs are not the image of any man, but of God.  2dly, Adam
is never propofed in Scripture as the pattern or author of holinefs, but as the perfon by whom fin entered into the world,
Rom. v. 12.  3dly, The image of holinefs, reftored in the parent by grace, is never propagated to the fon by natural generation.  Things natural are propagated, but things fupernatural are *alone of God that fheweth mercy*, Rom. ix. 16.  But by
this likenefs of Adam, I underftand the vicious corruption of
his nature.  1ft. Becaufe the image of Adam, after Seth was
begotten, is fet in oppofition to the image of God, after which
Adam was created.  2dly, Becaufe the Apoftle, in like manner, oppofes 1 Cor. xv. 49. the image of the *earthy* Adam, as
confifting of fin and pollution, to the image of the *heavenly* A-
dam, which confifts in holinefs and glory.  3dly, Becaufe the
whole analogy of Scripture evinces, that *a clean thing cannot be
brought out of an unclean*, and that *what is born of the flefh is flefh*,
Job xiv. 4.—John iii. 6.

XVIII. This turpitude of fin is by Paul called the *old man*,
Eph. iv. 22.—Col. iii. 9.  *Man*, becaufe it overfpreads the
whole man, and defiles both foul and body; in the foul it has
poffeffion of the underftanding, will and affections.

XIX. It has involved the underftanding in horrid darknefs,
whereby it is grofsly ignorant of divine things, Eph. iv. 18.  So
that the ἄνθρωπος ψυχικος the natural or animal man, or he that
has no other fpirit but his foul, and deftitute of the Spirit of
God, Jud. v. 29. *receiveth not the things of God, neither can, he
know them*, 1 Cor. ii. 14.  And as he difcerns no wifdom in
divine things worthy of God, fo, with intolerable prefumption,
he reprefents them under thofe difagreeable notions, which his
own foolifh, and felf-conceited wifdom hath devifed; and
while he attempts to correct the wifdom of God which he cannot underftand, he transfigures it as much as he can to down-
right folly, and this is that which is faid, Rom. i. 22, 23.
*Profeffing themfelves to be wife, they became fools: and changed the
glory of the incorruptible God, &c.*

XX. But

XX. But the finner is not only under blindnefs, but is in love with his blindnefs. He glories that he really fees, even when he is moft blind, John ix. 40, 41. And when, to the utmoft of his power, he refifts the true light, though difcovering itfelf in a moft pleafing manner, by the works of divine providence, by the word of God, and by fome fparkling rays of the Spirit; *he loves darknefs rather than light; hateth the light, neither cometh to the light*, John iii. 19, 20. Of fuch Job witneffeth, *that they are of thofe that rebel againft the light*, Job xxiv. 13. They have an averfion to all light, both that which is natural, which hinders them from perpetrating their crimes in the fight of the world, and that which is moral, which convinces them of the duty they ought certainly to perform, but which they wickedly neglect. They endeavour to ftifle it by difputing both againft the word of God and their own confcience. Hence thofe impious expreffions of fome, who wifh that this or the other truth that oppofes their lufts, was not to be found in the word of God.

XXI. And yet thofe very perfons that are fo foolifh in that which is good, are moft fubtle and crafty in that which is evil, Jer. iv. 22. They commit evil by that art which is exactly conformable to the pattern of the infernal fpirits. Emphatical is that of Micah on this head, Chap. vii. 3. על רצ כפיס להיטיב, * *both hands are upon evil, that they may do it well*. They are not flothful in evil, but apply both hands, exert all their ftrength. And they take care to do it well, according to the rules of that fatanical art, carefully obferving all the contrivances of wickednefs: nay, they have learned to frame and contrive it with fo much art as to impofe it on the incautious under the appearance of good.

XXII. Nor is the will, lefs corrupt; for, 1ft, It is averfe to all that is truly good, Job xxi. 14. " Therefore they fay unto God, depart from us, for we defire not the knowledge of thy ways. And when the great things of the law are written to them, they are counted as a ftrange thing;" as of no very great moment, and what they have no concern with, Hof. viii. 12. And how can it be otherwife? For fince by reafon of their blindnefs, they do not difcern the excellency of true virtue, but on the contrary find many things in the practice of it which are oppofite to their unruly lufts, their mind is averfe to it: " they hate the good," Micah. iii. 2.

XXIII. Secondly, It is driven on to evil with great impetuofity: " They love the evil," Micah iii. 2. to a degree indeed that not fome, but *every imagination of the heart of man;* not at

B                                                fome,

---

* Our verfion renders that text, *that they may do evil with both hands earneftly.*

fome, but *at all times;* not in fome, but in every meafure, " i
only evil," Gen. vi. 5. Now this is to be underftood, no
only of the giants in the firft ages, as appears by comparin;
this place with chap. viii. 21. where almoft the fame word
are ufed concerning men in future periods of time. *I will no
again,* fays God, *curfe the ground any more, becaufe,* or *though th.
imagination of man's heart is evil from his youth.* Whereby it i;
intimated, *that evil imagination* is the common blemifh of all
mankind. To this alfo may be referred, what Paul writes,
Rom. viii. 7. *το Φρονημα της σαρκος, the carnal mind the wifdom of
the flefh,* that which it willingly imagines, lufts after as wifdom,
or that action, which the carnal mind contrives, *is enmity a-
gainft God; for it is not fubject to the law of God, neither indeed
can be.*

XXIV. Nay, 3dly, The defire of evil is fo great, that it is ir-
ritated by that very law of God which forbids it, and is more
impetuoufly hurried on to things forbidden only becaufe they
are prohibited. Without the driving or impelling force of the
law fin lies dormant and lifelefs; but when the commandment
comes it revives and is put in motion, and taking occafion by
the commandment, works all manner of concupifcence to a
pitch, that every check being hurtful, " by the commandment
fin might become exceeding finful," Rom. vii. 8, 9, 11, 13.
Chryfoftom beautifully fays, *όταν τινος επιθυμωμεν, οταν κωλυωμεθα,
αιρετα' μαλλον της επιθυμιας η φλοξ. When we luft after any thing
and are afterwards reftrained, this only blows up the flame of luft
to a higher degree.*

XXV. Surprifing and lamentable is the depravity in the affections. For, firft, when the underftanding does not lead
them on to things holy, fpiritual, heavenly and eternal, they
are bafely and madly bent upon things corporal, carnal, fading
and finful, and mifpend all their vigour on things beneath and
unworthy a man. 2dly, In all their emotions they are fu-
rioufly toffed, and not waiting for the direction of the underftanding, but throwing off the reins of reafon, and having no
reftraint, they rufh headlong with a blind and wicked violence,
and bafely rack and wound the foul, never allowing them any
reft, nor that calmnefs, which would otherwife be her peculiar
happinefs, but continually crying, " like the daughters of the
horfe-leach, give give," Prov. xxx. 15. Hence God elegantly compares " the wicked to the troubled fea which cannot reft, whofe waters caft up mire and dirt," Ifa. lvii. 20.
3dly, They are obftinately bold and luftful, both againft the
will of God's decree and of his command, ever lufting after

what

that is contrary to it, with that eagerness that they can scarcely bear that God and nature should not be subservient to their desire, and all rules of religion not be framed and modelled to their liking. These are those *πάθη ἀτιμίας, vile affections*, mentioned Rom. i. 26. Which though they do not rage with equal fury in all, yet they reside in the soul as in a stable; and being restrained to no purpose, burst out at times with the greater fierceness.

XXVI. Nor indeed is the body itself free from the tyrannical dominion of sin: the members are agitated by such an inordinate flow of blood and spirits, that they easily carry away the mind, while it is forgetful of her own dignity. And, indeed, that pleasure which the members have in sin, or which they seek for by sinning, is the cause of most sins, even spiritual sins not excepted, and of their reasoning against the law of God. This perverseness and corruption is by the apostle called *the law in the members*, that power and efficacy of sin dwelling in the body, which had frequently forced it to a criminal compliance, and had *warred against the law of his mind;* that is, against the law of God inscribed on the mind by nature and grace, and in which the mind delights, *and had brought him into captivity*, and having once taken hold of him, does not let him go, Rom. vii. 23. Certainly the members seduce and prove offensive, which Job, being afraid of, *made a covenant with his eyes, that they should not look upon a maid*, Job xxxi. 1. And David prayed, *turn away mine eyes from beholding vanity*, Ps. cxix. 37. And wisdom advises, to *put a knife to thy throat if thou be a man given to appetite*, Prov. xxiii. 2. All these plainly declare the danger, arising to religion from the members.

XXVII. As therefore this corruption wholly overspreads all the parts and faculties of man, it is therefore called *man*. But it goes by the name of the *old* man: 1st, Because it sprung up in Paradise itself at the beginning, by the infection of the tempting serpent, and owes its original to that old dragon mentioned, Rev. xii. 9. 2dly, Because it is cotemporary with every man in particular, Pf. li. 7. and if not always in order of time, yet of nature, precedes man's gracious regeneration. 3dly, Because we ought to abolish, reject and abhor it, as a worthless and antiquated thing, which is wore out and disfigured by long use; just as *old things pass away, that all things may become new*, 2 Cor. v. 17.

XXVIII. This corruption is sometimes held forth under the emblem of an unseemly, filthy, and loathsome garment; and then it is said *to be put off* and laid aside by sanctification, Col.

iii. 9 ; and Eph. iv. 22. Sometimes under the emblem of a monſtruous body, which deſtroys by a horrid ſlaughter every thing in man; and then it is ſaid to be *mortified*, Col. iii. 5. and *crucified*, Gal. v: 24. Now this *putting off* and *mortification* of the old man is nothing elſe but the deſtruction of the dominion of ſin, and the purging of corruptions : ſo that; 1ſt, We be vexed at the heart and grieved becauſe of them ; for nothing dies without pain and anguiſh. 2dly, That we abhor them as we do a rotten carcaſe. 3dly, That we have them in execration as things which have put God and man to * torment. 4thly, That we ſuppreſs all their motions, as far as poſſible, both in the ſoul and the body, and never ſuffer them to revive again, Rom. vi. 6. *Knowing this, that our old man is crucified with him, that the body of ſin might be deſtroyed ;* not only ſome actions and parts of it, but that entire compound, made up of depraved habits, thoughts, luſts, words, and actions ; as a body is made up of its members, *that henceforth we ſhould not ſerve ſin.*

XXIX. By another phraſe, the godly are ſaid *to be dead to ſin*, Rom. vi. 2. The meaning of which is, that as a dead body is not a fit habitation for the ſoul, ſeeing it has not thoſe organs and that diſpoſition of parts, by which the ſoul operates, ſo believers with reſpect to ſin and its motions, are dead bodies, uſeleſs and motionleſs organs, in which it can no longer lodge, live, and exert its efficacy.

XXX. Not much different is that expreſſion of Paul. Gal. vi. 14. in which he ſays, the world was crucified to him, and he *to the world* ; intimating, that he was no more delighted with the vanities of the world, than a good man would be with the rotten carcaſe of a malefactor, who was juſtly condemned to a ſhameful death ; and on the other hand, that the world was unable to act upon, or affect him with any greater efficacy, than objects of ſenſe affect a dead perſon.

XXXI. This putting off, and this mortification of the old man is always accompanied with the putting on, or *vivification of the new man,* by which are denoted all thoſe qualities wherein the excellency of the divine image is placed. *Theſe* come under the appellation *man*, for the ſame reaſon, we juſt gave of the depraved qualities : becauſe
they

---

* The author's expreſſion here is very ſtrong ; *ut cruciarii Deo et hominibus erant ;* and I think, he alludes to the crucifixion of Chriſt, who is God as well as man, and who was put to the torture of the croſs for the ſins of his people : and they alſo are generally brought to anguiſh and pain when their old man is *crucified* with him.

they overspread the whole man, so that there is nothing in
the sanctified person, no part, no faculty, that remains un-
touched, or neglected, by the sanctifying Spirit, and unadorn-
ed with new habits.  And as the citadel and throne of virtue
stands in the mind and inward. parts, therefore Paul.speaks of
the *inward man*, Rom. vii. 22. and Peter, 1 Pet. iii. 4. of the
*hidden man of the heart.*

XXXII. A new and gracious light shines upon the understanding.  The eyes of the mind are enlightened, Eph. i. 18.
by which he sees divine truths, not under false and confused
ideas, but in their native form and beauty, *as the truth is in*
*Jesus,* Eph. iv. 21. so that the sanctified person really beholds
in those truths, the manifold wisdom of God, the depths of his
perfections, and the unsearchable riches of Christ ; nor does
he see them only, but in a manner not to be expressed, feels
them penetrating themselves into his inmost heart, embraces
them with a glowing affection of piety, exults in them, and
desires, that what is truth in Christ may be also truth in him,
and that he may be modelled to the likeness of those truths,
and cast, as it were, into the very shape of them.  In fine,
that knowledge of God, which flutters not in the brain only,
but *brings forth the fruit* of every good work, *from the day that*
*it hath truly heard and known the grace of God,* is a part of the
new man, Col. i. 6, 9, 10. Whereas that other knowledge,
which puffs up and boasts itself, and charges the wisdom of
God with folly is vain ; and the more boldly it counterfeits
the new man, the more it appears to be *earthly, sensual and*
*devilish,* Jam. iii. 15.

XXXIII. Among other things, the understanding of a
sanctified person beholds so much purity in God, who is the
pattern of the rational creature, so much equity in the law of
God, which is the rule of every virtue, so much holiness in
Christ Jesus, who exhibited himself to us as a living law so
much beauty in virtue, or holiness itself, which is, as it were,
the native image of the Deity, that he reckons nothing more
excellent than exactly to resemble that pattern, that rule and
that image.  He sees nothing in any of these, that he would
correct, nothing he would have otherwise appointed, neither
does he imagine that any thing can be better framed ; and
thus *he consenteth to the law, that it is good,* Rom. vii. 16.  This
is, what Paul calls, *a being filled with the knowledge of his will,*
*in all wisdom and spiritual understanding,* Col. i 9.

XXXIV. And as the eyes are with difficulty diverted from
a pleasing object, so to him whose mind is enlightened by the
Holy

Holy Spirit, nothing can be more defirable, nothing more pleafant, nothing more charming, than to dwell on the contemplation of God, and the meditation of divine things.   He loves to join the night to the day, Pf. i. 2. and then he entertains himfelf, then he is delighted, then he exults, and feems by his earneftnefs, to enjoy heaven itfelf; for when he is deeply engaged in this facred meditation, and at the fame time forgetting himfelf, is plunged, as it were, in the immenfe gulf of the divine perfections and myfteries.

XXXV. Nor is the enlightened mind fatisfied to tafte things alone by itfelf, nor envioufly to conceal its treafure, but it difcovers thofe facred truths to the will, to which it frequently prefents them, as things moft precious which are far more valuable than gold and filver, or even than pearls, which are ftill more highly efteemed, that the will alfo may be united to them by the indiffoluble band of love, and with the utmoft readinefs, be in holy fubjection to them.   This is the activity of the fanctified underftanding.

XXXVI. Now the will cannot poffibly reject fo great a good, which is conftantly pointed out to it by the underftanding as fuch.   It is therefore ravifhed with the love of it, Pf. cxix. 97. *O! how love I thy law!* Rom. vi. 22. *It delights in the law of God.*   Pf. xl. 8. *I delight to do thy will, O my God!* For, what is truth in Chrift becomes alfo truth in its order and degree in thofe who are Chrift's.   The will is never eafy, never fatisfied, when it finds it has difpleafed God and departed from his will.

XXXVII. Hence arifeth a fteady and fixed purpofe of heart, to be conformable in all things to God, Pf. cxix. 106.   To whom the will wholly refigns itfelf up, to be fwallowed, as it were, in his will? eftablifhing this into an inviolable and facred law for itfelf, to have the fame inclinations, the fame averfions with God.   And God himfelf declares, that the true reverence or fear of the Deity lies in this, Prov. viii. 13. " The fear of the Lord is to hate evil; pride and arrogancy and the evil way, and the froward mouth do I hate."   He that truly fears God will hate what he knows to be hateful to God; and on the contrary love what God loves, Pf. cxxxix. 21, 22.

XXXVIII. And feeing the will commands the inferior faculties, as they are called, and in its meafure, even the underftanding itfelf; hence, with the greateft alacrity, it makes all things to be ready at the will and pleafure of God and of Chrift.   So that the foul of one who is fanctified, is like a well marfhalled army, in which every individual will, in his place

and

and order, directly move upon the first word or sign of command. This is that *willing mind* by which we are acceptable
to God, 2 Cor. viii. 12.

XXXIX. The underſtanding and will being thus ſet in order,
the tumult of the wild affections gradually comes to ſubſide;
which being forced into order, learn to wait the commands of
reaſon before they take a ſingle ſtep; and in proportion to
the object, act either more intenſely, or more remiſsly; moreover they exert themſelves in a right and proper manner with
reſpect to ſpiritual and heavenly things, with which before
they were wont to be ſcarcely, if at all, affected: In ſhort,
they calmly reſign themſelves to be governed by the Holy Spirit,
receiving from him, with full ſubmiſſion, the law of motion
and of reſt. When formerly furious luſt held the reins they
were accuſtomed to run mad after wordly, carnal, and vitious
objects, now they ſuffer themſelves to be led as circumſtances
require, and being ſublimated to a higher pitch, and having obtained a more generous and noble guide, they ſtrongly by their
native vehemence, excite or puſh forward, the mind, otherwiſe
ſlow in its motion, objects that are holy, heavenly and becoming a Chriſtian.

XL. In the mean time, this admonition is continually inculcated upon them, that they muſt not conſult with their affections, whenever they are called to comply with or ſubmit to
the will of God, whether that of his decree or that of his precept. In that caſe, they are enjoined to a perfect ſubmiſſion. He
who is ſanctified, does not preſume ſo much as to wiſh, that
God would regulate either his precepts or purpoſes from any
regard to his deſire, hope or fear. That ſelf-denial, which is
the firſt leſſon in Chriſt's ſchool, commands all the affections
to be ſilent, and unlimited obedience obliges them to be reſigned
to God. It is not lawful for a Chriſtian to will that any
thing that God has done or ſpoken ſhould be otherwiſe than
it is; and whenever that fooliſh ſelf-love which is not yet
quite rooted out begins, thro' its unmortified luſts and vain anxiety to go away from God to other things, then the ſuperior
faculty of the ſoul, under the conduct and direction of the
Spirit, repeats that pious ejaculation, " And thou, my ſoul be
ſilent unto [wait thou only upon] God," Pſa. lxii. 5. This is
to compoſe the ſoul and keep it in quiet;" Pſ. cxxxi. 2. that it
may look upon it as unlawful, either to wiſh or mutter any
thing againſt the will of God.

XLI. Moreover, that holy diſpoſition of ſoul communicates
itſelf to the members of the body, which, being before " in-
ſtruments

struments of unrighteousness unto sin, are now instruments of righteousness unto God," Rom. vi. 13. In a sanctified person, the eyes, the tongue, the ears, the hands, and the feet, are not only restrained from giving the least occasion to entice and disturb the mind, as Paul said of himself, that he " kept under his body, and brought it into subjection," 1 Cor. ix. 27. but all of them are ready, and inclined to obey God, to whom they yield themselves, in order to the practice of *righteousness*, and even as *weapons*, by which the kingdom of sin and Satan may be strongly opposed. For so long as the most eminent virtues lie concealed in the inward recess of the mind, they cannot edify our neighbour and gain him over from sin to holiness; but when they are exercised by the members of the body, when the tongue lays itself out in the praises of God, and the commendation of virtue or holiness; the hands and feet in assisting his neighbour, and the other parts of the body, according to their several capacities, in the practice of religion; it is then he fights manfully for extirpating vice and promoting virtue. Nor can it be doubted but the Apostle's expression imports all this.

XLII. From all this it is now evident, that even the new man 'no less than the old, possesses the old man both soul and body, according to the command of Paul, 1 Cor.vi. 20. " Glorify God in your body, and in your spirit, which are God's;" and his prayer, 1 Thes. v. 23. " And the very God of peace sanctify you wholly, and your whole spirit, and soul, and body, be preserved blameless unto the coming of our Lord Jesus Christ." Interpreters differ with respect to the distinction between *spirit* and *soul*, and the signification of each term. We agree with those who, by *spirit*, understand the *mind*, the ἡγεμονικον, or leading faculty of man, called by Philo de Mundo, ἰξαιρετον ἀνθρωπου γερας, *the select ornament of man*, in which his principal excellence above the other creatures consists; and elsewhere called by the apostle νους, *mind*, Eph. iv. 17. but by *soul*, the inferior faculties, not as if there were two souls, but that in the manner commonly received among philosophers, Paul distinguishes the faculties of one and the same soul. And by BODY, it is plain, is denoted the receptacle of the soul. And the whole man will at last be sanctified, when the spirit shall think nothing, the soul desire nothing, the body execute nothing, but what is agreeable to the will of God.

XLIII. Now, these spiritual qualities of a man, are called the NEW MAN. 1st, Because they succeed upon the departure

of

of the old man, 2 Cor. v. 17. *Old things are paſſed away, be-hold all things are become new.* 2dly, Becauſe they are quite other than, and very different from the former. In which ſenſe Chriſt ſaid of the Apoſtles, Mark xvi. 17. *They ſhall ſpeak with new tongues ;* that is, other tongues, Acts ii. 4. different from their mother-tongue, and from thoſe they had learned before. And certainly theſe good qualities are not only different from the former, but alſo quite contrary to them. *For what fellowſhip hath righteouſneſs with unrighteouſneſs ? And what com-munion hath light with darkneſs?* 2 Cor. vi. 14. 3dly, Becauſe rare, excellent, and unparalleled. For as new things uſually attract and are eſteemed valuable, as being preferable to old things which are worn out by long uſe ; ſo that which is ex-cellent and ſurpaſſing in its kind, is alſo called *new.* In this ſenſe God promiſes a new name to the godly, Iſa. lxii. 2. Rev. ii. 17. and iii. 12. that is, a condition far more excellent than what ever they yet had. And, indeed, nothing excels this new man which Peter declares, 1 Pet. iii. 4. *to be in the ſight of God of great price.*

XLIV. Sometimes ſanctification is called, *the putting on of the new man,* as Eph. iv. 24. Col. iii. 10. Sometimes *vivification,* or the *quickening* of the ſame. Thus theſe laudible qualities may be conſidered either as a precious ornament of the ſoul, 1 Pet. iii. 3, 4. Pſ. xlv. 14, 15. and Pſ. xciii. 5. and Pſ. cx. 3. Prov. i. 9. and then they are ſaid to be put on : or, as a new creature made conformable to the example of Chriſt, which is all activity and life, and then he is ſaid to live in us. Theſe expreſſions denote the productions of thoſe new qualities in us, and their continual increaſe and growth, and their being in-centives to action : all which have here the nature of a term to which they tend.

XLV. We may view the parts of our ſanctification in this order : 1ſt, If we conſider them in their whole compaſs or ex-tent, they are cotemporary. For ſin is expelled, virtue or holineſs is introduced by the ſame work, juſt as he who at the ſame time by his motion and progreſs, leaves the term from which he ſet out, and draws near to the term whither he at firſt intended. 2dly, If we conſider its commencement, the vivification, or quickening of the new man, is firſt in the order of nature. For all the virtue and efficacy againſt ſin proceeds from a principle of a new and ſpiritual life. Death is removed only by life, darkneſs by light, poverty by riches, nakedneſs by clothing, deformity by beauty, hatred of God by love. 3dly, If we conſider each act a part, we find a mani-fold

fold variety in the order. The illumination of the underſtanding, which is a part of the vivification of the new man, does undoubtedly go before our being diſpleaſed with ourſelves, and our ſorrow for ſin, which properly belong to the mortification of the old man. And this ſorrow again precedes that holy alacrity of the ſoul, whereby it rejoices in God : and ſo of the reſt. 4thly, If we view its conſummation, the final deſtruction of the old man, which is effected at the diſſolution of the body of ſin, that is, of the body, by whoſe luſts we are polluted, and in which we ſin, Rom. vi. 6. is prior to the complete ſanctification of the whole man.

XLVI. Hence it appears, that ſanctification does not conſiſt only in the amendment of the actions, according to the Socinians and the favourers of Pelagianiſm, who do not ſincerely acknowledge the corruption of our nature ; but in the conferring of new habits, which ſucceed to the old ones, which gradually give way. Thus Peter, among theſe precious promiſes which we obtain, mentions the *communication of a divine nature,* a large meaſure of thoſe virtues, *which if they be in us, they make us that we ſhall neither be barren nor unfruitful in the knowledge of our Lord Jeſus Chriſt.* 2 Pet. i. 8. And Paul, Gal. v. 22. ſpeaking of *the fruits of the Spirit,* ſays, that they are *love, joy, peace, long-ſuffering,* &c. All which virtues or graces are habitual, inherent, and permanent in the ſoul, 1 Cor. xiii. 13. *And now abideth faith, hope, charity, theſe three.* Nay, ſometimes the Apoſtle uſes the very term *habit,* Heb. v. 14. *Who διὰ τὴν ἕξιν, by reaſon of uſe ( habit ) have their ſenſes exerciſed.* The increaſe indeed of this habit is acquired by repeated acts of a vigorous endeavour ; though its beginning is infuſed by the Holy Spirit, who *fills the elect with the knowledge of the will of God, in all wiſdom and ſpiritual underſtanding,* Col. i. 9.

XLVII. The author and *efficient cauſe* of ſanctification is God. Increated infinite holineſs is the ſource of that which is created and finite, Ezek. xx. 12. *that they might know, that I am the Lord that ſanctify them.* 1 Theſſ. v. 23. *And the very God of peace ſanctify you wholly.* Iſa. lxiii. 11. *Who put [the ſpirit of his holineſs] his holy Spirit within him.* He is the author of ſanctification.

XLVIII. For, by a ſpecial appropriation, according to the œconomy of the divine operations, this work is immediately aſcribed to the Holy Spirit, 2 Theſſ. ii. 13. *through ſanctification of the Spirit.* Tit. iii. 5. *renewing of the Holy Ghoſt :* and ſo in many other places. This is not however done, as if the Holy Spirit alone was immediately concerned in the production of ſanctification,

and

and the Father and Son fanctified only mediately by the Spirit. For that power by which holiness is produced in the elect, is common to the undivided Trinity. Nor do the Father and Son operate less immediately therein than the Holy Spirit : and as the power of each divine person is the same, so also the action of all is one. That saying, δι ὖ τὰ πάντα, *by whom are all things*, equally belongs to the Father and the Son, as it does to the Holy Spirit. Nor does one person act by the other, as by *a mean*, or instrument. But the reason of this appropriation seems to be this : because the fanctification of a sinner, follows upon the grace and merit of Christ ; and seeing the Holy Spirit follows the Son, in the hypostatical order of subsisting and operating, and is therefore also called *the Spirit of the Son*, Gal. iv. 6. To whom then can the application of the grace and merits of the Son be more properly ascribed than to him, who is next to the Son in order ? Sanctification is such a divine operation, as supposes the will of the Father, making a testament concerning the seed which was to be given to the Son ; and the will of the Son claiming by right that holy seed : Who then can better claim that operation than the Holy Spirit, who is of the Father and of the Son, and who *takes of the things of the Son*, all that he gives unto them ? John xvi. 14.

XLIX. However Christ, the Mediator, acts here a special part both as to *impetration* and *application*. Christ impetrated, or purchased by his merit, the fanctification of the elect. For this cause he himself came *in the likeness of sinful flesh*, Rom. viii. 3. *appeared under the load of sin*, Heb. ix. 28. for this end also himself *was made sin*, 2 Cor. v. 21. *that he might fanctify his church*, Eph. v. 26. The image of God being defaced and lost, could not possibly be restored to sinful man, unless he who is the personal image of God the Father, should first assume the image of man, and that of a sinner and a slave, and so expose himself to the unjust hatred of men, and the most righteous vengeance of God, as if he had been the greatest of all criminals : and thus he is made unto us by his merit, *fanctification*, 1 Cor. i. 32.

L. But that which he impetrated. He *applies*, he unites the elect to himself by his Spirit : and then the virtue of his death and resurrection flows from him to them ; *so that being planted together in the likeness of his death, they shall be also in the likeness of his resurrection ; and their old man crucified with him, and they being dead with Christ shall also live with him*, Rom. vi. 5, 8. and, *by the cross of Christ, the world is crucified to them and they to the world*, Gal. vi. 14. This is the effect of meditating on the cross of Christ. And *the power of his resurrection*,

Phil. iii. 10. produces a new life in them. For, he himfelf being raifed from the dead, has received, not only for himfelf a new and a glorious life, but a fountain of a new and holy life for all his people; from which, by a continued influence, the moft refrefhing ftreams flow to all his members; hence, from his own life, by a moft conclufive argument, he inferred the life of his people, John xiv. 19. *Becaufe I live ye fhall live alfo.*

LI. Moreover, that work of God which produces our fanctification, is performed by a real fupernatural and moft powerful efficacy, reaching to the full effect as we have already intimated, when treating on effectual calling and regeneration. *For, we are his* ποιημα, *workmanfhip, created in Chrift Jefus unto good works,* Eph. ii. 10. By the very fame power, which was difplayed and exerted in the work of the old creation, he forms his own people to good works, or which is the fame thing, he fanctifies them. *He gives an heart to perceive, and eyes to fee, and ears to hear,* Deut. xxix. 4. *He puts his fpirit within them, and caufes them to walk in his ftatutes, and to keep his judgments,* Ezek. xxxvi. 27. *He gives them one heart and one way, that they may fear him for ever,* Jer. xxxii. 39. And certainly none is fit to form again the image of God in man, but he who at firft made man after his own image; the one being a work of no lefs power and excellence than the other.

LII. And hence, the gangrene of the Socinian divinity difcovers itfelf, according to which, if a man has got fuch a full difcovery of the will of God as is made in the Gofpel, with a promife of eternal life, he will then have that, whence he may receive ftrength to perform that very will. They fome times mention internal affiftance for form fake, but place it only in this, that the promifes of God are infcribed and fealed on the mind; and they will have this to be the cafe of none, unlefs he has firft made a right ufe of that external aid. They are truly ignorant of any fupernatural influence and real efficiency of God. So much have a fond felf-admiration, and their infatuated arrogant boafting of the powers of nature infatuated them.

LIII. But fome among the Heathen have really fpoken far better concerning the divine affiftance, though unacquainted with the excellency of Chriftian holinefs. *Plutarch de ftoic. contradict.* " If God give not virtue to men, but that which they attribute to their own choice; and give them riches and health without virtue, he certainly gives things to thofe who fhall not ufe them well, but ill." Plutarch adds; " if the Gods can beſtow virtue but do it not, they are not good and gracious ; for if they cannot render men good, neither can they profit them ; ſince without virtue nothing can be good or profitable. To the ſame purpoſe is the twenty-ſecond diſſertation of *Maximus Tyrius,* entitled, *whether any one can be made good by God ;* in which there are very many things worthy of attention, but too long to be tranſcribed. Theſe things he borrowed from his maſter Plato, in whoſe Menon is extant this notable diſſertation ; whether in the whole of his preſent diſcourſe, we have properly enquired into, and made it appear, that virtue is neither obtained by nature, nor by teaching, but by divine appointment. See Clemens Alexandrius, ſtromat lib. 5. p. 588.

LIV. Nature itſelf and man's conſcience teach him theſe two things : 1ſt. Our inability for virtue. 2dly, The all-ſufficiency of God, whereby he is the fountain and the author of all true good. Of the former Epictetus apud Arrianum, lib. 2. c. 11. ſays, *the beginning of philoſophy to thoſe who enter into it by the gate as they ought, is a ſenſe of their own impotence and inability.* Of the latter, *Maximus Tyrius Diſſert.* 22. *We are not to imagine, that any good can befal men but what comes from God : as there is no good to men which derives not its original from God.*

LV. From thoſe generals, the Heathen themſelves have proved theſe more particular propoſitions : 1ſt, That to the acquiſition and practice of virtue, men ſtand in need of divine aſſiſtance and grace. Hierocles, a Pythagorean philoſopher has excellently taught this in theſe words : *We are not ſo much as to preconceive, that virtuous actions are ſo in our power as to be performed without divine aid : we ſtand in need of the aſſiſtance of God, both for eſcaping evil and acquiring good.* 2dly, That from a ſenſe of our own impotence, we are to aſk it of God, Epictet. apud Arrianum, lib. 2. c. 18. *Noble is the ſtruggle and divine the enterpriſe, the ſubject a kingdom, liberty, happineſs, calm of mind unruffled by paſſions. Are all concerned? therefore remember God, call him in for thy aſſiſtant, thy aſſociate.* See alſo Seneca, Epiſt. 10. and 41. and Marc. Antonin. lib. 2. § 40. 3dly, That we are to thank God for it, *Epictet. apud Arrian.* lib. 4. c. 4. *Then I ſinned, now I do not,* THANKS BE TO GOD.

LVI. But they did not imagine, that this divine aſſiſtance conſiſted only in moral ſuaſion, or in preſenting ſuch objects whereby a man may be excited to virtuous actions ; but in divine ſuggeſtions, aids and inſpirations, as the emperor Antonine ſpeaks, lib. 1. §. 17 : who, in the ſame place, declares, that he had a good diſpoſition of mind from the Gods, which he aſcribes

fcribes to their beneficence : lib. 9. §. 40. he mentions their
co-operation ; *for, if they can at all co-operate with men, they al-*
*fo can in this,* namely, in the practice of virtue. But if a-
ny fhould except, that thefe relate to things in our own power,
he anfwers, *who has told thee that the Gods do not affift even in*
*thefe ? Set about afking thefe things of the Gods by prayer, and*
*you will fee the confequence.*

LVII. And they maintained, that the fame divine aid was
fo neceffary to virtue, that even the beft difpofed fouls could not
be without it. Maxim. Tyr. Differt. 22. p. 228. fays, " but
they who have acquired the very beft natural difpofition of
foul, halting between the higheft virtue and the loweft vice,
ftand in need of the divine aid, to give the proper bias and direction to the better fide. For their natural weaknefs makes them
eafily take the worft path. This by means of pleafures and
lufts, flatters even well-difpofed fouls, and hurries them into the
fame paths of vice.

LVIII. It is therefore really a fhame that heathen writers
have entertained more humble fentiments of the infirmity and
inability of our nature for good, and clearer conceptions of the
divine affifting grace, and have faid finer things about imploring it by prayer, than thofe profeffors of the excellency of the
Chriftian religion, who ought to have put a due value on the
holinefs of true virtue. Thus they who are Pagans, will, in
the day of judgment, rife up againft thofe falfe Chriftians,
the ungrateful enemies of the grace of God, no lefs to their
condemnation, than the queen of the South, to that of the unbelieving Jews.

LIX. Moreover, feeing the Spirit of God, the author of
holinefs, is highly generous and noble, and therefore by David
Pfal. li. 12. called *free* (ingenuous) *fpirit,* hence that holinefs,
with which he adorns the elect is alfo fuch ; as highly furpaffes
all the painted virtue of the Gentiles, in whatever manner it
difplays itfelf, and all the fcrupulous diligence of the Scribes
and Pharifees. Which if it does not exceed thefe it is not acknowledged to be genuine holinefs by Chrift our Lord, Mat.
v. 20.

LX. When the children of God recollect their glorious and
heavenly pedigree, they endeavour to excel others both in a beautiful difpofition of foul and manner of life, Pfalm xlv. 13.
" The king's daughter," that is the daughter of the heavenly Father, who is alfo the Bride of the king's fon, e-
very believing foul " is all glorious," adorned with a holinefs not only glorious to herfelf, but alfo to the Father and
the Bridegroom, and is the beginning of a heavenly glory.
and that chiefly within not only when fhe appears abroad and
                                              prefents

presents herself to the view of men, but also when she sits in the inner bed-chamber in the secret exercises of religion, in which she in private pleases the Father and the Bridegroom, who having a regard to the inward man, she above all endeavours to keep that pure and chaste. Her clothing is of gold; in comparison of which whatever excellency natural men were ever possessed of, is but a shining vanity: nay it was *wrought;* gold curiously beautified with various resemblances, which represents the perfections of God himself; and of different colours, on account of the different yet harmoniously corresponding graces of the Holy Spirit: or, of needle work of the phrygian embroiderers, or rather the work of the cunning workman, mentioned Cant. vii. 1. Nor is the spouse only beautiful within, but also without; holding forth the word of life, Phil. ii. 16. she practises charity, glorifies Christ, edifies her neighbour: and in this manner she is brought unto the king worthy to be presented to him. This is the only way, by which we are to endeavour to obtain familiarity with him, and the sweetest intercourse of the chastest love, both on earth and in heaven.

LXI. That which we have in Psal. cx. 3. is not very different from this encomium : " Thy people, O Jesus Christ, which " were given thee by the Father, purchased and redeemed by " thee, who acknowledge thee for their Lord, and are bound to " thee by a military oath, is *extremely willing,* being devoted to " thy service with the greatest readiness of soul, alacrity, incli- " nation and voluntary obedience. Nor are they willing only, " but *willingness* itself in the abstract; nay, willingnesses in the " plural number, the highest and most excellent willingness: all " which add an emphasis, and such it is חילך ביום *in the day of thy* " [*valour*] *power,* in which thy generous spirit laying hold on " them, animates them to some grand and bold enterprize. Then " they go forth in the beauties of holiness, by which they are " a terror to the devil, a delight to God and angels, and a mu- " tual edification to one another."

LXII. These brave soldiers of Christ are not without their ambition, which Paul describes, 2 Cor. v. 9. Διὸ καὶ φιλοτιμούμεθα εἴτε παρόντες εἴτε ἀπόντες, *wherefore we [make it our ambition] labour to be accepted of him.* God never beholds himself without the highest complacency; above all he is delighted with his own perfections, and with holiness, which is the glory of them. When he sees any delineation of this in his creatures, there he in a manner stands still, and delights his eyes with so pleasing an object, and declares by words and actions, that nothing can be more acceptable to him. And this is the holy ambition of believers, so to behave

behave in the whole courfe of their life, and to have their mind fo difpofed, as in both to pleafe God. Of old, Satan infpired a wicked ambition into our firft parents, to labour after the image of God in a falfe way, by attempting what was forbidden them. But the heavenly Spirit is the author of a more generous ambition, which ftirs the man up, to imitate God in the habits of his foul, and the actions of his life, that he may, upon earth, prefent fomething before God, in which he may take pleafure, as in a lively image of himfelf. Nothing can be more noble than this holy ambition.

LXIII. What is faid Canticles i. 9. is very remarkable, " I have compared thee, O my love, to a company of horfes in Pharoah's chariot." For the underftanding this paffage, we are to explain, 1ft, Why the church is compared *to a horfe*. 2dly, Why to *an Egyptian horfe*. 3dly, Why *to a horfe in the king's chariots*. As to the *firft*: 1. An horfe fuffers itfelf to be eafily managed and led, not only with fpur and bridle, but alfo with the whip. Thus Strabo writes, lib. 17. that the " Maffæfilians and Lybians, made ufe of horfes fo fwift and manageable, that they could be governed by the whip only :" hence Martial fays, lib. 9. Epigr. 23. " Et Maffylæum virgo gubernet equum. And manage a Maffylean horfe with a rod." Wherefore the very learned Bochart, Hierozoic, lib. 2. c. 6. refers the Hebrew word סוס to a word ufed by the Arabs, which fignifies *to manage* and *govern*. See what Lipfius has collected, Centur. 3. ad Belgas, Epift. 56. concerning the nature, fidelity, and natural affection of horfes. Such alfo are the godly : for as they have renounced their own will, fo they are docile and manageable at the leaft command of God, faying, Speak Lord, for thy fervant heareth. 2. An horfe is a very ftrong creature, and hence it is, Jer. viii. 16. and xlvii. 3, called אביר, *ftrong*. Whence the very learned perfon ingenioufly conjectures, that Epirus, a country famous for horfes, had its name. In like manner, the godly " go in the ftrength of the Lord God," Pf. lxxi. 16 : they can do all things through Chrift which ftrengtheneth them," Phil. iv. 13. And perform fuch things in overcoming the world and conquering fin, as far exceed the ftrength of other men. 3dly, An horfe is a generous animal, to which God himfelf gives an illuftrious encomium as an emblem of warlike prowefs, Job xxxix. 22, &c. Bochart l. c. chap. 8. has given us a very diftinct explication of that paffage. And certainly there is fomething heroical in the godly, which, whenever Chrift, falvation and piety are concerned, difcovers itfelf in a manner, that may aftonifh thofe who behold it, For tho aged,

aged, the young, the helplefs of both fexes have been often feen to behave with fuch courage and bravery for Chrift, and undergo with fo much refolution, the moft cruel deaths in the caufe of religion, that it was evident, they were actuated by a fpirit above that which is human. And they were " as mighty men, which tread down their enemies in the mire of the ftreets in the battle; and they did fight becaufe the Lord was with them, and the riders on horfe were confounded." Zech. x. 5.

LXIV. Moreover, Egypt was formerly famous for its horfes, of which we frequently read in Scripture, 2 Kings xviii. 24. If. xxxi. 1. Nay, the law itfelf prohibited the kings of Judah too much to multiply their horfes, leaft, by that means, they fhould bring the people back to Egypt, Deut. xvii. 16. However Solomon had his horfes from thence in very great numbers, 1 Kings x. 28, 29. 2 Chron. ix. 28. We may then infer from this, that they were extraordinary beyond others. But to fuch Egyptian horfes the church is compared, to fhew her excellent courage and boldnefs: for the Egyptian horfe was the fymbol of this, and in their enfigns they preferred it to the lion, as Clemens Alexandrinus Stromat. lib. 5. p. 567. informs us: " for of ftrength and force the lion is their fymbol, but of courage and boldnefs the horfe."

LXV. Nor are they compared to this alone, but alfo to the horfes in king Pharoah's chariot, which doubtlefs were the moft excellent, and felected from his whole kingdom. For as the royal chariot excelled, fo who can doubt, that the king's horfes excelled all others? All thefe comparifons are adapted to fet off the noblenefs of Chriftian piety.

LXVI. Nay, God does not ftop here: but as if it was too mean to compare his elect to a company of horfes in Pharoah's chariot, he promifes to prepare them רוח מצרים " as the horfe of his majefty, his goodly horfe in the battle," Zech. x. 3. Than which nothing could be fpoken with greater magnificence. The holy perfon is really as a horfe prepared for the battle of the Lord, and the horfe of the fupreme commander of the divine majefty, which, on account of its ftrength and valour, is worthy to be mounted by the king of heaven himfelf. Wherefore even he who had his name written on his vefture and on his thigh, *The King of kings and Lord of lords,* was feen by John fitting on *a white horfe,* Rev. xix. 11. by which is denoted the genuine profeffors of truth, and fincere followers of holinefs, with whom Jefus fights, and in whom he refts and is glorified.

LXVII. But that this pre-eminence of Chriftian virtues may appear more evidently, three things are diftinctly to be confidered : 1ft, Their original. 2dly, Their rule. 3dly, Their end, for in thefe things their fuper-excellence confifts above all the virtues or graces of the unfanctified.

LXVIII. As to their original, the virtues of the Heathen, and the actions proceeding from thence, have their rife from fome remains of the divine image, ftill left in man fince the fall ; fuch as innate notions, fome love of honefty, the incentives of a natural confcience ; befides thofe, fome have had a liberal education, applied themfelves to the ftudy of philofophy, and enjoyed fome fpecial benefits of the common providence of God, repreffing, reftraining and curbing innate corruption, and on the other hand, exciting them to the practice of a much more regular life, than the common herd of mankind, fo that thefe virtues had no higher nor better original than *nature*, excited by the affiftance of common providence, Rom. ii. 14, 15. " the Gentiles do by nature the things contained in the law, and fhew the work of the law written in their hearts."

LXIX. But the practice of Chriftian holinefs has its rife, 1ft, From *the Spirit of grace*, which Chrift has merited for, and beftows on his elect; " whom the world cannot receive, becaufe it feeth him not neither knoweth him," John xiv. 17. who feeing he is the Spirit of Chrift, excites in the elect, even the very fame motions and inclinations of foul, which are in Chrift, and moulds and forms the whole life of Chrift in them: fo that they act, not by their own virtue or ftrength, nor by any innate principle of natural life, but by fupernatural grace, and the virtue of Chrift, 1 Cor. xv. 10. " not I, but the grace of God, which is with me;" and Heb. xii. 28. " let us have grace, whereby we may ferve God acceptably."

LXX. 2dly, From faith, " without which it is impoffibe to pleafe God," Heb. xi. 6. For, ἐναρεστῆσαι, *to pleafe*, fignifies here to walk before God, as is evident from the foregoing verfe, where the Apoftle fays, that Enoch, *before his tranflation, had this teftimony, that he pleafed God*. By which words he undoubtedly has an eye to what we have, Gen. v. 24. " And Enoch walked with God, and he was not, for God took him." For to walk with God, the Septuagint every where tranflate, ἐναρεστειν τῷ Θεῷ, *to pleafe God;* they alfo in fome places, render *ηνω. to ferve*, by the fame word. The Apoftle here imitates their way of fpeaking ; in like manner, as Tit. ii. 9. where he enjoins fervants, ἐν πᾶσιν ἐναρεστους εἶναι, *in all things to pleafe them*, that is, fo to behave as in every thing to do what is well-pleafing to their mafters.

LXXI.

LXXI. But faith, without which nothing can be done, that is acceptable to God, is that virtue or grace, which is the beginning of the spiritual life, or the first work of the Holy Spirit uniting us to Christ. And there are various ways to prove that without this a man can do nothing that is good. 1st, 'Seeing faith apprehends and applies to itself all the efficacy of Christ's merits, it has a power " of purifying the heart," Acts xv. 9. But so long as that fountain of the heart is impure, nothing pure can flow from it: For " unto them that are defiled and unbelieving is nothing pure !" not even their food; " but their mind and conscience is defiled," Tit. i. 15. On the contrary, ' The end of the commandment is charity, out of a pure heart, and of a good conscience, and of faith unfeigned, 1 Tim. i. 5. 2dly, By faith we are justified, and are restored to the favour of God. But it is necessary that the persons of sinners be acceptable to God in Christ, before their works can be so. For how can the work of that man please God, who is an abomination and execration to him? First, God had respect to " Abel, then to his offering," Gen. iv. 4. Be it far, says Augustine, lib. 4. contra Julianum, c. 3. " that any one should be really virtuous, who is not righteous. But be it far, that he should be truly righteous, who does not live by faith: for the just shall live by faith ;" 3dly, It is not possible, that any can truly love God, and endeavour from a principle of love to do what is acceptable to him, unless he know him to be such, as he manifests himself in Christ the Mediator. But it is the proper work of faith to behold God in Christ; and thus faith worketh by love, Gal. v. 6. 4thly, As faith first unites us to Christ, so it continually draws virtue, efficacy and life from him, by a spiritual suction and attraction, whereby we may be enabled to act in a holy manner: "The life which I live, I live by the faith of the Son of God, Gal. ii. 20."

LXXII. But besides that common faith, which is the fountain of all spiritual life, another more special faith is requisite to the goodness of our actions, consisting in a certain persuasion of mind, that the work we undertake is good and holy, or at least lawful, and no where prohibited. For whoever does any thing, about which he is not certain that it is acceptable to God, does by that very action shew, that he is not affected with a due reverence for the Deity, nor endeavours, as is fit, to avoid the displeasure and indignation of God. And to this I imagine, the Apostle has an eye, Rom. xiv. 23. he that doubteth, that is, who is not persuaded in his conscience, that he may lawfully eat of any food ; " is condemned if he eat ;" that is, is judged to have acted amiss; " because he eateth not

of

of faith; for, whatfoever is not of faith, is fin." For, here the
Apoftle preffes what he had enjoined, verfe 5. let every man
be fully perfuaded in his own mind.

LXXIII. 3dly, The practice of Chriftian holinefs flows from
*the love of God*, and confifts in that *very ambition*, which we
have recommended from 2 Cor. v. 9. of doing what is acceptable to God. And in this, Chriftian holinefs furpaffes all the
virtuous actions of the Heathen, who were very juftly commended, if what they did proceeded from the love of that virtue they were acquainted with; but as that love did not afcend
to God himfelf, but centered in a created, nay, and a very de-
fective thing, fuch as their virtue was, it was not a holy love
but a vicious affection, which indirectly and finfully terminates
in man himfelf.

LXXIV. Janfenius lib. 4. *de ftatu naturæ lapfæ.* c. 11. *feq.*
has treated diftinctly and at large on this fubject; where he
fpeaks to this purpofe: " This therefore was the proper defect of philofophical virtue even when pureft, that being delighted with a certain ruinous height of virtue, they earneftly
defired it for this end, that they might be great in their own
efteem, delight, and pleafe themfelves; whereas it became
them to pleafe God or the truth, as Auguftine fpeaks; this
vice of felf-pleafing fo clofely adheres to thofe who feek not to
pleafe either God or men, that it is not poffible fuch perfons
fhould not fall into it." To which he immediately fubjoins:
" whoever lifts not up his eyes to God in order to pleafe him
from the beauty of virtue, but admires it alone as the end of
good, the faireft and the moft exalted, it is impoffible that either
defiring it he fhould not thence pleafe himfelf, or not willing
thence to pleafe himfelf he fhould defire it. Seeing it is altogether neceffary the foul of man fhould delight in fomething.
With what other object, pray, can a foul alineated from God
be delighted, and looking down as we fuppofe, with contempt
on the other meaner creatures, than with what he imagines to
be moft excellent among created things? but this is the
mind itfelf now adorned with virtue; which ornament it judges
the moft becoming of all. He therefore neceffarily pleafes
himfelf from his virtue, who defires not by it to pleafe either
God or other men." All which is found and folid.

LXXV. Chriftian virtue therefore has a deeper and better
original than any love of virtue whatfoever, or than any complacency in one's own actions. But faith, which reprefents
God to the foul, as infinitely good and perfectly holy, and the
moft bountiful rewarder of good actions, as alfo his laws as
full

full of equity and juftice, enflames the foul with the love of a gracious God, and of his moft equitable laws, and to deem nothing preferable to, nothing more valuable than by a conformity to thofe laws, to refemble him in his meafure in holinefs, and in that refemblance to pleafe him. That God looking down as it were out of himfelf, and from heaven, may alfo find upon earth what to delight himfelf in as his copy; which is the higheft pleafure of a holy foul. So that it loves not virtue for itfelf alone, but for God whofe image it is, and whom in the practice of virtue it pleafes. From this love to God fprings the practice of true holinefs.

LXXVI. I cannot but tranfcribe an excellent paffage of Clemens Alexandrinus to this purpofe, who Stromat. lib. p. p. 532. thus gives us the picture of a holy perfon. " He who obeys the bare call fo far as he is called, labours after knowledge neither from fear nor from pleafure; for he does not confider whether any profitable gain or external pleafure will enfue, but being conftrained by the love of what is truly amiable, and thereby excited to his duty, he is a pious worfhipper of God. Were we therefore to fuppofe him to have received from God a liberty to what was forbidden, without any apprehenfion of punifhment; nay moreover, had he a promife of receiving the reward of the bleffed, and befides was he perfuaded that his actions fhould efcape the notice of God, (which by the way is impoffible) he could never be prevailed with to act contrary to right reafon, after he had once chofen what is really lovely and eligible of itfelf, and on that account to be loved and defireds." Than which nothing can be faid more fublime.

LXXVII. He would have a holy or fanctified perfon do every thing from a principle of love. " It becomes him who is perfect to be in the exercife of love, and fo endeavour after the divine favour and friendfhip, while he performs the commandments by love." But this love has not renown, nor any other advantage but virtue itfelf, pure virtue for its object; fo he frames his life after the image and refemblance of God, no longer for the fake of renown, or as the philofophers fpeak, *similans of a fplendid name; nor from the view of reward, either from God or men.* Moreover, what renders virtue amiable to him, is not that philofophical agreement it has with right reafon, but becaufe he beholds in it a refemblance to God, than which nothing can be imagined more amiable: for thus he defcribes it, what is *truly good*, he calls *truly defirable*, faying, *it is good by an affimilation to God to become impaffive and virtuous.*

LXXVIII. Yet we are not fo to underftand thefe things as

if

if in the practice of holinefs, we were not allowed to pay any regard to our own advantage, and that all love of ourfelves ought in this cafe quite to difappear. We are not only allowed but commanded to love ourfelves; nor are we bound to love our neighbour without a love for ourfelves. And this is not written, but a natural law which we have learned from no other quarter, but have received it from nature herfelf: " no man ever yet hated his own flefh, but nourifheth and cherifheth it," Eph. v. 29. We may alfo be lawfully ftirred up to the diligent practice of holinefs by this love of ourfelves. God himfelf by this enticing motive invites his people, promifing that " their labour fhall not be in vain in the Lord," 1 Cor. xv. 58. And to what, pray, tend all thofe promifes by which he has recommended his commandments to us, but that being excited by a defire of them we fhould more chearfully obey him? Not to love the promifed good, is to throw contempt on the goodnefs of a promifing God. By the love of them not to be ftirred up to piety, is to abufe them to fome other purpofe than God ever intended. David himfelf confeffed, that the commandments of God were even on that account, " more to be defired than gold, yea, than much fine gold; fweeter alfo than honey, and the honey-comb; becaufe in keeping of them there is a great reward," Pfa. xix. 10. 12. And the faith of Mofes is for the fame reafon commended, becaufe " he had a refpect unto the recompenfe of the reward, Heb. xi. 26. Nay, that faith is required as neceffary for all who come to God, whereby they may believe that " he is a rewarder of them that diligently feek him," verfe 6.

LXXIX. But then here alfo the love of ourfelves ought to fpring from the love of God, be fubordinate thereto, and rendered back to him. We muft not love God on our own account, fo as to confider ourfelves as the end, and God as the means, by which we are made happy in the enjoyment of him: but becaufe we are God's property, whom we ought to love above all, and therefore for his fake we are bound to ourfelves. We are further to feek our own good, that therein we may tafte the fweetnefs of the Lord, and that thereby we may be fo much the more improved and enriched as God's peculiar treafure. Thus the love of ourfelves is at laft fwallowed up in that ocean of divine love. Of this we fhall fpeak a little prefently.

LXXX. Let us now confider the *rule* or ftandard of holinefs. Philofophers made *the nature* of man, right *reafon*, and the *examples* of excellent men the rule. A few of them fpoke of the precepts of God, and of the example which he gives us, but that, indeed, in a very slender manner. Of the *nature* of man the emperor Marc. Antonine, speaks thus, lib. 8. §. 11. " wherein consists a happy life? In doing those things which human nature requires." They are for ever talking of *right reason*, and of the examples of illustrious men, see Seneca, Epist. 6. 11. 25.

LXXXI. Epictetus speaks things more sublime concerning the precepts of God than could well have been expected from a Heathen. He protests, Arrian. lib. 3. c. 24, towards the end, that he would live and die before God; " As thou hast required, says he, that as free as thy servant, as knowing what thou commandest and what thou forbiddest." And a little after, " Do not I wholly tend towards God and his precepts and commands?" And lib. 4. c. 7, " I am set at liberty by God, I know his commandments." And in the same book, c. 3. " I am set free, and am the friend of God, that I may willingingly obey him." And a little after : " Wherefore I cannot transgress any of his commands." And to conclude; " These are edicts, I must be the interpreter of, must obey them, before the precepts of Massurius and Cassius."

LXXXII. Sometimes also they have spoken of *the imitation of God*, and of conformity to him. Seneca de benefic. lib. 7. c. 31. " Let us imitate the Gods." Marc. Antonin. lib. 5. §. 27. " We must live with the Gods:" and lib. 2. §. 5. " live a divine life." Clemens Storm. lib. 2. p. 403. " Plato the philosopher defining happiness, says, it is an assimilation to God, as far as may be." See above, chap. 5. sect. 2.

LXXXIII. These things are spoken in a lofty strain; nevertheless, as they had not the knowledge of any other laws of God but what nature suggests, and are inscribed on the conscience, which prescribe the duties of holiness only in general and in a very confused and imperfect manner; and as they knew not the true God in his perfections, nor ever beheld him in his sanctuary; what they had for the rule of their virtues was very defective.

LXXXIV. But Christian holiness has a far more excellent rule to go by, whether we consider its *precepts or examples*. Its precepts are taken from the most perfect law of God; not only that of which the rubbish, and as it were, the faint resemblance or shadows like a passing image, still remain in the conscience of a natural man ; but also that which with so much magnificence of heavenly glory, God formerly published before the full assembly of his people, wrote with his own finger on tables of stone,
enlarged

enlarged with the plaineft expofitions of the Prophets and inſpired penmen, and which, by the fecret efficacy of his Spirit, he writes on the hearts of the elect: which is the moſt exact expreſſion not only of his moſt holy will, but alfo of his nature and perfections, fo far as they are imitable by man; nor does it only regulate and order the external actions and converfation, but alfo reaches to man's moſt inward parts, directs the inmoſt receſſes of the heart, and roots out the fibres of vice, even to the very firſt motions of rifing concupifcence; which in fine, raifes man to a perfection worthy of God.

LXXXV. This is that law, which God gave in charge to Iſrael, Pf. cxlvii. 19; "by which יגדיל he made them great and glorious," Iſa. xlii. 21; fo that, in an aſtonifhing manner, they excelled other nations, Deut. iv. 6, 7. in which are רבים μυγαλια the moſt ample inſtructions [great things written], Hof. viii. 12. the excellency of which, and not their excellency alone, but alfo their moſt exact perfection, the Pſalmiſt has nobly fet forth, Pf. xix. 8, &c. and indeed, fo great was the perfection, that he could find no end to it, as he found in other perfections, Pfal. cxvi. 96. And certainly the more a man is engaged with an attentive mind, in the profound meditation of this law, the more diſtinctly he will underſtand that he is far from forming in his mind a perfect notion of that holinefs prefcribed by it. The Lord Jefus has faid all in a few words, and comprifed the whole fummary of the law, calling out to his difciples (but who can underſtand the full force of thofe words?) "Be ye perfect, even as your Father which is in heaven is perfect," Mat. v.48.

LXXXVI. Befides thofe moſt holy laws, the believer has illuſtrious examples of virtues for his imitation; and thofe not of one kind or order. And the firſt that here occur are the SAINTS THAT ARE IN THE EARTH, "and the excellent, in whom is all his delight," Pfal. xvi. 3. we have no occafion to prefent you with a Socrates, a Zeno, a Cato, or a Lælius, whom Seneca recommends for this purpofe. We have men actuated by the moſt noble and generous Spirit of God, Patriarchs, Prophets, Apoſtles, and the like heroes of both fexes, whom God himfelf honoured with familiarity, with encomiums and commendations; whofe manner of life he took care to have exactly defcribed in the moſt facred volumes of our religion, and whofe number is fo great that Paul calls them a cloud of witneſſes, by whofe example we may be animated to run with conſtancy, the race of piety, Heb xii. 1. Thefe are propofed to us for our imitation, 1 Cor. iv. 16. and xi. 2. Phil. iii. 17. Jac. iv. 10. Heb. xiii. 7.

LXXXVII.

LXXXVII. However as the most excellent saints on earth
have had their blemishes prudence is necessary in this case,
that we may propose, for our imitation, only those actions of
theirs, which are the most consonant to the standard of the
divine law; where they have departed from the rule, let us be
admonished by their mistake, and learn to walk uprightly. For
this end Nehemiah wisely proposes the example of Solomon *,
Neh. xiii. 26. And it is of singular use to us, that the back-
slidings of the holy men of God are recorded in holy writ.
Spots appear no where more disagreeable, than when seen in
a most beautiful face, or on the cleanest garment. And it is
expedient to have a perfect knowledge of the filthiness of sin.
We also learn from them to think humbly of ourselves, to depend on the grace of God, to keep a stricter eye upon ourselves, least perhaps we fall into the same or more grievous sins,
Gal. vi. 1.

LXXXVIII. But our Lord would not have us without perfect examples, and therefore he raises the meditations of his
people to the inhabitants of heaven, the choirs of angels, and
spirits of just men made perfect, whose conversation he recommends even in our daily prayer, *as it is in heaven.* These
being filled with the clearest light, and flaming with the purest
love, and continually beholding the face of God, and being altogether conforming to him, incessantly shew forth the praises
of their Creator, and execute his commands with incredible alacrity. Isa. vi. 2, 3. Psf. ciii. 20. Rev. iv. 8, 9, 10, 11. The
sacred writings testify all this concerning them. And faith not
only believes, but sees all this; for, being endowed with the
quickest sight, it penetrates within the veil of the heavenly sanctuary, and, as if mixed with the consort of the heavenly inhabitants, views those exercises of the most consummate holiness,
with the love of which the believing soul cannot fail to be inflamed.

LXXXIX. But yet, as it is very desirable to have likewise
an example of perfect holiness upon earth; so God has not
suffered us to be without one; for he sent his own Son from
heaven, who hath left us the brightest pattern of every virtue,
without exception, *that we should follow his steps,* 1 Pet. ii. 21.
It was a part of Christ's prophetical office, to teach not only by
words, but by the example of his life, that both in his words
and actions he might say, *learn of me,* Mat. xi. 29. The imi-

* Did not Solomon king of Israel sin by these things? Yet, among many nations,
was there no king like him, who was beloved of his God, and God made him
king over all Israel; nevertheless even him did outlandish women cause to sin.

tation of him is often recommended by the Apoftles, 1 Cor. xi. 1. 1 Theff. i. 6. 1 John ii. 6.

XC. It has been very well obferved by a learned perfon, that we are to diftinguifh between *imitation*, whereby we are faid to be μιμηται, *imitators* of Chrift, 1 Cor. xi. 1.; and between *following*, by which we are commanded to follow Chrift ; between *follow me*, Mat. xvi. 24. and *follow after me*, Mat. x. 38. For, the former denotes a conformity to an example : the latter, the attendance of fervants, going after their mafters : which words are generally confounded by writers in their own language, though they ought by no means to be fo.

XCI. As we have already often inculcated, that Chrift is not to be confidered in a threefold refpect, as *man*, as *Mediator*, and as *God* : fo we are to enquire in what relation or refpect he is given us as an example. And firft, we are not to doubt, that as he reprefented, in his human nature, the image of God, in which the firft man was created, and poffeffed and practifed all the virtues due by a rational creature, without any defect ; in fo far as he is, in the moft perfect manner, propofed to our Imitation. Certainly this world was hitherto deftitute of fuch a pattern ever fince the fatal apoftacy of our firft parents, viz. to have a man, who being untainted with vice, *holy, harmlefs, undefiled,* might, as a living and breathing law, converfe among his brethren : fuch a one, God hath exhibited to us in Chrift. It is a pleafure to him who loves holinefs, to behold a moft exact delineation of it in the written law of God. But what is that delineation but only a picture ? It is indeed, exact, and painted in natural colours ; but then it is a picture only, without flefh and blood, without life and motion. How much greater therefore, the pleafure to behold the fame holinefs which is pourtrayed in the law, living as it were, and animated in Chrift ?

XCII. What was peculiar and proper to his mediatorial office, as the honour of his mediation, whereby we are reconciled to God, and that eminent dignity, by which he has the peculiar honour of being prophet, prieft and king ; in fum whatever belongs to that more excellent name, which was beftowed on Chrift above his fellows ; all this we are neither to imitate nor follow the example of thofe who pretend to be imitators ; " there is one mediator between God and men, the man Chrift Jefus. 1 Tim. ii. 5.

XCIII. Neverthelefs, believers, after the example of Chrift, and from a participation of his unction, have the honour of being prophets, priefts, and kings, Joel ii. 28. 1 Pet. ii. 5.

Rev.

Rev. i. 6. And confequently, it is incumbent upon them, to conform to the example of Chrift, in the fpritual difcharge of thofe offices. In which, however, there is fo great a difference, that befides partaking of the name, and fome fmall analogy, fcarce any coincidence can be obferved. The prophetical, facerdotal, and regal offices of Chrift are of a far different nature from ours.

XCIV. But thofe virtues which Chrift difcovered in the difcharge of his offices, are by all means, propofed for our imitation; as the demonftration he gave of his humility, faithfulnefs, love, patience, zeal, and conftancy in the whole difcharge of his offices; as alfo his not intruding into them without a call, Heb. v. 4, 5. his faithfulnefs to him who had appointed him, Heb. iii. 2. his not feeking his own advantage or profit, Phil. ii. 4, 5. his not finking under the reproaches and contradiction of finners, Heb. xii. 2, 3. his zeal for God's houfe that had eaten him up, John ii. 17. his not feeking his own but the glory of his Father in all things, John viii. 49, 50. and a great deal more to the fame purpofe.

XCV. In fine, even *as God*, he, together with the Father and Holy Spirit, is a pattern to us of the pureft holinefs, Levit. xi. 44. and xix. 2. Mat. v. 48. Eph. v. 1. 1 Pet. i. 15, 16. The holinefs of God is fo great an ornament of his other perfections, that without it all the reft would be unworthy of God. Hence he is faid to be *glorious in holinefs*, Exod xv. 11. and we are particularly commanded to celebrate the memorial, *or give thanks at the remembrance of his holinefs*, Pf. xxx. 4. and lxxix. 12. after the example of the feraphim, who having repeated the threefold praife of the divine holinefs, added, *the whole earth is full of his glory*, Ifa. vi. 3. God invites his people to imitate this holinefs, he has fet it before them in his word for their contemplation; that while they admire its beauty, they may be inflamed with the love of it, and gradually transformed to that image.

XCVI. In the third place, we propofed to fpeak of the END of Chriftian virtues or graces; which muft needs be of all others the moft excellent. The true believer does not there apply himfelf to the practice of holinefs, to gain praife and reputation with men, which was the crime of the Heathen and the Pharifees, of whom our Lord teftifies, Mat. vi. 5. *That they have their reward* He does not aim only at his own advantage, either in this or in the life to come, from a mercenary felf-love, which all thofe do, who, endeavouring to eftablifh their own righteoufnefs, profefs that all motives to piety are deftroyed, if the merits of good works are exploded. He does not only purfue after that tranquillity of foul, which is pleafed with what it has done, and which virtue or holinefs, when properly efteemed, ufually beftows on thofe who love it. The intention of the godly is far more pure and fublime, whereby they are carried out both towards *God, themfelves* and their *neighbour*.

XCVII. Above all, they feek *the glory of God*. This they love, defire its enlargement, and promote it with all their might : *Let fuch as love thy falvation, fay continually, the Lord be magnified,* Pf. xl. 16. Hither all their exercifes tend, going on *without offence, until the day of Chrift ; being filled with the fruits of righteoufnefs, which are by Jefus Chrift unto the glory and praife of God,* Phil. i. 10, 11. They who have the love of God for the fource and principle, cannot but have the glory of the fame God for their end. For whoever has an ardent love to God, will likewife, above all things, love what is moft beloved by him. But fuch is the love that God has to his own glory, that whatever he does is with a view to, and for the fake of that : wherefore all things are *of him,* in order to be again *to him,* and *to him be the glory for ever,* Rom. xi. 36. In this refpect the faints are truly like to God, for in all their actions they have the glory of God before their eyes. *Whether therefore ye eat or drink, or whatfoever ye do, do all to the glory of God,* 1 Cor. x. 31.

XCVIII. Yet thefe things are not fo to be underftood, as if in all and every particular, even the moft minute actions of life, it was neceffary to have that explicit intention of glorifying God before them. For this is not practicable in the prefent ftate of things : however it ought univerfally to be the firm and fixed difpofition of the children of God, that they be fo confecrated and dedicated to God, as, for the future, neither to think, fpeak, meditate, nor do any thing, in which fome expreffion of the perfections of God and manifeftation of his glory may not appear. For what is facred or devoted, cannot without a confiderable injury to him, be applied to profane ufes. They are not their own : therefore it is unlawful for them to propofe to themfelves this end : only to feek what they imagine will be profitable to the flefh. They are not their own : let them therefore, as far as may be, forget themfelves and theirs. They are God's : let them therefore live and die to him. They are God's : let his wifdom therefore over-rule all their actions. They are God's : let therefore all the parts of their life tend to him as their only lawful end. And in this fincere felf-denial and furrender of ourfelves to God, that we may firmly propofe to do all our works with a holy refpect to him, confifts this glorifying of God we now fpeak of.

XCIX.

XCIX. For inftance, a perfon then eats and drinks to the glory of God, when, confeffing himfelf unworthy to enjoy this life and the conveniencies of it, he praifes that bountiful favour of God, which abundantly beftows all things upon him, and above all admires that immenfe love of the Lord Jefus, who willingly was deftitute of all the dainties of life, and fubmitted to drink vinegar and gall, that his people, thro' the favour of God, might eat the fat and drink the fweet : when alfo he does not delight fo much in the creatures and the gifts of providence, as in the Creator himfelf and the giver ; tafting, to his unfpeakable pleafure, how fweet the Lord is ; when he fincerely propofes faithfully to employ his life, which is lengthened out by thefe means, and all his faculties, which are thus continually refrefhed, to the fervice of God, who gave and preferves them, when in fine he rifes in meditation, from the delights of this natural life, to the almoft unfpeakable pleafures of a future and heavenly life ; and having a prelibation of them in thought and faith, with a grateful heart, tunes up a fong of love to God ; " Lord, if thou doeft fuch things in this dark dungeon, what wilt thou not do for us, when admitted into thy palace of light !"

C. Here I choofe to tranfcribe fome things from the Jewifh catechifm of " Rabbi Abraham Ben Chanania Jagel, publifhed firft at Venice in 1595, under the title נשׁ תפׁ, afterwards reprinted at Amfterdam 1658, and at laft exhibited to the Chriftian reader, with a Latin verfion by John Benedict Carpzovius, entitled, Introductis in Theologam Judiacam, c. 9. p. 74. Where the Hebrew Catechift inftructs his Difciple in this manner ; " Let all thy works be done to the glory of the divine name, and to the honour of the bleffed Creator. In all thy ways think of him ; when thou walkeft in the way, when thou rifeft up or lieft down. For inftance, when thou eateft, know, that the bleffed God has, by the power of his wifdom, created thy food, and given it virtue to be converted into the fubftance of him who is to be nourifhed by it ; when thou goeft to fleep in thy bed, confider with thyfelf that God ordained fleep for the benefit of man, that his body might reft, and his ftrength be recruited, and himfelf rendered fit and found for ferving his Creator. And thus, in all thy other bodily actions, take care to give glory and praife to God ; for, by this means, all thy works fhall be to the glory of the divine name, whofe providence will keep clofe to thee and direct all thy actions."

CI. Next to this glory of the divine name, a holy perfon may alfo in the exercife of his virtues, or graces, have a regard to
himfelf,

himself, and endeavour, 1st, To have the affurance of his own eternal election by God, his internal vocation, his faith and communion with Chrift, 2 Pet. i. 10. 2dly, To rejoice in the teftimony of a confcience void of offence, and in that compofure of mind, which is the confequent thereof, 2 Cor. i. 12. 3dly, That, by proving the fincerity of his love towards God by holy actions, he may enjoy for himfelf that love and familiarity of God, which Jefus, John xiv. 21. 23. has gracioufly promifed to thofe that love him. 4thly, That he may gradually become in the habits and difpofitions of his foul, and the actions flowing therefrom, more like the Supreme Being, and fo more glorious and happy, 2 Cor. iii. 18. 5thly, And that by proceeding in this way of holinefs to eternal glory, he may live at eafe, and in affurance of his falvation, 1 Cor. ix. 24—27.

CII. Neverthelefs Chriftian holinefs teacheth us to defire all thefe things, but not to reft in them as our ultimate end, but even to direct them to the glory of God. For, the more abundantly any one has attained to what we have juft now only mentioned, the brighter will the fplendor of the divine perfections fhine forth in him: the goodnefs and bounty of God magnificently difcover themfelves in this reward of virtue: the beloved fpoufe of Chrift, whom he will one day prefent without fpot, and glorious to God the Father, fhall be the more adorned: the high value of his fatisfaction and merits, will be duly efteemed from the happinefs beftowed on the faints. The faints themfelves fhall be enriched with thofe rewards of their virtues, and be better fitted for celebrating the praifes of their God. And thus it is, that, while they pioufly aim at the happinefs promifed to them, and feek their own glory in the proper order and meafure, they, at the fame time, " rejoice in hope of the glory of God," Rom. v. 2. For then they are made happy, " when God is glorified and admired in them," 2 Theff. i. 10.

CIII. In fine, the works of piety are alfo adapted to gain over our neighbour to God. The holy foul never fatisfies itfelf in glorifying God, but defigns to have many companions employed in the fame work: to obtain which, " he caufeth his light to fhine before men, that they may fee his good works, and glorify his Father which is in heaven," Mat. v. 16. And having a hearty defire for the falvation of his neighbour, he very willingly employs every means to bring him to the good old way. For this purpofe, as nothing is more effectual than a holy life, fo Peter calls upon Chriftian wives to apply thereto, " that if any obey not the word, they alfo may, without the word

word, be won by the converfation of the wives, 1 Pet. iii. 1. And certainly, whoever are made partakers of that extraordinary grace of God, and tranflated out of darknefs into his marvellous light, will labour, by the reflected rays of divine love, alfo to enlighten, enflame and make others partake of the fame happinefs with themfelves. And who can conceive any thing more holy, more praife worthy than this?

CIV. This is that generous holinefs which the Spirit of grace powerfully operates in the elect, and which he promotes by the ufe of various means. Though the ufe of thefe means is required of man, yet their efficacy depends on the bleffing of God alone. Nor indeed is it without the interpofition of God, that man can and will favingly ufe thofe means. For daily experience teacheth us, how dull and languid we ufually are in thofe things, when the influence of the Spirit either ceafes, or is but fmall. Among thofe means of fanctification, the following deferve to be moft recommended.

CV. We juftly give the firft place to the word of God, and the devout meditation of it. "God fanctifieth us through his truth, his word is truth," John xvii. 17. For as it proceeds from the Holy Spirit, the characters of the divine holinefs are imprinted upon it, and as in every part, it fends forth the moft fragrant odour of holinefs, fo it infpires the pious reader with it, though perhaps he may not underftand all that he readeth : which Chryfoftom has likewife obferved in Orat. 3. in Lazar. " Even though thou doeft not thoroughly underftand the contents, yet even the reading begets a very great degree of fanctification."

CVI. And whatever is contained in the word of God, is directed to this end. The precepts of the law, which exhibit the exacteft delineation of holinefs, are adapted to inflame the foul with love to it, Pf. cxix. 8, 9, 10. The threatenings annexed to the law, and the recorded inftances of thofe judgments, by which God has punifhed fin, are fo many powerful dehortations from it, 1 Cor. x. 6. 11. The very ample promifes made to godlinefs, and the bleffings wherewith the liberal goodnefs of the deity has enriched the godly who love and worfhip him. are fo many incentives to holinefs, Ifa. lii. 2, 3. The examples of the faints both teach and allure at the fame time, Heb. xii. 1. Their very ftumblings and falls remind us of our weaknefs, inculcate humility, teach us to take heed to ourfelves, and point out what things we ought to avoid, Neh. xiii. 26. But nothing more effectually perfuades to piety, than the doctrine of grace revealed in the Gofpel, Tit ii. 12. and whoever abufe it to lafcivioufnefs,

nefs, never knew the truth as it is in Jefus: " for the word of the truth of the Gofpel, is all the world bringeth forth fruit, fince the day they heard of it, and knew the grace of God in truth," Col. i. 5, 6.

CVII. But in order to obtain this fruit of holinefs from the word of God, it is, 1ft, To be diligently, daily and carefully attended to, and as Chryfoftom fpeaks, it is to be read *with a myftic filence,* or profound attention John v. 39. 2dly, Diligently heard: for the public preaching of the word has very excellent promifes, Rom. x. 14, 15, 17. 3dly, When read and heard, it is to be laid up in the inward treafure of the foul, there to be kept as the moft valuable treafure, Job xxiii. 12. Pfa. cxix. 11. Luke ii. 19. 4thly, But it is not to be kept in fome remote corner of the memory, there to rot in mouldinefs and duft, but at times it is to be brought forth, and made the object of holy meditation: whereby the foul, by ruminating and fucking as it were, extracts and turns into its own fubftance, that quickening and nourifhing juice that is to be found in the word of God, Pfa. i. 2. Jof. i. 8. 5thly, It is expedient to have always at hand fome powerful ftriking paffages of fcripture, wherewith we may be armed againft the attacks of fin, and excited to duty. This was what the Lord meant when he ordered Ifrael to bind his word as a fign upon their hand, and to be as frontlets between their eyes, Deut. vi. 8. Why between their eyes? To be a rule of life continually before their mind. Why bound upon their hand? to put them in mind that knowledge was to be reduced to practice.

CVIII. Very wifely, indeed, did the emperor Antonine addrefs himfelf thus, Lib. 3. §. 13. " as furgeons have always their inftruments ready for fome unexpected operation, fo have thou at hand thy philofophical principles, in order to diftinguifh between things divine and human." Similar to this is what Seneca has de Benefic. Lib. vii. c. 1. " Demetrius the cynic was wont to fay very well, that it is more beneficial to have a few precepts of wifdom in readinefs for practice, than to learn a great deal and not have it at hand for ufe." And c. 2. " Our Demetrius orders the proficient to hold thefe things faft and never let them go; nay, to imprint them on his mind, and make them a part of himfelf; and by daily meditation to bring himfelf to that pitch, that what is ufeful fhall fpontaneoufly occur, and what is wanted fhall, upon all occafions, directly prefent itfelf." What they fpoke concerning the precepts of wifdom, which Epictetus called πρόχειρα βοηθήματα, *ready aids,* we may affirm concerning fome ftriking paffages of Scripture, which it is

expedient

expedient to have in such readiness, that, on any occasion, they may spontaneously cast up to the mind.

CIX. *Secondly,* The attentive consideration of the Lord Jesus is a most powerful mean of sanctification. The vileness and hideous nature of sin no where more clearly appears, than in the meanness, humiliation and sufferings of Christ. For, what was it that clothed the Lord of glory with the contemptible form of a servant? What overwhelmed the mighty lion of the tribe of Judah with horror and anguish, that he was almost ready to sink under them? What roused the cruel bands of hell to arms against him? What turned the flowing rivers of heavenly consolations into the most melancholy dryness? What mixed those bitterest of bitters in the cup of the divine fury, with which the Son of God's love was almost struck with astonishment and amaze? Sin certainly was the cause of all, Isa. liii. 5. Who can reflect on this, and not be inflamed with the most irreconcilable hatred to it? Will he not endeavour to avenge himself of that hideous monster, which so cruelly afflicted his most beloved Lord, and which, unless it be first slain, will, with the same fierceness, rage against all those that give it a favourable entertainment? Who can prevail on himself to be again enslaved by that tyrant, from whose chains, burning with hell-fire, he seriously believes and considers, he could not have been delivered but by the accursed death of the Son of God? And thus the meditation of the sufferings of Christ makes us, that, " being dead to sin, we should live unto righteousness," 1 Pet. ii. 24.

CX. Nor did the incredible love of God towards wretched mortals ever on any occasion, more evidently present itself to view, than in Christ Jesus, which may melt down the most frozen hearts, and kindle them into the brightest flames of mutual returns of love ; " for the love of Christ constraineth us, &c," 2 Cor. v. 14, 15. Whoever is deeply engaged in the meditation of this, will he not cry out with admiration ? " Wast " thou, most loving Jesus, scorched no less in the flames " of thy love for me, than in those of the divine wrath " against my sins, and shall I be lukewarm in returns of love " to thee? Didst thou die for my salvation, and shall I not " live to thy glory? Didst thou descend to hell on my account, " and shall not I at thy command cheerfully walk in the way " to heaven? Didst thou give thyself up for me to be torment- " ed with hell-pains, and I not render myself to thee, to bear " thy yoke which is easy, and thy burden which is light ?" It cannot be expressed, how much the pious soul, while intent

Vol. II.                    F                    on

on such meditations as these, will be displeased with his own lukewarmness; and wish he had a soul a hundred-fold more capacious, to be all filled with the love of Christ.

CXI. And never does virtue or holiness itself charm us with a more beautiful aspect than in Christ, which, we have also formerly intimated is seen painted in the law, but here alive and breathing; in such a manner, that the more frequently it is viewed by the eyes of the mind, it transforms the beholder into the same image, 2 Cor. iii. 18. When Moses had been admitted into familiar converse with God, in the holy mount where he spent forty days, the skin of his face shone with such effulgence, that the eyes of the Israelites could not bear it, Exod. xxxiv. 29, 30. Thus it is with those who view Jesus the king of glory in his beauty, with open face. The rays of the heavenly Spirit, plentifully issuing from him, pervade the inmost parts of the soul, and conciliate to them a new vigour of spiritual life. To which the intent contemplation of the Lord Jesus greatly contributes. The oftener that a believer beholds him in spirit, the more clearly he knows his perfections, of which his holiness is the ornament. The more clearly he knows them, the more ardently he loves them. The more ardently he loves them, the more like to them he desires to become. For love aspires after a likeness to the beloved: nay, in love itself there is already a great similitude: "for, God is love," 1 John iv. 8. Moreover, the more ardently he loves God, he will both the more frequently, the more willinlgy and attentively behold him; and thus often running round that circle of beholding and loving, for ever returning into itself, he gains by every act a new feature of this most glorious image.

CXII. *Thirdly,* To this contemplation of the Lord Jesus, add *the practice of* devout *prayer,* by which we may draw from the most exuberant fulness of Christ, and which he is ever most ready to impart, and grace for grace. God has promised to give all things to those that ask according to his will, 1 John. v. 14. But we can ask nothing more agreeable to the will of God, and which he more willingly gives, than his Spirit, Luke xi. 13. Who, as he is the principal cause of our sanctification, so is the author and finisher of it. Let this therefore be our daily prayer to God; "Teach me to do thy will; let thy good Spirit lead me into the land of uprightness," Ps. cxliii. 10. "Keep back thy servant also from presumptuous sins, let them not have dominion over me: then shall I be upright, and I shall be innocent from the great transgression. Let the words of my mouth and the meditation of my heart be acceptable in thy sight, O Lord, my strength and my redeemer," Ps. xix. 13, 14.

CXIII.

CXIII. *Fourthly*, Whoever seriously endeavours to be a proficient, must in all things give himself up to the government and guidance of the Holy Spirit. Whenever he begins to work internally by his suggestions, impulses, and emotions; we are with care and solicitude, to observe them; and above all beware, that we do not despise and grieve the Spirit, or stifle his operations, Eph. iv. 30. 1 Theff. v. 19. For, the Spirit of God is a delicate thing; he deals by us as we deal by him. If, with care and alacrity, we follow his conduct, he will manifest himself to us with a more cheerful and serene countenance, will carry us forward to higher attainments, bring us nearer to God and to heaven, and, abundantly favouring us with his joys, make us cheerfully, and without weariness, run the race that is set before us. But if we indolently neglect his influences, he will not bear that affront, but will withdraw with those his sweetest suggestions, leave us to ourselves, justly expose us to be harrassed by the devil and the flesh, and himself disquiet us with his terrors: till we are brought to observe, how ill we have regarded our own interest by this indolent carelessness, and how we are nothing without him, we have again reconciled him to us by means of humble prayer and supplication. Let us therefore readily spread all our sails, while this heavenly breeze continues to blow, lest this prosperous gale should shortly die away, or the storm come on, and so our failing to the fair haven of salvation be intercepted.

CXIV. *Fifthly*, It his also expedient, that we *renew* our *covenant* with God, and *those promises* by which we formerly bound ourselves to the sincere observance of his commandments; frequently saying, " I have sworn, and I will perform it, that I will keep thy righteous judgments," Pf. cxix. 106. It was an excellent advice of Epictetus apud Arrianum. Lib. i. c. 14. You ought to swear to God, as soldiers to their general. And to what are you to swear? That you will always obey him, never accuse him, nor find fault with whatever he is pleased to bestow, &c. And certainly that oath being thus renewed, if no other advantage attend it, will be of use, 1st, To restrain the soul from sin, by being put in mind of its late promise. 2d, To quicken its indolence into zeal; 3d, To raise it when fallen, and teach it to mourn for its sins, with more than ordinary bitterness, especially as the guilt of treachery and perjury is added to all the rest.

CXV. *Sixthly*, Holiness is greatly promoted, if by a careful and frequent *examination of conscience*, you recollect your deeds and words, nay and your very thoughts, that, with shame and sorrow, you may confess to God, what you have done, either altogether wrong, or not sufficiently right, and endeavour to reform for the time to come ; or if, by glorifying God for what you have done well, and rejoicing in the testimony of a quiet conscience, you are animated with chearfulness, to pursue that course of religion, you have entered upon. David declares, that he acted in this manner, to the great improvement of holiness. Pf. cxix. 59. " I thought on *my* ways, and turned my feet unto thy testimonies."

CXVI. The heathens themselves have recommended this examination of conscience, and if they made not a false profession, were not negligent in the practice of it. Antonin. Lib. 5. §. 31. " Recollect with thyself, how thou hast hitherto behaved towards the Gods, thy parents, brethren, wife, &c. Whether thou hast commited any thing towards any of them, either in deed or even word, which did not become you, Lib. 8. §. 2. In every action ask thyself, how far is this proper for me, may I not have cause to repent of it ? Seneca Lib. 3. de Ira, c. 36. The foul is to be called to a daily account. This SEXTIUS did, at the close of the day, when, before he went to sleep, he would ask his foul ; What evil of thine hast thou cured to day ? What vice hast thou resisted ? In what respect art thou become better ?—what therefore can be more excellent than this practice of convassing the whole day ? What sleep is that which ensues on the review of ones self ? How calm, how excellent and free, when the foul is either commended, or admonished, and a secret spy and censor of herself takes cognizance of her manners ?" As to what Seneca adds concerning himself, the reader may see in the author. It is all excellent and divine. But the chosen people of God are to endeavour not to be put to the blush in this respect by the heathen.

CXVII. *To conclude* (for should I expatiate on every particular, this chapter would swell to a large volume), whoever would make progress in holiness, must willingly and thankfully suffer admonition and reproof. *It is peculiar to God and above human nature, never to commit sin,* said Gregory Nazianzen formerly, *Orat.* 15. *in plagam grandinis.* But to cure this evil, no remedy is more salutary than prudent and friendly admonition. " As an ear-ring of gold, and an ornament of fine gold, so is a wise reprover upon an obedient ear," Pro. xxv. 12. Hence faithful reproof is acceptable to the godly. " Let the righteous smite me, it shall be a kindness ; and let him reprove me, it shall be an excellent oil, which shall not break my head ; for yet my prayer also shall be in their calamities," Pf. cxli. 5. It was finely spoken by whoever he was, whether Gregory Nazianzen

uzen or Methodius (for the author is not agreed on, as Gataker has observed on M. Antonine, Lib. 6, §. 21), " I think it a greater happiness to be reproved, than to reprove, as it is much greater for ones self to be delivered from evil, than, to deliver another."

CXVIII. There can be no doubt, but whoever carefully walks in this way, shall make very great progress in sanctification, and daily arrive more and more at a nearer conformity to the pattern set before him. However we are not to imagine, that ever any one, in this life, can attain to that perfection, which the law of God requires, that being without all sin, he should wholly employ himself in the service of God with that purity, that intenseness of all his powers, that the divine holiness itself could find nothing in him, but what was agreeable to it. The contrary is evident, 1st, From express testimonies of scripture, in which it is asserted, that none liveth, who sinneth not, stumbleth and falls not, 1 Kings viii. 46. Eccl. vii. 28. Prov. xx. 9. Jam. iii. 2. 1 John i. 8. 2dly, From the humble and sincere confession of the saints, who every where own their blemishes and failings, Psa. xix. 12. Rom. vii. 18, 17. Phil. iii. 13, 14. Isa. lxiv. 6. 3dly, From an induction of particular examples. For there are none, even of the most excellent among the saints, whose actions are more largely described, but have also some blemishes recorded, which in some measure, throw a shade on the light of the most shining virtues. These things are more notorious than need to be repeated here: nor do we with pleasure mention them. So far are we from taking any delight in the infirmities of the most excellent men of God, or wishing to detract from their heroic virtues, when we sometimes speak of their faults, that on the contrary, we have an inward horror at the remembrance of them, and deservedly tremble at the consideration of our own weakness, because, the latchets of their shoes we are not worthy to loose.

CXIX. The principle and proper cause of this imperfection is to be found in ourselves. And is the still indwelling flesh, or corruption which, though really subdued by the efficacy of the Spirit, with respect to its reign, Rom. vi. 14. yet vexes the godly; and, as that unhappy incumbrance retarded * Atalanta

---

* For the benefit of the common English reader, I would observe, that Witsius seems here to refer, to the fabulous story of Atalanta the daughter of Schœnus king of the island Scyrus, who being wearied with the importunity of her suitors, consented to have the man that could out run her; but on this condition, that he was to die who lost the race. This being the fate of several, others were discouraged. But Hippomanes receiving three golden apples, ventured to run with her, and at proper times, when she was like to get the start of him, threw the apples, which she stooping to gather, lost the race.

lanta, fo alfo believers are retarded by this corruption in their Chriftian race! while the flefh continually lufts againft the fpirit, it hinders the elect from chearfully performing what otherwife they would earneftly defire to do, Gal. v. 17. Rom. vii. 15, 16. By the Spirit the renewed man certainly tends upwards: but the flefh foon with great ftruggling pulls him down again, like a heavy ftone tied to the feet of one of the fowls of heaven. With a courageous boldnefs believers enter upon all the exercifes of every virtue or grace, Pfa. cxix. 128. Acts xxiv. 26. and while they go on in all the ftrength of the Lord their God, Pfa. lxxi. 16. they undertake what far furpaffes the capacity and power of natural men, and thus, at a great pace, they prefs forward to perfection, like thofe who hunt down fome wild beaft in hopes to poffefs it, Phil. iii. 14. But inherent corruption, innate perverfenefs, heightened by fo many vicious acts, " the fin that eafily befets us," Heb. xii. 1. again fpoils and taints all. And this abides in man till his death: *It dwells, but reigns not, abides, but neither rules nor prevails; in fome meafure it is rooted out, but not quite expelled: caft down, but not entirely caft out,* as Bernard elegantly fpeaks in Pf. xc. Serm. x. According to the law of Mofes, when an earthen veffel was once ceremonially unclean it remained impure, till it was broken, Lev. xi. 33. Such earthen veffels are we, 2 Cor. iv. 7. for after we are defiled with fin, we do not attain to perfect purity, till the earthen veffel of our body is broken by the ftroke of death.

CXX. When the Apoftle fpeaks of the conflict between the fpirit and the flefh in a fanctified perfon, we are not to think, that the conflict arifes only from this, that the *glandula pinealis* can be impelled on one fide by the foul, on the other by the animal fpirits, and that thefe two impulfions are often contrary; fo that the flefh may be then judged to prevail, when the animal fpirits prove the ftronger; but the fpirit to predominate, when the foul, by a determinate judgment, proves more powerful in the impulfions of that pineal gland. For though it is a very great truth, that the inordinate motions of the animal fpirits excite very many vicious thoughts and appetites in the foul, yet the conflict of the fpirit with the flefh does not confift in that of the foul with the body. As new habits are put into the foul by the fanctifying Spirit; fo there are likewife in the foul itfelf the remains of the old man: thefe are two diftinct principles of action. But fometimes when the man is left to himfelf, he may think, reafon, defire, from that vicious principle; at other times, he is excited by the Spirit of God, he acts from a new principle

principle of grace, which has not yet expelled all the power of sin; from these opposite principles, and their reciprocal actings arises that warfare we are speaking of, which is principally carried in the soul itself; according as it is either depressed to earth by inherent corruption, or raised to heaven by a principle of a more noble life, produced by the Spirit. And when the Scripture speaks of flesh, it does not mean the body of man, but all the remaining corruption, which in its measure doth really abide in part in the body and its members, while it still has its principal seat in the soul itself, which is the proper immediate subject both of virtue and vice. The enemies therefore in this combat, are not soul and body, but the grace of the sanctifying Spirit, and the remains of natural corruption.

CXXI. But known to God are the reasons of his conduct, in dispensing the operations of the Spirit of grace in believers, so that the remains of the flesh are not entirely expelled in this life, For, 1st, He would by this, shew the difference between earth and heaven, the time of warfare and of triumph, the place of toil and of rest, that we may the more earnestly long for our translation out of this valley of sin and misery into the heavenly country, where every thing shall be made perfect; and may with open arms, embrace death, which will bring us to that perfection, crying out with the apostle; "O wretched man that I am who shall deliver me from the body of this death?" Rom vii. 24.

CXXII. 2dly, He is willing to exercise and accustom his people to patience, humility, and sympathy or fellow-feeling. As in old time, he suffered the Amorites and Philistines to remain in the land of Canaan, for the exercise of the Israelites; to prevent their growing indolent through a slothful ease, and dissolved in too much prosperity and quiet: so in like manner, he exercises his saints by the remains of the flesh. For, nothing teaches them to think more lowly of themselves than a daily sense of so many infirmities: nothing is more effectual to bring them to patience, than the constant assaults of those most wicked enemies, from whom, to their considerable grief, they have often experienced blows and wounds. Nothing, in fine, is more adapted to render them more sympathising, with respect to the failings of others, both in judging concerning their state, and their general conversation, than the consciousness of their own defects, Gal. vi. 1.

CXXIII. 3dly, By this means he strongly convinces all that the salvation of his people is owing only to his most free grace. For who, that is conscious of his own infirmities, and daily

daily failings, but muſt be obliged to acknowledge, that he obtains life from God, not as the judge of merit, but as the beſtower of pardon? The rigour of the law excluded from the prieſthood the blind, the lame, the disjointed in any member, or thoſe, who had any ſuch blemiſh, Lev. xxi. 18. What then can we infer, but that the grace of the Goſpel is unmerited, which admits to the heavenly prieſthood, and does not refuſe acceſs to the holy of holies made without hands, to thoſe who have far worſe diſorders of mind? If, notwithſtanding ſuch imperfection, it be ſcarce, if at all poſſible, to baniſh the arrogance of merits out of the church, what would it be ſhould we teach the poſſibility of perfection?

CXXIV. 4thly and laſtly, It becomes the wiſdom of God to raiſe his people by degrees to the higheſt pitch of holineſs. As in the creation of the firſt world, he began with a rude chaos and indigeſted maſs, which in ſix ſucceſſive days, he faſhioned into this beautiful frame, till, having given the finiſhing hand, he reſted on the Sabbath, Gen. ii. 2. So, in the creation of the new world of grace, beginning with nothing, he gradually leads his people higher and higher, till on the expiration of this earthly week, on the dawn of the heavenly ſabbath, he crowns them at once with holineſs and glory.

CXXV. It cannot indeed be denied, that ſometimes the ſcripture makes mention of ſome, who are ſaid to be *perfect* even in this life. But it is to be obſerved, that the term *perfection*, is not always uſed in the ſame ſenſe. For, 1ſt, there is a perfection of SINCERITY conſiſting in this, that a man ſerves God with an unfeigned heart, without any reigning hypocriſy. In this ſenſe it is ſaid of Job, that he was תם וישר, " perfect and upright, and one that feared God and eſchewed evil," Job i. 1. In the ſame ſenſe, Hezekiah proteſts that he had walked before God " in truth and with a perfect heart, and done what was good in his eyes," Iſa. xxxviii. 3. 2dly, There is a perfection of PARTS, and that both *ſubjective* with reſpect to the whole man, in ſo far as he is " ſanctified wholly, in ſpirit, ſoul and body," 1 Theſſ. v. 23. And *objective*, with reſpect to the whole law, when all and every one of the duties preſcribed by God are obſerved without exception. Of this David was ſpeaking, Pſa. cxix. 128. " I eſteem all thy precepts concerning all things to be right; and I hate every falſe way." And it is ſaid of Zacharias and Elizabeth, Luke i. 6. and they " walked in all the commandments and ordinances of the Lord, blameleſs." 3dly, There is a COMPARATIVE perfection aſcribed to thoſe, who are advanced in knowledge, faith and ſanctification, in

compariſon

comparison of those, who are still infants and untaught : in this manner John distinguishes *little children, young men,* and *fathers*; John ii. 12, 13. In that sense Paul speaks of the perfect, 1 Cor. ii. 6. and Phil. iii. 15. 4thly, There is also an EVANGELICAL perfection, or with a veil or covering of grace, according to which, these persons are looked upon as perfect, who sincerely endeavour after perfection; God; for the sake of Christ, graciously accepting the attempts of a ready mind, and accounting every thing to be done, because what is not done is forgiven. The Apostle speaks of this 2 Cor. viii. 12. " For if there be first a willing mind, it is accepted according to that a man hath, and not according to that he hath not." Thus " we are complete in Christ," Col. ii. 10. his most perfect righteousness covering all our defects. However this is to be understood in a proper manner : for the judgment of God is always according to truth : he so judges of us and our actions, as they are : and seeing we ourselves and our actions are imperfect, he cannot but judge us to be so. This is what we would say agreeable to scripture, that God, on account of the most perfect obedience of Christ, graciously accepts the sincerity of his people; not less bountifully rewards them, than if their holiness was in every respect complete. 5thly and lastly, There is also a 'perfection of DEGREES; by which a person performs all the commands of God, with the full exertion of all his powers without the least defect, having rooted up every depraved lust. This is what the law of God requires. And this is that perfection which we deny the saints to have in this life, tho' we willingly allow them all the other kinds above mentioned. **•**

CXXVI. It is certainly true, that when God enjoins us by his law, to love him with *our whole heart, soul, and strength,* these expressions denote an absolute perfection, both of degrees and parts. Nor can he require any thing less than the most perfect obedience of man, even of sinful man, as we shewed; book. 1. chap. 9. sect. 11, &c. But when it is said of Josiah, 2 Kings xxiii. 25. " And like unto him there was no king before him, that turned to the Lord with all his heart, and with all his soul, and with all his might, according to all the law of Moses," this is to be understood in a certain diminutive sense; so as to denote his sincerity, and the beginnings of, and endeavours after a due perfection, and to signify God's gracious esteem of him in the Messiah. In the same sense, the Jews in the time of Asa, bound themselves by an oath to seek the God of their fathers, " with all their heart, and with all their soul," 2 Chron. xv. 12. All which are said to have been done, v. 15. But yet none will say that the Jewish people completely fulfilled all the holinefs that the law required, feeing the high places were not taken away out of Ifrael, verfe 17. And then who will imagine that the condition of an entirely perfect obedience was exacted of the defcendants of David, before. they could come to be partakers of the promifes that were given them ; yet this the words of God feem naturally to import, 1 Kings ii. 4. " If thy children take heed to their way, to walk before me in truth, with all their heart, and with all their foul." And that the commendation given Jofiah cannot be taken in its full import, appears from comparing it with 2 Kings xviii. 5. where it is faid of Hezekiah, " After him was none like him among all the kings of Judah, nor any that were before him. If thefe words be taken in both places in their full import, and are not reconciled by a favourable interpretation, they involve a manifeft contradiction. Wherefore it is evident that in both places there is a kind of hyperbole, or the commendation of both kings is not to be underftood abfolutely, but conditionally, in the order taken for the reformation of the public worfhip ; in which the one may be faid in a different refpect, to have done fomething more than the other.

CXXVII. We beg, indeed, in the Lord's prayer, that God's will may be done in earth, as it is in heaven, in which confifts the utmoft perfection of piety ; nor did the Lord Jefus prefcribe to us that part of the prayer in vain : and John fays, 1 John v. 14. " Whatever we afk according to his will, he heareth us :" But we cannot infer from hence the abfolute perfection of holinefs in this life. For the particle ai, does not in this petition denote an abfolute equality in degrees, but a fimilitude in the thing, and the manner of it, in the fincerity, readinefs, and alacrity of fubmiffion to the will of God, as well his commanding as his decreeing will ; for it is ufed both in the fourth petition, and Mat. v. 48. in the fame fignification. The godly are indeed allowed, nay are commanded to afpire to perfection, and to endeavour to come the neareft to it poffible ; it is alfo acceptable to God to exprefs that love of perfection in their prayers ; however feeing God has exprefsly declared, that he does not give his people abfolute perfection in this life, it is the duty of all to acquiefce in this difpofition of the divine will, nor are they allowed to beg of God, to grant them that perfection here, which they know he has not appointed for this, but for the other life.

CXXVIII. We very well know, that our Lord, Luke xv. 7. fpeaks of " one finner that repenteth, and of ninety and nine juft perfons, which need no repentance." But neither does this
favour

favour the pretended perfection of this life : for there is a twofold repentance. The first universal, whereby the human sinner who is estranged from the knowledge and worship of God,
and all true religion, betakes himself or turns to God, and to the
practice of virtue : the second renewed and particular, to which,
as a sacred anchor, the regenerate themselves are often obliged
to have recourse. And of this again there is a three-fold difference, For 1st, It is possible that they who are sanctified, may
fall into some grievous sin, which lays them under the necessity
of the greatest sorrow and a very extraordinary degree of repentance. 2dly, It is also possible that such may, for a time, fall
into a kind of spiritual faintness and listlessness, and for some
space continue in that *state*, which may expose them to very
many sins ; from which they are to rise by a renewal of repentance. 3dly, Should this not be the case, yet in the very best,
there are sins of daily infirmity cleaving to their actions, words,
and thoughts, from which no one who accurately examines
himself, will dare to declare he is free. Now let us apply these
distinctions to our present purpose. When our Lord speaks of
a sinner causing joy in heaven by his repentance, it is evident
he treats either of that first and universal, or of the renewed repentance from some more grievous fall, and a state not so commendable. This, he says, the just need not, because they have
already performed the first ; and are solicitously careful that
they be under no necessity of the latter ; yet he does not say
that they are free from all necessity of repentance ; for, though
perhaps there may be some just persons, who for a considerable
time are careful to be kept from more gross sins, or from falling into that sluggish state we have just described, and so not
to stand in need of those ways of repentance ; yet there is none
upon earth, who, on account of his daily failings, is not bound
daily to renew his repentance. In a word, what our Lord says
comes to this : That there is greater joy in heaven, on account
of great sinners when they are first converted ; or for the regenerate when returning after a shameful backsliding ; than
for those, in whom, on account of their constant practice of
a more strict piety, there is no such remarkable and conspicuous change to be observed.

CXXIX. It might here not improperly be asked, why a
greater joy is said to be in heaven for the conversion of one re-
penting sinner than for the constancy of ninety and nine persons in holiness ; seeing a greater good may justly cause a
greater joy ; as it is certainly better to have kept a steady course
of piety than to return to the right way after great backsliding.
I answer, 1st, That when our Lord made use of parables, and ac-

cording

cording to his cuſtom, ſuited himſelf to the capacity of his hearers, he ſpoke of divine things after the manner of men. But it is evident, that when any good comes of a ſudden, it cauſes greater joy than any other greater good one has for ſome time been in quiet poſſeſſion of; and that the recovery of things loſt more ſtrongly affects the mind than in the uninterrupting keeping of others. The ſame alſo in its meaſure is the caſe here. The angels doubtleſs rejoice, that the juſt labour after and preſs on to happineſs; but they have for a long time been reſcued from the ſnares of the devil. But when a wicked perſon is newly delivered from the ſnares he was in; that converſion, and the ſalvation of the converted, which was the conſequence of it, by how much the more it was unexpected, muſt alſo yield ſo much the greater pleaſure. 2dly, Here our Lord ſpeaks according to the old Jewiſh divinity. The Jews affirmed, " That when a Hebrew ſins, the angels weep:" our Lord ſays, that on the converſion of any perſon, the angels rejoice. The Jews ſaid, " The dignity of the penitent is greater than that of the perfectly juſt. And, in ths place where the penitents ſtand, there the perfectly juſt ſtand not." Which teſtimonies Druſius and Ludovicus Cappellus and Grotius, have long ago produced. The reaſon of which is this : becauſe it is more difficult to break off a cuſtom or habit of vice, than after being brought to a commendable courſe of life, to go on without ſtumbling. It yields a greater pleaſure when virtue is ſo very conſpicuous. 3dly, The glory of the wiſdom, power, and mercy of God, and the efficacy of the merits of Chriſt ſhine with greater glory in the converſion of a deſperate ſinner, than in the preſervation of thoſe who walk in the way of righteouſneſs. As therefore the devil is more enraged when that prey is ſnatched from him, which he imagined he would have held faſt for ever; ſo, in like manner the angels juſtly rejoice more, when their and the enemy of their Lord is mortified to ſuch a high degree. 4thly, And generally theſe are warmer in the practice of righteouſneſs, who are inſtigated by the ſorrow of a paſt life. An equable tenour of virtue is moſtly more remiſs; but they who are ſuddenly brought over from a very bad to a very good courſe, by the powerful arm of God, uſually outſtrip others by a quicker pace. They dread ſin more who were deeper plunged therein : have a more ardent love for religion, to whom its beauty has more unexpectedly appeared. And none prize the grace of God towards them more than thoſe who know themſelves to be the moſt unworthy of it. And it is not poſſible but this ſenſe of ſo great a love muſt kindle the moſt ardent flames of a reciprocal love. As is evident from the example of Paul, and

and the woman who was a sinner, Luke vii. 40—48. All which yield matter of greater joy to the angels.

CXXX. Seeing we have now made a frequent mention of repentance μετανοια, we will subjoin something concerning the proper signification of this word. The very learned Beza, either was the first or among the first, who observed on Mat. iii. 2. that the term μεταμελεια is properly never put but to denote a good; and that συμφερμος is always joined with μετανοια; but that μεταμελεσθαι is expressive of *a solicitude and anxiety after the doing of a thing* : for which the Latins say *pænitere* ; and that it is also used to denote an evil, though simply signifying a kind of solicitude, and δυσαρεστησις, *a displicency*, which makes us wish the thing that is done, whether good or bad to be undone, even though it be out of our power to correct it. Hence he thinks that μεταμελεσθαι is denoted by the Hebrew word נחם as μετανοειν is rather denoted by the word שוב, whence comes נשוב, *conversion*. Peter therefore having said, Acts iii. 19. μετανοησατε *repent*, immediately subjoins, και επιστρεψατε, *and be converted*, in order to explain the former. The same thing Paul does, Acts xxvi. 20. In this the venerable Beza has been followed by very many commentators, especially when they treat of the μεταμελεια, repentance of the traitor Judas.

CXXXI. But it may be doubted, whether there is any solid ground for this distinction. For it can neither be deduced from the etymology of either of these terms, nor confirmed by the authority of approved authors, nor proved from the constant style of Scripture, nor in fine, concluded from the corresponding Hebrew terms, which we are now to shew in order.

CXXXII. As to their etymology, μετανοεω is a word compounded of μετα, *after* and νοεω, *I understand*, and as *Henr.* Stephanus in his Thesaurus translates it, *postintelligo*, and thus it is opposed to the term προνοεω *ante intelligo*. Very elegantly says, Clemens Alexandrinus Stromat. lib. 2. Ει εφ' οις ημαρτε μετανοησεν, ὁ συνεσιν λαβων, εφ' οις εσταισε, και μετεγνω, οπερ εστι, μετα ταυτα εγνω. Βραδεια γαρ γνωσις μετανοια. " If he has repented of his sins, recollect in what he has offended, and acknowledged it, that is, afterwards known it : for μετανοια is a slow kind of knowledge that comes after something is done." But μεταμελεια, according to its etymology, signifies " solicitude, after having committed, or omitted any thing." And thus μετανοια, which is properly an act of the *understanding*, reflecting on itself and its actions, in order of nature, goes before μεταμελεια, which rather belongs to the *will* and *affections*.

CXXXIII. Both words are so used in the best authors, as indifferently to denote an after-sorrow of mind, whether in good

or

or in evil. Hesychius explains μεταμελεῖσθαι, by μετανοεῖν. Suidas in like
manner μεταμέλει, μετανοεῖ. And in the *Etymologicum magnum*,
μεταμέλομαι, μετανοῶ, μεταγινώσκω are used promiscuously. *Gomarus*
on Mat. xi. 20. adduces a remarkable passage from Plutarch,
'περι ευθυμιας, where he varies the terms, μεταμελεία and μετανοία, as
words of the same signification, and describes μετανοια, as δακνο-
μενην, συν αισχυνη της ψυχης, και κολαζομενην ὑφ' αυτης ; *remorse and
torture to itself with shame of soul*: which the venerable Beza will
have to be appropriated to μεταμελεία. Nay, I have observed
instances, where μετανοια denotes a simple displicency ; as in
Marc Antonin. lib. 8. §. 2 ; καθ ἑκαστην πραξιν ερωτα σεαυτον, πως
μοι αυτη εχει, μη μετανοησω επι αυτη ;" In every action, ask thyself, how
it affects me, shall I have reason to repent it ?" Ibid. §. 10. η μετανοια εστιν επιληψις τις εαυτου, ως χρησιμον τι παρεικότος : *repentance is a
kind of reprehension of ourselves, as having omitted something useful*.
On the contrary, μεταμελεια is sometimes of the same signification with επιφρονησις, *amendment*.   In which sense Plutarch said
παντη γης 'η μεταμελεια συντομα δαιμων, *amendment is quite a salutary
genius*.

CXXXIV. Nor does the scripture use of these words differ.
For even their μεταμελεια sometimes denotes a sincere repentance ; as Mat. xxi. 29. υστερον δε μεταμεληθεις απηλθε, *but afterwards
he repented and went :* and verse 32. where our Lord upbraided
the Jews for not having true repentance, says : ὑμεις δε ιδοντες 'υ
μετεμεληθητε υστερον, τω πιστευσαι 'αυτω, *and ye when ye had seen it, repented not afterwards, that ye might believe him.*   Where μεταμελεισθαι answers to John's invitation, expressed by μετανοειν. And
on the contrary, μετανοια sometimes signifies mere sorrow. Thus
Christ, Luke xvii. 3. treating of some degree of sorrow, for of-
fending a brother, says, εαν μετανοηση, *if he repent*, and verse 4. if
he shall say, μετανοω, *I repent*, I could wish it undone. And
Mat. xiii. 41. μετανοια, is affirmed of the Ninevites, and their repentance was external only, not internal ; civil, not spiritual ;
temporary, not persevering.

CXXXV. Besides, it is not universally true, that μεταμελεια
answers to the Hebrew נחם ; and μετανοια to שוב.   For tho' perhaps the Syriac interpreter of the New Testament renders
μετανοειν constantly by תוב ; yet the Septuagint promiscuously
translate נחם by μεταμελεισθαι or μετανοειν.   I shall single a few examples of each out of many ; as, 1 Sam. xv. 35. *and the Lord
repented* (נחם) *that he made Saul king.*   The LXX. και κυριος μετε-
μεληθη.   In verse 29. of the same chapter, נחם לא: the LXX.
ουδε μετανοησει, *nor will he repent,* Again, Ps. cx. 4. נחם ולא: the
LXX. και 'υ μεταμεληθησονται, *and will not repent.*   On the contrary,

τραте, Joel. ii. 14, שוב נחם : the LXX. 'επιτρέψω και μετανοήσω, _he will return and repent._ In like manner, John iii. 9. Jer. iv. 28: and viii. 6. and xxxi. 19. and in very many other places, they have translated נחם by μετανοεῖν. Whence it is evident, they thought these Greek words were synonymous.

CXXXVI. To conclude, it cannot be proved from Acts iii. 19. or Acts xxvi: 20. that μετάνοια constantly answers to נחם, as the contrary may be deduced from these passages. For επιστρέψατε expresses the Hebrew שוב, as we just shewed from Joel ii. 14: As μετάνοια properly denotes the act of the soul recollecting its own actings, so in the order of nature, it does before conversion, and is justly presupposed thereto by Peter and Paul. Let these hints therefore suffice concerning these words: If any desire more, they may consult Grotius on Mat. xxvii. 3. Scultetus, Exercitat. Evangelic. c. 19. Gataker advers: Miscel. c. 29. and Suiceri Thesaurus.

---

# CHAP. XIII.

## Of * Conservation:

I. THOSE to whom God has freely given faith and holiness, he likewise keeps with such solicitous care, that it is impossible for any true believer totally and finally to fall away from that holiness when once it is begun, and thereby forfeit the salvation appointed for him. " The Lord is faithful, who shall STABLISH you, and keep you from evil," 2 Theff. iii. 3.

II. CONSERVATION " is a gracious work of God, whereby he so keeps the elect, the redeemed, the regenerated, the faithful and the sanctified, though in themselves weak and apt to fall away, internally by the most powerful efficacy of his Spirit, externally by the means which he has wisely appointed for that purpose, that they shall never quite lose the habits of those graces once infused into them, but be certainly brought, by a stedfast perseverance, to eternal salvation."

III. They whom God preserves and enables to persevere, are ELECTED persons, or persons appointed, by the immutable counsel

* Though this word is not very commonly used, yet it is of a very extensive signification, and conveys to us the idea, not only of perseverance, but of the manner of it, viz. their preservation by God. Accordingly our author makes perseverance, a branch of conservation.

counsel of God, not only to some external communion of a
national covenant, Deut. viii. 6. but to an internal glory, Eph. i.
4, 5. They are REDEEMED by Chrift : not only bought by *that
mafter of a family*, who obtains very great, tho', only common
benefits for fome, and takes them into his family in the capacity
of fervants ; who, *in that great houfe*, are at length found to be
" veffels to difhonour," 2 Tim. ii. 20; of whom Peter fpeaks,
2 Pet. ii. 1. but alfo redeemed from the bondage of fin, by the
precious blood of Chrift the Lord, 1 Pet. i. 18. 19. They are
REGENERATED ; who have not only acquired a name to live,
whereby they impofe on themfelves and others, by fome external actions, which refemble the fpiritual life, Rev. iii. 1.
but who have a prinicple of fpiritual life implanted in them
by the Spirit of life which is in Chrift, Rom. viii. 2. They
are FAITHFUL, or believers having not only that faith which
confifts in a bare affent, nor that called temporary by our Lord,
and having no root ; but that which is unfeigned, 1 Tim. i. 5.
which influences the whole foul, and, being rooted in Chrift,
brings forth the fruits of holinefs. They are SANCTIFIED, not
only by a *federal* holinefs, which gives a right to the facraments
in the vifible church, 1 Cor. vii 14. nor by that external holinefs, whereby one has " efcaped the pollutions of the world
through the knowledge of the Lord and Saviour Jefus Chrift,"
2 Pet. ii. 20; while yet they ftill retain ther nafty cannine and
fwinifh nature, v. 22. but by *a true* and *thorough* holinefs,
whereby righteoufnefs and true holinefs, are brought into the
foul, Eph. iv. 24.

IV. All thefe things are to be well obferved, leaft any one
fhould object to us, that either the *covenant-breaking* Ifraelites,
who were really chofen to the communion of an external covenant, but diftinguifhed from thofe who were *elected to glory*,
Rom. xi. 7. " or the falfe prophets who deny the mafter who
bought them," and who are far different from thofe, whom not
the *mafter*, but the Lord not only *bought* for any kind of benefits,
but *redeemed* by his precious blood, 1 Pet. i. 18. " or thofe branches of Chrift, who abide not in him, but are caft forth and wi-
thered," John xv. 6. For though they may be faid to have
been in Chrift, as to the knowledge and profeffion of him, and
the external communion with the church, the myftical body of
Chrift, and in fo far with Chrift himfelf ; yet they were always without the quickening communion of Chrift, and the
nourifhment of his vivifying Spirit, or thofe temporary believers mentioned Mat. xiii. 21. whofe faith, though it may be
faid in a fenfe to be true, becaufe by a mafk of a feigned profeffion they do not counterfeit what they have not in their heart;

but

but fincerely profefs what they believe concerning Chrift; yet this is not that true faith eminently fo called, " which knoweth the grace of God in truth," Col. i. 6. and which alone confti-tutes the true difciples of Chrift, John viii. 31. or in fine, thofe who " trample under foot the blood of the covenant by which they were fanctified," Heb. x. 29.   For if that fanctification is to be referred to thofe profane men (which yet is not neceffary, as we have elfewhere fhewn), it is altogether to be underftood of a federal, a facramental; and an external fanctification, fuch as is alfo found in the dogs and fwine mentioned by Peter.   It was proper to premife thefe things concerning the genuine object of a gracious confervation, becaufe by this very means, we obviate many objections of adverfaries, arifing from the improper manner of handling this fubject.

V.   It is true, elect believers confidered in themfelves, and in their internal principles are weak, and may fall away; nor are they alone fufficent to furmount the affaults of the world and the devil.   Indwelling fin " which eafily befets them," Heb. xii. 1. ftill refides in their members.   " They are often tempt-ed by the flattering lufts of the flefh," Gal. v. 17.   The very habits of engrafted graces are exceedingly imperfect in this life; and frequently fome degrees of floth and drowfinefs fteals even up-on the wife virgins and the chafte fpoufe of Chrift, Mat. xxv. 5. Cant. v. 2. while the devil that cunning and powerful enemy, watcheth thefe opportunities of acting, that he might eafily bring them under his power were they left to themfelves alone. The perfeverance therefore of thofe, who are fo weak in them-felves, is owing partly to the *internal* principle of immortal life, which God has gracioufly beftowed upon them; and partly to the *external* fuperadded divine protection, guardianfhip, and fup-port, which the immutability of the divine covenant caufes to be perpetually, though not equally prefent with them.

VI.   That which God preferves in his people is the *the effence of the fpiritual life,* and *the habits of the Chriftian graces.*   For as to the acts, we really own it to be poffible, that a true be-liever may gradually fink to fo torpid a ftate, in which the ac-tivity of that excellent life may feem almoft to ceafe, and him-felf to be like trees almoft killed by a long and fevere winter. For the church of God has alfo its alternate changes of win-ter and of fummer, Cant. ii. 11.   Nor is that remarkable prophe-cy, Jer. xvii. 8. any objection to this affertion which experience has fo often proved, " He fhall be as a tree planted by the wa-ters, and that fpreadeth out her roots by the river, and fhall not fee when heat cometh, but her leaf fhall be green, and fhall not be careful in the year of drought, neither fhall ceafe from yielding fruit." For that promife is not univerfal, nor the lot of all believers in whatever fpiritual ftate they may be, feeing it is certain they are fometimes like a *bruifed reed*, Ifa. xlii. 3. which certainly differs very much from fuch a fruitful tree. Neither by *heat*, and *withholding of rain*, is here underftood *fpiritual drynefs*, arifing from reftraining that myftical influence which is the caufe of vigour in believers; for on the contrary, the abundance of that influence is fuppofed when this tree is faid to be planted *by the waters* and *to fpread out her roots by the river :* whereby he intimated, that it is not without the watering of the ftream that waſhes it, from which the root may draw its juice and fap. The words therefore of God in Jeremiah contain a defcription of a believer, who being filled with the grace of the Spirit of God, brings forth the fruits of righteoufnefs moft abundantly, in the midft of adverfities, and in the want of external things.

VII. We add, that it is poffible, a fanctified perfon may be guilty of fome acts, which are directly oppofite to fpiritual life, and to the habits of Chriftian graces. And experience, as well as fcripture has proved, that the moft eminent men of God have frequently fallen into grievous and atrocious fins; by which they not only deferve to be entirely deferted of God, difinherited and fpiritual death; but alfo actually very much grieve the Spirit of grace, wound the fpiritual life, and very greatly diminifh the affurance of faith: nay would entirely ftifle the principle of life, unlefs their guilt being taken away by the blood of Chrift, his quickening Spirit gracioufly prevented this their mortal efficacy.

VIII. Nor do we difown, that habits themfelves, as to the facility and readinefs of acting, are fometimes impaired, and fpiritual life itfelf fometimes undergoes fo violent a fainting fit, as to feem to be juft at the point of death. This is thought by fome practical writers to have been the cafe of Heman, when he complained, Pf. lxxxviii. 15. " I am afflicted and ready to die from my youth up: while I fuffer thy terrors, I am diftracted."

IX. When we therefore fpeak of confervation, we mean that God fo continues to cherifh, by his gracious influence, the principle of fpiritual life once ingrafted, and the habits of Chriftian graces once beftowed, that though they may be many ways fhaken by various temptations, and fometimes by very grievous fins, yet they are never quite extinguifhed; but afterwards refuming ftrength, and renewing faith and repentance,

                                                              they

they shall at last triumph over all their enemies, and continue stedfast unto death.

X. Neither do we assent to those, who teach, that the salvation of the elect is so secured, that death shall not come upon them, while they are destitute of faith; yet they think that the spiritual life is sometimes quite destroyed, but may afterwards be restored by some new and singular act of the grace of God; so that they admit a *total* defect of spiritual life sometimes in the regenerate, but deny equally with us a *final*. They are indeed to be commended, in that they refuse not the certainty of the salvation of the elect; but are to be blamed, in that they would overthrow the stability of faith.

XI. The absurdity of this opinion, not to mention other things, appears from this, that should the believer wholly apostatise from his faith, he would then no longer have any interest in Christ, to whom we are united by faith alone, would be brought under the power of the devil, become his child, and be entirely excluded the communion of God for that time: which would be effects and indications of the grievous wrath of God towards the believer under the guilt of great wickedness. But now if the wrath of God could be so great towards his children, while as yet believers, as to deprive them of the faith and right of children; I would ask, after they shall be altogether wicked and enslaved to the devil, what shall bring them again into favour, that being anew adopted and restored, they may obtain the gift of faith? For if he shall be so offended with his own children, as, for their condign punishment, to deprive them of life, and seclude them wholly from the communion of the Lord Jesus, in whom alone he can be reconciled (which yet is not at all suitable to the goodness and clemency of our heavenly Father) there can be no reason given, why he should again receive them into his favour, when they are neither reformed, nor yet lament their past sins, which they cannot do without the preventing grace of God. For on that account could they, who are thus disinherited, be received into favour? No probable cause can be assigned, but the satisfaction and intercession of Christ. But if that can procure the restoration of those who are already cast out of their Father's house, disinherited, and enslaved to the devil; shall it not rather procure that they whose sin is pardoned, shall never be ejected, disinherited, or brought under the power of the devil, but rather be corrected in measure by their most gracious Father according to their fault? This is much more probable, and far more becoming God.

XII. The whole adorable TRINITY concurs to that conserva-

tion of believers above defcribed. The FATHER has, by a
fure and immutable decree, predeftinated them to eternal falvation, which we proved at large, chap. 4. Sect. 14. feq. But
they cannot obtain falvation, unlefs they perfevere in faith and
holinfs. Neither can they perfevere unlefs the are fupported by
the power of God. Hence Chrift himfelf infers the impoffibility of the feduction of the elect, from their election,
Mat. xxiv. 24. " They fhall fhew great figns and wonders, in
fo much that (if it were poffible) they fhall deceive the very
elect." It is plain, that the Lord Jefus there treats of the
elect after their calling, and being brought to the knowledge
of the truth: and fpeaks, not of any feduction whatever, but
of that which is total and final; whereby, having forfaken
Chrift, they gaye credit to the moft falfe and lying deceivers.
He, moreover, foretels, that fuch would be the efficacy of
thofe falfe prophets to deceive, that they would not only feduce
thofe, who at leaft make fome flight attempts after faith, but
impofe on the very elect, if (as it is not) the power of any
feduction was fo great, as to overthrow the faith of fuch. But
that thofe words, *if it were poffible*, intimate a real impoffibility
from the fuppofition of the divine decree, is evident from this,
becaufe if it was poffible for any of the elect to be feduced,
which our adverfaries fuppofe; it would alfo happen, according
to our Lord's expreffion, that fome of the elect might be actually
deceived by the falfe prophets; which is contrary both to the
intention of Chrift, to experience, and all found reafoning.

XIII. Yet our adverfaries infift and pretend that the phrafe,
*if it were poffible*, does not always denote an abfolute impoffibility, but often the difficulty of doing a thing; and bring, for
that purpofe, various places of fcripture; as Acts xx. 16.
where Paul is faid *to have hafted*, " IF IT WERE POSSIBLE for
him to be at Jerufalem the day of penticoft." Rom. xii. 18.
" IF IT BE POSSIBLE, as much as lieth in you, live peaceably
with all men." Gla. iv. 15. " I bear you record, that, IF IT
HAD BEEN POSSIBLE, ye would have plucked out your eyes,
and have given them to me." Mat. xxvi. 39, " O my Father,
IF IT BE POSSIBLE, let this cup pafs from me."

XIV. But the anfwer is at hand; 1ft, If the thing fpoken of
fhould really happen, then the expreffion *if it be poffible*, would
denote, the great difficulty of executing the fame; if it fhould
not, its real impoffibility is then intended. Paul was in doubt,
whether it was poffible for him, at fo great a diftance, to be at
Jerufalem on the feaft day: which was very difficult, nay impoffible, unlefs he made more than ordinary expedition. It is

impoffible

impossible, considering the great perverseness of mankind, to live always in peace with all men. It was impossible for the Galatians, to pluck out their own eyes and give them to Paul, that they might become his, and be of service to him. They could not do it, without supposing them out of their senses, thus without advantage to any, to exercise such an act of cruelty on their own body ; and without supposing Paul to be out of his mind, who, for his own honour, would permit and commend it. In fine, it was impossible for that cup to pass from Christ, without his drinking it. Impossible, I say, not absolutely, in which sense Christ says, " O my Father, all things are possible to thee ;" but from the supposition of the divine decree, the suretyship he had undertaken, the prophecies and types by which he was foretold and perfigured. For, Christ was to make satisfaction to the utmost farthing. Which satisfaction is represented by his drinking the cup. 2dly, Should we grant our adversaries, what they strenuously contend for, that *impossible*, sometimes denotes what is difficult ; and *possible*, what is easy ; yet that sense would not suit this passage. For, should any transform our Saviour's words, thus : " They will shew signs and wonders, so as to deceive (if it might be easily done), the elect themselves ;" he would render that most wise sentence impertinent and foolish.

XV. *Secondly*, the Father *gave* believers to Christ, John xvii. 6. for his *inheritance*, and as the reward and price of his labour, Psa. ii. 8. But the Father will neither suffer the inheritance of his only begotten Son to be alienated, nor him to lose his purchase. Christ was secure as to this, when he said, Isa. xlix. 4. " Surely my judgment is with the Lord, and my work with my God :" and, John x. 29. " My Father which gave them me, is greater than all, and none is able to pluck them out of my Father's hands :" that is, neither Satan, nor the world, nor the flesh, which three are the enemies of Christ's sheep, shall ever have so much power, as to make them unwilling to abide under the saving protection of the Father : for, they cannot be pulled away against their will. This violent taking them away consists in the alone change of the will. Whence it appears, that these persons trifle in a matter of serious importance, who would have this condition understood, viz. unless they willingly depart from God. For, the tendency of Christ's discourse is to assure believers, that their enemies shall never be able to make them foolishly steal away from God. We are to attend to Christ's manner of arguing, which runs thus : " I give life to my sheep, nor shall they ever perish, because none can pluck them out of mine, or my Father's hands." But if our adverfaries anfwer be true, that they may ceafe to be fheep, and of their own accord, by their fins fly out of his hands, though not plucked out of them; then Chrift's reafoning would be weak and inconclufive. It is the greateft abfurdity to reftrict thefe words of Chrift to thofe who have died in the faith; and that the plucking them out of Chrift's hand, denotes the detaining them under death and condemnation, and preventing their being raifed by Chrift from death to eternal life. For, 1ft, Chrift here fpeaks of the fheep, which hear his voice, and follow him; the voice of a ftranger they hear not, but fly from him: all which belong to the ftate of this life. 2dly, It is evident, that Chrift here comforts believers againft thofe temptations, by which they are moft of all annoyed. But what believer is much difquieted by the thought, that when he is dead in the faith of Chrift, and his foul is received into the heavenly manfions, he fhall be detained under death and condemnation? Who once doubts, but his happinefs is then firmly fecured? 3dly, Nothing can be fpoken more indigefted, than that they, who have *died in the faith of Chrift, are detained under death and condemnation*; as the babbling apologift for the Remonftrants is pleafed to fay. What? are thofe who have died in the faith of Chrift under a condemnation under which they can apprehend they may be detained?

XVI. 3dly, The Father has, by an immutable covenant and teftament, promifed to take care, that the elect fhould not fall away from him to their eternal deftruction. But to doubt of the faithfulnefs of God, promifing and bequeathing by teftament is blafphemous. To this purpofe is Ifa. liv. 10. " The mountains fhall depart, and the hills be removed, but my kindnefs fhall not depart from thee, neither fhall the covenant of my peace be removed, faith the Lord, that hath mercy on thee." By which words, God not only in general declares, that he will faithfully adhere to what he has promifed in behalf of his children; but intimates the ftability of the covenant of grace, which he calls the covenant of peace, beyond the covenant of works. Certainly, God would have performed what he had promifed in the covenant of works, provided man had perfevered in his obedience; but in the covenant of peace he abfolutely promifes, that his goodnefs fhall not depart from his covenant-people, becaufe it was that which was to preferve them in holinefs, and fo to bring them to happinefs. And in this fenfe alfo, it may be faid of the new covenant, that it " is better and eftablifhed upon better promifes," Heb. viii. 6. namely, fuch as are abfolute, without depending on any uncertain condition

XVII.

XVII. The fame thing is more fully inculcated, Jer. xxxii; 38, 39, 40. " and they fhall be my people, and I will be their God: And I will give [put within] them one heart and one way, that they may fear me FOR EVER. And I will make an EVERLASTING COVENANT with them, that I WILL NOT TURN AWAY FROM THEM TO DO THEM GOOD; but I will put my fear in their hearts, that THEY SHALL NOT DEPART FROM ME." The very fame thing we have Jer. xxxi. 31, 32, 33. On thefe teftimonies we are to obferve, ift, That God here, in explaining his gracious covenant, propofes it by way of *teffa-ment*, while he abfolutely promifes, what he is to do, requiring to conditions to be performed by man. 2dly, That this cove-nant or teftament is faid to be perpetual, or everlafting, with an exprefs oppofition to another covenant, which depended on a mutable condition, broken by man, and abrogated by God, Jer. xxxi. 32. 3dly, That there is not only a promife of the conftant affection of God towards them, whereby he will ne-ver turn away from doing them good, to which promife fome condition might be underftood; but alfo of that fear of God whereby they fhall not depart from him. Which being fuppof-ed, nothing further can be required. 4thly, That God fays not, he will invite them by his word, by the greateft promifes, and by very many benefits to a conftant fear of himfelf, and thus, by moral fuafion, incline their minds, as much as in him lay; which the *remonftrants* repeat after the Socinians; but that he would actually and by the invincible efficacy of his Spirit, put his fear in their hearts; the confequence of which would be, that *they fhould not depart from him.* Could this al-mighty confervation of believers be poffibly promifed in clearer terms ?

XVIII. *Almighty*, I fay: for what we are *fourthly* to obferve is, that God exerts his fuper-eminent power in the perfor-mance of thofe promifes, for their confervation: that power, by which he is *greater than all*, as we juft heard our Saviour declaring. Of this Peter fpeaks, 1 Pet. i. 5. " who are kept by the power of God [as a garrifon] through faith unto falva-tion, ready to be revealed in the laft time." There Peter tefti-fies, 1ft, That the elect are kept unto falvation by the power of God. It is not therefore poffible, they fhould per-ifh. 2dly, He compares that power to a ftrong garrifon, which may not only bravely repulfe all external violence, but alfo eafily quell all commotions of inteftine rebellion; for both thefe are incumbent on foldiers in garrifon. 3dly, He fhows the means of their confervation, namely, faith, whereby we can-

not

not be preserved unless it also be preserved in us. Thus far of the Father.

XIX. Now let us take a view of the Son. And *first* consider, at what rate he purchased the elect; not with gold or silver, but with his precious blood, with dreadful horrors of soul, and tortures of body, with an accursed death, accompanied by the pains of spiritual and eternal death. Can any one think it probable, that Christ would suffer those whom he purchased at so dear a rate, to be taken away from him, and to fall into the power of another, and even of him, who is our most enraged enemy? What? Will not Jesus protect them, who are now become his peculiar property? Why was he willing to be at such expence for their purchase? Why are they called λαος εις περιποίησιν, *a people purchased,* 1 Pet. ii. 9. and λαος περιούσιος, *a peculiar people,* Tit. ii. 14. For περιποίησις and περιουσία are interpretations of the Hebrew word סגלה *Segullah,* which signifies a peculiar treasure, a thing of value, that is, a thing acquired by one's labour and expence, and therefore exempted from all foreign right and power, to be carefully kept by the purchaser, and its loss to be deemed a great detriment and damage. Elegantly, says Moses Gerundensis, on Exod. xix. 5. " Ye shall be in my hands a purchase, a beloved thing, which one puts not into the hands of another." See what we have more fully said on these words in *the preceding chapter,* sect. 7. Or can he not keep them, unless they also themselves are willing? But he who could act so powerfully by his inclining efficacy on their will, when beset on every hand by the devil, as with full bent of soul towards him to rest, by faith and love, upon him; why can he not, by the same inclining efficacy, cause them, after having fully tasted his incredible sweetness, to abide with him with a fixed purpose of soul? Nay, he is both willing and able to keep them, and actually does so: " Those that thou gavest me, I have kept, and none of them is lost," John xvii. 12. From what our Lord adds, " but the son of perdition," we are not to conclude that Judas was, in the same manner, given to Christ, as the other Apostels were; namely to be redeemed and saved. For, " Christ knew who were his." had long before known that Judas was a devil. John xiii. 18. and John vi. 70. It is therefore plain, that we cannot conclude, from the ruin of Judas, the perdition of those who are given to Christ to be redeemed, and whom he actually has redeemed with his own blood.

XX. *Secondly,* It is evident, that the Lord Jesus is heard by his Father in all things, especially in those things, which he asks is our interceffor, John. xi. 42. But he prays the Father for all believers, that *he would keep them from the evil*, or the evil one, John xvii. 15, 20. Our adverfaries, by a ridiculous fophiftry endeavour to fubvert this invincible argument, by affirming, that Chrift has no where prayed for the abfolute perfeverance of believers in the faith ? nay, would not have prayed fo earneftly for their perfeverance, had God abfolutely determined it fhould be fo. This affertion, together with the reafon annexed, is very rafh and extremely falfe. It is a rafh affertion : for, 1ft, Where in this petition of our Lord, is there the leaft fign of a conditional prayer ? It is not for us to frame conditions at our pleafure. And then, 2dly, What condition is underftood, when Chrift fays, keep them from the evil, or the evil one ? Is it this ? unlefs they become willing to join themfelves to that evil one ? But their confervation confifts in this very thing, that they fhall be conftantly unwilling to do that. 3dly. The remonftrants themfelves deny not, that Chrift prayed for the abfolute perfeverance of Peter, Luke xxii. 32. But that immunity from defection, which he prayed for in behalf of his difciples, he alfo prayed for in behalf of all who were to believe by their miniftry, John xvii. 20. The *reafon* they gave is moft falfe, becaufe it fuppofes that none earneftly prays for what he knows to be certainly decreed by God. The contrary appears in David, 2 Sam. vii 27. 28, 29. *for thou, O Lord, haft revealed to thy fervant, faying, I will build thee an houfe: therefore hath thy fervant found in his heart to pray this prayer unto thee.* And in Daniel; who, when he had found from the prophecies of Jeremiah, that the determined period for the Babylonifh captivity was feventy years, immediately *fet his face unto the Lord God, to feek by prayer and fupplications*, that he would do, what Daniel knew from Jeremiah, was certainly decreed by God, Dan. ix. 3. And laftly, in Chrift himfelf, who certainly knew, that it was a thing fixed and decreed, that he was to be glorified with the glory, which he had with the Father before the world was : and yet with no lefs earneftnefs does he afk for that in this very prayer, than he did for the confervation of his own people, John xvii. 5.

XXI. *Thirdly*, We have Paul's authority to affert, that Chrift Jefus built the church for his own houfe, Heb. iii. 3. But Chrift himfelf fpeaks of that building in order to fhew, by the ftrongeft reafons, its impregnable ftability, Mat. xvi. 18. " upon this rock I will build my church, and the gates of hell fhall not prevail againft it." From which place we argue thefe three ways, 1ft, The building or houfe of Chrift confifts

of " lively ſtones," 1 Pet. ii. 5. fitly joined together, and com-
pacted by that which every joint ſupplieth, Eph. iv. 16.    But
ſhould it happen (which our adverſaries pretend, it ſometimes
does) that ſome lively ſtones die away, and that the dead are
removed from their place, the work would be interrupted,
the towering walls totter, and the edifice of the greateſt artiſt
be diſgraced with many flaws.    2dly, A houſe built upon a rock
ſtands ſecure againſt all the ſhocks of ſtorms, ſtreams and tem-
peſts, Mat. vii. 25. But what rock is that ? Here let that of the
Apoſtle directly ſtrike out mind; 1 Cor. x. 4. " That rock was
Chriſt. Who is a rock ſave our God ?" Pſ. xviii. 31. " yea, there
is no (rock) God, I know not any," Iſa. xliv. 8. Chriſt therefore
is, at the ſame time, under a different metaphor, both the
architect and the foundation of this houſe, 1 Cor. iii. 11. And
ſeeing he his *the rock of ages*, Iſa. xii. 3. not only, becauſe he
is from everlaſting to everlaſting, but alſo becauſe he gives a
bleſſed eternity and an eternal ſecurity to all thoſe who are
ſpirtually united to him : it is not poſſible, that they ſhould be
torn by any violence, or by any ſtratagem from that rock, on
which they are built.

XXII. 3dly, What our Lord adds is moſt emphatical: " And
the gates of hell ſhall not prevail againſt it." *Hell*, in Greek αδης
*Hades* in Hebrew שׁאול *Shoel* in ſcripture ſtile, ſignifies the *place
and ſtate of the dead*, αδης properly ſignifies, τω αδη τοπον, the *unſeen
place*, in which they who are, do not appear: שׁאול denotes that
place, in which he who is, is to ſeek; whom you may ſeek, but
not find. This place the Scriptures ſet in the lowermoſt part,
and oppoſe it to the high heavens, Mat. xi. 23. Sometimes it
ſignifies not ſo much a place, as a ſtate, as Gen. xxxvii. 35.
where Jacob ſays, " I will go down שׁאולה εις αδην into the grave
(Hades) unto my ſon mourning;" though he imagined his ſon
was devoured by beaſts. In like manner, Pſal. xlix. 14. " like
ſheep they are laid שׁאול εις αδη in the grave" (Hades). Who
yet are neither laid in a burying place, nor carried away to a
place of eternal torments. It therefore denotes the *ſtate of the
dead:* thus alſo, Theophylact on Luke xvi. defines it, according
to the opinion of many, *the tranſlation of the ſoul from the ſtate
in which it appears* (namely by its operation), *into that which neither appears nor is ſeen*. Moreover, both the place and the ſtate
of the dead may be conſidered, either with reſpect to the body
or the ſoul ; and both are called *Hell* or *Hades*. Hezekiah
ſpoke of the former, Iſa. xxxviii. 10. *I ſhall go to the gates of*
(Shoel or Hades) *the grave:* and the ſacred writers very frequently. The profane writers place all the ſouls both of the
juſt

just and unjust in *Hades.* Diodorus Siculus explains the fabulous figment of Hades, by *the torments of the wicked and the elysium, or flowery meadows of the pious.* And Jamblichus says, *we shall obtain in Hades, as the wise poets assert, the rewards of virtue.* Grotius on Luke xvi. has collected very much to this purpose. Yet I do not recollect, that the Scriptures ever place the soul of the righteous in *Hades.* It therefore remains, that *Shoel* and *Hades,* when applied to the soul, denote a place of torments; and I can see no reason, why some very learned men should deny this. For, both Luke xvi. 23. and Prov. v. 5. persuade us of this; where Solomon says of the adultress, " her steps take hold on hell." Her steps are not directed to that which is truly life, but to [Shoel] the place of eternal misery, and Prov. vii. 27. " her house is the way to hell (Shoel): compare 1 Cor. iv. 10. and Rev. xxi. 8. where whoremongers are excluded the kingdom of heaven, and thrust into the place which burns with fire and brimstone. To this purpose also is Prov. xv. 24. " The way of life is above to the wise, that he may depart from hell (Shoel) beneath:" which the Septuagint translate, *ινα εκκλινη εκ της αδου αυτος,* that *declining from hell (Hades) he may be saved.* The wise man's meaning is, that he may ascend to the heavenly mansions, where true life is enjoyed, and never sink down to hell, the place of eternal death. We see then, what *hell* signifies in Scripture; namely, in general, the state and place of the dead; and more especially the state and place of souls spiritually dead, who are associated with devils.

XXIII. But what mean *the gates of hell?* I think it may be far better learned from Scripture than from the expressions used by the profane poets. 1st, Gates are the defence of a town, where bands of soldiers, and arms, and whatever may be necessary in sallies for repelling force, are usually kept in readiness. Hence we read of " the gates of the foundation," 2 Chron. xxiii. 5. which 2 Kings xi. 6. is called, " the gate of retreat," whither one may safely retire. 2dly, In the gates they formerly held courts of justice, Amos v. 15. " establish judgment in the gate." 4thly, In the gates was held the solemn assembly of the citizens, where they deliberated on difficult matters, and the elders gave prudent counsel; hence Ruth iii. 11. " all the city (gate) of my people doth know:" that is, the whole assembly, which usually meets in the gate; and Lament. v. 14. " the elders have ceased from the gate." The gates of hell therefore signify, 1st, All the power of death, and of him, who hath the dominion of it, that is the devil. 2dly, The bloody edicts past, and cruel sentences of death pronounced

ced, at the inftigation of the devil, by the princes and dreaded tyrants of the world, on the confeffors of the Chriftian truth. 3dly, All the craft and cunning of evil fpirits, exciting each other mutually to deceive the godly.

XXIV. It is not to be doubted, but thefe gates of hell have great ftrength and power; and yet they fhall not *prevail* againft the church. No poffe of the devil, though ever fo ftrong, tho' he fallies out with his powers from the gates of hell againft believers, no edicts of emperors, kings and princes, though never fo cruel, that are paffed againft them; no arts and deceits framed in the very council of hell, fhall be able to fubdue and force the faints from their faith in, and union with Chrift. And hence it is, that neither death, nor he that hath the power of death, can either bring, or detain them under his dominion. This to us feems to be the fulleft meaning of that faying.

XXV. *Fourthly,* Chrift unites believers to himfelf, fo that he is the head, and they collectively taken are the body; and every one in particular is a member of his body, Eph. v. 23. From this likewife we have a twofold argument, 1ft, As it is impoffible, any member fhould be torn from the natural body of Chrift, who is now in a ftate of glory; fo it is no lefs impoffible, that any fuch thing fhould befal his myftical body. Becaufe as Chrift, by the merit of his humiliation, obtained for himfelf a conftant immunity in glory from all harm; fo by the fame merit, he alfo obtained, *that he might prefent to himfelf* his whole myftical body *glorious,* Eph. v. 27. that is, the true church, and each fpiritual member thereof. But this he could not do, were any of his members to be wholly cut off. 2dly, As the animal fpirits, which produce motion in the members, by means of the nerves, inceffantly flow from the head to the lower parts; fo that power and efficacy, wherein fpiritual life both confifts and is exercifed, flows continually from Chrift to believers: and though it unequally moves them to produce fpiritual actions, he at leaft preferves that life, and will not fuffer it altogether to be ftifled.

XXVI. There is no ground to object the inftance of David, as if, when he defiled himfelf by his adultery with Bathfheba, and was joined to her, "he had taken a member of Chrift, and made it a member of an harlot, according to 1 Cor. vi. 15. For, 1ft, It is certain, that David was neither finally nor totally cut off from Chrift. For, the fpiritual life, which inceffantly flowed from Chrift, being exceedingly oppreffed, and almoft ftifled with the poifon of fin, did, in its appointed time, powerfully exert itfelf by the evidence of a fincere repentance.

Hence

Hence he begged of God " not to take his Holy Spirit away from
him," Pf. li. 11. intimating, that though he was indeed very
much grieved and 'oppreſſed, yet not quite taken away. 2dly,
Paul's words run thus; αρας ὀν τα μιλη τῦ χριſῦ, ποιησω πορης μιλη,
ſhall I then take the members of Chriſt, and make them the members of
an harlot ? But the verb αρω does not always ſignify to take
away, but to take upon ones ſelf, to attempt, or enterpriſe ſomething therewith. And ſo the meaning is, ſhall I take upon me
to put the members of Chriſt to ſo vile a uſe ? 3dly, The Apoſtle
does not ſay, that a perſon is ſo eſtranged from Chriſt by one
act of incontinence, as to become one with the harlot : but
ſpeaks of him, who is joined to an harlot; being as much inclined towards her, as a huſband, by the command of God, towards his lawful ſpouſe. In ſum, " he declares the natural
conſequence of whoredom, and the uſual caſe of thoſe who
do not deſiſt from it : but he does not limit the grace and
mercy of God; as if he who has joined himſelf to a harlot,
could not for ſome time, be continued in union with Chriſt.
Theſe are the words of Amas in his Anoiſynodalia, de perſever.
ſanct. c. 5.

XXVII. The HOLY SPIRIT, by an inſurmountable efficacy,
taking poſſeſſion of the hearts of the elect, which was the place
Chriſt had deſigned for him, and having vanquiſhed and expelled the evil ſpirit, keeps his throne conſtantly there alone,
and never quite forſakes his habitation; according to what
Chriſt ſays, John xiv. 16, 17. " And I will pray the Father, and
he ſhall give you another Comforter, that HE MAY ABIDE WITH
YOU FOR EVER; even the Spirit of truth, whom the world
cannot receive, becauſe it ſeeth him not, neither knoweth him :
but ye know him, for HE DWELLETH with you and SHALL BE
in you." This promiſe was not made to the Apoſtles alone,
nor does it treat of that effect of the Spirit only, by which they
were rendered infallible, in preaching the goſpel : but regards
all believers. For, iſt, it is propoſed as the fruit of our Lord's
aſcenſion to heaven, and of his ſacerdotal interceſſion ; the
benefit of all which redounds to all the elect. 2dly, He is
not ſpeaking concerning the Spirit as the author of infallibility
in teaching, which the Apoſtles and ſome other evangeliſts
had ; but as an advocate and Comforter, which belongs to all
the faithful. 3dly, They to whome the Spirit is promiſed, are
not diſtinguiſhed from other believers, as teachers are from
the common people; but from the world of reprobats, who
neither ſee nor know the Spirit, and conſequently cannot receive him. - Nor are we to think, that this continual indwelling

ing of the Spirit is fo promifed to the whole church, that every
member of it cannot claim it to himfelf; for, by thefe words
our Lord comforts every one of his difciples in particular; for
being grieved for his approaching departure, he gives them the
promifes of fuch a prefent of the Spirit that fhall never at any
time be entirely taken from them. But fo long as the Spirit of
Chrift dwells in any perfon, fo long it is felf-evident, he is
Chrift's nor can he belong to the devil. We indeed, allow,
that the Holy Spirit, when he is ill treated and grieved by believers, will fometimes depart, as to the influences of his confolations and their having cheerfulnefs in the fpiritual life; yet
abides with them as the fource of their life, and the band of
their union with Chrift.

XXVIII. Nor is there any reafon to object David's prayer,
Pf. li. 11. where he fo earneftly entreats, that God would not
take away his Holy Spirit from him; which he would not have
done, had he been affured, he was never taken from the elect.
For, 1ft, We have proved already, fect. 20. the falfehood
of that hypothefis; namely, that none prays fervently for what
he is well affured will be granted him. 2dly, After a believer
has fallen into fo horrid a fin, his faith and his full affurance
are ufually fo much fhaken, that he dare not always fecurely
promife himfelf the continuance of divine grace in that ftate:
hence thofe fighs, and anxious ejaculations of foul to his God.
3dly, When David prays, that the Spirit of God may not be
taken from him, it may be underftod. (1.) Of the fpirit of royal
wifdom, and military prowefs; of which he had feen a melancholy inftance in Saul. (2.) Of the prophetic fpirit, which had
before fpoken by his mouth, 2 Sam. xxiii. 2. (3.) Of that
operation of the fpirit, which fhould prevent his commiffion of
other fins in the adminiftration of government, whereby the
wrath of God would be kindled againft Ifrael. (4.) Of thofe
motions of the fpirit, whereby he now found his heart pricked,
and which he fincerely wifhed, that they might not be ftifled
again, but heightened by new acceffions, fo as to end in a true
and folid repentance.

XXIX. The cafe is different as to what we read, Ifa. lxii. 10.
" but they rebelled, and vexed his Holy Spirit; therefore he
was turned to be their enemy, and he fought againft them."
For he is not there fpeaking of elect believers, but of the rebellious Ifraelites. God had placed among that people his
Holy Spirit, who fpoke by the prophets and fanctified the elect.
The rebellious refifted that Spirit, rufhed upon him like wild
beafts, Acts vii. 51. by perfecuting the faithful fervants of
God

God and his dear children, * Ifa. lxvi. 5. In this manner then "they vexed his Holy Spirit;" who dwelt not in them, but in the prophets and other holy perfons; that is, they gave him occafion to do thofe things, which are the effects of wrath, and which are ufually done by him; who avengeth the injuries he has received: or; if we may explain it of the Spirit working in thofe rebels, then it is to be underftood of the convictions of natural confcience, excited by the Spirit; which they impioufly oppofed. Therefore it was, " that he turned to be their enemy," and rejected that people; and took their kingdom from them, and gave them up to hardnefs of heart: and fought against them, as well externally by his armies, which flew them, and deftroyed their city and polity; as internally by terrors and anguifh of confcience, Deut. xxviii. 65. All which is no proof of the total departure of the Holy Spirit from believers:

XXX: As that Spirit continually abides in believers, fo he is alfo in them as the fpring of eternal life. For, he is " the Spirit of life," Rom. viii. 3. His holy and comfortable energy is the life of the foul: for death reigns in a blind and depraved mind, John xvii. 3. " This is LIFE ETERNAL, to know thee the only true God, and Jefus Chrift whom thou haft fent." Spiritual life confifts in knowing, loving, revering the grace and truth of God the Father and of Chrift, and in the joy which arifes from thefe; which is called ETERNAL, becaufe, when it is begun in this world, it is carried on by the continual influence of the Spirit, and brought to perfection in the world to come. In another place it is called " a root within," Matt. iii. 21. " The anointing which abideth," 1 John ii. 27. " the feed that remaineth," 1 John iii. 9. " a well of water fpringing up into everlafting life," John iv. 14.

XXXI: The nature of that life, which is infufed into the elect in regeneration, is far different from that, which was in Adam in innocence, though even that was holy, and from the Holy Spirit. For, 1ft. In that ftate, man was left to himfelf, without any promife of the conftant inhabitation of the Spirit; fuch as, we have juft proved, the elect have now. 2dly, That caufe which firft produced this life, feems alfo to be the fame which makes them perfevere therein; but this life is implanted in man, who refifts it and takes pleafure in fpiritual death, and

fets

* Hear the word of the Lord, ye that tremble at his word, your brethren that hated you, that caft you out for my name's fake, faid, let the Lord be magnified. The author evidently applies this text of Scripture, to make it appear, that nothing is a greater evidence of rebelling againft and vexing the Holy Spirit, than the perfecuting thofe in whom he dwells, efpecially when they pretend to be acted by zeal for the glory of God, John xvi. 2.

fets himfelf with all his might againft God: it is infufed, I fay, by the invincible efficacy of the Spirit, which Paul has fo highly commended, Epft. i. 19. As therefore that efficacy of the Spirit, has notwithstanding, overcome and fubdued thof: that refifted and oppofed his operations; fo, in like manner, after he has once fettled himfelf in fouls thus vanquifhed and fubdued, he conftantly keeps the place he has once occupied: and fhould any thing arife, either from within, or from without, that fhould attempt to weaken it; the more violent the attack, the more carefully it will collect its whole force and prepare for a refiftance. And what fhould retard its progrefs, when its enemies are now vanquifhed; feeing nothing could withftand its power, in the beginning, when every thing was againft it?

XXXII. Moreover, 3dly, This life flows from the life of Chrift, Gal. ii. 20. " neverthelefs, I live; yet not I, but Chrift liveth in me." Moreover Chrift, by his death, has obtained, that he fhould live for ever, Rev i. 18: " I am he that liveth, and was dead, and behold, I am alive for evermore." But Chrift lives not only in glory with the Father, as to his perfon but alfo by his Spirit in the elect. The Spirit of life, which refiding in him as the fountain, flows from thence to his people, and he is the author of the fame glorious life in them, which fhall be perfected in their feveral degrees. And hence he argues from his own to our life, John xiv. 19. " becaufe I live, ye fhall live alfo." This life therefore of Chrift in us is different from the life implanted in Adam by creation. For, that was given him for the trial of his conftancy, and might therefore be loft. But after his conftancy was at length tried he might expect a confirmation in a holy and bleffed life, as was the cafe with the bleffed angels. Whereas the life of Chrift in believers is the fruit of his fatisfaction and merits, and therefore muft be everlafting and eternal, that he might not lofe the pains he had been at: and is to be compared, as to its duration, not with the life of Adam, when in a ftate of probation, but with that life, which he was to obtain, had he happily finifhed the courfe of his trial.

XXXIII. That expreffion of Paul is very memorable, which we have, Col. iii. 3. " ye are dead, " namely, to the devil, the world, fin and yourfelves, " and your life is hid with Chrift in God; " every word of this fentence is fufficient to prove the perpetuity of this life. *Life* here denotes that holy and bleffed energy, or activity of believers, which refult from the communication of the Spirit of Chrift, which begins in this life, and

is

is perfected in that which is to come. That life is *hid*, 1st, From believers themselves, who do not fully conceive the manner, in which the Spirit now worketh in them; and still less that inexplicable knowledge, that perfect holiness, that unshaken love, that unspeakable joy, which is ready to be revealed in the last time, 1 Pet. i. 5. 1 John iii. 2. 2dly, For the world. For as Christ who is our life is not seen by the world, so neither does the world know how we live in Christ and Christ in us; but reckons these mysteries of our Christianity, as a kind of melancholy madness. 3dly, From the devil; * whose mortal blows and victories can have no access to it. The life of God's children, like a most precious treasure, is laid up in a secret place; from which the evil spirit cannot take it away, neither by open violence, or secret stratagem. In this sense it is said, Psal. lxxxiii. 3. " They have consulted against thy hidden ones," whom thou protectest in thy bosom. This life is hid *with Christ*, to whose care and custody it is entrusted; " who is able to keep that which is committed unto him against that day," 2 Tim. i. 12. As Christ therefore, though invisible to the world, actually sits at God's right hand, and will be really revealed; so in like manner our life is with Christ, and is really kept for us. In fine, the same life is hid *in God:* that is, is contained in the decree and love of God, who, in his own time, will make it manifest, for what end he loved us in Christ. The bosom of God, is that most sacred repository, in which that treasure is kept safe.

XXXIV. The same Spirit, who is the author of this everlasting life, is the seal, wherewith believers are sealed, Eph. i. 13. The Apostle compares believers to *an epistle, written, not with ink, but with the Spirit of the living God*, 2 Cor iii. 3. Now that epistle contains God's testament. And whenever the elect have received the promises of that testament by a lively faith, then, in some measure, they have the Spirit to write them on their minds. Moreover, God ratifies that inscription with the stamp of his seal. That *seal* is the Spirit of promise, not only with respect to the extraordinary gifts, which formerly abounded in the church (for these were neither conferred on all, nor on true believers only, neither were they an earnest of the heavenly inheritance) but chiefly with respect to saving gifts or graces. It is called " the Spirit of promise," either because he was promised, or because it is his office to intimate to, write and seal the promises of the gospel upon the hearts of

* A thing may be said to be hid for safety and security, as well as for concealment, and it is with respect to this, that our author here speaks.

believers. A *fealing* is the impreffion of the image, which is
on the feal upon the thing fealed; whereby we both affure
the perfon to whom we write of the author thereof, and
more ftrongly confirm the contents of the epiftle or teftament,
fo as he may have no doubt about the truth of the thing. This
myftical fealing, therefore, by the feal of the Spirit, confifts in
the effectual communication of that divine light, purity, holinefs, righteoufnefs, goodnefs, bleffednefs and joy, which are
found in the Holy Spirit. Of which the firft lines are drawn
at the beginning of regeneration, and this is the writing on
the heart by the Spirit. But after faith in Chrift comes to be
ftrong and operative, all thefe things are confirmed, ftrengthened, incrafed, and more deeply imprinted by the fame Spirit;
and in this deeper impreffion confifts the fealing; by the view
and fenfe of which believers have affurance that they are the
children of God.

XXXV. Moreover, this fealing of the Spirit is a proof of the
unfhaken fteadinefs of believers, for the Apoftle himfelf with
good reafon, joins their eftablifhment with this fealing, 2 Cor.
i. 21, 22. " he which STABLISHETH us with you in Chrift,
and hath anointed us, is God; who hath alfo SEALED us."
For, 1ft, The promifes of the eternal teftament are confirmed
and ratified to us by that feal. The wonderful and almoft incredible goodnefs of God fhines forth in this matter. He not
only promifes the elect, that he will never depart from them,
but will fo order it, that they fhall never depart from him.
And he likewife ratifies the fame in the facred and inviolable
writings of both teftaments; but this is not all, for he alfo
engraves the fame promifes, by the finger of his Spirit on the
hearts of the elect. Nor does he ftop here: but he adds the
feal of the fame Spirit whereby they are affured in the higheft
degree, of the donation of thefe excellent promifes. 2dly,
This fealing denotes a firm and indelible impreffion of the graces
of the Holy Spirit. For, who can efface God's own feal, which
he has appended to his eternal teftament, and deeply impreffed
on the hearts of his people? 3dly, By this fealing, the fealed
are rendered inviolable or facred. Thereby God declares, that
they are his peculiar property, which he will never fuffer to be
alienated, Rev. vii. 3.

XXXVI. We cannot here omit that remarkable paffage,
2 Tim. ii. 19. " neverthelefs the foundation of God ftandeth
fure, having THIS SEAL, the Lord knoweth them that are his:
and let every one that nameth the name of Chrift depart from
iniquity." Chryfoftom, by the *fure foundation of God*, underftands,

*thefe*

*these stedfast souls, who stand firm and immoveable.* Which exposition is suitable both to this context and to the language of
scripture.   It is agreeable to this context; for the sure foundation of God is distinguished from those men, who suffered
themselves to be drawn aside from the doctrine of the true
faith, by the new doctrines and deliriums of deceivers, such
as were Hymenæus and Philetus.   And it is agreeable to the
language of scripture, where the believer is called *an* עולם יסוד
a foundation of ages, or " an everlasting foundation," Prov. x.
25. and " a pillar in the temple of God; which shall go no
more out," Rev. iii. 12.   To this also might be referred, Isa.
xxviii. 16. where Christ is called מוסד מוסר אבן יקרת, which
may be translated *a precious corner,* (corner-stone) *of the surest
foundation.*   For, Christ is the corner-stone of his church, which
being built upon a rock, has the surest foundation : therefore
the church of the faithful is the foundation.   And as none but
God can lay such a firm foundation, it is therefore called the
foundation of God.   " Ye are God's building," 1 Cor. iii. 9.
That foundation of God stands *sure,* and unshaken against all
temptations.   But what is the reason and cause of that stability?
Believers have it not of themselves, but from *the seal* of God :
of which seal a two-fold use is here proposed, 1st, To set a
mark on the elect, as those who are known to and beloved by
God, and on whom he imprints characters as 'his peculiar
treasure, which he highly esteems and choicely keeps, and as
testimonies of his dominion and property : of this it is said,
" the Lord knoweth them that are his." 2dly, To imprefs upon them the likenefs of that holinefs which is in the feal, that
is, in the Holy Spirit; whereby they are made to be diligently
on their guard against iniquity and defection.   To this purpose
is the caution; " let every one that nameth the name of Chrst,
depart from iniquity."   For, whoever has this law inscribed
within, so that it becomes the proper law of his heart, which
he frequently repeats to himfelf; and as from this he may know
that he is chosen and beloved of God, so he carefully referves
himfelf for God, to whom he belongs.

XXXVII. In the last place, this Spirit is ἀρραβὼν τῆς κληρονομιας
ἡμῶν, *the earnest of our inheritance,* Eph. i. 14. Grotius has learnedly observed on this place, that the word αρραβων (earnest)
is not of Greek, but Syriac origin ; but we say, it is of Hebrew
derivation, as appears from Gen. xxxviii. 17. where Thamar
asks ערבון, Arabon *a pledge of Judah.*   It is probable, the Greeks
had this word from the Phenicians, with whom they carried
on much commerce.   But *Arrabo* an earnest, or, as the Latins
express it shorter, *arra,* is a part of the price given beforehand,

hand, as an affurance, that the whole fhould afterwards follow. And Chryfoftom fays, ὁ ἀξιαβῶν μυχῆϛ) τῦ παντὸς *an earneft is part of the whole.* In like manner, thofe gifts of the Spirit, of which we have juft fpoken, are a part of the future happinefs, and of the principal thing that is to come after; and they clearly refemble that earneft, which the bridegroom gives to the bride in teftimony of her communion with him in all his poffeffions. For, who will not readily believe, that there is a reference here to the ceremony of betrothing? To which there is certainly an allufion, Hof. i. 21, 22. Moreover, that poffeffion, of which the Spirit is an earneft, is called " the inheritance of the children of God;" becaufe it is perpetual and never to be alienated from the poffeffors; whoever has it, has it continually from the firft moment of poffeffion through all the ages of eternity. Therefore we conclude, that it is not poffible, that they, who have once received the Holy Spirit, can forfeit the heavenly inheritance; becaufe otherwife, which God forbid, the Spirit of truth would be a falfe and fallacious earneft.

XXXVIII. Thus far we have fhewn, that the whole adorable trinity contribute their part to the confervation of believers: whence it appears, that their falvation is fecure under fuch guardians. Let us now further enquire into the method which God takes for their confervation. Firft, then, he employs that infinite and *fupernatural power*, by which he at firft infufed the beginning of the fpiritual life into elect fouls, fo that it may be cherifhed and maintained for ever by no lefs efficacy, than it was at firft produced. To this purpofe is what we have advanced, fect. 18. Concerning the power of God difplayed in this affair.

XXXIX. But as it becomes God to deal with a rational creature in a way fuitable to its nature, fo he fuperadds to that fupernatural power fome means, acting morally as they commonly fpeak, by which the elect themfelves are excited carefully to keep themfelves under God's protection. Here he ufes the miniftry of his *word*, which *is the incorruptible feed*, and " the word of God, which liveth and abideth for ever," 1 Pet. i. 23. He fets before them *the excellence of faith* and godlinefs, thereby *confirming the fouls* of his people, and *exhorting them to continue in the faith*, Acts xiv. 22. He gives *the promifes* of a great reward to thofe and only thofe who perfevere, Mat. xxiv. 13. Rev. ii. 10, 11. He fubjoins the threatenings of a dreadful vengeance againft backfliders and apoftates, Ezek. xxxiii. 13, 14, 15. and at times awakens dull and drowfy fouls with his chaftening rod, and reminds them of their duty, Pf. cxix. 67. " before I was afflicted

afflicted, I went aftray; but now have I kept thy word." Thefe
admonitions, promifes, threatenings and the like actions of God
towards the elect, are fo far from giving the leaft ground to
conclude any thing againft their perfeverance; that, on the
contrary, they are powerful means for their confervation.

XL. For, when God, by the power of his Spirit, excites
the mind attentively to confider thefe things, a certain holy
fear and trembling are produced on man, Phil. ii. 12. which
ftir him up to be diligently upon his guard againft the flefh,
the world, and the devil, and all their fnares, leaft, by being
impofed upon by their deceits, he fhould do any thing prejudi-
cial to his own falvation.    And fhould it happen, that he has departed from God by fome abominable iniquity; the fenfe of
the wound he has given his confcience, and which, unlefs
timely cured, muft at laft iffue in eternal death, does not fuffer
him to be eafy, till, by renewed repentance, he has returned
to God, and obtained with many tears, the pardon of his fin
from his infinite mercy.    And as every believer is confcious
of his own weaknefs, therefore with humble dependence on
the affiftance of divine grace, he is earneft in devout prayers,
for the continual influences of it, in order to his confervation
and corroboration; praying, according to our Lord's direction,
" Lead us not into temptation, but deliver us from evil."    And
in this manner all true believers, being excited and affifted by
God, alfo perfevere and preferve themfelves; " we know that
whofoever is born of God, finneth not : but he that is begotten of God, keepeth himfelf, and that wicked one toucheth him
not," 1 John v. 18.    And indeed whoever forms a right judgment of the vilenefs of fin, the torments of hell, and the greatnefs of divine wrath : whoever has had but the flighteft tafte
of the beauty of religion, the pleafantnefs of grace, the honour
of eternal glory, and the incredible fweetnefs of the love of
God; it is not poffible, he fhould not exclaim; " Lo! they
that are far from thee, fhall perifh; thou haft deftroyed all them
that go a whoring from thee : but it is good for me to draw
to God," Pfa. lxxiii. 2, 28.    This is " with purpofe of heart
to cleave to the Lord," Acts xi. 23.

XLI. Hence appears the falfehood of the calumny of our
adverfaries, that, by this doctrine concerning the almighty confervation of God, a wide door is opened to profanenefs and carnal fecurity.    That it is highly ufeful and effectual for the
confolation of believers, provided it is true, will not be contra-
dicted even by thofe who deny it.    But nothing can be effectual for the confolation of the faints, which, at the fame time

is

is not effectual for the promoting of holiness. For, in every
confolation, there is a demonftration of the beneficent love of
God towards the wretched finner, who is folicitous about his
falvation ; and the clearer that demonftration of divine love is,
and the more particular the application, the ftronger alfo is the
confolation. Befides, nothing is more powerful for inflaming
our hearts with love to God, than the knowledge, fenfe and
tafte of the divine love fhed abroad in them. Whoever therefore moft amplifies the powerful grace of God in his confolation, which impudence itfelf will not deny we do, prefents to
the faints the moft powerful motives to divine love and the
confequences thereof.

XLII. But let us more particularly fhow, that our doctrine
is far more adapted to promote piety, than what our adverfaries
maintain concerning the unftable happinefs of believers. And
firft, Our doctrine doth certainly moft of all illuftrate the glory
of God, which the oppofite tends to obfcure. We celebrate
the infinite POWER of the deity, whereby he can not only ref-
train our outward enemies from overthrowing our falvation,
but alfo fo fix the wavering difpofition of our will, that it may
not depart from the conftant love of holinefs : alfo his TRUTH
in the promifes of the covenant of grace, on which we fafely
and fecurely rely, being affured, that he who hath promifed,
will alfo perform : and his GOODNESS, whereby he does not altogether reject, or difinherit his children, or cut them off from
the communion of Chrift, even when they have fallen into
fome grievous fin, but by his fatherly chaftifements, gracioufly
recovers them from their fall, and ftirs them up to repentance
and his HOLINESS, to which it is owing, that he hides his face
from his children, when for fome time, they feem to give too
much way to fin, fo that he does not grant them familiar accefs to himfelf, nor the influences of his confolations, but rather fharply ftings, and thoroughly terrifies their confcience
with the fenfe of his indignation, leaft he fhould appear to be
like the finner, or could bear with fin in his own people without refentment : and the EFFICACY OF THE MERITS AND IN-
TERCESSION OF CHRIST, whereby he has acquired and preferved for himfelf an inheritance never to be alienated. In fine,
we celebrate the invincible POWER OF THE HOLY SPIRIT who fo
preferves his myftical temple, that it neither can be deftroyed
nor be made an habitation of impure fpirits. But as the fum of
our religion confifts in glorifying God, fo that which illuftrates the glory of God in this manner, does moft of all promote godlinefs.

XLIII.

XLIII. But as the opposite doctrine separates the immutable bent of the free will to good, from the efficacy of divine grace ; as it maintains, that God does not always perform what he has promised ; as it will not grant, that God's children, when they fall into some grievous fin, are chastised with rods, but disinherited, and punished by spiritual death ; as it asserts, that the impetration of salvation by Christ may be perfect, and, in every respect, complete, though none should happen actually to be saved thereby, and that Christ was not always heard in his prayers ; and that the Holy Spirit is sometimes constrained, by the mutability of the human will, to give up his habitation to the evil spirit ; the opposite doctrine, I say must, in many respects, be injurious to the power, truth and goodness of God the Father ; to the merits and intercession of God the Son, and to the invincible efficacy of the Holy Spirit.

XLIV. Secondly, Our doctrine is excellently adapted to allure the unconverted, seriously to endeavour after conversion and repentance : for, the more sure and stable that happens it, which is promised to the penitent, the more effectual is the motive taken from the consideration of it. The scripture every where dissuades men from searching after the good things of this world, and encourages them to seek those good things, which are spiritual, from this argument, that the former will perish, but the latter endure for ever, John vi. 27. " Labour not for the meat which perisheth : but for that meat which endureth unto everlasting life," 1 John ii. 15, 17. " Love not the world : the world passeth away, and the lust thereof : but he that doth the will of God, abideth for ever." And indeed, what can be more powerful to excite to repentance than this reflection ? " As long as I am distracted " with the anxious cares of this life, let my success be ever so " great, I can only amass perishing treasures, of which I may " perhaps be deprived in this very life, and the remembrance " of which shall certainly torment me in the next. But if I " diligently pursue the work of my conversion, I shall, from " the very first moment of that, obtain that love of God in " Christ, from which nothing shall ever be able to separate me " again : and the sooner I enjoy that, the sooner I acquire that " supreme good, which is possessed without any danger of hav- " ing my misery renewed."

XLV. But the opposite doctrine is adapted to procrastinate endeavours after repentance. For, when it is inculcated on a man, that a child of God by regeneration, after having for some time been engaged in the practice of holiness, not only may, but actually has often fallen away, and become a child

of

of the devil, been difinherited by his heavenly Father, and is, with greater difficulty renewed to repentance, the further progrefs he had made in holinefs : this thought will eafily be entertained by thofe, who hear of exhortations to repentance, that there is no occafion to prefs the matter of their converfion fo ftrenuoufly in their tender years, leaft perhaps, confidering the great inconftancy of unftable youth, they be overtaken by fome great fin, and their condition be far worfe than it was before : that it is more advifeable, to wait for thofe years (for we generally promife ourfelves long life), in which both our judgment is riper, and the mind ufually purfues, with more conftancy, what it has once applied to, enjoying in the mean time the delights of this world. Now, nothing can be more peftilential, than this thought, which yet this doctrine fuggefts.

XLVI. *Thirdly,* Our doctrine is alfo very powerful to confirm the elect, already converted, in the fpiritual life, and to quicken them to the conftant practice of religion. Which may be proved various ways : 1ft, All the arguments, which are raifed from the poffible apoftacy of the faints, are taken from the fear of punifhment, and the terror of dreadful threatenings; but thofe taken from God's moft powerful confervation, breathe nothing but his love and the incredible fweetnefs of divine grace. Moreover, it is certain, that the children of God," who have not received the Spirit of bondage again to fear ; but the Spirit of adoption, whereby they cry, Abba, father," Rom. viii 15. are more powerfully drawn by the cords of love, than driven by the fcourge of terror: for, " the love of Chrift conftraineth us," 2 Cor. v. 14. 2dly, All our religion is nothing but gratitude: but it is clear, that that perfon more effectually promotes gratitude, who proves by cogent arguments, that the happinefs beftowed from grace fhall be perpetual, by the help of the fame grace, than he who maintains, that though it be truly great, yet it may be loft. 3dly, It is equitable, that the better fecured the reward of our duty is, we fhould be the more diligent in the practice of religion. For, the confideration of the reward is among thofe things which render the commands of God fweet, Pf. xix. 10. But we affure the faithful worfhippers of God, from his own word, that from their very firft entrance on the courfe of fincere godlinefs, their reward is fure ; calling upon them with the Apoftle, 1 Cor. xv. 58. " therefore my beloved brethren, be ye ftedfaft, unmoveable, always abounding in the work of the Lord, FOR AS MUCH AS YE KNOW, that your labour is not in vain in the Lord." But our adverfaries, unhappily difcourage all diligence, while they teach, that we know not, whether our labour

fhall

ſhall be in vain or not, ſince it is poſſible, we may fall away, and ſo have all along laboured for nothing.

---

## CHAP. XIV.

### Of Glorification.

I. AS all God's works tend to his glory, ſo alſo to the GLO-RIFICATION of his choſen people. This doubtleſs is the glory of God, to manifeſt himſelf in his elect, to be what he is to himſelf, the fountain of conſummate happineſs. When he does this, " he is glorified in his ſaints, and admired in all them that believe," 2 Theſſ. i. 10. Believers exult in this hope of their ſalvation, which is ſo connected with the glory of God that it is called by that very name in the holy ſcripture : " we rejoice in hope of the glory of God," Rom. v. 2. Our glorification is called the glory of God, not only becauſe it comes from and is freely beſtowed on us by God ; but alſo becauſe the magnificence of the divine majeſty diſplays itſelf no where more illuſtriouſly than in that glorious happineſs, which he makes to ſhine in his beloved people.

II. Some would prove, that we are called to this by God, from 2 Pet. i. 5. " who hath called us to glory and virtue :" but the Greek runs, διὰ δόξα καὶ ἀρετῆς, by glory and virtue ; which may be underſtood either of our glory and virtue, or of the glory and virtue of God, and of Chriſt. If we underſtand it of ours, the meaning will be, that God had called us to communion with himſelf, by ſuch a clear diſplay of the glory to be revealed in the ſaints, and by the propoſal of true virtue, which is made in the goſpel, that none can be acquainted with it, but muſt be inflamed with a deſire after it. But it will be better to apply them to God, as Peter elſewhere calls them, τὰς ἀρετὰς τῦ καλέσαντος ἡμᾶς, the virtues (praiſes) of him who hath called us, I Pet. ii. 9. And ſome manuſcripts have διὰ δόξα καὶ ἀρετῆ, his own glory and virtue : and then the meaning will be, he hath called us by his own glorious virtue : or, what I take to be fulleſt, the Lord Jeſus hath called us by glory, while he preſents unto us a glory in himſelf, as of the only begotten of the Father, and by virtue, while he diſcovered a life full of every inſtance of virtue, which, as they are ſet forth in a preached goſpel, clearly ſhew, that he was the Son of God and Saviour of the world. And thus we keep to the proper ſigniſication of the particle *δια*, which I have not yet seen proved by any example, to signify the same as *εις to*. Indeed, the venerable Beza adduces Rom. vi. 4. where Christ is said to be raised from the dead, *δια της δοξης του πατρος*, that is, says he, *to the glory of the Father*. But such an explication is unnecessary; let us say, as the words bear *by the glory of the Father*. Which admits a twofold sense, and both of them very agreeable. As first, *by glory* to mean the strength, and glorious power of God, for sometimes the Greek word *δοξα* answers to the Hebrew עז, Isa. xlv. 24. Thus God is said to " have raised Christ *δια της δυναμεως αυτου* by his own power," 1 Cor. vi. 14. in the same sense. Again, if by glory we understand the display of the divine supereminent excellency, we will say, that Christ was raised by the glory of the Father, because it was for the Father's glory, that the only begotten and righteous Son of God should live a glorious life in himself, and a holy life in his members.

III. But whatever be Peter's meaning, it is evident, we are both *called* and *justified*, in order to glory; and for that end powerfully preserved by God. Paul speaks of our *calling*, 1 Thess. ii. 12. " who hath called you unto his kingdom and glory:" of *justification* he says, Rom. viii. 30. " whom he justified, them he also glorified:" of *conservation* Peter speaks, 1 Pet. i. 5. " who are kept by the power of God, through faith unto salvation, ready to be revealed in the last time.

IV. GLORIFICATION is the gracious act of God, whereby he actually translates his chosen and redeemed people, from an unhappy and base, to a happy and glorious state. And it may be considered, either as *begun in this life*; or, as *consummated in the next*. The *first-fruits of the Spirit*, Rom. viii. 23. who is *the Spirit of glory*, 1 Pet. iv. 14. are even in this life, granted to the children of God : not only, that by these they might comfort themselves in adversity ; but also that, from these, they might in some measure, infer what and how great that future happiness is, which is reserved for them in heaven; and that, having had a foretaste of that great reward they expect, they may be the more chearful, in the course of faith and holiness : now, these first-fruits consist in the following things.

V. *First*, In that most excellent *holiness*, which is freely bestowed on the elect, and was described, chap. XII. For, as there is the greatest filthiness in sin, it being contrary to the most just and righteous law of God ; and the greatest vileness and misery, as it makes man most unlike the infinitely glorious and blessed God. Accordingly these two things are conjoined, " they have sinned, and come short of the glory of God," Rom.

iii.

iii. 23. and fin is called " that fhameful thing, Jer. iii. 24.
On the contrary, in righteoufnefs and holinefs, there is not only fome moral goodnefs, in fo far as they agree with the law
and with God, the pattern of them ; but alfo an excellent
glory, in fo far as there is in them a refemblance of the moft
bleffed God ; whom Mofes reprefents as באדר בקדש magnificent,
glorious in holinefs, Exod. xv. 11. Accordingly, the image and
glory of God, 1 Cor. xi. 7. are connected. See what we have
faid chap. VIII. fect. 9. To fay nothing now about that incredible fweetnefs and boldnefs with God, which the con-
fcioufnefs of fanctification gives thofe who endeavour after it.
On which account David defcribed " the ftatutes of the Lord,
to be the rejoicing of the heart ; fweeter than honey and the
honey-comb," Pf. xix. 8, 10.

VI. Secondly, in that vifion of God,-with which he honours
the faints even in this life. We fhall prefently hear, that the
complete happinefs of the life to come confifts in the perfect
vifion of God. That vifion therefore, which is the privilege
of believers here, is certainly the beinning of that other. Now
God prefents himfelf here to be feen. 1ft, By faith ; which,
indeed is mere darknefs, when compared with the light of glory,
and in that refpect, is diftinguifhed from fight, 2 Cor. v. 7.
and faid to be the evidence of things not feen, Heb. xi. 1. yet it
is a clear and fhining light, in comparifon of the ignorance of
unbelievers, " in whom the god of this world hath blinded
their minds," 2 Cor. iv. 4. Hence Mofes is faid by faith " to
have feen him, who is invifible," Heb. xi. 27. By faith alfo,
" we all with open face behold as in a glafs the glory of the
Lord," 2 Cor. iii. 18. Nor does the faith of believers behold
the perfections of God, only in general, as they are in him,
but it likewife beholds them, as belonging to them, and
become theirs for the fake of Chrift Which certainly has
no fmall influence on our falvation. He that believes,
and by faith views God, and that, as his own, not only
expects, but already has eternal life, and through that very
" faith he is faved," Eph. ii. 8. according to that of our
Lord, John v. 24. " verily, verily, I fay unto you, he that heareth my word, and believeth on him that fent me, hath everlafting life." 2dly, God is alfo feen by an experimental fenfe of
his goodnefs, which intimately infinuates itfelf into the foul,
in the holy ufe of the creatures. So that he not only knows by
reafoning, that God is good, not only believes it on the authority
of infallible teftimony : but has the experience of it both by
fight, fenfe and tafte, while God himfelf, by means of his

creatures,

creatures, wonderfully delights the foul. To this purpofe is
the invitation of the Pfalmift, Pf. xxxiv. 8. "O! tafte and fee,
that the Lord is good." 3dly, He is feen ftill more *immediately*,
when he reveals himfelf to the foul, while deeply engaged in
holy meditation, prayer and other exercifes of devotion, as the
fountain of life and the fource of light; fo as wonderfully to
affect it with the immediate darting of his rays into it. This,
I imagine, was what David defired, when he fought " to behold the beauty of the Lord, and to enquire in his temple," Pf.
xxvii. 4. And this, I am apt to think, he obtained, when he
fung, כן בקדש חזיתיך " to fee thy power and thy glory, fo as I
have feen thee in the fanctuary," Pf. lxiii. 3. 4thly, Something
peculiar is at times imparted to fick and dying Chriftians, in
whofe *imagination* God fometimes draws fo diftinctly the bright-
eft images of heavenly things, that they feem to fee them before their eyes; nor are they otherwife affected, than if the
things themfelves were prefent before them. The nearer the
foul is to heaven, it is alfo enlightened with the brighter rays
of fuperceleftial light, flowing from him, who, being light itfelf, dwells in light inacceffible. Of which there are not a
few inftances in the hiftory of the life and death of godly perfons, and very many experiences offer in our daily vifitation of
the fick. This is a kind of defcent of heaven into the foul, before the foul is taken up to heaven.

VII. Maimonides, the wifeft among the Jews, feems to
have had fomething to his purpofe in his mind, when, in
*More Nevochim*, p. 3. c. 51. towards the end, he fpeaks thus;
- " The more that the faculties of the body are impaired, and
" the fire of luft is extinguifhed, the more is the underftand-
" ing ftrengthened, its light increafed the apprehenfion purified
" and the more it rejoices at what it apprehends: fo that when
" the perfect man is arrived at mature age, and juft approaching
" to death, the apprehenfion, the joy arifing from that appre-
" henfion, and the love of the thing apprehended, are, in an
" extraordinary manner, heightened, fo that the foul, as it were
" is in a ftate of feparation from the body, during the time
" of that high pleafure. To this our wife men had an eye,
" while they fay, that, at the death of Mofes, Aaron and
" Miriam, thefe three died בנשיקה, *in the kifs*, or *by the kifs*.
" For, fay they, what is faid, " fo Mofes the fervant of the
" Lord died there in the land of Moab על פי יי AT THE MOUTH
" OF THE LORD," Deut. xxxiv. 5. which fhews, that he died
" in the act of kiffing, בנשיקה. and fo it is faid of Aaron, AT
" THE MOUTH OF THE LORD, *and he died there*, Num. xxxiii.

38.

" 38. They also affirm of Miriam, that she died בנשיקה, in the
" act of kissing: but yet the Scripture does not say of her,
" AT THE MOUTH OF THE LORD, because, being a woman,
" that parabolical mode of speech was not suitable.  But the
" meaning is, that they died from excessive love, in the plea-
" sure of the apprehension thereof.  As to the phrase itself,
" our wise men borrowed it from the song of songs, where the
" apprehension of the Creator, conjoined with the supreme
" love of God, is called נשיקה, kissing, let him kiss me with the
" kisses of his mouth, Cant. i. 2." Thus far that learned Jew.

VIII. *Thirdly, In the gracious possession and enjoyment of God :*
when God himself, according to the promise of his covenant,
holds communion with them, and gives them not only to see
him, but also to possess and enjoy him in the manner we explained, Chapter X. section 33. and in this consists salvation.
" Happy is that people, that is in such a case ; yea, happy is
that people, whose God is the Lord," Ps. cxlv. 15. He may
justly glory of riches, who is admitted into the possession of
such great happiness.  " The Lord is the portion of mine inheritance, and of my cup ; thou maintainest my lot.  The lines
are fallen unto me in pleasant places; yea, I have a goodly
heritage," Ps. xvi. 5, 6. But that fruition of God consists in that
sweet and frequent delight the soul takes in him as its treasure,
Ps. lxxiii. 28. in its being enriched with his riches, fed with his
plenty, preserved by his power, directed by his wisdom, refreshed by his goodness, and, in fine, filled with his sufficiency ;
so that he knows of nothing he can desire, besides the perfect
fruition of him, of which he has now only the first fruits.
" Blessed is the man, whom thou choosest, and causest to approach
unto thee, that he may dwell in thy courts ; he shall be filled
with the goodness of thine house, even of thy holy temple."
Ps. lxv. 4.

IX. *Fourthly,* Such magnificent beginnings of glory beget
*all riches of the full assurance of understanding,* Col. ii. 2. and the
firmest certainty of consummate happiness, to be enjoyed in its
appointed time.  For when one has obtained the first-fruits
of the Spirit, and has so many and such evident signs of his
communion with God and Christ, why may he not say with
Paul ? " I know, whom I have believed, and I am persuaded,
that he is able to keep that which I have committed unto him
against that day," 2 Tim. i. 12. and again, " I am persuaded
that neither death, nor life, shall be able to separate us from
the love of God, which is in Christ Jesus our Lord," Rom. viii.
38, 39.  And indeed, I know not, whether there be any thing
                                                        more

more delightful and pleafant, can be defired in this life than that full affurance of our faith, which entirely calms the confcience, and delights it with the ineffable fweetnefs of confolations.

X. *Fifthly;* Thefe fo many and fo great benefits joined together, beget " a joy unfpeakable and full of glory," whereby Peter teftifies, " though now not feeing; yet believing, they rejoice," 1 Pet. i. 8. For that God, with whom they have fellowfhip as their God, is their exceeding joy אל שמחת גילי, *the God of the joy of their exultation,* Pf. xliii. 4. Nothing exceeds this joy in efficacy, for it penetrates into the inmoft foul, and is alone fufficient to fweeten the moft grievous of all afflictions, let them be ever fo bitter, and eafily difpel the greateft anguifh of foul: fo that the faithful martyrs of Chrift, who had tafted the fweetnefs of it, have gone, with joy and fongs of praife, to the moft cruel torments, as to the moft fumptuous feafts: Nothing is more pure. It does not difcompofe the mind, unlefs in a falutary, wife, and holy manner; that, having no command of itfelf; but being full of God; and on the very confines of heaven, it both favours and fpeaks above the capacity of a man, The more plentifully one has drank of this fpiritual nectar; though he may appear delirious to others; who are unacquainted with thofe delights, he is the more pure, and wife, and happy. Nothing, in fine, is more conftant; " everlafting joy upon their heads," Ifa. xxxv. 10. " your heart fhall rejoice, and your joy no man taketh from you," John xvi: 22. If it is not conftant as to the fecond effects, or after-acts, as they are called, yet it is fo at leaft, as to the foundation and firft act. For, though God, in this life, according to his infinite wifdom, mixes the communication of his fweetnefs with much bitternefs: yet believers have that in them, which proves the unexhaufted fountain of a joy fpringing forth at times, and of a delight, that is afterwards to continue flowing for ever. Nor does God at all times deal out this joy with a fparing hand: he fometimes beftows it in fuch plenty on his people, that they are almoft made to own themfelves unable to bear fuch heavenly delight on earth, and to fay with Ephrem Syrus; " Lord; withdraw a little, leaft the brittle vial of my heart fhould burft by the rays of thy favour darting too ftrongly." If God does fo great things for his people in the prifon, what will he not do in the palace ? If the firft fruits are fo plentiful, how abundant will the harveft be ?

XI. The glorification of *the future life* has again its feveral degrees and periods ; and is either of *the foul feparated* from its body before the laft judgment; or of *the whole* man after the refurrection.

surrection. We are here to take notice of the gangrene of the Socinian divinity; whose meaning it is hard to come at, these worst of hypocrites are so involved and dark. I shall give their own words, from the *compendiolum* they themselves drew up, and which the venerable Cloppenburg undertook to refute.

XII. *Their sentiments about the state of souls after death are these; that man by death undergoes such a* TOTAL DISSOLUTION, *as to be altogether* NOTHING: *unless that his spirit (even as the* SPIRIT *of the* BEASTS*) like a kind of wind or breath, returns to God, who gave it,* Eccl. xii———, *because that breath or spirit is a kind of* VIRTUE *or efficacy of him, to whom it returns———moreover, they infer from this, that souls after death have* NO SENSATION; *nay, do not indeed, actually* SUBSIST *in themselves, as persons do.* The whole comes to this; 1st, Since they contend, that the soul is not a substance, but a kind of virtue and efficacy, as strength, health, wit, skill, and the like; they deny that it any ways subsists of itself. 2dly, As they say, *it returns to God,* they ascribe nothing to it, but what it has in common with the spirit of beasts; dreaming, namely, of a kind of divine air or breath, a particle of which every man, and every beast enjoys; by which God inspires, vegetates and moves their bodies, and which, when it is breathed out at death, he receives, as a kind of virtue or efficacy of his own. 3dly, However that return to God hinders not man, *after death, from becoming altogether nothing,* as beasts are nothing after death; only with this difference, that the soul of man is rational, and has the hope of eternal life; such as the souls of the righteous who will actually live for ever. But then they mean that eternal life, which begins at the resurrection, by which the soul as well as the body, will be again brought into being; while the souls of the wicked will remain in the same condition, with those of the beasts, which are not to be reproduced by any resurrection. 4thly, Since they deny the souls surviving death to be substances, it is much more evident, that they deny them to be capable of rewards or punishments: which is down-right epicurism.

XIII. We are therefore to prove these three things in their order: 1st, That human souls *truly* survive after death. 2dly, That they live and think; for that life which is essential to the soul, consists in these; and consequently they either enjoy the beatific communion of God, with the highest delight, or are tormented with the gnawing worm of conscience, and the horrible expectation of a future judgment, with the utmost pain. 3dly, That the souls of the righteous (for we now treat of their

glory)

glory) are immediately, upon their quitting the body, received
not only into *heavenly joys*, but also into *heavenly manfions*.

XIV. As to the *firft*; that the foul, on being fet free from
the body, fubfifts; and that man, after death, is not reduced
into nothing, the facred writings fo evidently declare, that fcarce
any thing can be clearer. The Lord Jefus invincibly proves,
that Abraham, Ifaac and Jacob exifted, when, long after their
death, God declared, that he was *their God*, Mat. xxii. 32. compared with Luke xx. 38. For, how could he be *their God* when
themfelves had no exiftence? And if the foul, when feparated
from the body, could not at all fubfift, Paul would have ridiculoufly doubted, whether he was caught up into the third heaven in the body or out of the body, 2 Cor. xii. 2, 3. His words
alfo had been vain, Phil. i. 23. " I have a defire to be diffolved,
or depart, and to be with Chrift. " Indeed, he fays, to *be diffolved*, or depart, and not to be extinguifhed: nor can we refufe,
that he has a being, who is faid *to be with Chrift*. And how,
pray, *are we come not only to myriads of angels*, but alfo " to
the fpirits of juft men made perfect, " who " are in the heavenly Jerufalem," if none fuch exifted? Heb. xii. 23. To what
purpofe alfo is that well known parable of the rich man and Lazarus, but to acquaint us with the exiftence of feparate fouls, and
their different conditions? Luke xvi. To what end, thofe prayers of believers and of Chrift himfelf, by which they commended
their departing fpirit to God? Pf. xxxi. 5. Acts vii. 59. In a
word, feeing Chrift was true man, and in all things like unto
his brethren, whom thefe men reproach as a mere man, I afk,
what they think was become of his foul, during the three days
of his death? Did it alfo vanifh into thin air, and was Chrift
really annihilated after his death, till his foul was raifed together with his body? One or other of thefe they muft fay! either that the foul of Chrift was of a quite different nature from
ours, which they affert, can no ways fubfift, viz. in a ftate
of feparation; and fo they contradict Paul, who declares, that
" he was in all things like unto his brethren, yet without fin,"
Heb. ii. 17. and iv. 15. or that Chrift was annihilated during
the three days of his death; and fo they contradict Chrift
himfelf, who promifed the thief, that he fhould be with him
in paradife, immediately upon the death of both, Luke xxiii. 43.

XV. The Heretics, in like manner, pervert the meaning of
the Preacher, who fays, Eccl. xii. 7. " Then fhall the duft return to the earth, as it was; and the fpirit fhall return unto
God who gave it:" as if that return was nothng but a refolution into God, of, I know not, what virtue, which they call a
particle

particle of divine breath, proceeding from God ; almoſt in ſuch
a manner with God, as now received from the body, as it was
with him before it removed into the body : which are mon-
ſtrous opinions ! It is contrary as well to the nature of God, as
to ours, that either our ſoul ſhould be any part of God, or
God any part of our ſoul.    The meaning of the preacher is no
ways obſcure.    After the death of the man he ſays, that the
condition of the body is quite different from that of the ſpirit.
The body, when deprived of the ſoul, he calls *duſt* ; becauſe
the union of ſoul with body is the band, and as it were, the
cement whereby the parts of the body remain conjoined.    After the departure of the ſoul, the lifeleſs body, which at firſt
was formed out of the earth, is nothing but a heap of earthy
particles, into which alſo it reſolves in proceſs of time.    But the
condition of the ſoul is quite different.    It dies not, nor is diſ-
ſolved, as the body ; but *goes to God*, as to the judge, who is to
aſſign it its place, either of reward or puniſhment.    Nay, *it returns to God*, not as if it had actually been with God, before it
was infuſed into the body ; (for God *formeth the ſpirit of man
within him*, Zech. xii. 1.) but becauſe, in order of nature and of
efficiency, it was God's before it was man's : for God gave it
to, and made it for man.    What Euripides has elegantly ſaid,
as quoted by Philo in his book, *de Mundi immortalitate*, wonderfully agrees with this ſaying of the preacher,

> χωρεῖ δ᾽ ὀπίσω, τὰ μὲν ἐκ γαίας
> Φύντ᾽ εἰς γαῖαν; τὰ δ᾽ ἀπ᾽ αἰθερία
> Βλαστόντα γονῆς, εἰς οὐράνιον
> Πύλον ἦλθε πάλιν.

That is, as Grotius explains it.

> *Retroque meant, quæ terra dedit,*
> *Iterum in terram.   Quod ab ætherio*
> *Venerat ortu, cæleſte poli*
> *Repetit templum.*

In Engliſh thus :

*What ſprings from earth, goes back to earth again : but what from
heaven derives its high pedigree, thither again returns.    Similar
to this is that of Epicharmus, apud Plutarch. ad Appollon.*
Συνεκρίθη καὶ διεκρίθη καὶ ἀπῆλθεν ὅθεν ἦλθε πάλιν. γᾶ μὲν εἰς γᾶν πνεῦμα δ᾽
ἄνω : *they are joined together and afterwards ſeparated, and return
again from whence they came, earth to earth, the ſpirit to heaven.*

XVI. None fhould oppofe to this teftimony, the 19th verfe of the 3d chapter; " I faid in my heart——that which befalleth the fons of men, befalleth beafts, even one thing befalleth them : as the one dieth, fo dieth the other; yea, they have one breath, fo that a man hath no pre-eminence above a beaft; for all is vanity. " For, it is evident, that the comparifon between man and beaft is only made with refpect to what is external, and ftrikes the eye; in as much as man equally with the beafts is deprived of that life, whereby he can enjoy the pleafures of this world: He does not here confider the condition of the next world, which is apprehended by faith. And it is plain, that thefe words cannot be underftood abfolutely, but only relatively, as to the privation of animal life, becaufe otherwife man and beaft would have the fame kind of fpirit; and that man has no pre-eminence above the beafts, none who is not out of his fenfes, will affirm, and who, by giving up all pretence to folid reafon, has willingly turned himfelf to a beaft.

XVII. When the Scripture affirms, that the dead *are no more;* Pf. xxxix. 13. Jer. xxxi. 15. it does by no means fay, that nothing of them furvives more, including even the foul in the fame condition; which the adverfaries themfelves will fcarce venture to affirm : but that they are not to be what they were before; namely, living men confifting of foul and body united; nor, *where* they were before בתון בהא *in the land of the living;* and becaufe all their converfe with the living is cut off, fo that with refpect to that intercourfe it is much the fame, as if they had no exiftence : fee Gen. v. 24.

XVIII. Now let us proceed to what we undertook to prove in *the fecond place.* That the foul not only furvives after death, but alfo lives, underftands and feels, either the favour or vengeance of God. Not only Scripture, but even reafon fhould perfuade us of this : for, the faculty of thinking, in which the life of the foul confifts, is fo effential thereto, that the foul cannot exift without it. Though we really approve not their way of fpeaking, who affirm, that the foul is *thought*; yet it is evident, that thought is fo effential to a rational foul, that a foul which cannot think, is not, indeed, to be deemed a foul. And if the foul has lived in the body, without deriving its life from the body; why fhould it not live when it is freed from the prifon of the body ? Will it, when it comes to God, the fountain of life, lofe its own life ? Nay on the contrary, the nearer it comes to God, it is agreeable to think, that it will live in a more excellent manner. Some of the heathen philofophers have fpoken much more juftly of the foul than thofe who are

the

the reproach and disgrace of the Christian name.  Plato said
the soul was *αὐτοκίνητος, self-moving, or endowed with spontaneity;*
Alcinous de doctrina Platonis, has best explained the meaning of
that word, c. 25. *αὐτοκίνητον δὲ φησὶ τὴν ψυχὴν; ὅτι σύμφυτον ἔχει τὴν
ζωὴν, ἀεὶ ἐνεργοῦσαν καθ' αὑτήν; he affirms the soul to be self-moving,*
*because it has a connate life, ever active in itself.*  Aristotle, in
like manner, lib. 3. *de anima texto septimo: τὸ μὲν αἰσθάνεσθαι ἐκ ἄνευ
σώματος, ὁ δὲ νοῦς χωριστός: The act of sense is not performed without a
body; but the mind is separable therefrom,* also, *textu decimo novo
& vicessimo: χωρισθεὶς δὲ ἐστι μόνον τοῦ' ὅπερ ἐστι, καὶ τοῦτο μόνον ἀθάνατον
καὶ ἀΐδιον: the soul alone, whatever that be, is separated, and that a-
lone is immortal and eternal.*  See Vossius de Idololat. lib. 1. c.
10.  Thus the philosophers ascribe life to the soul, even in the
state of separation, and a faculty of acting independent of the
body.  But nothing, from a mere heathen, can exceed in
grandeur, those words of Maximus Tyrius: " How then shalt
thou be able to emerge out of this sea, and obtain a view of
God? Then only, and that perfectly, when thou shalt be called
by him; which will soon be the case, only tarry thou, and
wait, till he call.  Old age will presently come, which shall
conduct thee thither: death, which cowards, or the faint-heart-
ed deplore, and tremble at its approach, will soon be here.
Whoever, on the contrary, longs to be joined to God, expects
it with joy, receives it with undaunted resolution."  And a-
gain, Dissert. 2. 25. *ὃν γὰρ Καλοῦσιν οἱ πολλοὶ θάνατον, αὐτὸ τοῦτο οἱ
θανασίας ἀρχὴ, καὶ γένεσις μέλλοντος βίου: what the generality call death,
is the very beginning of immortality, and a birth to a future life:
while the body, indeed perishes, by the very law of its nature, and drops
in its appointed time; τὰς δὲ ψυχῆς ἐπὶ τὸν αὑτῆς τόπον καὶ βίον ἀνα-
καλουμένης, but souls are recalled to their proper element and life.*
See also Dissert. 28.  For, it would be too tedious to transcribe
all.

XIX.  But let us take a view of the Scripture-testimonies:
the Lord Jesus expresly declares, that Abraham, Isaac, and
Jacob, after death, " do all live unto God," Luke xx. 38.
Which is not only to be understood of that happy life of the
entire compound, which they are to obtain by the resurrection
from the dead; but of the blessed life of the soul in a state of
separation, which our Lord ascribes to them in the present
time.  In order to prove the resurrection, he proceeds in this
manner, as first, he concludes that the soul survives and lives,
and then from that infers the resurrection of the body: because
God's covenant was not made with souls, but with entire persons.  And what is clearer than that testimony of Paul? Rom.

viii. 10. "and if Chrift be in you, the body is dead, becaufe
of fin; but the fpirit is life, becaufe of righteoufnefs." He
oppofes the fpirit to the body: to this laft he attributes
death, as the effect of fin: to the former, life, flowing from
the life of Chrift, even while the body is dead. Add, that
not only Elias, who without death was taken up to heaven;
but alfo Mofes. who it is evident died, appeared to the difciples in difcourfe with Chrift, Matt. xvii. 3. which could not poffibly be without the life of the foul. But what kind of body
Mofes appeared in, is not for us to determine, as the Holy
Ghoft is filent about it.

XX. And why had Paul a defire *to depart and to be with
Chrift*, and thought it *far better* for him? Phil. i. 23. why did
he judge it *gain to die?* ver. 21. and why are believers actuated by the fame fpirit, " willing rather to be abfent from the
body, and to be prefent with the Lord?" 2 Cor. v. 8. if, after
death they are altogether to be deprived of that moft holy and
fweet communion with God in Chrift, which they enjoy in
this life? Can it be imagined, that believers expected no happinefs, but what they were only to obtain at the laft day? As
Smalcius impertinently talks. But what fhould oblige them to
wifh therefore for death, which was to bring them no nearer
to that day? Paul longed for death, and reckoned it gain; believers were willing rather to be abfent from the body. Say,
Smalcius tell us, why Paul defired it, why believers chofe it,
if they had nothing to expect before the laft day? Certainly
death in that cafe is not any gain, but an ineftimable lofs, as
it deprives of fo many and great bleffings we fo lately defcribed, and brings them no manner of advantage.

XXI. But by what cavil will they elude what is afferted, Rev.
xiv. 15. "Bleffed are the dead, who die in the Lord, from henceforth; yea, faith the Spirit, that they may reft from their labours,
and their works do follow them." This teftimony contains
many things. 1ft, That the dead in the Lord are *bleffed*. But
to fuppofe any bleffednefs without knowledge or feeling, is
only for thofe to affirm who are deftitute of all fpiritual knowledge and feeling. 2dly, That the dead are happy ἀπαρτι, from
*henceforth:* which is to be underftood either of that time when
John heard that voice from heaven, and was ordered to
write thefe things; or of that time when believers die in the
Lord. But pray, what new change was introduced in the
dead from that time in which the Revelation was made to
John; that the dying fhould then be happier than thofe who a
little before had died in the Lord? Unlefs perhaps it be intended

tended to shew, that at what time the everlasting gospel shall
be again preached, ver. 6. after convicting Antichrist and
purging the church, there will, from that time, be preached
and written in the church what we contend for, concerning
the happiness of believers after death; the fiction of a purga-
tory being quite exploded. But it seems more natural to
think, that *straight* from *thenceforth* denotes the moment of their
death; because, from that time the more perfect happiness of
their souls shall commence. 3dly, That they then *rest from
their labours :* which rest consists not in a sleep, that deprives
them of all sense; but in a freedom from all vexations, and in
the most calm and never to be interrupted participation of the
divine glory; and in a word, in a continued serenity of conscience. 4thly, That *their works follow them :* that is, that they
enjoy the free reward of their good actions, which can then,
as little as afterwards, be unattended with any sensible feeling
of the intelligent soul.

XXII. Nothing more plausible is advanced by our adversaries against this truth, than that reasoning of Paul, by which
he proves the resurrection of the dead from this consideration;
because otherwise, they who believe in Christ would to no
purpose stand in jeopardy every hour, in vain undergo so many
calamities for Christ; and because Christians would of all
men be the most miserable, 1 Cor. xv. 19, 30, 31, 32. Certainly say they, this would be false, should the souls of
the righteous immediately upon death enjoy the happiness of
heaven, and of the wicked feel the torments of hell : for the
former would not bear their calamity in vain; nor the latter
pursue the pleasures of the flesh with impunity. And the pious
would be much more happy than the wicked, though their
bodies should never rise. But it is to be observed, 1st, That they
whom Paul refutes, did not only deny the resurrection of the
body, but also the immortality of the soul; just as the *Sadducees*
did, against whom Christ disputed concerning the resurrection.
And this is the reason why both our Lord and his faithful servant, reason in such a manner, as to draw both conclusions at
once. This appears from the points which the Apostle undertook to refute, v. 18, 19, " They which are fallen asleep in
Christ, are perished. If in this life only we have hope in Christ,
and v. 32. let us eat and drink, for to-morrow we die." All
which tended to persuade men that there was nothing after death
either to be feared or hoped for. If that be true, says the A-
postle, that all who die perish, if our hope be confined to this
life, if the soul neither survives, nor the body is to be raised;

in

in vain are fo many calamities undergone for Chrift, and Chriftians of all men are the moft miferable : which is not a falfe
or deceitful, but a folid way of reafoning, and worthy of an
Apoftle.    2dly, As the dangers and calamities the Apoftle
here fpeaks of, principally concern the body, he juftly argues
that the body feems to have been in vain employed for the.
Lord, if it alfo was not to be raifed in its appointed time to a
participation of the reward : fo that no inference can be deduced from this againft the immortality of the foul.

XXIII. Let us now, *in the laft place* fhew, that when the
fouls of the godly are feparated from the body, they are received not only into *heavenly joys*, but alfo into heavenly *manfions*.
The Apoftle affures us of this, 2 Cor. v. 1. " For we know,
that if our earthly houfe of this tabernacle were diffolved, we
have a building of God, an houfe not made with hands, eternal in the heavens."    He affigns a twofold receptacle for the
foul ; one earthly, that is, the body in which it refides during
this animal life, and from which it departs at death ; the other
heavenly, which it poffeffes immediately on quitting the former.
For here he fpeaks of that eternal receptacle for man which
death makes way for, and which is faid to be eternal in the
heavens.    In the fame *heavenly Jerufalem* he places the *fpirits
of juft men made perfect.*; where are *myriads of angels*, and *Jefus
the Mediator of the new covenant*, Heb. xii. 22, 24.    In like manner alfo, *John faw a throne fet in heaven, and round about the
throne four and twenty elders*, who are the patriarchs (or reprefentatives) both of the Old and New Teftament church, fitting
on fo many thrones, Rev. iv 2, 4.

XXIV. Nor are we to doubt but this was Chrift's meaning
when he faid to the penitent thief : " Verily I fay unto thee,
to-day fhalt thou be with me in Paradife," Luke xxiii. 43.
Thefe words are an exact anfwer to the petition of the thief,
who prayed that Chrift would *remember him* : Chrift anfwers,
I will not only remember thee as abfent, but promife that
thou fhalt be in my prefence in everlafting glory : *thou fhalt be
with me.*    The thief fixed the time in which he defired his petition might be granted, viz. *when thou comeft unto thy kingdom.*
Chrift informed him not only of the *place* where he was to
reign, which he calls *Paradife*, that is, the *third heavens*, compare 2 Cor. xii. 2, 4.    A very common way of fpeaking among
the Jews, who place the fouls of the godly deceafed גן בעדן *in
the garden of Eden* ; but alfo of the *time* in which he was to enter
on his kingdom, TO-DAY : *and it was about the fixth hour*, the
noon of the day, before the expirations of which the death of
                                                           both

both interveening, that our Lord promised him thefe joys. But becaufe fuch a fudden change of condition feemed to be ftrange and almoft incredible, Chrift confirms his promife by an affeteration, * AMEN verily. Thefe things are plain. Whereas on the other hand, the interpretations of our adverfaries are ftrained and foolifh. They imagine the words may be thus pointed or diftinguifhed, *I fay unto thee to-day, thou fhalt be with me in Paradife;* as if Chrift did not fix the time when the thief was to be with him in Paradife, but only declared the truth of what he promifed. And they refer to Deut. xxx. 11, 15, 17, 18. where Mofes fays, *I command thee this day, &c.* But how weak is this? For firft, The thief could not be ignorant of the time; when Chrift faid this to him; he did not want to have that inculcated. 2dly, It is not our Lord's faying *to-day*, but his faying *Amen, verily,* that declares the truth of the promife. 3dly, *To-day* denotes a time, and anfwers to the † *when*, which was in the petition of the thief. 4thly, Maldonat himfelf looks upon this expofition as infipid and weak: Bellarmin accounts it ridiculous from the fame arguments almoft with ours. See *Riveti Catholicus Orthodoxus, queft* 60. 5thly, The phrafeology of Mofes is of a different nature, *I command thee this day; I denounce unto you this day;* for befides, that the words there cannot be otherwife conftrued, here they both may and ought: Mofes there prophefies of things that were to come to pafs afterwards, and would have the Ifraelites mindful of that time in which he had foretold them in fuch a pathetical proteftation; and therefore *this day* or *to-day*, has a remarkable emphafis in the difcourfe of Mofes; but renders the difcourfe of Chrift, if conftrued as our adverfaries would have it, weak and infipid. Moreover, what they contend for, that the thief underftood by *Chrift's coming into his kingdom,* his *coming to judge the quick and the dead,* is afferted without any proof, nor will they ever be able to prove it. He had certainly been miftaken if he imagined, that Chrift's kingdom was to be deferred to the laft day. Chrift had reigned long before, notwithstanding the vain rage of all his enemies: And Chrift's kingdom is fo far from beginning at the laft day, that Paul declares he will then *deliver up the kingdom to the Father,* 1 Cor. xv. 24. But a groffer impiety than any Chriftian could well be imagined guilty of, is what the heretic fubjoins: that *from all thefe things, there is not the leaft pretence to couclude* THAT
CHRIST

---

* I the Amen, who am truth itfelf, infallibly affure thee, that what I fay unto thee fhall comft to pafs this day.

† Lord remember me WHEN thou comeft into thy kingdom.

CHRIST IN ANY RESPECT LIVED AFTER DEATH, or *that other men live after death.* These things are blasphemous, and cannot be either read or heard without horror.

. XXV. Let us add Luke xvi. 22. " and Lazarus was carried by the angels into Abraham's bosom." It is the general opinion of the Jews, that God uses the ministry of angels in carrying home the souls of the pious. Thus they relate concerning Moses; that when the moment of his death was come, God said to Gabriel משה של נשמתו מבא אתה *go and bring me the soul of Moses.* And Christ confirms the opinion about the ministry of angels by his own authority. But whither was the soul of Lazarus conveyed? *Into Abraham's bosom.* From which expression, it is certainly manifest; that the place and state of the blessed are understood; from the opposition to the place and state of the miserable, in which the rich man was. But the learned are not agreed about the derivation of that metaphor. Some think, that this present life is compared to a tempestuous sea, the condition of the pious soul after death to a calm haven, signified by the term, *bosom.* Thus in Virgil:

*Nunc tantum finus, et statio malefida carinis.*

It is now only a bosom, or bay, and an unsafe harbour:

And James Capellus has observed, that what the Latins called *navem appellere, to bring a ship to land,* the Greeks express by καλλω; from which Eustathius remarks is derived καλπος, a bosom, or bay, which is the word that Luke uses here. But Ludov. Capellus thinks, that the bosom of Abraham is an expression borrowed from the custom of parents, who cherish their dear infants in their bosom, in which they also sometimes sweetly rest and sleep: just as the godly are said to sleep when they die, and to rest from their labours: but where can they be said more properly to rest and sleep, than in the bosom of Abraham their spiritual father? For confirming this interpretation, we may add, that little ones thus tenderly treated, are called by the Greeks αγκαλιδια βρεφη, children in the *bosom:* see also John i. 18. " the only begotten Son, which is in the bosom of the Father, that is, who is most intimate and familiar with, and extraordinarily beloved by the Father. But if I mistake not, they explain that expression best who think that here, as also, Mat. viii. 11. and often elsewhere, eternal happiness is represented under the similitude of some splendid and sumptuous feast. For, it was customary, that whoever of the guests was allowed to lean on the bosom of the master of the entertainment, was

accounted

accounted the moſt honourable perſon. Thus John xiii. 23.
" There was leaning on his boſom. one whom Jeſus loved."
Moreover, there is no doubt, but the Jews aſcribed to Abraham,
the father of the Gentiles, the principal place among the righteous. Here then is denoted the very great honour conferred on
Lazarus, who, in that bleſſed abode, was placed next to A-
braham. See Cameron and Grotius on the place. I conclude
in the words of Auguſtine, lib. 2. *de Origine Animæ*, c. 4.
" Was you then ſo very ignorant of this ſound and very wholeſome article of faith, that ſouls are judged upon their departure out of the body, before they come to that other judgment,
in which they muſt be judged at the reſtitution of their bodies,
and that they are either tormented, or glorified, in that very
fleſh in which they lived ? Who has with ſuch obſtinacy of
mind been ſo deaf to the goſpel as not to hear, and upon hearing, not to believe theſe things in the inſtance of that poor
man, who, after death, was carried into Abraham's boſom,
and in that of the rich man, who was conſigned to eternal torment ?" What the opinion of the ancients was concerning the
boſom of Abraham, Martyr has with great learning explained
at large, *Claſſis Tertiæ Loc.* 16. § 7. ſeq.

XXVI. When we aſcribe to ſeparate ſouls, not only a change
of ſtate, but alſo of place, and new habitations or manſions,
we ſpeak agreeable to the Scriptures, which aſſign *manſions*
and a *place* to heaven, John xiv. 2, 3. and *everlaſting habitations*,
Luke xvi. 9. and a *houſe*, 2 Cor. v. 1, 2. Yet we do not
think that ſouls are in a place in the ſame manner that bodies
are : nor do we conceive that they conſiſt of ſome very ſubtle
corpuſcles, whoſe particles are commenſurate to the parts of
the ſpace in which they are included. The very learned Park-
er, *de deſcenſu ad inferos*, p. 106, 107 has given undoubted
teſtimonies, that a great many of the ancients were of this opinion. But we think, that not only with reſpect to their external operations, but even as to their ſubſtance, they are in
that part of the created world, where Chriſt is bodily preſent, ſo
as not to be on the earth. We diſtinguiſh the eſſence of the ſoul,
which is a ſpiritual and immaterial ſubſtance, from all operations
whatever, whether internal or external, as an agent is diſtinguiſhed from its action. Nor do we only enquire about the actions of the
ſoul, in what place they may be exerted, but alſo about its ſubſtance,
in what place it may exiſt. Seeing it ceaſes not altogether to be,
it ought to be ſomewhere; and as it is not infinite, it cannot be e-
very where. It is therefore in ſome place; for inſtance, in ſome

part of heaven or of hell, not indeed locally, as if it had parts
commenfurate to the parts of fpace ; but in a way fuitable to a
fpiritual nature : fo that while it is in this place, it cannot be in
another. Nor is it in this place, becaufe it operates therein ;
but on the contrary, operates in this, and in no other place, becaufe it exifts in this place. Hence the prefence of the foul, as
to its fubftance is in order of nature, prior to its prefence, as to its
operation. And when the fcripture afferts that fouls are in heaven, we are to underftand that of their fubftance, even fecluding every confideration of their external operations. We would
rather be content with this plain way of fpeaking than to fay with
fome, that *the foul confidered in itfelf, without any operation ad extra,
cannot be conceived to be in any ubi or place*, from which it would follow, that if the foul does not operate without itfelf, it has no
*ubi*, and is incapable of every change of place after death. But
we do not remember, that any has explained, whether, and
what it then operates without itfelf. Of a kin to this is that
inference from the fubjeft relating to the condition of the feparated foul, *that by heaven and hell, we are only to underftand
the ftates of happinefs and mifery*, which is crude and indigefted.

XXVII. We need not be very folicitous about the place of
thofe feparate fouls, which were foon to be reunited to their
bodies, by a miraculous refurreftion : nor here give too
great a loofe to our curiofity : nor venture to *intrude into thofe
things which we have not feen*, Col. ii. 18. The facred writings
fay nothing diftinftly on that fubjeft. The fafeft courfe is to
commit thofe fouls to the hands of God ; who has wifdom a-
bundant to affign them a proper place of reft for that time, and
of whofe goodnefs and juftice we need entertain no apprehenfion, that he will do them any injuftice. This is their
glory, this their falvation, that, in whatever place they are,
they are ftill for the glory of God, and in his favour and grace.
This is the language of modefty, to determine any thing per-
emptorily, would be only prefumption.

XXVIII. Let us now fee, what happinefs the fouls of the
righteous enjoy, when they are fet free from the body in heaven. And *firft*, It is their happinefs, that they are *with God
and Chrift in glory*, John xii. 26. *where I am there fhall alfo my
fervant be*, John xvii. 24. *Father, I will, that they alfo whom
thou haft given me, be with me where I am.* Believers even here
are with Chrift by faith and love : *Chrift with the Father cometh
to them, and manifefts himfelf to them*, John xiv. 21. And they find
an incredible reft to their fouls, in that gracious prefence of
God and of Chrift. *It is good for me to draw near to God*, Pf.
lxxiii.

lxiii. 28. But the greateſt nearneſs, they are favoured with
in this life, is mere diſtance from God, if compared with the
future ſtate of the ſoul ; *whilſt we are at home in the body, we
are abſent from the Lord*, 2 Cor. v. 6. And hence it was, that
*Paul had a deſire to depart, and to be with Chriſt*, Phil i. 23.

XXIX. *Secondly*, Being in the preſence of God, they ſhall
*alſo ſee him in the light of glory*. That is, they ſhall attain to
that knowledge of the moſt bleſſed God, which ſhall be ſufficient both to perfect and content the underſtanding, and with
reſpect to this, that viſion of God, which is allowed them in
this world, is mere darkneſs and blindneſs, as we have formerly hinted. Of this viſion our Lord ſpeaks, Matt. v. 8. *Bleſſed are the pure in heart, for they ſhall ſee God*. And they ſhall
ſee God, 1ſt, In the works of glory, which are now made
known in heaven, wherein his moſt illuſtrious perfections will
ſhine forth with far greater clearneſs, than in the works both of
nature and grace. 2dly, In the face of Jeſus Chriſt, whom they
will continually contemplate face to face, and very familiarly
and intimately know, John xvii. 24. *that they may behold my
glory, which thou haſt given me*. 3dly, More immediately, in
himſelf ; ſo far as man is capable to approach to God ; in a
degree and meaſure incomprehenſible to us.

XXX. *Thirdly*, This viſion of God, who is eſſential truth,
ſhall be accompanied with the moſt holy, and, at the ſame time,
the moſt delightful *love* of the ſame God, who is alſo perfect
goodneſs : nor can it otherwiſe be. For, when the underſtanding beholds, and, without interruption, contemplates God
himſelf and his moſt deſirable perfections, not in a fallacious
appearance, nor with obſcure and confuſed ideas, as here, but
in their native light, the holy will cannot but be enflamed with
moſt ardent love to them. That happy ſoul, not only in the
light of God, beholds God as the fountain of light, but is, on
every hand ſurrounded with the flames of divine love ; by
which it continually gives love for love. And that love makes
it feel neither wearineſs, nor uneaſineſs in the preſence, contemplation and fruition of God ; while new pleaſures, one after another, ariſing from the intimate poſſeſſion of the chief
good, ſupremely beloved, and its unvaried complacency, charm
the ſoul. For, that love is not a love of longing, but of fruition that had long been wiſhed for. And this is that charity
which the Apoſtle, 1 Cor. xiii. 8. declares, abides for ever,
when even faith and hope are no more.

XXXI. *Fourthly*, To perfect love is conjoined the moſt

perfect *conformity* of the foul to God, in holiness and glory.
If *Moses* was fo favoured, that rays of unufual light fhone from
his face, after his familiar converfe with God in the mount,
which yet can fcarce be compared with that familiarity or intimate accefs, which the blefled enjoy in heaven ; how great,
do we think muft that effulgence of divine glory be, which the
infinite goodnefs of God communicates to the fouls, who are
the objects of his love, and who perfectly love him ? What
the firft-born Son of God is, in a moft eminent degree, and
in a way altogether peculiar to himfelf, viz. *the brightnefs of
the Father's glory,* Heb. i. 3. that alfo they fhall be in their
meafure ; even perfectly according to that ftate, tho' only fo
far as mere creatures can be, that Jefus *may be the firft-born a-
mong many brethren,* Rom. viii. 29.

XXXII. *Fifthly,* From all thefe things taken together, a *joy*
arifes more than inexpreffible, more than glorious ; of which
that joy, we have already defcribed, Sect. V. is but a faint and
tranfient image. For, as the bleffings of grace are infinitely
exceeded by thofe of glory, fo the foul alfo in a ftate of glory is
capable of thofe that are more excellent, is a far better judge
of them, and enjoys them much more perfectly : hence alfo
the joy flowing from them muft be much more excellent. In
Mat. xxv. 21. it is called, *the joy of the Lord.* Becaufe, 1ft,
It proceeds from, and is freely beftowed by the Lord. 2dly,
It has the Lord for its object, Pf. xvi. 11. *in thy prefence is
fulnefs of joy, at thy right hand there are pleafures for ever more.* 3dly,
and laftly, It is the moft excellent and worthy of the Lord.

XXXIII. There can be no doubt, but the things we have
thus far mentioned, are moft excellent : yet they are not the
complete fulnefs of that ftate ; nor do they fully contain that
abundance of happinefs and glory, which the Gofpel commands
us to hope for. And for this reafon, the frequent confummation of our happinefs, till the glorious coming of our Lord    as
2 Tim. i. 12. " I am perfuaded, that he is able to keep that
which I have committed unto him againft that day ;" and v. 18.
" the Lord grant unto him, that he may find mercy of the Lord
in that day." 2 Tim. iv. 8. " there is laid up for me a crown
of righteoufnefs, which the Lord fhall give me at that day."
1 Pet. i. 5. " the falvation ready to be revealed in the laft time."
And, 1 Pet. v. 4. " when the chief Shepherd fhall appear, ye
fhall receive a crown of glory that fadeth not away :" add Col.
iii. 4. and 1 John iii. 2. From thefe teftimonies we are,
by no means to conclude, that the fouls of the righteous fhall
be,

x, till then, without all fenfe of happinefs; but only, that
what they have till then been favoured with, is but a kind of
prelibation, till the work of falvation fhall be in every refpect completed. For certainly it cannot be denied, that there
is a great difference between that meafure of happinefs, which
the fouls of believers enjoy, while they are feparated from the
body, and that confummation of glory, which is to be revealed at the laft day; and that becaufe the happinefs of a part
is not to be compared with that of the whole, fince even that
part, which is already received into heaven, has not attained
to that perfection, which the gofpel has promifed; as we
will prefently more fully fhew. Hence alfo, the ancients
faid, that the fouls of believers have, indeed, a joy, but it is
only enjoyed in part; as finners have a forrow and a punifhment in part, while they are fhut up in prifon, they are referved for the coming of the judge, *Auctor quæft. & Refpos.
quæft.* 20. Who is faid to be Athanafius. And Chryfoftom
places thefe fouls as in a kind of *porch.* Bernard called it a *hall,
Serm.* 3. *de Sanctis*; diftinguifhing three ftates of men, or of
fouls, *the firft in the tabernacle; the fecond, in the hall; the
third, in the houfe of God.* Which, however, is to be underftood with caution, not that the fouls of believers are out of
heaven, and have not the vifion of God; but we are to think;
that then they will obtain their moft perfect happinefs, when
they fhall be reunited to their bodies.

XXXIV. The things, which the laft day will contribute to
the confummation of happinefs, we comprife chiefly under
three heads. *Firft,* the bodies of believers, when raifed in
glory, fhall be reftored to their fouls. The Apoftle has fully
treated on this fubject, 1 Cor. xv. The bodies indeed, fhall
be the fame, which believers, as was their duty, tenderly
cherifhed in this life, in which as in temples dedicated to the
moft holy God, they glorified God, and often underwent fo
many afflictions for the caufe of Chrift and religion. For,
both the juftice of God, the comfort of the godly, and the very
term *refurrection,* which can only be applied to what fell by
death, do require them to be the fame. But though they are
to be the fame as to fubftance: yet they fhall be fo changed as
to qualities, that they will feem to be altogether different:
" For this corruptible muft put on incorruption, and this mortal put on immortality, then fhall be brought to pafs the faying that is written, Death is fwallowed up in victory," 1 Cor.
xv. 53, 54. Great therefore fhall be the change of the body,
but the fame fubject fhall remain, which the Apoftle int-
mates by the term THIS, as if he had pointed to his own body.
And

And to what purpose is the repetition of the same particle, four several times, but to remove all ambiguity, and every cause of hesitation? And in fine, how otherwise can death be said to be *swallowed up in victory?* Ought it not rather to be said, that death swallowed up our bodies *us νικος* or as it is in the Prophet *נצח*, which may also be translated *for ever*, if the same numerical bodies do not rise?

XXXV. Moreover, we cannot here but admire the almost incredible goodness of God. The divine mercy was willing to bless our bodies also with a participation of heavenly felicity. But their present constitution renders them incapable of so great a glory. As herbs and flowers wither and fade by the excessive heat of the radiant sun, so also our bodies, such as we now carry about with us, are unequal to bear the heavenly glory; " Flesh and blood cannot inherit the kingom of God," 1 Cor. xv. 50. Where flesh and blood do not denote our nature, corrupted by sin, but the very substance of the human body, with those infirmities of animal life, which naturally follow it. Our flesh is from blood; blood from meat and drink: and in blood consists that animal life, from which the body is called animal, v. 44. By flesh and blood therefore is signified the nature of the human body, as it is nourished and preserved in this life, by taking in meat and drink, and by the circulation of the blood. But such flesh and blood is incapable of the heavenly glory. What then? Is God to diminish the heavenly glory, that our body may also be admitted to have some participation of it? By no means. He will rather change the qualities of our body, and of terrestrial, make it heavenly, and of animal, spiritual, so as thus to bear a suitable proportion to the glory, wherewith it shall be endowed, v. 40, 43. But who, while he still remains on this earth, can take in this heavenly language? Who can form an idea of such a spiritual body? And yet it is evident from undoubted testimonies of holy writ, that the righteous shall have this granted to them, and we are to look for it from our Saviour, the Lord Jesus Christ, " who shall change our vile body, that it may be fashioned like unto his glorious body, according to the working, whereby he is able even to subdue all things unto himself," Phil. iii. 21. that we may *shine forth*, not as to our soul only, but also as to our body, " as the sun in the kingdom of our Father," Mat. xiii. 43.

XXXVI. The *second* thing, in which the last day shall contribute to the consummation of our happiness, is such a great *effulgence of the divine perfections* in the works of glory, that a more illustrious neither the understanding can conceive, nor
the

the heart wifh for.   Undoubtedly the foul of man, immediately
upon its reception into heaven, moft diftinctly fees very many
things in and concerning God, which on earth it underftood
only by the faint glimmering light of faith: but yet God has
poftponed the full difplay of his glory to that day.   And therefore that vifion of God, which we maintain to belong to the
feparate foul, though more evident than we can now well conceive; is not yet fo perfect, but a greater meafure of new
light may be fuperadded.   For, as knowledge depends moft
of all on the revelation, or difcovery of the objects; fo that
knowledge cannot be brought to its perfection, while a great
part of the objects lie concealed.   But a great part of the
objects in the contemplation of which our mind fhall be employed, lie concealed, till a new heaven and a new earth are
made, wherein dwelleth righteoufnefs.   Indeed, the more
illuftrious the works of God are, with which the bleffed find
themfelves furrounded, the greater is the pleafure, with which
they contemplate the glory of God therein.   But what more
illuftrious, than to fee this vaft univerfe, delivered from the
bondage of corruption, and brought into the glorious liberty of
the fons of God, which this created world with earneft expectation waited for? Rom. viii. 19, 21.   What more noble
and divine, than that general judgment, in which they fhall
hear themfelves not only acquitted, their enemies not only condemned, but themfelves alfo appointed to judge angels in Chrift
their head? 1 Cor. vi. 3.   What more illuftrious, than that
general affembly of all the elect, from the beginning of the
world to the laft day, who, being cloathed with heavenly bodies,
fhall each of them fhine, as the fun in the kingdom of their
Father?  And with what pleafing aftonifhment may we imagine,
the foul will look upon its body, which it formely knew to be
fubject only to very many and great infirmities, but fhall then
behold it glittering with fuch a blaze of light, as that it may
feem, not indeed, equal to, but yet greatly refembling the
glorious body of Chrift?  And as, in all thefe things, it can admire nothing but the effulgence of the divine glory, may it not
be faid, while it beholds them, to fee God himfelf in a moft
eminent manner?  Hence John fays, 1 John. iii. 2: " but we
know, that when he fhall appear, we fhall be like him; for
we fhall fee him as he is."   And David in like manner promifes himfelf, only after the refurrection, that contemplation of
God, which gives the moft full fatisfaction, Pf. xvii. 15.  " As
for me, I will behold thy face in righteoufnefs: I fhall be fatif-
fied, when I awake with thy likenefs."   To this alfo we are to
                                                        refer

refer that of Paul; " For now we fee through a glafs, darkly ;
but then face to face : now I know in part, but then fhall I
know even as alfo I am known," 1 Cor. xiii. 12. That is, in a
manner moft perfect and altogether divine, a more excellent
than which cannot, it feems, be the portion of any creature.
For, both the object fhall be moft clearly reprefented, as well
in its moft glorious operations as in its immediate illapfe, or
entrance into the mind, in a manner which at prefent we cannot explain; and the fubject will be difpofed in the beft manner,
in order to behold and obferve in God, whatever can complete
its happinefs.

XXXVII. *Thirdly*, That day fhall bring the bleffed to that
*fruition of God*, which fhall be much more perfect and immediate, than whatever they had enjoyed before. As long as
there are fome believers, who are ftill in this miferable life ;
as long as the bodies of the elect, who are departed out of it,
are detained in the prifon of death, and lie hid in the duft,
the faints in heaven cannot be ignorant, that very many remains of that power, which fin had gained over man, muft
ftill fubfift. And confequently fomething muft be wanting
to the full perfection of their joy. And feeing the effects and
remains of fin are not yet abolifhed in their own bodies, and
in believers not yet made perfect, who, together with them
are members of the fame myftical body; which is the reafon,
why God does not communicate himfelf to them, but by
the intervention of a Mediator. But by the refurrection,
death itfelf, which is the laft enemy, fhall be abolifhed, 1 Cor. xv. 26. and caft into the lake of fire and brimftone, Rev. xx. 14. never more to have any power but
over the enemies of God and of believers. Nor fhall there
be any member of the whole myftical body of Chrift, which
fhall not be perfectly holy, and abfolutely fubject to him. And
after all the remains and effects of fin, fhall be entirely deftroyed, nothing fhall hinder God from communicating himfelf immediately to men without the intervention of a Mediator, as he
does to the holy angels. We are of the opinion, with the
beft interpreters, that this is the meaning of Paul, in 1 Cor.
xv. 28. and when all things fhall be fubdued unto him, then
fhall the Son alfo himfelf be fubject unto him, that put all
things under him, THAT GOD MAY BE ALL IN ALL.

XXXVIII. To this happinefs likewife belongs a boundlefs
and immutable *eternity*: without which, it would in reality be
no happinefs. For, no good, how great foever, that one is poffeffed of with a fear of lofing it, can, by its fruition, yield

that

that perfect and folid joy, which is requifite to happinefs. Wherefore happinefs is called eternal life, Matt. xxv. 46. Rom. i. 7. and *a crown of glory, that fadeth not away*, 1 Pet. v. 4. and *an incorruptible crown*, 1 Cor. ix. 25. and the Apoftle declares concerning the righteous, 1 Theff. 4. 17. that they *fhall ever be with the Lord*.

XXXIX. Here it is ufual to enquire whether there will be any difference of degrees among the bleffed. In this queftion, indeed (though we utterly difclaim the proud doctrine of the Romanifts concerning the difparity of glory, founded on the inequality of merits) the arguments of thofe, who think, that God will crown the unequal meafure of the gifts of grace with a difparity of gifts of glory, feem more probable to us. To this purpofe are thofe fcriptures, Rom. ii. 6. " who will render to every one according to his deeds," and 2 Cor. v. 10. " that every one may receive the things done in his body, according to that he hath done." By which words is not barely fignified the quality of the free reward, which fhall be granted the righteous according to their works ; but alfo the quantity of that reward, anfwering in a certain proportion to their works. Which is exprefsly explained by the Apoftle, 2 Cor. ix. 6. " he which foweth fparingly, fhall reap alfo fparingly : and he which foweth bountifully, fhall reap alfo bountifully." Moreover, that this harveft, and its diverfity, or different product, is erroneoufly confined to this life, appears from comparing this place with Gal. vi. 8. " he that foweth to his flefh, fhall of the flefh reap corruption: but he that foweth to the fpirit fhall of the fpirit reap life everlafting." To the fame effect is 1 Cor. iii. 8. " he that planteth and he that watereth are one : and every man fhall receive his own reward, according to his own labour." Where it is clearly enough declared, that the proportion of the reward will be adjufted to that of the labour. Nor unlike to this is the difcourfe concerning the refurrection of the dead, 1 Cor. xv. 40, 41. " there are alfo celeftial bodies, and bodies terreftrial ; but the glory of the celeftial is one, and the glory of the terreftrial is another. There is one glory of the fun, and another glory of the moon, and another glory of the ftars ; for one ftar differeth from another ftar in glory." Where firft, the bodies laid afide at death are compared with thofe affumed at the refurrection : and then, the celeftial bodies are faid to differ very much in glory from each other. As the fun, moon, and ftars, are all truly celeftial bodies, but greatly unlike in glory. And to what purpofe is that diftinct mention of fun, moon and

ftars, and of the unequal glory of each, if the Apoftle only
intended to teach us the difference of the terreftrial from the
celeftial bodies, while all the celeftial were notwithftanding
to have the fame degree of glory?

XL. It cannot, it feems, on any pretence, be denied, that
at leaft the principal leaders, Patriarchs, Prophets, Apoftles,
Martyrs, and diligent teachers of the Old and New Teftament
church, fhall have fome greater degree of glory affigned them.
What was faid to the Apoftles, was not faid to all, Mat. xix,
28. " when the Son of man fhall fit in the throne of his glory,
ye alfo fhall fit upon twelve thrones, judging the twelve tribes
of Ifrael." The meaning of thefe words, if I can form any
judgment, the illuftrious Grotius has beft of all explained.
It is, as if our Lord had faid, you fhall occupy the next place
of honour to me your king. *To judge*, here denotes, to be fet
over, or to prefide by a metalepfis, becaufe generally prefidents
are employed in paffing fentence. Whence a *prefidentfhip* or
province is called by the Hebrews מרה, Gen. xlix. 16. Zech.
iii. 7. The metaphor is taken from the ancient ftate of the
kingdom of Ifrael, in which the Phylarchæ, or heads of the
tribes, ftood in the next degree to the royal majefty, and are
fuppofed to have fat by the king's throne, in chairs of ftate, in
the public affemblies. But to confine this glory of the Apoftles
within the limits of the church militant in fuch a manner, that
in the triumphant, where they have the full reward of their
labours, they fhall quit their thrones, feems repugnant to reafon: nor does it agree with John's vifion, who faw in heaven
four and twenty thrones, and twenty four elders fitting on
them, that is, the Patriarchs of the Old and New Teftament
church, " Clothed in white raiment, and having on their
heads crowns of gold," Rev. iv. 4. And thefe things are fo
evident, that thofe very perfons, who, in other refpects, contradict the difparity of celeftial glory, own, that we are to diftinguifh between that happinefs, which fhall be the portion of
believers, as believers, and the commendation, which, in the
laft day, fhall be given to every one, in proportion to the diligence and fuccefs he fhall have laboured in promoting the kingdom of Chrift, and which it feems, is to be inequally diftributed. But becaufe it is a glorious thing, to obtain fuch a commendation from the mouth of Chrift, and the memory of that
teftimony fhall for ever abide in the minds of believers; they
cannot deny, but in the kingdom of heaven a difparity of degrees in that kind of glory may be admitted to take place a-
mong the bleffed. For certainly, it is not to be thought, that
                                                    then

then there will be many servants of Christ, who may, in that respect be compared with the Apostle Paul. See *Theses Amyraldi de vita æterna*, § 34.

XLI. The Apostle John seems to have given a check to other things, which are too curiously made the matter of enquiry, concerning the condition or state of the future world, when he said, 1 John iii. 2. " Beloved, now are we the sons of God, and it doth not yet appear, what we shall be. It is then more prudent and pious to endeavour to become hereafter partakers of that glorious life, than to gratify an itch of curiosity with insipid and vain speculations. This, however, we may look upon as a certain truth, that, " Eye hath not seen, nor ear heard, neither have entered into the heart of man to conceive, the things, which God hath prepared for them that love him," 1 Cor. ii. 9.

# THE

# ECONOMY

### OF THE

# *DIVINE COVENANTS.*

### BOOK IV.

### CHAP. I.

*Of the Doctrine of Salvation in the first age of the World.*

I. WE have thus far confidered thofe benefits that are
*effential to the covenant of grace:* let us now more particularly take a view of the two ECONOMIES, or the different
difpenfations under which that covenant was adminiftered.
And here, according to the plan laid down, Chap. III. of the
preceding book, we are more accurately to explain, firft, the
nature of the OLD TESTAMENT, and .then that of the NEW.
In the OLD, we will diftinctly confider *four* principal points.
I. The doctrine concerning the common falvation, as there
laid down. II. The benefits or privileges of that Teftament.
III. Its defects, or according to Paul, Heb. vii. 18. " The
weaknefs and unprofitablenefs thereof," on account of which
that covenant was not *faultlefs*, Heb. viii. 7. IV. Its abrogation. The DOCTRINE again, may be confidered, as expreffed
by WORDS, figured by TYPES, and ratified by SACRAMENTS.

II. Divine compaffion publifhed to wretched man, immediately upon his fall, the firft doctrine of grace; in fuch a manner,
indeed, as in few words, and thofe almoft enigmatical, fum-
marily to contain the whole gofpel: we have that firft promife,
Gen. iii. 14, 15. " And the Lord faid unto the ferpent becaufe
thou haft done this, thou art curfed above all cattle, and above
every beaft of the field: upon thy belly fhalt thou go, and duft
fhalt thou eat all the days of thy life. And I will put enmity
between thee and the woman, and between thy feed and her
feed; it fhall bruife thy head, and thou fhalt bruife his heel."

Luther

Luther long ago complained, that none of the ancient fathers and bishops, who were men eminent for knowledge and piety, had explained this passage as it deserved: their successors ought to use the greater diligence to do it with the more care : which several learned interpreters have indeed happily effected. Treading in their footsteps, we shall make it appear, that the principal articles of the gospel doctrine are summarily contained in this text.

III. We suppose, that the *devil* is condemned by this sentence, to whom the Lord addresses himself, under the appellation of the *serpent*, because he had abused that animal; in order to deceive man. For, it is dull and trifling to restrict that magnificent speech of the Deity, as if it had its full accomplishment in that animal alone ; for besides, that it might seem unbecoming the supreme Being, to address a brute beast, void of all reason, in such pomp of language, many things said here to the serpent, if interpreted literally, are natural to that beast : as *to go upon his belly* and *eat dust*. For, we are not to affirm without scripture, that the serpent, as the Jews vainly dream, went on feet or walked erect, or had other food formerly, different from what it has now : nor to imagine, that serpents now feed only on dust ; seeing Aristotle reckons them among the παμφάγα or *omnivorous*, that eat all kinds of things, and testifies, that they eat both flesh and herbs, and *that of all animals they are fond of the nicest delicacies*. *Dust* is said to be *the serpent's food* ; because, since it creeps upon the ground, it cannot but take dust into its mouth, along with its other food. Just as David complains in his mourning, that he ate ashes like bread, Pf. cii. 9. for while he lay on his face in the ashes, he ate the bread, that was thrown to him on the ground. Moreover what is here said of the serpent going on the belly and eating dust, is common to many kinds of worms, as the very learned Bochart has shewn, Hierozoic. l. 1. c. 4. But how could that be a curse to the serpent, which is natural to other animals, whom Satan never abused in this manner ? And then its being detestable to man is owing to its dangerous poison, which it has also in common with other beasts ; who, after sin, became a horror and dread to man. But some serpents are commended for their philanthropy, or love to men. See *Vossius de Origin. Idololat. Lib.* 6. *c.* 58 : some also are fit to be eaten, and accounted a royal dainty, ibid. c. 62. In a word it is of no great consequence to man, whether any animal goes on its feet or on its belly ; whether it feeds on herbs or flesh or dust. But certain it is, that by this condemnation of the serpent,

ferpent, God intended to comfort our firft parents in their
wretched eftate. To what purpofe then is it to interpret the
words in fuch a manner, as to yield very little or no comfort
at all to man, who now ferioufly deplored his own unhappinefs ?

IV. But the principal confideration is, that the fcripture
exprefsly calls the devil, *ϕιν, the ferpent,* 2 Cor. xi. 3. and
*τον οϕιν τον αρχαιον, the old ferpent,* Rev. xii. 9. and his defeat is
called *the bruifing him under our feet,* Rom. xvi. 10. And tho'
we grant, that both thefe things were primarily and literally
faid to the animal, the inftrument which Satan fpoke by; yet
it is evident from the nature of the thing, that both might and
ought rather to be faid to the principal feducer. For, as
Chryfoftom argues well; *if the inftrument experienced fuch a degree of indignation, what punifhment can we probably imagine the
devil incurred?*

V. Nor can it be objected, that what is faid to the ferpent,
*all the days of thy life,* cannot be applied to Satan, who, it is
evident, is an immortal and never-ceafing fpirit. For even Satan has a peculiar death, referved for him; namely the judgment of the laft day: in which he, together with death, will
be thrown into the lake of fire and brimftone, Rev. xx. 10.
The devil lives, when he works effectually in the children of
difobedience, and thereby fhews himfelf to be *τον κοσμοκρατορα the
prince of this world.* He fhall die when he will no longer be able, to ufe any of his inftruments in or againft the kingdom of God.
Thus the Lord Jefus *ftills the enemy and the avenger,* Pf. viii. 2. and
*deftroys him that had the power of death,* Heb. ii. 14. The days
therefore, of the devil's life, are thofe antecedent to the laft
judgment: which yields us an ufeful doctrine, as we fhall prefently fee.

VI. But God was pleafed to pronounce thofe words, (the
fource of all confolation to wretched man) againft the devil in the prefence and hearing of man. 1ft, To mortify that
wicked and arrogant fpirit, who was conftrained to hear his
own condemnation, in the prefence of fuch weak feeble creaures,
whom he had fo eafily brought under his power, and over whom
he thought to domineer for ever. 2dly, That he might revive
and charm our firft parents, with the fweeteft confolations, to
whom not only that juft vengeance ought to be moft acceptable, which God promifed to take of their enemy; but who alfo, in the condemnation of the devil heard their own abfolution. 3dly, To fhew that this fentence had the nature of a
laft or unchangeable will. For, as God by a peremptory and irrevocable

vocable fentence, condemns, without farther enquiry, the devil, when he was taken in the very fact, which hecould neither
deny nor transfer to another; fo thofe bleffings or privileges,
which are made over to the elect in this condemnation of
the devil are made over to them, by the laft and immutable will
of God, which does not depend on any uncertain condition.

VII. Now let us take a more diftinct view of the things,
contained in this fentence. And they are the following : I.
The *bleffings* : or benefits promifed to man.  II. *The author* of
thofe good things.  III. Their *meritorious caufe*.  IV. *The manner of acquifition*.  V. The *heirs*.  VI. The *mean* of acquifition.

VIII. The *evils* which God pronounces againft the ferpent,
are fo many BENEFITS, or bleffings to man : and they are four.
The *firft* is the " curfe of the ferpent ; becaufe thou haft done
this, thou art curfed above all cattle, and above every beaft of
the field."  All beafts are fubject to deftruction : " natural
brute beafts, made to be taken and deftroyed," 2 Pet. ii. 12.
And it is for man's fin, that beafts, as the property of man,
are made more miferable ; for they cannot be excluded
from being a part of this world, which is not willingly
fubject to vanity, Rom. viii. 20. and among them there are
thofe, called *evil beafts*,  But the curfe threatened againft the
ferpent, is fuch as renders him inferior to, viler and more miferable than all beafts : importing, 1ft, An invincible folly
and malice ; fo that he can be neither wife nor good : worfe
than a " horfe or mule, which have no underftanding," Pf.
xxxiii. 9.  2dly, The very worft degree of vilenefs, whereby he,
who impioufly attempted to be equal to God, and feemed to
have acquired a dominion over man, the nobleft of God's creatures, is depreffed below the beafts of burden.  3dly, A ftate
of never ending mifery.  The beafts die and perifh, and never
come into judgment.  But the ferpent accurfed above the
beafts, cannot efcape judgment ; " everlafting fire is prepared
for the devil and his angels," Matt. xxi. 41.  It could not but
be acceptable to man, to hear that fentence pronounced, by
which that enemy, who had made him obnoxious, is himfelf
doomed to be accurfed.

IX. The *fecond* benefit is the *deftruction of his power :* expreffed
by three feveral phrafes. The firft, " upon thy belly fhalt thou
go :" that is, thou fhalt be conftrained to creep on the ground,
nor fuffered any longer to fly at man, twift thyfelf round him,
and kill him with thy envenomed embraces.  Pareus fays judicioufly : " He himfelf alfo is forced to creep on his breaft ; becaufe

caufe being once thrown headlong down from heaven, he is now condemned to creep for ever on the ground amidft earthly filth, nor able any more to raife his head to heaven." Thus Rev. xii. 9. " the judgment of the old ferpent, the devil, by which he is now bound faft, is called his cafting out into the earth; where, in a hoftile manner, he perfecutes, but cannot overpower the woman."

X. The other expreffion *duft fhalt thou eat*, doubtlefs denotes a ftate of the greateft degradation. For, the fcripture phrafe, *to lick the duft*, is applied to conquered enemies, who lie proftrate at the conqueror's feet; Pfal. lxxii. 6. " his enemies fhall lick the duft;" Micah vii. 17. " they fhall lick the duft like a ferpent;" Ifa. xlix. 23. " they fhall bow down to thee with their face towards the earth, and lick up the duft of thy feet." But there feems a much greater emphafis in thefe words, when the ferpent is commanded *to eat duft*; as alfo when it is faid, Ifa. lxv. 25. " and duft fhall be the ferpent's meat." Which, if I miftake not, fignifies in general three things. 1ft, The reftraining the devil's power to earthly minded men, who are glued to the earth, and feek their good and happinefs in earthly things. Thofe alone he fhall be able to devour, without having any right over others. And this tends much to the great benefit of the church. For, when the wicked are devoured by the devil, offences are removed out of the way of righteoufnefs, the church is delivered from their vexations, and Satan's kingdom diminifhed in this world. 2dly, As to the elect, it fignifies the reftricting the power of the devil to their bodies, which, on account of fin, is faid to be duft, and to return to duft. That body the devil will devour, that is, bring down to death, and keep under the power thereof, till the refurrection: he fhall have no power over the fouls of the elect. And even that deftruction of the dufty body is of benefit to believers: for, at the fame time the old man is deftroyed, who had hitherto harboured in their members. 3dly, It denotes that wicked pleafure, which the devil takes in drawing the reprobate to fin, and confequently to eternal deftruction, and in vexing the godly as much as he can. It was the *meat*, that is the delight, of the Lord Jefus, " to do the will of him that fent him," and to turn men to God, John iv. 34. On the contrary, it is the delight of Satan to pufh on the wicked to evil, and to vex the beloved children of God. Which as it is the greateft wickednefs, fo alfo the higheft degree of mifery.

XI. Leaft any one fhould hifs this expofition off the ftage, as if it was new and never heard of before, I fhall fubjoin the comments

comments of Fagius and Pareus. Fagius writes thus, " If we
" now, as we certainly ought, refer thefe things to that fpiritual
" ferpent, I mean Satan, whom the Hebrews call נחש הקדמוני,
" *the old ferpent*, who acted in the ferpent, a brute animal, as
" in an inftrument, they fignify, that this our old crafty enemy,
" who before walked, as it were in ftate, is now thrown down
" and confounded; *to eat duft* fignifies to confume earthly
" minded men, who are enflaved to their affections. Satan is
" a fpirit, fuch therefore muft be his food; here are fins to
" ftay his hunger. For, as the ferpent creeps on the earth,
" lives on the earth, broods on the earth; fo the difpofition of
" Satan is to entice men to the earth, to hurry them to earthly
" things, and draw them afide from thofe that are heavenly."
Thus far, Fagius: from whom Pareus does not greatly differ.
His words are thefe. " He is alfo condemned to eat earth,
" that is to feed on the earthly naftinefs of vice and wickednefs
" as the filthy fwine feed on excrements. Which that impure
" fpirit does, when he not only pollutes and delights himfelf
" with the defilements of the world, as fwine with wallowing
" in the mire; but alfo plunges the reprobate into the fame,
" and deftroys them with himfelf: this is Satan's fweeteft food.
" For, wherewith any one is delighted, that he accounts his
" meat and his pleafure, according to that faying, *envy is the*
" *beft food: again envy feeds on the living,* &c. Auguftine
" advances no unelegant doctrine; where he fays, *the finner*
" *is earth; the finner therefore is given up to the devil for food:*
" Let us not be earth, if we would not be devoured by the
" ferpent:" thus far Pareus. Ambrofe, Lib. i. *de pœnitentia*,
c. 13. quoted by Rivet, Exerc. 35. in Gen. explains *duft* by
the flefh of men, and maintains, that the devil is permitted by
God to feed on this flefh, that is, to torment and tear the bodies
of believers, but not to have any power over the foul.

XII. The third expreffion, by which the deftruction of the
devil is fet forth, is *the bruifing his head*. In the head of the
ferpent are his poifon, craft, ftrength and life. The head of
the ferpent therefore fignifies the crafty fubtilty of the devil,
his venomous power, and all that tyrannical dominion, which,
by fin, he has acquired over man. The bruifing his head is
the abolifhing of all his power, according to the Apoftles explication, Rom. xvi. 20. " and the God of peace fhall bruife
Satan under your feet fhortly." The fymbol of this bruifing
was that extraordinary power granted to the difciples of Chrift,
mentioned Luke x. 19. " Behold, I give unto you power to
tread on ferpents and fcorpions, and over all the power of the

Vol. II.           P           enemy;

enemy; and nothing ſhall by any means hurt you. And Mark xvi. 18. " they ſhall take up ſerpents;" namely, without being hurt, as appears from the hiſtory of Paul, Acts xxviii. 5. Which power of depriving ſerpents of their venom, and of bruiſing their heads without harm, Tertullian as quoted by Grotius on Luke x. 19. 'teſtifies was not quite extinct in his time among Chriſtians. Though the devil imitated this miracle in the temple of Iſis in Egypt, as Bochart has remarked from Allian Hierozoic, lib. 1. c. 4. at the cloſe; yet our Lord expreſsly declares, that the deſtruction of his kingdom was thereby ſignified, when to ſerpents and ſcorpions, he adds, " all the power of the enemy." Thus the devil was conſtrained, by his juggling tricks and deluſions, to give a prelude of his own deſtruction.

XIII. The *third* benefit, God promiſes here, is " the putting enmity between the ſerpent and the woman and her ſeed:" theſe words include man's ſanctification. For, when man becomes an enemy to the devil, then he abhors and avoids all intercourſe with him, hates and deteſts his works, endeavours to deſtroy him and his kingdom in himſelf and others, and moſt willingly does, what he knows ſhall mortify the devil. And though the devil, on that account, wages war againſt him, becauſe he endeavours after godlineſs: yet he is ſo far from ſuffering himſelf to be thereby diverted from that which is good, that, on the contrary he goes on, with the greater alacrity to oppoſe him. While a man continues unſanctified, he cultivates peace with the devil, and calmly ſubmits to his dominion: enmity and hoſtility againſt the devil can only proceed from an infuſed principle of holineſs. And this is what God promiſes to man, when he ſays, " I will put enmity, &c.;" he not only commands the woman, to have no intimacy or friendſhip with the devil, or to have any commerce with a ſworn enemy; nor, by this ſanction, did he again open a door of repentance for our firſt parents, as Pareus obſerves on this place; but he alſo promiſes, that, by the unſurmountable efficacy of his power, he would perform and bring it about: namely, that *he would put* that enmity againſt the devil, which cannot ſubſiſt, where there is not the love of God. Rivet ſays well, Exerc. 36. in Gen. " When a ſtate of enmity is foretold, in the ſame breath " it is alſo foretold, that men ſhall return to ſuch ſoundneſs of " mind, as diſpleaſed with that grievous yoke of Satan's tyranny, " to ſeek the ſhaking it off: and having once happily ſucceeded, " afterwards to watch by a continual ſtruggle againſt being " entangled therein again." But fulleſt of all, Cloppenbergius,

Schol.

Schol. Sacrific. p. 75. " There could have been no enmity be-
" tween the woman and the devil, without removing, by jufti-
" fication, the enmity with God, which the devil, by his fe-
" duction, had brought the woman and her pofterity to; and
" without conquering and fubduing, by fanctification, the do-
" minion of fin in the woman. Putting therefore that enmity
" againft the devil, he appoints a covenant of peace and friend-
" fhip, whereby he promifes to the woman the grace of juftifi-
" cation and fanctification."

XIV. The *fourth* benefit is the refurrection of the body,
which was brought to duft, by his means who hath the power
of death : this is more obfcurely intimated, when it is faid, that
" the ferpent fhall eat duft all the days of his life;" which we
have fhewn, fect. V. to be the days preceding the laft judgment.
From which we concluded, that the time of the devil's power,
and of his going about to devour, is limited, and to have a final
period. And, when that is elapfed, the bodies of the righteous
fhall be raifed from the duft, and all the effects and remains of
the power of the devil, and of fin, by which he acquired his
power, be entirely abolifhed; that he may not detain, under
his power, the duft of our bodies, which ought to be temples
of God, and of his Holy Spirit, in a ftate of glorious holinefs.
Nor was this, indeed, altogether unobferved by Fagius, who
thus fpeaks : " the days of Satan's life are the whole time to
the confummation of the world, and the coming of Chrift.
For, then he and all his fervants fhall be thrown headlong into
everlafting fire," Mat. xxv. 41.

XV. JEHOVAH GOD, who fpeaks to the ferpent, and declares,
that he would put that enmity, of which we have been fpeaking, takes the honour to himfelf of being the AUTHOR of all
thofe benefits. Though we are not to deny, that the conferring
fo great a benefit is to be afcribed to the whole undivided
Trinity; yet, in the economy of our falvation, the Father, who
is firft in order, holds the principal place. And whereas the
eternal furetyfhip of the Son, according to the tenor of the
covenant between the Father and the Son, on the fuppofition
of fin, began immediately to exert its efficacy, thefe words are
not improperly referred primarily and immediately to the Father, who, on account of the furetyfhip of the Son, appoints his
grace to the finner; and who exprefsly enough diftinguifhes
himfelf from the Mediator, or the feed of the woman. And
indeed, " God was in Chrift reconciling the world to himfelf," -
2 Cor. v. 19. that is, the Father in the Son, the Mediator.

XVI. The MERITORIOUS CAUSE of thofe benefits is the SEED

OF THE WOMAN, eminently so called. I own, indeed, when the seed of the woman is opposed to the seed of the serpent, and between both an enmity established, both seeds are to be understood collectively: that by the seed of the serpent, all the wicked are intended, who Mat. iii. 7. are called the *generation of vipers*: by the seed of the woman, elect believers, together with Christ their head: yet it is without all doubt, that, in this seed, there is some eminent one, to whom that name does chiefly belong, and by whose power the rest of the seed may perform the things that are here foretold. Just as the seed of Abraham is sometimes to be understood more largely, at others more strictly; sometimes denoting his posterity by Isaac and Jacob, as Gen. xvii. 8. " I will give unto thy seed the land wherein thou art a stranger:" sometimes more especially believers of his posterity, who walk in the steps of the faith of their father Abraham, and to whom the promise of the inheritance of the world, by the righteousness of faith, is made, Rom. iv. 12, 13: sometimes, most especially, that eminent one in the seed of Abraham, who was to be the spring of every blessing, as Gen. 21. 18. " in thy seed shall all the nations of the earth be blessed; which is Christ," Gal. 16. Thus also the things here said are, in their measure, common to all believers; but then some effects are primarily and principally to be ascribed to him, who, in this seed, is the eminent one, namely, Christ: as the Apostle also distinguishes the seed *that sanctifieth*, and that which is *sanctified*; both which are of one, Heb. ii. 11.

XVII. But the reasons, for which Christ is called the seed of the woman, seem to be chiefly these two: one peculiar to Christ, the other common to him with other men. That which is common, is his being of the same blood with us, that we might know him to be our brother and next kinsman. For, men, in Scripture-language, are called, " born of a woman," Job xiv. 1. and Job xv. 4; and xxv. 4: " born of women, Mat. xi. 11. But then, we must add that which is peculiar to himself, that though Christ, indeed, had a woman for his mother, being " made of a woman," Gal. iv. 4. yet he had no man for his father, being " without father," Heb. vii. 3. See Jer. xxxi. 22. " a woman shall compass a man." For, though this last reason holds not in believers, who are likewise called the seed of the woman, for another reason, to be explained directly; yet, seeing Christ holds the principal place in this seed, as he bruises the head of the devil in one sense, and believers in another; so therefore he is called the seed of the woman in a different sense

from

from them.  The fame words are indeed, ufed of both; but becaufe, Chrift is far more excellent than they; therefore when they are applied to Chrift, they have a much more illuftrious meaning.

XVIII. It, is indeed true, that Chrift is the feed of Adam whofe fon he is called, Luke iii. 38. alfo the feed of Abraham, and the fon of David, becaufe he was born of a virgin, who defcended from them.  Yet there was great reafon, why he fhould be here called the feed of the woman, rather than of Adam.  For, Adam, in Scripture, is reprefented as the origin of fin and death.  Eve, indeed, was firft in the tranfgreffion: but as it was not Eve, but Adam, who was exprefsly conftitued the federal head of all mankind; fo fin and death are faid to have entered into the world by Adam, Rom. v. 12, 14. Wherefore he who delivers us from fin and death, ought not to be confidered as fubordinate to Adam, and as his fon: but, as the fecond Adam, and the head of another family, oppofed to Adam.  However, as he was to be our kinfman and brother, it was neceffary he fhould be born of a woman; and that Adam, as his fon by the fpirit and by faith, fhould be fubordinate to him.  For, fince God fays here, that he would put enmity between the woman and her feed, and between the ferpent and his feed, without any mention of Adam: it muft be, that either Adam is excluded this promife, or comprized under the feed of the woman.  The refpect and regard we ought to have for our parent, who was the author and teacher of the true religion to his pofterity, forbids our faying the firft.  Nor do I think we fhould fay the fecond: becaufe it is agreeable to reafon, that the woman fhould be comprized under, and accounted in the man; not, on the contrary, the man under the woman.  It therefore remains, we fay the third; namely, that Adam, as he was the origin of fin and death, is oppofed to Chrift; as himfelf was faved, is to be accounted to the feed of the woman, whofe head is Chrift, and fo to be fubordinate to Chrift.  Chrift therefore is called the feed of the woman, becaufe, being the origin of a better ftock, he is oppofed to Adam as the root of a corrupt race.  And it is hinted, that Adam himfelf owes his falvation to the woman, on account of her feed.

XIX. Paul, if I miftake not, leads us to this, 1 Cor. xi. 11, 12. " Neither is the man without the woman, neither the woman without the man in the Lord.  For, as the woman is of the man, even fo is the man alfo by the woman: but all things of God."  I do not remember to have feen a fuller explication of this place, than what I fhall give from the *Thefes* of a certain

tain very learned perfon.  That the man and the woman may
BE IN THE LORD, partakers of the grace and redemption purchafed by Chrift, they are mutually indebted to one another,
for fomething common to both, which the one neither had,
nor could have obtained without the other.  For, as the woman is *ἐκ τῷ ἀνδρος* OF THE MAN, from whofe rib fhe was formed,
and who could not have been in the Lord, had it not been for
the man, without whom fhe could not have fo much as exifted :
fo the man is in the Lord *διά τῆς γυναικος* BY THE WOMAN, for the
woman was appointed to be the firft enemy of the ferpent, and
the Mefliah is called the feed of the woman: but the man obtains
the fame happinefs by the woman, as by faith he lays hold on
the Mefliah, who was to defcend from her in virtue of the promife.  The woman is OF THE MAN, materially and naturally :
not fo the man *of the woman* (which yet might be faid ; if we
only mean ordinary generation, according to the manner that
children are of a woman, Mat. i. 3, 5, 6. and Chrift himfelf, Gal. i. 4.)
But BY THE WOMAN; becaufe not materially, but fpiritually and
fupernaturally, by grace and faith.  Thus therefore the man is the
origin of *being* to the woman, the woman of *well being* to the man.
But to prevent pride on either hand on this account, and their arro-
gating any thing to themfelves, it is added, *but all things are of
God :* by whofe wifdom and moft free difpofal it was ordained,
that the woman fhould derive her natural origin from the man;
the man his fupernatural from the woman ; and become mutually debtors to one another : but the glory of both thefe privileges to remain entirely to God alone, the fupreme caufe.

XX. Hence it is evident, fuch a Saviour is promifed, who
was to be man, and the Son of man.  But feeing he is defcribed as ftronger than the devil, who, by fin, had acquired a
right over man ; it follows, that he is alfo true God.  For the
bruifing of the ferpent's head is afcribed to him : and this he
does, 1ft, By the merit of his fatisfaction; and therefore he
muft have been of fuch dignity, as to be able to pay a fuitable
ranfom for all the elect.  2dly, By the efficacy of his Spirit,
which gradually abolifheth every power of the devil, and fo
fhews himfelf to be *ftronger than the ftrong man.*

XXI. God declares the MANNER in which this Saviour
was to purchafe falvation, by faying to the ferpent, *thou fhalt
bruife his heel.*  In which words there is, 1ft, A denunciation
of fufferings, to be inflicted on Chrift by the devil and his inftruments, whereby he would be thrown down for a time.
While he himfelf bruifes with his foot the ferpent's head, and
ftrips him of all his power ; the ferpent by his envenomed fting,
will

will grievously wound his * heel, and conftrain him to ftagger
and fall. For a man in an upright pofture, ftands on his heels,
which being grievoufly wounded he is thrown down. 2dly,
A prophecy of his refurrection. For his *head* will not be
bruifed, nor his *heart* wounded, nor any vital part grievoufly
affected; but only his *heel* hurt; nay, not both but only one.
Though he was therefore thus to be thrown down, yet he was
foon to rife again, on refuming ftrength, and fhew himfelf a
conqueror to the whole world.

XXII. The fufferings here denounced are not only WARLIKE,
as a certain author calls them, with which the ferpent together
with his feed, from a hatred to holinefs and righteoufnefs, af-
faulted Chrift; but even JUDICIARY being inflicted by the moft
righteous fentence of God on the Son the furety, to fhew his
righteoufnefs by which he could not pardon fin without a due
fatisfaction. For God here perfonates a judge: pronounces
fentence againft the devil, declaring his deftruction at the
appointed time. But the fame fentence alfo condemns the
furety of men to undergo thofe vexations of the devil, which, as
a conqueror, he could have inflicted on finful men. He had
indeed acquired his dominion over man by evil practices. Yet
after man, by forfaking God, his lawful Lord, had enflaved
himfelf to the devil, the juftice of God in every refpect, required his being fubject to the devil, as God's jailor and execu-
tioner, for his torment, punifhment, and condemnation. In
which fenfe the devil is faid to " have the power of death,"
Heb. ii. 14. and that even by virtue of the law and fentence of
God: for *the fting of death is fin ;* that is, fin introduced death,
and the inftruments of it, and made them fharp, mortally to
wound man : *but the* [ftrength] *power of fin is the law';* that is,
the power that fin has of putting man to death, is in virtue of
the divine law, which threatened the finner with death, 1 Cor.
xv. 56. Whence it follows, that the power of the devil over
finners of mankind is fo far lawful, becaufe the devil obtains
the power of death over man, but death its power from fin,
and fin from the law. But as that law is moft righteous, life
cannot be granted to the finner in prejudice thereto. It is
therefore neceffary, that fatisfaction be made to it from fome
other quarter ; and that the devil fhould exercife that power of
death, which he had acquired by fin, either on the finner himfelf, or on his furety. Yet in fuch a manner, that, while he
                                                        puts

---

* Some have obferved, that this expreffion of bruifing Chrift's heel, was not altogether an obfcure reprefentation of his death on the crofs, to which his feet were
nailed.

puts the furety to death, he lays violent hands upon himfelf, and lofes all his dominion over the elect; for full fatisfaction is made, by the death of the furety, to that divine juftice by which the devil had obtained power over the finner. Thefe words therefore fhew, how the devil in a way agreeable to divine juftice, may be deprived of all that power over the elect, which juftice had granted him over finners: namely, becaufe the devil was to exercife that power over the furety of men, by biting his heel, or putting him to death. So that thofe fufferings, which was here foretold to endure, are in the higheft degree, judiciary or fatisfactory. Compare thefe things with what we have faid, Book II. Chap. VI. Sect. 23, 24.

XXIII. The HEIRS of thofe benefits or bleffings, are, 1ft, *The woman* herfelf, *noun*, with the demonftrative particle *he*, namely, that woman whom the ferpent had firft attracted and conquered. She is here mentioned, but not in exclufion of her hufband; but becaufe fhe, having been enticed by the flatteries of Satan, feemed to have contracted a greater familiarity with him; and therefore her enmity to the devil was to be a moft admirable effect of divine power and goodnefs. But then it was alfo a remarkable contempt put upon the proudeft of fpirits, that he fhould be vanquifhed not by the man, but the woman, *that very woman*, whom he had fo eafily fubdued by his delufions. In fine, from this it moft clearly appears, that the whole work of our falvation is owing to divine grace. For if Adam had here been exprefsly fet in oppofition to the ferpent, becaufe he was ftronger and more prudent by nature, and was laft overcome by the devil; this thought might by degrees have eafily gained upon mankind, that by the remains of virtue and wifdom, which were in Adam, he had undertaken a new combat with the ferpent and with better fuccefs. But feeing the commencement of the enmity is afcribed to Eve, the woman, who was both weaker by nature and firft overcome, it is clearer than noon-day, that the grace of God alone is here all in all.

XXIV. 2dly, *The feed of the woman.* By which is fignified not all mankind but elect believers; as appears from that diftinction, by which that feed is oppofed to the *feed of the ferpent.* For it is evident, that wicked men, who " are of their father the devil," John viii. 44. 1 John iii. 8. and " the children of the wicked one," Mat. xiii. 38. are the feed of the ferpent. The feed of the woman therefore, is the godly pofterity of Eve: namely, the children of the promife, who " are counted for the feed," Rom. ix. 8. And perhaps this is the reafon

why

why the godly are called the feed of the *woman*, and not the
feed of the *man* : becaufe as the woman was wholly indebted
to a gracious promife, that fhe was appointed to oppofe and
fight againft the ferpent, not without the defired fuccefs : fo
alfo, it was not thofe children in general, who were to be born
of her, according to the law of nature, by matrimonial commerce ; but thofe only, whofe mother fhe was to be by the
fame gracious promife, who are here accounted for her feed.
For, though Eve, as fhe was joined to Adam in marriage is
the natural mother of all mankind, even of thofe, who are called the feed of the ferpent. Yet the fame Eve, being, by virtue of this divine promife, fet in oppofition to the ferpent, by
whom fhe was overcome, is the mother only of the blefled
feed ; which was to proceed from her, not according to the
law of nature, but in virtue of the promife of grace : this is
therefore called the feed of the woman ; even of that woman, who is, and in fo far as fhe is, placed in oppofition to
the ferpent.

XXV. The MEAN, by which the appointed heirs become
actually partakers of the promifed benefits, is *faith* in the furety, as is intimated by a twofold enigma or dark faying.  1ft,
As all the heirs are called by the common name, feed ; this
denotes the myftical union and communion of the feed, which
is fanctified, with that which fanctifies ; fo that what the latter has done or fuffered, the former is accounted to have done
or fufferd in him.  But the band of that union is faith, by
which we receive Chrift, adhere to him, and become one fpirit
with him, 1 Cor. vi. 17.  2dly, As the bruifing the ferpent's
head is afcribed to the feed : which, indeed, Chrift alone does
by the merit of his obedience, and the infinite efficacy of his
Spirit ; yet the elect alfo in Chrift, and by the power of Chrift,
conquer him through faith.  Chrift is the general in this combat, the feed of the woman by way of eminence, who overthrows and triumphs over the enemy : but next to Chrift, and
under him, believers alfo fight and overcome by his power,
" And they overcame him by the blood of the Lamb," Rev. xii.
11.: that is, becaufe on that very account the blood of the Lamb
was fhed for them.  The victory, which the reft of the feed
gains over the ferpent, cannot but follow upon the fhedding
of the blood of the Lamb, who is the feed of Eve.  Moreover,
that victory is obtained only by faith ; " whatfoever is born of
God overcometh the world," (confequently the devil, who is
called the prince and god of this world, Eph. vi. 12. 2 Cor. iv.

4.). " And this is the victory, that overcometh the world, even our faith."

XXVI. It is not to be thought improbable, that so many and so great mysteries of faith are expressed in few words. For, the words are both very proper to signify, and elsewhere in scripture do signify what we have here said, and it became the wisdom of God, to lay before the primitive church some short abridgement, which, by its well contrived brevity might comprehend the sum of the things to be believed; and then it is our duty, to form high and honourable thoughts of what God speaks. Neither is it unreasonable, that the whole should be wrapped up in some enigmatical or obscure expressions. For, the bright shining light reserved for noon-day, was not suitable to the first dawn of the day of grace. Moreover, God had not then desisted from appearing to our first parents; but explained to them, by frequent instruction and the gracious illumination of their mind, those things which belonged to faith and godliness. And indeed it was wholly reasonable, that above all they should carefully keep this promise of salvation, as a most valuable treasure, diligently meditate thereon, and explain it by mutual conversation to each other and to their children. Some other things seem to belong to this subject, which being briefly related by Moses, we shall explain a little more particularly.

XXVII. Moses, having distinctly related, what God had said to the serpent, to the woman, and to Adam, subjoins Gen. iii. 20. " and Adam called his wife's name EVE, because she was [or was constituted] the mother of all living." It is not necessary, we here suppose with some a * proteron-hysteron, as if this name had been given before the fall; at the same time, when Adam called that help, which had just been given him, Ischah woman; for-there is no reason, why we should contend, that things were done at the same time, which Moses relates on different occasions, and after other intermediate narratives. We own, indeed, that sometimes a thing is related after, which had been done before: but this is not usual, unless the affinity of the subject with what goes before or follows makes it necessary. But there is no such affinity here; unless we would say, that this denomination bears some respect to the words of God, before narrated by Moses, in the sense we are presently to shew. Nor can we prove, that the word rendered, *and he called*, is to be rendered in the preterpluperfect tense, *and he had called*; that Moses's meaning should

be

---

* A way of speaking, when we place that after, which should come before.

be, Adam was greatly deceived, who had promifed life to himfelf and his pofterity from his wife ; whom he afterwards found
to prove the caufe of death.   For, 1ft, The following words,
which explain the reafon of this denomination, are not the
words of Adam, deceived in his expectation : but of Mofes,
fhewing the truth of the matter.   2dly,  If we will have them
to be the words of Adam, we ought to change חַוָּה, *fhe was*,
into תִּחְיֶה, *fhe will be*, and to have fomething underftood as,
*ie imagined*, or the like ; to this effect, Adam had called her
name Eve, becaufe he imagined, fhe would be the mother of
all living, but, from the event, he learned the reverfe.   But
we do not take upon us fo boldly to make free with the facred
text : let us therefore difmifs this ungrounded προθυτερον.

XXVIII. But why was fhe called *Chavah, Eve ?*  Some
of the Rabbins ridiculoufly derive that name from חַוָּה,
which in Piel denotes to *fignify* or *difclofe*, " becaufe fhe was
a great talker, according to Baal Hatturim.  Fagius writes, the
Jews thus exprefs it, becaufe fhe was a great talker and uttered many empty words to the ferpent, till being enfnared in her
talk fhe finned ; and as foon as fhe made her hufband to fin,
he called her *Chavah*, or *Eve*, as we render it.   But thefe
things are repugnant to the exprefs declaration of the Holy Spirit, who gives a quite different reafon for the name; for he
fhews, that this name is derived from חַוָּה *to live*, not from
חַוָּה ; and the *jod* is changed into *vau*, to put fome difference
between the name of the woman and of a beaft, which in Hebrew is called חַוָּה as Aben Ezra has not improperly obferved.

XXIX. No lefs ridiculous is Lyranus, who fays, that Eve
in Hebrew denotes life, but fubject to penalties ; moft of all
Peter Comeftor, author of the Scholaftic hiftory; that Adam
then deploring the mifery of his pofterity, called his wife Eve,
alluding to the cries of infants ; the male newly born crying A,
but the female E ; as if we fhould fay, all born of Eve will fay
A or E.   This perhaps might be pardonable in poor Comeftor,
and in the age in which he lived : but it is highly ridiculous,
that amidft fo great a light of knowledge, Cornelius a Lapide, in
his commentaries fhould not blufh to call fuch trifling. by the
name of pious contemplations.   There is nothing in the word
חַוָּה, that can denote anguifh or penalty.   But let us proceed
to what is ferious.

XXX. Mofes explains the reafon of the denomination in
thefe words; " becaufe fhe was, or was conftituted, the mother
of all living."   By all living, fometimes is underftood all men
in general, as Pfal. cxliii. 2.  And it is certain, that, except

Q 2                                                Adam

Adam, all that ever did, do now, or fhall hereafter live, derive their origin from our mother Eve. But if this alone was intended, here it might be afked, 1ft. Why Adam chofe to call his wife the mother, rather than himfelf the father of all living, as the natural origin of all is equally due to both? 2dly, Why as we have fhewn from the feries of the Mofaic hiftory, he gave this name to his wife, not till after the fall; feeing, if we attend to natural generation only, fhe became the parent, not fo much of the living as of the dead? 3dly, Was this a thing fo very worthy of notice, fince it was felf-evident, that all, who were to exift, were to defcend from her, who was the only woman in the world.

XXXI. It feems therefore more advifeable, and more becoming both the faith and piety of Adam, and the wifdom of the Holy Spirit, who accurately relates thofe things, to underftand by all living, both the Lord Chrift, who is the fountain of life, and the elect, who, being united to him, are quickened by his Spirit. The woman was conftituted the mother of thefe living, by the word of promife, by which fhe was exprefsly appointed to have that feed, who was to bruife the ferpent's head. Wherefore Adam, who by fin became the father of all who die, 1 Cor. xv. 22. called his wife Eve, from his faith in God's promife, believing, according to the word of God, that no man fhould have true life, but what would be derived from her. However the original of this was not in the woman herfelf, but in the principal feed, that was to defcend from her. This name therefore contains a confeffion of Adam's faith, and fhews, what Adam taught his children, and to what hope he formed them by the word of God: who, in the very name of his wife, as often as he repeated it, would have a lafting monument both of the promife of God and of his own hope.

XXXII. Peter Martyr, that moft excellent interpreter of of fcripture, faw and taught thefe things long ago: who thus comments on the place. " Adam knowing that her feed, would bruife the devil and death, juftly and with propriety, chofe to call her by that name, by which this falutary promife of God might at all times occur to his mind. Now Adam had entertained hopes of life by Chrift, and when he perceived, that his wife was to be the mother of him, and of all thofe who were to be quickened by him, called her name Eve, becaufe fhe was the mother of the living." Fagius in like manner: " we doubt not but Adam, by giving that name to his wife, had a view to the promife concerning the feed, that was to bruife the ferpent's head :

head ; by which he hoped, that his wife was to be that person.
Wherefore he named her *Chavah*, which we call Eve, as
if you would say an enlivener ; because dead mankind was to
be made alive by her offspring." See also Paræus and others,
all agreeing in the same thing.

XXXIII. Eve discovered the same hope, when, upon bringing forth her first-born, she cried out, יהוה את איש קניתי, Gen. iv.
1. which words are variously rendered by interpreters. That
which we think most agreeable, is, with Reuchlin, Pelicanus,
Fagius, Forsterius, Luther, Clarius, Scindlerus and many o-
thers, to take את, as usual, for the sign of the accusative case,
and the meaning be, *I have gotten a* MAN JEHOVAH. Remarkable is the Chaldæ paraprase of Jonathan. " And Adam
knew Eve his wife, who was taken with a longing for that
angel, and conceived and bore Cain, and said, I have gotten
the man, that angel of the Lord." Certainly our pious mother
continually revolving in her mind that promise of God, which
was the ground of all her consolation, as soon as she bore that
male child, observed in his birth a sign or token, that the promise would be performed. She therefore joyfully exclaims, she
had now obtained that *promised seed:* not that she imagined Cain
was that seed, but that, in his birth, she could see the first
multiplication of mankind, and, in that multiplication, an argument for her hope concerning the seed, eminently so called,
who was to arise in his appointed time. Seeing she laid hold
of this with a great assurance of faith, and made it, as it were
present to her mind, she now so speaks, as if in the birth of
Cain, she was actually possessed of that seed, which, by an
argument taken from that birth, she expected with an assured
faith. For, had she thought that Cain was the promised Messiah, and Jehovah himself, she would have paid him, though
her own son, religious worship, and by this means incurred
the guilt of a horrid idolatry ; till being apprized, either by
the vicious disposition of the child; or by some other means,
she had owned her mistake. Which our pious respect to our
common parent forbids us to believe. She moreover publishes
an eminent confession concerning the person of the Messiah,
whom she acknowledges to be God-man. She declares him
to be man, by calling him *man;* at the same time pointing out
his excellence above other men : for, אדם *Adam* and איש *Ish*
are usually distinguished, so that the last viz. *Ish*, implies excellency ; and the first, viz. *Adam*, meanness. Christ, indeed,
in his humiliation, was " a worm and no man," Ps. xxii. 6. but
considered in himself he is " the man of the right hand of the
Lord,"

Lord," Pf. lxxx. 17. and " the m n his fellow," Zech. xiii. 7.
She alfo makes profeffion of the divinity of the Meffiah, when
fhe calls him JEHOVAH ; and fignifies, that both natures fhould
be united in one perfon, by joining thefe two, Paul calls him,
" God manifeft in the flefh," 1 Tim. iii. 16.

XXXIV. To this explication three things are principally
objected. 1ft, If Eve intended this, fhe would have faid
doubling the fign of the accufative cafe : as in the following
verfe, τον αδελφον αυτου τον Αβελ. 2dly, את often fignifies the
fame as עם. with; את יהוה therefore fignifies with Jehovah, as
συν Θεω with God. In this fenfe, Jonathan is faid to have
wrought אלהים עם. with God, 1 Sam. xiv. 45. that is, under the
conduct and direction, or by the affiftance and help, of God.
3dly, Filial refpect prompts us to entertain right fentiments concerning the faith of our mother Eve; namely, that fhe knew and
believed, the Meffiah was not only to be God-man, but alfo the
feed of the woman, that is, the fon of a virgin; for, without this
her faith had been a miftaken, not a true faith, nor yielded her
any comfort. She could not therefore think, fhe got in Cain
the Meffiah ; as fhe was perfectly well affured, that Cain was
not the fon of a virgin.

XXXV. We anfwer, to the firft : that the repetition of that
particle, is indeed frequent, but yet not univerfal: for we have inftances of the contrary, 1 Kings xi. 23. If. viii. 2. Ezek. iv. 1. 1 Sam.
xv. 4. Where the fign of the accufative cafe is placed between
two nouns, without a repetition. To the fecond: we deny not, that
את is often equivalent to עם but there is no inftance to prove, that
what the Greeks fay, συν Θεω, the Hebrews exprefs in their
language by את יהוה or אל חים: as it is well known, they ufually
exprefs it by כיהוה or כאלהים. What is adduced from 1 Sam.
xiv. 45. is not to the purpofe. For, there we have עם but not את.
For, tho' thefe particles, are fometimes equivalent, yet they ought
not to be confounded. And then, with God, does not fo much
fignify with God's affiftance as God difapproving. Compare, Ifa.
xxxvi. 10. With greater fhew of reafon might be urged Mic. iii. 8.
I am full of power by the fpirit of the Lord, that is by the help of that
fpirit; and Hab. iii. 13. Thou wenteft forth for the falvation of thy
people, even for falvation with thy Meffiah, that is, falvation to be procured by his means. But the former paffage is very properly rendered, I am full of power with the fpirit of Jehovah; full of power
no lefs than full of the fpirit. And the latter fhould feem to be
thus pointed, that God may be faid to go forth with Chrift for
falvation. To the third it might be anfwered, that there would
be no abfurdity to fuppofe, that Eve was not fo well acquainted with every thing, regarding the condition of the Meffiah.

Who

Who can affert, fhe knew, the Meffiah was to be born of a
virgin, when the bleffed virgin herfelf did not know it, when
fhe heard it from the mouth of an angel, as appears from her
words; " how fhall this be, feeing I know not a man," Luke
i. 34. We deny not, that the Meffiah is eminently called the
feed of the woman, becaufe he was to be born of a virgin:
which the the Holy Ghoft afterwards more clearly foretold.
But it is no crime to doubt, whether our mother Eve could
have gathered this from..thofe words; fince; in the facred
language, even they are faid to be born of a woman,
who are conceived in matrimony, as we fhewed fection
XVII. One may affert this, and not tranfgrefs againft that
refpect due to our common mother; as it is certain, God
gradually brought his people to the knowldge of the Meffiah:
nor does it overturn the faith of Eve, which might have been
genuine and faving, though it was under this imperfection;
ignorance and miftake; as Peter had a true faith concerning
Chrift, that is a faving, and not a hypocritical, though he imagined through miftake, that Chrift could be the Saviour of his
people, without fufferings, Mat. xvi. 22. But we are under
no neceffity to be obliged to fay any of thefe things, for we do
not affert, our mother Eve received Cain, for the very Meffiah:
but only we are of opinion, that, in the birth of Cain, fhe obferved a fign or token of God's performing the promife, and
fomething to fupport her faith, which fhe was willing to
declare and preferve the memory of, by giving him that name:
and confequently that argument does not affect us.

XXXVI. And we are not to pafs over in filence, that when
fhe afterwards brought forth another fon, fhe called his name
" Seth, ﬡﬡ becaufe God (ﬡﬡﬡ) hath appointed me another feed
inftead of Abel, whom Cain flew," Gen. iv. 25. A fentence
full of fpiritual affurance and of prophecy. She calls him feed,
having a view to the promife, and foretelling, that he would
not only carry on the enmity with the ferpent, but alfo that
from him, that eminent feed would come forth, by whofe
power the ferpent's head was to be bruifed. The feed fhe proclaimed was given by God; as a fon not of nature only, but
alfo of grace and promife, and accounted by God himfelf for a
feed: nor only given, but alfo appointed of God, that is,
eftablifhed and fecured by the council of God that he fhould
not be flain, but be the foundation of the future church, to
be propagated in an uninterrupted fucceffion in his pofterity,
and preferved down to Chrift. For the word to appoint, denotes a determination and fteadinefs, as John xv. 16. " I have
chofen

chosen you, and ordained (appointed) you, that ye should go
and bring forth fruit. She therefore acknowledges Seth for
the chosen seed, and the parent of him, in whom all the elect
are chosen.

XXXVII. This doctrine of salvation flourished both in the
mouths and in the hearts of believers, who began קלרא־בשׁם יהוה,
that is, as Aquila translates it, Καλῖσθαι ὁ ὀνόμαϊι Κυρίυ to be called
by the name of the Lord, Gen. iv. 26. and they were called the
sons of God, as distinguished from the sons of man. Above
all, the prophecy of Enoch is very remarkable, which the a-
postle Jude relates in his epistle, not from any apocryphal book,
nor from the mere authority of any unwritten tradition, nor
by a sagacious conjecture from the history of Moses; but by the
inspiration of that same Spirt, who prompted Enoch to pro-
phesy, v. 14. 15. in these words : " and Enoch also, the seventh
from Adam, prophesied of these, saying, behold, the Lord
cometh with ten thousand of his saints, to execute judgment
upon all, and to convince all that are ungodly among them," &c.
That Lord, of whom Enoch speaks, is the Messiah, in unity
of essence the same Jehovah with the Father and the Holy
Spirit ; to whom also all power is given in heaven and in
earth, and whose peculiar property the elect are on a
special account. He foretels his coming by a verb of the pre-
terperfect tense, to express the undoubted certainty of the thing,
and the full assurance of his own faith, he prophesies, that the
Messiah, at that coming, will be attended with myriads of angels.
Which happened, when he came down upon mount Sinai to give
the law, Deut. xxxiii. 2. and when he came in the flesh, to visit
his people : for, then a multitude of the heavenly host, declaring his nativity, was seen and heard in the country of
Bethlehem, Luke iii. 13. but this will be the case in a most
illustrious manner when " he shall come in the clouds of heaven,
and all the holy angels with him," Mat. xxv. 31. The end of
this coming will be " to execute judgment upon all : for, the
Father hath committed all judgment to the Son," John v. 22.
and to convince all that are ungodly, by inflicting the punishments
due to their impiety. These things Enoch preached to the
people in his days, who, giving a loose to their lusts, impiously
denied the future coming of the Lord. And seeing that prophecy contains an universal truth, it is applicable to all, who
walk according to their lusts. And these are the things, which
the scripture testifies, were delivered concerning the doctrine
of salvation, in the first age of the world.

C H A P.

# CHAP. II.

## *Of the Doctrine of Grace under Noah.*

I. AS Noah was the patriarch of the new world, we are now to explain, what was handed down to us in his time, concerning the doctrine of salvation ; as soon as he was born, his father Lamech called him *Noach,* saying, " this same shall comfort us concerning our work and toil of our hands, because of the ground, which the Lord hath cursed," Gen. i. 29.

II. And here, in the first place, we are to take notice of the name given to the child, both with respect to its etymology, and the reason assigned by the pious parent for that name. The name is Noah, which if we follow the rules of grammar, is derived from the root to *rest* or *be quiet* ; to which word, both as to letters and signification, *be comforted,* is near of kin, which Lamech used in assigning the reason of the etymology. They who keep close to grammatical niceties, endeavour to correct the words of the text, and, instead of ‏נחמנו‎ would have us read ‏ינחמנו‎ as the Septuagint, in order to come nearer to the etymology of the word, and to the name והave also rendered it, ΔΙΑΝΑΠΑΥΣΕΙ ημας *this same shall refresh us.* But seeing the Hebrew copies, the Chaldee paraphrast, Jerome, &c. constantly read it otherwise we dare not rely only on our own judgment, or be willing to have any thing altered. In proper names, derived from a verb, commonly some letter or other is either added, taken away, or transposed, and the accuracy of grammatical etymology not constantly observed : which the celebrated Buxtorf has shewn, by several examples, in his *Vindiciis veritatis Hebraicæ,* p. 267. Whence the Hebrew doctors generally incline to derive, from by cutting away the last letter. But Mercer's opinion appears more probable, who affirms, here only is a resemblance of words, but not a reason taken from etymology ; because the verb both in sound and signification, comes near to the noun, which signifies *rest* and *comfort :* And as Aben Ezra learnedly says, " comfort also is rest from grief of heart." And then the Hebrews usually have a greater regard to the sense than to the sounds of words. As therefore the reason of the name is thus expressed, *he shall comfort us,* it is altogether the same as if he had said, *he shall make us to rest ;* because to the same purpose, whoever comforts, causes rest from trouble. But these are

rather niceties, tho' not to be overlooked, in order to preserve
the integrity of the Hebrew copies inviolable. This one thing
is evident, that Lamech, in the name of his son, intended a
standing monument of his own wishes and hopes.

III. Let us therefore see, what he intended by this name.
" This same," says he, " shall comfort us concerning our work
and toil of our hands, because of the ground which the Lord
hath cursed." Three things are contained in this sentence :
1st, The *evil*, under which, with other pious people, he groan-
ed. 2dly, The *good* opposed to that evil, which he had the hope-
ful prospect of. 3dly, The *author* of that good.

IV. He makes the evil, he complains of, to consist *in our
work, in the toil of our hands*, and in *the ground which God hath
cursed*. The carnal Jews generally restrict this to that fatigue
of body, which men are forced to .bear, in the culture of the
earth, occasioned by the curse of God, and that these words
only contain a prophecy concerning an easier method of agri-
culture, which Noah would discover. But his pious parents
were not so delicate, and so much taken up with the conveniencies of this life, as to place the greatest part of their misery in those fatigues of the body. These things have a higher
view. By ‏עמל‎, *our work*, are principally to be understood
those evil works, which bring grief and sorrow to the soul.
For, these are *our* works, opposed to the *work of God* in us.
These produce an unspeakable trouble and fatigue to the godly,
" as an heavy burden, they are too heavy for them," Ps. xxxviii.
4. These were at that time visible every where, men being arrived at the utmost pitch of wickedness. Whence Peter, 2 Pet.
ii. 5. calls the men of that generation, *the world of the ungodly*.
But to those evil works was added *the toil of their hands*. To
this I refer all the labour, misery and calamity of this life, which
were to be undergone in the sweat of our brow. This is ac-
compained with dwelling on the *earth which is cursed* ; so that
while man lives there, he cannot possibly enjoy a full state of
holiness and tranquillity of soul, and see the light of God's
face in glory. For, " whilst we are at home in the body, we
are absent from the Lord," 2 Cor. v. 6.

V. The *good* opposed to this evil, which he desired, and was
in expectation of, he calls *consolation* or *comfort*. This consists
in the applying some effectual remedy against, and in the very
removal of those evils. The *comfort* against *our vicious works*
consists in the expiation and remission of them, in the intimation of that gracious sentence, by which they are pardoned on
the account of the Messiah ; and finally, in the purging them
away by the Spirit of sanctification. *Comfort* from the miseries

of

of this life or *from the toil of our hands*, is partly a leffening of
that affliction, by granting a more profperous and happy ftate
of things, partly the delighting the foul with an inward relifh of
divine goodnefs, whereby it is enabled to bear all thofe toils,
with which God is pleafed to exercife his people, willingly and
with cheerfulnefs, from a fenfe of the love of God. *Comfort,
as to the ground, which God hath curfed*, confifts in the beginnings
and preludes of the heavenly glory, which the elect are even
here favoured with; but chiefly, in a freedom from the body
of death, and the tranflation of the foul into a better ftate and
manfion. Lamech breathed after thefe bleffings, defired them
and hoped for them : and was willing to have a monument of
this defire and hope in the name of his fon.

VI. But whom did he point to, as the author of this great
bleffing, when he faid to his fon, when he was born,
this fame fhall comfort us ? Some think, that being miftaken
in the perfon, he flattered himfelf that Noah was the Meffiah.
And indeed, as the believers of that age, with the greateft and
moft affured hope, preffed earneftly, after the accomplifhment
of the promife made in paradife, and prepoffeffed it in their
longings, but not having any certainty about the time when it
was to be fulfilled, it is not fo very improbable, that, in the
warmth of defire, they promifed to themfelves the expected feed
in the perfons of the fons, which were born to them. But what
we lately obferved concerning the expectation of our mother Eve,
are objections to this. It feems therefore fafer to believe, that,
on occafion of this fon, he comforted himfelf with the hope of
the fpeedy coming of the Meffiah, and confidered him as a
forerunner and type, and an extraordinary herald of the Meffiah. Finely fpeaks Martyr to this purpofe : " I would rather
imagine, they acknowledged their fons to be fhadows or types of
Chrift, and therefore diftinguifhed them by fuch names. But
Noah was not only a fhadow of Chrift, &c. Though a genuine
and real confolation proceeds alone from the Meffiah and his
Spirit, yet Lamech truly prophefied of Noah, that he alfo
would be a comfort to wretched mortals. And he was fo, 1ft,
By preaching, with an extraordinary zeal, the righteoufnefs of
faith; of which prefently. 2dly, By obtaining a refpite of the
imminent deftruction by means of his prayers, and exemplary
holinefs of life, till the ark fhould be completed : for, Ezekiel
claffes him, with Daniel and Job, as one, who was very pre-
valent by his deprecations, Ezek. xiv. 14, 20. 3dly, By preferving the remains of the perifhing world in the ark, which
he had built at God's command, and performing very many
things, in which we might fee him, as a type of the Meffiah,

and

and of the fpiritual and heavenly benefits to be obtained by him.
Of which we are to fpeak more fully hereafter.

VII. We have juft now faid, that Noah was a preacher of
righteoufnefs. This we learn from Peter, who calls him κηρυκα
της δικαιοσυνης a preacher of righteoufnefs, 2 Pet. ii. 5. But righteoufnefs fignifies not only that virtue of man, which confifts
in rectitude and conformity to the rule ; but alfo that obedience
of the Meffiah, whereby the ungodly is juftified ; " the righteoufnefs which is of God," and oppofed to " our own righteoufnefs," Rom. x. 3. Noah was a preacher of both thefe.
He not only pathetically exhorted the men of his time to a
holy life, and to the practice of religion, in order to efcape the
wrath of God, that was hanging over them, but alfo preached
that righteoufnefs of the Meffiah ; which, as it is the fame
with refpect to its efficacy, yefterday, to day and for ever, fo
it is alfo " witneffed by the law and the prophets," Rom. iii.
21. and of which himfelf was heir, as Paul affirms, Heb. xi.
7. For, feeing he was not ignorant of fo great a benefit ; nay
and even enjoyed it ; it is quite inconfiftent with the piety of
the man, and the zeal; with which he was animated for the
glory of God, and for the falvation of his brethren, to fuppofe
he would conceal it from them.

VIII. Here we are to explain another paffage of Peter, 1
Pet. iii. 19, 20. Where he thus fpeaks of Chrift, who was
quickened by the Spirit: Εν ω (πνευματι) Και τοις εν φυλακη πνευμασι
πορευθεις εκηρυξεν, απειθησασι ποτε, " by which" (Spirit) " alfo he
went and preached unto the fpirits in prifon ; which fometime were difobedient, when once the long fuffering of God
waited in the days of Noah while the ark was a preparing."
It is to no purpofe to fay, how varioufly this paffage has been
treated by interpreters ; though if it be well confidered, the
meaning will appear eafy and plain. The Lord Chrift, fays he,
who was raifed from the dead by the infinite power of his Spirit,
formerly *went*, came out of heaven, not indeed in the flefh affumed, and perfonally united to himfelf, but in the demonftration of his *Spirit*, by which he formed the prophets, and a-
mong them alfo Noah. By the miniftry of thefe prophets,
who were ftirred up by his Spirit, he *himfelf preached*. For,
not fo much the prophets, as the " Spirit of Chrift, which was
in them, fpake, 1 Pet. i. 11. By that preaching, he invited
the *fpirits* to faith and repentance, that is, thofe fouls of men,
which are now feparated from the body, and fuch are ufually
called *fpirits*, Heb. xii. 23. and now are *in prifon*, in brw, according to the Syriac interpreter, *in hell* ; compare Rev. xx.
7.; becaufe they were *difobedient*, and rejected the preaching
of

of Chrift by Noah, when the divine goodnefs and long-fuffering
called them to repentance. Peter therefore declares, that
Chrift formerly, and efpecially in the days of Noah, preached
by his Spirit, by the prophets; and what elfe did he preach,
but himfelf, and faith and repentance, whereby they might
come to him? In this fenfe alfo Peter writes chap. iv. 6. that
the " gofpel was preached to them that are dead;" namely,
when they were formerly alive. Thus to the fame purpofe,
Naomi faid to her daughters-in-law, Ruth i. 8. " as ye have
dealt with the dead and with me."

IX. Neither improperly, nor without authority does Peter
refer the preaching of the prophets, and efpecially of Noah, to
Chrift. For Chrift, who calls himfelf *Jehovah the redeemer*,
exprefsly proclaims, " I have not fpoken in fecret from the beginning," Ifa. xlviii. 16, 17. And what elfe can the meaning
be, but that I have publicly preached, from the very beginning?
Nor is it altogether improbable, that Peter had a view to Gen.
vi. 3. " and the Lord faid, my Spirit fhall not always ftrive
with man," that is, " I will not always contend againft their
wickednefs by fruitlefs exhortations and rebukes, made by my
prophets, actuated by my Spirit; but for the determined fpace
of a hundred and twenty years, will invite them to repentance
by my long-fuffering and forbearance of wrath; but when that
term is once expired, I will deftroy them all by a deluge."
From this it appears, that, in the time of Noah, Jehovah con-
tended with men by the preaching of his Spirit. That Spirit,
by whofe infpiration, the word of life was declared, is by Peter
juftly called *the Spirit of Chrift:* not only becaufe he is the
Spirit of the Son no lefs than of the Father; but alfo becaufe
it is owing to the furetifhip of Chrift, that the word of grace
is propofed to finful man. The Spirit therefore, preaching
that word, may by a peculiar appropriation be pointed out as
the Spirit of Chrift the furety. All this is to inform us, that
the fame doctrine of falvation concerning the fame Chrift, and
through him, was, by means of the prophets, preached from the
remoteft antiquity.

X. I cannot here but take notice, how ftrangely Grotius
perverts and corrupts this eminent teftimony of Peter. He
feems to envy us, and refufe, that we can find Chrift and his
works in the ancient ages of the world: and therefore he applies what Chrift is faid to have performed in the time of Noah,
to what was done by the apoftles, and to the preaching of the
gofpel to the Gentiles. By *the fpirits in prifon* he underftands
*the fouls of men in the body, as in a fheath.* But how does he
prove it think you? Peter, fays he, borrows a fimilitude from
the

the times of Noah. Then God faid, בשגם היה רוח ירין לא, that is, if we regard the propriety of the words, *my fpirit fhall not be fo detained in man as in a fheath*, that is, the foul, which I gave him (Wifd. xii. 1.) fhall not be ufelefs, as a fword in its fheath, which by no means anfwers the end it was made for. Let us proceed. A *prifon* is ufually called φυλακὴ; but the *fheath* is, as it were, *the prifon of the fword*, the Chaldees calling a fheath נדן. The fame name they give to the body of a man, as Dan. vii. 15. and the *Talmudifts* often. But on the words *who were difobedient, &c.* he obferves. They were fuch as the " fouls, who did not obey formerly in the times of Noah; he fpeaks as if they had been the fame: and they were the fame fpirits or fouls, not numerically, as Ariftotle fpeaks, but generically; that is, fouls equally ufelefs to God; namely as thofe, who did not obey the preaching of Noah. Men altogether alienated from God, did not believe Noah, did not believe Chrift." If I rightly take the meaning of the intricate difcourfe of this otherwife illuftrious perfon, the fum of his opinion comes to this. Chrift, by the Spirit, put into the apoftles, preached the gofpel to the Gentiles, whofe fouls were fhut up in the body, as in a prifon and fheath, and who are juftly accounted the fame with the difobedient men, who lived in the days of Noah, the fame, I do not fay numerieally, but by imitation of their wickednefs. I tremble at the reading fuch things, and imagine, I fee in them a fpirit, which will not have the Holy Ghoft to have faid, what he actually has, and which fhamefully mifapplies its learning: let us now make this appear.

XI. 1ft, The explication of the words of God, Gen. vi. 3. though countenanced by fome Jewifh and Chriftian doctors, is abfurd. Among others fee Buxtorf in Vindic. Verit. Hebrace. p. 639. For, the foul of man is no where in fcripture, called the Spirit of God. It is, indeed formed in man by God, Zech. xii. 1. yet not called the Spirit of God, but " the fpirit of man," Ecclef. iii. 21. and " the fpirit of man which is in him," 1 Cor. ii. 11. In vain are alledged to the contrary, Ezek. xxxvii. 14. and Pfal. civ. 30.; for, there the Spirit of God does not denote the foul, or life of the creatures, but the author of that life. Nor does the grammatical analogy admit the deriving ירין *Jadon* from נדן, for, in that cafe, the points ought to be altered: the letter *daleth* ought to have a *dagefch forte*, becaufe *nun* is excluded, and under *jod*, a *Chirek*. Not to mention, that neither in the Talmudifts nor Chaldee, nor books of the Old Teftament, is there any word derived from נדן, which fignifies to *be detained in a fheath*: fo that this explication is rafhly urged, without either reafon or authority. 2*dly*, The
application

application of thofe words to the words of Peter is ftill more
abfurd, as if hence we could underftand, what is meant by the
*fpirits in prifon.* For, certainly the *Spirit* of God is one thing,
the *fpirits of difobedient men* another. And fhould we grant,
which yet we do not, that there is in Hebrew a verb derived
from נרה, a *fheath ;* this נרה, a *fheath* is certainly not the thing
which the Septuagint render Κολεὼ, 1 Chron. xxi. 27. and φυλακὴ
another, which, according to the venerable Beza's obfervation,
when it does not fignify the *fourth part of the night,* always denotes a prifon. To conclude, what method of commenting is
it? That the words of Peter, namely *the fpirits in prifon,* fhall
be explained from Gen. vi. 3. יחר חיר; and חיר moreover explained from נרה; and again נרה denotes a prifon, becaufe a
fheath is the prifon of the fword; and then the body be the
prifon of the foul: and therefore the *fpirits in prifon* in Peter,
fhall denote the fouls contained in the body, as in a fheath.
How far fetched, uncertain and trifling is all this? 3*dly,* It is
moft abfurd of all, to make the Gentiles, to whom the apoftles
preached, the fame with the difobedient, who lived in Noah's
days, who were not only men of another age, but, by an inter-
val of many ages, men of another world. Indeed, Grotius refers us to his book *de jure* B. and P. Lib. 3. c. 9. Sect. 3.
where he proves, that a people is accounted to be the fame at
this day, which they were a hundred years back, as long as that
community fubfifts, which conftitutes a people, and binds them
together by mutual ties. Though this be true, it is nothing to
the purpofe: for, the Gentiles, to whom the apoftles preached,
were knit by no tie of mutual union to the fame fociety with
the cotemporaries of Noah. They who were difobedient, when
the ark was a preparing, were all of them entirely deftroyed by
the deluge, nor from any of them did any of the Gentiles derive their origin; fo that it is inconceivable, how they could
coalefce into one people with the Gentiles. And Peter is fo
far from making the unbelievers of his time to be one body
with thofe, who lived in the time of Noah, that, on the contrary, he calls the old world " the world of the ungodly,"
2 Pet. ii. 5. and chap. iii. 6, 7. oppofes " the world that then
was, to the world which is now." A fimilitude of manners is
not enough to make them the fame people. Who, that trem-
bles at the word of God, can afcribe fuch a weak and foolifh
fpeech to the divine apoftle, as to think he could fay; that
when the apoftles preached to the men of their time, they
preached to thofe who were difobedient in the time of Noah?
Be it far from us thus to trifle with facred writ. The reader
                                        may

may be pleafed to fee a very folid defence of this paffage in *Difputat. Placæi, Difput.* ɪʏ.

XII. Memorable alfo is that blefling, with which Noah blefſed his pious fons, containing many doctrines of the true religion, Gen. ix. 26, 27. " Blefſed be Jehovah the God of Shem, and Canaan fhall be his fervant. God fhall enlarge" (or allure) Japheth, and he fhall dwell in the tents of Shem." When he calls Jehovah, *the God of Shem,* he gives an intimation of that covenant, which was to fubfift between the fupreme being and the pofterity of Shem, above other men. For, Abraham and all Ifrael were defcended from Shem. Thefe God had chofen to himfelf for a peculiar people. Whence, with a remarkable compellation, Shem is called the " father of all the children of Heber," Gen. x. 21. that is, of the Hebrews. He alfo publifhes the piety of Shem, who was conftantly to adhere to the worfhip of the true God, and to oppofe, to the utmoft, the fpreading of idolatry ; teaching, both by his doctrine and example, that he acknowledged none to be God but Jehovah. Generally interpreters alfo obferve, that thefe words fet forth, that the Meffiah fhould defcend from the pofterity of Shem, fince he does not celebrate fo much Shem himfelf, on the account of his piety, as he transfers the whole praife to God, faying, *blefſed be Jehovah,* he fhews, that God is the author of every good inclination of the foul, and pious action of the life, to whom therefore all the glory of them is due. He had denounced a curfe on the guilty in his own perfon, on account of the crime he had committed ; becaufe the fuel and fource of evil is in man himfelf. But being pleafed with the piety of Shem, he was willing rather to blefs God ; that he might not feem to afcribe too much to his fon, or to facrifice to his own net, and attribute any thing to his good education. He gives thanks to God, who had heard his vows, and had abundantly blefſed the pains he had taken in forming the morals of his fon. Nor is it without a myftery, that though Japheth was the firft born of his three fons, yet Noah fhould, by the fpirit of prophefy, prefer Shem before him ; to teach us, that, in election, God has no refpect to age, and that the order of grace is not the fame with the order of nature. He was therefore juftly called שם that is, *famous and of a great name,* becaufe he was eminent for fo many and fo great privileges above his brethren ; and efpecially becaufe with him and his pofterity " Jehovah put his name," as it is, Deut. xii. 5. Noah adds, *and Canaan fhall be his fervant;* providing him with a fervant, after he had provided him a Lord. This prophecy was not fulfilled till eight hundred years after, when the Ifraelites,
who

who defcended from Shem, invading the land of Canaan, vanquifhed above thirty kings of the Canaanites, and having utterly deftroyed the greateft part of the inhabitaints, made flaves
of the reft, laying a heavy tribute upon them.  And they employed the Gibeonites in cutting wood, and drawing water for
the fervice of the tabernacle, down to the days of David who
changing their name called them *Nethinim,* that is, *dediti-
tious,* or perfons given or offered, Ezra viii. 20. becaufe they
willingly furrendered themfelves.  See Bochart. Phaleg. lib.
2. c. 1.

XIII. What is faid to Japheth is varioufly explained.  The
verb from whence Japheth is derived, as alfo the term *Japht,*
which Noah here ufes by an elegant *paronomafia,* or illufion,
fignifies in Chaldee to *enlarge.*  Hence in the Chaldee paraphrafe on Pf. civ. 25. is the *wide fea ;* and 1 Kings iv. 29. *largenefs
of heart.*.  But in Hebrew, the fame verb fignifies in *kal* to *be
allured,* in *piel* to *allure,* and is generally taken in a bad fenfe, to
denote an *alluring* or *feducing* into error : tho' fometimes in a
good fenfe, as Jer. xx. 7. *thou haft perfuaded me, and I was perfuaded,* and Hof. ii. 14. or according to another divifion, v. 16.
*behold, I will allure her* or *perfuade her.*  Both fignifications are
applied by great men to this paffage.

XIV. They who contend, that the fignification is to *enlarge,*
infift on the following arguments.  Firft, that Noah makes
ufe of the conjugation *hiphil,* which is never ufed to fignify
*alluring ;* nor does it elfewhere occur in *hiphil* but in the Chaldee,
where נות fignifies to *enlarge.*  Secondly, that פתה is a verb of
a common fignification, neverthelefs it is almoft always taken
in a bad fenfe, excepting in one or two places.  The Greeks
generally render it απαταν by a manifeft allufion, but which
rightly expreffes the force of the word.  Thirdly, that פתה when
it fignifies to *allure,* always governs an *accufative :* but here it
is joined to the *dative,* for *lamed,* prefixed to Japheth is the fign
of the *dative.*  Seeing therefore it cannot be faid, *God fhall
allure to Japheth,* we muft render it, God *fhall enlarge to Japheth* place or habitation being to be underftood.  For, thus the
Hebrews fpeak : as Gen. xxvi. 22. *the Lord hath made room for
us,* and to the fame purpofe generally elfewhere.  Moreover
this explication is very confonant to the event.  For, in the
divifion of the earth, the largeft portion fell to be inhabited by
Japheth.  For befides Europe in all its extent, Afia the lefs
belongs to the portion of Japheth ; and Media and a part of
Armenia, and Iberia and Albania, and thofe vaft regions towards the north, which the Scythians formerly occupied, and
the Tartars poffefs at this day ; to fay nothing about the new

world, to which, it is not improbable, that the Scythians formerly paſſed over by the ſtraits of Anian, as Fuller in his Miſcellan. Scar. lib. 2. c. 4. has ſhewn at large.

XV. But others, who contend for the ſignification to *allure*,
can make uſe of theſe reaſons.   1ſt, That Noah did not ſpeak
in Chaldee, but in Hebrew, in which language מתה has ſcarce
if at all, any other ſignification, but to *allure*.   2dly, That not
without reaſon he uſed the conjugating *hiphel*, though occuring
no where elſe in ſcripture; namely, to render the *paronomaſia*
or alluſion the more elegant, which in *piel* cannot come ſo near
to the name Japheth.   And that a change of conjugation does
not neceſſarily infer a change of ſignification.   3dly, That from
the inſtances above alledged, it appears מתה is alſo taken in a
good ſenſe: and that it is not to the purpoſe, whether more rarely
or more frequently ſo. And indeed, the word πιθω, uſed by the a-
poſtle, 2 Cor. v. 11. when he ſpeaks of the doctrine of the goſpel
has a greater affinity with απαταω than the verb απαταω.   4thly, Buxtorf ſhews, by many examples, that the change of the *dative*,
for the *accuſative*, with active verbs is frequent. Theſaur,
Grommat. lib. 2. c. 12. And more eſpecially, that though verbs
of *commanding* are indeed often conſtrued with the accuſative
yet alſo ſometimes with the dative, as Numb. ix. 8. Iſa. xxxviii.
1. As is alſo נשא to *ſeduce*, conſtrued ſometimes with the accuſative, Jer. xlix. 16. at other times with the dative, Jer. iv. 10.
And why not the ſame thing hold in מתה?   5thly, That neither
did the event diſagree with this explication; ſeeing upon rejecting the Jews, the goſpel, by which they are allured to
the communion of God in Chriſt, was more than to all others
revealed to the poſterity of Japheth, and that in their own
language.   And as this was a far greater bleſſing than the
poſſeſſion of the whole earth, why not rather think, that by
thoſe words was predicted what they may moſt conveniently
ſignify?

XVI. Now what follows, *and let him dwell*, or *he ſhall dwell
in the tents of Shem*, may be applied either to God, or to Japheth.
They who apply it to God, as among the ancients Theodoret,
in Gen. quæſt. 58; among the moderns, Fuller in Miſcellan.
Sacr. lib 2. c. 4. *Muſculus in commentar* and others, have a regard to the word שכן whence שכינה, *Shekinah* εκηνωσις; by which
words, the inhabitation of the divine majeſty, is generally ſignified.   The Shechinah was in the tabernacle of the Iſraelites,
in mount Sion, and in the temple built there; of which God
ſ² ſaid, that he would dwell in the thick darkneſs," that is, in
an amazing cloud, the ſign of the divine glory, which filled
the houſe, 1 Kings viii. 11, 12.   And the city, where either
the

the tabernacle or temple ſtood, was called the "place which the Lord choſe to place his name there;" Deut. xiv. 23. But above all the Shechinah is in Chriſt, in whom "dwelleth all the fulneſs of the Godhead bodily," Col. ii. 9. and by whom manifeſting himſelf to the Iſraelites, and travelling over their country, God dwelled in the tents of Shem. To which John ſeems to allude, John i. 14; "the Word was made fleſh and" *σκηνωσε* *tabernacled*, "dwelt among us," and Rev. xxi. 3. behold, ἡ σκηνὴ τᾶ Θᾶ, *the tabernacle of God is with men, and σκηνωσει he wilt dwell with them.* Onkelos, the Chaldee paraphraſt, led the way to our writers in this explication: Who ſpeaks thus: "may God enlarge to Japheth, and may his SHECHINAH, majeſty, dwell in the tents of Shem." Hence Erpenius's Arab. interpreter, "and may his light," that is, the glory of God "dwell in the tents of Shem." Which is certainly, a beautiful explication, and contains a prophecy of Chriſt's walking and dwelling in the land, given to the poſterity of Shem.

XVII. They who explain this prophecy, not of God, but of Japheth, who was to dwell in the tents of Shem, affirm, that it was fulfilled partly *literally*, partly *myſtically*. LITERALLY, becauſe it is apparent, that the Greeks and Romans, who deſcended from Japheth, invaded a great part of Aſia, the lot of Shem; as alſo Balaam propheſied, that Chittim, the poſterity of Japheth ſhall afflict Aſur, and afflict Eber, that is, the Aſſyrians and Hebrews, the poſterity of Shem, Numb. xxiv. 24. MYSTICALLY, becauſe the poſterity of Japheth were, by the preaching of the goſpel, brought to dwell in the ſame church with the Jews who belived; or to ſucceed the unbelieving Jews, who were caſt off. And the church is compared to *tabernacles*; not only becauſe the patriarchs lived in tabernacles or *tents* as ſtrangers, Heb. xi. 9.; but alſo becauſe this is the condition of all belivers in this life, 2 Pet. i. 13. 2 Cor. v. 1. Moreover, theſe *tabernacles* are ſaid to be Shem's, becauſe the church, even to the coming of Chriſt, was confined to the family of Shem. And to them the believers of the Gentiles are united by him, who made *both one*, Eph. ii. 14. In fine, the poſterity of Japheth is the principal part of the church of the Gentiles. For, though God excludes neither the poſterity of Shem nor of Cham from the church, in which "there is neither Greek nor Jew, Barbarian, Scythian; but Chriſt is all and in all," Col. iii. 11.: yet it is certain, that the faith of Chriſt from the days of the apoſtles, has chiefly flouriſhed in Europe, and in thoſe parts of Aſia, which fell to Japheth's lct.

XVIII. But indeed, ſeeing both theſe things, the habitation of God by Chriſt in the tents of Shem, and the habitation of

Japheth

Japheth in the same tents, and having joined not only in time, but also that the latter is a consequent and effect of the former, that is no reason why we may not affirm that both are included in the latitude of the words: and the meaning to be, that the time should come when God would visibly dwell by Christ in the church descended of Shem: and this extraordinary grace be preached through the whole habitable world with such powerful persuasion, that many nations, and among these, chiefly the descendants of Japheth, should by a true faith be united with the church of the Israelites.

XIX. Lastly, it is added, that Canaan should also be the servant of Japheth. And history testifies, that those parts of Asia, which had been long possessed by the Canaanites, were conquered by the Greeks and Romans. And that if any remains of the Canaanites continued, supposing Tyre built by the Sidonians, Thebes by Cadmus, and Carthage by Dido, they were all of them destroyed either by the Greeks or by the Romans. Here I again recommend to the reader Bochart's Phaleg, lib. 3. c. 1.

XX. Let us now take a summary view of the doctrines pointed out by this prophecy of Noah. 1st, We find that the praise of every virtue and of every good action is to be ascribed to God as the supreme author thereof; whom therefore Noah blesses on account of the piety of his son. 2dly, God by a special covenant, laid claim to Shem and his posterity, as his peculiar people, so as to be called their God. 3dly, In the election to grace and glory, and in the bestowing of spiritual benefits external prerogatives are of no manner of avail. For Shem, who was younger than Japheth, is preferred to the elder. 4thly, The heinous crimes of parents are sometimes visited on their descendants unto several generations. For Canaan with his posterity, is on account of the sin of Cham, condemned to be slaves to the descendants of Shem and of Japheth. 5thly, Godliness has the promises even of this life, as well as of that which is to come; and obtains for its reward not only blessings for the soul, but also for the body: for a large part of the earth is promised to Japheth, if we derive his name from *enlarging:* and a large dominion over the Canaanites to Shem and to Japheth   6thly, The word of grace, published in the gospel, has a great power of alluring and persuading. 7thly, Such is the condition of the church on earth, as to resemble tabernacles, expecting a fixed habitation in heaven made without hands. 8thly, The divine majesty shining forth in the Messiah, who was to arise from the posterity of Shem, was afterwards to dwell in his tents. And then, 9thly, the Gentiles, especially the descendants of Japheth, who were before aliens from the
covenants

covenants of promife, were to be allured by the preaching of the gofpel to the communion of the church of Ifrael.

XXI. We are alfo here to take notice of the longevity of the patriarchs in this period; by which means, the doctrine of grace could be very conveniently and fafely propagated by them. For our father Noah, not to mention now the others, lived to fee all the Antediluvians, excepting the firft three: and his fon Shem who alfo had feen the firft world, lived to the fifty-firft year of Jacob. But as thefe teftimonies, concerning the doctrine of the ancient church, were in that period, both more obfcure and fparing, we have been the fuller in treating of them: we fhall therefore ftudy more concifenefs in the others, where the luftre of divine grace was made known in greater plenty and perfpicuity.

---

### C H A P. III.

*Of the Doctrine of Grace from Abraham to Mofes.*

I. **W**E are now got to the days of ABRAHAM, to whom as God revealed himfelf *at fundry times and in divers manners*, fo leaft our prefent work fhould exceed all proper bounds, we fhall only briefly confider the principal heads: and, firft treat of the *appearances* made to Abraham; and then of the *covenant* folemnly entered into and frequently renewed between God and him. For, both thefe contribute to fet the doctrine of the church, during that period in a clearer light.

II. The fcriptures teftify, that God appeared eight times to Abraham I. At Ur of the Chaldees when he commanded him to leave his country and kindred, and go elfewhere. Gen. xii. 1. compared with Acts vii. 2. II. Near Sichem, at the oak of Mamre, Gen. xii. 67. III. In Bethel, Gen. xiii. 3, 4. IV. When he promifed him a fon and heir, Gen. xv. 1. V. When he gave him circumcifion, Gen. xvii. 1. VI. When he entertained him as his gueft, Gen. xviii. 1. VII. When he approved Sarah's propofal to caft out Hagar and Ifmael, Gen. xxi. 12. 8thly, When he commanded him to offer up Ifaac in facrifice, Gen. xxii. 1.

III. There was, in thefe appearances fuch an evident manifeftation of the divine majefty made to the conviction of confcience, that the godly could as eafily diftinguifh them from the delufions of evil fpirits, as a fober man can diftinguifh

fleeping

fleeping and waking. But the fcripture does not always determine, in what form God appeared to Abraham. It is however
clear, that fometimes it was in a human form, by way of prelude, it feems, and fymbol of the future incarnation. Nor are
they miftaken, who imagine, that generally it was the Son of
God, who appeared to Abraham, as he did afterwards to the
other patriarchs, and to Mofes. To which may be referred
John viii. 56. " your father Abraham rejoiced to fee my day :
and he faw it and was glad." He faw that day in the promife
of the feed, in illuftrious appearances, in Ifaac the type and
pledge of the Meffiah, who was to come, and in fine by faith,
the property of which is to exhibit things future, as if they
were prefent : in all thefe things he had a profpect of the incarnation of the Son of God.

IV. Among the other appearances, that mentioned, Gen.
xviii. 1. is very eminent. Where it is faid, that " Jehovah appeared unto Abraham," and ver. 2. and immediately fubjoined, that he faw three men : whence the pious ancients concluded, that the adorable Trinity appeared to Abraham in a vifible
form. *Ambrofe, in Proemio in lib.* 2. *de Spirtu Sancto,* fpeaks
thus : " but Abraham was not ignorant of the Holy Spirit.
He really faw three, and adored one; becaufe one Lord, one
God and one Spirit. And therefore, there was an unity of
honour, becaufe an unity of power." Auguftine lib. 2. de
Trinit. c. 11. 12. alfo lib. 3. *contra maximinum,* c. 26. is more
full on this head. With whom agrees Pafchafius the Roman
deacon, *lib.* 1. *de fpir. fancto, c.* 5. : and others cited by *Forbes.
Inftruct. hift. Thol. lib.* 1. *c.* 14. See *Chriftiani Schotani Biblio-
theca, in hift. Abrahami, p.* 155. *Seq.* MUSCULUS. though of a
different opinion, yet in his commentaries writes : " this paffage was ufually quoted in the church, when the myftery of
the facred Trinity and unity was treated of." MUNSTER, after
reciting the words of Aben Ezra, who in vain attacks the
doctrine of the Chriftians, adds : " this is certain, that Abraham faw three, and addreffed himfelf to one, O my Lord, if
I have found favour in thine eyes; whatever the Jews may idly
talk to the contrary. Had not Abraham acknowledged that
myftery, he would have faid MY LORDS, if I have found favour
in YOUR eyes, &c. The prophets reprefent a plurality of perfons in God, &c." FAGIUS infinuates that it is a common argument of our divines, when he fays, " our authors, infer the
myftery of the Trinity from the appearance of angels. Though
MARTYR is of the fame opinion with Mufculus, yet he thinks
he fhould not conceal, that both the ancient Latin and Greek
fathers, ufually produced this paffage in proof of the Trinity ;

and

and adds, that the inculcating thefe things is not altogether unpleafant to godly perfons.

V. We indeed acknowledge, that the church has ftronger
arguments, whereby to eftablifh this fundamental article of our
faith; yet we imagine, the pious zeal of the fathers in this fubject, is on no account to be exploded. The text affords them
wherewith to defend themfelves. And why fhall we fo far
gratify our adverfaries, as to go about to overturn no contemptible reafons for the truth? Firft, we are to obferve, that after
Mofes had faid, ver. 1. " and Jehovah appeared to him," he
immediately adds, ver. 2. " and he lift up his eyes, and looked,
and lo, three men ftood by him." Which words really feem
to contain the explication of the manner, in which God appeared to Abraham. Nor fhould it be thought unfuitable, that
even the Father and the Holy Spirit appeared in human form;
for Ifaiah faw the whole Trinity, like a king fitting on a throne.
This vifion is, actually explained of the Son, John xii. 41. and
alfo of the Holy Ghoft, Acts xxviii. 25. and, I imagine, none
fhould exclude the Father. Daniel alfo faw the ancient of
days fitting on a throne, and another, like the fon of man, who
came to him, Dan. vii. 9, 13. Which interpreters commonly
explain of the Father and Son, and, as I think, not improperly.

VI. Moreover, we find that Abraham addreffes thefe three;
as if they were one, faying, in the fingular number: " O my
Lord, if I have found favour in thy fight, pafs not away from
thy fervant. He was accuftomed, perhaps, to fee God in a
like form, or was inftructed in that matter by the Holy Spirit;
and therefore in the Trinity he immediately obferved an unity:
for, what fome object, that Abraham addreffed himfelf to one
of the three, becaufe, by his more auguft appearance, he difcovered himfelf to be the Lord of the others, is faying a thing
without proof and befide the text. Nay, the words of the Patriarch are fo put together, that they not only exprefs a civil
and common refpect, but a religious homage. For, he ufes
the appellation *Adonai* with *kametz* under the letter *nun*, which
being thus pointed, (unlefs, perhaps, on account of the accent,
*patach* may be changed into *kametz*), is among the epithets of
the fupreme being, as the orthodox agree. Nor is it any objection, that he entertained them as men. For, feeing they
behaved themfelves as fuch, he was unwilling to deny the duties of humanity, due to the perfon they fuftained. But it was
fomething above common civility, that while they were eating,
he himfelf fhould ftand by them as a fervant under the tree,
ver. 8.

VII. It is added, that when three men appeared to Abraham,
one

one of them is conftantly called Jehovah, ver. 13, 17, 20, &c. and the others, angels, Gen. xix. 1. fent by Jehovah to deftroy Sodom, ver. 13. Becaufe the name, angel, cannot agree to the Father, who is never fent; but may to the Son and Holy Spirit, who are fent by the Father. Auguftine fays well, *lib.* 2. *de Trinit. c.* 13 : " though I do not recollect, that the Holy Spirit is any where called an angel ; yet it may be gathered from his office. For, of him it is faid, he will annunciate or declare unto you, things to come : and certainly angel is interpreted meffenger; but we very evidently read concerning our Lord Jefus Chrift in the prophet, that he is called the angel of the covenant ; though both the Holy Spirit and the Son of God is God and Lord of angels. Nor does Epiphanius differ in his fentiments, in Ancorato §. 70. " for, as the Son is the angel of the covenant, fo alfo the Holy Spirit." But that thofe angels, which Lot faw, were not miniftering fpirits, may be gathered from the religious honour, which he paid them, Gen. xix. 18, 19. &c. And the anfwer, full of authority and divine majefty, they gave, ver. 21. What fome pretend, that, in the mean time, a third perfon intervened, who had remained with Abraham, and to whom thefe words are to be applied, is what is not in the text : nor do I fee, how it can be proved.

VIII. It does not militate againft this interpretation, that thefe angels are exprefsly diftinguifhed from Jehovah, ver. 13. They are, indeed, diftinguifhed from Jehovah the Father, not effentially, as we have fhewn, but hypoftatically or perfonally. Nor is it below the dignity of an increated angel to fay, לא אוכל לעשות, " I fhall not be able to do any thing, till thou be come thither," ver. 22.; becaufe that was faid, on the fuppofi- tion of a gracious decree and a promife already made to Lot. And this expreffion fhould be compared with John v. 19, 29. And laftly, Heb. xiii. 2. is but foolifhly objected, for the apoftle there recommends hofpitality on this account ; namely that " fome have entertained angels unawares ;" whereas if God himfelf had been entertained, that confideration fhould rather have been urged. But it is not for us to prefcribe to the Holy Spirit, what arguments or expreffions he is to make ufe of. If the apoftle had thought fit to fay, that Jehovah himfelf was en- tertained, he might certainly have done it, feeing Mofes ex- prefsly afferts it. And now when he fpeaks of angels, he, in like manner, imitates Mofes, who declares that angels turned into Lot. But feeing the term *angel* fignifies diverfe things, and may be applied both to an increated and to a created angel ; therefore from the bare appellation, angel, it cannot be proved, that the difcourfe only regards created angels. Moreover,
when

when he says, that some entertained angels unawares, he again
has an eye to Lot, who, inviting them to come under his roof,
imagined they were some honourable guests, till, from their
talk, or by the inspiration of the Spirit, he understood who they
really were. Nor is it any objection, that the apostle says in
the plural number, that *some* entertained angels. For an enal-
lage or change of number is frequent in such ways of speaking ;
and it is probable, that what happened to Lot, happened also
to many others. And now let it be sufficient, to have said these
things, in favour of the explication of the ancients, and of other
very excellent divines of the reformed church. Nor do I imagine, that equitable judges will blame me for having attempted
to shew, that those pious and learned men neither spoke incon-
siderately, nor, by their arguments, did any prejudice to the
good cause they undertook to maintain. But should any one
think otherwise, it is not our province to contend with him, we
shall use much stronger arguments than these with such a
person.

IX. Let us now consider that covenant which God entered
into with Abraham. Paul says, that its commencement was
four hundred and thirty years before the giving of the law,
Gal. iii. 17. As chronologers vary in their calculations, so it
is a matter of dispute among them, from what period to begin
these years ; the difficulty of finding the truth being such, that
Scaliger declared it to be unsurmountable. What seems to
come nearest, *Fridericus Spanhemius in Introduct. Chronologica
ad Hist. V. T.* has ingeniously, as is his manner, explained.
Whose calculation is thus : from the 75th * year of Abraham
in which he came out of Charan, Gen. xii. 4. to the birth of
Isaac in the hundredth year of his father, are 25 years. From
the birth of Isaac to that of Jacob, who was born in Isaac's
60th year, Gen. xxv. 26. and 15 years before the death of A-
braham, Gen. xxv. 7, 8, are 60 years. From that period to
the going down of Jacob into Egypt, in the 39th year of Joseph,
or about nine years after his exaltation in Egypt, Gen. xli. 46,
are 130 years, Gen. xlvii. 9. The years from Abraham's entering Canaan, to the going down of Jacob to Egypt, come to
be 215. And then the years of the dwelling or bondage of
the Israelites in Egypt, were as many, or 215 years ; and are
thus calculated. Joseph died in the 110th year of his age,

Gen.

---

* There is doubtless a typographical mistake in our author, who makes Abraham
to leave Charan in his 78th year, and that in the 28th year after, Isaac was born,
Whereas the sacred text says, he was but 75, to which we add 25, that will bring
us to Abraham's 100th year, when Isaac was born.

Gen. l. 26. from which, if you subtract 39, which was·His age
at the time of Jacob's defcent, there will remain 70 years.
From the death of Jofeph are to be reckoned·about 65 years
down to the birth of Mofes, the grandfon of Kohath, who went
down very young with his father Levi into Egypt, Gen. xlvi. 11.
and begat Amram the father of Mofes, when upwards of 60
years old ; but Amram, when he was 70, begat Mofes, who
was younger than Aaron, Exod. vi. 17, 19. From the birth
of Mofes to the bringing the people out of Egypt, are 80 years :
and thus the years of their continuing in Egypt, amount to
215. Which if added to as many years from Abraham's going
out of Charan, to his going down into Egypt, we have a period
of 430 years. And by fo many years did the federal promife
made to Abraham, go before the giving of the law.

X. But in this covenant we will confider. 1ft, The STIPU-
LATIONS. 2dly, The PROMISES. Which were, indeed, repeated at various times, and expreffed under different heads or
articles ; but which we fhall recite briefly and in order, for the
help of the memory.

XI. The STIPULATION contains chiefly three precepts. 1ft,
THAT OF LEAVING HIS COUNTRY, his kindred and father's
houfe : though he knew not whither God was to bring him,
Gen. xii. 1. This imports a denial of himfelf, and of thofe
things which are ufually moft dear and defirable; and in fine, an
univerfal furrender of himfelf to God. Compare Pf. xlv. 11. and
Luke. ix. 59, 60, 61, 62, and Mat. x. 37. 2dly, OF NOT FEARING,
Gen. xv. 1. By this, faith fecurely acquiefces in God, was enjoin-
upon him. For, fear is oppofite to faith, Mark v. 36. and
Mark. iv. 40. 3dly, OF WALKING BEFORE GOD, and being upright, Gen. xvii. 1. This is the precept of holinefs; which extends not only to the external actions, but alfo to the inward
motions of the foul, believing, that all muft be done as in the
prefence, and under the all-feeing eye of God. In·thofe few
words, the infinitely wife God has comprehended all the duties
incumbent on a religious perfon towards the Deity.

XII. The PROMISES annexed to the ftipulation, are of various
kinds ; fome are *fpiritual*, others *corporal*. The fpiritual, are
either *general* and common to all believers, or *fpecial* and peculiar
to Abraham.

XIII. The *general* promifes are thefe, Gen. xv. 1. " I am thy
fhield and thy exceeding great reward," and Gen. xvii. 17, 1, 7.
" I, who am EL-SHADDAI, God all-fufficient, will be a God
unto thee, and to thy feed after thee." In thefe words God
.promifes, 1ft, Protection againft every ·evil, while he calls himfelf a fhield. 2dly, A moft eminent reward and of infinite
                                      value,

value, feeing he makes over to him not only his benefits, in which he is moft affluent, but alfo himfelf, the fountain of every bleffing. In ike manner, as Eliphaz fays to Job, *the Almighty will be thy moft choice gold, and filver of ftrength will be to thee:* it therefore fignifies eminently " an exceeding and eternal weight of glory," 2 Cor. iv. 17. which we could not bear, unlefs, we were endowed with new powers. 3dly, The communion and fruition of this all-fufficient God, in grace and glory, in foul and in body. See what we faid of the word, Shaddai, Book III. Chap. 1. fect. 2. and of the expreffion, " to be the God of any one, ibid." chap. 2. fect. 5. 4thly, The continuance of that favour in the elect feed.

XIV. More *efpecially*, God promifed, *firft*, that Abraham fhould be the head, and honorary father of all believers, who in him as the type of the bleffing, were to obtain the bleffing. For, fo the words run, Gen. xii. 2, 3. " I will make of thee a great nation, and I will blefs thee, and make thy name great, and thou fhalt be a bleffing——and in thee fhall all families of the earth be bleffed." He not only makes the moft ample promifes of every kind, as well earthily as heavenly, but he likewife promifes a new and a great name, that he fhould be the *father of all believers*, Rom. iv. 11. than which fcarce a greater can be granted to any mere man. Nay, he declares, that he fhould not only be bleffed but *bleffing* itfelf ; fo that all the bleffing of God might be feen accumulated on him, and to refide in him, as the fountain and fource, but a fecondary and lefs principal ; and be the type and exemplar of every bleffing. For, it is added, " and in thee fhall all the families of the earth be bleffed. *In thee* may be fimply explained, *with thee*: as it is faid, **Gal.** iii. 9 " they which be of faith, are bleffed with faithful Abraham." For, ב of the Hebrews is fometimes the fame thing as *with*: as Exod. viii. 5, " ftretch forth thine hand" במטר WITH *thy rod*," and Exod. xv. 19. " the horfe of Pharoah went in ברכבו ובפרשיו WITH his chariots and his horfemen into the fea." But בר, *in thee*, feems to denote fomething more : for, in Abraham all the nations of the earth are bleffed. ift, Becaufe the Meffiah was in his loins, in whom every bleffing is contained. 2dly, Becaufe he was the head and prince of God's covenant, and the pattern of faith and bleffing to thofe who were to come after him.

XV. Paul has given a notable commentary on this place, Gal. iii. 6, 7, 8, " even as Abraham believed God, and it was accounted to him for righteoufnefs. Know ye therefore, that they which are of faith, the fame are the children of Abraham. And the fcripture forefeeing, that God would juftify the heathen

then through faith, preached before the gospel unto Abraham saying, in thee shall all nations be blessed." The Apostle there supposes, as a thing well known among Christians, that Abraham was the honorary father of all the blessed seed, and consequently, that there was no other mean of obtaining the blessing, that is justification and the favour of God, than that by which Abraham obtained it : but he obtained it by faith. Moreover, seeing it is foretold, that in him all the families of the earth are to be blessed, they must needs be united to him, and be accounted to him, as their spiritual parent. But, in order to that union, it is not sufficient, that there be even an association with his natural descendants by a communion of ceremonies, or of political laws: but a communion in the same faith is requisite. And seeing this promise extended to all the families of the earth, and consequently even to the Gentiles ; the Apostle has justly concluded, that the Gentiles also are to be joined to Abraham, by the imitation of his faith, and, by the same faith, become partakers of the same blessing with him.

XVI. *Secondly*, God especially promised him a SEED : which does not signify promiscuously, any one who was to descend from Abraham according to the flesh. For even Ishmael was *his feed*, Gen. xxi. 13. And therefore great, but carnal promises were also made to him, Gen. xvi. 10. and Gen. xvii. 20. But by *feed* we are to understand. 1st, ISAAC, who sprung from a father almost dead, and of a mother barren and past bearing. For, " in Isaac shall thy seed be called, Gen. xxi. 12. Moreover, Isaac was not only the stock, but also the type of the Messiah, who was afterwards to be born, and that of a virgin, who was certainly not more, if not less, capable than Sarah to bring forth a seed. And therfore, 2dly, the seed denotes also CHRIST, * that seed which was formerly promised in paradise, " he saith not, and to seeds, as of many; but to thy seed, which is Christ, Gal. iii. 16. Besides, as Isaac was born, not by the virtue or power of the flesh, but of the promise, he is also a type of all BELIEVERS, who, are indebted to the word of the promise of the gospel for their spiritual birth. And 3dly, Believers are also denoted by the feed ; " they which are the children of the flesh, these are not the children of God ; but the children of the promise are accounted for the feed, Rom. ix. 8.

XVII.

---

* This is more explicit and particular than the first promise, in the garden, concerning the *feed of the woman ;* for this determines the *family,* as well as the *race,* or kind ; that he should not only be in our nature, but descend from such a stock, even from Abraham, who was not only the father of the *Jewish* nation, but of all the *faithful.*

XVII. Here we have a difficulty to be refolved, which, it feems, cannot well be omitted. Seeing the word feed fometimes denotes not only, but alfo chiefly a multitude of men; and efpecially, as it was promifed to Abraham, that his feed fhould be as the duft of the earth, and fince it has juft been fhewn, that, by the promifed feed of Abraham, both Ifaac and all believers are to be underftood; how then could the Apoftle infift on the fingular number, in order from thence to make out, that by the feed we are to underftand Chrift? and which feems to be the lefs cogent, becaufe the facred writers of the Old Teftament, when treating of men, never ufe the word רע, in the plural number. This difficulty appeared fo great to Jerome, that not knowing how to untye the knot, he ventured, though not with fufficient piety, to cut it afunder. He obferves, that Paul only made ufe of this argument with the dull and ftupid Galatians, which he knew would not, in other refpects, be approved by the prudent and the learned, and therefore forewarned the prudent reader of this, wen he faid " brethren, I fpeak after the manner of men." Jerome's words are as follows : " whence it is evident, that the Apoftle performed what he had promifed, and did not make ufe of abftrufe meanings, but fuch as daily occur and are common, and which (had he not premifed," after the manner of men) " might difpleafe the prudent." But this is giving up the caufe to thofe, who defpife and ridicule the fcripture. The Apoftle certainly, by the expreffion mentioned by Jerome, was far from intimating, that by abufing the ftupidity of the Galatians, he would argue lefs accurately and folidly. This is highly unworthy the gravity of an Apoftle and the unfearchable wifdom of the Spirit of God, by whofe infpiration he wrote thefe things. Nor was this epiftle written only for the dull and ftupid Galatians, if we may call them fo, but alfo for the whole church to be a * directory of faith. He intimated only this, that, he was to draw a fimilitude, from human things in order to explain things divine, and thus compare great things with fmall.

XVIII. And, indeed, as all other things, fo thefe alfo, appear to me to have been moft wifely obferved by the Apoftle. It is certain, that the term *feed*, often fignifies a multitude, but it is a multitude collectively taken and united in one; at leaft with regard to the firft ftock cr origin. When he fpeaks of the feed of Abraham, as the feed of the promife ὃ ἐπήγγελται, *which he had promifed*, to which the fame bleffings are to flow
from

* The author's words are *in fidei cynofuram*, in which he refers to Cynofura, which was the leffer *bear-ftar*, by which the mariners of Tyre and Sidon, fteered their courfe.

from the fame fountain, it muft be confidered as one body. If
I miftake not, when the Apoftle fays, the promifes were made
to Abraham and to his feed, he points to the formula of the
covenant, which we have, Gen. xvii. 7. I will be a God unto
thee and to thy feed after thee." On this occafion the Apoftle
declares, that feeing all the families of the earth were, in their
proper time, to become partakers of this blefling, it was neceffary, they fhould be accounted to the feed of Abraham, and
united to him in one body, and, as he fpeaks, Eph. i. 10.
" gathered together in one in Chrift." But this is not done
by circumcifion, or the other Jewifh ceremonies. For befides
that the promife was made to Abraham, while he was yet un-
circumifed, and 430 years before the giving of the law ; thefe
ceremonies are the middle wall of partition, which feparate the
Ifraelites from the Gentiles, and therefore cannot be the band
of union. But this incorporation or coalition is effected by the
fpirit of faith, which indiffolubly unites believers to Chrift the
head, who is the principal feed, and with one another mutually : and thus they all form together one fpiritual feed of Abraham
a whole Chrift, with his myftical body. For, here we take
the word CHRIST in the fame fenfe, as 1 Cor. xii. 12. Seeing
therefore, as is evident, the promifes were made to the fpiritual feed of Abraham alone, exclufive of all others ; but that
fpiritual feed ought to have alfo the fame fpiritual ftock and origin; it muft needs form one myftical body, whofe head undoubt-
tedly is Chrift, from whom all the other members have the honour to be called. Well therefore did the Apoftle urge, that by
the appellation *feed*, an union was intended, not precifely of
perfon, but of fome myftical body, united by faith under the
head Chrift. See on this place Drufius, Cameron, Gomarus,
Diodati and others, who explain it of Chrift and his myftical
body.

XIX. But we are not to overlook a notable diverfity of expreffion, that occurs here. God feveral times repeats to
Abraham, " in thee fhall be blefled all families of the earth,"
Gen. xii. 3. and Gen. xviii. 18. But of the feed of Abraham
it is faid, " and in him fhall all nations of the earth והתברכו
blefs themfelves," Gen. xxii. 18. which is repeated, Gen. xxvi.
4. of the feed of Ifaac. But furely, we are one way blefled in
Abraham, and another in his feed, Chrift. In Abraham as the
type and exemplar; in Chrift, as the meritorious caufe and
real beftower of the blefling, Eph. i. 3. We are not only
blefled, but alfo *blefs ourfelves* in Chrift, acknowledging and
praifing him, as the fountain and fource of the blefling, flowing
down to us : אשר חמתברך בארץ יתברך באלהי אמן " that he who blef-
feth

feth himfelf in the earth, fhall blefs himfelf in * the God of truth," Ifa. lxv. 16.

XX. The *corporal* or external promifes made to Abraham are chiefly three.  (1.) " The multiplication of his feed by Ifaac," Gen. xiii. 16. and Gen. xv. 5. and Gen. xvii. 2. and Gen. xxii. 16.  (2.) " The inheritance of the land of Canaan," Gen. xii. 7. Gen. xlii. 15. Gen. xv. 17. and Gen. xvii. 7. which was fuifilled in the twelve tribes of Ifrael, efpecially under David and Solomon ; and afterwards, during the fecond temple, when all Palestine and Idumea were conquered and fubdued by the Jews.  (3.) " The deliverance from the Egyptian bondage," Gen. xv. 13, 14.  But we are to obferve, that thefe external promifes were types of fpiritual and heavenly things. · For, the multiplication of the carnal feed denoted the great number of fpiritual children, both from among the Jews and the Gentiles, that was to be brought to the faith, Rev. vii. 9.  And Canaan was a pledge of heaven ; and the deliverance from Egypt, fignified the deliverance of the church from fin, from the world, the devil and Babylon.

XXI. But we ought not to omit the fundamental doctrine of juftification by faith alone, which, at that time, was very much illuftrated by the example of Abraham, and the divine declaration concerning him.  For, thus it is faid, " Abraham believed in Jehovah, and he counted it to him for righteoufnefs," Gen. xv. 6.  This teftimony is the more to be obferved, becaufe the apoftle frequently ufes it, in order to affert the righteoufnefs of faith, Rom. iv. 3, Gal. iii. 6.

XXII. The faith of Abraham had, for its general object, all the promifes made to him.  " He gave glory to God, and was fully perfuaded, that what he had promifed he was able alfo to perform," Rom. iv. 20, 21.  He therefore believed, and, by faith, embraced the promifes of the heavenly and eternal bleifing, of the birth of a fon from his barren wife, of the multiplication of his feed, both the fpiritual and carnal, of the calling of the Gentiles, &c.  But more efpecially he believed that promife, whereby God engaged to be " his fhield and exceeding great reward," Gen. xv. 1.  That is, he relied on God, as the averter of every evil, and the beftower of every good.  But in a moft efpecial manner, he believed the promife concerning that feed, who was to be the repofitory and the caufe of the bleffing ; and he expected, that the Son of God would manifeft

---

* Or *in the God* AMEN ; fo that our author, with great propriety, quotes this paffage, as it is very evident, that the bleffed feed is called *amen*, even the AMEN, the true and faithful witnefs, Rev. iii. 14.

feſt himſelf in the fleſh, which he would aſſume from his poſterity, and thus his faith was in Chriſt: for, " he rejoiced to ſee Chriſt's day, and he ſaw it and was glad," John viii. 56.

XXIII. But this faith, this believing, was imputed unto him for righteouſneſs. Not that the faith of Abraham was by a gracious eſtimation, accounted by God in the room of perfect obedience, which the covenant of works required : but that by his faith, he laid hold on, and ſpiritually united or appropriated to himſelf, the promiſed ſeed, by virtue of which union, all the righteouſneſs of that ſeed was reputed to be his righteouſneſs. Thus in the book of God's accounts, the great bleſſings of God are written on one page, as ſo many talents beſtowed on men : and the ſins of men, not rendering to God the thanks due for ſo great benefits, as, ſo many debts : and laſtly, the condemnatory ſentence, by which they are declared guilty of eternal death. But as man's own righteouſneſs could not ſtand on the other page, the ſatisfaction and merits of Chriſt for the elect are inſcribed, and likewiſe their faith, as the gratuitous gift of God, and that by which the elect are united to Chriſt, and become partakers of all his righteouſneſs. And thus upon balancing the account, from their faith it appears, that all their debts are cancelled, and that they have ſufficient to give them a right to eternal life. Thus faith is imputed for righteouſneſs. See what we have conſidered at large, book III. chap. viii, ſect. 42.

XXIV. The promiſes made to the father, and eſpecially that concerning the ſeed, in which all nations of the earth were to bleſs themſelves, were not only confirmed to Iſaac the ſon of Abraham, Gen. xxvi. 4. but alſo the doctrine of gratuitous reprobation and moſt free election, was evidently publiſhed in the oracle concerning his ſons, Jacob and Eſau. For, Jehovah ſaid to Rebeccah, when with twins, " two nations are in thy womb, and two manner of people ſhall be ſeparated from thy bowels; and the one people ſhall be ſtronger than the other people, *and the elder ſhall ſerve the younger,*" Gen. xxv. 23.

XXV. We find, in ſcripture, that this propheſy was two ways fulfilled, the one hiſtorically the other myſtically; both regarding as well the ſtocks themſelves, as the nations, which were to ariſe from them. As to the ſtocks and heads of the nations, the elder ſerved the younger, that is, Jacob appeared more worthy than Eſau. (1.) In reſpect of the birth-right, which Eſau ſold. (2.) Of the inheritance of the land of Canaan, from which Eſau was excluded, as Iſhmael and the other children of Abraham had been formerly. (3.) Of communion in the covenant of God, which Eſau, by his profaneneſs, had forfeited. If we conſider the nations, they were often at war, and

and there was a time, when the Edomites feemed to prevail over the Ifraelites, " Edom purfued his brother with the fword and caft off all pity, Amos i. 11. fee Num. xx. 18, 19. But at laft the Ifraelites proved conquerors, when David put garrifons throughout all Edom, and the Edomites became David's fervants, 2 Sam. viii. 14. And they continued fo, until the reign of Joram, under whom they again fhook off the yoke, 2 Kings viii. 20. according to the prophecy of Ifaac, Gen. xxvii. 40. But afterwards, under the fecond temple, they were again conquered, and entirely fubjected to the Ifraelites. See *Jofeph. Antiq. Lib.* 13. *c.* 17.

XXVI. But thefe things had likewife a further profpect; for, as the inheritance of the land of Canaan was a type of the heavenly inheritance, and the national covenant included the fpiritual covenant of grace; fo alfo the exclufion from the national covenant and typical inheritance, was a fign of the exclufion from the covenant of grace and the heavenly inheritance. So that Efau and Jacob are here inftances of the moft free reprobation, and gratuitous election of God. And that this was the myftical fenfe of this prophecy, the apoftle fhews, Rom. ix. 10. and following verfes.

XXVII. God renewed the fame promifes made to the father and grandfather to Jacob, Gen. xxviii. 13—15. Though Jacob declared his twelve fons, the patriarchs, to be the heirs of thefe promifes; yet, by the infpiration of the Spirit of God, he gave the tribe of Judah fuch prerogative above the reft, that not only kings, but alfo the prince of kings, even the Meffiah, was to defcend from it, Gen. xlix. 10. " the fceptre fhall not depart from Judah, nor a lawgiver from between his feet, until Shiloh come, and unto him fhall the gathering of the people be." On which place we have illuftrious commentaries by the moft excellent perfons, which we judge foreign to our purpofe here to rehearfe. The plain meaning feems to us to be this. It is foretold concerning Judah, that his tribe fhould very much excel all the reft, both with refpect to the ornament of the fceptre and the fupreme government, and the feat of religion, the temple and fchools, where the moft famous *doctors of the law*, were to refide. It is alfo foretold, that חליש, Shilo, which I tranflate, the *quieter* or *peace-maker, faviour,* from the root חליש, *to be quiet* and *fafe.* As the Hebrew חליש and Latin *falvus* agree to it both in found and fenfe. This is doubtlefs the Meffiah, to whom is promifed the *gathering,* or *obedience of the people,* who were to believe in him, and fubmit to his precepts. The event ratified this explication. For, in very many things the tribe of Judah had the pre-eminence above the others: from that the royal family arose; there, for a long time, was the seat both of empire and religion, and lastly, from the term Judah, the whole nation of Israel had its name. It is also evident and well known, that " our Lord sprang out of Judah," Heb. vii. 14. about the time of whose birth, according to the intention of the oracle, the sceptre gradually departed. 1. When Judea was subdued by the victorious arms of Pompey, and Jerusalem taken, 2. When Herod the Idumean was raised to the throne. 3. When Judea was reduced to a Roman province, and annexed to Syria. 4. and lastly, When the city and temple, and the whole Jewish polity were destroyed and overturned by Vespasian. While in the mean time many nations flocked with emulation, from all parts of the world, to the standard of salvation, which was then erected, and gave up their names to Christ.

XXVIII. It will not be improper to inquire into the blessing of the tribe of Naphthali; to see whether we may not possibly find something even there concerning Christ, Gen. xlix. 21. " Naphtali is a hind let loose, he giveth godly words:" for, so the passage is commonly rendered. What the Jewish as well as Christian interpreters intended thereby, we leave others to find out. In words so very obscure, we apprehend, that he who conjectures best is the best interpreter. Jerome, after premising some things, says, it is better, that " we refer the whole to the doctrine, which our Saviour taught, for the most part, in the lot of Naphthali;" but he does not properly shew how the words can be applied to that. Let us attempt it. We suppose, that a part of Galilee fell to the lot of Naphthali; to which belonged the lake of Genesaret, and in the neighbouring territory Capernaum stood; as Lightfoot proves, *Centuria chorographica, Matthæo premissa, c.* 71 and 80; and as appears from Mat. iv. 13. where it is said to be " a town on the sea-coast, in the borders of Zabulon and Naphthali;" that is, in that part of Naphthali bordering on Zabulon. In that town Christ dwelt, and first preached the gospel, as he likewise did in the adjacent country, according to Isaiah's prophecy, there quoted by Matthew. And thither a great multitude came from their habitations, quitted their occupations, and flocked with the greatest ardour to hear Christ preach. Let us now see, whether that truth be not justly signified by this prophecy of Jacob. *A hind let loose,* of what can this be a more proper emblem, than of some multitude running, with the greatest eagerness of mind, to some place or other: especially, where they find fountains of living water to quench their parching thirst. As it is not unusual with the Holy Spirit, to compare believers to *hinds.* See Cant. ii. 7. Heb. iii. 19. Isa. xxxv. 6. And the Naphthalites may

may be called a hind *let loofe*, becaufe they were formerly engaged in other purfuits, which could not quench their thirft;
but now being ftirred up by the gofpel, which is the publication of liberty, and breaking through the entanglements of
worldly purfuits, they flocked to the Lord Jefus. But *by* him,
*who giveth goodly words*, who can more properly be underftood
than Chrift, into whofe *lips grace is poured*, Pfal. xlv. 2. whofe
*mouth is moft fweet*, Cant. v. 16. whofe *gracious words*, that is,
almoft literally אמרי שׁפר, aftonifhed the hearers, Luke iv. 22.
Moreover, it often happens that, in Hebrew, the abfolute ftate
is put for the conftructed; as Buxtorf proves by feveral examples, *Grammat. lib.* 2. *c.* 4. So that nothing hinders our con-
ftruing the words thus: " Naphthali is a hind of him that giveth
goodly words," that is, devoted to the moft lovely Jefus, and
hanging on his gracious lips. What favours this interpretation
is, that the two hemifticks do not otherwife appear to be well
connected; it not being the property of a hind to give goodly
words. But if we conftrue them, as I have faid, nothing is
forced into the text, nothing mean and low is expreffed by the
prophecy, nothing devifed inconfiftent with the genius of the
Hebrew language; but every word has a fignification, both
proper and highly emphatical; and feeing they undoubtedly fet
forth the bleffing of Naphthalites, why fhould we not rather
think of fome fpiritual privilege, they had by the Meffiah, than
of fome external and momentary bleffing under Barak and Deborah, in which Napthali had nothing diftinguifhing above
Zabulon? Nor is it fo certain, that the Naphthalites, as fome
would gather from this place, were more eloquent than the
other Ifraelites. On the contrary, the people of Galilee, a part
of which that tribe occupied, were fo impure in their language,
and rude in their manners, that they were the derifion of the
inhabitants of Jerufalem: as Buxtorf largely proves, efpecially
of that part of Galilee, in which the Naphthalites dwelt, *Lex.
Talm voce*. But Barak, fay they, was a Naphthalite, who, upon
the defeat of Sifera, fung together with Deborah that excellent
fong of triumph, which we ftill have in the fifth chapter of
Judges. As if it could follow, that the Naphthalites ftudied
eloquence of language, from this fingle inftance of a poem;
written not by Barak, but by Deborah the prophetefs, who was
defcended not of the tribe of Naphthali, but of Ephraim: as
*Bochart. Hierozoic. lib.* 3. *c.* 18. has learnedly obferved. Mafius
alfo in his commentaries on the book of Judges, Chap. xix.
No. 35. proves by feveral arguments, that thefe things cannot
be applied to Barak and Deborah; with whom Rivet on this
place agrees. Nor fhould any fcornfully reject this application,

made

made to the doctrine of Christ, as if it was a modern invention, because besides Jerome, the same application is made by Ambrose and Procopius, as quoted by Cornelius a Lapide. To whom may be added Eucherius bishop of Lyons, and Peter Martyr. And if Isaiah prophesied concerning Christ's preaching in the country of Naphthali, why may we not allow that Jacob prophesied concerning the same thing, when he foretold the fate of his children.

XXIX. It is not to be doubted, that these articles of the saving doctrine, which were so carefully handed down by the fathers, were not only preserved in Egypt, and inculcated upon their children, by these pious patriarchs: but also, that among the posterity of Lot, of Ishmael, of Esau and others, as long as the Gentiles were not entirely rejected, the remains of the same truth eminently shone forth, as appears from Job, from his friends, and from Balaam.

XXX. When Job, declared his confidence in God, he called him *the* NOTZER *of Adam* the *keeper* or *preserver of men*, Job vii. 20. Christ uses the same word, when he expresses his solicitous care for his church, Isa. xxvii. 3. *I Jehovah do keep it.* And the elect, whom Christ bears, as it were in his eyes and hands, are called *the preserved and the saved of Israel*, Isa. xlix. 6. The denomination Nazarene comes nearest to this term in Hebrew, נצר though it was given to Christ because he dwelt at Nazareth, yet we learn from Matthew that it was mystical, and belonged to the fulfillment of some prophecy. Mat. ii. 23. Interpreters endeavour to find this prophecy in more places than one. Some have recourse to the Nazarites of the Old Testament. But these are not called נצרים, with a *trade*, as the Jews constantly write the name, Nazarene; but נצרים, with a *zain*. Others observe, that the Messiah is called Isa. xi. 1. and Isa. lx. 21. *the branch*, from which the name of the town Nazareth is likewise derived. But amidst such diversity of opinions, it is astonishing, that but very few have recollected this passage of Job, where there is express mention of the Messiah, under the appellation *Notzer*. At least this passage of Job, and that of Isaiah, with which we compared it, are with no less probability applied to this purpose, than any thing else I have met with among interpreters. Job also professes excellent things concerning the person, offices and benefits of Christ, Job xvi. 25. *Seq.* But that passage we have already discussed, Book III. Chap. II. Sect. 19.

XXXI. Let us add Elihu's commendation of the Messiah, Job xxxiii. 23, 24. " If there be, [*an angel*] a messenger with him, an interpreter, one among a thousand, to shew unto man his

his uprightnefs : then he is gracious unto him, and faith, deliver [redeem] him from going down to the pit, I have found a ranfom." Elihu here fpeaks of a man, who was brought, by afflictions and difeafe, almoft to the gates of death; and fhews, how he may be faved from death both of foul and body. If Elihu had any knowledge of the Meffiah, certainly this was the place to fpeak concerning him. And fince every word is fo framed, as to fuit none more properly than the Meffiah, to whom can they be better applied than to him? Elihu fet forth in a conife manner. I. The *excellence* of the Meffiah. II. His *offices*. III. His *benefits*.

XXXII. He proclaims the excellence of the Meffiah, calling him, *one of a thoufand*. Where thoufand is a definite number put for an indefinite; as if he had faid, one above others, let them be ever fo many. There are indeed very many, who may be called angels and interpreters; and though thefe names may be given to thoufands, yet this perfon is not to be among the number of a thoufand others, becaufe he excells them all, in refpect of nature, dignity and efficacy, being *only one* among fo many others.

XXXIII. He firft fets before us, under a general appellation, the *offices* of the Meffiah, and then more particularly explains them. In general he calls him an *angel*, becaufe Chrift was fent by the Father, and fpoke and acted with men in the Father's name. In Mal. iii. 3. he is called the *Angel of the covenant*. Neverthelefs he is fo the *Angel* of *Jehovah*, that, at the fame time, he is himfelf Jehovah, Zech. iii. 1, 2.; in " whom is the name of Jehovah," Exod. xxiii. 21. and who " is by fo much more excellent than all other angels, as he obtained a more excellent name than they," Heb. i. 4. Chrift was called an Angel before his incarnation, becaufe he often appeared, as angels ufually did; and becaufe he then performed thofe things, which depended on his future miffion in the flefh.

XXXIV. But then more particularly 16. His prophetical office is fignified when he is called *interpreter*, a teacher, compare Ifa. xliii. 27. namely, becaufe he is *he that doth fpeak*, Ifa. lii. 6. ἱλογος τυ Θυ *the word of God*, whofe office is to " declare the Father," John i. 18. Nay, he who *fpeaks plainly*, and interprets dark fayings. For this is the meaning of מליצה a *clear faying;* to which is oppofed חידה a *dark faying*, Prov. i. 6. Moreover, it belongs to Chrift as a prophet, to *declare* unto man *his righteoufnefs*, externally by his word, internally by his Spirit, by which we may underftand, either the righteoufnefs of God, demanding fatisfaction for fin, and even chaftifing his elect on that account, or the righteoufnefs, of Chrift himfelf, or his

fatisfactory

satisfactory righteousness, which is the only meritorious cause
of our salvation; or in a word, the righteousness of man, that
is, the practice of faith and repentance. There is none of all
these things, which Christ does not teach his people.

XXXV. 2dly, The office of *redeemer*, because to him is
ascribed נאל or פדה, both signifying the same thing, and
פדה. The former word denotes *redemption from guilt*, from his
obligation to, and from the power of another; properly, indeed, that which is effected by a price, as Pf. xlix. 7. where פדה
and פדיון *price of redemption* are joined: improperly, that which
is brought about by a greater power, opposed to the power of
an unjust detainer, as Deut. ix. 26. " thou hast redeemed
through thy greatness;" that is, as it is explained, Neh. i. 10.
" by thy great power and by thy strong hand." Both these
ways of redemption are applicable to the Messiah; who, on
paying the price, purchases the freedom of his people, and by
a strong hand applies it to them. The term פדה generally
signifies a price, by which any one may be appeased, and the
punishment bought off. Christ paid that price, when he gave
his " life a ransom for many," Mat. xx. 28.

XXXVI. But interpreters are not agreed, whether those
words *deliver* or redeem *him*, are the words of Christ, inter-
ceeding with the Father; or the words of the Father addressed
to Christ. Those who maintain the former, explain them thus.
" Redeem him, that is, by thine infinite power deliver him
" from the evil with which he is pressed down, and which
" otherwise hangs over him; for I myself have undertaken to
" satisfy thy justice; and in that satisfaction there is λύτρον the
" ransom which *I have found*, that is, which I know to be full
" and complete; or which *I have found*, that is, have disco-
" vered to him, for whom I intercede, that he may apprehend
" it by faith." Compare Heb. ix. 12. " having obtained eternal redemption." They who choose the latter, think, that the
meaning of the words is this; " Do thou, O Christ, redeem
" this wretched man, apply to him the efficacy of thy merits,
" I have no longer any objection to his happiness; for *I have
" found a ransom*, I have considered and weighed the satisfac-
" tion thou hast made for man, and have found it to be such,
" as my justice required, that is, highly sufficient." Whatever way we take the words, they yield a very suitable
meaning.

XXXVII. There are two *benefits* mentioned. 1st, The mercy
of God, *if there be a messenger [an angel] with him, an interpreter;*
this is the *protasis*, or first proposition; *and*, or *then he is gracious unto him;* this is the *apodosis*, or latter proposition. He
shews,

shews, that it is not otherwise possible for man to obtain mercy of God, unless there be some angel intercessor, who, by his atonement and intercession, may restore him to the favour of God: nay, unless that angel be *with him*, עלו, by his gracious presence, and by his aid and assistance. For עלו is often the same as *with*; as Gen. xviii. 8. Judg. iii. 16. and other places: and here it seems most properly applicable to the man spoken of. If, among the numbers who surround the sick persons bed, and who can only comfort him in his sickness with medicines, that shall avail him nothing, or entertain him with frivolous idle discourse, this *one of a thousand* be present, by his counsel, help, and intercession, the man will then be exceedingly refreshed with the fruits of divine mercy; even *deliverance from the pit*, or *corruption*, that is, from death both temporal and eternal.

XXXVIII. None have occasion to despise these things as if they were modern inventions: for certainly, Gregory applies them at large to Christ. " For who," says he, " is that angel, but he, who, by the prophet, is called the angel of the covenant? For, seeing to evangelize in the Greek, signifies to declare as a messenger; our Lord who delivers his message to us, is called the angel." He also more clearly observes; " there are, who by angel, understand Christ, the angel of the great council, by whom we are justified." See above all, the commentaty of Sebastian Schmidius, a divine of Srastburg.

XXXIX. Let us add to these Balaam's prophecy concerning the Messiah, which he delivered in magnificent language, Numb. xxiv. 15—19. " Balaam the son of Beor hath said, and the man whose eyes are open hath said: he hath said, which heard the words of God, and knew the knowledge of the Most High, which saw the vision of the Almighty, falling into a trance, but having his eyes open: I shall see him (*it*) but not now: I shall behold him (*it*) but not nigh: there shall come a star out of Jacob, and a sceptre shall rise out of Israel, and shall smite the corners of Moab, and destroy all the children of Sheth. And Edom shall be a possession, Seir also shall be a possession for his enemies, and Israel shall do valiantly. Out of Jacob shall come he that shall have dominion, and shall destroy him that remaineth of the city."

XL. The author of this prophecy is Balaam, whom, from an ancient tradition of the Jews, Jerome and Eucherius will have to be the same with Elihu, whose testimony concerning Christ we have just explained. But Fridric Spanheim, the son, in his history of Job, c. 15. § 18, 19. has learnedly shewn the silliness of that tradition, and that there is no resemblance between Elihu and Balaam. Here Balaam mightily extols himself, in
order

order to gain the greater credit and authority to his prophecy, and though it is not without affectation and vain glory, that he uttered thefe haughty encomiums of himfelf, yet by them God was pleafed to ratify, what he refolved to teach us by the mouth of the prophet.  He calls himfelf *the man whofe eyes were open*, that is, endowed with prophetic light to difcern things, which were concealed from others: *hearing the words of God*, to whom God familiarly imparted his fecrets.  *Knowing the knowledge of the Moft High*, knowing from divine revelation, thofe things which in other refpects God alone knows.  *Seeing the vifion of the Almighty*, like a prophet of the true God, according to Numb. xii. 6.  " I make myfelf known unto him in a vifion. Falling into a trance, but having his eyes open," who falls into a fleep, or an extafy, and yet has the eyes of his mind open. Whatever be the cafe as to his other prophecies, it is certainly not to be doubted, but he delivered this prophecy by divine impulfe.

XLI. He premifes, that what he had a profpect of in fpirit, as not *nigh:* " I fee it but not now, I behold it but not nigh." He gives warning of this beforehand, in order partly to embelifh his prophecy, which reached forwards to things fo diftant; partly to fhun envy, and to comfort Balak, whom he endeavoured to gratify as much as he could.  However, he here alfo comes up to the ftile of the holy prophets ; who ufually refer what they prophefy concerning the Meffiah, to the *latter days.*

XLII. But what is the fubject of his prophecy ?  " A ftar," fays he, " fhall come out of Jacob, and a fceptre fhall rife out of Ifrael."  This might be underftood literally, and in a diminative fenfe, concerning David, who was, as it were, a kind of light fhining in darknefs, and who obtained the fceptre of Ifrael by a feries of aftonifhing providences : who alfo fmote the Moabites, and made them tributary, 2 Sam. viii. 2.  Hence he fays. " Moab is my wafh-pot," Pf. xc. 10. that is, does me the offices of the meaneft drudgery, is placed at my feet, as a veffel, in which I ufually wafh them.  But thefe things have a higher view.  And David in this refpect, can only be confidered as the type of a more excellent perfon.  The *ftar* therefore, and *fceptre* fignify Chrift the Lord, who is both the light of his people, by the demonftration of the truth, and their manifold confolation by his word and Spirit, " the bright and morning ftar," Rev. xxii. 16. and the SCEPTRED KING, " King of kings, and Lord of lords," Rev. xix. 16.  He came *out of Jacob* and rofe *out of Ifrael.*  For the Lord raifed up that prophet " from the midft of his brethren," Deut. xviii. 15. " and the

glorious

glorious one of Ifrael fhall be of him, and the governor fhall proceed from the midft of him," Jer. xxx. 21. " who is over all, God bleffed for ever; but from the fathers as concerning the flefh," Rom. ix. 5.

XLIII. The works afcribed to him are thefe two.  1ft, The *fmiting [breaking] of the fides or corners of Moab.* That is, the fubduing of thofe, who were before fworn enemies to himfelf and his church.  And that two ways, either by *grace*, when, by his word and Spirit, he fubdues them to the obedience of faith, fo that they willingly fubmit to his fceptre, " cafting down every high thing, that exalteth itfelf againft the knowledge of God, and bringeth into captivity every thought to the obedience of Chrift," 2 Cor. x. 5.  Or, in a way of *juftice* and *vengeance*, when he fubdues the obftinate and forces them, however unwillingly, to acknowledge his power and fupereminence, " breaking them with a rod of iron, dafhing them in pieces like a potter's veffel," Pf. ii. 9.  But the Moabites are here mentioned as an inftance; becaufe Balaam was, at that time, principally concerned with them.  2dly, *The deftruction of all the children of Seth.*  This fignifies his triumph over all men, whom he fhall fubdue to himfelf, either by his grace, or by his righteous vengeance.  Becaufe all men in the world are propagated from Seth; while the progeny of Cain, and of the other fons of Adam, perifhed in the deluge.  From Seth Noah defcended; and all mankind from Noah: fo that we are all the children of Seth.  But we fhall all be made fubject to Chrift, " who fhall deliver up the kingdom to God, even the kingdom to his Father: when he fhall have put down all rule, and authority, and power, 1 Cor. xv. 24.

XLIV. In the laft place, he fhews the time and nature of Chrift's kingdom; *when Ifrael fhall do valiantly* againft his enemies, by fhaking off the tyrannical yoke of Antiochus and others: when Edom and Seir a noted mountain of Idumea, fhall become the poffeffion of Ifrael; which happened under the fecond temple, when the Idumeans were fubdued, and fubmitting to circumcifion and the other Jewifh rites, were added to the republic of Ifrael: as not only Jofephus, but alfo Strabo relates, Geogr. lib. 16. " they joined themfelves to the Jews, and had laws in common with them." When, I fay, all thefe things fhall happen, " out of Jacob fhall come he, that fhall have dominion:" namely, that great ruler, that " mighty one of Jacob," Ifa. lx. 16. " whofe right it is, and I will give it him," Ezek. xxi. 27.  " He fhall deftroy him that remaineth of the city." He will overthrow the city and all human power, which shall made head against him to the utmost: " for he bringeth down them that dwell on high, the lofty city he layeth it low, he layeth it low, even to the ground, he bringeth it even to the dust. The foot shall tread it down, even the feet of the poor, and the steps of the needy," Isa. xxvi. 5, 6. And thus we have carried down the doctrine of salvation in one continued series to the times of Moses.

---

## CHAP. IV.

### Of the Decalogue.

I. THINGS had a quite different appearance under Moses. What was spoken here and there, and delivered only by word of mouth, was now enlarged with very many additions digested into one body, and, at the command of God, consigned to lasting records; which neither the rage of enemies, nor fire, nor sword, nor all-consuming time shall be able to abolish. But neither the nature of our design, nor our intended brevity will permit us to prosecute every thing at large, that comes under this head. In this chapter we shall treat concerning the *giving of the law*, and the *covenant* of God with the Israelites, founded on that law.

II. It was the prerogative of the people of Israel above other nations, that to them pertained the *covenants and the giving of the law*, Rom. ix. 4. And there were several kinds of laws given them, of which there are principally three mentioned by divines. The *moral*, or the *decalogue*, the *ceremonial*, and the *political*, or *forensick*. The people of Israel may doubtess be considered three ways. 1st, As *rational creatures*, depending upon God, as the supreme reason or cause both in a moral and natural sense. And thus the *law of the decalogue* was given them; which, as to its substance, is one and the same with the *law of nature*, and binds men as such. 2dly, As *the church of the Old Testament*, who expected the promised Messiah and happier times, when he should make every thing perfect. And therefore they received the *ceremonial law*, which really shewed, that the Messiah was not yet come, and had not yet perfected all things; but that he would come, and make all things new. 3dly, As a *peculiar people*, who had a polity or government, suited to their genius and disposition in the land of Canaan. A republic constituted not so much according to those

forms

forms which philofophers have delineated, but which was, in a peculiar manner, a *theocracy*, as Jofephus fignificantly calls it, God himfelf holding the reins of government therein, Judg. viii. 23.    Under that view God prefcribed them *political laws*.

III. We are firft to fpeak of the *decalogue* and its promulgation.    Mofes has accurately defcribed it, Exod. xix. and xx. The *law-giver*, or if you will the *legiflator*, is God himfelf. " The one law-giver, who is able to fave and to deftroy, James iv. 12.    Who has a right of dominion over the confciences of men.    As the fumpreme reafon or caufe, he is the rule of all reafonable creatures ; and as the fupreme Lord, is the ruler of all, and by taking Ifrael to himfelf for a people, in an efpecial manner fhewed himfelf to be their God.    In the firft words of the law, he afferts his own divinity, proclaiming, *I am Jehovah thy God.*

IV. But we judge it criminal for any to doubt, that this is to be underftood of the whole undivided trinity, whofe equal majefty, in one Deity, we are all bound to acknowledge and worfhip.    Neverthelefs, as the *Son of God* was then, in a certain peculiar refpect, the king of the people of Ifrael and of the church at that time ; the giving of the law is alfo, in a fingular manner, afcribed to him.    For Stephen, in exprefs words, declares, Acts vii. 38. compared with v. 35. that it was an angel who fpoke with Mofes and the fathers on mount Sinai, even that very angel, who appeared to Mofes in the bufh, and faid, that he was the God of Abraham, Ifaac, and Jacob.    But no Chriftian will deny, that this was Chrift.    And Chrift, certainly is, he " who afcended on high," &c. Pf. lxviii. 18. compared with Eph. iv. 8.    But he himfelf " went forth before his people in the wildernefs, when the earth fhook, the heavens alfo dropped at the prefence of God ; even Sinai itfelf was moved at the prefence of God, the God of Ifrael," that is, at the giving of the law, Pf. lxviii. 7, 8.    Certainly the Apoftle Heb. xii. 26. fays, that he *who fpoke from heaven, and whofe voice then* (namely, at the giving of the law) *fhook the earth*, was our Lord Jefus Chrift to whom we are now alfo to hearken ; as Zanchius has learnedly obferved T. IV. lib. 1. c. 12.    Who profeffedly and at large proves, that he who promulgated the law, was the Son of God, *de tribus Elohim, lib. 2. c. 3.*

V. What the celebrated Iac. Altingius has obferved on Deut. v. 6. from a catechifm of the ancient Jews very much deferves our notice.    The Jews fay, " three fpirits are united in one ; the loweft fpirit, which is called the *holy fpirit :* the middle fpirit *which is the intermediate*, and called *wifdom* and *intelligence ;* and this is the fpirit which proceeds from the midft of the moft

confummate

confummate beauty, *with fire and water:* the fupreme fpirit, which is abfolutely in filence, in whom all the holy fpirits, and and all the bright perfons confift," Rahanat. fol. 132. col. 3. They alfo fay, that אנ and חהוא and אהי, I and THOU and HE, are names of God, denoting three perfons, and, at the feaft of tabernacles, they all profefs it in their prayers: *I and* HE, *fave I pray.* Moreover, they fay, that when the law was promulgated, there were two perfons. For, quite to the end of the fecond commandment, the difcourfe runs in the 'firft perfon, " I the Lord thy God, *&c.* For I the Lord God, *&c.* of thofe that hate me, *&c.* of thofe that love me, *&c.*" In the third and following comandments, God is mentioned in the third perfon. " Thou fhalt not take the name of ' the Lord thy God, *&c.* The fabbath of the Lord thy God." Which having obferved, they proceed thus: " that the two firft words" or commandments, " were fpoke by the fupreme fpirit; but the other words, by his glory, called EL SCHADDAI, known to the fathers, by whom the prophets prophefied, who is called JAH, in whom is the name of God, the beloved of God, who dwelt in the temple, and the mouth of God, and face of God, and the rock, and that goodnefs which Mofes faw, when he could not fee God," Bechai fol. 88. col. 3, 4. Elfewhere they call him the " Schekinah, by whom there is accefs to God, by whom prayers are poured out to God: who is that angel, who has the name of God in him, who alfo himfelf is called God and Jehovah." I enquire not now, how folid thefe reafonings of the Jews are. It is fufficient to have mentioned thefe remarkable records of an ancient catchifm concerning the plurality of the divine perfons; of which there are alfo indications in the Decalogue itfelf.

VI. *Angels* were prefent, as *minifters,* at the giving of the law by the Lord Chrift. Whence Stephen fays, Acts vii. 53. that the " Ifraelites received the law by the difpofition of angels," ὡς διαταγὰς ἀγγέλων. Grotius obferves, that ὡς here fignifies amidft, and that διαταγὰς denotes troops, ranged in military order: that the meaning is, the law was given in a magnificent manner, amidft many troops of angels, and that there was a reference to Deut. xxxiii. 2. thefe things are not improper. But others would rather take διαταγὴ for a *command, ordinance,* and *fanction:* as * Rom. xiii. 2. And they render ὡς *at;* in which fenfe the Son is faid to act *at the pleafure of the Father.* *Ludovicus de Dieu* has learnedly expreffed that meaning; and as his words tend to explain feveral paffages, we fhall not fcruple to infert them as follows. ' Stephen had faid, v. 38. that
‘ the

---

* Whofoever therefore refifteth the power, refifteth τῇ διαταγῇ the *ordinance* of God.

' the angel fpoke with Mofes in mount Sinai, even the fame,
' who had appeared to him in the bufh, v. 35. who, though he
' was in himfelf God, yet is here economically confidered as
' the angel of God, and the captain of the other angels. He
' gave the law to Mofes, from the midft of the angels, who
' furrounded him on all hands. Of which there was a figur-
' ative reprefentation in the fanctuary, where God fitting be-
' tween the cherubims delivered his oracles—Hence Pf. lxviii.
' 17. when he had faid, the chariots of God are twenty thou-
' fand, even thoufands of angels, the Lord is among them; he
' adds, *Sinai is in the fanctuary:* to teach us, that as God,
' when formerly furrounded on Sinai with myriads of angels,
' and riding on them, as on chariots, gave forth the law, fo
' the fanctuary refembles mount Sinai, where God rides on a
' chariot of cherubims. Seeing therefore the law came forth
' from an affembly of angels, whofe prefident was the fupreme
' angel Jehovah, the Apoftle juftly faid, that it was *pronounced*
' *and ordained by angels.* Stephen, that it *was received by the people*
' *by the difpofition of angels.* Διαταγὴ ἀγγέλων is here the fame thing,
' as *the decree of the watchers,* and *the word of the holy ones,*
' Dan. iv. 17. The decree and mandate of the angelic fenate
' is underftood, over whom the Son of God prefided as fup-
' reme: in regard of whom the fame decree is called, v. 24.
' *the decree of the moft high.*" Thus far *de Dieu.*

VII. But what kind of miniftry did the angels perform to
God at giving the law? *Firft,* It is certain, that, with their
heavenly choirs they furrounded the mount, and added to the
majeftic pomp of the Lawgiver, and were witneffes of all that
was tranfacted. The confideration of this was capable of ftriking not only terror into the Ifraelites, but fhould alfo have infpired their minds with reverence, that the angels, in whofe
affembly the law was given, might not be witneffes of their
perfidy. To this purpofe is Deut. xxxiii. 2. " Jehovah came
from Sinai, he came with ten thoufands of faints; from his
right hand went a fiery law for them." *Secondly,* It is not improbable, that the found of thofe words, in which the law was
conceived, was formed in the air by the means of angels. For,
God properly ufes not a voice : this is a degree of imperfection :
but yet it is called the voice of God, formed in the air in fome
extraordinary manner, to exprefs the mind of God, for which
purpofe he ufes the miniftry of angels: namely, the law was
given in thunder and lightning; the thunder indeed, which
formed the matter of the voice, which proclaimed the words of
the law, muft certainly have had an articulation, fuperadded,
which was framed by the means of angels. Philo, *in ennarra-*
*tione*

*tione Decalogi* fays, God fpoke not by himfelf, but " filling a
reafonable mind with a diftinct knowledge, which moulding
and attenuating the air, and changing it to a flaming fire, he
gave forth an articulate found; as breath does through a trum-
pet." I know not, whether he intended the fame thing that
we do. We mean nothing, but what the apoftle faid, when he
calls the law, " the word fpoken by angels," Heb. ii. 2. Not
that it was any created angel, who faid, " I am Jehovah thy
God." Thefe are the words of God; but that the thunder, in
which God fpoke, was produced by the means of angels, and
articulated into words intelligible to man. They, who underftand *by angels*, only their prefence and attendance, as 2 Tim. ii. 2.
*Among many witneffes*, too much leffen the force of the apoftle's
comparifon, by which he prefers the gofpel to the law on this
account, that this laft was promulgated by the miniftry of angels, the former publifhed by the miniftry of the Son of God
manifefted in the flefh. See Cameron and Meftrefat on the
place. *Thirdly*, It is probable, that the tables of teftimony, on
which the law was written by the finger of God, were delivered
to Mofes by the intervention of angels: and to this I refer Gal.
iii. 19. " the law was ordained by angels in the hand of a
mediator."

VIII. Mofes was the other minifter of God at the giving of
the law. " Mofes commanded us a law, even the inheritance
of the congregation of Jacob," Deut. xxxiii. 4. " The law
was given by Mofes," John i. 17. And Mofes is that mediator; in whofe hands, as we have juft learned from Paul, the
law was ordained by angels. We can by no means agree with
a certain learned author, who denies, that Mofes was the mediator of the moral law, and maintains, that by the law we are to
underftand the ceremonial only; and he thinks, the hiftory of
the promulgation of the ten words or commandments removes
Mofes to fuch a diftance from the office of a mediator, that it
places him in the fame rank and order with the people, Exod.
xix. 25. " fo Mofes went down unto the people," &c. and
Exod. xx. 1. " and God fpake," &c. But if I miftake not, the
very learned perfon miftakes the cafe. Mofes indeed went
down from the mount, to put the people on their guard, not to
break through the boundary, by coming up to Jehovah: and
having executed that commiffion, he, together with Aaron his
brother, went up again, at the command of God, fome little
way at leaft, Exod. xix. 24. and ftood nearer, when God promulgated the laws. Which done, he again fpoke with the
Ifraelites. Very many confiderations fway with us, thus to
range thefe matters. Let us, firft, confider verfe 9. " and Je-
                                                    hovah

hovah faid unto Mofes, lo, I come unto thee in a thick cloud, that the people may hear when I fpeak with thee, and believe thee for ever." From this it appears, that from among the whole affembly, God called Mofes by name, and recommended him to the people, as the meffenger of God, when he promulgated this law. And Mofes himfelf declares this, Deut. v. 4, 5, 6. " Jehovah talked with you face to face in the mount, out of the midft of the fire. (I ftood between Jehovah and you at that time, to fhew you the word of Jehovah. For ye were afraid by reafon of the fire, and went not up into the mount) faying, I am Jehovah thy God," &c. And what is plainer than that of Stephen: " that Mofes was in the wildernefs with the angel, which fpake to him in the mount Sinai, and with our fathers, who received λόγια ζῶντα, the lively oracles, to give unto us," Acts vii. 38. Where Beza fays; " it is not to be doubted, but Luke calls λόγια, oracles, what the Hebrew calls דברים, the words, and has an eye to God himfelf, who is faid to have pronounced, and delivered them to Mofes, written with his own finger." And what appearance of truth is there, that by λόγια ζῶντα, lively oracles, we are only to underftand the ceremonial laws, and not thofe precepts of the moral law, which whoever does, fhall live in them ? And this very learned author himfelf has elfewhere obferved, that the words, משפטים חוקה, חקים, law, ftatutes and judgments are often fynonymous; but whenever they are thus joined together, they are diftinguifhed from each other by a peculiar fignification; and that by חוקה is underftood the moral law; by חקים, the ceremonial, and by משפט the forenfick law. But now thefe three are fo joined, as that each of them is afcribed to Mofes, Mal. iv. 4. " remember ye the law of Mofes my fervant, which I commanded unto him in Horeb for all Ifrael, with the ftatutes and judgments. You fee, that the law equally with the ftatutes and judgments are afcribed to Mofes. In like manner, Lev. xxvi. 46. " thefe are the ftatutes, and judgments, and laws, which Jehovah made between him and the children of Ifrael, in mount Sinai, by the hand of Mofes." Mofes therefore was the mediator even of the moral law, and his inftitutions are erroneoufly reftricted to the ceremonies.

IX. The time of the publication of the law is fuppofed to be the fiftieth day from the departure of the people out of Egypt, and from the celebration of the paffover. How to find out this number of days, fee Rivet on Exod. xix. 1. And thus the Ifraelites were taught, that they were not then to be at their own difpofal, when they were delivered from Egyptian bondage by a bountiful hand, fo as for the future to live at their own difcretion; but to enter into the fervice of God, and to apply

themfelves

themfelves to it with the greater earneftnefs, the more they
were fet at liberty from the bondage of others: as Zachariah
alfo prophefies, Luke i. 74, 75. " That being delivered out of
the hands of our enemies; we might ferve him without fear, in
holinefs and righteoufnefs before him, all the days of our life."
God likewife ordered three days to be fet apart for preparation :
becaufe none has accefs to familiar converfe with God, but he
who has duly confecrated himfelf to him.

X. The *place* was mount Sinai, fometimes alfo called Horeb,
Deut. v. 2. Exod. iii. 1. and fometimes " the mount of God,"
1 Kings xix. 8. " The law was given in the mount." Beda
on Exod. xxiv. " fays, that from the height of the place, we
may gather, how fublime, or how different from human inftitutions the law was, which Mofes received." That mountain
was fituated in the defarts of Arabia, an uncultivated and barren fpot, far from Canaan, oppofed to mount Sion, which was
greatly cultivated and very pleafant, Pfal. xlviii. 3. and fituated
in the heart of the promifed land, from whence came forth the
law of faith, Ifa. ii. 2, 3. For, the law cannot give life to finful man, render him fruitful in the practice of true holinefs,
and introduce him into the heavenly country. That is the province of the gofpel, " which is the power of God unto falvation," Rom. i. 16. We are not to defpife the obfervation of
Lud. Cappelus on Gal. iv. 25. That mount Sinai was fo called
from the word נסה, which both in Hebrew and Arabic fignifies
a *thorn*, *bufh*, *briers*. For, God fpoke here to Mofes *from the
bufh*. Mount Horeb, alfo denotes *drynefs* and *defolation*: for
God made choice of fuch places and names in giving the law,
with a particular purpofe, that the names might anfwer to the
things; and the things typified, to their types. The law, confidered in itfelf alone, is *more dry* and barren to finful man than
any rock or fandy defart, from which not even a drop of true
piety can penetrate into the heart of man; it alfo forms a horrid
wafte and defolation by its threats and curfes, with which, as
with fo many *thorns*, it pricks and wounds the confcience of the
finner. And what the moft excellent Lightfoot has remarked,
deferves alfo to be added, *Mifcellan. c.* 59. *The ceremonial law,*
which only regarded the Jews, was given (at leaft, as to a great
part of it) privately to Mofes in the tabernacle, Lev. i. 1. and
was demolifhed along with the tabernacle, when the vail was
rent. The *moral law* concerns the whole world, and was publifhed in the fight of all; namely, from the top of a mountain:
and ought to laft, as long as any mountain fhall ftand. *The
judicial law,* which is more indifferent and may ftand or fall, as
                                                                    fhall

shall seem most expedient for the common-weal; was not published so openly as the one, nor so privately as the other.

XI. Besides, though the people were, in their manner externally sanctified, yet they had not free access to the mountain. God commanded that the mountain and the people should be kept within bounds, and threatened those with death, who should dare to go up to the mountain, or to touch any part of it, Exod. xix. 13. This command appeared so severe, that Paul declares, *they could not endure it*, Heb. xii. 20. And as it is truly delightful and *good to draw near to God*, Psal. lxxiii. 28. so it is unpleasant and melancholy to be debarred from access to him. That command was a proof that the Israelites were impure, and unworthy of the presence of God. The very animals appointed for their service, were reputed impure. And therefore proclamation was made, " If even a beast touched the mountain, it should be stoned or thrust through with a dart." To such a degree were all things brought into the bondage of corruption by, and on account of sinful man, Rom. viii. 21.

XII. There were likewise awful *signs*, such as loud peals of thunder, quivering, flashes of lightning shining along the cloud of thick darkness which covered the top of the mountain, black vapours of smoke ascending up to heaven, the earthquake, the quaking of the very mountain, as if sensible of the approach of God, and many other circumstances recorded, Exod. xix. 16, 18. Deut. iv. 11. Heb. xii. 18. Now to what purpose was all this apparatus? It was first to proclaim the tremendous majesty of the-lawgiver, and to beget in the souls of men a reverence for his law; " God himself is come,—that his fear may be before your faces, that ye sin not," Exod. xx. 20. 2dly, To display the nature of the law, which, by demanding perfect obedience, and by the addition of dreadful threatenings, wonderfully strikes sinners to the heart, and without any mixture of gospel grace, leads to despair, and is to them *the ministry of death and condemnation*, 2 Cor. iii. 7, 9. But it is otherwise with the gospel, which, in this respect, is opposed to the law, Heb. xii. 18, 22. 3dly, To put the faith and constancy of the Israelites to the trial; whether this terror of God would bring them to humility and obedience, or whether through forwardness they would pour contempt upon him, or out of despair rebel against him, Exod. xx. 20. *that he might prove you.*

XIII. But notwithstanding this display of majesty, the Israelites saw no form or similitude of God, Deut. iv. 12, 15. This was on purpose to prevent them from entertaining gross conceptions of the God of heaven, or " corrupting themselves and making to themſelves a graven image, the ſimilitude of any figure, the likeneſs of male or female," ver. 16. For to what could they liken him, of whom they ſaw no ſimilitude? Iſa. xl. 25. " to whom then will ye liken me, or ſhall I be equal? ſaith the holy One."

XIV. The law, which God, in this manner publiſhed, conſiſts of *ten words* or *commandments*, Exod. xxxiv. 28. Deut. iv. 13. Wherefore the Greeks alſo called it δικάλογος the *decalogue*. Moreover the contents of thoſe ten words are various. 1ſt, There is the preſcription of certain duties; and in this the nature of a law as ſuch, properly conſiſts. 2dly, The threatening of divine vengeance againſt the tranſgreſſors thereof, as in the ſecond and third commandments: and this is the ſanction of the covenant of works, from which all threatenings are derived, as we explained at large, Book III. chap. i. ſect. 22. 3dly, The propoſal of divine grace and favour; and as this is made to ſinners, and that under a condition, not of perfect, but of ſincere obedience; ſo far it flows from the covenant of grace.

XV. All the duties required by the law, are comprehended under this one, viz. *love*, which is therefore called the *fulfilling of the law*, Rom. xiii. 10. and *the bond of perfectneſs*, Col. iii. 14. Moreover, ſeeing love either aſcends to God, who as the chief good, is to be loved above all, and with all our ſtrength; or extends itſelf to our neighbour whom we are bound to love as ourſelves, ſince he belongs to God equally with ourſelves; therefore Chriſt divides the whole law into theſe two capital precepts, Mat. xxii. 37—39.

XVI. The Moſt High God was not only pleaſed to publiſh his laws to Iſrael with a loud voice, in the preſence of the moſt auguſt aſſembly of the whole people, but he likewiſe engraved them with his own finger, on tables of ſtone, poliſhed by himſelf for that purpoſe, Exod. xxiv. 12. Exod. xxxi. 18. Deut. ix. 10. He choſe to write his law, in order to prevent the oblivion of it, and to perpetuate the memory of the giving and receiving it in Iſrael. And hence theſe tables are called הָעֵדֻת לֻחֹת, *the tables of teſtimony*, Exod. xxxi. 18. Exod. xxxiv. 29. Both becauſe they contained the declaration or teſtimony of the divine will, and becauſe the preſervation of them by the Iſraelites, was a teſtimony of the law given to, and received by them at Sinai. This writing alſo ſignified the purpoſe of God, to write the law on the hearts of his elect, according to the promiſe of the covenant of grace, Jer. xxxi. 33.

XVII. Nor is it for nothing that God himſelf would be the author of this writing, without making uſe of any man or angel. For this is the meaning of the Holy Spirit, when he ſays,

that

that the tables were written *with the finger of God*, Exod. xxxi.
18. and that the writing was *the writing of God*, Exod. xxxii.
16. The reasons were, 1st, To set forth the pre-eminence of
this law, not only above all human, but also above the other
divine laws, which he permitted to be written by Moses. 2dly,
To intimate, that it is the work of God alone, to write the
law on the heart, which is what neither man himself, nor the
ministers of God can do, but the Spirit of God alone. And
thus believers are " the epistle of Christ, written not with ink,
but with the Spirit of the living God," 2 Cor. iii. 3.

XVIII. It likewise merits our attention, that this writing of
God was not a drawing of certain letters on a plane, but חרות
חרות *an engraven writing*, by incision and * engraving, Exod.
xxxii. 16. The term חרות, which occurs no where else, seems
by a commutation of the letters of the same organ ה and ע to
be from חרט, which signifies a *graver*, graving instrument or
tool : so that חרט signifies *he cuts with a graver* or *style*, as R.
Soloman has observed. This signified not only the perpetuity
of the law, in respect of its obligation (for characters so engraved are with much greater difficulty effaced, than letters
drawn upon a plane) but also its deep engraving in the inward
parts of the elect, which Satan himself, with all his power
and stratagems, cannot eraze. If we consider ourselves, as
corrupted by nature, " our sin is written with a pen of iron,
and with the point of a diamond, it is graven upon the table of
our heart," Jer. xvii. 1. But the grace of God will cancel that
writing of sin, and in the room of it, with the graver of his
most holy spirit, will engrave on the same table of our heart
the characters of his law.

XIX. Nor must we omit, that God would not write his law
in paper or parchment, nay nor even on wood, but would engrave it on *tables of stone.* That was done, as Abrabenel well
remarks, " that the foundations of the law might always remain incorrupted, and this be a monument of the perpetuity of
the law." The other laws, which were to continue at least
till the time of the restitution, and whose abrogation was at hand,
" for the weakness and unprofitableness thereof," Heb. vii. 18.
were written by Moses on a less durable material. But this
law, which is of eternal obligation, was engraved by God himself on stone. And why may we not, on this occasion, reflect
on the stony hardness of our own hearts ; on which, however,
the characters of the divine law are imprinted by the spirit of
sanctification ? *Musculus in Locis communibus de Decalogo* says :

Y 2　　. " It

---

* The author says, *per incisionem et excavationem*, which last signifies a making
hollow.

" It was not enough to have heard the voice of God, unlefs
there was alfo a literary monument, written by the finger of
God, for the benefit of pofterity, and for the conviction of the
rocky confcience of a hardened people, and therefore tables of
ftone, and not paper, were ufed." See alfo *Jo. Gerhardi; Loc.
commun. de lege,* fect. V. §. 32.

XX. Thefe tables were two in number, enjoining the fanctification both of foul and body, the love both of God and our
neighbour.   They were alfo " written on both their fides ; on
the one fide and on the other were they written," Exod. xxxii.
15.   Which is either to be underftood thus, that the tables
fhut or clofed on each other like writing-tables, and were written on their two fides that faced each other : or, what appears
to be more fimple, that each table was filled up with writing
on each fide thereof, in the manner of that, which the Greeks
call ὀπισθόγραφα *opifthography.*   And thus provifion was actually
made againft a poffibility of either taking from, or adding any
thing to this law : which alfo God exprefsly charged upon his
people, Deut. iv. 2. and Deut. xii. 13.   Nor is it prepofterous
to think, that by this means, the fanctification of the whole
man was fhadowed forth.   As there was no part of thefe tables
left unwritten by God, fo there is no part of the believer, which
the Spirit, by his fanctifying influences, does not pervade,
1 Theff. v. 23.

XXI. But we cannot well determine, what number of precepts God infcribed on each table.   For, when we refer the
former precepts, treating of love to God to the firft table; and
the fix following, which treat of love to our neighbour, to the
fecond table; we do not fo much confider the manner of God's
writing, as the nature of the things; as Chrift alfo did, Mat.
xxii. We have juft heard, that the tables were written both fides;
and that they were of equal fize is very probable.   But the
four former precepts greatly exceeding the other fix in length,
it is fcarce credible, they were contained in one table.

XXII. When Mofes came down from the mount, with the
tables, written by God, in his hand, and, on his approach to
the camp of the Ifraelites, obferved the calf which Aaron had
caft or founded at their command, he was moved with a holy
indignation, and threw the tables out of his hand and broke
them, Exod. xxxii. 19. Deut. ix. 16, 17.   We are by all means
to conclude, that Mofes, fired with a zeal for God, broke
thefe tables confiftently with his duty.   For, this conduct tended
1ft, To ftrike the Ifraelites with fhame and terror, fince, by
*this alarming* action, he much more effectually convinced
them of their breach of covenant, than he could poffibly have
done

done by any vehemence or warmth of words ; by depriving them of that ineftimable treafure, whereby they had otherwife excelled all other nations of the world.   2dly, To demonftrate, that, by their breach of the moft folemn covenant, they made themfelves unworthy of the fymbol of the divine prefence : For, the words of the covenant were written on the tables, in order to their being placed in the ark, and that God might dwell upon the ark in the tabernacle.   Therefore, by this indignation of Mofes, . God fo ordering it, it came to pafs, that there was nothing which could be depofited in the ark ; and fo the tabernacle could neither be erected, nor the propitiatory or mercy-feat be in the midft of Ifrael.

XXII. Neverthelefs God, being entreated by Mofes, renewed the broken covenant, commanded Mofes to hew two other tables, like the former, on which God himfelf might write the fame word Exod. xxxiv. 1.   However he was pleafed to manifeft his grace, in fuch a manner, that fome token of his difpleafure fhould remain, leaft the facility of pardon fhould produce indolence and floth.   There was no art of man ufed in the former tables ; both the tables and the writing were God's.   But now, fome part of that fo great dignity was impaired ; fince Mofes was commanded to bring the ftones, when polifhed by the hands of man, that God might write the ten words upon them.   We are, however, taught, that the moft holy perfons can, indeed offer nothing to God (if even they can do that) but fmooth tables without any characters.   The whole writing is to be entirely afcribed to God the author of holinefs.

XXIV. While thefe things were doing, God again prohibited the Ifraelites from coming near the mount ; nor, indeed, did he fuffer either fheep or oxen to feed in fight of it, Exod. xxxiv. 3. becaufe, by their idolatry, they had made themfelves abominable in the fight of God.   We men perhaps, might have thought, that the miracle would have been more illuftrious, if the writing had been made to appear in an inftant on the bare tables in the fight of all : but now the writing was performed in fecret, before Mofes alone, in order to leave fome room for faith, to embrace even what it fees not.   However, God fufficiently obviated the cavilling of carnal reafon ; it being evident, that Mofes neither took any graving tool with him, nor could find any in the mount.   For, God fo orders the difpenfation of his heavenly doctrine, as to prove the obedience and docility of believers, and yet to leave no room for doubting ; as Calvin has ingenioufly obferved.

XXV. But there was another way, by which God afferted the authority of his law ; namely by that extraordinary fplen-

dour,

dour, which gliftered in the face of Mofes, when he came down from the mount, with the tables of the teftimony in his hands, fo that the Ifraelites were not able to look upon him, but he was obliged to put a vail on his face, when he fpoke with them, Exod. xxxiv. 30——. This alfo was a part of the ornament and glory of the law, as the apoftle intimates, 2 Cor. iii. 7. For, if Mofes himfelf, who was a minifter, appeared in fuch eminent glory, the miniftration itfelf could not be lefs glorious. But fince the Ifraelites could not bear that fplendour, that was to them an indication, how far they had departed from God by their ingratitude, who were fo much afraid at the fight of the fervant. This diftinction therefore might really humble them; fince Mofes was favoured with a nearer view of the glory of God himfelf, and with having the effulgence, of that glory in the fkin of his face; while they, being ftruck with terror ftarted back at the fight of a mortal man. Moreover, it being faid, that Mofes, when he fpoke to Ifrael, put a *vail* on his face, this was a proof, that the great myfteries and the true end of the law, which is " Chrift for righteoufnefs, to every one that believeth," Rom. x. 4. were concealed from them, 2 Cor. iii. 13. And finally, the apoftle obferves, that the glory of the face of Mofes was to be done away as ufelefs, 2 Cor. iii. 7. It might be, that this fhining fplendour of his fkin lafted not long; at leaft it vanifhed at death: which was a vifible proof, that the glory of the Mofaic miniftration was afterwards to have a period, to make way for the more eminent glory of the miniftry of Chrift.

XXVI. Thefe tables were depofited in the ark of the covenant under the mercy-feat, Exod. xxv. 16. Deut. x. 5. 1 Kings viii. 9. Not only to be kept there as a moft precious piece of furniture, and a fymbol of the divine covenant; but efpecially to fignify, that Chrift, who was typified by the ark, was to have the law of God in the midft of his bowels, or *within his heart*, Pfal. xl. 8. and to fulfil it perfectly for his people: likewife, that Chrift had not only the propitiatory or mercy-feat, whereby our fins are covered but alfo the law, which was to be the rule of life and directory of gratitude to thofe, who are reconciled with God.

XXVII. It has been formerly, and is to this day a matter of difpute in the church, whether the laws of the two tables, as they were given to the people of Ifrael by Mofes, are of perpetual obligation, and extend even to us Chriftians. *Hieronymus Zanchius Operum Tim. IV. lib. 1. c. 11.* Maintains at large and by feveral arguments, that we Chriftians have nothing to do with the moral precepts, as they were given to the Ifraelites

by

by Mofes; but only in fo far, as they agree with the law of
nature, common to all nations, and confirmed by Chrift, whom
we acknowledge to be our king.   And Mufculus writes to the
fame purpofe, *Loc. commun. de abrogatione legis Mofaicæ*.   But
while David Pareus gives his opinion about the oppofite opinions of Dominicus a Soto and Bellarmine, the former of whom
denied, that we are fubject to the law of the decalogue, as it
was delivered by Mofes; but the latter, on the contrary, maintained, that the law, as given by Mofes, was alfo binding on us;
though he premifes (*ad libri Bellarmini de juftificatione* IV. *c.* 6.)
that it is of fmall importance to difpute about the miniftry of
Mofes, by which the law was formerly promulgated, provided
the law, and the obedience thereof, be in vigour or force in the
church : yet he fays, that Bellarmine's opinion is to be retained,
as the fafer and more preferable.   *Rivet, in Explicat. Decalog.*
thinks, that the difference is not in the thing, but in the manner
of expreffion : for all agree, that all the moral duties contained
in the law, are of perpetual obfervance among Chriftians, in fo
far, as they are natural precepts, imprinted on the minds of all,
by God, the author of nature ; and as by way of inftruction
they are contained in the written laws, they are a great, nay a
neceffary help to our weaknefs and ignorance.   Yet he rather
feems to incline to the fentiment of Zanchius and Mufculus.
We fhall comprehend our own opinion in the following
pofitions.

XXVIII. 1. Seeing the decalogue contains the fum of the
law of nature, and, as to its fubftance, is one and the fame
therewith, fo far it is of perpetual and univerfal obligation.
And thus far all divines are agreed, the Socinians themfelves
not excepted.   See *Volkel. lib.* IV. *c.* 5.

XXIX. 2. We are not only to perform the duties, which it
requires, becaufe they are agreeable to reafon; and to abftain
from the contrary vices, becaufe reafon declares them to be
bafe and vile, but alfo under this formal notion, becaufe God
has enjoined thofe duties, and prohibited thofe vices ; that his
authority as lawgiver, may be acknowledged, and our goodnefs
have the nature of an obedience ; which, as fuch, is founded on
the alone authority of him who commands.   And who can
doubt, that it is the duty of a rational creature, to acknowledge
God as his fupreme Lord and governor, to whofe will, without
any further examination, he ought to fubmit ; faying, " Lord,
what wouldft thou have me to do ?"

XXX. 3. The Gentiles, who had heard nothing of the giving of the law in the wildernefs, were not bound to the obfervance of that law, as it was publifhed to the Ifraelites, but
only

only as infcribed on their own confciences.  Hence the Apoftle fays, " that as many as have finned without law," namely,
the written law, " fhall alfo perifh without law," Rom. ii. 12.
That is, fhall not be condemned in confequence of the law, as
delivered to Ifrael in writing, but of the violation of the natural
law.  However, if any of the Gentiles came to have any knowledge of the giving of this law, they were to believe, that the
precepts of it were fpoken to them no lefs than they were to
Ifrael; nor could they neglect them without throwing contempt on God, and incurring the forfeiture of falvation.

XXXI. 4. Though the precepts of common honefty, in fome
fpecial manner, and with fome particular circumftances, were
originally appointed for a peculiar people, yet they are ftill
binding by a divine authority, on all thofe who come to know,
that God formerly enjoined them to their neighbours.  For inftance, what Paul wrote to the Romans, is no lefs binding on
us, than it was on them; becaufe the obligation is founded on
the manifeftation or difcovery of the divine will and pleafure.
When therefore, God has faid to any particular perfon, that
this or that duty is incumbent upon him as a rational creature,
who ought to bear a refemblance to the divine image; all other
men who hear this, are as much bound to that duty, as he to
whom it was firft propofed; not only becaufe they apprehend
the matter of that precept to be confonant to reafon; but alfo,
becaufe that command was given by God, no matter to whom
it was given at firft.

XXXII. 5. Common precepts which bind all to whom they
are made known, on account of the authority of him who enjoins them, may be preffed upon fome by certain peculiar reafons.  For inftance, the precept concerning conftancy in the
faith of the gofpel, might be preffed on Jews and Gentiles
from different motives; and yet the precept remain common
to both.  Thus when God publifhed the decalogue to the Ifraelites, he annexed fome reafons, which, to the letter, were
peculiar to them alone: becaufe, what was a common duty to
all, he was pleafed in an efpecial manner, to recommend to
them.  Yet in his wifdom he publifhed thofe reafons, in fuch
a manner, as to concern others alfo, by way of analogy, and in
their myftical fignification.

XXXIII. 6. As the people of Ifrael conftituted the church
at that time, and as Jefus Chrift the Son of God, and king
of the church, prefcribed the decalogue to them, it follows,
that the fame law retains its force in the church, till it be abrogated again by the king of the church.  We are not to think,
that the church of the Old Teftament, which confifted of Ifraelites,

raelites, and that of the New, though for the greateſt part,
made up of Gentiles, were a quite different people. They
ought to be looked upon as one kingdom of Chriſt, who made
*both one*, Eph. ii. 14. and who graffed us, when wild olives,
into that fat olive, Rom. xi. 17. And conſequently, the laws
which were once given to the church by Chriſt the king, are
always binding on the whole church, unleſs Chriſt ſhall declare,
that he has abrogated them by ſome other inſtitution. But it
is abſurd to imagine, that Chriſt abrogated the moral law, in
ſo far, as he gave it by the mediation of Moſes to the church
of Iſrael, and directly confirmed the ſame law to the Chriſtian
church. For ſeeing it is the ſame law, of the ſame king, in
one and the ſame kingdom, though that kingdom is enriched
with new acceſſions and new privileges; why ſhould we ſuppoſe it abrogated and ratified again almoſt in the ſame breath ?
Nay, many conſiderations perſuade us to believe, that the law
of the decalogue was given to the church, in order to be à perpetual rule, from the manner in which it was given.

XXXIV. For, as theſe commandments were publiſhed before the aſſembly of the whole church, in the hearing of all,
while the other precepts were given to Moſes alone in his ſacred retirement : as they were engraved on tables of ſtone by
the finger of God to the end, that as Calvin remarks, this
doctrine might remain in perpetual force : and ſeeing they, and
they alone, were put in the ark of the covenant, under the
wings and guardianſhip of God himſelf; God plainly ſhewed
by ſo many prerogatives, that the reaſon of thoſe precepts was
far different from that of the others, which were only impoſed
on the church for a time.

XXXV. From theſe things the raſhneſs of a late Catechiſt
appears, who maintains that the ten commandments were written on tables of ſtone, to ſhew that they were to continue in
force while thoſe tables laſted; but, that when the tables were
loſt, the law that was written upon them was to be abrogated:
and that they were laid up in the ark of the covenant, to ſignify that they were of the ſame nature with that ark, and that
covenant, that is, of a fading or periſhing nature. But if this
was true, it will follow, that the Iſraelites from the deſtruction
of the firſt temple, when the ark with the tables of the law was
loſt, were ſet free from the binding power of the decalogue;
and that there was no difference between the decalogue and
the other ceremonies, the ark being as it were, the centre of
the ceremonies; nay, that the decalogue was in this reſpect inferior to the other ceremonies, as the latter continued to the
coming of Chriſt, but the decalogue was abrogated by the Ba-

bylonifh captivity. All which notions are fo falfe, and fo diftant from all found divinity, that they have almoft an air of
impiety.

XXXVI. We may add, that Chrift has declared, " he was
not come to deftroy, but to fulfil the law," Mat. v. 17. To
deftroy, fignifies there, to abrogate, and to free men from the
obligation of it, as appears from ver. 19. But that Chrift
fpeaks of the law of the decalogue, we gather from what follows, where he explains the precepts of that law, and recommends them to his difciples. And when Paul, Rom, xiii. 9.
and James, chap. ii. 8, 11. inculcates the precepts of the law on
Chriftians, in the fame terms in which they were delivered by
Mofes to Ifrael, they do not infift upon this confideration, that
they were agreeable to the dictates of right reafon, or were ratified again by Chrift, but that they were thus formerly publifhed and written by God. Nay, Eph. vi. 2. the Apoftle not only
infifts on the promife, that was annexed to the fifth commandment, but alfo on the order of the precepts, recommending honour or regard to parents from this argument, that this
is *the firft commandment with promife*. But if the decalogue, as
it was formerly delivered to the church of Ifrael, did not concern Chriftians, that argument of the Apoftle (which be it far
from us to fay), would have no force with Chriftians.

XXXVII. Finally, if the decalogue, as it was formerly given
to the church, was not now binding on the fame; it muft neceffarily have been revoked by God, and abrogated by Chrift:
both which is abfurd. For who will be fo bold, as to fuppofe
God to fpeak in this manner: " It is indeed my will, that you
" obferve thofe natural precepts, which I formerly commanded
" the Ifraelites, in the law that was publifhed with fuch fo-
" lemnity; but for the future, I will not have you bound to
" thefe, becaufe of my command, but becaufe nature requires
" it." And why fhould Chrift abrogate the precepts given to
the church of Ifrael, in order directly to give the very fame
precepts again to the Chriftian church ? Not to fay, that there
is not the leaft fign of any fuch abrogation in the facred writings.

XXXVIII. However, we do not refufe, that the law of the
covenant of works was abolifhed by Chrift in its *federal confideration*. 1ft, *As to its rigour*, which required of man himfelf an
obedience in every part and degree perfect, as the condition of
juftification, and that without any promife of the Spirit and of
fanctifying grace. 2dly, *As to the curfe*. which it threatens a-
gainft all who deviate from it in the leaft. And in this fenfe
Paul fays, " that we are not under the law, but under grace,"
                                                        Rom.

Rom. vi. 14. though as to its *normal* relation, or as it is the rule of life and manners, it was not even for a moment abrogated or abolished by Christ. "Do we then make void the law through faith? God forbid, yea we establish the law," Rom. iii. 31. In that respect, Christians are no less under the decalogue, than the Jews were formerly: and that not only because the precepts of it are just and holy, but also because they are commandments, which were formerly promulgated with so much majesty and pomp: or which is almost the very same thing, not only on account of the doctrine they contain, but also of the authority of the supreme governor.

XXXIX. Let us now consider the use of this law in all ages of the world : and this may be considered either *absolutely* and *in itself* or *relatively*, with respect to a *certain* condition or *state* of man. In itself, the law is, 1st, A representaion of true virtue, a delineation of internal and external goodness, and a copy of that holiness which is worthy of God. 2dly, A demonstration of the way, in which a rational creature can come to have glorious communion with God: " which if a man do he shall live in them," Lev. xviii. 5. " The commandment which was ordained to life," Rom. vii. 10. None attains to life but by this law, which must be fulfilled either by man himself, or a surety for him. 3dly, A command of the supreme ruler, binding every one to obedience under the threatening of eternal death, Lev. xviii. 2, 3, 4. Deut. xxvii. 26.

XL. The state of man, to which the law has its peculiar relations, is threefold; viz. his *first*, his *fallen*, and his *restored* state. In his *first* state, it was to man, first the rule of his nature and of all his actions, to which he willingly, and with the greatest complacency of soul conformed himself. 2dly, The most excellent beautiful ornament of man, as stamped and impressed by the creating hand of God on his mind. 3dly, The condition of the covenant of works, which man himself was to perform in order to obtain consummate bliss and happiness.

XLI. In *his fallen state* it serves, 1st, To discover and convince man of his sin, Rom. iii. 20. " by the law is the knowledge of sin. And the precepts of the law do this two ways. *First*, as in a mirror, they discover to man the vileness both of his life and actions, James i. 23. *Then* by its irritating virtue, whereby, on account of human depravity, they stir up sin, which otherwise lay dormant; so that, like one galled by a bridle, the more strictly sin is prohibited and restrained, the more vehemently it resists and makes opposition, every thing that would keep it under being offensive to it. The Apostle excellently

illustrates

illuftrates this, Rom. vii. 7, 13. 2dly, To denounce the curfe
againft man; which it does by its "comminations: now we
know, that what things foever the law faith, it faith to them
who are under the law; that every mouth may be ftopped, and
all the world may become guilty before God," Rom. iii. 19.
3dly, To be a reftraint upon men, and bring them to fome external honeft deportment, in order to preferve civil government,
and prevent the deftruction of mankind by adulteries, rapines,
oppreffions and the like heinous crimes. The Apoftle feems
particularly to intimate this office of the law, 1 Tim. i. 9, when
he fays, " that the law is not made for a righteous man, but
for the lawlefs and difobedient, for the ungodly and for finners, &c. For, he fhews, that it is a curb to thofe prevailing
lufts of the flefh, which otherwife would be immoderately extravagant. 4thly, To bring finners to Chrift : " for, Chrift is
the end of the law for righteoufnefs to every one that believeth,.
Rom. x. 4. The law was our fchool-mafter to bring us to
Chrift," Gal. iii. 24. This is not only true of the ceremonial,
but alfo of the law of the decalogue, which brings to Chrift
thefe two ways : firft, as it really keeps an elect perfon, while
in an unconverted ftate, in fome measure, in the way of his
duty, that he may not obftinately neglect all concern for righteoufnefs and his foul. For, where the Spirit of God does not
yet bear rule, finful lufts break forth there, in fuch a manner,
that the foul, which is obnoxious to them, is in danger of finking into forgetfulnefs and contempt of God : And they would
actually do this, did not the Lord put a bar thereto by this
remedy of his law. But principally the law brings to Chrift,
as it ftrips man of all confidence in his own goodnefs and righteoufnefs, and, by an acknowledgment of his mifery, deeply
humbles him, that fo he may be thus prepared to endeavour
after, what before he thought he did not ftand in need of.

XLII. In the ftate of *reftoration* it teacheth believers: 1ft,
How perfect the obedience was, which Chrift performed for
them, and how much they are under obligations to him, fince
he, who was Lord of the law, fubjected himfelf to it for them
not only to obey its precepts, but to endure the curfe, that he
might redeem them from the law, Gal. iv. 4, 5. 2dly, At
what diftance they ftill are from that perfection of holinefs
which the law requires; in order the better to bring them to
humility, and to a denial of all felf-righteoufnefs, Phil. iii. 8, 9.
and a longing after a bleffed perfection, Rom. vii. 24. 3dly,
What is the rule of their gratitude, and the mark at which they
ought to aim, Phil. iii. 12. 1 Tim. i. 5. 4thly, and laftly, it
bears witnefs to, approves and commends, the beginnings of
fanctification

sanctification, and comforts those as being true Israelites, who
" delight in the law of God after the inward man." The law
does this, not from its own authority, which can admit of nothing but what is perfectly holy, and condemns every thing,
that is stained but with the least spot; but from the authority
of the grace of Christ, to whom it is now subservient, and at
whose command it commends even the imperfect works of believers, declares them to be sincere, and so far approves of them
as conformable to itself: and in that sense the righteousness of
the law is fulfilled in those, " who walk not after the flesh but
after the spirit, Rom. viii. 7.

XLIII. Upon these ten words or commandments God entered into a *covenant* with Israel. " The Lord our God made a
covenant with us in Horeb," Deut. v. 2. So that the ten words
are called the words of the covenant," Exod. xxxiv. 28. and the
*covenant* itself, Deut. iv. 13, nay the tables, on which they were
written, are called the *tables of the covenant*, Deut. ix. 9. The
plan of this covenant is that contract, which God entered into
with Israel, a little before the law was given. Exod. xix. 5,
6, 8. Its solemn ratification was made by those signs, which
are recorded, Exod. xxiv. 3. *seq.*

XLIV. The *stipulation* on the part of God was published in
these words, Exod. xix. 5. 6. " Now therefore if ye will obey
my voice indeed, and keep my covenant, then ye shall be a peculiar treasure unto me above all people: for all the earth is
mine. And ye shall be unto me a kingdom of priests; and an
holy nation." We are not to think, that God, by these words,
required Israel to preform prefect obedience in all parts and degrees, as the condition of the covenant. For in that case, the
whole of this proposal would be nothing, but an intimation of
an inevitable curse. Seeing it is absolutely impossible for sinful
man to give such a perfect observance, even though he is regenerated and sanctified. But a conditional proposal upon an
impossible condition, is equivalent to an absolute denial. It is
indeed true, that the law, considered as a rule, cannot but enjoin a holiness absolutely perfect in every respect: Which we
have elsewhere professedly proved: but the case is different,
when something is required as the condition of a covenant.
The man indeed is still bound to perfect holiness, so far that
the least deviation is a sin: but yet supposing a covenant of grace,
among the benefits of which is remission of sins, God stipulates
with his people in this manner; if, with sincerity of heart, you
keep my precepts, and recover from your falls by renewed repentance, I will upon that give you an evidence, that I am
your God. Here therefore he requires a sincere, though not,
in every respect, a perfect observance of his commands.

XLV.

XLV. Upon that condition he promiſes to them not only temporal bleſſings, ſuch as the poſſeſſion of the land of Canaan, and a peaceable life there, abounding with all plenty of every thing deſirable, Exod. xx. 12. but alſo ſpiritual and eternal, when he ſays, that he will be their God and they his people, in that ſenſe which he promiſed the land to the pious fathers : " that he may eſtabliſh thee to-day for a people unto himſelf, and that he may be unto thee a God, as he hath ſaid unto thee, and as he hath ſworn unto thy fathers, to Abraham, to Iſaac, and to Jacob," Deut. xxix. 13. Compare Jer. vii. 22, 23. But that theſe words compriſe life eternal, and the reſurrection of the body, we learn from our Lord, Mat. xxiii. 32.

XLVI. To this ſtipulation of God the Iſraelites agreed, Exod. xix. 8. " And all the people anſwered together, And ſaid, all that the Lord hath ſpoken, we will do." Which they repeated upon the publication of the law, Exod. xxiv. 3. " and all the people anſwered with one voice, and ſaid, all the words which the Lord hath ſaid will we do." The pious among the Iſraelites, conſcious of their own inability and manifold infirmities, humbly promiſed, depending by faith on the gracious influences of divine ſtrength, and obedience, not indeed perfect, (for that would be to incur the guilt of a lie,) but yet ſincere, and by no means feigned. The others, as they did not duly attend either to the ſpiritual perfection of the law, or to their own natural inability, raſhly and confoundly bound themſelves to the obſervance of all the precepts. Yet ſo far theſe words were good and acceptable to God, as by them they teſtified ſome degree of readineſs of ſoul, Deut. v. 33, 34, 35.

XLVII. Now concerning this covenant, made upon the ten commandments, it is queried, whether it was a covenant of works, or a covenant of grace ? We judge proper to premiſe ſome things, previous to the determination of this queſtion. And firſt, we obſerve, that, in the miniſtry of Moſes, there was a repetition of the doctrine concerning the law of the covenant of works. For both the very ſame precepts are inculcated, on which the covenant of works was founded, and which conſtituted the condition of that covenant ; and that ſentence is repeated, " which if a man do he ſhall live in them," Lev. xviii. 5. Ezek. xx. 11, 13. by which formula, the righteouſneſs, which is of the law, is deſcribed, Rom. x. 5. And the terror of the covenant of works is increaſed by repeated comminations ; and that voice heard, " curſed be he that confirmeth not all the words of this law to do them," Deut. xxvii. 26. Now the apoſtle declares, that this is the curſe of the law, as the law is
oppoſed

opposed to faith, or the covenant of grace, Gal. iii. 10, 12.
Nay, as the requirement of obedience was rigid under the miniſtry of Moſes, the promiſes of ſpiritual and ſaving grace were
more rare and obſcure, the meaſure of the Spirit granted to the
Iſraelites, ſcanty and ſhort, Deut. xxix. 4. and, on the contrary,
the denunciation of the curſe frequent and expreſs; hence the
miniſtry of Moſes is called, " the miniſtration of death and condemnation," 2 Cor. iii. 7, 9. doubtleſs becauſe it mentioned the
condemnation of the ſinner, and obliged the Iſraelites to ſub-
ſcribe to it.

XLVIII. *Secondly,* we more eſpecially remark, that, when the
law was given from mount Sinai or Horeb, there was a repetition of the covenant of works.  For, thoſe tremendous ſigns of
thunders and lightenings, of an earthquake, a thick ſmoke and
black darkneſs, were adapted to ſtrike Iſrael with great terror.
And the ſetting bounds and limits round about the mount,
whereby the Iſraelites were kept at a diſtance from the preſence
of God, upbraided them with that ſeparation, which ſin had
made between God and them.  In a word, " Whatever we
read," Exod. xix. (ſays Calvin, on Heb. xii. 10.) " is intended
to inform the people, that God then aſcended his tribunal, and
manifeſted himſelf as an impartial judge.  If an innocent animal
happened to approach, he commanded it to be thruſt through
with a dart; how much ſorer puniſhment were ſinners liable
to, who were conſcious of their ſins, nay, and knew themſelves
indited by the law, as guilty of eternal death."  See the ſame
author on Exod. xix. 1, 16.  And the apoſtle in this matter,
Heb. xii. 18—22. ſets mount Sinai in oppoſition to mount Sion,
the terrors of the law to the ſweetneſs of the goſpel.

XLIX. *Thirdly,* we are not, however, to imagine, that the
doctrine of the covenant of works was repeated, in order to ſet
up again ſuch a covenant with the Iſraelites, in which they were
to ſeek for righteouſneſs and ſalvation.  For, we have already
proved, book I. chap. IX. ſect. 20. that this could not poſſibly
be renewed in that manner with a ſinner, on account of the
juſtice and truth of God, and the nature of the covenant of
works, which admits of no pardon of ſin.  See alſo *Hornbeck.
Theol. Pract. tom. 2. p.* 10.  Beſides, if the Iſraelites were taught
to ſeek ſalvation by the works of the law, then the law had
been contrary to the promiſe, made to the fathers many ages
before.  But now ſays the apoſtle, Gal. iii. 17. " the covenant
that was confirmed before of God in Chriſt, the law, which
was four hundred and thirty years after, cannot diſannul, that
it ſhould make the promiſe of none effect."  The Iſraelites were,
therefore, thus put in mind of the covenant of works, in order
to

to·convince them of their fin and mifery, to drive them out of
themfelves, to fhew them the neceffity of a fatisfaction, and to
compel them to Chrift.    And fo their being thus brought to a
remembrance of the covenant of works tended to promote the
covenant of grace.

L. *Fourthly*, There likewife accompanied this giving of the
law the repetition of fome things, belonging to the covenant of
grace.    For, that God fhould propofe a covenant of friendfhip
to finful man, call himfelf his God (at leaft in the fenfe it was
faid to the elect in Ifrael,) take to himfelf any people, feparated
from others, for his peculiar treafure, affign to them the land
of Canaan as a pledge of heaven, promife his grace to thofe
that love him and keep his commandments, and circumfcribe
the vengeance denounced againft defpifers within certain
bounds, and the like ; thefe things manifeftly difcover a covenant of grace : and without fuppofing the furetifhip of the
Meffiah, it could not, confiftently with the divine juftice and
truth, be propofed to man a finner.    Judicioufly fays Calvin on
Exod. xix. 17.  " by thefe words we are taught, that thefe prodigies or figns were not given, to drive the people from the
prefence of God ; nor were they ftruck with any terror, to ex-
afperate their minds with a hatred of inftruction ; but that the
covenant of God was no lefs lovely than awful.    For, they are
commanded to go and meet God, to prefent themfelves with a
ready affection of foul to obey him.    Which could not be, unlefs they had heard fomething in the law befides precepts and
threatenings."    See alfo *Tilenus Syntagm. p.* 1. *Difp.* 33. §. 18,
19, 20, 28, 29.

LI. Having premifed thefe obfervations, I anfwer to the
queftion.    The covenant made with Ifrael at mount Sinai was
not formally the covenant of works.    1ft, Becaufe that cannot
be renewed with the finner, in fuch a fenfe as to fay, if, for the
future, thou fhalt perfectly perform every inftance of obedience,
thou fhalt be juftified by that, according to the covenant of
works.    For, by this, the pardon of former fins would be prefuppofed, which the covenant of works excludes.    2dly, Becaufe God did not require perfect obedience from Ifrael, as a
condition of this covenant, as a caufe of claiming the reward ;
but fincere obedience, as an evidence of reverence and gratitude.
3dly, Becaufe it did not conclude Ifrael under the curfe, in the
fenfe peculiar to the covenant of works, where all hope of pardon was cut off, if they finned but in the leaft inftance.

LII. However the carnal Ifraelites, not adverting to God's
purpofe or intention, as they ought, miftook the true meaning
· of that covenant, embraced it as a covenant of works, and by
it

it fought for righteoufnefs. Paul declares this, Rom. ix. 31, 32. " but Ifrael which followed after the law of righteoufnefs, hath not attained to the law of righteoufnefs; wherefore? Becaufe they fought it not by faith, but as it were by the works of the law: for they ftumbled at that ftumbling ftone." To the fame purpofe it is, that, Gal. iv. 24, 25. he compares to the Ifhmaelites the Ifraelites, while they tarried in the defarts of Arabia, which was the country of the former, who are born to bondage of their mother Hagar, or the covenant of mount Sinai, and being deftitute of true righteoufnefs, fhall, with Ifhmael, be at length turned out of the houfe of their heavenly Father. For, in that place, Paul does not confider the covenant of mount Sinai as in itfelf, and in the intention of God, offered to the elect, but as abufed by carnal and hypocritical men. Let Calvin again fpeak: " The apoftle declares, that, by the children of Sinai, he meant hypocrites, perfons who are at length caft out of the church of God, and difinherited. What therefore is that generation unto bondage, which he there fpeaks of? It is doubtlefs thofe, who bafely abufe the law, and conceive nothing concerning it but what is fervile. The pious fathers, who lived under the Old Teftament did not fo. For, the fervile generation of the law did not hinder them from having the fpiritual Jerufalem for their mother. But they, who ftick to the bare law, and acknowledge not its pedagogy, by which they are brought to Chrift, but rather make it an obftacle, to their coming to him, thefe are Ifhmaelites (for thus, and I think rightly, Morlorat reads) born unto bondage." The defign of the apoftle therefore, in that place, is not to teach us, that the covenant of mount Sinai was nothing but a covenant of works, altogether oppofite to the gofpel-covenant; but only that the grofs Ifraelites mifunderftood the mind of God, and bafely abufed his covenant; as all fuch do, who feek for righteoufnefs by the law. See again Calvin on Rom. x. 4.

LIII. Nor was it formally a covenant of grace: becaufe that requires not only obedience, but alfo promifes, and beftows ftrength to obey. For, thus the covenant of grace is made known, Jer. xxxii. 39. " and I will give them one heart, and one way, that they may fear me for ever." But fuch a promife appears not in the covenant, made at mount Sinai. Nay; God, on this very account, diftinguifhes the new covenant of grace from the Sinaitic, Jer. xxxi. 31—33. And Mofes loudly proclaims, Deut. xxix. 4. " yet the Lord hath not given you a heart to perceive, and eyes to fee, and ears to hear, unto this day." Certainly, the chofen from among Ifrael had obtained this. Yet not in virtue of this covenant, which ftipulated obedience,

bedience, but gave not power for it: but in virtue of the covenant of grace, which alfo belonged to them.

LIV. What was it then? It was a *national covenant* between
God and Ifrael, whereby Ifrael promifed to God a fincere
obedience to all his precepts; efpecially to the ten words;
God, on the other hand, promifed to Ifrael, that fuch an obfervance would be acceptable to him, nor want its reward, both
in this life, and in that which is to come, both as to foul and
body. This reciprocal promife fuppofed a covenant of grace.
For, without the affiftance of the covenant of grace, man cannot fincerely promife that obfervance; and yet that an imperfect obfervance fhould be acceptable to God is wholly owing
to the covenant of grace. It alfo fuppofed the doctrine of the
covenant of works, the terror of which being increafed by thofe
tremendous figns that attended it, they ought to have been
excited to embrace that covenant of God. This agreement
therefore is a confequent both of the covenant of grace and of
works; but was formally neither the one nor the other. A
like agreement and renewal of the covenant between God and
the pious is frequent; both national and individual. Of the
former fee Jofh. xxiv. 22. 2 Chron. xv. 12. 2 Kings xxiii. 3.
Neh. x. 29. Of the latter, Pfal. cxix. 106. It is certain, that
in the paffages we have named, mention is made of fome covenant between God and his people. If any fhould afk me, of
what kind, whether of works or of grace? I fhall anfwer, it is
formally neither: but a covenant of fincere piety, which fuppofes both.

LV. Hence the queftion, which is very much agitated at this
day, may be decided: namely *whether the ten words are nothing
but the form of the covenant of grace?* This, I apprehend, is by
no means an accurate way of fpeaking. For, fince a covenant
ftrictly fo called, confifts in a mutual agreement; what is properly the form of the covenant fhould contain the faid mutual
agreement. But the ten words contain only a prefcription of
duty fenced on the one hand by threatenings, taken from the
covenant of works; on the other, by promifes, which belong
to the covenant of grace. Hence the fcripture, when it fpeaks
properly, fays that a covenant was made *upon* thefe ten words,
or *after the tenor of thofe words*, Exod. xxxiv. 27. diftinguifhing
the covenant itfelf, which confifts in a mutual agreement from
the ten words, which contain the conditions of it. The form
of the covenant is exhibited by thofe words, which we have
already quoted from Exod. xix. 5, 6, 8. I deny not, that the
ten commandments are frequently in fcripture called *the covenant
of God*. But at the fame time, no perfon can be ignorant, that
                                        the

the term *covenant*, has various fignifications in the Hebrew, and often fignifies nothing but a *precept*, as Jer. xxxiv. 13, 14. Thus Mofes explains himfelf on this head, Deut. iv. 13. " And he declared unto you his covenant, *which he commanded you to per-form*, even ten commandments." They are therefore called a covenant by a Synecdoche, becaufe they contain thofe precepts, which God, when he fet his covenant before them, required the Ifraelites to obferve, and to which the faid Ifraelites bound themfelves by covenant.

LVI. The ten words, or commandments, therefore, are not *the form of a covenant properly fo called*, but *the rule of duty* : much lefs are they *the form of the covenant of grace* : becaufe that covenant, in its ftrict fignification, confifts of mere promifes, and, as it relates to elect perfons, has the nature of a teftament, or laft will, rather than of a covenant ftrictly fpeaking, and depends on no condition ; as we have at large explained and proved, Book III. chap. 1. fect. 8. &c. And Jeremiah has fhewn us, that the form of the covenant of grace, confifts in abfolute promifes, chap. xxxi. 33. and xxxii. 38—40. In like manner Ifa. liv. 10.

LVII. Leaft of all can it be faid, that the ten words are *nothing* but the form of the covenant of grace, fince we may look upon them as having a relation to any covenant whatever. They may be confidered in a twofold manner. 1ft, Precifely, *as a law*. 2dly, As an *inftrument of the covenant*. As a *law*, they are the rule of our nature and actions, which HE has prefcribed, who has a right to command. This they were from the beginning, this they ftill are, and this they will continue to be, under whatever covenant, or in whatever ftate man fhall be. As an *inftrument of the covenant* they point out the way to eternal falvation ; or contain the condition of enjoying that falvation : and that both under the covenant of grace and of works. But with this difference ; that under the covenant of works, this condition is required to be performed by man himfelf ; under the covenant of grace it is propofed, as already performed, or to be performed by a mediator. Things, which thofe very perfons, with whom we are now difputing, will not venture to deny.

## CHAP. V.

### *Of the Doctrine of the Prophets.*

I. THE plan we formerly laid down, should now require to speak a little of those things from Moses himself and the succeeding prophets, which they have published concerning the person, natures, states, offices, and blessings of the Messiah. And it would be easy to shew, that nothing remarkable did befal our Jesus, nothing great was either said or done by him, which the prophets did not foretel was to come to pass. The prophets, I say, who " prophesied of the grace that should come unto us; searching what, or what manner of · time the Spirit of Christ which was in them did signify, when it testified beforehand the sufferings of Christ, and the glory that should follow," 1 Pet. i. 10, 11. and who all, with one consent, " give witness to Jesus, that through his name, whosoever believeth in him shall receive remission of · sins," Acts x. 43. The apostle Paul, who protested, " he had not shunned to declare all the counsel of God," Acts xx. 27. · at the same time protests, " he says none other things than those which the prophets and Moses did say should come, Acts xxvi. 22. And certainly, the body itself should exactly agree with the picture, that was long before presented to the view of the ancient church since it became the wisdom and goodness of God, to give such an exact description of the Messiah, with all his marks or characters, that he might be known by any thoughtful and attentive mind, and distinguished from all manner of impostors, who should impiously pretend to, or counterfeit his name. But this subject has been, both formerly and lately, considered by the learned, and treated with such accuracy, that I have nothing to add. If any would have a compendious view of these things, he may consult the preface to the New Testament, drawn up, with great judgment, by our divines.

---

## CHAP. VI.

### *Of the Types.*

I. SUCH is the inexhaustible copiousness of the Holy Scriptures, that not only the words are significative of things, but even the things, which are first signified by the words, do likewise

wife reprefent other things, which they were appointed to pre-figure long before they happened. Chrift principally, and Paul have informed us of this, when they apply moft of the things which happened under the old difpenfation to the Meffiah, and to the œconomy of a better teftament. And indeed, if the old inftitutions of the deity had not their *myftical fignifications*, they might defervedly be accounted childifh, ludicrous, and un-worthy of God. Thefe are things, which not only Chriftians require to be granted to them, but alfo were acknowledged by the ancient Jews, who befides a *literal*, or *plain meaning*, fought alfo a *myftical fenfe* in fcripture. And it was a conftant and re-ceived opinion among them, that all things were myftical in the law of Mofes, and therefore may be myftically explained.

II. Their myftical fignification points to Chrift, in his *perfon, ftates, offices, and works*, and in his *fpiritual body*, the church: for *Chrift is the end of the law*, Rom. x. 4. *the body*, or fubftance of the ceremonial fhadows, Col. ii. 17. and the centre of the prophecies, Acts x. 43. The doctrine of Chrift is *the key of knowledge*, Luke xi. 42. without which nothing can be favingly underftood in Mofes and the prophets. As is apparent in the Pharifees of old, and the Socinians in our day; who being tainted with falfe notions concerning the Meffiah, pollute for the moft part, all the teftimonies concerning the common falva-tion by their impure interpretations. It was very well faid by the ingenious Bifterfield, that " the Lord Jefus Chrift was the fpirit and foul of the whole, both of the Old and New Tefta-ment," *de Scripturæ eminentia*, §. 40.

III. It is an unqueftionable truth, that the Old Teftament believers, efpecially thofe who were favoured with a fuller mea-fure of the Spirit, applied themfelves with peculiar diligence, to find out the myftical meaning of the TYPES: in which ftudy they were very much affifted by the prophets and divinely infpi-red priefts. Thus David declared, that " he had feen God in the fanctuary," Pfal. lxiii. 2. that is, that he had, by the figures of the Levitical fervice, fearched by holy meditation, into the very truth of the things. This made believers fo chearful in the acts of external worfhip; not that they were very much taken with thofe minute corporal performances, but that " they beheld in them the beauty of Jehovah, and enquired in his temple," Pfal. xxvii. 4. They were not put off with mere fhadows, but were " fatisfied with the goodnefs of God's houfe, even of his holy temple;" and though it was but darkly, yet they heard him " fpeaking terrible things in righteoufnefs," Pfal. lxv. 4, 5.

IV. Though Chrift and the Apoftles, in order to illuftrate and prove the truth of the gofpel, argued from the types by
divine

divine infpiration, and the infallible guidance of the Holy Spirit: yet they did not lay the ftrefs of thofe arguments on their own bare authority, becaufe they were infpired, (for that authority was at times called in queftion, and upon fuppofing it, all reafoning would almoft feem fuperfluous), but on the evident demonftration of the truth to the confcience, which plainly difcovered to an attentive perfon, that it was worthy of God to reprefent fuch a truth by fuch types.

V. The ftrength of thofe arguments refts on this fuppofition, that God was pleafed to give the church at that time, in the memorable perfons of the Old Teftament, to whom fome remarkable things happened in an extraordinary way, and in the whole of his inftituted worfhip, a beautiful picture, and becoming the accuracy of fo great an artift, in which Chrift with his myftical body might be delineated. The apoftle, when he argued with the Jews in his epiftles to the Galatians and Hebrews, lays this down as a fundamental truth; and having laid that foundation, directly proceeds, with a kind of divine fkill, to the application of the types. For, when there is any thing in the antitype refembling the type, it is juftly affirmed, that God, who knows all things from the beginning, ordered the type in fuch a manner, that it might fignify beforehand that truth; which was in the antitype. Unlefs we would rather maintain, that the likenefs of an ingenious picture to the original, was rather the effect of chance, than of the intention of the artift; which is contrary to all reafon.

VI. It is not only lawful but the incumbent duty of teachers, even though not infpired, to tread in this very path, and to explain, in the fame method, the types of the Old Teftament. For, we muft not think, either that an infallible authority is neceffary to explain the types, or that all the types of the Old Teftament are explained in the New. Not the *former*; for, why fhould an infallible authority be required in interpreting the types, rather than in interpreting the prophecies and other dark expreffions in fcripture? Since it is manifeft, that it was the will of God to inftruct the church by types; and the explication of the types is now oftentimes far more eafy, on account of the diftinct knowledge of the antitype, than of many prophecies, which it is far more difficult to determine to what they refer. Not the *latter* for why fhould we believe, that all the types of Chrift were explained rather than all the prophecies concerning him? Efpecially, as the apoftle affirms, that he has not fpoken particularly of them all, Heb. ix. 5. We are therefore to maintain, that the infpired teachers have pointed out to us the way and method, in which we ought to proceed in explaining the types, and given us a key to open thofe myfteries which are contained in them.

VII. Now we fhall proceed in that way with fafety. 1. When we accurately confider the original, even the Lord Jefus, who is now prefented to our view without a vail, and from thence turn the eye of our mind to the type; then the greater, the fuller, and the more efpecial agreement we obferve and difcover between both; the greater glory we afcribe to the wifdom and truth of God, who made the type, fo exactly to correfpond with him who is figured by it. For, when we read the fcriptures, we are to judge beforehand, that then only we underftand them, when we difcover in them a wifdom unfearchable and worthy of God.

VIII. In every thing we are to proceed with caution, *fear and trembling*, left we devife myfteries out of our own imagination, and obftinately pervert to one purpofe what belongs to another. We do injury to God and his word, when we would have it owing to our fanciful inventions, that God feems to have fpoke or done any thing wifely. However, though there is a meafure in all things, I fhould think the miftake more tolerable in one, who imagines he fees Chrift, where perhaps he does not difcover himfelf, than of another, who refufes to fee him, where he prefents himfelf with fufficient evidence. For the one is an indication of a foul that loves Chrift, and is very much taken up with the thoughts of him, when the very leaft, or perhaps no occafion is given him: the other argues an indolent foul, and flow to believe; fuch as difcovers itfelf in the Socinians, and in Grotius, in other refpects a great man, who generally fo pervert very many paffages, that they make them appear to have no manner of regard to Chrift.

IX. When ever it is evident, that any perfon or thing is a type of Chrift, we are not to imagine, that every circumftance in that perfon or thing is typical. For, it may be that, in the fame context, fome things are peculiar only to the type, others only to the antitype and others common to both: for inftance, 2 Sam. vii, Solomon, is propofed as a type of Chrift. But it agrees to Solomon and not to Chrift, " if he commit iniquity, I will chaften him with the rod of men, and with the ftripes of the children of men," ver. 14. To Chrift, and not to Solomon in its full fignification, " I will ftablifh the throne of his kingdom for ever," ver. 13. For the kingdom of Ifrael became extinct in the pofterity of Solomon by the Babylonifh captivity. And it is applicable to both, *he fhall build an houfe for my name*, *ib*. We may confider other inftances in the fame manner.

X. Sometimes it is fufficient that there be a very faint refemblance

blance in the type of fomething moft excellent, in a moft eminent manner, in the antitype. Nay, the more noble and divine,
the thing fignified is, the refemblance of it muft of neceffity be
the more flender ; becaufe of the immenfe diftance there is between Chrift and the *poor creature*. For example : their being
no mention in Scripture either of the beginning of the days, or
the end of Melchifedec's life, that was fufficient to prefigure
the eternity of Chrift, Heb. vii. 9. And this, once for all,
fhould be a fixed principle in our minds, that, when the fame
things are afferted both of the type and the antitype, they are,
in a more excellent manner, true in the latter than in the former, fo that the truth of the thing, in its full import, is only
to be found in the antitype. Thus we are to explain that of
the Apoftle, Heb. i. 5. " To which of the angels faid he at
any time, thou art my Son----I will be to him a Father, and
he fhall be to me a Son ;" when it is evident, the fame was
faid concerning Solomon, but in fuch a diminutive fenfe with refpect to Solomon, that when his whole dignity, honour and
grandeur are compared with Chrift, it is plainly of no avail :
but it is true in Chrift, in fuch a large and extenfive fenfe, that
his dignity and honour exceeds that of all the angels, and cannot be communicated to any creature.

XI. Finally, the learned have likewife obferved, that a certain variation fometimes takes place with regard to the fignification of the type, in fo much that in fome refpects, it may be
applied to Chrift, and in others to the church, which is his
myftical body. Let Abraham's offering up his fon be an inftance of this. Ifaac, in carrying the wood, in being bound
by his father, and ready to fuffer death in obedience to his father and to God, was a type of Chrift, in his carrying his crofs,
being bound, and in obeying his Father even unto death. But
when the ram was offered in the room of Ifaac, the figure was
changed, and that *ram* reprefented Chrift, and Ifaac the church,
which is delivered from death by the death of Chrift. Thefe
things, I thought proper to premife in general, becaufe they
caft light on the whole of typical divinity, and will be of ufe to
us in the fubfequent obfervations.

XII. Moreover, the types are not all of one kind ; but may
very properly be divided into three claffes : fo that fome are
*natural :* fome *hiftorical :* and others *legal.* We fhall out of a
great number give a few inftances of each of thefe, according
to the three periods of time formerly mentioned.

XIII. By a *natural* type, I underftand the creation of this
vifible world, as Mofes has given us the hiftory of it ; which
was a type of the new creation of believers and of the conftitu-
tion

tion of the church. Hence *the new man* is said *to be after God, created,* Eph. iv. 24. and believers are said to be God's ποιημα, αυτοδουτες υχειςτ ῦ ἰησω *workmanship, created in Christ Jesus unto good works,* Eph. ii. 10. And the whole myftical body of Chrift is called a *new creature* or creation, 2 Cor. v. 17. Nay the whole method of our reftoration is expreffed in phrafes and fimilitudes from the moft part, taken from the firft creation. Though Adam in his innocent ftate could have no thoughts of that, nothing having been made known to him, either concerning his fall, or his recovery; yet God fo wifely ordered his works in the firft creation, that they might be, as it were, an exemplar of the fecond; and it is manifeft to any attentive perfon, that they are fo ; which will evidently appear by particularly comparing the one with the other.

XIV. The firft creation of the world was out of nothing ; fo nothing was prepared for the fecond, no good, no virtue, no previous difpofitions in the fubject : yea fomething indeed was in being, which had no place in the old, but that was only rebellion and enmity making vehement oppofition to the almighty grace of God.——The firft was performed at the command and will of God, the fecond in like manner. " Of his own will begat he us with the word of truth, that we fhould be a kind of firft fruits of his creatures," Jam. i. 18.——The rudiments of the firft was an indigefted mafs. "The earth was without form and void, and darknefs was upon the face of the deep," Gen. i. 2. In like manner, all things lie in bafe confufion in the foul, when it is to be adorned by the new creation : and depraved lufts are violently agitated every where, without any order. Thofe things, which fhould poffefs the upper place are depreffed to the loweft. There is alfo a furprifing emptinefs of every thing that is good, Rom. vii. 18. Neither are all things only furrounded with the grofs darknefs of ignorance, but the whole foul is nothing but darknefs itfelf, Eph. v. 8. When God was pleafed to adorn the world he had created, he began with the production of light, and he takes the fame method in this other creation. " God, who commanded the light to fhine out of darknefs, hath fhined in our hearts, to give the light of the knowledge of the glory of God in the face of Jefus Chrift," 2 Cor. iv. 6.——After the light, God made the expanfe or firmament, to divide the waters from the waters, or the waters under the firmament from thofe above it. He divided alfo the waters from the dry land. So alfo he brings every thing, by degrees, into order in our fouls. He places reafon, which was formerly depreffed by the affections, on the chief throne, and commands the affections to ftand at the foot-

ſtool of reaſon ; but then in ſuch a manner, that the ſame
Spirit, which of old moved on the face of the waters, has the
management of all here likewiſe.—When the dry land diſcovered itſelf from the waters, immediately flowers herbs and trees
with their fruit were produced : ſo after every thing is properly arranged in the new man, fruits meet for faith, and repentance appear, and the church of God is * " a paradiſe of po-
megranats," Cant. iv. 13. When the " rain is over and gone,
the flowers appear on the earth, the fig tree putteth forth her green
figs, and the vines with the tender grape give a good ſmell," Cant.
ii. 11, 12, 13.—But as God was pleaſed to divide the huge maſs
of light into unequal parcels, in order to diſtinguiſh years and
days in their ſeaſons, and the more commodiouſly to cheriſh
all things by a certain proportion of light and heat : ſo he likewiſe diſpenſes his light in the church in different degrees. She
has the ſtars of the prophecies twinkling in the midſt of darkneſs ; alſo the brighter day-ſtar of the Goſpel, the joyful harbinger of the perfect day, 2 Pet. i. 19. ſhe is as the moon in
the heavens of this univerſe, and the more abundant rays ſhe receives from Jeſus, who is her ſun, the brighter ſhe is, Cant.
vi. 10. Laſtly, in proportion to the approach or removal of
her ſun, ſhe enjoins the myſtical revolutions of day and night,
of ſummer and winter, Cant. iv. 6. and ii. 11. While the
heavens are ſpangled with ſo many ſtars, the inferior parts of
the creation are replete with various creatures, the air with
birds, the waters with fiſh, the earth with animals, as well reptile, as with feet. In the ſame manner, the grace of the
Spirit of God quickens the ſoul by his holy emotions ; ſome
ſouls ſeem to live, as it were, in the waters of pious tears ; o-
thers again, ſuiting themſelves to meaner attainments, creep
on the ground ; others, like lions, hold on a ſteady pace ; while
others, in fine, like eagles, ſoar aloft, and waft themſelves on
nimble pinions above all heavens.

XV. But the creation of man, which ſucceeded the former,
diſplays again new myſteries. The whole trinity addreſſed
themſelves to this by mutual conſultation. And manifeſt themſelves in a ſingular manner in the work of the new creation.
The Father from eternity laid the plan of that work in his Son.
The Son, in our nature, purchaſed our transformation into the
likeneſs of God. The Holy Spirit excutes the counſel of the
Father, and applies the merits of the Son to his choſen people,
in that new creation. " We are God's workmanſhip, created
in Chriſt Jeſus," Eph. ii. 10. and "born of the Spirit," John iii.

5.—

* Our verſion renders it an orchard, but the Septuagint and ſeveral other verſions
render it paradiſe.

5.—In the firſt creation, man was adorned with the beautiful image of God: the ſame is reſtored to him in the ſecond; at firſt indeed, ſtill this image is ſoiled with ſome ſtains; however it cannot be loſt, but ſhall gradually be perfeſted to the full likeneſs of God.—While Adam was aſleep, out of one of his ribs Eve was formed, whom he acknowledged to be fleſh of his fleſh, and bone of his bone. The death-ſleep of Chriſt gives life to his beloved ſpouſe. *This myſtery* of Adam and Eve *is great, regarding Chriſt and the church,* Eph. v. 32.—The firſt man had dominion given him over all things: which is reſtored to him far more glorious by grace, 1 Cor. iii. 22. And if perhaps this world, as being ſubjeſt to vanity, might ſeem unworthy of his dominion, God has framed another for his ſake, in which dwelleth righteouſneſs, 2 Pet. iii. 13.

XVI. When God had thus created all things for man, man for himſelf, and formed Eve for Adam while he was aſleep, he then *reſted* from all his work, and took pleaſure in it as good, and adapted to diſplay the glory of his perfeſtions. In this manner God ſtill proceeds in the work of grace, till his Eve, his church, ſhall be perfeſtly adorned for our heavenly Adam, and the whole body of the eleſt, gathered together into one: and then having finiſhed all his work, he will enter upon his moſt bleſſed reſt, and moſt ſweetly delight himſelf in the new world of glory. And as on that day on which God reſted, man, at the ſame time, entered into the reſt of God; ſo, in this other reſt of God, the church having happily gone through all her toils, ſhall for ever enjoy, in like manner, a moſt holy and delightful reſt. This is " that [Sabbatiſm] reſt which remaineth for the people of God, that they may enter into God's reſt, and ceaſe from their works as God did from his," Heb. iv. 9, 10. And this ſhall ſuffice concerning the natural types.

XVII. Let us now illuſtrate two *hiſtorical* types, in the *firſt age* of the world. And we have ABEL among the firſt, who was ſlain by his envious brother Cain, Gen. iv. 1ſt, Abel in Hebrew ſignifies *vanity* and *emptineſs;* and he was called by that name, though he was a ſon dear to his parents, a ſervant dear to God, and indeed the firſt of all mankind, whom we read of, that was honoured with the glory of heaven. Thus alſo Jeſus, though he thought it not robbery to be equal with God, *was to empty* himſelf, upon aſſuming the nature of man, who is *like unto vanity,* Pſal. lxii. 9. Nay, ſuffering himſelf to * be treated like a *worm;* which is inferior to a man. (2.) Abel was a ſhepherd: ſo the Meſſiah is that good Shepherd by way

B b 2                                    of

---

* The author refers to Pſ. xxii. 6. where the royal prophet, as a type of the Meſſiah, ſays, *but I am a worm and no man.*

of eminence, John x. 14. (3.) The religious service of Abel
was acceptable to God; and Christ " does always those things
that please him," John viii. 29. (4.) Abel offered the choice of
what he had to God, of the firstlings of his flock and of their
fat. Christ having nothing better, through the eternal Spirit
offered *himself* without spot to God, Heb. ix. 10. (5.) God
graciously looked upon Abel's offering: the offering of Christ
was for a sweet-smelling favour to God, Eph. v. 2. (6.) Cain
though a full brother, burned with ungovernable envy against
Abel. With the same fury the Jews were instigated against
Christ, though they were his brethren on many accounts. (7.)
Cain *conversed* with Abel, with a design to entangle him in his
words. How often did the Pharisees lay snares and traps for
Christ by their deceitful conferences? (8.) Abel at last was
slain by his brother, and by a bloody death, cut off in the very
flower of his age. Nor did the Jews cease, till they had cut off
Christ by an accursed death, nailing him to the cross. (9.) The
parricide Cain was accursed and banished from the presence
of the Lord. The deicide Jews are still under the same curse,
being banished both from heaven, and their native soil: and
the blood of Christ which they shed, calls aloud for the vengeance, which they, with mad fury, imprecated on themselves
and their posterity: though in other respects, the blood of
Christ speaks better things than that of Abel, Heb. xii. 24.

XVIII. As Abel typically represented Christ in his state of
*humiliation:* so ENOCH was a type of his *glorification.* (1.) Enoch,
signifies * *instructed, devoted,* being one who was consecrated to
God, and from his early years, instructed in the doctrine of
godliness. Compare, Prov. xxii. 6. " train up, initiate, [in-
struct] a child in the way he should go," instill into him the
first principles of heavenly wisdom. If ever any one, surely
Christ was consecrated and devoted to God, and when he was
scarce twelve years of age, he appeared as a doctor amidst the
greatest doctors in Israel. (2.) Enoch walked with God, that
is, according to the Apostle, Heb. ix. 5. *pleased God.* This also
Christ perfectly did, " in whom the Father was well pleased.
(3.) Enoch prophesied of the glorious coming of the Lord, with
ten-thousands of saints, Jude ver. 14. Christ often and very expressly foretold this, and that even when he was charged with
blasphemy, and stood before the tribunal, Mat. xxvi. 64. (4.)
Enoch, after he had walked with God, and declared the counsel
of God to the men of his generation, was taken up alive to
heaven, in soul and body, without seeing death, Heb. xi. 5.

for

* Ainsworth says, it is in the Hebrew chanoch, that is *dedicated* or *catechised.*

for he was not to conquer it for the falvation of others. But Chrift, having fuffered death for the elect, and purged away our fins by himfelf, was made higher than the heavens, and fat down at the right hand of the majefty in the higheft. (5.) Enoch was the feventh from Adam; Chrift the feventieth from Enoch, as appears from his genealogy in Luke. (6.) Enoch was the third perfon, that we read of, who departed this world: Chrift the * third of thofe, who afcended to heaven. (7.) As in Abel we have an inftance of a violent death, in Adam of a natural; fo in Enoch, an example of that fupernatural change, which thofe of the elect fhall undergo, who fhall be alive at the laft day. (8.) And laftly, God was pleafed, before the law, to give the world in Enoch an inftance of an afcenfion to heaven; under the law, in the perfon of Elias; under the Gofpel, in Chrift; to fhew, that believers, in every period, become partakers of the fame falvation.

XIX. Let us next, under the *fecond period*, explain two types of the fame kind. The firft is Noah; the fecond Ifaac. Peter declares, 1 Pet. iii. 20, 21. that Noah the Patriach of the new world, the ark, which he built, and the waters of the deluge, had all their myftical fignification: where he teacheth us, that baptifm is the antitype of thofe things, which happened under, and by the direction of Noah. Antitype there denotes a type correfponding in the fame fignification to fome other type. For order's fake, we will diftinctly confider three things. I. Noah himfelf. II. The ark. III. The deluge.

XX. As to Noah. 1ft, His name fignifies *reft*. And as that was not altogether expected in vain, fo he could not beftow it fully, and in a manner, that was proper to anfwer the import of that name. But Chrift freely beftows this on all thofe, who being burdened with the load of fin, and betake themfelves to him, Mat. xi. 29. having calmed the ftorm of divine wrath, that was hanging over our guilty heads, brings his church, amidft the ftorms and tempefts of adverfities, to the wifhed-for haven of reft. (2.) Noah was *a juft man in his generation;* Chrift was *holy, harmlefs, undefiled,* and feparate from finners, knew no fin, neither was guile found in his mouth; nay, he is Jehovah our righteoufnefs. (3.) Noah was a *preacher of righteoufnefs;* Chrift preached this much more diftinctly, both that righteoufnefs, by which we muft be juftified before God, and that, which we fhould endeavour after as a teftimony of our gratitude. (4.) Noah, in building the ark, prepared a fafe retreat for his family againft the impending waters of the deluge.

---

* Enoch himfelf was the first, Elijah the fecond, and fo Chrift was the third.

deluge. Concerning Chrift it is faid, Ifa. xxxii. 2. " And a man
fhall be as an hiding-place from the wind, and a covert from
the tempeft." (5.) Noah preferved his family, which confifted
only of eight fouls: Chrift preferves the children, whom God
has given him; who, in comparifon of the great number of
thofe that perifh, are but a little flock. (6.) As Noah was the
prince of the fecond world; fo Chrift is the head of that new
world, which was formed by means of the ruin and deftruction
of the former. For as, whatever belonged to the former world
was deftroyed in the time of Noah; fo whatever takes its rife
from the firft Adam, ought to be abolifhed, in order to give
place to the new creature, which is from Chrift. 7thly, Noah
offered to God a facrifice of a fweet favour; Chrift offers that
facrifice of a fweet fmelling favour, by the virtue of which
God is reconciled to the world. 8thly, After God had fmelled
a fweet favour from the facrifice which Noah offered, he
promifed, that he would no more deftroy the world by a new
deluge; but only collect that quantity of vapours in the air,
which being beautifully painted with the folar rays, might form
in the heavens the variegated rain-bow. By the efficacy of the
facrifice, which Chrift offered, God was reconciled to his elect,
and promifed, that he would never punifh them in his anger;
but only chaftife them with flighter paternal ftripes, amidft
which the rays of his grace would fhine.

XXI. The *ark*, which Noah built, fignified both Chrift and
the church of Chrift. It was a type of Chrift; for (1.) As the
ark fecured all who entered into it, from the defcending rains,
and from the waters of the great abyfs, as they broke out from
beneath: fo Chrift gives a fecure refuge to all who fly to him,
both againft the wrath of God, which is revealed from heaven,
and againft the rage of their infernal enemies. (2.) As it appeared ridiculous to the ungodly world, who were hardened to
their own deftruction, that the feeds of a new univerfe fhould
be preferved in fuch an ark; fo the glad tidings of falvation
which we are to feek for only in Chrift, is to the Jews a
ftumbling-block, and to the Greeks foolifhnefs. (3.) As the
ark had its juft dimenfions of length, breadth and depth, and
in a word, was fo large as to be able to contain fo many animals together with their food: fo in like manner, there is in
Jefus Chrift that length, breadth, depth and heighth of delightful love, which is abundantly fufficient for faving all the elect
for ever. 4thly, That pitch, with which, according to God's
appointment, the joints of the ark were pitched over, within
and without, to prevent all ingrefs of the water, is called in
Hebrew *cophir*, which likewife fignifies *expiation*, and *a price of
redemption.*

*redemption.*  Was not this an elegant and fine reprefentation of the expiation and redemption of Chrift, to which alone we are indebted, for our being fecured from the deluge of divine vengeance.

XXII. But this fame ark was alfo a figure of the *church.* (1.) As the ark contained all the hope of the fecond world; fo in like manner, the church contains that affembly of the firft-born, who are to be the heirs of the new world.  (2.) As the profane Ham alfo entered into the ark with the godly, and many unclean beafts with the clean: fo many impure hypocrites creep into the external communion of the church.  (3.) As the ark remained unhurt and unfhattered amidft all the fhocks of ftorms and tempefts, the tops of houfes and craggy cliffs of mountains and rocks: fo neither fhall the gates of hell prevail againft the church.  (4.) As the ark floated fecurely on the waters, without fails, oars, or rudder, by the providence of God alone, even when Noah was afleep: fo the church, when deftitute of all human aid, and while they, to whofe care fhe is committed, are often afleep, is guided by the watchful eye of Chrift, and at laft happily brought into the haven of falvation. (5.) As the ark, upon the retiring of the waters again into their abyfs, refted upon the mountains of Ararat, where Noah, when he debarked and fet his feet on dry land, offered facrifices of thankfgiving to God: fo, in like manner, the church, after it has paffed through the trials, dangers and oppofitions of this prefent world, fhall reft in the heavenly Zion, where, with uninterrupted thankfgivings, fhe will fing the praifes of her great God and Saviour.

XXIII. Again, the *waters of the deluge* have a reference both to Chrift and the *church.*  (1.) As the waters, which defcended from heaven, and violently iffued out from beneath, covered the ark, and encompaffed it on every fide, fo Chrift was alfo to grapple with the wrath of his heavenly Father, with the bands of hell let loofe upon him, and with the unrelenting cruelty of malicious men.  In fhort, "the forrows of death compaffed him, and the floods of [Belial] ungodly men made him afraid," Pfal. xviii. 4.  (2.) As thofe waters did indeed cover, but did not fink, the ark; nay the deeper they were, the more they lifted it up on high, and brought it nearer to heaven; fo Chrift in like manner, "was put to death in the flefh, but quickened by the Spirit," 1 Pet. iii. 18.  And the more grievous his fufferings were, to the higher pitch of glory did God exalt him, 2 Pet. ii. 9.  (3.) As the waters of the deluge deftroyed the world of the ungodly, but preferved the ark, 1 Pet. iii. 20. which being lifted up on high was placed above the tops of

houfes

houfes and turrets, againft which it might be dafhed, while, in
the mean time, all the devices and inftruments of art were
overthrown: fo the afflictions, which are fent by God are indeed to confume the ungodly, and drive them headlong into
hell; but appointed to purge and prepare the godly for falvation, that they may not perifh with the world, 1 Cor. xi. 32.
(4.) As the waters of the deluge, by drowning finners, wafhed
out the crimes of the old world; that the church being delivered
from thefe notorious crimes, might, with greater purity, ferve
God (by which the fame thing is fet forth as by the water of
baptifm, 1 Pet. iii. 21.) So, by the blood and Spirit of Chrift,
our fins are wafhed away, the old man mortified, that the new
man may, with the greater alacrity, be employed for God.

XXIV. Laftly, It is not for nothing, that notice is taken of
the *dove*, which Noah fent out, and which returned in the evening with an olive-leaf plucked off. For, (1.) As Noah was a
type of Chrift, fo *that dove* was a type of the Holy Spirit, which
defcended upon Chrift, when he was baptifed at Jordan. (2.)
As that dove brought the olive-branch to thofe who were in
the ark, from which they might infer, that the waters were
now dried up; fo, in like manner, the Holy Spirit affures thofe,
that are in the church, of the peace of God, the fymbol of
which was the olive-branch. (3.) As the dove carried that
olive-leaf in her *mouth;* fo the Holy Spirit publifhes that myftical, or fpiritual peace by the mouth of the prophets, apoftles,
and evangelifts. (4.) As the dove came to the ark in the evening, fo, in the evening of the world, the gifts of the Holy Spirit
are more plentiful and abundant.

XXV. Omitting for the prefent, the illuftrious type of Melchizedec, which Paul has accurately explained, Heb. vii. we
fhall take a fhort view of the hiftory of Ifaac, who was a type
of Chrift: I. In his perfon. II. In his offering. III. In his
deliverance and the glorious confequence thereof.

XXVI. As to his perfon. (1.) He is called Ifaac from *laugh-
ing*, becaufe he was a fon of joy and exultation to his parents,
Gen. xxi. 6. But Chrift is the joy of the whole world, and at his
birth the angels proclaimed to the fhepherds good tidings of
great joy, which fhall be to all people, Luke ii. 16. (2.) Ifaac
was the *fon of the promife*, being defcended in a miraculous manner from Abraham, who was old, and from Sarah, who was
barren and paft bearing, by the alone efficacy of the word of God,
whereby " he calls things that are not, as if they were," Rom.
iv. 17. So Chrift, not according to the order of nature, nor
by virtue of the general bleffing, *increafe and multiply*, but by
the efficacy of a gracious promife, was born of a virgin mother,
by

by a strange and surprising miracle. (3.) Isaac was the *only*
son of Abraham, Gen. xxii. 2. by a lawful and free wife, and
in whom *his seed was to be called,* Gen. xxi. 12. though he likewise had Ishmael, and afterwards begat sons of Keturah; so
Christ is the only begotten Son of the Father, John iii. 16.
though he also has brethren, but of a far more inferior order
and condition, Rom. viii. 29. (4.) Isaac was the head of Abraham's family, and, in his measure, that is, typically, the origin
of the blessing. Christ is the head of God's family; " of whom
the whole family in heaven and earth is named," Eph. iii. 15.
And " in him we are blessed with all spiritual blessings," Eph.
i. 3.

XXVII. In the *offering* of Isaac, the analogy is in the following particulars: 1st, Abraham could not possibly have given a
more illustrious instance of his love to God, than by offering
to the death his son, his only son Isaac, whom he loved, in
whom all his hopes were placed.   Nor was it possible for God
to give a more illustrious display of his love to men, than by
delivering up for them his beloved and only begotten Son to
the most dreadful tortures of many deaths in one, John iii. 16.
(2.) It was an extraordinary instance of Isaac's obedience, to
submit to his father in such a dreadful case, without a repining
murmur. And who can, as it justly deserves, relate, with what
cheerfulness Christ obeyed his Father unto the death, even the
death of the cross? Phil. ii. 8.   (3.) As Isaac went out of his
father's house to the place, which God had appointed; so
Christ went out of Jerusalem, in order to suffer without the
gate, Heb. xiii. 11.   (4.) Isaac carried the wood: and Christ
carried his cross.   (5.) Isaac's hands were tied: in like manner were Christ's.   (6.) Isaac was laid on the wood: and
Christ was nailed to the cross.   (7.) Isaac was offered on mount
Moriah, which was either the same with, or at least near to
Calvary, where our Lord was crucified.

XXVIII. We are further to observe these coincidences in
his deliverance. 1st, Isaac was already dead in his father's
opinion, and Abraham received him from the dead in a figure,
Heb. xi. 19.   So Christ, being truly dead was restored to life,
2dly, Isaac was dead in his father's intention, from the moment he received the command to offer him up, until the third
day, on which he was forbid to lay hands on the lad.   On the
third day also Christ arose.   3dly, When Isaac was restored to
Abraham, he dwelt with his father, and became the parent of
a numerous seed.   So when Christ rose from the dead, he entered into his Father's house, and saw his seed, Isa. liii. 10.

XXIX. When a ram was substituted for Isaac, who was

otherwife to have been offered ; by inverting the figure, Ifaac reprefents the *church*, and the ram is a figure of Chrift.   (1.) Ifaac was, by the command of God, brought to be offered, which was near put in execution by Abraham. Thus the feverity of the divine judgment againft fin was fhadowed forth; whereby, unlefs the fatisfaction of Chrift had interpofed, all mankind muft have perifhed.   (2.) That ram was not of Abraham's fold, but was fuddenly at hand, and got ready for that purpofe, by a remarkable difpenfation of divine providence. Thus alfo Chrift was given by a peculiar gift of God to us, who could never have found, among any thing belonging to us, a facrifice fit for an expiation.   (3). That ram's being caught by the horns in the thicket, feems to be a reprefentation of all thofe calamities, in which Chrift was involved, through the whole courfe of his life : and why may we not here call to mind that crown of thorns, which was put round his head ?   (4.) Abraham did not fee the ram before he was called upon by God. None fees Chrift by faith but by the efficacy of the gofpel call. (5.) After the ram was offered Ifaac was fet at liberty.  Chrift having died for the elect, they alfo fhall live for ever.

XXX. Under the Mofaic *period*, no perfons were more illuftrious than MOSES himfelf, and AARON his brother.  But Mofes fuftains a two-fold character or relation.   1ft, That of a law-giver, whofe office it was ftrictly to inculcate the law with its appendages.   2dly, Of an interpreter and *teacher of the promifes* made to the fathers concerning a Saviour and falvation. In the former refpect he is oppofed to Chrift, and is a type of the law.   In the latter, he remarkably reprefents Chrift.

XXXI. To the former relation belong the following particulars.   1ft, His flow fpeech and ftammering tongue, Exod. iv. 10. fignified, that the doctrine of the law is difagreeable and harfh to the finful man, (quite the reverfe of the doctrine of grace, which Chrift declares, whofe mouth is therefore faid to be *moft fweet*, Cant. v. 16.) and can by no means juftify him, but rather condemns him, that " every mouth may be ftopped," Rom. iii. 19.   2dly, That the people were forbid to draw near to the holy mount, on pain of death, and their being fecluded from familiar converfe with God, while he himfelf alone was allowed a nearer approach to the deity, reprefented, that his legal miniftry could by no means unite finners to God, but was rather an evidence of that feparation, which is between God and man.   (3.) When, being actuated by a holy zeal, he broke the tables of the covenant, and ftirred up the treacherous Ifraelites to mutal flaughter, he actually fhewed, that his miniftry was the " miniftration of death and condemnation," 2 Cor.

iii.

iii. 7, 9. (4.) That his covering his face with a vail, when he was to fpeak to the children of Ifrael, was a figure, that the glorious doctrine of grace was not a little obfcured among a carnal people by the covering of his ceremonies; for being wholly intent on the vail, they did not penetrate into the glory, that was concealed behind it. (5.) Though, among the many miracles he performed, a variety of judgments were indeed, inflicted upon his enemies, by which they were deftroyed, but not fo much as one was raifed from the dead. Is not this a confirmation of what we juft faid, that the law is a *killing letter*, 2 Cor. iii. 6. in contradiftinction to the " law of the Spirit of life, which is in Jefus Chrift," Rom. viii. 2. (6.) and laftly, That he himfelf died in the wildernefs, without being able to bring the people into the promifed land, but was obliged to leave that work to Jefus [Jofhua] the fon of Nun. Is not this a plain proof, that falvation is not of the law? But is only to be looked for from our Jefus, who is alfo the end of the law, which was publifhed by Mofes, and whom Mofes recommended to the people to hear, preferably to Jofhua.

XXXII. But as in that refpect Mofes was oppofed to Chrift, fo in another he clearly prefigured him, both in his *perfon* and *offices*. As to his perfon. (1.) The birth both of Mofes and of Chrift was rendered famous by the tyrannical flaughter of infants. (2.) Both of them having undergone immediately on their birth, a cruel perfecution from their enemies, did not efcape but by a miracle of the fingular providence of God. (3.) Mofes, when he might have enjoyed the pleafures of the Egyptian court, refufed to be called the fon of Pharaoh's daughter, choofing rather to partake in the reproach of his brethren. In like manner, though Chrift thought it no robbery to be equal with God, yet, vailing his majefty, he chofe contempt and poverty, in order to honour and enrich his people. (4.) Mofes had not his equal among men, for meeknefs, Num. xii. 3. fo Chrift left an example of the moft perfect meeknefs to his people, Mat. xi. 29. 5thly, When Mofes came from converfing with God in the holy mount, he dazzled the eyes of the fpectators, with a kind of radiancy iffuing from his face. Chrift is the " brightnefs of the Father's glory," Heb. i. 3. " and we beheld his glory, the glory as of the only begotten of the Father," John i. 14. And when he was transfigured before his difciples, " his face did fhine as the fun," Mat. xvii. 2.

XXXIII. Mofes fuftained a three-fold *office*. I. That of a *deliverer*. II. Of a *mediator*. III. Of a *prophet*. In each he was a type of Chrift. He is called λυτρωτης a *deliverer* (redeemer) Acts vii. 35. For, by the power of God, he delivered the peo-

ple from Egyptian bondage, by deftroying the firft-born 'of E-
gypt, by preferving the Ifraelites by the blood of the pafchal
lamb, by enriching them with the fpoils of their enemies, and,
in fine, by drowning Pharaoh and all his hoft. In like manner,
Chrift redeems (delivers) his elect from the tyranny of the
devil, overthrows all the power, which oppofes the liberty of
his brethren, taking fuch a vengeance on his enemies, as contains an exprefs charge of guilt: with his own blood he
fprinkles the hearts of the elect, and fcreens them from the
deftroying angel, brings into the church the glory and honour
of the nations, Rev. xxi. 26. and in a word, having fpoiled
principalities and powers, he makes a fhew of them openly,
triumphing over them, Col. ii. 15.

XXXIV. Mofes himfelf declares, that he was a *mediator*,
Deut. v. 5. " I ftood between Jehovah and you at that time :"
and he acted as a mediator in a twofold refpect. (1.) As the
meffenger of the covenant, propofing the commandments and
promifes of God to the people, and bringing the words of the
people back to God, Exod. xix. 7, 8. and in a folemn manner
ratifying the covenant in the name of both parties, Exod. xxiv,
8. (2.) As interceding for the people with God, praying, that
if divine juftice could not otherwife be fatisfied, himfelf might
rather be blotted out of the book of God, and the people fpar-
ed, Exod. xxxii. 32. In all thefe things, he reprefents Chrift,
who, in a far more excellent manner, is the Mediator between
God and man : not only the angel of the covenant, and the
meffenger of the everlafting teftament, but alfo the fponfer and
furety of a better covenant, than that of Mofes, Heb. vii. 22.
not only in the name of God undertaking with men for their
falvation, and all things appertaining thereto, but alfo in our
name, undertaking with God, to cancel by his death, to the
utmoft farthing all our debts; and being admitted by God to
the difcharge of that office, he by his death and interceffion
became the procurer of an everlafting peace.

XXXV. Laftly, As Mofes was the greateft *prophet* of God's
people, whofe equal no age produced, Deut. xxxiv. 10. fo
Chrift in this alfo was like to Mofes, Deut. xviii. 28. nay, fo
much greater than Mofes, as a fon is greater than a fervant,
and " he who hath builded the houfe than the houfe," Heb.
iii. 3, 5, 6. More efpecially. *Firft*, whereas God made himfelf known unto the other prophets *in a vifion or a dream*, with
Mofes *he fpoke mouth to mouth*, and gave him to behold *the fimili-*
*tude of the Lord*, Num. xii. 6, 7, 8. But who did ever more
clearly fee God, than his only begotten Son, who is in the bofom of the Father, and was therefore only qualified to declare
the

the Father unto us, John i. 18. *Secondly*, None of the prophets were so famous for miracles and wonders as Moses. And yet Christ, by his miracles, struck every one with astonishment, and obliged even the most refractory Jews to confess, that nothing like or even equal to them was ever seen in Israel, Mat. ix. 33. *Thirdly*, Moses made great alterations in the external polity or form of worship, and, at God's command, made many additions to it. Christ again, by the same will of God, having abrogated the former institutions, made the church appear in a more excellent form, and delivered those words, which God had reserved to be spoken in the last days. *Fourthly*, " Moses was faithful in all the house of God, for a testimony of those things which were to be spoken after," Heb. iii. 5. proposing all these things briefly and obscurely, which were to be spoken and taught through the whole house of God, in every period of time. But Christ with his apostles spoke those things clearly, to which Moses bore witness as to things afterwards to be spoken, John v. 46. Acts xxvi. 22.

XXXVI. To Moses let us join Aaron, whose typical relation we cannot here, however, explain without intermixing some things from the legal types. *First*, He, being born before Moses, was sanctified, at God's command, to be the high-priest of the people in things pertaining to God, Exod. xxviii. 1. and xxix. 1. Heb. v. 1. In like manner, Christ the first-born among many brethren, and the only begotten Son of God, is the " high-priest of our profession," Heb. iii. 1. " who glorified not himself to be made an high-priest; but he that said unto him, Thou art my Son, to-day have I begotten thee," Heb. v. 5. *Secondly*, When Aaron was to be installed in his office, he was anointed with the most fragrant oil, even with that, which was appointed for the most sacred uses, Exod. xxix. 7. and xxx. 31, 32. This was so plentifully poured on his head, that it run down upon his beard, and to the skirts of his garments, Psal. cxxxiii. 2. In like manner, " God anointed Christ with the Holy Ghost and with power," Acts x. 38. " not by measure," John iii. 34. and his gifts descend plentifully upon all his chosen people, 1 John ii. 30. Whence *his name* is *as ointment poured forth*, Cant. i. 3. but the elect only partake of it; for the profane *world receiveth not this Spirit*, John xiv. 17.

XXXVII. *Thirdly*, Aaron was likewise clothed with *holy garments*, (1.) He had a mitre of the finest linen on his head, to which was fastened on a blue lace, a plate of pure gold, having engraven upon it *holiness to Jehovah*, Exod. xxviii. 36, 37. and by this was signified the most unspotted holiness of Christ, both as to his divine and human nature, Heb. vii. 29. And likewise
that

that Chrift was the perfon, who " bears the iniquity of the
holy things, ver. 38. that is, expiates the fins, with which our
moft holy actions are otherwife polluted.　(2.) He was alfo
clothed with a *blue robe*, upon the hem of which were pome-
granates and golden bells interchangeably, quite round, Exod.
xxviii. 31, 33.　That reprefented the *robe of righteoufnefs*, with
which Chrift was himfelf clothed, and with which he clothes
his people, Ifa. lxi. 10. as alfo the moft acceptable found of the
gofpel, to be preached by him, whitherfoever he fhould come,
together with the moft fweet and fragrant fruits thereof.　(3.)
He alfo had on the *ephod* *, or fhort cloke of moft curious workmanfhip, on the fhoulders of which were joined two onyx-
ftones with the names of the children of Ifrael, Exod. xxviii.
6, 9.　By which was fignified, that his chofen people would
be very dear to Chrift our high-prieft, whom he was to carry,
as it were, on his fhoulders into the heavenly fanctuary, Ifa.
xl. 11. nay and to carry them with care, as a precious ftone,
סגלה *fugullah*, a peculiar treafure, and as his own inheritance.
(4.) There was likewife the holy *breaft-plate of judgment*, with
twelve precious ftones fet therein, on each of which was a
name of a tribe of Ifrael, Exod. xxviii. 15, 17.　Many are
pleafed to call this the *Urim* and *Thummim*, Lev. viii. 8.　This
fignified, that Chrift is he, " whofe is the judgment," Ezek.
xxi. 27. to whom " the Father hath given authority to execute
judgment," John v. 27. with whom is the light of the moft
perfect wifdom, and the perfections of the moft confummate
holinefs, and who bears his chofen people on his heart, and
prefents them by name, by his interceffion with his Father.
Nor has it without reafon been obferved by the learned, that,
when under the New Teftament we likewife read of twelve
precious ftones; the *jafper*, which had the laft place in the Old,
has the firft in the New, Rev. xxi. 19. as if it was the band or
connection of both Teftaments, intimating to us, that both having the fame fcope; namely Chrift, whofe cherifhing never
failing grace is elegantly reprefented by the greennefs of the
jafper.　(5.) and laftly, To omit other particulars, Aaron's
ephod, which otherwife hung loofe, was bound clofe with a
girdle of gold, blue, &c. interwove with fine linen, in a moft
curious manner, ver. 8. Which fignified with what alacrity and
readinefs, together with the moft confiderable prudence, Jefus
undertook his office.

XXXVIII.

* There was a common ephod, which was not peculiar to the high-priefts, but
to other priefts alfo.　We read that Doeg the Edomite flew 85 perfons, who did
wear a linen ephod, 1 Sam. xxii. 18. but our author here fpeaks of the facred
ephod, which none but the high-prieft was to wear, and none were to make any
like it.

XXXVIII. 4thly, The authority of Aaron's priesthood was ratified by the miraculous buds, blossoms, and fruits of the rod, which was cut from the almond-tree, which was the only one of all the other rods, that suddenly budded, Numb. xvii. That rod signifies Christ, who not only " came forth out of the cut stem of Jesse," Isa. xi. 1. but was also " cut off out of the land of the living," Isa. liii. 8. yet budded again immediately after his death, and became a tree of life, having at the same time buds, blossoms, and fruit, yielding new fruit every month, Rev. xxii. 2. It also represents the perpetual fresh and flourishing efficacy of Christ's priesthood, who is a priest " after the power of an endless life," Heb. vii. 16.

XXXIX. 5thly, Aaron by the legal sacrifices, expiated the sins of the people, and by his prayers interceded for them, Numb. xvi. 43. especially on the solemn day of expiation, when, with the blood of the slain sacrifice, he entered into the holy of holies. So Christ in like manner " through the eternal Spirit offered himself without spot to God, entered not into the holy places made with hands, which are the figures of the true, but into heaven itself, now to appear in the presence of God for us; nor with the blood of others, but with his own, he obtained eternal redemption," Heb. ix. 14, 24, 25.

XL. These are a few instances, from among many, of the *historical types;* to which we shall subjoin two of the *legal types* from a great number of others. And in the first place, let us consider the mystery of the *ark of the covenant,* which is, as it were, the centre and compendium of all the ceremonies. The construction of this ark is described, Exod xxv. 10. It was made of *shittim-wood,* or as is generally thought of, the most excellent cedar. That wood, when made into the form of an ark, was over-laid within and without, with the purest gold. The ark had a crown or cornice of gold around it. Four rings of gold were put in the sides: and into these two staves made of cedar wood, but overlaid with gold, to carry the ark by, and were never to be taken out of the rings, even while it remained in its place. In the ark the tables of the testimony were put: but the covering mercy-seat of pure gold, was placed above on the ark. And two cherubims of gold, made of one piece with the mercy-seat, covered it with their wings, having their faces so turned towards each other, as, at the same time, to look downwards to the mercy-seat. The figure of these cherubims is a matter of much dispute among writers. The description which Josephus gives of them is not amiss, Antiq. lib. 3. c. 6. when he says, that they were *winged animals, resembling nothing that was ever seen by men.* That they came the nearest

to

to the shape of an ox, may be gathered from Ezek. i. 10. compared with Ezek. x. 14. For in the latter place, what is called
the *face of a cherub*, is in the former, called the *face of an ox*.
Further, כרב, whence the name *cherubim* is derived, signifies in
the Chaldee, Syriac, and Arabic, to *plough*, for which oxen
were formerly much employed. On the mercy-seat, between
the two cherubims, was the throne of the divine majesty, from
whence answers were given to the enquirers. The ordinary
place of the ark was within the vail, in the holy of holies, Exod.
xxvi. 33. but in such a manner, that the ends of the staves were
seen from the holy place, towards the front of the holy of holies, 1 Kings viii. 8. While the tabernacle stood, the ark was
taken out of it, when the Israelites were to march, that it might
search out a resting place for them, Numb. x. 33. and be to
them as the symbol of the divine presence, for their comfort;
but a terror to their enemies, ver. 34, 35. But after it was
once brought into the temple, it was not taken from thence,
till that was destroyed, Psal. cxxxii. 13, 14. 2 Chron. v. 9. Now
let us enquire into the meaning of all this.

XLI. This ark principally signified, or was a type of Christ.
1st, Its *matter*, being partly of wood, and partly of gold, was
proper to represent the two natures of Christ : the wood might
denote his human nature, according to which he is *the fruit of
the earth*, Isa. iv. 2. And that it was incorrupted, free from all
putrefaction, even when it was dead and laid in the grave, Psal.
xvi. 10. as Pliny ascribes *eternity to cedar*, lib. 13. c. 5. Gold
was accounted a symbol of divinity, in respect of solidity, purity, brightness, and value; and so that represented the eternity, holiness, and glory of Christ; and at the same time, shewed
us, how valuable he ought to be in our eyes; even of such value, as *to count all things else but loss and dung*, in comparison of
him, Phil. iii. 8. But as the gold only was conspicuous and
not the wood which was within and without overlaid with
gold; did not this signify, that Christ was not then manifested
in the flesh, but his manifestation, which had hitherto been
wrapped up in the most precious promises of God, was reserved
for a happier period? 2dly, The *form* of the ark, by which it
was capable to contain a great treasure, denoted that Christ
was the person, in *whom are hid all the treasures of wisdom and
knowledge*, and of all manner of happiness; from *whose fulness*
the elect may *receive grace for grace*. 3dly, The *cornish*, or crown
*of gold*, which encompassed the ark, seems to be a type of the
crown and kingdom of Christ. 4thly, The tables of the covenant, which were put into the ark, signified, that Christ was
to have the law of God in the midst of his bowels, or within

his

his heart, and to fulfil all the righteousness of it for his chosen people.

XLII. 5thly, But the *propitiatory covering*, or the *mercy-seat*, in an especial manner, signified Christ, as taking away the guilt of our sins. For " God is in Christ, reconciling the world to himself," 2 Cor. v. 19. Formerly that propitiatory or mercy-seat, being placed in the holy of holies of the tabernacle, or temple, behind the vail, was concealed from the eyes of all, because the expiation was not yet made: but God has now *set forth* Christ, exposed him before the eyes of all believers, and openly exhibted him to their view, as *a propitiation in his blood,* Rom. iii. 25. The mercy-seat being of pure gold, but laid upon the ark of wood, teacheth us, what it was that added worth and value to the obedience and sufferings of the man Christ; namely, the infinite dignity of his God-head. The tables of the law were covered by the mercy-seat: which the men of Beth-shemeth venturing to look into, when the cover was but a very little removed, brought a fearful destruction upon themselves, 1 Sam. vi. 19. By Christ's propitiation all our sins are covered, Psal. xxxii. 1. but should we venture to view the law without this, we should find nothing there, but the sentence of eternal condemnation. On the mercy-seat God displayed the presence of his majesty, and from thence gave gracious answers to his people. In Christ a throne of grace is erected, to which every believer may approach with boldness; and be assured, that if he pray according to the will of God, he shall not pray in vain, but there " find grace to help in time of need," Heb. iv. 16. There God dwelt *in the cloud*, Lev. xvi. 2. amidst the darkness of which, the rays of divine effulgence shone forth: which indwelling the Hebrew doctors have expressed by the famous term, שכינה, *Shechinah*, and what else does this signify, but the fulness of the God-head, that was to dwell bodily in the man Christ, and through Christ graciously in us? Col. ii. 9. *The Word was made flesh, and ἐσκήνωσεν tabernacled*, or dwelt as in a tabernacle (observe the elegant allusion to the Hebrew word) *ἐν ἡμῖν in, among us*, John i. 14.

XLIII. 6thly, The *cherubim* over the propitiatory or mercy-seat, represented the holy angels who descended upon Christ to minister unto him, while in this world, John i. 51. And with myriads of whom he is now surrounded, while sitting on a throne of glory, Dan. vii. 10. Isa. vi. 2. Psal. lxviii. 17. They were of the same piece with the mercy-seat, because Christ, by his propitiation, has brought about a coalition of the elect from among men, into one heavenly society with the angels. For,

by his means " we are come unto the heavenly Jerufalem, and
to myriads, an innumerable company of angls," Heb. xii. 22.
The cherubim viewed the ark with their faces downward *defiring
to look into* the myfteris of our redemption, 1 Pet. i. 12. They
were two in number, with their faces towards each other,
neverthelefs each might alfo view the ark : this their pofition
reprefented the duty of blievers, both of the Old and New Teftament, who, with eyes of a like precious faith and mutual love,
view one another, but they jointly fix their eyes upon Chrift.
For the angels are often propofed to us as examples.

XLIV. I dare not affirm with fome, that the cherubim were
directly an emblem of believers: it being certain, that by them
in fcripture angels are reprefented. God committed the guard-
ing of paradife to the cherubim, Gen. iii. 24. Riding upon a
cherub he flies, Pf. xviii. 10. But I have not yet feen any
fcripture-teftimony, to prove that believers are called cherubim.
The only one produced, with any fhow of probability, is that
from, Rev. v. 8, 9, 10. where it is thought, that the fame fong
is afcribed to the four living creatures, which are the cherubim,
together with the four and twenty elders, in which they proclaim their being redeemed by the blood of the Lamb out of
every kindred : which is not true of angels, but of believers,
But I anfwer. 1ft, If by the four living creatures, believers are
here to be underftood, I could wifh it was fhewn, why thefe
living creatures are generally placed before the four and twenty
elders, who are the patriarchs and predeceffors of the univerfal
church ; nay, and who lead and go before them in their facred
fongs, as may be feen, Rev. iv. 9, 10. As every reafon would
perfuade, that the patriarchs of the univerfal church fhould have
the precedency before the promifcuous affembly in celebrating
the divine praifes. Alfo, how the church of believers fhould
introduce John to the vifion and knowledge of things to come,
which certainly knew nothing about them but by means of
John: and yet they are faid to have done this, Rev. vi. 1, 3, 5,
7. Certainly, angels, and not men, ufually perform that office
to the prophets. 2dly, The former claufe of verfe 8, namely,
" the four living creatures, and the four and twenty elders fell
down before the Lamb," is affirmed of both conjointly. But
we need not underftand what follows, " having every one of
them harps, &c. ver. 9. And they fung a new fong, &c." of
any other, but the four and twenty elders. I will not now fay,
with a very learned perfon, that this appears from the Greek
conftruction; becaufe, as εχοντας ἑκαϛος, *having every one,* is of
the mafculine gender, it cannot be referred to ζωα, *living creatures,* which is neuter; for I know that is of little weight : But

I

I shall confirm this expofition by fome paffages altogether fimi-lar, Neh. xiii. 1, 2. it is faid; "therein was found written, that the Ammonite and the Moabite fhould not come into the congregation of God for ever: becaufe they met not the children of Ifrael with bread and with water, but hired Balaam againft them, &c." the firft thing afferted, viz. That they met not Ifrael, is common both to the Moabites and Ammonites : but the latter, about hiring Balaam, is applicable only to the Moab-ites, as appears from, Numb. xxii. 3. In like manner, Jer. xxi. 7. " I will deliver Zedekiah king of Judah, and his fer-vants and the people, &c. into the hand of Nebuchadnezzar king of Babylon, &c. who fhall fmite them with the edge of the fword." What is faid in the former claufe about delivering Zedekiah and his fervants and the people into the hand of Ne-buchadnezzar, is true of all: but what is afterwards added, who will fmite them with the edge of the fword, muft be under-ftood of the fervants and people of Zedekiah, not of himfelf, who died a natural death, Jer. lii. 11. So in like manner here, it is true, that both the living creatures and the elders, fell down before Chrift, whom angels as well as men adore. But the harps, and vials full of odours and the fong belonging to the elders, not to * the living creatures. At leaft it cannot be proved from this place. But let us return to the ark.

XLV. The STAVES, which were put into four rings of gold for carrying the ark, fignified, that Chrift with all his grace and glory fhould be, as it were, carried by the preaching of the gofpel to the four quarters of the world. The faithful preach-ers of the gofpel may juftly be called χϱιϛοφόϱοι, † bearers of Chrift. Thefe ftaves were never to be taken out of the rings, even while the ark refted, after it was fet up in its place. The found of the gofpel has never been altogether fuppreffed: and no country can be affured, that Chrift with his gofpel may not depart from it. The place in which the ark refted, was the

D d 2                                              holy

* There are many and various opinions concerning thefe *living creatures*. Se-veral think, that they reprefent the angels: but fuch things are faid of them, that feem to be inconfiftant with this. None of the angels could fay, that Chrift had redeemed them by his blood, and made them kings and priefts unto God. Befide chap. vii. 11, 12. It is faid, that all the angels.ftood round about the throne, and about the elders and the *four living creatures*, which are confequently diftinguifhed from the angels. Others therefore, with greater probability, think, that the living creatures were the reprefentatives of the minifters of the gofpel, and the twenty-four elders, the reprefentatives of the whole church, both of the Old and New Teftament ; and this may account for the placing the living creatures before the elders. Had our author therefore taken things in this view, he would have at once confuted the opinion he oppofes ; though upon his own principles his reply is ju-dicious and ingenious.

† Thus the Lord faid in vifion to Ananias, that Paul was to bear Chrift's name before the Gentiles, and kings, and children of Ifrael.

holy of holies within the vail. The place of Chrift's reft is in the fanctuary not made with hands, Heb. ix. 24. after he entered into that within the vail, Heb. vi. 19, 20. But the ends of the ftaves being feen in the holy place, fignified, that though Chrift indeed is in heaven out of the reach of our bodily eyes; yet he reveals himfelf to the eyes of our faith by a manifeftation of his manifold grace. That, during the ftanding of the tabernacle, the ark was carried fometimes to one place, and fometimes to another, but was not removed from the temple, till the deftruction of it; might not this fignify to believers, that Chrift fhould afterwards come forth from the fanctuary of the divine decrees and promifes, and fo from heaven itfelf, and while he paffed through the country of Ifrael, was feen fometimes in one place, and fometimes in another, but after he was again received into heaven, he fhould continue there until the time, " in the which the heavens fhall pafs away with a great noife, and the elements fhall melt with fervent heat," 2 Pet. iii. 10. " Whom the heavens muft receive, until the times of the reftitution of all things," Acts iii. 21.

XLVI. It was not without a difplay of divine wifdom, that there was to be a time, when the ark was not in the houfe of God; namely, under the fecond temple; as Jeremiah foretold fhould happen; " they fhall fay no more, the ark of the covenant of Jehovah: neither fhall it come to mind," Jer. iii. 16. For by this they might be admonifhed, to expect another, and indeed, a far more noble habitation for God; another mercy-feat, far more excellent, to which the former was commanded to give place, as the fhadow to the body. However, it is not without a myftery, that John faw again " the temple of God opened in heaven," and that there was feen in his temple the ark of his teftament," Rev. xi. 19. And that, at the time, in which the kingdoms of the world were become the kingdoms of our Lord, and of his Chrift, ver. 15. John faw thefe things *in heaven*, becaufe heaven was the place, where he was favoured with thefe vifions, Rev. iv. 1. Not that every thing he faw was to be in heaven. For furely that war, which he defcribes, Rev. xii. 7, 8. was not to be there, but in the church on earth. But what did he now fee? *The temple opened*. This, if I miftake not, fignifies a free, open and unobftructed entrance for all into the church of Chrift. Into which the nations of the world, or as Paul fpeaks, Rom. xi. 25. " the fulnefs of the Gentiles had come in;" and whofe doors now ftood open even for the Jews, againft whom they had been fhut for a great while. In that temple he fees again the *ark*, which was a fymbol of the covenant formerly entered into with the Jews: by
which

which is signified a new habitation for Chrift among the Jewifh
nation, not by an external fymbol, but by internal and fpiritual
grace; and as they fhall enjoy this, they will readily and with
gladnefs be without an external fymbol.  See what Jonas le
Buy, whom Bochart, Hieroz, lib. 3. c. 9. calls *an excellent
perfon and highly fkilled in thofe matters*, has wrote on this place.

XLVII. Near the ark was laid up the *pot of manna*, and Aaron's
rod which budded, Numb. xvii. 35.  To reprefent the incredible
and permanent fweetnefs of that fpiritual food, which Chrift beftows on his people, and which himfelf prefers, on fo many accounts, to the manna, given by Mofes, John vi. 48, &c. and
which, by an evident allufion to what was contained in this pot,
is called the *hidden manna*, Rev. ii. 17. And, at the fame time,
to fhew the perpetual verdure and eternal efficacy of Chrift's
priefthood, by virtue of which our buds alfo may come to blow,
and humble fhrubs to fweet balfam.  So much fhall fuffice
concerning the ark of the covenant.

XLVIII. Let us now confider the things, which the high-
prieft was to perform on the folemn *day of expiation*, in order
to give another inftance of a legal type, the ceremonies of which
are defcribed, Lev. xvi.  Aaron was to put on the linen garments, appropriated for that day, and only during thofe mini-
ftrations, which were to be performed within the fecond vail,
ver. 4.  And after he was ordered to make an atonement for
himfelf and his houfe, by offering a young bullock, he was
commanded to take from the congregation of the children of
Ifrael two kids of the goats for a fin-offering, and a ram for a
burnt-offering, ver. 5.  Thefe kids were to be procured at the
common expence of all, out of the treafury appointed for de-
fraying the charges of the facrifices, and other things neceffary
for the worfhip of God.  Both, inftead of one offering, belonged
to one facrifice for fin.  Both were an expiatory facrifice, in
the room of Ifrael-finners, bearing their fin.  Thefe goats were
to be prefented to God before Jehovah, at the door of the tabernacle of the congregation; they were facred to God and
devoted to his worfhip, ver. 7.  Lots were to be caft upon both;
one lot for Jehovah, and the other for Azazel *, ver. 8. this,
according to the Jews, was done in this manner.  The high-
prieft ftood before the goats between the Sagan, or the prieft
next the high-prieft, and the head or chief perfon of the principal family; then out of a box he drew the lots, which were
at firft of wood; and under the fecond temple of gold: on one
of thefe was infcribed, *for Jehovah*, on the other *for Azazel*:
the

---

* Or, as our tranflation renders it, for the *fcape-goat*.

the lot, drawn out with the right-hand, was put on the head of
the goat, opposite to that hand; and that drawn with the left,
placed on the head of that opposite to the left.   See Ainsworth
and Altingius.   That which fell to Jehovah, was to be prepared
for a fin-offering; which was directly done, not by killing immediately, but by declaration.   For, the lot being laid upon it,
the high-priest called it the *fin for the Lord*, that is, appointed
to be a facrifice for fin; and he offered it, that is, put it in
the place of flaughter, at the north fide of the altar.   But what
fell to Azazel was again prefented alive before Jehovah to make
an atonement over it, by confeffion and impofition of fins, ver.
9, 10.   Then that which was Jehovah's was to be killed for the
fins of the people, and its blood carried within the vail, with
which blood the high-priest was to fprinkle both the mercy-feat,
and before the mercy-feat.   Thus an atonement was to be
made for the holy place, and for the tabernacle of the congregation, becaufe of the uncleannefs of the children of Ifrael, ver.
15, 16.   Then again the live-goat, which by lot fell to Azazel,
was to be brought forth: and the high-priest laid both his
hands on his head, and confeffed over it the iniquities of the
children of Ifrael; generally in this form, according to the Jews:
" Lord, I befeech thee, thy people, the houfe of Ifrael, have
tranfgreffed, been rebellious, and have finned before thee.  Lord,
I befeech thee, forgive now the trefpaffes and rebellions and
fins, which thy people, the houfe of Ifrael have trefpaffed, and
in which they have been rebellious; as it is written in the law
of Mofes thy fervant, becaufe on this day he will make atonement for you, to cleanfe you from all your fins," Joma, c. 6.
And the priests and people, who stood in the porch, upon hearing the name Jehovah pronounced by the high-priest, kneeled,
with their faces downward, adored and faid; " Bleffed be the
Lord, and let the glory of his kingdom be for ever."   In this
manner all the iniquities of the children of Ifrael, and all their
trefpaffes of what kind foever, greater and fmaller, fins against
knowledge, or fins of ignorance, were laid upon the goat, which
was fent away *by the hand of a fit man* into the wildernefs,
bearing the iniquities of the children of Ifrael, *into a land not
inhabited*, ver. 21, 22.   But the bullock, which Aaron offered
for himfelf, and the goat, which he offered for the people, were
to be carried without the camp, that their fkins and their flefh
and their dung might be burnt, ver. 27.   Before we inquire
into the myftery of thefe things, fome difficulties are first to be
cleared up.

XLIX. And *first*, it is indeed very obfcure, what we are to
underftand by AZAZEL: I have chiefly met with four opinions
of

of the learned concerning this word. The *firſt* is, that by A-zazel we are to underſtand the very goat, which was ſent forth into the wilderneſs. And they ſuppoſe, this may be gathered from the etymology of the word, which is ſaid to be com-pounded of ע, a *goat*, and אזל, *went away*. And according to them, the words of Moſes are thus to be underſtood. One lot for Jehovah, that is, for the goat to be offered to Jehovah; the other for Azazel, that is, for the goat that was to go into the wilderneſs. But though the Hebrew word may ſignify a goat going away, yet it cannot thence be concluded, that by that name the goat itſelf was ſignified : as it is poſſible, that, on occaſion of the goat's going away, the place to which it was led, might be ſo called, which Kimchi in Radicibus contends for : *that place was ſo called*, ſays he, *becauſe the goat went thither*. But the main thing is, that this explication of the lots is very perplexed : whereas the words of Moſes are clear, that the lots were caſt for the goats to know which of them ſhould fall to Jehovah, and which to Azazel. Nor does it appear, that one of the goats could be called Azazel, unleſs we ſuppoſe, the other goat was called Jehovah, which is abſurd.

L. Thoſe of the *ſecond* opinion will have it, that Azazel was a ſteep and rugged mountain in the wilderneſs. Thus Jona-than, Saadias, Gaon, Jarchi, Kimchi, and moſt of the Jews. But it has been well obſerved by others : 1ſt, That Moſes no where mentions Mount Azazel, as he mentions the *mountains* of Ararat, mount Abarim, mount Ebal, mount Gerizim, &c. 2dly, That it does not ſeem probable, that, in a country ſo often travelled over, and ſo exactly deſcribed, none ſhould ever make mention of mount Azazel, and point out its ſituation. For, what a certain anonymous author mentions in Aben Ezra, that it was mount Sinai, will never have weight with thoſe, who know what vaſt deſarts lay between Jeruſalem and Sinai : whereas a goat was yearly led from that city to Azazel.

LI. The *third* opinion is, of thoſe who contend, that Azazel is the *devil :* and they will have one of the goats to have fallen to the devil, not as if it was offered to the devil, (for it was de-voted to God, and brought before him to the tabernacle) but that, at the will of God, it was expoſed to be tormented by the devil. This ſentiment is ſupported by ſuch arguments as theſe. 1ſt, It is the received opinion of the Jews, that Azazel is one of the names of the devil, juſt as Sammael, Azael, and Macha-zael. In like manner a Chriſtian poet thus ſings againſt Mar-cus the diſciple of Volentinus, who was thought to deceive the ſpectators by his juggling tricks,

A

*A ον χέρηγῦ σὸς πατὴρ σωτὼ ἀεὶ,
Δι 'ἀγγελικῆς δυνάμεως Ἀζαζὴλ πεπῖν.*

*Hec tu ille Satanæ fretus auxilio Patris
Azazelique mira defignas ope.*

*Which thy Father Satan ever enables thee to perform by the angelic
power of* Azazel. Thefe verfes are cited by Epiphanius, Hæres,
34. 11. The etymology favours this. For, *the goat which went
away;* that is, the creature which kept not its firft eftate, but
revolted from God. Elfewhere in fcripture the devils are called
*goats,* as Lev. xvii. 7. 2 Chron. xi. 15. Kimchi in his Lexicon
gives the reafon of it: *they are called goats,* fays he, *becaufe they
appear in the fhape of goats to their votaries. Maimonides in more
Nebochim, lib.* 3. *c.* 46. fpeaks much to the fame purpofe. To
this may be referred the ancient mythology concerning Pan,
Faunus and the Satyrs, who were likewife called goats. Since
then devils have indifputably been called goats, elfewhere,
why may not the devil here likewife be emblematically fignified
by Azazel, that is, *the goat which went away;* or, as Ben Nachman fpeaks, *the prince who rules in defart places?*

LII. The *fourth* opinion is that of Bochart, who, though he
owns, he can advance nothing certain on the head, yet offers
his conjecture, which is thus: the Arabic verb *azala* fignifies
*to remove* and *feparate.* Which he proves by many inftances.
And he thinks that Azazel is derived from that, and fignifies
*feparation* and *feceffion.* The goat, therefore, whofe lot is to
Azazel, to feceffion, was that, which by lot was appointed for
retreat, in order to be led into a feparate place of the wildernefs,
which, ver. 22. is called *a land cut off or feparated.*

LIII. But leaving every one to judge for himfelf, the third
opinion pleafes me not a little, becaufe it feems to reft on the
firmeft grounds, and gives us a difcovery of a great myftery:
and I fcarce fee, what can be objected to it, unlefs this one
thing which Bochart advances: namely, that ש and עז agree
not in gender, the former being feminine, the latter mafculine: and therefore, fays he, the word could not be made
up of both. But that reafon is of no great weight: for, 1ft,
In compound names, grammatical analogy is not always regarded: for inftance, in the word שאול, which at full fhould be
שאולאל, *afked of God,* the letters א and ו and ל are ftruck out,
and ש is joined with אל by a *fchurec,* whereas analogically it
ought to be joined by a *tzere.* Inftances to this purpofe are
numerous. 2dly, A change of genders is common among the
Hebrews,

Hebrews. We have a fimilar inſtance in Gen. xxx. 38. ותחמנה in the feminine; and ver. 39. ויחמו הצאן, in the maſculine. Buxtorf has collected a great many examples to this purpoſe in his ſyntax. 3dly, Though צאן be feminine in ſignification, yet it is maſculine in termination, as alſo the plural צאים; and therefore it is no wonder, it be joined with a word of a maſculine termination; which is alſo done, Lev. xxii. 27. עז כשב רחם, where a double maſculine is joined to the word עז. But neither is Spenſer's obſervation to be overlooked, that עזאזל may be explained, by *the ſtrong one going away*. For עז, ſignifies *ſtrong*. And as the true God is ſaid Pſal. xxiv. 8. to be, *ſtrong and mighty;* ſo alſo the devil was called Azizos by the Phenicians; in the goſpel, Luke xi. 21. *the ſtrong man*.

LIV. *Secondly*, It is worth enquiring what might be ſignified by Aaron's laying his hands on the head of the goat: which was not done here only, but alſo upon other occaſions, Lev. i. 4. Lev. iii. 2. and Lev. iv. 4. and Herodotus ſays, this was likewiſe in uſe among the Egyptians, lib. 2. c. 39. See Outrom de Sacrif. lib. 1. c. 15. § 18. and c. 22. § 5. ſeq. Bochart, if I miſtake not, has given us the beſt explication of the reaſons of this. 1ſt, The offerer, by this rite delivered up the victim to God, and, as it were, manumitted, or releaſed it, profeſſing, he gave up all the right he had in that animal, exempted it from his own dominion, and devoted it to the ſervice of God. Juſt as the Romans formerly held in their hand the ſlave they were to ſet at liberty, uttering theſe words, *I will that this man be free*. 2dly, By this very ceremony, the ſinner deprecated the wrath of God, and prayed that it might fall on the head of that victim, which he put in his own ſtead. By this ceremony, therefore, the ſins of all Iſrael were laid on this goat, in order typically to bear them, and carry them away far from Iſrael.

LV. *Thirdly*, Let us enquire what is *the land of exciſion*, or ſeparation, into which that goat was to be carried. I do not think, that any particular place was preciſely ſignified: for it is not credible, when the ſacred ſervices were performed at Jeruſalem, that the goat was carried to the ſame place, to which it was carried, when Aaron performed that ceremony for the firſt time in the wildernefs. In general, therefore, it ſignifies a place remote from the reſort of men; ארץ גזרה, *a deſolate place*, ſays Jonathan; ארעא לא יתבא, *an uninhabited land*, according to Onkelos. The Greeks call γῆν ἄβατον it *wayleſs, or inacceſſible*. Abarbanel explains it, *a land of the decree*, meaning that country, concerning which, a decree was made, that the captive Iſraelites ſhould be ſent away thither.

LVI. *Fourthly*, We may enquire who is that איש עתי *fit man*, who was to carry away the goat? We meet with the Hebrew word עזאזל no where else. The Greeks render it ἑτοῖμος, *ready*, עז, crtainly fignifies *time*, the fame that the Chaldee, זמן. Hence they inferred, that עז with the Hebrews, is the fame with the זמן of the Chaldees, *ready, furnifhed*. It would not be improperly rendered Καίριος or εὐκαιρος, *feafonable, opportune*. Abarbanel will have it to be, *a man of great dignity in his age and time*, at leaft in the application of the type. Whatever be in this, it is very plain, that God appointed no particular order of men for this office. The Rabbins tell us, that any one was fit for it, if he was appointed by the high-prieft; and that formerly fcarce any, but a ftranger, was employed in this fervice.

LVII. *Laftly*, We are to enquire what became of that goat at laft. The Jewifh doctors have a conftant tradition, that the prieft faftened a piece of fcarlet cloth in the fhape of a tongue, weighing two fhekels, to the head of the fcape-goat, which the conductor of the goat, when he was come to the place appointed, divided in two, and faftening one part to the rock, to which he had driven the goat, and the other to the horns of the goat, he pufhed the goat down from behind, which falling head-long, was crufhed to pieces before it reached half-way down the precipice. But Jonathan infifts, it was pufhed down by fome divine power. Moreover, if this fcarlet tongue turned white, which they fay, was generally the cafe, they looked upon that as a happy omen; and thence conjectured, their fins were forgiven; according to that, Ifa, i. 18. " Though your fins be as fcarlet, they fhall be as white as fnow." But thefe things are either falfe, or doubtlefs uncertain, which borders upon falfehood. Others therefore are of opinion, that it was let loofe in the wildernefs, to feed where it lifted: and Bochart proves, that both the ancient Greeks and Romans had animals confecrated to God, which were called ἄφετα ζῶα, *animals let loofe*, and the words of the text favour this, ver. 22. " and he fhall let go the goat in the wildernefs."

LVIII. Let us now fearch into the myftical meaning of all this. That folemn day reprefents to us Chrift's death, refurrection and afcenfion into heaven; and principally, our reconciliation with God, in virtue of his fatisfaction and interceffion. Aaron, we fee, performed, thofe facred rites in linen garments, of lefs value indeed, yet white and very pure. This was to reprefent Chrift's humiliation, which was never lower, than when he was moft engaged in making atonement for our fins: and likewife fhewed his moft holy purity, unftained with the fpot of the leaft fin. In this refpect, our Lord is certainly greater than Aaron, and all the other high-priefts; becaufe he ſtood in need of no offering for his own ſins, for he had no ſins, on account of which an offering was neceſſary, Heb. vii. 26, 27. When the Iſraelites ſaw Aaron firſt offering for his own ſins, they might thence eaſily conclude *the weakneſs and unprofitableneſs* of that earthly prieſthood. For what real good could that prieſt do the people, who by a ſolemn expiation, publicly declared, that he himſelf, together with the people, was in the number of the guilty? But our Lord Jeſus, having no occaſion to offer for himſelf, gave himſelf, as is evident, out of pure love for his people.

LIX. Chriſt, who is frequently in other places called the Lamb, is repreſented here by the emblem of *a goat*. For as on account of his meekneſs, patience, and holineſs, he merits to be called the Lamb; ſo on account of our ſins, which as ſurety he undertook for, and of his coming in the likeneſs of ſinful fleſh, Rom. viii. 3. he is typified by the ſymbol of a vile and wanton goat. That goat was given to Aaron by the people; Chriſt was given to men by God: yet what he offered, namely, his human nature, he took from men, being raiſed up by God *from the midſt of his brethren,* Deut. xviii. 15. Chriſt was bought with thirty pieces of ſilver, which were taken from the treaſury, in order, it ſeems, to be an expiation for the whole people. Both the goats were preſented to the Lord at the door of the tabernacle of the congregation. Chriſt willingly preſented himſelf to God; ſaying, "Lo! I come: I delight to do thy will, O my God," Pſal. xl. 7, 8.: and his offering was made in the view of the whole church, and at the inſtigation of thoſe who were the principal men of the tabernacle. The goat, which by lot fell to Jehovah, was ſlain. But as divine providence alone undoubtedly orders the diſpoſal of the lot, Prov. xvi. 33. So Chriſt alſo was delivered to death, by the *determinate counſel of God,* Acts ii. 23. and iv. 28. The ſlain goat was burnt in the ſacred fire: Chriſt, in like manner, was ſcorched and burnt, both by the fire of the divine wrath kindled againſt our ſins, for which he undertook to ſuffer, and by the flames of his own love for us, and of his zeal for the glory of God. The burning of the fleſh and ſkin of this goat was performed without the camp: Chriſt alſo ſuffered without the gate; and we are likewiſe to go out to him without the camp, bearing his reproach, Heb. xiii. 11—13. namely, we are courageouſly to bear it, if, for the ſake of Chriſt, we are expoſed to loſe the advantages of this world. Thus Chriſt's *humiliation* was typified by this *goat*.

LX. But let us alſo take a view of a type of his *exaltation*. Aaron entered into the ſanctuary with the blood of the goat,

which

which was given by and for the people. Chrift having made an offering for our fins, entered into heaven, and " fat down on the right hand of the majefty on high," Heb. i. 3. Aaron entered within the vail with the cenfer and incenfe. Chrift afcended into heaven, " to appear and intercede there in the prefence of God for us," Heb. ix. 24. And there was no entrance poffible for Aaron without the blood of the expiatory facrifice : neither did Chrift enter into the holy place without blood ; blood, I fay, not of goats or bulls, but his own, whereby he obtained eternal redemption for us, Heb. ix. 12. Nor is there any other way, by which we can enter into the fanctuary, but by the blood of Chrift, whereby he hath confecrated for us a new and living way thereto, Heb. x. 19, 20. The vail, which gave way to the prieft, who was to reprefent the atonement made, returned to its former place and ufe, when he went out again ; becaufe an expiation was made for fin, not in reality, but in figure only, Heb. x. 5. But, when Chrift was to enter into the heavenly fanctuary, the vail not only yielded to him for a time, but was rent by the hand of God, Mat. xxvii. 50, 51. having obtained a redemption of eternal efficacy and value. The blood of the goat was to be fprinkled on and before the mercy-feat ; and fo that blood remained in the holy of holies. Chrift appears always in heaven with his blood, which is the " blood of fprinkling fpeaking better things than that of Abel," Heb. xii. 24. Hence it is, that John faw before the throne " a Lamb ftanding, as if it had been flain," Rev. v. 6. For, though Chrift was once dead and liveth for ever more, Rev. i. 18. yet he is reprefented in heaven as flain, on account of the virtue and efficacy of his death, which is ever frefh. Nor is the interceffion of Chrift any thing elfe, but a continual reprefenation of his merits and death before his Father. But that an expiation was to be made by blood for the holy place itfelf, and for the tabernacle of the congregation, fignifies, that God's indwelling in the finner man cannot be in a holy manner, without the facrifice and blood of Chrift ; and that heaven itfelf would be polluted, if, which is impoffible, finners were to be admitted there without an expiation. Thus Paul affirms, Heb. ix. 23. " the heavenly things are purified with better facrifices." Not that there is any impurity in heaven, but that it is not confiftent with the divine holinefs to admit finners, unexpiated by the blood of Chrift, into the communion or participation of his glory, nor for him to dwell in them. Thefe things concerning the firft goat are fufficiently evident.

LXI. There is greater difficulty about the myftery of the fcapegoat : concerning which we may modeftly propofe, what we
imagine

imagine comes neareſt the truth, without prejudice to any.
And here I find two different opinions among divines, that de-
ſerve our conſideration.  For, it is not worth while, to trouble
ourſelves, in refuting the opinion of thoſe who, by the ſcape-
goat, underſtand Barabbas or Antichriſt ; though Cornelius a
Lapide ridiculouſly ſays, that ſuch *ſpeak more diſtinctly and perti-
nently*, than others concerning *this figurative repreſentation*.  But
ſome learned men think, that, by the ſcape-goat, the rebellious
Jews were prefigured: others will have it to be a type of
Chriſt.

LXII. The former ſpeak to this purpoſe.  Whereas the ſend-
ing the goat away into the wilderneſs, was done after the purification of the tabernacle, and it did not fall into the Lord by
lot : ſo the diſobedient people, and not the mediator of the
teſtament, ſeems to be ſet forth by the baniſhed goat.  For, the
wicked are called goats, Mat. xxv. 33.  They controverted
Chriſt's right of *acceſs to God*.  The determination between both
was made by a divine lot.  Chriſt by his blood, was introduced into the heavenly ſanctuary: over the others hung that curſe
in Deut. xxix. 21.  " and Jehovah ſhall ſeparate him unto evil
out of all the tribes of Iſrael."  Are not alſo the Jews ſent a-
way and diſperſed among the nations ? They are given up to
Azazel, or, according to the ancient Rabbins, they are fallen
as a portion to Samael (for the *Serpent* may eat the *duſt*, Gen.
iii. 14.)  In a word, they are given up to the power of the devil.
And how juſtly are the veſſels of wrath, ſaid to *bear the ſins
of the faithful people*, is evident.  For, though there is no procuring cauſe of juſtification in them, yet in them the ſeverity of
God is ſeen ; thus all the blood ſhed from the beginning of the
world, and ſo every ſin, at any time commited, is avenged.
*For, they who refuſe to confeſs their own ſins,* in order to ſubmit
to the juſtice of God, make the ſins of all others their own.
What is ſaid of the goat to be ſent away, namely, its being to
be *preſented before the Lord to make an atonement*, ſignifies, that
they alſo, as ſanctified in the root, *are preſented to God by Chriſt
the Prieſt*, that even from them may ariſe a *holy ſeed*, Iſa. vi. 13.
and children of the promiſe.  In a word, that the time ſhall
come, when all Iſrael ſhall be ſaved, and at laſt be expiated by
Chriſt the Prieſt, Rom. xi. 26, 27.

LXIII. It always did, and ſtill does appear ſtrange to me,
after the cloſeſt and moſt ſolicitous meditation, that learned
men could ſeriouſly give into ſuch idle imaginations; than
which I apprehend, nothing could be ſpoken more foreign to
the myſtery of this ceremony; becauſe it is altogether inconſiſtent
with the end and ſacred intention of this day.  For, who can
think it probable, that, on the ſolemn day of propitiation,

which

which was set apart, for making an atonement for all the sins of the whole people, the rejection of the same people should be so solemnly inculcated by an anniversary symbol? The whole people fast, afflict their souls, confess their sins, pray for the forgiveness of them : the high-priest is wholly taken up in procuring an expiation : God promises to *the whole congregation of Israel; ye shall be cleansed from all your sins before Jehovah.* Can we believe, that, at the same time, and by the very same sacred rites, the high-priest and the believers among the people, should be commanded to lay their sins by direful ceremonies on the goat, representing the far greatest part of their brethren according to the flesh, in order to be punished in them, by a most severe instance of a divine curse; the like to which was never afterwards seen among men. I allow that the punishment of the rebellious Israelites was foretold in awful prophesies : nor would I deny, that there were some Mosaic institutions, which prefigured that punishment. But at that time when the typical expiation of all Israel from all their sins was to be procured by those rites, it appears to me of all things the most improbable, that, at the same time, and by the very same ceremonies, the dreadful curse of God for the sins of all, which could not be separated from the imposition of sin, was represented as resting on the greatest part of Israel, and that according to the imprecation of the expiating priest, and of believers who prayed for expiation. I know, it is said, that " the godly, who were mixed with the ungodly among this people, might have the consolation of beholding, on this day, a sign, or token of their happier lot beyond the disobedient. But none, I imagine, will deny, that even this consideration must have yielded the greatest grief, which would have been an exceeding damp to the joy they had conceived from the pardon of their sins; and that the pious would rather intercede in behalf of the perishing than lay their own sins upon them with an imprecation. Certainly, Jesus himself deplored, with bitter tears, the impending destruction of the most abandoned city. And Paul calls not only his conscience, but also Christ and the Holy Spirit to witness, that he had great grief and continual anguish of heart, when ever he reflected on the deplorable state of his brethren, according to the flesh ; and was so far from wishing to make them a curse for himself, by the imposition of his sins, that he rather wished himself separated from Christ, to become a curse for them, Rom. ix. 1, 2, 3.

LXIV. Moreover, as the interpretation, we are now examining, is foreign to the end and intention of that day, so almost all the ceremonies, that were then used, strongly dissuade us from it. 1st, Aaron was commanded to receive both goats from

. the

the congregation of the children of Israel, and that *for sin*, that is, to expiate and take away sin, ver. 5. " But the goat which was given by the people, shews that what was from them, is offered for them :" as these learned men themselves speak very justly. If that be true of the one goat, why may it not be said of the other, even that it represented its being from the people, in order to take away sin ? For, so far both are on a level. Both being from the people ; both bought at the common expence ; both of them for sin : thus far there was no distinction in the types. What can then constrain us to imagine, there was so great difference in the signification ? Is it consonant to reason, that what was appointed to represent their eternal curse, was bought at their expence ; that is, with their consent and approbation ? And was the rebellious nation of the Jews given to the rest *for sin*, that in this respect, they might be joined together with the Lord Christ ? Be it far, says the learned person, they should thus be joined along with Christ, *for whose honour we are too much concerned, to speak so impertinently.* We are thankful to God, that he speaks so far piously. But he denies, that one of the goats was taken for sin. He says, " that is asserted of both which is true only of one. Before the lot distinguished them that could be affirmed collectively of both, which, after the lot, was to be the case only of one." But I think, we are by no means to depart from the plain meaning of the words ; nor to understand only of one, what is affirmed of both. Though we are to understand, with some difference, what the following words of the law intimate : namely, both goats were for sin, which the law expresly affirms ; yet with this difference ; the one was sin, because it was slain for sin, the other, because by bearing the sins of the people, it took them away. To sum up all in a word, the whole of this sacred expiation consisted of two parts : first, the slaying of the one goat, whose blood was shed to expiate the sins of the people : and then the sending away the other goat, which took away the sins which were laid upon it, by virtue of the sacrifice just offered. Both therefore concurred, in their place and order, to the solemn atonement.

LXV. *Secondly*, Aaron was commanded to present both before Jehovah at the door of the tabernacle of the congregation, ver. 7. By which both were declared to be equally devoted to God. Without all controversy Aaron is here a figure of Christ as priest ; the goat to be slain, signified Christ as the sacrifice. For, he presented himself to God, when " he went up to Jerusalem, that all things, that are written by the prophets concerning the Son of man, might be accomplished," Luke xviii.

xviii. 31. But how did our high-prieſt, when he was about to
to make an atonment, at the ſame time preſent before God the
the rebellious Jews, who were to be given up to the devil?
To ſay, that they were preſented before God, ſo far as they were
ſanctified in the root, and were to be the fathers of the ſons
of the promiſe, is quite from the purpoſe. For, the rebellious Jews, conſigned to the devil, are to be wholly diſtinguiſhed
from the holy root, from which thoſe degenerate branches took
their riſe, and from the children of the promiſe, who were to
deſcend from them in their appointed time. *Theſe*, certainly,
the prieſt daily preſented to God in the names of the twelve
tribes, which he wore on his breaſt: the very ſame he alſo now
preſented to God, though without that ſymbol. But it cannot be explained, how the high-prieſt, when making atonement, could preſent *thoſe* to God, if by this goat they were repreſented, as the portion of the ſerpent.

LXVI. 3dly, After both the goats, which were purchaſed
for God at the common expence of the whole people, were
conſecrated to God, by bringing them before Jehovah, to the
door of the tabernacle of the congregation, Aaron was commanded to find out by lot, which was for *Jehovah*, and which
for *Azazel*, becauſe this was unknown both to the people, and
the prieſt, till the lot determined it. But it ſcarce admits of a
favourable meaning, if that, which fell to Azazel, was the figure of the rebellious Jews. For, that ſortition, or deciſion by
lot, muſt be referred either to the figure, or to the thing repreſented. That it cannot to the thing repreſented is plain. For
the Iſraelites neither ought, nor could have any doubt, which
ſhould fall to the devil, Chriſt or the rebellious Jews, ſo there
was no need to make a trial of it by lot. What pious ears
would not be offended, to hear any perſon aſſert, that the high-
prieſt, at the command of God, caſt lots between Chriſt and
the rebellious Jews, whether he or they ſhould be offered to
the Lord? I imagine none will contend with me on this point.
Though the wicked Jews had a controverſy with Chriſt concerning the prieſthood, yet it was not proper for that to be decided by lot, but, as was really done, by a demonſtration from
the ſacred writings. It therefore follows, that the caſting of
lots here, regarded the goats themſelves, ſince it was unknown,
what each of them was to prefigure. Moreover, as both were
purchaſed at the common expence, for the benefit of the whole
people of Iſrael, and conſecrated to the ſervice of God; neither
the one nor the other ſeems adapted ſymbolically to repreſent
thoſe, who were to be given up to the devil. For, though the
goat fell by lot to Azazel, yet it ceaſed not to be the Lord's.

The

The very learned Frifmuthus fpeaks to the purpofe, *de hirco Emiſſar, Diſſert.* 2. §. 14. " We muſt not think, that the former goat alone was confecrated to God. For as both were ufually prefented before him, it is evident, that the goat, on which the lot fell for Azazel, was alfo the Lord's, as even R. Nachman has granted. But that the one, on which the lot fell for the Lord, did peculiarly and by fpecial right become the Lord's, was becaufe it was flain upon the altar. Such a facrifice offered in honour of God is called, in the Hebrew phrafeology, the bread of God, Lev. xxi. 6. Which appellation could not be given to the other, that was to be fent to Azazel, it being appointed to be feparated from the flock, and carried to remote places, to be expofed, perhaps, to the teeth of wild beafts. The goat therefore, which is, and in the whole ceremony, remains confecrated to God, feems not adapted to be allotted for a fymbol of thofe, who on all accounts were to be the flaves of the devil.

LXVII. 4thly, A ftrong argument may be taken likewife from the impofition of the hands of the prieft, of the fins of Ifrael, with thofe prayers of the high-prieft and applaufe of the people, we mentioned, *ſeƈ*. 48. which are very eafily applied to Chrift; when he bore, according to his own and his Father's will, and the wifhes of all the godly, the fins of the whole myftical Ifrael. And if any thing was to be reprefented to the Jews, on the day of expiation, certainly this was the thing, which is the alone foundation of a true expiation. But very difficultly, nay indeed in my judgment, on no account, can that which is fignified, in the facred ceremonies, by the impofition of hands and of fins, be referred to the rebellious Jews, whom the faithful Ifraelites never conftituted to ftand in their room and ftead. Do they, the moft abandoned of mankind, " who pleafe not God, and are contrary to all men," 1 Theſſ. ii. 15. bear the iniquities of all Ifrael, laid upon them by the prieft, into an uninhabited land, carrying them far away from Ifrael? Why do we yield fo much to that moft peftilent feƈt the Socinians, as to go to overturn an argument for the fatisfaƈtion of Chrift, hitherto happily defended from this rite, by this extravagant fiƈtion.

LXVIII. In fine, who can digeft fo hard a faying? *It appears, how juſtly the veſſels of wrath may be ſaid to bear the ſins of the faithful.* Which of the prophets or apoftles, ever faid fo? Is this to fpeak with the Scriptures? Who has to this day ever heard, that *thoſe make all the ſins of all men their own, who refuſe to confeſs their own?* or, that *all the ſins ever committed, are avenged on the rebellious Jews?* This is an imputation of fin, altogether new and unknown in the fchools of divines. Certainly, our modefty forbids us to difpute againft that right of God, whereby he punifhes the fins of parents in their children, and pofterity, which he himfelf, fuch is his clemency, ufually confines to the third and fourth generation of thofe that hate him. Nor is it lawful for us to deny, that the feverity of God's anger may at times burn to a farther degree, if the fins are above meafure atrocious; and pofterity fhall, for a long feries, not only equal, but even exceed their anceftors·in wickednefs. God was pleafed to give us an example of this in the wicked Jews, according to that threatening prophefy of Chrift, Mat. xxiii. 35. Luke xi. 50. " So that from this inftance his wrath might be feen, burning from the beginning of the world againft hypocrites, enemies of righteoufnefs, and murderers;" as the learned perfon very well fpeaks elfewhere. But, that " all the fins of all men are punifhed in fome one perfon or people," I do not remember, that I ever read or heard till 'now: neither that " the wicked bear the fins of the faithful." I know that, when God, in pathetic language, Ifa. xliii. 3, 4. commends his love towards Ifrael, he declares, that he gave the Egyptians, Ethiopians, and Sabeans for their ranfom, and *other men and people for their life*. But, as our Calvin judicioufly obferves, the prophet borrowed that way of fpeaking from the common method of men, as if he had faid, " the Egyptians, Ethiopians and Sabeans, have been fubftituted for thee, and, as it were, by way of exchange, forced to undergo that deftruction, which was hanging over thee: for that I might fave thee, I have deftroyed them; and turned againft them the power of the enemy, that was ready to fall upon thee." Or, to return to the learned perfon's own words: " the meaning of that paffage is; fuch is my efteem for thee, that I am to bring to nought the greateft and moft flourifhing empires of the world, in order to relieve and comfort thee." This certainly, is quite different from bearing the fins of the faithful, as was typically done by the goat.

LXIX. It is with joy we learn from Paul, that the time will come, when all Ifrael fhall be faved, after the fulnefs of the Gentiles is come in. But we think, this cannot be inferred from thefe words, " the fcape-goat fhall be prefented alive before Jehovah, to make an atonement with it. The learned perfons themfelves teach us that בָ fometimes fignifies an *inftrument*, as Gen. xxvii. 40. Deut. xiii. 3. And why not here? That the meaning fhould be, *to make an atonement with* or *by it*. We fhall prefently fhew how this is done by the live-goat.

LXX. Others therefore, and, if I can form any judgment, to better purpofe, affirm, that this fcape-goat, no lefs than that

which

which was killed, was a type of Chriſt.  But theſe again run
into different ſentiments.  Some maintain, that here are repreſented the two natures of Chriſt, the human, to be expoſed to
miſery and torment; the other the divine, as being impaſſible,
to remain free and to live for ever; which Cornelius a Lapide
relates, was the opinion of Theodoret, Iſychius and Cyril.
Others ſay, that the twofold ſtate of Chriſt, before and after
his reſurrection, was here ſet forth.  Thus the ſlain goat was
the type of Chriſt, lifted upon the croſs, but that ſent away
alive, of the ſame Chriſt, raiſed from the dead, and living for
evermore.  Of this opinion, after Auguſtin and Procopius,
were Bochart and other celebrated divines.  Yet two things
ſeem very much to oppoſe this ſentiment: 1ſt, That the ſins of
Iſrael were laid upon the live-goat: but Chriſt roſe from the
dead, and entered into glory *without ſin*, Heb. ix. 28.  2dly,
That the ſame goat, as loaded with ſin, was accounted unclean,
ſo that the perſon who conveyed it into the wilderneſs, ſtood
in need of cleanſing, ver. 26.  But no uncleanneſs can ſo much
as be conceived to be in Chriſt after his reſurrection.

LXXI.  Others therefore, to whom I readily yield, imagine
that a twofold relation of Chriſt the mediator is ſignified; the
one to God the judge, to whom ſatisfaction was to be made by
the merit of his death; the other, to the devil his enemy, with
whom he was to encounter by the efficacy of his life.  With
reſpect to the former, the goat to be ſlain, fell to God: in the
latter reſpect, the live-goat fell to Azazel.  Let us add, that,
in the ſlain goat, a true expiation of ſin was repreſented, which
is performed by ſhedding of blood and undergoing puniſhment:
but in the other, the effect of this expiation; namely, the removing and taking away of ſin, by the bearing it away ſo far as
never to come into the ſight of God againſt us.  And this ſeems
to be the reaſon of the order, why, after ſlaying the former
goat, ſins were laid on the other, to be carried a great way off.
Becauſe there could be no taking away of ſin *without ſhedding
of blood*.  Both indeed was done in the ordinary ſacrifices: but,
becauſe the latter was not ſo evident in the other ſacrifices,
God was pleaſed to ſet it forth by a peculiar ſymbol in this
ſolemn feſtival, for the greater conſolation of his people.  And
thus the riches of the divine goodneſs and wiſdom manifeſtly
appear, when he laid before the eyes of his people, by different
types, all the relations of Chriſt the Redeemer, which could
not be diſtinctly exhibited in one ſingle piece or picture.

LXXII.  But let us more particularly illuſtrate the analogy.
1ſt, The ſins of Iſrael were laid on this goat that he might bear
them.  Chriſt truly bears, and by bearing takes away the ſins

of

of the whole world. And as Aaron laid both his hands on the head of the goat, fo the hand of God lay very heavy and grievous on our furety. 2dly, This goat was appointed by lot for Azazel: not that this brute creature, which was confecrated to God, might be offered to the evil fpirit, but expofed to be tormented by the devil, who very much refides in folitary places, Mat. xii. 43. Now the firft promife fhews, that Chrift alfo, by the divine will, was to be given up to the Serpent who deceived Eve, Gen. iii. 15. " Thou fhalt bruife his heel." And Chrift himfelf fays, John xiv. 30, 31. " the prince of this world cometh, and hath nothing in me, but that the world may know, that I love the Father; and as the Father gave me commandment, even fo I do." That is, " the devil indeed has no right " in me, who am, and as I am, perfectly holy, nor can he ever " prevail againft me: yet he is come out to combat with me, " to vex and even to flay me, becaufe I have interpofed in the " room of thofe who deferve death. But I go cheerfully to " meet him; to the end, my obedience and love to my Father, " may appear to all the world." 3dly, The goat was to be fent to a wildernefs, and a land not inhabited: and fuch was the whole world, fuch, above all, was Judea, when Chrift came to fuffer there. Scarce any harveft of faith, truth, and piety, was to be found there; nothing but unfruitfulnefs, every where the thiftle and prickly thorn arofe. And why may we not apply to this, what Matthew relates concerning Chrift, when he was carried by the Spirit into the wildernefs, there to be tempted by the devil? Mat. iv. 1. For the wildernefs, into which the goat was driven, could not lefs typify the wildernefs in which Chrift was tempted, than the wood on which the ferpent was raifed, typified the wood on which Chrift was lifted up. 4thly, The hand of a fit man, by which the goat was fent away (which, by a conftant tradition of the Jews, might be done as well by a ftranger as by an Ifraelite) feems to denote the power of thofe, who rofe up againft Chrift, namely, *the Gentiles and people of Ifrael*, Acts iv. 27. and above all, Pilate, who had caufed Chrift to be carried without the gate, loaded with the crofs, the fymbol of a curfe, when he was to encounter with the devil for the laft time.

LXIII. I acknowledge I have learned thefe things, partly from Turretin *, partly from Cocceius himfelf; the former explains

---

* Turretin concludes § 5. with thefe words. But, as I formerly faid, it feems to be more fimple, that the two goats fignify nothing, but the perfect expiation, which Chrift made, who not only bore our fins in his death, but took them away by his refurrection; not only fatisfied by the offering of himfelf, but demonftrated

plains this opinion in a large difcourfe, and with cogency and fuccefs defends the argument deduced from it, for the fatisfaction of Chrift againft the Socinians, de Verit. fatisfact. Chrifti, p. 3. § 22, 23.  But the words of the latter in Comment. ad Heb. c. 9. § 25, *feq.* as far at leaft as they are to our purpofe, very well deferve to be inferted here.  He fays, " it is evident " from Ezek. xx. 35.  That Chrift was to come to Ifrael, when " Ifrael was, as it were, *in the wildernefs*, but that was, when " Judea was a Roman province, and had a Roman governor : " for then it was a part of the *wildernefs of the people.*  And it is " plain enough, that by the *dragon*, Rev. xii. is reprefented the " Roman people.  He made himfelf ready to devour Chrift, " as foon as he was born.  Moreover, *the firft promife declares,* " Gen. iii. 17.  *That Chrift was to be given up into the hands of* " *the devil*, who deceived Eve, under the appearance of a fer- " pent.  The Jews afcribe this to Sammael.  As therefore the " flaying of the one goat reprefents the death of Chrift, and " the fheding of his blood : *fo the fending away of the other goat* " *into a place uncultivated and defart, denotes, the delivering of* " *Chrift into the hands of the devil, who has the power of death;* " *in order to vex and difquiet him;* and that by the hands of fin- " ners, and of fuch men, to whom the land was fubject, like " the reft of the wildernefs of the people, and a part thereof. " That this was done by the appointment and will of God, " *Chrift himfelf declares*, John xiv. 30, 31.  As if he fhould fay, " the prince of this world, who has nothing in me, is come to " exercife his cruelty upon me ; which will happen, to the end, " my obedience may appear to the world.  We have therefore " a figure of a twofold delivering up of Chrift.  Firft, Of that " by which he delivered up himfelf as prieft.  Secondly, Of " that, by which he was given up into the hands of finners, or " the Gentiles."  Thus far Cocceius.  To the like purpofe, the very learned Momma Oeconom. Temp. t. 1. lib. 2. c. 11. § 36. *feq.*  Where, after explaining the fame opinion with neat- nefs and elegance, and proving it from Scripture, he then fub- joins : *we might reft contented with thefe things, and proceed to* *others.*  Let therefore none be offended, that being fatisfied with thefe things, which exhibit a doctrine found and certain, I pafs over other things, in which I find neither that foundnefs, nor that certainty.

LXXIV.

the perfection and truth of his fatisfaction by his difcharge, whereby we are affured, that our fins, being tranflated from us and laid upon him, are carried away, fo that there is now no condemnation to them who are in Chrift Jefus, Rom. viii. 1. and that of Paul is fulfilled ; that he was delivered for our offences and raifed again for our juftification, Rom. iv. 25.

LXXIV. Very lately were published the Varia Sacra of the very famous John Vander Waeyen, in which are two differtations concerning the goat Azazel; the former of which is principally levelled at me. But I would neither have my reader, nor the illuftrious author ignorant, how much I have profited by the perufal of that differtation. By it I was really brought under a kind of neceffity, to confider more accurately the whole of this fubject. Which I have alfo endeavoured to do with a mind fo free from, and divefted of all prejudices, as if I had never written any thing on the point before. Nor do I conceal, that from thence I had an opportunity to explain fome things more clearly, others alfo more diftinctly, and to fet a keener edge on my arguments, than I had done in the former editions of this book. On that account therefore, if he will accept of it, I return him my thanks. But then he muft fuffer me to fay, that I have not found reafons cogent enough in his differtation to render his opinion more probable, or mine lefs fo. While he oppofes my fentiment, and feems to charge it with many inconveniencies, he oppofes what Dr Cocceius himfelf has dexteroufly explained and confirmed by Scripture teftimonies, and as far as I know, never condemned or difapproved; though he fuperadded another opinion. But I could never yet think it probable, that one and the fame ceremony fhould fignify things fo very remote from one another. As for my particular, I leave the entire decifion of this controverfy with the equitable reader; who, if he is not wifer than us both, may profit by our writings. But as to the manner in which the illuftrious perfon manages the difpute, I imagine, I have very weighty grounds of complaint. Whoever happens to enter the lifts with him, contend indeed on unequal terms. While he thinks, he may fay what he will againft others, he gives no quarter to any expreffion of his opponent, if it has but the leaft appearance of harfhnefs in it; and affuming to himfelf, what is the prerogative of God alone, canvaffes not only the heart and inmoft principles of the thoughts, but alfo boldly pronounces what fentence upon them he thinks proper. Indeed, I fhould appear ridiculous, was I ferioufly to ward off from myfelf the grudge conceived againft Cocceius, as the origin and the caufe of this diffention. Every page in my book fhews my efteem for that celebrated perfon. And though I cannot affent to him in every particular with an implicit faith, yet I never once dreamed of charging him with herefy; much lefs in this controverfy, where the difpute is not fo much about a doctrinal point, as about the myftical fignification of fome Mofaic inftitutions, without any detriment to our common faith. In which kind of fubjects, if

I

I may not be allowed, for John Vander Waeyen, the liberty to dissent, in what pray shall I be allowed it? But I will suffer no mortal ever to deprive me of this liberty. But, good sir, whenever I am to dispute, I desire my method of writing may be as different from yours as possible. While your language breathes nothing but harshness, mine shall be all mildness. As in this dispute, I have struck out every word, that had but the least tendency to harshness, and substituted softer. And let this suffice, by way of specimen, concerning the types.

---

## CHAP. VII.

### *Of the Sacraments of grace down to Abraham.*

I. WE have explained with what wisdom and condescension, God saw it proper to confirm and seal the promises of his covenants by certain sacred symbols. As he did this under the covenant of works, so especially he was likewise pleased to do the same upon introducing the covenant of grace. To which, under whatever œconomy it stood, he appended, as it were, certain peculiar signs and seals, which the church has, now for many ages past, been accustomed to call sacraments. In some of the types, which we have already explained, and in others of the like nature, there was also, indeed, something sacramental; as they prefigured the Messiah and the spiritual benefits he was to procure for his people: yet more especially we call by the name of sacraments, those things, which were given by God to man, to be seals of his covenant, or earnests and pledges of his favour.

II. And these again, were indeed, very different; consisting either in things *natural*, on which God inscribed that character in order to be vouchers and seals of his testaments. To which Calvin refers Noah's ark, Instit. lib. iv. c. 14. § 18. Or in things *miraculous;* such as the manna, which was rained down from heaven, and the water issuing out of the rock, which constituted the miraculous meat and drink of the Israelites in the wilderness: or in certain *ceremonies,* and sacred rites, instituted by God to represent spiritual things. Some were also *extraordinary,* in favour of some certain persons, and but of a short continuance. Others *ordinary,* given for the use of the whole church, and not to cease but with that particular œconomy of the covenant. And hence it is, that in reckoning up the sacraments of

the

the Old Teftament, divines are not agreed; for fome take the
term in a.larger extent, and others in a more reftricted fenfe.
We are not inclined to confine ourfelves within too narrow
bounds: but fhall freely and calmly confider, according to our
capacity, what has any relation to a facrament, in every period
of time.

III. Some would.have the firft facrament of the covenant of
grace to be the *ejection of man out of paradife*, and blocking up
his accefs to the tree of life, leaft he fhould put forth his hand
and eat of it, thinking that he fhould thereby obtain eternal
life. For man being deprived of this farcrament of works, was
at the fame time, given to know, that righteoufnefs was to be
fought for from another covenant; and thus he was led by the
hand from the covenant of works to the covenant of grace. But
we cannot be fatisfied with thefe things. 1ft, Becaufe man's ejection out of paradife, and exclufion from the tree of life were the
effects of the divine wrath and vengeance againft his fin, as appears from that truly holy, but ftinging irony; *behold the man is become as one of us*. But the inftitution of a facrament is an act of the
higheft goodnefs and mercy. We deny not, that man was already
received into favour, and had the hopes of eternal life: neverthelefs, fome things were inflicted upon him becaufe of his tranfgreffion, that he might, by his lofs, experience the direful nature
of fin, and God's hatred of it. Among thefe was this ignominious ejection out of paradife. It was an inftance of grace and favour, that God placed him in paradife immediately upon his
creation, but of wrath, that he turned him out, when he had
finned. 2dly, This ejection doubtlefs declared, that man could
not now obtain falvation by the covenant of works, and that
he, who was deprived of the thing fignified, was unworthy to
ufe and enjoy the fign; and that it was in vain, and to no purpofe, for him to pleafe himfelf with the thoughts of it. But
it by no means fhewed, that there was another covenant, by
which righteoufnefs could either be fought for, or obtained.
Adam was to know, and he did know this elfewhere. 3dly,
Every thing, upon the fuppofition of the promife of the covenant of grace, that, by convincing man of his own impotency,
leads him to that covenant, is not to be efteemed a facrament
of it. For then every demonftration of God's wrath from
heaven againft finners, and every fign, which is proper to give
us an intimation of the curfe of the covenant of works, in a
word, every chaftifement, as all thefe are appointed to bring
the elect to Chrift, fhould be called facraments of the covenant
of grace.

IV. According to my judgment, the learned have much
                                                        more

more probably ranged them in this manner: that God firſt of
all dealt with fallen Adam about ſacraments; that is, when the
aprons of fig-leaves, which man ſewed together, were not at all
ſufficient to cover the ſhame of his nakedneſs, he himſelf clothed Adam and his wife with coats of ſkins, Gen. iii. 21.    And
it is very probable, theſe were the ſkins of thoſe beaſts, which
were ſlain for ſacrifices.    But it is a vain controverſy, which
ſome make about the matter of thoſe garments: ſince the Hebrew word ‫עור‬ is never uſed in ſcripture to ſignify any thing, but
the outward ſkin of animals.    And as this is the moſt ſimple
and plain, ſo it is the moſt ancient kind of clothing.    See Job
xxxi. 20. Prov. xxvii. 26.    Hence the ancient heroes among
the Greeks were clothed with the ſkins of a wild boar, or a
tyger, or a lion, or the ſkin of the Lybean bear, or the ſkin
worn by the Bacchæ or female prieſts of Bacchus, which was
that of a fox.    And who now is ignorant, that the progenitors
of the Romans were clothed with ſkins, and were of a rude
diſpoſition of mind.    See Voſſius, de Idololatriæ lib. 3. chap.
70.    It is a curious obſervation of Mr. Cloppenburg Schola
Sacrificiorum, p. 12.    Here we may ſee the original of that law
in Lev. vii. 8. by which the ſkin of any man's burnt offering is
appropriated to the prieſt, who offers it.    And who will deny,
that God's clothing our firſt parents was a ſymbolical act?
Do not Chriſt's own words very clearly allude to this? Rev. iii.
18.    " I counſel thee to buy of me white raiment, that thou
mayeſt be clothed, and that the ſhame of thy nakedneſs do
not appear."    Compare Joh. Henrici Urſini Annalecta, lib. 6.
chap. 15.

V. The myſtical ſimilitude of theſe things is this.    1ſt, As
that clothing, which man contrived for himſelf, could not
cover him, ſo as to appear before the eyes of God.    In like
manner, nothing that a ſinner can work or toil by his own in-
duſtry, or wiſdom falſely ſo called, can produce any thing
that can procure him a juſt and well grounded confidence, by
which he may appear before the tribunal of God.    " Their
webs, which are ſpiders webs, ſhall not become garments,
neither ſhall they cover themſelves with their works," Iſa. lix.
5, 6.    2dly, Proper garments for men, were the gift of God's
mercy, and ſo that righteouſneſs, by which our ſins are covered, is of God, Phil. iii. 9. contrived by God, perfected by
Chriſt, who is God, and applied to us by the Spirit of God
through faith.    3dly, The bodies of our firſt parents were
covered with the ſpoils of mortality and the ſkins of ſlain
animals.    The garment of grace, whereby the body of ſin is
covered, is owing to the very death of Chriſt, without which

that righteoufnefs, which makes us acceptable to God, could not have been performed. 4thly, That fimple clothing of the firft man was, in its appointed time, to be changed for one more convenient and fine. And this garment, which we have from God, while we are under the crofs and partakers of the death of Chrift, and which in external appearance is mean and defpicable, fhall afterwards be changed. For fince we fhall be partakers of Chrift's refurrection, no longer in hope, but in reality; fo the garment, which now appears to be mean and contemptible, fhall be then moft neat and beautiful, and worthy to be accounted the nuptial robe. See *Peter Martyr* and *Mufculus.*

VI. The other farcament of that firft period, were the *facrifices* which were flain at God's command, after the very firft promulgation of the covenant of grace, as appears. 1ft, Becaufe " Abel offered by faith," Heb. xi. 4. That is, he knew that himfelf and his facrifice were acceptable to God, and in his offering he looked by faith to the future offering of the Meffiah. But fuch a faith plainly prefuppofes the divine inftitution of facrifices, and a revelation about their fignification. 2dly, Becaufe God gave that teftimony to the facrifices of the ancient patriarchs, whereby he declared they were acceptable to him, *ibid.* But, in the matters of religion, nothing pleafes him, but what himfelf has commanded. All will-worfhip is condemned, Col. ii. 23. 3dly, Becaufe there was a diftinction between clean and unclean animals before the deluge, which was not from nature, but from the mere good pleafure of God, and has a particular refpect to facrifices. And it is probable, that this was the cafe of every kind of facrifices, even of thofe that were of a propitiatory nature, by which the promifes of the covenant of grace were more clearly and diftinctly ratified, than by all the others. For, while Mofes fhews, that the patriarchs offered fuch facrifices, as he himfelf offered, and that they were adapted to fignify the fame things, it is not for us to reftrict, what is faid in general, to certain particular kinds, in exclufion of others. Certainly Job offered burnt offerings for the fins of his children and friends, Job i. 6. and Job xlii. 8. which doubtlefs were propitiatory.

VII. But thefe facrifices were feals of God's covenant. For, though there is a difference between facrifices and facraments formally confidered; becaufe facraments are given by God to men, but facrifices are offered by men to God: neverthelefs, there is no reafon, why the confideration of a facrament and facrifice may not, in different refpects, concur in one and the fame thing. For, even facrifices are given by God to men, that

is,

is, are inftituted by divine authority; that, by thefe ceremonies, the coming of the Son of God in the flefh, and his bloody death, and the remiffion of fins thereby, might be fignified and fealed. And believers, in the ufe of them, declared for that worfhip and veneration, that is due to God. Auguftin, de Civit. Dei, lib. 10. c. 5. fays, " the vifible facrifice is a facrament, that is, a facred fign of an invifible facrifice." To make this more evident, let us diftinctly confider.  I. The prieft offering.  II. The animal offered.  III. The ceremony of offering.  IV. The empyrifm, or burning it by fire from heaven.  V. The expiation, which is the confequent of the facrifice.  VI. The facred feaft, annexed to facrifices.

VIII. The priefts were in a manner, typical fureties, in fo far as they approached to God in the name of the people; being " ordained for men in things pertaining to God," Heb. v. 1. And they became fureties, when ever thy took upon them to offer facrifices for fin.  For, by that offering, they performed what God, at that time, required for the expiation of fins. Lev. i. iv. and Lev. iv. 26, &c. and Lev. xvi. 34.  And thus believers were affured, that Chrift is the furety of an eternal teftament; who, immediately, on man's firft fin, undertook to fulfil the whole will of God, at the appointed time, and to offer a facrifice, which fhould be the caufe not of a typical, as formerly, but of a true and faving expiation.  By which will of God and of Chrift *we are fanctified*, Heb. x. 10.

IX. In the *animal*, which is offered, we fhould confider, 1ft, That it was to be clean, without fpot or blemifh: that it might fignify that moft unfpotted purity of Chrift, " as of a lamb without blemifh and without fpot;" 1 Pet. i. 19.  2dly, That it was to be fuch, as was given to man for food, by the ufe of which food, man continues to be what he is.  And therefore fuch an animal might be fubftituted for man himfelf, and, in the typical fignification, be a fponfer, partaking of the fame flefh and blood with us.  3dly, That it was to be fuch, as men fet a great value upon: " The goats are the price of the field," Prov. xxvii. 26.  Of old, flocks and herds were the only or principal riches.  Accordingly Columella, in prefat. lib. 7. conjectures, that the names *pecunia*, (money) and *peculiam* (private property) feem to be derived from *pecus* (a beaft), which not only the ancients poffeffed, but are, at this day among fome nations, reputed the only kind of riches.  By this was reprefented, that Chrift was to be offered for men; and as he is the choice and beloved of his Father, and his blood infinitely more precious than gold and filver; fo he fhould alfo *be moft precious* to us, *who believe*. 1 Pet. ii. 4, 6, 7.  4thly, That it be an animal, dumb before its shearer and slayer, in order to be an hieroglyphic of that unspeakable patience, which was illustrious in Christ. 5thly, That the firstlings were most acceptable to God; which therefore Abel offered, and God afterwards required under the law, Exod. xiii. 12. By this emblem we may discern that pre-eminence of Christ, whereby he is the first-born among many brethren, both as to inheritance and dignity. For, none comes to the inheritance but by Christ, nor to any other inheritance, but what was his before.

X. These following particulars belong to the rite of offering. 1st, The priest laid upon the propitiatory sacrifices the sins of these, for whom they were to be offered, which is plain from the names, *sin* and *guilt*, by which the sacrifices themselves are usually called, and the thing itself shews it. For, as in reality none but the guilty are punished; so in the type also, that, which is appointed to die for sin, is typically under the guilt of sin. And thus far the priests represented God, as laying sin upon Christ; and the sacrifices were a figure of Christ, as suffering for sin. 2dly, The blood of the sacrifices was shed, when they were slain, to be a symbol of Christ shedding his blood, when he was put to death. 3dly, The slain sacrifices were burnt on the altar. This represented that Christ was to be consumed by the flames of his love for his Father and his elect, and, at the same time by the flames of the divine wrath against sin, which he had undertaken to bear. 4thly, Together with the flames and smoke, there was a sweet-smelling savour, that ascended up to heaven; on which account, sacrifices are said to be acceptable to God; nay, also the food of God. This shadowed forth that most grateful fragrancy of Christ's sacrifice, by the efficacy of which all the severity of the divine vengeance is changed into the most tender love for the elect.

XI. The *accension*, or miraculous consuming the sacrifices by fire, seems to be cotemporary with sacrifices themselves: and the opinion of some excellent divines is very probable, that God had such a regard to Abel's gift, as in this manner to set it on fire, while Cain's was neglected. For, at the time, when sacrifices were in use, God generally testified, by fire from heaven, that they were acceptable to him, when offered in faith. "A burning lamp passed between the pieces," Gen. i. 5, 17. See also Lev. ix. 24. Judges vi. 21. 2 Chron. vii. 1. And this burning of the sacrifices by fire from heaven, being the most certain token of the divine acceptance, was prayed for, Psal. xx. 3. *remember all thy offerings, and accept* (reduce to ashes) *thy burnt-sacrifice.* This fire from heaven signified the Holy Spirit, by whose flames whatever is not set on fire, cannot be an acceptable

ceptable sacrifice to God; and by which Christ also offered
himself to God without spot; by which, in fine, he baptizes
his people, that both they, and their actions may be pleasing
to God.  We may see what John the Baptist says; " he shall
baptize you with the Holy Ghost and with fire," Mat. iii. 11.
For, this burning of the sacrifices, we are now speaking of, was,
in all respects, a typical baptism of fire, that came suddenly
from heaven, after the other typical baptism of water, wherein
the hands and feet of those, who approached the altar, were
washed, Exod. xl. 30—32. as Cloppenburg has ingeniously observed, *Schol. Sacrific. p. 65.*

XII. When the sacrifice was duly performed, the *expiation*
followed; which consisted in this, that God was satisfied with
the sacrifice, which he graciously accepted, and that, when the
guilt of the sin, laid on the sacrifice, was, together with the
sacrifice, typically abolished, the wrath of God was appeased,
the raging plague stayed, and God gave tokens of his favour to
the sinner.  For this reason, the atonement for the soul is ascribed to the sacrifices, Lev. xvii. 11. namely, a typical and
sacramental.  See what we advanced, *sect.* 8.  *Sacramental,* I
say, because that typical expiation was a sacrament or sign of
the true expiation, which all believers obtain in Christ.  And
those types prefigured, that God, from the very first notification
of the gospel, acquiesced in Christ's undertaking to make satisfaction for sins, in the fulness of time, by which they might be
truly expiated.  And in this sense, Paul declares, that the blood
of Christ purges the conscience from dead works; as the blood
of bulls and of goats sanctified formerly to the purifying of the
flesh, Heb. ix. 12, 13.  For this last prefigured and sealed the
former on supposition of the faith of the offerers.

XIII. There was, last of all, a sacred *feast* kept before Jehovah, upon the offered gifts and sacrifices, which were not entirely consumed by fire: this under the Mosaic law, was the
case especially with those sacrifices, which were called שׁלמים,
*peace-offerings,* Lev. vii. 15.  Which word the Greeks have
rendered ιρηνικα, the Latins, *pacifica :* others prefer Ευχαρισια.
But *confession* or *thanksgiving,* is one of the kinds of this sort of
sacrifices, Lev. vii. 12. and these were also *propitiatory ;* as appears from the imposition of hands, which denotes the imposition of sins, Lev. iii. 2, 8, 13.  And therefore, it has not been
improperly observed by a learned person, that the reason and
notation of the name seems to be; that, in this sacrifice, there
was in some measure a *perfection,* a *consummation.*  For, burnt-
offerings were entirely consumed, and no body eat of them : of
the others the priest ate; of the last, even any private person,
whose

whose sacrifice it was, Deut. xii. 6, 7. To which the apostle
has an eye, 1 Cor. x. 18. " are not they, which eat of the sacrifices, partakers of the altar ?" This was a sacrament of communion, which they who approach to God, have with the altar
and the true Priest : and a symbol of that communion, which
all believers have among themselves in Christ ; whereby Christ
and all his benefits, and all the gifts of every believer in particular, are the gifts of all, as belonging to the same body.
Paul intimates, that to this feast, the holy supper answers, as
an antitype, 1 Cor. x. 16—18. In this manner the grace of
God and the benefits of Christ were signified and sealed to believers in the sacrifices.

XIV. But there was in them no less a *reminding of the duty*,
which believers owe to God, and to which they bound themselves by the use of the sacrifices. *First*, There was in sacrifices a confession of sin and guilt. For, there were no sacrifices
before the fall. And the animals, which the offerers substituted
for themselves, as oxen, sheep, goats, &c. signified some fault.
For, the ox is an emblem of ignorance, Isa. i. 3. the sheep, of
wandering, Isa. liii. 6. the goat of petulence and mischievouf-
ness, Mat. xxv. 33. And the slaying and burning the sacrifices
extorted from man a confession, that he deserved eternal death,
and to be scorched in the flames of divine justice.

XV. *Secondly*, There was likewise in sacrifices an excitement
to the practice of holiness and real goodness. 1st, It was not
lawful to offer any thing to God, but from among clean animals,
which were given to man for food. Thus, " pure religion and
undefiled before God and the Father is this, to keep himself
unspotted from the world," James i. 27. 2dly, Nothing was
to be offered, but what was found, without blemish, or defect
in any part, not the blind, the deaf, the maimed, the lame, the
languid and the sick, Mal. i. 13. Thus, which will also be a
thing acceptable to God, we ought to serve him with all our
faculties, with all attention and intention, with a right judgment, a *found heart*, a cheerful will, and to consecrate all our
members to him : because God requires *perfection*, Mat. v. 48.
3dly, The animals, appointed for sacrifice, had something peculiarly adapted to represent those virtues, which ought to be in
those, that approach to God. Oxen are both patient in labour,
and obstinately resist what is hurtful to them : sheep and goats
know their shepherd, and hear his voice, without listening to
that of a stranger, John x. 4, 6. Polybius, lib. 12. not far
from the beginning, relates a remarkable story concerning goats,
with respect to this particular. And then they are led to the
slaughter, without a murmur or noise, Isa. liii. 7. All these
things

things should in a spiritual sense be in those, who are devoted to God.

XVI. *Thirdly*, by the offering of the sacrifice is signified, 1st, That our old man with all his lusts should be slain to the honour of God. 2dly, That it is equal and just, that the whole man, who endeavours to please God, should present himself before him in the exercise of faith and love, and with his heart inflamed, or a desire to have it inflamed with zeal, as " a living sacrifice; holy and acceptable unto God, Rom. xii. 1. 3dly, As sacrifices consumed with strange fire, were displeasing to God: so is every act of worship, that has not the Spirit of God for its author, or does not proceed from heavenly love. They who " kindle a fire, and compass themselves about with sparks, shall go into the fire, and the sparks they have kindled," Isa. l. 11. " Though one should give his body to be burned, and has not charity, it profiteth nothing,". 1 Cor. xiii. 3. 4thly, That we ought to consecrate to God not only ourselves, but also our all: for, as we hinted above, riches formerly consisted chiefly in herds and flocks, and Paul tells us, that the " doing good and communicating are sacrifices, with which God is well pleased," Heb. xiii. 16. 5thly, That our very lives ought not to be dear to us: but when God calls us to it, we are willingly to lay them down for his glory, Phil. ii. 17. " yea, and if I be offered upon the sacrifice and service of your faith, I joy and rejoice with you all."

XVII. We are next to speak of the RAINBOW, which was given for a sign of the covenant made with Noah, Gen. ix. 12 —16. And here we are, first to consider, what covenant it was: and then, how the *rainbow* was a sign of the covenant.

XVIII. Concerning the *covenant*, we observe the following things. 1st, That it was not formally and precisely the covenant of grace. For here, there is no mention of a spiritual and saving benefit; and then the promises of this covenant are not only made to Noah and his elect seed, but to all men, to every living creature without exception, fowl, cattle and every beast of the earth; an universality this, not to be found in the covenant of grace. God indeed says, when he speaks of the covenant of grace made with the church, Isa. liv. 9. *for this is as the waters of Noah unto me, &c.* nevertheless by these words, God does not declare, that the covenant made with the church was, in every respect, of the same nature with that universal covenant, which secured the world from being destroyed by a deluge. He only runs the parallel between both, with respect to permanency and stability: just in the same manner, that he compares his covenant made with Israel, with the covenant concerning day and night, Jer. xxxiii. 25.

XIX.

XIX. 2dly, However, it would not be confiftent with the divine perfections, to make fuch a covenant with every living creature, but on fuppofition of a covenant of grace, and with a refpect to it. For all the patience of God, in the prefervation of the world, which was ftained with fo many crimes, and of men, who more than deferved an avenging deluge, was ordained for the elect, whofe falvation God intended, and for whofe fake all other things are preferved, to be fubfervient to the promoting their falvation, 2 Pet. iii. 9. "It is a queftion," fays Pareus, "whether it is a different covenant from the former, in Gen. vi. 18. and from the covenant of grace? *Anfwer*, Certainly it is another with refpect to the earthly promife which is common to men, beafts, and the earth, and as to its peculiar fign. Yet the fame as to origin and grace; for God would not have adopted the fons of Noah into that covenant, unlefs he had firft received them into the covenant of grace. It is therefore an appendage of the covenant of grace with regard to an earthly promife."

XX. 3dly, Nay, in this covenant there is a confirmation and a typical reprefentation of the covenant of grace. I fhall here ufe the words of Peter Martyr, "This we are carefully to remark; though in this covenant, God promifed to deliver men, as to their bodily life, that they fhould not perifh in the waters; yet in this there was a fhadow or type of the deliverance from eternal death; namely, they fhould not be overwhelmed with eternal damnation. And befides, as this is held forth by a fhadow, believers may alfo form an argument to this purpofe: if God thus provides for thofe that truft in him, as to give them affurance, without doubting of their deliverance from the waters; how much more will he deliver their fouls, their better part, not from a momentary, but from an eternal death. If he is fo careful in thefe things of lefs moment; how much more, about what concerns the fum of our happinefs?" See Owen's Theologumena, lib. 3. c. 1. And fince we fhould obferve, that previous to this, there was a fymbol of the covenant of grace, whofe antitype was baptifm, 1 Pet. iii. 21. in the deluge and the ark of Noah, which contained as it were, the univerfal feeds of the whole world: why fhould we not take notice of a confirmation of the covenant of grace in the promife, that no deluge fhould any more come upon the earth?

XXI. Concerning the *rainbow*, we remark thefe following things: 1ft, As that covenant, of which the rainbow was given to be a fign, was not precifely and formally the covenant of grace, fo the rainbow fhould not be accounted a facrament, ftrictly and properly fo called; and it is alfo very impertinent,

to

to call it a third facrament of the New Teftament. However, the figns of the covenant of grace, in a way of proportion, bear the very fame relation, that the rainbow bore in fealing or ratifying this covenant: and therefore our writers effectually argue from this topic againft Bellarmine, who obftinately denies, that the promifes of the covenant are fealed, or ratified by the facraments.

XXII. 2dly, But then, as this covenant prefuppofed, and in its univerfality, implied the covenant of grace, we are not to deny, but the promifes of it were alfo fealed to believers by the rainbow. Hence John mentions a rainbow, Rev. iv. 3. and Rev. x. 1. Which he faw *round about the throne and the head of Chrift :* " That we may acknowledge," fays Rivet, Exercit. 60. in Genefin, " that Chrift's throne is encompaffed with mercy, and that he fhews it on his countenance, whenever he manifefts himfelf. But efpecially, that in his face we have that rainbow, by which we are affured, not only that the waters fhall no more overflow the whole earth; but efpecially, that we are not to be afraid of the deluge of divine wrath, feeing Chrift has reconciled the Father, fo that while God beholds him, he remembers his mercy and his promifes, which in him are yea and amen. Chrift therefore appears crowned with a rainbow, as the meffenger of grace and peace." *For he is* " the prince of peace, and our peace," Ifa. ix. 6. Eph. ii. 14.

XXIII. 3dly, Every fign fhould have fome analogy with the thing fignified. This, in fuch facred figns, which by divine inftitution, reprefents fuch and fuch figns, doubtlefs, chiefly depends on the good pleafure of the inftitutor. However fome natural coincidence or agreement with the fpiritual thing fignified, is generally fuppofed, as appears from an induction of all the ordinary facraments. What is natural to the rainbow, was likewife fo * before the flood; but its virtue of fignifying and fealing the promifes was fuperadded to it by divine inftitution. We are therefore to take notice of fuch things in the rainbow,

Vol. II.　　　　　H h　　　　　as

* Some have thought that their was no rainbow before the flood, becaufe it had been fmall comfort and affurance to the new world, to fee that which had been feen before; but according to others, it is not likely, that in the fpace of fixteen centuries, which were expired before the deluge, the fun fhould never have darted his rays upon the water in the clouds, in fuch manner as was neceffary to produce a rainbow. Befides, it is not effential to an arbitrary fign, that the matter of it did not fubfift before its eftablifhment; it is enough if it did not fubfift as a fign. The rainbow therefore might have often appeared before the flood, but God had never joined to it, that idea which he communicated to Noah, *viz.* that it was appointed for the future, to feal the covenant he had made with him, and in his perfon with all mankind. Saurin.

as are proper to reprefent the patience and grace of God: and they are either *general* or *more efpecial*.

XXIV. Mufculus has judicioufly taken notice of the general analogies. 1ft, God would have this to be an *everlafting cove-nant*, to continue to the end of the world: and therefore ap-pointed a fign, which not only Noah and his family might view at that time, but alfo his pofterity have before their eyes, while the covenant endured. 2dly, That covenant has the nature of a teftament and laft will, is abfolute, without depending on any condition of our righteoufnefs and piety. And therefore he hath alfo added fuch a fign to it, which we can neither make nor repeat, but can only be produced in the courfe of the feafons, and being formed by himfelf, be propofed to the view of our eyes only, and the meditation of our minds. 3dly, We are alfo to confider, *where* he placed the *bow*, the fign of his covenant; and *when* he produces it. For he placed it, where it may be feen by all; namely, *in the heavens:* not in any place of the heavens whatever, but *in the clouds;* he does not produce it but only in time of rain, when thick clouds hang over the earth, and either threaten or actually pour down their fhowers. Here we muft be obliged to acknowledge the fingular providence of God; whofe goodnefs calls aloud to every one from thofe very watery clouds; " be from henceforth not afraid of them: be-" hold in thofe very clouds, the rainbow, the fymbol of my " favour, and the fign of the covenant between me and all " flefh: what was formerly the inftrument of my vengeance, " fhall now prefent you with a token of my perpetual grace."

XXV. But Peter Martyr affigns a more efpecial analogy from the Jewifh doctors, as well in the *figure* as in the *colours*. The bow, fays he, is a military inftrument. Upon making leagues, and concluding a peace, neither arrows nor the ftring bent, are to be feen; but the foldiers carry it, with its horns or extremi-ties down to the earth; but it is otherwife in the time of battle: then they draw its horns together towards their face, that aim-ing with the eye, they may throw their arrows at the enemy. In like manner, God being reconciled, has taken out the ftring, removed the arrows, and turned its horns down to the earth; thereby affuring us, that his anger is appeafed.

XXVI. Concerning the *colours* he goes on as follows: from the matter, which is water, and from the nature of the colours, which reprefent both the light and darknefs of water, it appears to be a fuitable fymbol. For by this, God has promifed, that for the future, he would fo order the waters, that they fhould not deftroy all things: but what repreffes or reftrains waters more than heat, both contained in, and fignified by light? This

fign,

sign, which is mixed with water, has something to give it a check, I mean the light of heaven, whereby God restrains its violence. Grotius observes, that the three colours of the rainbow represent the severity, mercy, and goodness of God. Another learned person thinks, that the colours of the rainbow, red, fiery, and green, signify a mixture of holiness, and mercy by means of blood; that both these being manifested by the shedding of blood; may render God venerable and lovely in our eyes on account of these perfections of his nature. The same person elsewhere would have us behold in the rainbow, the colour of fire, blood, and green grass, and in them to reflect on the zeal of God, the blood of Christ, and on mercy and life: for the zeal of God is unto life, by the blood of Christ. Another likewise has observed, that the rainbow, with which John saw the throne of God encompassed, was only of one colour, *in sight like unto an emerald*, Rev. iv. 3. To set forth that God's gracious covenant with the church is different from the general covenant made with all mankind after the flood. For in this covenant God indeed promised, he would no more cover the whole earth with water; yet, at times he hath reduced whole countries to ashes by avenging flames : and therefore the symbol of this covenant was painted out in various colours, the red or fiery colour flashing out between the bright and green. But the sign of the covenant of grace made with the church is of one colour only; namely, green or emerald; to represent, that this covenant was always one, and always yielding joy to those who are truly in covenant. For in the kingdom of God there is nothing but *peace and joy in the Holy Ghost*, Rom. xiv. 17. These observations of learned men, are curious and judicious, and may be matter of pious meditation : but I doubt whether they will meet with the assent of those of a difficult and nice taste. It is enough, that we have related them. Let the prudent and pious reader judge for himself.

---

## CHAP. VIII.

### *Of Circumcision.*

I. LET us now speak of *circumcision*. Concerning which we shall take notice of the following things. I. The outward ceremony. II. The divine institution. III. The subject of it. IV. The necessity. V. The minister. VI. The time. VII. The spiritual signification. VIII. Its abrogation,

　　　　　　　　II.

II. The *rite* of circumcifion was, according to God's appointment, as follows: The extreme cuticle or thin fkin of the *glans* was cut off with a fharp knife. This, from its natural ufe, was called עֹרְלָה by the Hebrews, Gen. xxxiv. 14. from the verb עָרַל to *clofe* or *ftop up*. The Greek interpreters of the Old Teftament, and the writers of the New, exprefs it by an elegant term ακροβυσια, becaufe το ακρον της βαλανε βυει, *it covers the extremity of the glans*. Gomarus ad Luc. 2, 21. has made many learned remarks on this word. The Latins call it *præputium*, a word of uncertain derivation. On account of circumcifion, the Jews were, by way of contempt, and in derifion, called Apellæ and Recutiti, becaufe they had not that pellicle or fkin. But it pleafed God, in order to confound all the wif om of the flefh, and to try the faith and obedience of his people, to give them for a fign of his covenant, a rite fo much to be blufhed at and almoft afhamed of; juft as he alfo laid the ground-work of all our falvation in what appears no lefs fhameful to flefh, namely, the crofs of Chrift.

III. The *inftrument* of circumcifion was any knife they could procure, made of any matter, that was fit to take an edge; namely, of ftone, glafs, or wood. Yet Buxtorf in Synagoga Judaica fays, that it was generally one of iron, and that very fharp, as furgeon's inftruments ufually are; fome think, that knives of ftone were formerly ufed, becaufe the inftrument of circumcifion, mentioned Exod. iv. 25. is called צֹר which in Ezek. iii. 9. denotes a *ftone*: and in Jofh. v. 2. the knives of circumcifion are called, *fwords of ftone*. But that inference is not fo certain, For the word fignifies not only a ftone, but alfo an *edge*; as is manifeft from Pf. lxxxix. 43. " thou haft turned the edge of his fword?" nor formerly did they fight with fwords of ftone. Hence the Chaldee paraphraft tranflates Jofh. v. 2. *fharp knives*.

IV. The firft *inftitution* of circumcifion, Gen. xvii. 11. was in the houfe and family of Abraham, about the year of the world * two thoufand. Circumcifion was not immediately given, to be a public and univerfal facrament to the whole church in thofe times, but was confined to Abraham's family. The remnant of the ancient fathers, fatisfied with their facrificial facraments, could exercife their faith, and pleafe God, in uncircumcifion, without being obliged to fubmit to this rite. But, after the expiration of about four centuries, when the vifible churches, without Abraham's family, gradually apoftatifed to
heathenifm,

* According to the chronology of the learned archbifhop Ufher, circumcifion was inftituted in the year of the world 2107 and before Chrift 1897.

heathenism, the godly remnant being removed to the heavenly assembly; and when the republic of Israel, in the mean time, wonderfully increased, and the measure of iniquity among the nations being now full, the church was confined to Israel, and the rest of the world was rejected; and all that feared God, were bound to join themselves in communion with them by a participation of the same rites. Well says Maimonides, in Issure Bia, c. 13. " Whenever any Gentile would betake himself to the Israelitish covenant, and put himself under the wings of the divine majesty, and take upon him the yoke of the law, there were required circumcision, baptism, and a voluntary offering." From that time, circumcision became an universal sacrament of the church. Thus the Lord Jesus distinguishes it, as it was *of the fathers*, to them it was a family institution, and as *given by Moses*, an universal sacrament of the church, that was to be constituted or set up, John vii. 22.

V. Moreover, circumcision was not only enjoined upon Abraham and Isaac, but also on all the descendants of Abraham, whether by Sarah, Hagar or Keturah, and even on all his domestics, bought with his money, and strangers, Gen. xvii. 25, 26, 27. For though, even at time, God had determined to form a peculiar people to himself from the posterity of Isaac alone, not indeed from all of them; nevertheless the time was not yet come, when he would have his church confined to one particular people. Nor are we to doubt, but he had his chosen people among the other sons and descendants of Abraham. And nothing is more certain, than that, within the compass of these four centuries, circumcision, and with it, the visible church, was propagated among all those eastern people, who derived their origin from Ishmael, from the sons of Keturah, from Esau, and the proselytes who were circumcised in Abraham's family. But I would observe by the way, that most of the Jewish Rabbins will have it, that Keturah was Hagar herself, while others of them sometimes deny it, and at other times call it in question. As may be seen in Selden, de Syendr. Lib. 2. c. 3. Those churches therefore, which, from among Abraham's posterity, had the sign of circumcision, as well as the uncircumcised churches, from the pious remnant of the other fathers, together with the Israelites, whom God began to claim to himself by a nearer relation, made up the universal church of those times. Nor should they, in the mean time, be accounted strangers from the covenant of God, confirmed with Abraham in Christ, but rather brethren, and fellow-professors of the same religion. To this purpose we may apply Deut. xxiii. 7. " thou shalt not abhor an *Edomite*, for he is thy brother."

ther." And as circumcision was at firſt enjoined even on ſtrangers in Abraham's family, this ought afterwards to have put the Iſraelites in mind of the future calling of the Gentiles.

VI. Meanwhile, among the nations that deſcended from Abraham, the uſe of circumciſion continued much longer than the true religion. For, while they revolted by degrees from the God of their fathers, ſo they polluted themſelves with horrible idolatries, and were rejected by God, and baniſhed from his covenant: but ſtill they retained circumciſion. Accordingly authors of every kind ſpeak of many circumciſed nations, beſides the Iſraelites. Grotius has drawn up a catalogue of them, in Notis ad lib. 1. de Veritate Relig. Chriſtianæ. And Selden, in a place already quoted, has much to this purpoſe.

VII. It is then certain, that other nations, beſides the deſcendants of Abraham, were circumciſed; as Herodotus in Euterpe teſtifies of the Egyptians, the Ethiopians, and the inhabitants of Colchis. Grotius indeed ſays, that the Ethiopians were deſcended from the poſterity of Keturah; and that the Colchians and neighbouring people, are the deſcendants of the ten tribes, which were carried away by Salmanaſſar. But Bochart, Geograph. Sacr. lib. 4. c. 26 and 31. has made it appear, by cogent arguments, that both the Ethiopians and Colchians owe their origin to the Egyptians. And Diodorus Siculus, whoſe fidelity on this point Grotius vainly attempts to weaken, relates, that the rite of circumciſion paſſed from the Egyptians to their colonies, and *ancient offspring*, as Ammianus, lib. 2. calls the Colchians. The ſame thing we are to believe concerning the Colchians. What Ambroſe, de Patriarcha Abrahamo, lib. 2. c. 11. relates of the Egyptians, is both remarkable and ſurpriſing. The Egyptians, ſays he, " circumciſe their males, at fourteen years, and at the ſame years, their females. Namely, becauſe at thoſe years, the paſſions of the male begin to rage, and the monthly courſes of the females to take their riſe." But Gomarus, ad Luc. 2. 21. Has juſtly obſerved: that we may very well doubt of the truth of that narration (unleſs he probably ſpeaks of his own time), on account of its diſagreement with ancient hiſtory. Beſides, we can ſcarcely allow the leaſt doubt, that the Egyptians had learned circumciſion from the Iſraelites, when they dwelt among them, and were acceptable gueſts at firſt.

VIII. Here it ſeems proper to ſay ſomething concerning the circumciſion of the Ethiopians, which they ſtill retain, notwithſtanding their having embraced Chriſtianity. Zaga Zabo,

an Ethiopian bifhop, and ambaffador from his prince at the
court of Portugal, afcribes the firft rife of it to the queen
Maqueda. He will have her to be fame whom the facred writings tell us, came to Solomon, being excited thereto by the
fame of his wifdom. He fays, that being with child by Solomon, fhe brought forth a fon, called Meilech.  When he was
grown up, fhe fent him to Jerufalem to his father, to be inftructed in the law of God.  After Solomon had carefully performed this, he folemnly anointed this his fon, before the ark,
king of Ethiopia, changing his former name to that of David.
After his return to his own country, with a great retinue, a-
mong which was Azarias the fon of Zadok (who preparing
himfelf for the journey ftole out of the ark, and, for the fake
of the new king, carried away with him the two tables of the
law, and perfidioufly placed falfe ones in their room) the Gyn-
ecocracy, or government of women, was entirely abolifhed,
and, it was ordained, that the male defcendants alone, in a
right line from this David, fhould fway the fceptre ; that circumcifion fhould be introduced, that of the women being added
by the queen Maqueda.  But they proteft, they retain it, not
from any religious view, but as an herditary and political fymbol of their nobility.

IX. But who does not fee, that thefe are foolifh ahd trifling
ftories ? Not to mention other things, the abfurdity and grofs
falfehood of which lie open to view of every one.  They arro-
gantly brag, that it was their queen who went to Solomon,
when it can be eafily proved, that it was the queen of Arabia
Felix. ift, She is called in fcripture the queen of Sheba, 1
Kings x. 1.  But Philoftorgius fays, that this *was the name
which the Greeks gave to* Abrabia the great and happy.  It is
otherwife called Homeritis, from an Arabic word.  The Nabi-
an Geographer relates, that this queen reigned there, whom
he calls Belkis, and the wife of Solomon.  2dly, Chrift calls
her *the queen of the fouth.*  But Sheba, or Arabia Felix, is not
only fouth of the land of Ifrael, but is alfo in Arabic called
*Alejman,* that is, the *fouthward,* as Drufius, ad Mat. xii. 42.
has obferved from Judæus Salmanticenfis and Aben Ezra.  And
Benjamin, in his Itinerary, p. 73. fays, *Sheba* is *Aljeman.*
When Chrift therefore called her queen of the fouth, which
in Syriac, is queen of Timena, he fpoke after the vulgar, fo
that he might eafily be underftood by any one.  3dly, Chrift
adds, that this queen *came from the uttermoft parts of the earth ;*
which much better agrees to the Sabeans, than to the Ethiopians ; for the moft extenfive countries lie beyond Meroe, the
metropolis of Ethiopia ; whereas the Sabeans occupy, on the
ocean,

ocean, the utmoſt parts of Arabia towards the ſea, conſequently of the earth.   4thly, There is much greater plenty of gold and ſpices, with which this queen is ſaid to have loaded her camels, 1 Kings x. 2. in Arabia, than in the country of the Ethiopians, and therefore called by the Greeks Αρωματοφοροι, *ſpice-yielding*.   5thly, What Joſephus ſays, Antiq. lib. c. 2. concerning the queen of the Ethiopians, and her royal city, formerly called Saba, afterwards Meroe, is not only uncertain, but alſo bewrays very great ignorance in hiſtory, as Bochart, who may be conſulted on this head, has invincibly ſhewn, Geograph. Sacr. lib. 2. c. 24.   As therefore the queen of the ſouth is not the queen of the Ethiopians, the modern Ethiopians vainly boaſt, that they received circumciſion, and therewith Judaiſm, on occaſion of that queen.   It is much more probable, they received it long before that time, from the Egyptians, whoſe deſcendants they are : but it is more likely, the Sabeans, who according to Philoſtorigus, were circumciſed the eighth day, were taught it by their queen, who viſited Solomon.

X. It is intolerable, by whoſoever introduced, that ſome attempted, out of a human device, to obtrude a kind of circumciſion, or ſomething analogous thereto, on women : as we juſt heard concerning Maqueda, that fictitious queen of the Ethiopians, and the Egyptians.   For, God enjoined circumciſion expreſsly to the males only : women are accounted in the men, and in and with them reckoned to be in covenant.   Nor was this without its myſtery.   1ſt, Thus they were taught, that ſalvation depends not on circumciſion.   2dly, It ſignified the imperfection of that œconomy, which was afterwards to give place to one more perfect, in which perſons were to be initiated by a more eaſy and common ſacrament, of which women themſelves were alſo to partake.

XI. But in all other nations, who were ſtrangers to the true worſhip of God, circumciſion was nothing but a mere ſuperſtitious practice, and a wretched imitation of a ſacrament given by God to his covenant people.   But he would have thoſe in covenant with himſelf, ſtrictly to be bound by this tie, Gen. xvii. 14. " and the uncircumciſed man-child, whoſe fleſh of his foreſkin is not circumciſed, that ſoul ſhall be cut off from his people, he hath broken my covenant."   I am not now inclined to tranſcribe what the learned have long ago obſerved on נכרת, or *the cutting off a ſoul from his people*.   Among many others may be ſeen Fagius ad Exod. xii. 15.   Amama in Antibarbaro, lib. 3. towards the end.   Seldenus de Synedriis, lib. 1. c. 6. and de jure Naturali, lib. 7. c. 9.   L'empereur in notis ad
                                                          Bertramum

Bertramum de Republ. Hebræor. lib. 1. c. 2.  And Hen. Ainf-
worth ad Num. xv. 30, 31.  Hottingerus ad juris Hebraic.
præceptum 227.  Owen in proleg. ad Hebr. p. 289.  And
very lately John a Mark, Exercit. Juvenil. Difp. 1 and 2.  I
do not think it improbable, that the cutting off a foul from the
people fignified a feclufion or feparation, from the church, and
from the folemnites and prerogatives of the people of God, to
which is oppofed *to enter into the congregation*, or church, *of Jehovah*, Deut. xxiii. 2.  To this purpofe is Exod. xii. 19. *even
that foul fhall be cut off from the congregation of Ifrael*, that is,.
fhall be removed from the fellowfhip of the faints, Ezek. xiii. 9.
*they fhall not be in the council*, or myftical affembly, *of my people,
neither fhall they be written in the writing of the houfe of Ifrael:*
namely, he who *has broken* my covenant, which *I made* with
him, *fhall be cut off* from among this covenant-people, and fhall
not partake of their privileges.  Befides this ecclefiaftical death,
there fometimes was added to it death by the fentence of the
judge, Lev. xx. 6. compared with ver. 27. fometimes by the
immediate hand of God, and other grievous calamities inflicted
by him, fee Exod. iv. 24, 25. fometimes a being childlefs, Lev.
xviii. 29. compared with Lev. xx. 20, 21. and at laft, unlefs
the finner repented, the eternal deftruction of his foul.'  Abarbanel does not fpeak amifs, as his words are quoted by L'empereur:  " the foul fhall be cut off from that fupreme bundle of
life, and fhall not obtain the fplendor of the divinity, that is,
the pleafure and reward of a foul."   And why may we not include all thefe in this general expreffion ?  But by this threatening, God would guard the command of circumcifion, leaft a
facrament, in other refpects full of fhame and pain, fhould be
either flighted or neglected.  It was his will, that his covenant
fhould be in fuch efteem, that its yoke, though hard, might be
cheerfully fubmitted to.   Aben Ezra has obferved, that, in the
whole facred Scripture, he finds twenty-three places, where
God threatens *extermination* to thofe who tranfgrefs the negative
precepts ; but with refpect to the pofitive he only found with
regard to the precepts of circumcifion, and the due folemnizing
the paffover.  From which it is evident, it was the will of God
to bind his people to thefe facraments by the ftricteft tie.

XII. But yet we are, on no account, fo to underftand thefe
things, as if all infants, dying uncircumcifed after the eighth
day, were configned to condemnation ; which, after fome popifh
writers, I wonder that Chamierus fhould have adopted, *lib*. 3.
*de Sacram. c.* 2.  But the meaning is, as Perkins has well obferved, *Tract. de Sacram. Baptifmi*, " whoever has not been circumcifed in his infancy, and being come to years of difcretion

and knowledge, fhall then refufe circumcifion, his foul fhall be cut off from his people." And therefore this is faid of adults, not of infants, who cannot break the covenant. There are the following reafons for this explication: 1ft, Becaufe the words of the orginal text are active, אשר לא ימול את בשר, *be who fhall not have circumcifed the flefh of his forefkin*. Where את, the fign of the accufative, fhews, that the word ימול is not here of the form *niphal*, from מול, but of the form *kal*, from מול. Whence I conclude, thefe words are not addreffed to him, who, in the act of his circumcifion, unknowingly fuffers any thing; but to him who can procure his own circumcifion, and yet deliberately neglects it. 2dly, Becaufe it is added, *he hath broken my covenant*. In which words he is charged with a culpable action, who only before could be charged with a culpable deficiency. But an infant who is without circumcifion, not through his own default, does not thereby render the covenant of God of no effect. 3dly, The occafion and end of this fanction lead to this: namely, circumcifion was enjoined to Abraham, when ninety-nine years old, to his fervants and domeftics, when grown up, to Ifhmael, a lad thirteen years old. But as it would have been difficult to perfuade grown perfons to that act of cutting away, or of mutilation, conjoined with fo much fhame and pain; for this reafon that threatening was added, that, for fear of a greater evil, they might obfequioufly fubmit to the command. As this could only be ferioufly confidered by grown-up perfons, fo it regards them only. 4thly, We may add this inconvenience; if infants dying uncircumcifed after the eighth day, are, on that account, configned to condemnation, as covenant-breakers; there can be no reafon, why the fame thing may not be faid concerning the infants of Chriftians, who die before baptifm; becaufe baptifm, no lefs than circumcifion, is a fign of the covenant. And that this was alfo the conftant opinion of the Jews, fee in *Selden de Synedriis, lib. 1. c. 6.*

XIII. The *minifter* of circumcifion was every mafter of a family, Gen. xvii. 23. or any other perfon, qualified for that office, and fubftituted in the mafter's place. Nor does it appear that Zacharias, though a prieft, circumcifed his fon John with his own hands, Luke i. 59. At leaft, it appears not, that God confined the adminiftration of this ordinance to any particular order of men. But yet, that women were not called to do it, may be gathered from the example of Zippora, Exod. iv. 24, 25. Becaufe amidft the confufion, arifing from a prefent danger, neither fhe nor Mofes feem fufficiently to have attended, by whom circumcifion was to be adminiftered, if it was only done. And it is plain, that God really approved that circum-

cifion;

cifion ; but it does not appear, that he approved the manner of it.

XIV. The *day* appointed for circumcifion was the eighth from the birth. Though the principal reafon of this is, the will of him who commands ; yet other reafons are likewife probably added. 1ft, That thus a regard might be had to the tender ftate of infants, who, before the eighth day, are fcarce able to bear the pains of circumcifion, under which grown perfons themfelves almoft fink, Gen. xxxiv. 25. 2dly, Becaufe infants juft born, are with their mother, accounted unclean till the eighth day. This reafon *R. Simeon, the fon of Jochi*, gives in *Pefkta, fol.* 16. *col.* 3. " Why has the law appointed circumcifion on the eighth day ? Circumcifion is put off, till the woman in child-bed be cleanfed from her uncleannefs," *Lightfoot ad Luc.* 2. 21. And this reafon feems to be grounded on Lev. xii. 2, 3. Certainly the infant was initiated by circumcifion, and offered up, as it were, to God by the fhedding of his blood. And it was after the feventh day, before God admitted of any facrifices from among brute animals, Exod. xxi. 30. Lev. xxiii. 27. 3dly, This was fo appointed, that we might not imagine falvation depended on an external fign ; for otherwife a good and gracious God would not have deferred it till the eighth day, before which time many muft needs have died. Upon this account alfo Abraham himfelf was juftified in uncircumcifion, Rom. iv. 10.

XV. I will not fay with fome (who yet, I own, can defend themfelves by the authority of Cyprian and fixty-fix bifhops affembled by him in council. See Cyprian's epiftles, *lib.* 3. *Epift.* 8. which in Pamel's edition is the 59th) that this myftery prefigured the day of Chrift's refurrection, which in the order of the days is the eighth, and on which the true circumcifion and our falvation were entirely completed and perfected. 1ft, Becaufe Chrift is no where faid to have rifen on the eighth day; but either on the third from his death, or on the firft day of the week. But this day, with refpect to circumcifion, is no more the eighth than any other day. Nor is it ufually called the eighth from the firft day of the preceding week, as the week is clofed with the feventh day ; from which the firft of the new week is reckoned. 2dly, Becaufe circumcifion was not a type fo much of the refurrection, as of the fufferings and death of Chrift ; as we fhall directly fhew. 3dly, Neither does it feem an accurate way of fpeaking, to fay that the true circumcifion and our falvation, were entirely completed and perfected on the day of Chrift's refurrection. For, as to the impetration or purchafe of our falvation, that indeed was perfected by the death of Chrift. The complete application of the purchafed falvation not only requires the refurrection of Chrift from the dead; but his afcenfion into heaven, and waits for his return to the general judgment. There is therefore no reafon, why thefe days ought not, as much as the day of his re-furrection, to be prefigured. We are carefully to be on our guard, not to run into extremes in allegorizing.

XVI. The fpiritual *fignification* of circumcifion is as excel-lent, as the fign itfelf feems mean and almoft fhameful. In general it was a " fign of the covenant of God with Abraham," Gen. xvii. 11. And therefore, by a facramental phrafe, it is called the *covenant* itfelf, ver. 10, 13. Nay it was not only a *fign*, but alfo a *feal:* for not only Paul has declared this, Rom. iv. 11. but alfo the Jewifh mafters, Lightfoot ad Mat. 28. 19. Whofe words, from the Jerufalem Talmud, Tract. Berachot are as follows: " Bleffed be he, who fanctified the beloved from the womb, and put a fign in his flefh, and *fealed* his fons with the *fign* of the holy covenant." God promifed to give the Mef-fiah, and with him all manner of bleffings, earthly, fpiritual, heavenly, to Abraham and his feed, and that all thefe fhould come from his feed. God required of Abraham by covenant, that he fhould walk before him. Circumcifion was the fign and feal of this covenant; fo that all, who duly fubmitted to this, according to God's prefcription, were folemnly declared by God himfelf to be partakers of the promifes made to Abraham: and, at the fame time openly avowed, that, by a lively faith, they received the promifed Meffiah, and expected from him bleffings of every kind. And thus circumcifion became to them a feal of the righteoufnefs of faith, Rom. iv. 11. And the cir-cumcifed perfon was faid *to enter, and to have a fafe ftation, under the wings of the divine majefty*. And by the fame act, they alfo bound themfelves to the fincere obfervance of the whole of re-ligion, and confequently of all the precepts of God, as became thofe in covenant with the fupreme being. It is not to be doubted, but from the remains of ancient piety is that prayer, which the Jews, at this day, ftill ufe in the circumcifion of their young infants, *Buxtorf. Synag. Judg. c.* 2. " As thou haft made this young child to enter, or haft received him, into the covenant of Abraham our father; fo make him enter into the law of Mofes, into the ftate of matrimony, (which Selden de Jure Nat. lib. 2. c. 2. renders, into protection or fafe-guard) and into good-works."

XVII. More efpecially thefe three principal heads of the whole of our religion are held forth by the figure of circumci-

fion:

tion: namely, our *misery*, our *redemption*, and our *returns of gratitude*.

XVIII. Man's *misery* confists partly in *sin*, partly in the *punishment* of fin. Both thefe are fignified by circumcifion. For the forefkin, that is the extreme pellicle of the generative member, which was to be cut off by circumcifion, denotes that vicioufnefs or corruption of the whole man, inherent in him from his very firft origin, and frequently in fcripture is called the forefkin of the heart, or an uncircumcifed heart, Deut. x. 16. Jer. iv. 4. Lev. xxvi. 41. Jer. ix. 26. And the painful cutting away of that flefhy part fignified, that the whole man deferved to be feparated for ever from the communion of God and all his faints, with exquifite and intolerable torments both of foul and body.

XIX. Here the *Redeemer* and the *redemption* of men are no lefs clearly difcovered. For, this facrament fignified and fealed, 1ft, That from Abraham, now circumcifed, was to arife Ifaac, Gen. xvii. 16. the father of that bleffed feed or of the Meffiah, who was to take upon himfelf, and to expiate, all our fin and all our guilt. 2dly, That this Meffiah was to fhed his blood for men, without which the covenant of grace could never be fealed, and to commence his fufferings from the very beginning of his life. 3dly, That he was to partake of the fame flefh and blood with us, Heb. ii. 14. to be cut off from the land of the living, Ifa. liii. 8, in order to the prefervation of his body, the church, Eph. v, 23. as in the carnal circumcifion a part of the body was to be cut away, that the whole man might not be cut off from his people. 4thly, That he would freely enable us to cut away and to put off the fins of the flefh, by regeneration and fanctification, which are perfected in glory, Col. ii. 11. This, I imagine, was the meaning of the ancient Jewifh doctors, when they faid, that, *whenever one becomes a profelyte, he is like a new-born child.* This being fo very common in the mouths of their mafters, Chrift juftly replied to Nicodemus, when he fo impertinently inquired about being born again, " art thou a mafter of Ifrael and knoweft not thefe things ?" John iii. 10. They taught, that a new foul, which came under the wings of the divine majefty, and was received into the embraces of the fupreme Being, dropt down from fome heavenly palace on him, who was circumcifed. By fuch dark and myfterious expreffions it is probable, the ancient Jewifh doctors defcribed fpiritual regeneration; which, not being underftood by the more modern, was by them changed into mere empty found: fee *Selden, de jure nat. lib. 2. c. 11.*

XX.

XX. Laftly, By the ufe of this facrament, they were put in mind of the duties of a becoming *gratitude.* 1ft, That they were to apply themfelves to internal, fecret, and fpiritual piety, juft as circumcifion was performed on a fecret member of the body, which is to be vailed, Rom. ii. 28, 29. 2dly, To mortify their members, which are upon the earth, Col. iii. 5. that is, to renounce their lufts, even thofe that formerly were moft dear to them, and beloved by them. 3dly, To have no longer any intimate friendfhip with the world which lieth in wickednefs; as the defcendants of Abraham were feparated by circumcifion from other nations, and renounced their friendfhip: as appears from the open declaration of the fons of Jacob, Gen. xxxiv. 14, 15. Though indeed they fpoke this from an evil intention, yet what they faid was right: compare Acts x. 28. A circumcifed perfon, fay the Jews, *has withdrawn himfelf from the whole body of the nations.* And indeed, circumcifion was a great part, and as it were, the foundation of the middle wall of partition. 4thly, They were cheerfully and willingly, at the command of God, and for his glory, to fubmit to every thing however difficult, grievous, and painful, and however improper, foolifh, and ridiculous, in the eyes of the world: not to account their reputation, nor even their life dear in comparifon thereof.

XXI. God has determined the *duration* of circumcifion in thefe words, Gen. xvii. 13. " and my covenant fhall be in your flefh for an everlafting covenant." This is not to be underftood of a perpetual duration even to the end of the world. The diftinction is well known of עולם הזה, *of this age,* as they fpoke formerly, which comprifed the whole oeconomy of the Old Teftament, and of עולם הבא, *of the age to come;* which by the Apoftle, Heb. ii. 5. is called ὁ μίλλων αἰὼν, *the age to come,* or ἐκκυμίνη μίλλυϊνα, *the world to come,* to which age belong the *days of the Meffiah.* But the prophecies conftantly fay, that what was inftituted for the covenant of the former age muft not be extended to the latter age, whofe face or ftate and oeconomy were to be quite different.

XXII. Moreover, that circumcifion was to be abrogated in the days of the more joyful difpenfation of the covenant may thus appear. 1ft, Becaufe it is a part of thofe fhadows, which, becaufe they prefigured the body that was to come, ought now to give place to it, fince it is come, Col. ii. 17. 2dly, Becaufe it was a great part of that middle wall of partition which feparated the Jews from the Gentiles, and whofe enclofure was to be broken down by the death of Chrift, " having abolifhed in his flefh the enmity, even the law of commandments, contained in ordinances: for to make in himfelf, of twain, one new man, so making peace," Eph. ii. 15. It was certainly foretold of old time, that the Gentiles were to be fellow-heirs, and of the same body with Israel, and partakers of the same promise, Eph. iii. 6. see Deut. xxxii. 43. Isa. xix. 24, 25. and Isa. lx. 3, &c. But this *concorporation*, or being of the same body, was not to be brought about by enclosing the Gentiles with Israel, within the same enclosure of rites and ceremonies (for that enclosure was appointed to establish a separation and enmity) but by destroying the same : " for in Jesus Christ, neither circumcision availeth any thing, nor uncircumcision, but faith which worketh by love," Gal. v. 6. *They which are of faith*, whether circumcised or not, *the same are the children of Abraham*, Gal. iii. 7. 3dly, Because circumcision plainly shewed, that the blood of the New Testament was not yet shed, that the Messiah was not yet born of the seed of Abraham, or at least not yet cut off for the salvation of his mystical body. But when the world was made to know, by the preaching of the gospel, that these things were done; it was necessary, that what testified they were not yet done should be abrogated; least any institution of God should be found to bear witness against the truth. To this purpose is that of Paul, Gal. v. 2, 3, 4. " Behold, I Paul say unto you, that if ye be circumcised, Christ shall profit you nothing : for I testify again to every man that is circumcised, that he is a debtor to do the whole law." The meaning is, whoever submits to circumcision, as a necessary part of God's instituted worship, or as a mean of justification thereby renounces Christ. 1st, Because he would have that sign to be still necessary, which testifieth, that every thing is not yet accomplished by Christ. 2dly, Because, as circumcision cannot be separated from the rest of the ceremonial law, to which it was as the porch, so he who submits to circumcision, thereby binds himself to the observance of the whole ceremonial law. But that is in effect to deny the coming of Christ, and the time of reformation and liberty. 3dly, Because, as the righteousness of man before God, must either depend wholly on his own works, or wholly upon Christ, and these two cannot be conjoined, Gal. ii. 21. and Gal. iii. 12, 18. whoever seeks for righteousness in circumcision, as his own work, is fallen from the righteousness of Christ ; and so, if he would obtain salvation, it is necessary, that he keep the whole law: which being impossible for him to do, he knows, he is cut off from all hopes of salvation.

XXIII. But the abrogation of this rite of circumcision had its several degrees. It was first in a languishing state, then it was dead, and at last became pernicious. 1st, It began to languish at the circumcision of Christ, who by submitting himself to the law for the elect, and solemnly teftifying that fubjection, by taking upon him the fymbol of circumcifion, made it appear, that he was that fingular feed of Abraham, whofe future nativity circumcifion was originally appointed to prefigure. From the time therefore, that he appeared, circumcifion, which fignified that he was to come, loft a great part of its fignification. 2dly, It was further weakened, after Chrift had, in the thirtieth year of his age, manifefted himfelf to Ifrael, and was pointed out by John, as the Lamb of God which taketh away the fins of the world, and was publicly owned by the Father as his beloved Son, to whom all were to hear and obey. For then the gofpel of liberty and of the kingdom began to be preached, and baptifm, a fign oppofed to circumcifion, was ufed, as a facrament of initiation into a better covenant, whereby circumcifion came to lofe much of its dignity. 3dly, It began to die at the death of Chrift. For when he was cut off from among his people, for the falvation of the whole myftical body, and had fealed the New Teftament by his blood, every thing relating to the future Meffiah, which circumcifion prefigured, and to which Chrift by his own circumcifion bound himfelf, was fulfilled. And thus the hand-writing, which was againft Chrift the furety, and againft believers, was torn afunder in his crofs, Col. ii. 14. 4thly, It came to be quite dead after Chrift, by his refurrection from the dead, had received from the Father a difcharge, in witnefs that the fulleft payment was made, and exhibited it to the view, as it were, of the whole world. Yet believers had fo little knowledge of the liberty purchafed for, and offered to them, that Peter himfelf wanted to be taught it by a heavenly vifion, Acts x. 28, 34, 35, 47. 4thly, It was not yet deftructive, but fo long as the church was not fufficiently inftructed in her liberty, it might at times, to avoid giving offence to the weak, be prudently, yet freely ufed, not from a principle of confcience, but from the dictates of charity and prudence, leaft the Jews, who were too tenacious of their peculiar and paternal rites, fhould be alienated from the Chriftian religion : juft as Timothy was circumcifed, being the fon of a Jewefs, Acts xvi. 1, 3. 6thly, But after the nation of the Jews, on rejecting the gofpel, were caft off by God, and continued obftinately to infift on circumcifion, as a neceffary part of religion, nay, of righteoufnefs, and the church was fufficiently inftructed in her own liberty, circumcifion came to be deftructive, as being a character of fuperftition and a badge of Jewifh infidelity, and a renunciation of Chriftian liberty, as we have fhewn from Gal. v. 2, 3.

XXIV. It is not now difficult to determine that queftion ; namely, whether the nation of the Jews, when they fhall in the

last

laft times be fully converted to Chrift, will religioufly retain the circumcifion of infants? Without any hefitation, I think, we are to anfwer this queftion in the negative, for the reafons juft given. As they are fuch as evince, that not only the Gentiles, but alfo the Jews were made free, under the liberty of the New Teftament from circumcifion, which is the band of the whole yoke. And in every refpeɛt, the reafon of both ought to be altogether the fame. Though *the pre-eminence of the Jew* was formerly great, yet now he has none at all. None under Chrift has wherein to glory: Paul accounted it as lofs and dung, Phil. iii. 7, 8. In Chrift there is no difference of Jew and Greek, of circumcifion and uncircumcifion: but Chrift himfelf is all in all, Col. iii. 11. all pre-eminece of whatever nation being totally removed. *Henceforth*, faith the Apoftle, 2 Cor. v. 16. *know we no man after the flefh*, that is, we have no greater efteem for him on account of his pedigree from the holy fathers; *yea, though we have known Chrift after the flefh*, that is, though we have looked upon our carnal relation to Chrift, as any prerogative; *yet now henceforth know we him no more*; we now place all our happinefs [not in that, but] in our fpiritual union with him by faith. And fince God is now in no fenfe *a refpeɛter of perfons*, Aɛts x. 34. we can never be allowed " to have the faith of our Lord Jefus Chrift the Lord of glory, with refpeɛt of perfons, James ii. 1. or, in the kingdom of Chrift, to put a greater value on the defcendants of Abraham, as fuch, than on Barbarians or Scythians, " who have obtained like precious faith with us," 2 Pet. i. 1. In a word, the circumcifion of the believing Ifraelites in the laft times, would be either a future privelege, or a burden and yoke. But can be neither: not the latter, becaufe that would be repugnant to the liberty purchafed by Chrift, which, as is meet, fhould be exceeding glorious in that happy period: not the former, becaufe the gofpel of the kingdom hath removed all pre-eminence of one above another, *hath made both one*, Eph. ii. 14.

XXV. Yet I have heard of two arguments againft this, which have the appearance of ftrength, and but the appearance only. The one is taken from the New Teftament, the other from the Old. From the New, that fpeech of James and the elders to Paul, Aɛts xxi. 21. has been propofed to my confideration by a learned perfon: " and they are informed of ●ee, that thou teacheft all the Jews, which are among the Gentiles, faying, that they ought not to circumcife their children, neither to walk after the cuftoms." But when this made a great commotion among thofe who were zealous of the law, and yet believed in

Vol. II.        K k        Chrift,

Chrift, James authorifed Paul to do fuch things, from which all might know, "that thofe things, whereof they were informed concerning him were nothing, but that Paul himfelf alfo walked orderly, and kept the law," ver. 24. Paul complied with this advice. From this it might be concluded, that the true fenfe of Paul's doctrine was; that though the Gentiles were not indeed bound to circumcifion and the other ceremonies, yet the Jews, even after they embraced the faith of Chrift, were to circumcife their children, and to walk after the cuftoms; becaufe Paul, at the perfuafion of James, by this compliance removes from himfelf the fufpicion of his teaching a contrary doctrine.

XXVI. But we are here to confider diftinctly three things. 1ft, The true doctrine of Paul. 3dly, The calumny invidioufly fixed upon him. 3dly, The prudential advice fuggefted to him by James and the elders. Indeed Paul, who was an excellent preacher of Chriftian liberty, fet both Jews and Gentiles, who had fubmitted to the gofpel, at liberty from the neceffity of fubmitting to circumcifion and the other ceremonies: for he proclaimed to all, that "circumcifion is nothing, and uncircumcifion is nothing, but the keeping of the commandments of God," 1 Cor. vii. 19. And he compares the law to a tutor, under whofe tuition the Old Teftament church was placed, being then in a ftate of bondage: but now the kingdom of heaven being fet up in the world; he declares that the fame church was come to age, which no longer ftanding in need of a tutor, was not again to be given up to bondage under thofe firft elements of the world, Gal. iv. 1. Which certainly comprife both Jews and Gentiles. He every where publifhed this privilege of the New Teftament freely and openly. Neverthelefs he was not againft making fome allowances for the weaknefs of the Jewifh brethren, in the exercife of that liberty; in cafe there was not a fpirit of contention, nor an opinion of neceffity and righteoufnefs, in ftanding up for the practice of the ceremonies. Calumny put a quite different conftruction on this conduct; as if he acted thus to the reproach of the law, and taught apoftafy from Mofes, and did not agree in this doctrinal point, who with others, maintained the Chriftian faith. But the cafe was certainly the reverfe: for it is no reproach put upon the law, to teach, that Chrift made fatisfaction to it: any more than it is a reproach put upon a hand-writing, that on payment being made, it is cancelled. Nor is it any apoftafy from Mofes, to preach that Chrift is the beftower of liberty, fince Mofes himfelf commanded him to be heard: nor did Paul difagree with the other Apoftles; becaufe they alfo taught

according

according to the decree of the fynod of Jerufalem, an immunity from that yoke; and Paul, in the exercife of that liberty, by no means difowned, that charity and prudence were to be regarded. Neverthelefs the calumny gained ground; and many of the bre-thren, who were not truly informed of the Apoftle's doctrine, entertained groundlefs fufpicions of him. Hence arofe the ad-vice, that he himfelf fhould openly perform fome certain cere-monies: not in order to create any prejudice to that Chriftian right and liberty, which he had preached; but to fhew publicly, that he had done nothing inconfiderately, which could give rife to any juft indignation: that it was a vile calumny, by which he was defamed, as entertaining lefs reverent thoughts of Mofes, and teaching the Jews a contempt of the law. With this ad-vice the Apoftle complies, not that he approved the violence of thofe zealots, but to wipe off a calumny, and to fuit himfelf prudently and friendly to the weak. Thus, " unto the Jews he became as a Jew, that he might gain the Jews; to them that are under the law, as under the law, that he might gain them that are under the law," 1 Cor. ix. 20. Thefe things being duly confidered, it is evident, nothing can be concluded from this paffage for the continuance of circumcifion among the converted Ifraelites.

XXVII. From the Old Teftament is objected Ezek. xliv. 9. Where the Lord, defcribing the ftate of the church after the the converfion of Ifrael, thus goes on; " no ftranger, uncircum-cifed in heart, nor uncircumcifed in flefh fhall enter into my fanctuary." By which words, all who have a right to enter into the fanctuary, are required to have the circumcifion both of flefh and heart. If the queftion was about uncircumcifion in general, we might very plainly explain it of the depraved dif-pofition of the unregenerate heart. Nay if the uncircumcifion of the flefh was exprefsly mentioned, nothing could hinder us from taking a prophetic expreffion, borrowed from the rites of the Old Teftament, in a fpiritual fenfe. But when the cir-cumcifion both of flefh and heart is diftinctly mentioned, it feems altogether neceffary, we fhould underftand the one, cer-tainly fpiritually, but the other literally.

XXVIII. In anfwer to this reafoning I offer the following confiderations. 1ft, That the whole context of Ezekiel con-cerning the building of a new temple, is myftical and allegori-cal, and is expreffed by fimilitudes, borrowed from the Old Teftament, all which, as is fuitable to the ftate of the New Teftament, are to be explained fpiritually. 2dly, That though the uncircumcifion of flefh and heart are diftinct, yet they are both myftical. Surely uncircumcifion myftically fignifies any depraved difpofition of man. Hence we read of *uncircumcifed lips*, Exod. vi. 12. and *ears*, Jer. vi. 10. Acts vii. 51. Nay, any impurity, even of thofe fruits, which God had forbid to be eaten, is called uncircumcifion, * Lev. xix. 23. The uncircumifion therefore of the heart, in the myftical language of Ezekiel, fignifies the impurity of the heart and inward affections; the uncircumcifion of the flefh, the impurity of the outward actions, performed by the body, according to the diftinction of Paul, 2 Cor. vii. 1. Both kinds of impurity are to be laid afide by him, who would be reckoned to belong to the communion of the people of God. " Who fhall afcend into the hill of the Jehovah ? And who fhall ftand in his holy place? He that hath clean hands and a pure heart," Pfal. xxiv. 3, 4. But we are efpecially to take notice, that the difcourfe here is not concerning the Ifraelites, but concerning the ftrangers, who were to be admitted into the fanctuary. They certainly fhall have their proper place in this new temple, Ifa. lvi. 6, 7. and not have reafon to complain ; " Jehovah hath utterly feparated me from his people," ver. 3. But to impofe upon them, in the latter days, the neceffity of circumcifion, from which they were free, all the intermediate time, is, as has been fhewn, diametrically oppofite to the doctrine of the Apoftles.

---

## CHAP. IX.

### *Of the Paffover.*

I. THE whole doctrine of the *paffover* has been learnedly and copioufly, above what can well be expreffed, unfolded by the very laborious Samuel Bochart, Hierozoic. lib. 2. c. 50. But becaufe that moft excellent and invaluable book is rarely to be found in the hands of the youth under our tuition, we have thought proper in this chapter, to exhibit what he has handled at large, in a compendious way. Yet in fuch a manner, as to follow at times our own judgment, and now and then interfperfe what obfervations we have made from other authors.

* The words are. " and when ye fhall come into the land, and fhall have planted all manner of trees for food, then ye fhall count the fruit thereof as uncircumcifed: three years it fhall be as uncircumcifed to you, it fhall not be eaten of." The meaning in general is, it fhall be unclean, and not to be eaten of, but caft away, and counted abominable, as the forefkins were.

authors. We will therefore briefly run over thefe feven par-
ticulars. I. The appellation of the paffover. II. Its time.
III. Its place. IV. Its minifters. V. Its guefts. VI. Its rites.
VII. Its myftery.

II. The *name pafcha* is Chaldee, as Philo juftly obfervs. In
Hebrew it is called חספ *pefach*, by the ancients *phafe* and *phafec*.
The root חספ, fignifies to *paffover*. Jofephus renders it ὑπερβασια:
Philo διαβατηρια. Juft as there were alfo *facrifices* called *for paf-*
*fage* at *Lacedemon*, that is, for the happy progrefs of an expedition. But is thus called *pafcha*, becaufe God, while he
flew the firft born of the Egyptians, *paffed over* the doors of
the Ifraelites, on feeing the pofts thereof fprinkled with the blood
of the lamb, Exod. xii. 13. Thus Ifa. xxxi. 5. God delivers
Jerufalem, by *paffing over* it, while he takes due vengeance on
other people. But the term *pafcha* is of various acceptations,
denoting: 1ft, The paffing over of the angel, who while he
fmote the firft-born of the Egyptians, paffed over the houfes of
the Ifraelites. 2dly, The lamb, which was flain in memory
of this deliverance, Exod. xii. 21. " kill the paffover ;" Luke
xxii. 7. " then came the day of unleavened bread, when the
paffover muft be killed." 3dly, The facrifices then ufually
offered to God along with the lamb, Deut xvi. 2. " Thou
fhalt facrifice the paffover unto the Lord thy God, of the flock
and the herd." 4thly, The feftival days on which thefe things
were folemnized, Luke xxii. 1. " now the feaft of unleavened
bread drew nigh, which is called the paffover." Seeing Chrift
our Lord fuffered at that time, hence fome of the ancients,
who were not acquainted with Hebrew literature, derived the
name *pafcha* from the Greek πασχω, *I fuffer*.

III. The *time* is exprefsly fpecified, Lev. xxiii. 5. " in the
fourteenth day of the firft month, at even" (between the two
evenings) " is the Lord's paffover." Where obferve. (1.) The
month. (2.) The day. (3.) The hour or time of the day.
The *month* Abib is mentioned Exod. xiii. 4. elfewhere called
Nifan, Neh. ii. 1. Eft. iii. 7. Abib fignifies in Hebrew an *ear*
*of corn*, as yet *frefh* or green. Hence was the name of the
month ; becaufe in thofe warmer countries, and efpecially in
Judea, in that month, which anfwers partly to our March,
partly to our April, and ftanding corn neceffary for the fupport of life, are, according to Philo, beginning to ripen ; and
at that time the Ifraelites began to put the fickle to the ftanding
corn, Deut. xvi. 9. and on the fecond day of the pafchal folemnity, they offered to God a handful of the firft fruits. But
why the fame month is in Chaldee called Nifan, is not fo evident. A great man conjectures, it ought to be written Niffan,

as is done by Jofephus; or the *dagefch* ftruck out of the latter
פ to be made by a long vowel; as נוסי, Nifin is often put for
נוסי, Nifin that is *ftandards*. And thus the appellation Nifan is
very properly taken from the warlike enfigns or ftandards, with
which, in that month, they firft took the field. And this very
time the Jews underftand to be intended, 2 Sam. xi. 1. " and it
came to pafs, that after the year was expired, at the time when
kings go forth to battle." For a like reafon, the two former fpring
months were called by the Bithynians Στρατιος and Αρμος, as by
the Romans *Martius Mars*. But this month is called the *firft;*
namely, of the facred or ecclefiaftical year, from the Exodus
out of Egypt; being otherwife the feventh of the civil year, whofe
beginning was about autumn, and whofe firft month was called Tifri. And there was the exprefs command of God for
this, Exod. xii. 2. " this month," namely Abib, compare, Exod.
xiii. 4. " fhall be unto you thee beginning of months, it fhall be
the firft month of the year to you."

IV. The *day* of this firft month, fet a part for the paffover,
was the fourteenth. The *hours*, or time of the day, was *between*
*the two evenings;* the one of which was a little paft noon, when
the fun began to defcend, the other a little before the fetting
of the fun. Not only the Hebrews diftinguifhed their evenings in this manner, as may be feen in Buxtorf's lexicon under
the word ערב; but alfo fome of the Greeks, according to the
teftimony of Euftathius, ad lib. 17. Odyfs. " According to
the ancients the evening is twofold : for, the late evening, according to them, is the latter part of the evening towards fun
fet : the other the early evening, the firft of the evening, following juft upon noon. See alfo Hefychius under the word
Δυλη. Within the compafs therefore of that time, in which the
fun begins to decline, and in which he fets, the paffover was
to be flain and roafted, that it might be eaten on the beginning
of the fifteenth day, which was at fun fet. Jofephus fays, that
the Pafchal lambs were killed, *from the ninth hour till the eleventh*,
that is, from three in the afternoon till five, Bell. Jud. lib.
7. c. 17.

V. As to the *place;* the paffover was celebrated the firft time
in Egypt, Exod. xii. 21. then in the wildernefs of Sinai, Numb.
ix. 5. And in Egypt, indeed, every one flew it in his own
houfe, as there was no altar, no place fet apart for God there.
But after the Exodus, none were allowed to kill the paffover
any where, but in the place which God had chofen : as is exprefsly enjoined, Deut. xvi. 5, 6. But that place was not Jerufalem only, after Solomon built the temple there, but alfo
the very court of the temple where they ufually killed the other
facrifices,

sacrifices. For God placed his name, and caused it to dwell
not so much in the whole city, as in the temple. The Jews all
agree in this: "they kill the passover as they do other sacrifices
only in the court of the temple," says Maimonides, lib. de Pasch.
c. 1. Sect. 3. And a very learned English author has shewn,
that this is confessedly the opinion of the Karaites or scriptura-
rian doctors of the Jews.

VI. And the reason is obvious: for every one knows, it was
not allowed to kill the sacrifices but in the court of the temple.
But that the *passover* was a real *sacrifice*, is evident from the
following arguments. 1st, Because the scripture in express
words calls its זבח, *sacrifice*, Exod. xii. 27. " it is the *sacrifice*
of Jehovah's passover." Though this word, in other places,
denotes any feast whatever, made up of slain animals, as Prov.
xvii. 1. yet that it is here to be taken in its most common and
sacred sense, we gather from this; because the paschal sacrifice,
was a type of that most real sacrifice of Christ, concerning
which, Paul says, 1 Cor. v. 7. " Christ our passover ἐτύθη is
sacrificed for us." Josephus and Philo likewise every where call
the paschal lambs θυσίαι or θύματα, that is, according to the interpretation of Ruffinus, *hostia*, *sacrifices*. 2dly, Because the persons, celebrating the passover, are said to " offer the offering
to Jehovah," Numb. ix. 7. 13. 3dly, Because the blood of
the paschal lamb, as of a true sacrifice, was offered to the Lord.
Which may be gathered from the words of Moses, Exod. xxiii.
18. " thou shalt not offer the blood of my *sacrifice* with leavened bread, neither shall the fat of my *sacrifice* remain until the
morning:" of my sacrifice, that is, of my passover, as even
Onkelos has it *the blood of my sacrifice*, and Jonathan, *the blood
of the libation* of my passover. Add a parallel passage, Exod.
xxxiv. 25. " thou shalt not offer the blood of my sacrifice with
leaven, neither shall the *sacrifice of the feast of passover*, be left
unto the morning." 4thly, Because the blood of the paschal
lamb was sprinkled as well as the blood of the other sacrifices.
In 2 Chron. xxx. 16. speaking of the passover, it is said, that
the priests sprinkled the blood, which they received from the
hands of the Levites: also chap. xxxv. 11. " and they killed the
passover, and the priests sprinkled the blood from their hands."
And none is ignorant, that this belongs to a sacrifice. Maimonides observes well on this occasion, that the sprinkling is
of great importance, as being the foundation of the offering.
And Peter alluding to this, says, that we are elected, " unto
sprinkling of the blood of Jesus Christ," 1 Pet. i. 2. As therefore we have a more clear representation of the sacrifice of
Christ in the passover, besides so many arguments, it is plain,
we

we are by all means to affert, that the paffover was a true facrifice. And if fo, it could not be properly killed any where, but in the court of the temple.

VII. The ftraitnefs of time and place is in vain objected; as if it was not poffible, within the compafs of the two evenings, to prefent and offer at one altar, fo many thoufand lambs. Concerning the prodigious number of thefe, fee an extraordinary hiftory or fable in Lightfoot on John xii. 12. For, that the court of the temple was very extenfive appears from the twenty-two thoufand oxen, and a hundred and twenty thoufand fheep, which Solomon offered there at the dedication of the temple, 1 Kings viii. 63. and the facrifices without number offered by the reft of the people, 2 Chron. v. 6. moreover, there were very many and expeditious priefts at leifure, for four hours, if circumftances fo required, to be employed in offering thefe lambs. And thofe very perfons, who tell us, there was fuch a prodigious number of pafchal lambs, at the fame time tell us, that the number could not be afcertained, but by the calculation made by the priefts, who offered in the court.

VIII. The *minifters* here were (1.) The common people. (2.) The Levites. (3.) The priefts. It belonged to the *common people* not only to bring the pafchal facrifices to the priefts, but alfo, if they pleafed, to kill them. Which Philo, after the manner of orators, exaggerates, when he writes, *lib. de decalogo:* " that at the feaft of the paffover every one indifcriminately facrificed, the law granting, on one extraordinary day once a year, the office of prieft to the whole people, to offer facrifices for themfelves." God himfelf feems to have granted that privilege to all the people, Exod. xii. 6. " and the whole affembly of the congregation of Ifrael fhall kill it." Nor was this peculiar to the paffover, as Philo fpeaks, but allowed to the common people in the cafe of any other facrifice, namely, to kill the facrifices, even the moft holy, whether for themfelves, for private perfons, or for the whole congregation; as Maimonides has more accurately obferved than Philo, *de Ingrefs. Sacred. in Sanct. c. 9. §. 14.* and the thing is clear from fcripture. See concerning the burnt-offering, Lev. i. 3, 4, 5. concerning the peace-offering, Lev. iii. 2. and concerning the fin-offering, Lev. iv. 24.

IX. But when private perfons did not choofe to kill the paffover, or were not allowed on account of uncleannefs, the *Levites* were fubftituted for this work, in their room, becaufe they were more fkilful and expeditious. We have an example, 2 Chron. xxx. 17. " for, there were many in the congregation that were not fanctified; therefore the Levites had the charge of the killing of the paffovers, for every one that was not clean, to fanctify them unto the Lord." Similar to this is the paffage, Ezra vi. 20.

X. The bufinefs of the *priefts* was to fprinkle at the altar the blood received from the common people or the Levites, as we have already fhewn from 2 Chron. xxx. 16. and xxxv. 11. They alfo alone burnt the fat on the altar, as the Jews conftant-ly affert.  Inftead of all others let us only hear Maimonides, *de pafcha, c.* 1. §. 14.  Who, after he had defcribed a long circle of priefts around the altar, with bafons of gold and filver, adds, when any of them had killed the paffover, the blood was re-ceived in a bafon by the next prieft, who was to deliver it to a fecond, and fo on, till it came to the prieft next the altar, who poured it out at once at the bottom of the altar, and returned the bafon empty, which he had received full.  After the blood was poured out, as he fays elfewhere, v. 6. they ftrip the paf-chal lamb of his fkin, and opening his belly take out the fat on the inwards and burn it leifurely as in every facrifice.  Which they might do during the whole night, till the morning dawn. Which is a further confirmation, that the paffover was a true facrifice.

XI. As to the *guefts*; they were, in the firft place, all true born Ifraelites, if they were not excluded by legal uncleannefs. For, Exod. xii. 6, 47. *all the congregation of Ifrael* is commanded to folemnize the paffover.  And then the profelytes, who *were circumcifed and became Jews*, Eft. viii. 17. whether they were bond-men born in the houfe, or bought with money, or mer-cenary, or inmates of the land of Canaan, fubject to no bond-age; or in fine, thofe, whom they called profelytes of righteouf-nefs, who upon being circumcifed alfo, had a right to eat the paffover, Exod. xii. 48. " And when a ftranger fhall fojourn with thee, and will keep the paffover to Jehovah, let all his males be circumcifed, and then let him come near and keep it ; and he fhall be as one that is born in the land: for, no uncir-cumcifed perfon fhall eat thereof.

XII. It is a queftion, whether women were likewife excluded by the fame law, that the uncircumcifed were; efpecially as the law commanded the males only to repair to the three fefti-vals, Exod. xxiii. 17. and xxxiv. 23. Deut. xvi. 16.  It would feem, they were not.  1ft, Becaufe women cannot be numbered among the uncircumcifed, nor accounted as fuch, for circumci-fion did not belong to them, but they were reckoned along with their circumcifed parents, or hufbands.  2dly, Becaufe all the congregation of Ifrael, as we have juft fhewn, is commanded to celebrate the paffover.  But the women make a part of this congregation, Deut. xxix. 11.  3dly, That the women together

with the men celebrated these solemn festivals, appears from the
example of Elkanah, who yearly carried with him his two wives,
with his sons and daughters to Shiloh, to the solemn festivals,
1 Sam. i. 3, 4. Joseph also and the holy virgin repaired yearly
to Jerusalem to the feast of the passover, Luke ii. 41. From
which it appears, that the same thing may be concluded concerning all the pious women in those times. 4thly, From a
parity of reason: because in other eucharistical sacrifices, or
peace-offerings, women also had their portion: thus Elkanah
gave to his wife Peninnah, and to all her sons and daughters,
parts of the sacrifice; but to Hannah, whom he loved, a worthy,
a double portion, 1 Sam. i, 4, 5. When David likewise offered
eucharistical sacrifices, he dealt out a part of them to all Israel,
as well to the women as men, 2 Sam. vi. 18. And the daughters of the priests ate of the sacred food, Numb. xviii. 11, 19.
And why may we not suppose, that women also partook of the
passover, which was a kind of eucharistical sacrifice, or peace-
offering? 5thly, We add the testimony of Maimonides, who
says, that women were not only admitted to the paschal feasts,
but also at times there was a company, which consisted only of
women, _de Pasch. c. 2. §. 5._

XIII. We must not, however, omit here the observation of
the Rabbins, who distinguish between the command concerning
the passover, and concerning the not eating leavened bread,
They say, that all were absolutely bound to this last, females
as well as males, This law, not to eat leavened bread, Exod,
xiii. 3. is, say they, " at every time and in every place, equally
binding on males and females." See _Hottinger. jus. Hebr. Sect._
4. §. 22. But the command concerning women's appearing at
Jerusalem to keep the passover is no where to be found in express terms. Hence it is said in _Talm. Hierosol. Tract. Kidduf-
chin, fol. 61. col._ 3. " the passover of women is a discretionary
thing." But those women, who were led by a zeal for religion,
were accustomed to present themselves before God, in order to
partake of this sacrifice, _Lightfoot ad Luc._ 2. 43.

XIV. The guests, who partook of the paschal lamb, are commanded to meet, by houses, or families, Exod. xii. 3. " They
shall take to them every man a lamb, according to the house of
their fathers, a lamb for an house." But if a house had not a
number sufficient to consume a lamb, the neighbours were to
be called in, till a just number was made up, ver. 4. The
Jewish masters took care, that the number of guests should not
be under ten, nor above twenty. Which Jonathan's paraphrase
on Exod. xii. 4. and Josephus, _de Bell. Jud. lib._ 17. _c._ 7. observe.
In those companies or societies, called φρατρίαι by Josephus, by
the

the Hebrews firmly, men and women sat down together, old men and young, whole and sick, masters and servants; in fine, every Jew, that could eat a morsel of flesh, not excluding even young children.

XV. They who were legally unclean, whether by touching a dead body, or by a leprosy, or whose seed went from them, or by any other accident, and women in their monthly courses, were debarred from the passover, Num. ix. 6. Persons thus polluted, till the time for their purification was elapsed, were not permitted to taste the flesh, either of the paschal lamb, or of any peace-offering, under pain of being cut off, Lev. xxii. 3, &c. And therefore the Jews, being to eat the passover, would not enter the judgment-hall, least they should be polluted, John xviii. 18. But under king Hezekiah, many tribes of Israel broke this law, for a great part of them had not sanctified themselves as they ought. Yet God being appeased upon the prayer of the pious king, forgave those who were truly converted, 2 Chron. xxx. 17, &c.

XVI. But least they who were unclean, at the time of that passover, should be deprived of such an excellent sacrament for a whole year, a second passover was, at God's command, appointed for them in the second month; on which a person on a journey afar off, was bound to attend, if he was not able to come to Jerusalem at the stated time of the passover, Numb. ix. 10, 11. The Jewish masters fix * a journey afar off, at fifteen miles without the walls of Jerusalem; so that a person at that distance from the city, on the fourteenth day of the month, might lawfully keep the second passover. But why should he not rather set out on the preceding day, in order to be at the feast, and not suffer himself to be straitened in time? For if any one who set out on a journey, was retained by the invincible slowness of his beasts, or by a disorder in his feet, or any accident of the like nature, such a person was not accounted to be on a journey afar off, but to be ϵϖϗ, *detained by force.* Philo therefore, de vita Mosis, lib. 3. seems to have better understood the meaning of this law, when he applies the following things to those, " who on account of a journey afar off, are hindered from sacrificing with the rest of the nation. For, *says he,* they who travel, and live, in other parts of the world, are

* Ainsworth makes the following remark upon this. The Hebrew of this word *afar off,* hath extraordinary pricks over it for special consideration. Hereby the Lord might signify, that we Gentiles who were unclean, even dead in trespasses and sins, and *afar off,* Eph. ii. 1, 13. should be made nigh by the blood of Christ, and so partakers of him, the second passover, who now *is sacrificed for us,* 1 Cor. v. 7.

not guilty of any fin, for which they are deprived of the common honour with the reft. Efpecially, as one country cannot contain fo populous a nation, but is obliged to fend out colonies into many places. Concerning this fecond paffover of the unclean, there are fine things in Selden, de Synedriis, lib. 2. c. 1.

XVII. In the *rites* prefcribed by Mofes, there are five things to be obferved. (1.) The appointment of the pafchal lamb. (2.) The preparation. (3.) The flaying. (4.) The roafting. (5.) The eating of it.

XVIII. The pafchal beaft was to be שׂה, *a fmall cattle* or *beaft*, *a lamb* or *kid*, Exod. xii. 3. for that name is common to both, Deut. xiv. 4. ye fhall eat *a fmall beaft, of fheep, and of goats:* thus alfo, Exod. xii. 5. it is emphatically added, *ye fhall take it out from the fheep, or from the goats.* However, it is probable, that the pious ufed this liberty, in fuch a manner, that they more frequently offered a lamb, as a more acceptable facrifice to God, becaufe, in fheep there is a greater degree of meeknefs, docility, and innocence. And therefore it is, that though Chrift is in fo many different places, propofed to us, under the type of a lamb, yet we never once obferve, that he is pointed out under the denomination of a kid. And therefore, Theodoret, Quæft. 24. in Exod. feems not to have given a bad explication of the meaning of the lawgiver: *that he who has a fheep, fhould offer it; but he who has none, fhould offer a kid.*

XIX. We are not to think, that oxen were made ufe of in the pafchal facrifice, ftrictly fo called; though in fcripture, even they are called by the name of the *paffover:* as Deut. xvi. 2. "thou fhalt therefore facrifice the paffover unto the Lord thy God, of the flock, and the herd;" and 2 Chron. xxxv. 8. "they gave unto the priefts for the paffover offerings two thoufand and fix hundred fmall cattle, and three hundred oxen:" and again, ver. 9. "they gave unto the Levites, for paffover offerings, five thoufand fmall cattle, and five hundred oxen." The appellation paffover, when it comprehends oxen, is taken in a larger fenfe, and then denotes thofe peace-offerings, which were killed at the paffover feftival, in order to feaft on them with joy before Jehovah. Thus in the folemn paffover under king Hezekiah, "they did eat throughout the feaft, feven days, offering peace-offerings," 2 Chron. xxx. 22. To this alfo, it feems, we fhould apply what John relates, John xviii. 28. that the Jews would not enter the judgment-hall leaft they fhould be defiled; *but that they might eat the paffover:* not certainly, the pafchal lamb which they had eaten at the fame time that Chrift did the day before; but the facrifices that were ufually offered for the feven days of the feaft, which were hence alfo

called

called *paffover*. We therefore infer, that the facrifice appropriated to the paffover, confifted of a lamb, or a kid only.

XX. The lawgiver requires three things in the lamb, or kid to be offered; that it be found, *a male*, and *of the firft year*, Exod. xii. 5. To be *found*, fignifies, to be without defect and blemifh, Lev. xxii. 19—21. The blemifhes in a facrifice are defcribed at large, ver. 22. God would have a *male*, becaufe the more excellent things are to be offered to him; but a male is more excellent than a female, Mal. i. 14. In fine, it was to be *the fon of a year*, or of the firft year. By which expreffion is not meant a lamb come to, but fhort of his firft year. For every beaft was, from its eighth day, pure or fit for facrifice, Exod. xxii. 30. Lev. xxii. 27. From the eighth day therefore, if we regard this general law, a lamb might be offered, till it completed its firft year. After which, the Jewifh mafters exclude it from facrifice. Yet to me it feems more natural, by a lamb of the firft year, to underftand that which is almoft a year old, at which time it is come to its proper fize, and its moft grateful relifh. Nor can I imagine, that the ancient believers were fo minutely nice in calculating the time that they accounted their lambs profane, directly on the commencement of the fecond year; or that they fet down the nativity of their cattle in journals, leaft they fhould miftake in a minute.

XXI. The *preparation* of the pafchal lamb, confifted in the keeping it up, or fetting it apart, which was done on the tenth day, and continued until the fourteenth, on which it was to be killed, Exod. xii. 3. The Jews give the following reafons for this command. 1ft, Leaft they fhould forget it if they delayed it, and took no care about it, till the very moment of their departure, fince they would then be hurried with a variety of bufinefs. 2dly, That they might more exactly obferve whether the lamb had any blemifh. 3dly, That they might have an opportunity, from the fight of the lamb, to converfe together concering their redemption out of Egypt. 4thly, That they might have time to prepare themfelves for keeping the approaching folemnity.

XXII. The *killing* of the lamb, followed upon its feparation, Exod. xii. 6. " And the whole congregation of the children of Ifrael fhall kill it." The blood was to be received in a bafon, and a bunch of hyffop to be dipt therein, with which they were to ftrike or fprinkle the lintel, and the two fide-pofts of the houfe, ver. 22. The lintel, I fay, not the threfhhold, leaft thofe that paffed, fhould trample under foot the facred blood, which was inftead, both of a facrifice and a facrament. For why fhould not true religion have the fame effect on them, that

fuperftition

fuperftition had on the people of Afhdod, who, for a long time, would not tread on the threfhhold of their temple, after Dagon had fallen on his face upon it? 1 Sam. v. 5. God himfelf fhews the reafon of this fprinkling, Exod. xii. 13. " And the blood fhall be to you, for a token upon the houfes where you are: and when I fee the blood, I will pafs over you, and the plague fhall not be upon you, to deftroy you, when I fmite the land of Egypt." Not that there was any natural effi-cacy in the blood of the lamb, or that God ftood in need of a fign to diftinguifh his own people: 2 Tim. ii. 19. But this fign was given to the Hebrews, that thereby they may be con-firmed and affured of their deliverance, Heb. xi. 28. " through faith Mofes kept the paffover, and the fprinkling of blood, leaft he that deftroyed the firft-born, fhould touch them.

XXIII. God gave a command about *roafting* it, Exod. xii. 9. " eat not of it raw, nor fodden at all with water, but roaft with fire." Firft, God forbids the eating it *raw*. Not that this is to be underftood of what is quite raw: for the Ifraelites knew this of themfelves. They were not fo voracious, as ufually to feed on flefh altogether undreffed. It is therefore, meant of that which is not fodden or roafted *enough*, as the Jewifh maf-ters well explain it. For in that great hurry, with which the firft paffover was enforced, and in fo great a number of pafchal lambs, it might eafily happen, that fome of them might be only half done, or fcorched, unlefs the lawgiver had provided againft it by an exprefs command. A thing not without its myftery, as we fhall prefently fee. But it was not fufficient to have the lamb perfectly done, unlefs alfo done in that manner which God prefcribed, namely, *roafted*, not *boiled*. This was quite otherwife, than in the other peace-offerings, whofe flefh was cuftomarily boiled, in order to be eaten both by the people and the priefts, even at the pafchal folemnity. Wherefore, 2 Chron. xxxv. 13. thefe things are accurately diftinguifhed: " and they roafted the paffover with fire, according to the ordinance, but the other holy offerings, fod they in pots, and in caldrons, and in pans." Where obferve, that in both cafes the word בשל is ufed, to fhew that it is applied both to boiling and roafting, ac-cording to the nature of the fubject.

XXIV. The roafting is followed by the *eating* it. Where firft, we are to obferve the drefs or attire of thofe who were to eat it, which they were to do, with their loins girded, their fhoes on their feet, and their ftaff in their hand, Exod. xii. 11. which is the drefs of travellers, and of thofe, who un-dertake fomething laborious. For the garments of the orien-tals, being long and flowing, and generally ungirded, were to
be

be tucked up, when either they addressed themselves to a journey, or some laborious work, that they might be no impediment to them, 2 Kings iv. 29.   And a *person girded*, does not
seldom denote an *industrious person*, whom the Greeks call
*ἄζωνος ἀνὴρ, a man well girded*, and the Hebrews יזמ   And none
is ignorant, that a *staff* is proper for a journey, as travellers are
supported in dangerous places, and defend themselves with it
against aggressors and wild beasts; see Gen xxxii. 10. Mark v. 8.
Nor was the rod of Moses, which is so celebrated, any thing
but a traveller's staff, Exod. iv. 2.

XXV. Their being commanded to eat the passover with *shoes
on their feet*, seems to be to the same purpose.   For it is probable, while the Israelites were in Egypt, they were generally
without shoes; at least they did not use them daily, during
their severe bondage.   As in the flourishing state of the Jews,
we have examples of persons being unshod even in Judea.   As
this want of shoes was less hazardous to the Israelites in Egypt,
God was pleased to provide them with shoes, when they were
now to undertake a tedious, hard, and rough journey: In other
cases, one's being bare-footed, was a sign of submission and devotion, Exod. iii. 5.   Hence that saying of the Pythagoric
school, " do thy religious worship and adoration bare-footed."
And Bernice, the sister of king Agrippa, *came bare-footed before
the tribunal*, to prefer her suit to Florus, who exercised great
cruelties against the Jews, Joseph. de Bell. Jud. lib. 2. c. 15.
This putting on of shoes, was not therefore a part of religious
worship, but a symbol of their approaching journey.

XXVI. We shall not grudge to subjoin, because of the affinity of the subject, what Zaba Zago relates, in *Damianus a
Goes*, concerning the manners of the Ethiopians.   He affirms,
they cannot enter their churches, but unshod.   Because, says he,
" the Ethiopic churches are not like that country, where the people of Israel eat the paschal lamb on their departure out of Egypt,
in which place God commanded them to eat it with shoes on
their feet, and their loins girded, on account of the defilement
of the country; but are like mount Sinai, where God spoke to
Moses; saying, Moses, Moses, put off thy shoes from off thy
feet, for the place whereon thou standest is holy ground.   And
this mount Sinai is the parent from which churches have derived
their origin; just as the apostles from the prophets, and the
New Testament from the Old."   Thus far he: but the observation appears to me, to be idle and silly: like those to which the
easterns are too much addicted.

XXVII. But to return from this digression.   Moreover,
God was, Exod. xviii. pleased to command them to eat the
                                                            passover

paſſover with *unleavened bread, and bitter herbs*. Plutarch relates, that among the Romans, the Flamen Dialis, or prieſt of Jupiter was forbid the uſe of leaven, in Quæſt. Roman. Becauſe, as leaven ariſes from a ſtate of corruption, ſo alſo when it is mixed, it corrupts the lump. Nor was only the paſchal lamb to be eaten with unleavened bread, but God commanded the Iſraelites to abſtain from leaven, for whole ſeven days, Exod. xii. 15. Since the five intermediate days of theſe ſeven were working-days, God ordered the firſt and laſt to be accounted feſtivals : for as on the firſt they we ſet at liberty, from ſuch a hard and grievous bondage, ſo on the ſeventh, the Red Sea ſwallowed up Pharoah and all his hoſt. And this divine inſtitution was ſerved to perpetuate the memory of both theſe among his people. But of what ſort theſe bitter herbs were, we are neither much inclined to enquire, nor is it of great importance. Whoever would know the opinions of the Jewiſh maſters on this head, may conſult our great author (Bochart.) We haſten to other matters.

XXVIII. God alſo forbid them, to break ſo much as a bone of the paſchal lamb, Exod. xviii. 46. Numb. ix. 12. This law ſeems likewiſe to have a reference to their being commanded to eat it in haſte ; for they who are in hurry do not ſpend time in breaking and taking the marrow out of the bones. But a myſtery alſo lay concealed in this law, of which preſently.

XXIX. There was another law, not to leave any of the fleſh of the lamb until the morning, but to burn what remained thereof, Exod. xii. 10. Of this kind, were the laws, in all ſacred feaſts, ſee Exod. xvi. 19. Lev. vii. 15. and Lev. xxii. 30. excepting only the fleſh of the offering of a vow, or a voluntary offering, Lev. vii. 16, 17. The deſign of theſe laws, was to preſerve the ſacred food, from corruption, and from being put to profane uſes. In the lamb, they were to take ſpecial care, that its remains ſhould neither hinder nor clog the Iſraelites, who were now to depart : nor yield matter of deriſion to the Egyptians nor become a prey to dogs. And perhaps alſo to prevent their becoming an object of idolatry, as the brazen ſerpent was.

XXX. Moreover, God commanded, that none ſhould go out of the door of his houſe until the morning, Exod. xii. 22. leaſt they ſhould meet with the deſtroying angel, who, indeed, could have diſtinguiſhed the Iſraelites, even out of their houſes ; but they were to be taught, that their ſafety conſiſted in keeping themſelves, as it were under the protection of the blood of the lamb, with which they had ſprinkled the poſts of their doors.

If

If they had rejected this facrament of their fecurity, they would thereby have alfo rendered themfelves unworthy of the grace that was reprefented by that fign.

XXXI. In fine, it was ordained to be eaten in one houfe, and none of the flefh to be carried out, Exod. xii. 46. This law feems to be joined with ver. 4. in which thofe families, which were fo fmall, as not to be able to eat a whole lamb, are commanded to join with their neighbouring families. But here left any fhould think, that the lamb could be halved, and one half carried out to the abfent family, the law directs two families joining together, to eat the lamb in one houfe, and carry none of its flefh abroad. Becaufe fo falutary a victim could not be divided : and nothing but an entire lamb in every houfe, could refcue that houfe from the imminent deftruction.

XXXII. But we are to obferve, that fome of thofe ceremonies, were perpetual; as the killing, roafting, and eating the lamb, with unleavened bread, and bitter herbs, without breaking a bone, &c. others again were ufed only once, and no where elfe but in Egypt. To this may we reckon. 1ft, The law concerning the keeping up the lamb for the fpace of four days, before it was to be killed. God would have this done in Egypt, leaft the Ifraelites, when among their enraged enemies, fhould not have lambs, if they were obliged to look out for them, only at the very laft : but in Judea they had nothing to fear of this kind : and it would have been no eafy matter for thofe who came a great way to the city, to provide themfelves precifely at that time, as the greateft part, did not come till the preparation for the feaft, or at moft, the day before, and then purchafed from thefe who ufually expofed lambs to fale in the temple. John ii. 13, 14. It alfo appears, from the hiftory of Chrift's laft paffover, that the difciples afked their mafter, only on the firft day of unleavened bread, " where wilt thou that we go and prepare, that thou mayeft eat the paffover ?" Mark xiv. 12. Confequently they had not kept up a lamb four days before. 2dly, The law concerning ftriking the lintel, and fidepofts with the blood of the lamb: becaufe the reafon which God gave for this command, could only refpect Egypt, Exod. xii. 12, 13. And from 2 Chron. xxx. 15, 16. and chap. xxxv. 5, 6, 10, 11. we learn, that in Judea, the pafchal lambs were killed in the court of the temple, and there their blood was poured out. Nor does it appear that any part of this blood was carried into private houfes, to be fprinkled on their doorpofts. 3dly, The law concerning the eating the paffover, with their loins girded, with fhoes on their feet, a ftaff in their hands, and with hafte. Becaufe thefe things had a refpect to that long and tedious journey, they were in a few hours to take : but after they had performed that journey, they ate it quietly and ungirded, not ftanding, but fitting. not in hafte, but at lei- fure ; as is plain from the example of Chrift, who fat down on a couch, in an upper room with his difciples. 4thly, The law not to ftir abroad out of their houfes, leaft they fhould meet the deftroying angel: as in like manner appears from the ex- ample of Chrift, and his difciples, who, in that very night, in which they kept the paffover, repaired to the mount of Olives, Mat. xxvi. 30.

XXXIII. It now remains, that we explain, and briefly fhew, the *myftery* of the paffover, and to what all this pomp of cere- monies tended. And in general, it is certain, that two benefits were fhadowed forth thereby ; the one temporary, and peculiar to the people of Ifrael ; the other eternal, and common to all true believers in Chrift. On the former we fhall curforily hint a few things: on the latter be more diftinct and explicit.

XXXIV. And, 1ft, The very name *pafcha*, which, as we have faid, fignifies a paffing over, reminded the Ifraelites of the angel, who paffed over their houfes, without touching them, in that night, in which he fell on the Egyptians, in fuch a manner, that not a houfe was free from the flaughter, Exod. xii. 30. 2dly, The bitter herbs, with which they were to eat the lamb, fignified, the *bitter life* they had led in Egypt, *under hard bond- age, in mortar, and in brick,* Exod. i. 14. fo that they juftly might cry out, as they afterwards did in the Babylonifh captivity, Lam. iii. 15. that they *were filled with bitternefs, and made drunken with wormwood.* This they teftified in the paffover, faying to each other, as Maimonides de Pafch. c. 2. §. 40. re- lates, " we have eaten that bitter thing, becaufe the Egyptians embittered the life of our fathers in Egypt, as it is written," Exod. i. 14. 3dly, The unleavened bread alfo, which was but little grateful to the palate, was eaten for the fame end. Wherefore the mafter of the family, when he diftributed the pieces of it to his domeftics, addreffed them thus : " this is the bread of affliction, which our fathers did eat in the land of E- gypt," in the very words of Mofes, Deut. xvi. 3. They there- fore fet down the unleavened bread only in pieces, becaufe not whole, but pieces of bread are given to the poor. 4thly, Moft of the other rites fignified to the Ifraelites, that, being now called to liberty by God, they were as foon as poffible to betake themfelves out of that ftate of bondage. And therefore they are commanded to eat in a ftanding pofture, with their loins girded, with fhoes on their feet, and leaning on their ftaves, and in hafte, becaufe that very moment they were to depart. They were

were not to eat it boiled, but roasted, that being sooner done: and with unleavened bread, that they might not slip the opportunity of departing, should they stay, till the lump was leavened. 5thly, However, as it is necessary to explain dumb signs by words; so, when their children asked what this ceremony meant, they were commanded to answer; " this is the sacrifice of the Lord's passover, who passed over the houses of the children of Israel in Egypt, when he smote the Egyptians, and delivered our houses," Exod. xii. 27.

XXXV. But a deeper mystery was vailed under these things, of which we are now to speak. And that we may do it with greater exactness, we will shew, that four things are represented by this sacrament. I. The very person of Christ. II. The sufferings he bore for us. III. The fruits of his sufferings. IV. The manner we are made partakers of them.

XXXVI. The scriptures frequently represent the *person* of Christ under the type of a *lamb*, John i. 29, 36. On account of his meekness and humility, Mat. xi. 29. the simplicity of his manners, 1 Pet. i. 19. his extraordinary patience, Isa. liii. 7. which was the more amazing in him, that though he was able to take vengeance and deliver himself, yet he voluntarily submitted, and, by an astonishing transformation from the lion of the tribe of Judah became a lamb: and thus Samson's riddle was fulfilled in Christ, " out of the eater came forth meat, and out of the strong came forth sweetness," Judges xiv. 14. This same lamb feeds us with his flesh, gives us his blood to drink, and in fine, clothes us with his wool, Rom. xiii. 14. Gal. iii. 27. But there were peculiar circumstances in the paschal-lamb.

XXXVII. For *first*, as the lamb was taken out of the flock, so also was Christ from among his brethren, Deut. xviii. 15. being a " partaker of flesh and blood, and in all things like unto his brethren," Heb. ii. 14, 17. *Secondly*, The lamb was to be perfect; Christ in like manner, is " a lamb without blemish and without spot," 1 Pet. i. 19. " who through the eternal Spirit, offered himself without spot to God," Heb. ix. 14. *Thirdly*, The same lamb was to be a male, a symbol of vigour, strength and excellency. So Christ also is that *man*, Jer. xxxi. 22. the *man-child*, Rev. xii. 5. *Fourthly*, It was to be of the first year, that is, young and of a most grateful savour, and of the greatest vigour: in order to represent, (1.) That Christ was not to continue long among men, but to be cut off in the flower of his age. (2.) That he is the sweetest food of the soul, beyond all the dainties of this world, Cant. v. 16. (3.) That his sacrifice is of perpetual, and of the greatest efficacy. *Fifthly*, Nor is it in vain, that the lamb was, for the space of four days, separated from the fold. Thus also it was with Christ, if we reckon prophetic days, for years: see Ezek. iv. 6. For at his thirtieth year, he left his mother's house, as a fold, where he was born and brought up, and was crucified the fourth after. But it likewise deserves observation, that Christ came to Jerusalem to the feast, and to his last passover, on that very day, on which God had commanded the lamb to be kept up in Egypt; namely, the tenth of the month Nisan. For, six days before the passover, he came to Bethany, John xii. 1. That is, on the ninth of the month Nisan: the day after he went to Jerusalem, ver. 11. to present himself to be offered to God.

XXXVIII. Let us now consider the *sufferings* of Christ, the manner, place, and time, these being all signified by the passover.

XXXIX. As to the *manner*. 1st, The lamb was to be killed, and that by the whole multitude of the congregation of Israel. So the priests, scribes, and pharisees, with the whole body of the people conspired to the slaying of Christ; for not being satisfied with mockings, smitings, and scourgings, they ceased not, till he was given up to death, Luke xxiii. 18. and " they cried out, all at once, saying, away with this man. 2dly, There is likewise an argument as to the kind of death. For, as the blood of the lamb, so that of Christ was also shed: both for the people. Nor was the blood of the lamb poured out on the ground, but, as something precious, received in a bason; because it represented the " precious blood of Christ, as of a lamb without spot," 1 Pet. i. 19. For, that blood is the perpetual treasure of the church, which Christ even at this day offers to the Father,' and is for ever to offer, or present. 3dly, The lamb was not to be eaten raw, or not sufficiently done. Christ was also to suffer indeed, and not in a superficial manner. His cup was not to pass, till it was drunk up to the bottom. 4thly, The roasting of the lamb at the fire, expresses the burning heat of divine wrath, justly kindled against sinners, with which Christ, who presented himself as surety for sinners, was to be scorched. Hence those complaints, Psal. xxii. 14, 15. " My heart is like wax, it is melted in the midst of my bowels: my strength is dried up like a potsherd, and my tongue cleaveth to my jaws." See what we have observed concerning the peculiar manner of this roasting, Book II. Chap. 10. §. 26.

XL. The *place*, where both the passover and Christ was slain, is exactly the same. For the paschal lamb, was, from the days of David, to be killed at Jerusalem; the place which God had chosen for himself, to cause his name to dwell there. But it was there that Christ suffered, as himself foretold. " It cannot
be

be that a prophet perish out of Jerusalem," Luke xii. 33. And Luke xviii. 31. " Behold, we go up to Jerusalem, and all things that are written by the prophets concerning the Son of man, shall be accomplished." '

XLI. There is also a manifest similitude with respect to the *time.* The passover was killed in the middle of the month Nisan, at the full moon, between the two evenings, that is, according to Josephus, from the ninth to the eleventh. hour. On that very month, day and hour, Christ was cut off; as is remarked, not without reason, by Matthew, chap. xxvii. 46, 50. Some observe, that, in the month Nisan,' after the equinox, the days come to be longer than the nights; to signify that a new light then arose upon the world, when Christ dispelled the darkness of error, and ignorance. And there are others, who, by the full moon, will have the fulness of time, and by the two evenings, the evening of the world, and the last times to be shadowed forth, in which Christ offered himself a sacrifice, according to that of the apostle, Heb. ix. 26. " once in the end of the world hath he appeared, to put away sin by the sacrifice of himself." Which, are at least ingenious, if not solid reflections.

XLII. It now follows, that we consider the consequences and *fruits* of this sacrifice; and indeed, they are most excellent and abundant. For, *first,* the posts and lintels of the Israelites were sprinkled with the blood of this lamb, that they might avoid the common calamity, and be preserved from the destroying angel: to teach us, that the justice of God spares all, whose consciences are sprinkled with the blood of Christ, Isa. lii. 15. " he shall sprinkle many nations." This is that *sprinkling of the blood* of Christ, this is that *blood of sprinkling,* spoken of by Peter and Paul, 1 Pet. i. 2. Heb. xii. 24. We are therefore no longer to dread the sword of the avenging angel. For, whether an angel of darkness, " God hath delivered us from the power of darkness, through the blood of his Son," Col. i. 13, 14. or an angel of heaven, " having made peace through his blood, he hath reconciled all things unto himself, whether they be things in earth, or things in heaven," ver. 20.

XLIII. *Secondly,* On the night the lamb was slain, the Israelites received full power to deliver themselves from the Egyptian bondage: to teach us, that Christ, by his blood, has redeemed us from the bondage of the devil, the world and sin, in order to call us to the glorious liberty of the sons of God, Heb. ii. 14, 15. John viii. 36.

XLIV. *Thirdly,* In that very night the God of Israel inflicted his judgments on the gods of the Egyptians, Exod. xii. 12.

Numb.

Numb. xxxiii. 4. namely, four judgments, if we may credit Jonathan, whofe words in his paraphrafe are thefe: " Their molten images were melted down, their idols of ftone cut down, thofe made of earth, ground to powder; in fine, thofe of wood reduced to afhes." Though we cannot avouch this for truth, as the fcripture is filent; yet it is certain, God's threatenings were not without their effect. And whatever they fignified, we fee an illuftrious fulfilment of them in the death of Chrift; whereby, the middle wall of partition being broken down, by which many nations, who had been feparated from the Jews, being called to the knowledge of the true God, caft their idols to the moles, and to the bats, Ifa. ii. 20.

XLV. *Fourthly*, As the month Abib, before the inftitution of the paffover, was the feventh month of the Jewifh year: but when God inftituted the paffover, he commanded, that it fhould for the future, be accounted the firft, and from it begin to reckon their facred or ecclefiaftical year. This month began with the fpring; at which time, when God fendeth forth his Spirit, all things are created, and the face of the earth is renewed, Pfal. civ. 30. And this may alfo be applied to Chrift, who introduced a new age, and abolifhed old things, in order to change them for the better: *behold*, fays he, *I make all things new*, Rev. xxi. 5. So that now we juftly reckon time, not from the firft creation of the world, which feems to have happened on Tifri, the firft month of the civil year, but from the rifing of a more aufpicious ftar, at the illuftrious epiphany or manifeftation of our Saviour: for, fuch new miracles of divine goodnefs caufe former things, in comparifon of *thefe, not to be remembered, nor come into mind*, Ifa. lxv. 17.

XLVI. Moreover, we are to fhew, in *what manner* the Ifraelites were made partakers of the benefits they obtained by means of the lamb. And here two things were required. 1ft, That they were to fprinkle the lintel and door-pofts of their houfes with the blood of the lamb. 2dly, To eat its flefh. For if any of the Ifraelites neglected either of thefe, they thereby rejected the grace annexed to thefe commands.

XLVII. By the door-pofts of the houfes are meant our hearts, becaufe God fprinkles thefe with the blood of his Son, Heb. x. 22. " our hearts fprinkled from an evil confcience." And the hearts of men lie as open before God, as the door-pofts of our houfes to us, 1 Sam. xvi. 7. the doors of our hearts are to be fet open, that by them the king of glory may come in, Pfal. xxiv. 7. Rev. iii. 20. But we may be faid to fprinkle our hearts with the blood of Chrift, when, by a ftedfaft faith, we embrace the doctrine of the crofs, and apply to ourfelves the merits of

his

his fufferings. We are however, to take care that we do not fprinkle on the threfhhold, what we are commanded to fprinkle on the lintel, and pofts of the door, that it may not be trampled under foot, leaft the apoftle's threatenings fhould be executed on us, which he denounced againft thofe, who " tread under foot the Son of God, and account the blood of the covenant, wherewith they were fanctified, an unholy thing," Heb. x. 29.

XLVIII. By the fame faith alfo, the flefh is to be eaten. For why haft thou teeth, and a ftomach ? [Is it not to eat?] Believe, and thou haft eaten. This eating is abfolutely neceffary to falvation, John vi. 53. " Verily, verily, I fay unto you, except ye eat the flefh of the Son of man, ye have no life in you.

XLIX. The flefh of the lamb was to be eaten neither altogether raw, nor half done. And they are guilty of this crime, who digeft not thefe myfteries by proper and diligent meditation : meditation is to the foul, what concoction or digeftion is to the ftomach. Hence according to Petronius, to publifh to the public indigefted thoughts, is to publifh things not yet properly concocted and digefted by an attentive meditation.

L. The whole lamb was likewife to be eaten, that nothing might remain : neither is it fufficient to receive Chrift in part : as if one would be willing to enjoy his glory, but not partake of his fufferings. Or to have him for his Redeemer, but not for his Lawgiver and Lord : or as if one, not thinking it fufficient to truft in the merits of Chrift, fhould place his hope of falvation, partly in his own works, or in the interceffion and mediation of others.

LI. What remained that could not be confumed, becaufe of the fmall number of guefts, was not fuffered to be referved to the next day ; but was to be burnt with fire. This may be applied partly to the type, partly to the thing fignified. The type was not to be referved to another time. From the day the light of the gofpel appeared, what regarded the fhadows, was to ceafe and be abolifhed. As to the thing fignified, whoever feeds upon Chrift by a true faith, will not be found empty, or hungry on the morrow; nor does he ftand in need of a new Chrift, or a new offering of him. For as " by one offering he hath perfected for ever them that are fanctified," Heb. x. 14. fo " he that cometh to him fhall never hunger, and he that believeth on him fhall never thirft," John vi. 35. Wherefore, thou art under no neceffity to referve any thing of thine own for thyfelf, with which to make up a deficiency in Chrift, when thou haft once apprehended him by faith.

LII. In the mean time, they were fo to eat the flefh of the lamb,

lamb, as not to break a bone of it. To break the bones of the lamb, is to pry and search into things that exceed our capacity. As if it was not sufficient for faith to be fed with things obvious, unless we attempted to search into those things, the knowledge of which is forbidden, and the discovery dangerous. To pry into such things, is to come off with damage in the attempt. This brings to mind, that saying of Moses, Deut. xxix. 29. "the secret things belong unto the Lord our God; but those things which are revealed, belong unto us and to our children for ever:" and that excellent saying of Jerome, Prov. xxv. 27. though not so agreeable to the Hebrew, "the curious pryer into his majesty, shall be overwhelmed with his glory."

LIII. The bitter herbs, with which the lamb was to be eaten, signify the necessity of communion with him in his sufferings, Phil. iii. 10. if we would have communion with him in his glory: we are to wear a crown of thorns with Christ, that a crown of glory may succeed; "if we suffer, we shall also reign with him," 2 Tim. ii. 12. Nor are these things to be applied only to the external afflictions of the body; but also to the internal distresses of the vexed soul, grieving for sin in a godly manner, fearing the wrath of God; without which the sweet consolations of the Lord Jesus, which he applies only to the mourners in Zion, Isa. lxi. 3. are usually neither tasted nor felt.

LIV. Nor is it in vain, that leaven is so often, and so expressly forbid those, who are invited to eat of the lamb. For in Scripture leaven is the symbol of corruption, and especially of hypocrisy, Luke xii. 1. Paul has writ very properly to this purpose, 1 Cor. v. 7, 8. "Christ our passover is sacrificed for us: therefore let us keep the feast, not with old leaven, neither with leaven of malice and wickedness, but with the unleavened bread of sincerity and truth." Leaven might also be applied to pride, because the leavened lump directly rises or puffs up; or to hatred and animosity, which embitter the soul. Now whoever has communion with Christ, ought doubtless to be purged from all these vices; because he, in whose mouth was found no guile, 1 Pet. ii. 22. cannot endure hypocrites; nor he, who became obedient even unto the death of the cross, Phil. ii. 8. the proud; nor he, who is our peace, Eph. ii. 14. the contentious; and therefore he offered himself, in order to reconcile us both to God, and to one another.

LV. But strangers, the defiled, the uncircumcised, were excluded from the paschal lamb: because righteousness hath no fellowship with unrighteousness, nor light any communion with darkness, nor Christ any concord with Belial, 2 Cor. vi. 14, 15. Nevertheless whoever he be, that from a sense of his

own

own uncleannefs, humbly has recourfe to the grace of God in Chrift, ought not therefore to defpond ; for, " the good Jehovah pardoneth every one that prepareth his heart to feek God, Jehovah the God of his fathers, though he be not cleanfed according to the purification of the fanctuary," 2 Chron. xxx. 18, 19.

LVI. Again, the Ifraelites in Egypt were commanded to eat the lamb, girded, fhod, and leaning on their ftaves. To which rites we may fee frequent allufions in Scripture. Chrift, Luke xii. 35. Paul, Eph. vi. 14. and Peter, 1 Pet. i. 3. commands us to have our loins girded about: to fignify that the fouls of believers are to be girded about with truth and fobernefs ; to be ready for the heavenly journey, for the work of the Lord, for the conflict with fpiritual wickedneffes in heavenly places ; to all which undertakings, flowing, and trailing garments, are an impediment. Paul, Eph. vi. 15. fpeaks of feet fhod with the preparation, or promptitude, of the gofpel of peace. For the gofpel is to be preached with cheerfulnefs, and confeffed and walked in without ftumbling. God himfelf is the believer's ftaff, on whom he leans, and to whom he commends his foul. Faith alfo is inftead of a ftaff, becaufe by it we are faid to ftand, Rom. xi. 20. 1 Cor. vi. 13. But we are to take particular notice, that this is the attire of travellers, which is the condition of all who are partakers of Chrift For, in this life they are ftrangers, and in their way to a better country, Pf. xxxix. 13. 1 Pet. ii. 11.

LVII. The Ifraelites were alfo commanded to eat it in hafte, becaufe there was danger in delay from the Egyptians, who were foon to prefs them to be gone. And this is alfo applicable to us ; becaufe many enemies have a defign upon us, the journey is long, the time fhort, and we feeble and eafily apt to flag. Wherefore, as Lot was to go out of Sodom, and the Ifraelites out of Egypt, fo we are commanded to make hafte, to ftretch every nerve in order to efcape the jaws of the devil, imitating thofe violent who take the kingdom of heaven by force, Mat. xi. 12. and remembering Lot's wife, who perifhed by her delay, Luke xvii. 32.

LVIII. Laftly, We are to obferve, that the lamb was to be eaten in one houfe, out of which it was not lawful to go, for fear of meeting the angel of death. This houfe is the church, out of which there is no falvation, no communion with Chrift. Let the falfe Nicodemifts take notice of this, who imagine they can fkulk in fafety among the Egyptians, and think it fufficient if they believe in their heart, though with their mouth they confefs not the Lord Jefus, feparating what the apoftle has joined together, Rom. x. 9. And therefore, if they be wife, let them not forfake the affembling themfelves together with us, Heb. x. 20. And having once entered this houfe, let them never leave it, leaft they be condemned for apoftates; concern- ing whom Paul fpeaks, Heb. vi. 4—6. and chap. x. 38, 39. and Peter, 2 Pet. ii. 20, 21.

---

## CHAP. X.

*Of the extraordinary Sacraments in the Wildernefs.*

I. **B**ESIDES the *ordinary* and *univerfal* facraments of *circum- cifion* and the *paffover*, fome extraordinary fymbols of divine grace were granted to the Ifraelites in the wildernefs, which, in the New Teftament, are applied to Chrift and his benefits, and faid to have the fame fignification with our facraments. And they are in order thefe: I. The *paffage* in the cloud *through the Red Sea.* II. The *manna* which was rained from heaven. III. The *water* iffuing out of the *rock.* IV. The *brazen ferpent* erected by Mofes for the cure of the Ifraelites.

II. The facred hiftory, Exod. xiv. very particularly relates, how Pharaoh with mad rage at the head of a vaft army, pur- fued the Ifraelites, who were juft departed from Egypt, and as he imagined, were entangled on every hand, through a miftake of the way, in unpaffable deferts: how in the firft place, a miraculous cloud, interpofing between them and the Egyptians, protected the Ifraelites, who were trembling with fear, and calling out to heaven for help: next how the channel of the weedy or Red Sea, was made paffable, as on dry land, by the waters giving way on each hand, being divided by the rod of Mofes and by a ftrong eaft wind. How, in fine, the Egyptian monarch did not delay to purfue them clofe as they retreated, entered the fea as it opened a way for them, and was deftroyed with all his army, the waters immediately returning upon them. For the better underftanding of all this, we fhall briefly explain thefe five heads. I. Why that fea, which Mofes, Exod. xiii. 18. and xiv. 4. called סוף ים, or the *weedy fea;* is by Paul, Heb. xi. 29. and generally by writers, called η ερυθρα θαλασσα, *the Red Sea?* II. Whether that drying up of the waters was natural, or altogether miraculous? III. Whether the Ifraelites paffed over the whole breadth of the fea, and landed on the Arabian fhore over againft Egypt, or only marched as far through it, as was enough

enough to overwhelm the Egyptians, and returned again on foot, by taking a femicircular compafs, to the fame fhore? IV. In what fenfe the apoftle might fay, the "Ifraelites were baptifed unto Mofes in the cloud and in the fea." V. What may be the myftical fignification of thefe things?

III. The reafon is obvious why this is called the weedy fea; namely, becaufe of the plenty of fea weeds, with which it a-bounds, heaps of which being raifed like mountains near the fhore, and laid clofe together by the continual heat of the fun, afford the convenience of houfes to the inhabitants there, who from their eating of fifh are called *Ichthyophagi*. And Aga-tharcides fays, that fome of them live *under the ribs of fifh, covered over with fea weed*. *Bochart in Phaleg. Lib. 4. c. 22.* may be confulted on this fubject.

IV. Why it is called the Red or Erythrean Sea, was formerly not fo well known. The ancients generally referred it to the colour of the water; which fome think was derived from the reflection of the folar rays; others from the circumjacent mountains being made red by the fcorching heat, from which waters impetuoufly defcended into the fea, and tinged it of a like colour; others, in fine, from the red fand that lay on its fhore, or channel: not to mention any thing now about the fable of Perfeus, who, after having killed the fea-monfter, to which the daughter of Cepheus had been expofed, is faid there to have wafhed away the blood, with which he was all over ftained. But the undoubted experience of mariners fhews the falfehood of all this. Ludovicus Vartomannus, who failed over the whole of it almoft from its extremity to the mouth of the ftraits, fays, " it is a thing fufficiently confeffed by all, that the faid fea is not red, but like other feas, *Navig. lib. 1. c. 21.* The fame thing Pietro della Valle, a noble Roman, an eye-witnefs, teftifies; who fays the waters are clear, tranfparent and blue, and the fand of the ufual colour, nay, whiter than ours, *Itiner. p. 1. c. 30.* Diodorus Siculus writes, that *in co-lour it is altogether green*. Not that fuch is the nature of the water, but on account of the quantity of mofs and fea-weed floating theron. What is therefore faid of the red colour is all fable, this prejudice having arifen from an erroneous interpre-tation of the name.

V. They come nearer the truth, who derive its name from king Erythras or Erythrus, who had this fea within the bounds of his empire. But who this Erythras was, all the profane writers are abfolutely ignorant. The Scriptures alone inform us of this: from which *Nic. Fuller, Mifcellan. lib. 4. c. 20.* boafts that he made the firft difcovery: namely, that this Erythras

was

was Efau, furnamed Edom or Red, both from the hairy rednefs, with which he was born, Gen. xxv. 25. and from that red pottage, for which he fold his birthright, ver. 30. This Edom, who, according to the genius of thofe times, having the whole authority in thofe parts, gave name to the country reduced under his dominion and power, fo that it was alfo called *the land* of Edom, and even fimply Edom, namely of the feminine gender, Jer. xlix. 17. His pofterity, proud of fo great an original of their nation, lived on the borders of the fea, we are now treating of: and hence it had its name: the Hebrew Edomi or Idumean Sea, the Greek ἐρυθραῖον, and the Latin *Mare rubrum* differ therefore only in language. See among others *Voffius de Idololat. lib.* 1. *c.* 34.

VI. We are on no account to imagine, that what we are here told, befel the waters of the Red Sea, was either altogether, or for the greateft part natural: as if Mofes, who had great fkill in the knowledge of nature, took the opportunity of an ordinary reflux, which, on the blowing of an eaft wind, was both more impetuous and lafting than ufual; ventured in the prefent imminent danger, to attempt the paffage, and perfuaded the Ifraelites to follow his example: but Pharaoh, who was ignorant of thofe things, and delaying too long, was drowned on the return of the flood. For, the whole of this hiftory is full of miracles; which none but the *enemies of the Scripture,* as *Scaliger, de Subtilitat. Exercit.* 52. juftly calls them, can doubt of. 1ft, It was a miracle, that the extraordinary cloud, which went before, and pointed out the way to the Hebrews, fhould now place itfelf in the middle, between them and the Egyptians, Exod. xiv. 19. 2dly, It was a miracle, that when Mofes lifted up his rod, and ftretched out his hand, the fea fhould not only go back, but was alfo divided; and giving way on each hand, yield a fafe paffage to Ifrael amidft the waters, ver. 16, 21. which never was, nor could be done by any natural reflux. 3dly, It is a miracle, that the waters, naturally fluid, fhould be collected together into very high heaps, and ftand like a wall on the right and left of the Ifraelites, ver. 22. 4thly, It was a miracle of miracles, that when Mofes again ftretched out his hand and rod towards that part of the fea, where the Egyptians were purfuing them, the waters fhould return to their natural force, and drown all the Egyptians; while the children of Ifrael had now either almoft finifhed, or were ftill profecuting their journey on dry land, through the midft of the fea, ver. 26, 27, 29. Can any mortal have fo much impudence, as to dare to compare thefe things with the daily flux and reflux of the fea? It is indeed true, that God here made ufe of the wind, but it is

alfo

alſo evident, that the ſame God exerted an extraordinary power, both by raiſing the wind ſo ſeaſonably, and by executing ſuch things by it, as could not be effected by any natural cauſe, by its own virtue. And therefore the Iſraelites deſervedly admired in this work, *that great hand of their God*, ver. 31.

VII. The inhabitants on the coaſt of the Arabian Gulf, though barbarous to the higheſt degree, preſerved the memory of this prodigy for many ages after; as Diodorus Siculus vouches, *lib.* 3. where he writes as follows. " The neighbouring Ichthyophagi have an ancient tradition, handed down to them by their anceſtors, that, upon a certain great receſs of the ſea, all the parts of this bay being dried up, and the ſea falling back to oppoſite parts, the channel appeared of a green colour, and that again the ſea, returning with a ſtrong tide, was reſtored to its former place." In theſe words, who does not ſee that this miracle of Moſes is deſcribed, the memory of which theſe barbarians did, though ſomewhat obſcurely, propagate to their poſterity ?

VIII. But it is a more intricate point, which is even at this day made the ſubject of debate among the learned; whether the Hebrews paſſed the ſea ſtraight forward, from the ſhore of Egypt, to the oppoſite coaſt of Arabia; or whether they fetched a ſemicircular compaſs in the midſt of the ſea, and returned to the ſame ſhore, from which they ſet out ? The former opinion is by far more commonly received; and reſts on thoſe arguments, collected by Rivet in Exod. xiv. 21. 1ſt, The words of the hiſtory ſeem to bear this meaning; and it tends very much to ſhew the greatneſs of the miracle. The Scripture ſays, that the " Iſraelites paſſed through the Red Sea;" but what others alledge was not a *tranſit* or paſſage, but a *circuit*. 2dly, It appears from the map of the country, that it muſt have been ſo. For, in order to come from Egypt to mount Sinai, as the Red Sea lies between that mountain and Egypt, it muſt of neceſſity be paſſed over. For, though the foot paſſage from Rameſes to Sinai is direct, leaving the Red Sea on one ſide, yet ſo blocked up, and every where ſo rough on account of rocks, as not to be fit for the journeying of ſo great a people. 3dly, The ſame is concluded from Numb. xxxiii. 8. " and they departed from before Pi-hahiroth, and paſſed through the midſt of the ſea into the wilderneſs;" which ſeems to denote quite a different thing, from their returning by a circuit, or compaſs to the wilderneſs. 4thly, Add the authority of Joſephus, who declares, that the Iſraelites paſſed over to the oppoſite ſhore, Antiq. lib. 2. c. ult.

IX. But the contrary opinion has alſo great names, and no
mean

mean arguments to fupport it. 1ft, They defire us to take notice of the intent of the paffage through the fea: which was, the drowning of the Egyptians, and by that means to manifeft the glory of God to the people all around. And therefore it is probable, the Egyptians were thrown out on that part of the fhore which was neareft to Egypt, that the judgment of God might be manifefted to that kingdom. 2dly, They obferve, that the part of the Red Sea, which the Ifraelites paffed over, is diftant from the oppofite fhore at leaft fix, others fay, fifteen leagues: which journey, it feems, could not poffibly be accomplifhed by fo great an army, together with their children, women, and baggage, in the compafs of a fhort night as was done here, ver. 21, 23. 3dly, It appears from Exod. xiii. 20. that before the Ifraelites entered into the fea, they encamped in the wildernefs of Etham, in the border of the wildernefs. And yet after their coming out of the fea, they again proceeded to the wildernefs of Etham, Numb. xxiii. 8. They confequently returned to the fame fhore, but at a greater diftance from the place, from which they fet out. This argument cannot be anfwered, but by faying, either that there were two wildernefles of the fame name, on each fide of the Red Sea, which Lyranus does, or that the whole country, quite to mount Sinai, went under the fame appellation, according to Rivet: but whether this can be proved, is matter of inquiry. 4thly, They add, that the Red Sea does not lie between Egypt and mount Sinai, but that the journey by land is directly performed with camels and other cattle. Of this may be feen the *Itinerarium of della Valle* p 1. c 27, 28. 5thly, The argument for the contrary fentiment, taken from its being faid, that the Ifraelites *paffed* through the Red Sea feems to be of little weight. For, the facred hiftory ufes very general terms, " and they went into the midft of the fea," Exod. xiv. 22. " they walked upon dry land in the midft of the fea," ver. 29. it is, indeed, faid Numb. xxxiii. 8. *and they paffed through.* But befides, the word fometimes fimply fignifies *to go on before*, as Gen. xxxiii. 3. and he paffed over (went on) before; the Ifraelites may very properly be faid to have paffed through the waters of the fea, though by taking a femicircular compafs they returned to the fame fhore. For in every journey there is an *intermediate paffage* from the term *from which*, to the term *to which*. Nor is it neceffary, that every paffage fhould be in a direct line. 6thly, Nor is it more convincing, that they are faid to have walked *in the midft of the fea*, though others oppofe this very reafon. For certainly they who had the fea both on their right and left, muft have walked in the midft of the fea by what way foever, or whitherfoever they went. So that it appears, nothing certain

can

can be brought from Scripture for the oppofite opinion.   The
decifion of the queftion depends principally on an exact plan or
map of the country.   Whoever wants more on this head may
confult Fagius in Exod. iv. and Chriftian. Schotanus, my honoured predeceffor in the chair at Franeker, Biblioth. Sacr. T. 2.
p. 142. add Genebrardus in Chron. p. 66. Gregor. Turon. Hift.
lib. 1. c. 10. Abulenfis, and Grotius on the place, and who is
more full on the fubject, Ludovicus de Tena ad Hebr. 11. Difficult. 19. and laftly, Ufher, Epift. 105.

X. The Apoftle alluding, 1 Cor. x. 1, 2. to this hiftory, fays,
" that all the fathers were under the cloud, and all paffed through
the fea, and were all baptifed unto Mofes in the cloud and in
the fea." Here are three difficulties to be cleared up : firft, it is
enquired, how the apoftle could write, that they were *under
the cloud*, fince the facred hiftory declares, that the cloud went
*behind them*, Exod. xiv. 19.   But this is of little weight : for it
was behind them in fuch a manner, that it hung a great way
over them, and extending to a vaft breadth, and height, encompaffed them under its protection : as there is an allufion to this,
Ifa. iv. 5. " and Jehovah will create upon every dwelling place
of mount Zion, and upon her affemblies a cloud by day."

XI. The other difficulty is fomething more confiderable ;
namely, how the Ifraelites could be *baptized in the cloud and in the
fea*, fince they were not dipt in the water of the fea, nor wetted
by the cloud.   But we are to know.   1ft, That the apoftle ufes
the term baptifm here in a figurative fenfe.   For, becaufe the
Corinthians gloried of baptifm, the apoftle applies the name
of baptifm to thofe things, of which the Ifraelites might glory,
as much as the Corinthians could of baptifm, and which were
to them inftead of baptifm.   2dly, There is alfo fome fort of
agreement in the external fign : a cloud differs very little from
water, and the fea is water already : the cloud hung over their
heads, fo alfo water hangs over baptifed perfons.  'Compare
this with what we fhall prefently advance from Gregory of Nyffa, concerning the cloud.   The fea furrounded them on all
fides ; fo does water alfo, thofe that are baptifed. 3dly, This fign
fignifies the fame that baptifm does: and fo baptifm is the antitype of it, as on a like fubject Peter faid, 1 Peter iii. 21.   See
Cameron in 1 Cor. x.   And the ancient Jews have obferved,
that, in the baptifm of the Ifraelites, there was indeed a
peculiar refpect had to the pillar of cloud.   In Pirke R.
Eliez. c. 44. R. Zacharias fpeaks thus : " the pillar of cloud
furrounded the camp of the Ifraelites, as a wall furrounds a town ;
nor could an enemy or foe approach to them."   But, " the
cloud preferved thofe who wanted true baptifm, even without
the

the camp, which was holy." Gul. Vorſtius has ingenuouſly
compared this paſſage with this place of the apoſtle. But
what we have ſaid concerning the paſſage of the Iſraelites
through the ſea, and the baptiſm therein, appears much more
probable to us than the judgment of Selden, in other reſpects
a learned man, who by the ſea underſtands here any receptacle
of water, and will have the paſſing through the ſea to be the
ſame, as to be dipt in water, *de S,:nedr. lib.* 1. *c.* 3. But this
intricate way of ſpeaking ſeems not to agree with the ſimplicity of the apoſtle.

XII. Thirdly, it is proper to enquire, in what ſenſe they may
be ſaid to be *baptiſed unto Moſes ;* ſince that ſeems to be too
great an honour to be conferred on a ſervant, or any mere
man ? 1 Cor. i. 13. I anſwer, it is one thing to be baptiſed
*unto a perſon ;* another, to be baptiſed *in the name of a perſon.*
In whoſe name ſoever we are baptiſed, we are baptiſed by his
authority and command ; we acknowledge him for our king,
who alone can inſtitute public ſeals; we devote our obedience
and worſhip to him, ſo as for the future to be called by his
name ; from him we, by faith, expect that ſpiritual grace,
which is ſealed by baptiſm. Paul carefully diſclaimed this
honour, becauſe it was greater than became a man. To be
baptiſed unto any perſon, is by far of a lower degree; for either, it ſignifies ſimply, to be baptiſed by the miniſtry of any
one ; or thus, that by receiving baptiſm, we acknowledge ſuch
a perſon to be a faithful ſervant of God. Both may be here
with propriety joined together. *They were* baptiſed unto Moſes ; that is, according to the Syriac, *by the hand of Moſes ;* or,
as Auguſtin reads on Pſalm 77, by Moſes. For, Moſes, by
his prayers, obtained for them this protection of the cloud, and
this paſſage through the ſea. Moſes, by ſtretching out his rod,
divided the water; Moſes, firſt entered the channel of the ſea,
and both led and encouraged the reſt to venture with him.
And thus they were baptiſed by the means of Moſes. But
there is more implied in this manner of ſpeaking. As theſe
miracles were ſacraments of divine grace to the true and ſpiritual
Iſrael, ſo they were alſo ſymbols, by which God confirmed the
miniſtry of Moſes, and proved him to be a typical deliverer and
mediator. And therefore in the place, where we read of their
paſſing through the ſea, the people is ſaid " to have believed
Jehovah, and his ſervant Moſes," Exod. xiv. 31. : and in ſo far
the people did well ; for, Exod. xix. 9. when God himſelf ſet
forth the authority he had beſtowed on Moſes, he ſays, " lo I
come unto thee in a' thick cloud, that the people may hear
when I ſpeak with thee, and believe thee for ever." And thus
they

they were baptifed unto Mofes, becaufe by this fign God taught them to acknowledge Mofes for a faithful prophet, and an eminent type of the Meffiah, by whofe intervention thofe benefits fhould be conferred upon them, which were both great in themfelves, and earnefts of the greateft bleffings to be conferred by the Meffiah. And in this refpect Mofes had fomething peculiar above other minifters.

XIII. This very paffage of Paul leads us to meditate on the myftery of this fign: for, it teaches us, that, in its fignification, it anfwers to our baptifm. *Tertullian, lib. de Baptifmo* fays; " firft, when the people went out of Egypt, and, by paffing through the water, efcaped the tyranny of the king of Egypt, who with all his hofts was overwhelmed. Which figure is more evident in the facrament of baptifm. The nations are delivered from the world, namely by the water, and leave the devil, their old tyrant, funk in the water." But let us defcend to particulars.

XIV. This miraculous cloud was: 1ft, A fymbol of God's gracious prefence: For, " God was in the cloud," Exod. xiii. 21. " and the angel of God," Exod. xiv. 19: namely " the angel of the covenant, the angel of his prefence," who had appeared to Mofes in the bufh, and led the Ifraelites through the wildernefs, Ifa. lxiii. 9. 2dly, It prefigured the future incarnation of the Son of God: for, as the Son of God vailed the infinite glory of his majefty in this cloud, fpoke from it, wrought miracles, and protected his people, fo in like manner he was, in due time, to conceal his majefty under the affumed form of a fervant, Phil. ii. 7. but in fuch a manner, that the rays of his glory, might at times fhine forth in his divine difcourfes and miracles, which no age ever faw either like them, or equal to them, John i. 14. 3dly, It fignified God's protection towards the elect, and his pointing out the way, through the wildernefs of this world, to the heavenly Canaan. For, as Gregory of Nyffa finely fays of this cloud, *de Vita Mofes.* " It was fuch a miracle, that while the fhining rays of the fun were hot and fcorching, it defended the people like an interpofing fcreen, and tempered, with its fhade and the gentle drops of dew, that were diffufed, the heat of the air: but in the night it became a fire, and by its own light afforded the Ifraelites, as it were a torch or flambeau from evening till the rifing of the fun." Such is the protection and guidance, that we have in Chrift, who, by his fhadow, fcreens us from the heat of divine wrath, Ifa. iv. 5, 6. and enlightens us by his word and Spirit, " as the light of the world, which whoever followeth, fhall not walk in darknefs," John viii. 12. who, in

a word, is the " author and finisher of our faith," Heb. xii. 2,
4thly, As this cloud placed itself in the middle between Israel
and the Egyptians; so Christ takes upon himself those evils, which
threaten his people, and "the glory of the Lord is their reward,"
Isa. lviii. 8.

XV. We may observe in the *passage* through the Red Sea, the
following things. *Pharaoh* and the *Egyptians* are the figure or
emblem of the devil and sin, who use their utmost endeavour,
to keep the elect under their yoke of bondage, and when ever
with a generous mind, they aspire to liberty, to pull them back
again. But they shall lose their labour, and in the end dearly
pay for their wickedness, in a way answerable to their crimes.
Because Pharaoh commanded the young children of the Israelites to be drowned in the river, Exod. i. 22. himself with all
his hosts, is, by the law of retaliation, drowned in the sea. The
angel of the waters publishes a similar procedure of divine justice, Rev. xvi. 6. " because they have shed the blood of saints
and prophets, thou hast given them blood to drink: for they are
worthy."

XVI. Moses was a type of Christ, our deliverer and Saviour,
(1.) Moses, by his prayers, interceded for the people, and obtained for them this great salvation. Christ is our advocate
with the Father; and all the good that befals us, is owing to
his intercession. (2.) Moses with his rod, as a moral instrument, divided the waters: Christ, with the wood of his cross,
hath opened a new and living way to heaven. (3). Moses was
the leader of the people, and went before them, through a
way, by which none ever went before, Christ, also went before us in the road of sufferings, " leaving us an example, that
we should follow his steps," 1 Pet. ii. 21. (4.) Moses with the
rod, with which he divided the waters, that the Israelites might
pass through, got the waters to return and drown the Egyptians. The same cross of Christ, which " unto them which
are called, is the power of God, is unto the Jews a stumbling-
block, and to the Greeks foolishness," 1 Cor. i. 23, 24. " to these
the favour of death unto death; but to those the favour of life
unto life," 2 Cor. ii. 19.

XVII. The *waters* of the Red Sea signify afflictions, and even
death itself: so likewise do the waters of baptism, the fellowship in the sufferings, death and burial of Christ, Rom. vi. 3, 4.
But as the Israelites marched to their deliverance through the
midst of the waters, as through the midst of death: so, in like
manner, the sufferings, which we undergo for Christ, work for
us a far more exceeding weight of glory, 2 Cor. iv. 17. and
death itself is the passage to eternal life, John. v. 14. The

waters

waters which faved Ifrael, deftroyed the Egyptians. The death
of our body, which prefents our fouls pure before God, as a
flock of fheep newly fhorn, which come up from the wafhing,
Canticl. iv. 2. entirely deftroys in us all the remains of the devil
and of fin, in fo much, that our eyes fhall never more behold
thofe enemies, to whofe troublefome and malicious affaults we
have been expofed even to the very laft.

XVIII. That ftrong *eaft wind*, which by its violence drove
the waters before it, for the benefit of the Ifraelites, was an
emblem of the Spirit of Chrift, John iii. 8. of Chrift, I fay, who
is * " the dawning, day-fpring from on high," Luke i. 78. and
applies to us, by the efficacy of his Spirit, the virtue of his
merits; by removing all hindrances, nay directing them to the
falvation of his people: " not by might, nor by power, but
by my Spirit, faith Jehovah of hofts," Zech. iv. 6. By the fame
Spirit of his mouth he will hereafter confume that wicked one,
who oppofes his kingdom, 2 Theff. ii.8.

XIX. The *Ifraelites*, when juft come out of Egypt, are a
figure of believers, who having no fooner renounced the devil,
and by the power of Chrift recovered their liberty, are immediately expofed to the perfecution of Satan and the world,
who endeavour to bring them back again to bondage. And
though they have now happily furmounted the firft danger, yet
they have ftill a wide fea to crofs, lofty tops of mountains to
pafs over, and in fine, an unpaffable wildernefs to go through,
before they obtain that full falvation, which is the mark they
aim at and defire. When every thing feemed to be given up
for loft, and no way of efcape appeared, then God came to
Ifrael's help, and opened a way through the midft of the fea.
So in an efpecial manner, he comes by his grace to the relief
of his church, when fhe is deftitute of all human affiftance,
and nothing but the moft certain deftruction feems to hang
over her, Ifa. xliii. 2. " When thou paffeft through the waters,
I will be with thee; and through the rivers, they fhall not
overflow thee." This deliverance happened to Ifrael, when
they did nothing at all towards it, Exod. xiv 14. " Jehovah
fhall fight for you and ye fhall hold your peace;" but only
believe, and behold the mighty hand of God: Heb. xi. 29.
" by faith they paffed through the Red Sea." It is thus alfo,
that God works out eternal falvation for us; for us, I fay,
" not working, but believing in him, that juftifieth the ungodly,"
Rom.

* The word αναῆολη, which our tranflators render day-fpring, is the fame, which
the Septuagint ufe, Jer. xxiii. 5. Zech. iii. 8. and .vi 8. Where the Meffiah is
fpoken of under the name of the Branch.

Rom. iv. 5. The Ifraelites, after their paffage through the fea, and the deftruction of their enemies, fung a joyful fong of triumph to the praife of God their deliverer : thus alfo John in the Revelation, chap. xv. 2, 3. faw the faints, who, having got over the fea of glafs, which was mixed with fire, fung the fong of Mofes the fervant of God, and the fong of the Lamb. And thus far of the paffage through the Red Sea.

XX. We are next to fpeak of the *manna*, where we are to confider. (1.) The name. (2.) The thing itfelf. (3.) Its origin. (4.) Its adjuncts. (5.) The duties of the Ifraelites concerning it. (6.) Their fin. (7.) The myftery of it.

XXI. The furprize of the Ifraelites gave rife to the *name*. When they firft faw it, they faid to one another, Exod. xvi. 15. MAN HU *it is manna ; for they wift not* MA HU, *what it was,* and *v.* 31. *and the houfe of Ifrael called the name thereof manna.* We can on no account affent to thofe, who render מן הוא, *what is this ?* For, מן never fignifies in Hebrew *what*, and here it is very exprefsly diftinguifhed from מה: nay, it is not very common in Chaldee taken in that fenfe, as they ufually fay מן of a perfon, not of a thing. I will not however conceal it, that they fpeak with greater freedom, than they ought who abfolutely deny, that מן in Chaldee is applied to a thing. Drufius ad Joh. vi. 31. hath given fome examples to the contrary. But the Ifraelites fpoke then in Hebrew, not in Chaldee. I know not, whether they are in the right who affirm, that מן is an Egyptian word, and is equivalent to an interrogative pronoun ; but though they are, yet it does not feem probable that the Ifraelites would exprefs a thing fo facred by a term borrowed from a nation fo odious, not only in that firft furprize, but alfo ever after. And then, it is altogether trifling to fay, that the food which God gave to the Ifraelites, was always called *what ;* only becaufe, when at firft they did not know it, they afked, *what is this ?*

XXII. It is much more agreeable to derive the word from מנה, *he prepared, appointed, determined :* and hence the name *manna, portion,* even of the food allotted for any perfon, 1 Sam. i. 4, 5. Neh. viii. 10, 12. and generally elfewhere. But from *manna* it is eafy to form *man* by an * *apocope,* efpecially in the exclamation of perfons under a furprize, and when *he* is the next letter that begins the following word. And this is the more probable, as fuch an apocope is often to be met with in the word *manna:* once in the imperative, *prepare* (or appoint)
" mercy

* A figure which takes away the laft fyllable, or letter of a word.

" mercy and truth," Pf. lxi. 7. and again, in the * preterit,
Jonah i. 17. " and Jehovah prepared a great fish ;" and what
comes neareſt to the point in hand is, when an allotment of
food is ſpoken of as in Dan. i. 5. " and the king appointed
them a daily proviſion." As therefore both. the form of the
term agrees to it, and the ſignification is very ſuitable; what remains, but that we ſay with the moſt learned of the Jews, that
*man* ſignifies the food appointed, prepared for, and given to
Iſrael as their portion ? Such a name became this miraculous
food. And what is added is no objection ; namely, that the
Iſraelites knew not what it was. For, in general, they knew
from the prediction of Moſes, that they were to be ſatisfied
with bread, ver. 12. from which they conjectured, that what
they ſaw, was the portion, which was intended for them from
heaven ; and this they expreſſed by the name, *man*. But they
did not diſtinctly know, what it would be, nor had they any
peculiar name, by which to expreſs it. To this the author of
the book of *Wiſdom* ſeems to have alluded, when chap. xvi. 20.
he calls " manna, bread prepared from heaven." And therefore this name has ſo far prevailed, that it has remained unvaried in all languages, and is even given alſo to things, which
have any ſimilitude with that food of the Iſraelites.

XXIII. As to the *thing* itſelf, naturaliſts well know there
are three things reckoned among watry meteors; namely, dew,
honey, and manna. But the learned are not agreed about the
original of manna. Chriſtophorus Vega apud Jonſtonum de
admirandis Meteorum, c. 10. is of opinion, that the manna of
the ſhops is the work of certain ſmall bees, like thick-bodied
gnats, from which, as they ſit in cluſters on trees, ſomething
flows down in drops, like a kind of ſweat. Voſſius Phyſiolog.
Chriſtanæ, lib. 5. c. 21. ſays, it is the ſap of the larch-tree,
or of the aſh, and that Matthias Lobelius was the very firſt
who ſaid ſo. The more common opinion is, that it is a kind
of aerial honey ſprinkled with dew which in the ſummer months,
during the ſcorching heat of the ſun in the day-time, runs to-
gther by the nocturnal cold into cluſters, and is rounded into
grains, from the flowing down of the dewy humour, and from
the moiſture of the air ; and generally ſettles on trees, herbs,
and ſtones, as Lemnius de herbis Biblicis, c. 3. deſcribes it.
. But it has a kind of medicinal virtue, by which it looſens, and
gently purges.

XXIV.

---

* The author's words are indeed, *iterumque in futuro, and in the future*, but I
imagine there is certainly a miſtake, as the words quoted are rendered in the
preterite tenſe.

XXIV. Now the queftion is, whether the manna of the If-raelites was of the fame fpecies and nature with the common? It is fufficiently agreed on, that fome miraculous circumftances attended the manna of the Hebrews; but there is no folid rea-fon to conclude from this, that the thing itfelf was altogether new, and was never produced by natural caufes at any time, or in other places: fince God could fo multiply the dew con-veyed in great plenty from fome other quarter, to be matter fit for the production of manna, as to be fufficient for the daily fupply of that great multitude; and fo difpofe it, as to be en-dowed with thofe wonderful adjuncts, we are hereafter to fpeak of. It is certain, Jofephus thought it was a natural manna, and relates, that in his time, it ftill continued to be plentifully rained down about mount * Sinai, Antiq. lib. 3. c. 1. And Francifcus Vallefius Philofoph. Sacr. c. 57. infifts at large, that the manna of the Ifraelites, was altogether the fame with the common. Cardan alfo de Subtilitate, lib. 21. relates, that in the defert of Traga in Lybia, there is fo much of it gathered in a day, efpecially about the town Agadez, as that a pound, of 28 ounces, is fold for twopence, and adds, the inhabitants by eating it, live found and healthy, though the air be pefti-lential. They who are of this opinion, likewife obferve, that they do not undervalue the favour granted to the Ifraelites, in fuch an extraordinary manner, when they fearch into the natural caufes of things; but praife the infinite wifdom of God, who difpofes all things in fuch a way, that even the moft extraordi-nary, may in a good meafure feem to have happened according to the ordinary courfe of nature; as Vallefius fpeaks in the place above quoted. Others again think, that the manna of the Ifraelites was fomething extraordinary, never feen before, and after it ceafed, was never after to be met with; and when it is called angels' food, and every where fpoke of in the holy fcripture, as prepared by the fpecial hand of God, they think a natural caufe ought pioufly and religioufly to be excluded in this cafe: thus Rivet in Exod. xvi. 13.

XXV. Our judgment is, that there is no reafon, why we may not conclude, that God, in the production of this manna made ufe of natural caufes, as he had before ufed the wind in drying up the Red Sea. And it is very probable, this manna took its rife from the fame, or the like caufes, from which the ordinary is produced: and fo far it may be called natural. Yet the continued and daily concurrence of thofe natural caufes,

for

* They have, fays he, in that country to this very day, certain dews and rains, that feem to be fomewhat of refemblance to this that fell upon the interceffion of Mofes.

for the production of it, in such quantities, was miraculous, and altogether extraordinary: thus far then I say, it was miraculous. We add, that, at this day, no manna is known, which in every respect, is of the same nature with the manna of the Israelites. For, to omit other things, the manna of the Israelites was of a consistent substance, supplied the place of corn, and was given to the people for food. The common manna is a medicine, not a food; and cannot be the ordinary food of any people, without a miracle.

XXVI. To the manna of the Israelites, the Polish comes nearest, which was not long ago found strewed in the fields, it was small and like sugar; and when it is boiled up with butter and a little sugar, may easily vie with the most delicate Italian jellies or dainties, as Keckerman describes it, Physic. lib. 6. c. 10. A Lapide in Exod. xvi. 21. treats more largely on this, and declares, that from the constant accounts of the Poles, it rains down in the nights of the months of June, and July, and settles on the herbs like a dew: that before the sun is up, it is gathered in sieves, sifted, pounded, mixt with water, and made into a kind of hasty pudding. But if the sun begins to be hot, the husk of it dissolves, and the grain of the manna, inclosed therein, is lost. He adds, that he had seen the grains, and that they resembled millet, are only longer and of a ruddy colour, and found the taste of it like that of * panick. But even this manna is different from that of the Israelites. 1st, In figure, for it is oblong; whereas that of the Israelites was round like coriander seed. 2dly, In colour, being ruddy, whereas the other was white. 3dly, The Polish is included in a husk, whereas the other had none. 4thly, The manna of the Hebrews melted before the sun, and vanished; only the husk of the other is dissolved, but the grain is hard and falls to the ground.

XXVII. However, there are many concurring circumstances, which here proclaim, that a miracle must by all means be admitted. For, (1.) The manna, which is commonly known, is gathered only at certain seasons of the year; but this came down daily. (2.) During so long a time, none fell on the sabbath, but in a double quantity on the day before. (3.) It was found daily in such quantities, as to suffice to feed so many thousands. (4.) If it was kept till the next day, it spoiled: except that which was the portion of the sabbath. (5.) And yet that part of it, which God commanded to be laid up, remained untainted for some ages after. (6.) It fell in all places, where ever

---

* This is a grain like unto millet, with a knob full of corn.

ever the Ifraelites encamped; but was not known among the
neighbouring people, at leaft not ufed for food, much lefs for
their daily food. (7.) It ceafed, after they paffed over Jordan,
and they had got a full fupply of ordinary bread : and perhaps
there are more circumftances to the fame purpofe.

XXVIII. The *origin* of the manna was from God, as the
principal caufe. It is every where afcribed to him, as a fingular
privilege, which be beftowed on his people Ifrael, Exod. xvi.
4, 8, 16. Deut. viii. 3, 16. Neh. ix. 15, 20, 21. But God
formed this bread in the air, from the vapours or exhalations,
properly prepared by the fun, and by the other ftars, if they
contributed any thing towards it. Whence it is faid, " that he
commanded the clouds from above, and opened the doors of
heaven, and gave them of the corn of heaven," Pf. lxxviii. 23,
24. But the air, which is the feat of meteors, is called heaven;
as *the fowls of heaven;* and in Lucretius, *the air which is called
heaven*. And as the angels are miniftring fpirits, Heb. i. 14.
whofe miniftry God very frequently ufed in the whole œconomy of the Old Teftament, and who upon other occafions, fupplied God's fervants with food, 1 Kings xix. 5, 6, 7. I fee not
why a celebrated expofitor of our day, who in other things
makes the church of that age fubject to angels, can deny, that
this food was prepared by angels. Suidas fays, " manna is a
food fupplied from above. And is called the bread of angels,
becaufe they fupplied them with it."

XXIX. And yet I doubt, whether any fufficient argument
can be formed from Pf. lxxviii. 25. for the miniftry of angels
in this particular. We there, indeed, find לחם אבירים, which
the feptuagint tranflate ἄρτον ἀγγέλων, *the bread of angels* : juft as
the author of the book of *Wifdom* calls it τροφὴν ἀγγέλων, chap.
xvi. 20. *angels food*. And R. Solomon in like manner להם חלאכם.
But firft, we are under no neceffity to underftand angels by
אבירים, which fignifies *the ftrong*. For that is a general name,
and is applied to men of valour, or *heroes* among men, Jer.
xlvi. 13. Lam. i. 15. Let it therefore be called *the bread of the
ftrong*, becaufe it made the Ifraelites robuft and and ftrong ;
as fupplying the place of ordinary bread, by which the heart is
fupported, though, at firft fight and tafte, it might feem light;
or, what I would choofe, the bread of *heroes*, that is, fuch as
even the greateft nobles would reckon delicious. God is alfo
called, *the [hero] mighty one of Jacob*, or of Ifrael, Gen. xlix. 24.
Ifa. xlix. 26. Nor is it unufual in fcripture, when fpeaking
of God, to ufe the plural number ; of which they who have
but a fmall fhare of learning, are not ignorant. Why may we
not therefore be allowed to explain it of the *bread of God*, which
the

the hero *of Jacob* gave them, and which alfo fpiritually was a
reprefentation of himfelf? Drufius alfo has obferved this on
John vi. 13. Again, fhould we grant, that angels are meant,
yet I do not recollect, that they are called אבירים in Scripture,
but I well remember, that they are reprefented as גבורים, *ex-
celling in ftrength*, Pf. ciii. 20. yet the matter would ftill remain
undecided, fince it might be called the bread of angels, becaufe of its excellence and fpiritual fignification: for, it fignified, that God, who is the life and joy of angels, was to defcend
from heaven, in order in like manner to become the food, that
is, the joy and life of men.

XXX. Mofes here alfo acted his part; who, it is very probable, interceded with God by prayer, that he would give food
to the ftarving people. Jofephus fays, thefe were poured forth
on a high rock, adding of his own fancy, that the manna firft
fell, and thickened on the palms of his hands, as they were
ftretched out to heaven, when he returned thanks to God: and
that Mofes, fufpecting what it was, tafted it and joyfully, upon
the difcovery, fhewed the people the favour God had beftowed
on them. That the people, having feen their food rained down
from heaven, imagined it fnowed, the feafon of the year com-
porting with this. But thefe things neither agree with reafon,
(for it is beyond all probability, it fhould fnow in that hot climate
in the month of May, when thefe things happened) nor with
Scripture, which fpeaks exprefsly of fome perfons, who went
out of the camp at break of day, and firft obferved the manna,
Exod. xvi. 15.

XXXI. The Gemarifts go too far, when they fay in Taanith,
Fol. 9. col. 1. " that the Ifraelites had three good fhepherds,
Mofes, Aaron, and Miriam; and three benefits given them by
their hands: the fountain, the cloud, and the manna. The
fountain, for the merits of Miriam: the pillar of cloud for the
merits of Aaron, and the manna for the merits of Mofes." But
what Chrift fays contradicts this affertion, John v. 32. " Verily, verily, I fay unto you, Mofes gave you not that bread from
heaven: but my Father giveth you the true bread from heaven."
Nor was the typical bread from Mofes, but from God. Mofes
was only the meffenger, not the meritorious caufe of the divine
gift: and much lefs did the antitype Chrift, with his grace, the
bread which came down from the third heavens, proceed from
Mofes. This, however, Mofes did; having by his prayers obtained the favour of God, he told the people in God's name,
what fhould happen with refpect to their food, and explained
the whole defign of the manna. Philo has prudently obferved,
that, God, indeed, gave his people comfort, but difcovered it

firſt to Moſes : " the one, indeed, on account of his natural be-
nignity and affection towards men, but the other becauſe he
would put honour on the leader, whom he himſelf had appointed."

XXXII. The *adjuncts* of the manna are either *internal* or *external*. To the former belong the figure, colour, taſte. Of the
*figure* it is ſaid, 1ſt, That it was " a ſmall thing, as hoar-froſt
on the ground," Exod. xvi. 14. ſmall indeed, at firſt ſight, yet
precious in itſelf, and of the greateſt efficacy ; as God uſually
diſplays his wonderful power in the ſmalleſt things. 2dly, That
it was מחספס ; a word which we no where elſe meet with in Scripture, and therefore diverſely explained. The Vulgate has, *quaſi
pilo tuſum*, " as if pounded by a peſtle," that is, of ſuch minute-
neſs, that it ſeemed to be brought to that ſmallneſs by ſome art,
and as in a mortar. Others tranſlate it, *decorticatum*, peeled ;
Junius, *rotundum*, round, as alſo Erpenius Arabic interpreter ;
and Kimchi ſays, it ſignifies the ſame thing as *round*. Other
Jews tranſlate it *rete&um*, diſcloſed.; and imagine, the manna
was ſhut up in the dew, which was over and under it, as in a
coffer, and the upper dew aſcending, by the more advanced
elevation of the ſun above the horizon, the manna appeared in
ſight. But all this, to ſpeak in the ſofteſt manner, is uncertain.
3dly, That " it was like coriander ſeed," ver. 31. Not in
colour, ſince coriander ſeed, is black; but becauſe it was ſmall
and round. Well ſay the *Talmudiſts in Joma c.* 8. fol. 73. *col. a,
round as coriander, and white as pearl.*

XXXIII. With reſpect to its *colour*, it is ſaid Exod. xvi. 31.
that it was *white*, and Numb. xi. 7. " the colour thereof as
the colour of bedola," but what that was interpreters are not
agreed. The Jews inſiſt, it was a kind of precious ſtone; but
are oppoſed by Junius and Marcus Marinus Brixianus; becauſe
Gen. ii. 12. it is ſaid, " there is bedola and the onyx-ſtone;"
wherefore, as the name *ſtone* is, by way of diſtinction, added to
the word onyx, they conclude, that bedola cannot be a ſtone.
Others imagine, it was *cryſtal*, and conſequently the colour of
the manna was bright and tranſparent. Moſt of the moderns
following Joſephus, from the affinity of the word, contend,
that it was bdellium : concerning which Serapion, quoted by
Druſius, ſays, that " the Jewiſh bdellium is the gum of a tree
that grows in Arabia: and that the better ſort, is that of a good
flavour, tough within, and ſoon diſſolving, inclining to white,
not having any bits of wood or other impurities," in it, &c.
Pliny adds, it is tranſparent, and like to wax, lib. 12. 9. See
Salmas. Exercit. Plinian p. 806, and *de homonymis hyle Iatreeq. c.*
109. From this they conclude, that the grains of the manna
                                                      / were

were tranfparent and of a whitifh-caft: which is a fign of its great purity and perfect digeftion. But I muft not conceal, that Bochart in Hierozoic. p. 2. lib. 5. c. 5. has by his arguments convinced me, that bedola is a *pearl*, for which they ftill very frequently fifh in that place, which Mofes has defcribed, Gen. ii. 12. as Patrus Texeira an eye-witnefs, and Benjamin in Itinerar. p. 105, teftify. Befides, both the manna and the pearl are of the fame colour, namely white: and both of them are round: nor is the obfervation of Junius or Brixianus to the contrary of any weight. Since it does not follow, that becaufe the onyx is called a ftone, bedola is not a ftone likewife. Not to mention now, that the lawyer alfo excepts pearls from the clafs of ftone and gems *lege, qum aurum* 19. §. *Gemma-autem,* 17. *and feq. ff. De auro and argento legato.* And though pearls are ufually called ftones by the Hebrews, yet they are of a quite different kind from thofe ftones, produced in the earth; fuch as gems properly fo called. They who contend for bdellium, having fcarce any other argument but the affinity of the appellation, which is often fallacious: in other refpects bdellium and manna have no fuch agreement.

XXXIV. Its *favour* or tafte is likewife highly commended, Exod. xvi. 31. *Sicut epichyti ex melle,* as *Eunius* tranflates, *as of a wafer made of honey,* or according to the *Vulgate, quafi fimila in melle, as of fine flour in honey.* And, Num. xi. 8. *as the tafte of frefh oil.* As the Scripture thus determines the tafte, the fictions of the Jews are very trifling, which the papifts too greedily catch at, the better to put a varnifh on their monfter of tranfubftantiation; as that the manna had all kinds of taftes, and that every individual Ifraelite tafted in it whatever he pleafed; youny men, bread; old men, honey; youny children, oil; as the Jewifh mafters trifle in Schemoth Rabba, fect. 25. with whom the author of the book of *Wifdom,* chap. xvi. 20. feems to agree. It is aftonifhing, with what nicety the papifts difpute on this matter: namely, whether this was only the privilege of the pious, or common to them with the wicked; Tirinus after Auguftin, Abulenfis, and Hugo Cardinalis, ftands up for the former; but is oppofed by *Corn. a Lapide.* This being obferved, there are other queftions alfo ftarted; and among the reft, whether the manna changed not only its tafte, but alfo its fubftance, at the defire of thofe who eat of it, fo as to be turned into an egg, a pullet, or lamb, as often as fuch things were longed for; or whether a change only was made in the qualities? In either of thefe ways, they find fomething in the manna to fupport their doctrine of tranfubftantiation. For, if the former, as has feemed good to doctors of great reputation,

we have an evident example of a tranfubftantiation. If the
latter, with the Jefuit *a Lapide*, hence at leaft may be concluded,
that accidents may remain without their fubftance; becaufe, as
a different talte ufually accompanies a different fubftance, the
fubftance of the manna remaining, the talte was changed at will
and proved nourifhing: whence it follows, that the accidents
of bread may alfo remain, and prove nourifhing in the tranfub-
ftantiated wafer. But thefe are the dotages and fond fportings
of men, who fhamefully abufe their wit, and are overturned
by three arguments from Scripture. 1ft, As it accurately defcribes the peculiar tafte of the manna. 2dly, As it mentions
the induftry of the Ifraelites in the different ways by which
they prepared it for their more convenient ufe. 3dly, As it
gives an account of their loathing it, Num. xi. 6. which could
not happen, did the manna yield the palate any tafte at pleafure.

XXXV. However have we not yet got over all the difficulty: for, as the tafte of honey differs from the tafte of oil, we
may enquire, how manna can be compared to both in tafte?
But this difficulty may be obviated three ways: if we fay firft,
that the tafte of the manna was fomewhat different, when it
was eaten in a plain manner, from what it was, when differently dreffed and prepared by the Ifraelites: the one may therefore be underftood of manna undreffed: the other of that which
was boiled. And again, which I would prefer, it might, in a
different refpect, be compared both with honey, and with oil;
not that in all refpects the tafte of it refembled either oil or
honey; but partook of fomething of both, the fweetnefs of honey, and the fatnefs of oil; in general a tafte mixed of both.
It might be added; as honey is * the *chief of fweet things*, as
the fon of Syrach fpeaks; whatever things are fweet to the
tafte, may be compared with honey. And fo manna may be
faid, to have the tafte of honey, that is in general, to be very
fweet. Wherefore the author of the book of *Wifdom*, chap.
XIX. 21. calls it a *kind of* † *Ambrofial, food that could eafily melt,*
ἔντακτον γίνος ἀμβροσίας τροφῆς.

XXXVI. The external adjuncts or circumftances are place
and time. The *place*, where God fed the Ifraelites with manna
was the wildernefs. The favour of heaven fupplied them with
what the barrennefs of the foil denied: and when they were
                                        deftitute

---

* The author of Ecclefiafticus, fpeaking of the bee, fays, " her fruit is the chief
of fweet things.

† Our Englifh verfion renders it a kind of heavenly meat, that was of nature apt
to melt.

deftitute of ordinary bread, produced from the earth, they were fatisfied, with bread, which came down from heaven. Finally fays Jofephus ; " fo divine and admirable was this food, that it fupplied the want of all others to thofe that partook of it ;" and truly believers may go every where with fafety, when God leads the way even through the wildernefs, and a land not fown, Jer. ii. 2. " The young lions do lack and fuffer hunger : but they that feek Jehovah, fhall not want any good thing," Pfal. xxxiv. 10.

XXXVII. We are to obferve the following things concerning the *time* when the manna was given.  As 1ft, That the Ifraelites had none before they left Egypt : Then they happily exchanged their cucumbers, pompious, garlick, and every fervile food, for the bread of heaven, and the dainties of angels. 2dly, That this bread was for the firft time rained down from heaven, when there was nothing in the land to ftay their hunger. Thus God ufually provides for his own people in due feafon, and where ordinary means fail, employs extraordinary. While a famine raged in all places, the rapacious ravens carry a daily portion to Elias, 1 Kings xvii. 6.   3dly, That the manna was rained every day, except on the fabbath: when none was to be feen on the ground: but a double portion was gathered the day before, for the fupply of the following : Thus the goodnefs of God is new every day : neither will the obfervance of his commands, efpecially that of the fabbath, prove detrimental to any. 4thly, That the manna continued forty years, till the Ifraelites came into Canaan ; where they could eat of the fruits of the land, Jof. 5. 12.   For where ordinary means are within our reach, we are not to defire, or expect extraordinary.

XXXVIII. The Ifraelites were to perform the following *duties* with refpect to the manna.  *Firft,* They were to gather it very early, becaufe it would melt, when the fun was more advanced.  So hateful to God is floth, that when raining down bread from heaven upon his people, without their labour, he commands them to rife with the fun to gather it.  Man was not fuffered to be idle even in paradife.

XXXIX. *Secondly,* They were to gather it by certain meafure, an homer for each : a quantity, it is probable, fufficient to fatisfy even the moft robuft, and thofe of the largeft appetite. For, an homer was a large meafure, concerning which may be feen *Waferus de Antiq. Menfur. lib.* 2. *c.* 3. where he fhews, that an homer contains as much as forty-three fhells of eggs and a half.  Tirinus has computed, the allowance of each to have been about fifty of our ounces.  God ftinted them to a certain meafure, to fet bounds to their exceffive appetite ; but indulged

ed them in such a meafure as fhould fhew the riches of his
bounty.

XL. But the account here given by Mofes deferves particular confideration, namely, that fome of the Ifraelites gathered
more, others lefs; but that afterwards when it was meafured
by the homer, he who had gathered more, had nothing over,
and he ·who had gathered lefs, had no lack, Exod. xvi. 17.
Some have conceived a twofold miracle here; one about the
gathering of the manna; the other about the confuming it.
They imagine, if any had gathered lefs than the appointed quantity, before it came to be meafured, what was lacking, was
miraculoufly added by an angel; but if more, the overplus
was taken away by an angel, and invifibly added to what others
gathered. They alfo imagine, that every one confumed an entire homer of manna a-day: but as this was not poffible in
fuch a diverfity of ages and health without a miracle, they boldly pronounce, God very unequally attempered the nutritive
efficacy of the manna in equal quantities to the ftrength and
appetite of every perfon: and befides, heaped the manna clof-
er in the homer for the more voracious, but loofer for the weaker
and the young.

XLI. But all thefe things are framed at pleafure; nor are we
to multiply miracles without neceffity. As to the gathering,
the manner of it feems to have been thus. Every one gathered as much as he could: and, as is ufual in fuch cafes, fome
gathered more, others lefs, as fome were more diligent than
others. But what was collected by all, who lived under the
fame tent, feems to have been thrown into one heap; from
which the mafter of the family taking the appointed meafure,
fo diftributed to each his portion, without paying any regard
to the labour or diligence employed, but to the divine appointment, fo that each had an equal portion. For, fo much could
with eafe, be jointly gathered, as that every one might have an
equal portion. Thefe thoughts have, in my opinion been judicioufly fuggefted by the moft excellent Rivet; and may be
confirmed from 2 Cor. viii. 14, 15. where Paul exhorts the
rich to fupply the wants of the poor out of their abundance, by
this argument; becaufe " it is written, he that had gathered
much, had nothing over; and he that had gathered little, had
no lack." As if he had faid, " as formerly it was the will of
" God, that, among the Ifraelites, they who had gathered
" much manna, fhould fupply the wants of thofe who had
" gathered lefs, that there might be an equality: fo among
" Chriftians, it is but juft, that thofe, who, by the bounty of
" God, are poffeffed of an affluence of good things, fhould fup-
" ply

" ply the wants of thofe, for whom a more fcanty provifion
" is made."

XLII. I am alfo of Rivet's opinion with refpeCt to their eating the manna; namely, that every one had really fuch a quantity allowed him, as was fufficient even for the largeft appetite,
yet that each was at liberty to eat as much as he pleafed : and
therefore that moft of them had more food, than either neceffity required, or than they could well eat. But that, as they
were not allowed to keep what was over till the next day, they
might throw it away towards evening; that fo they might profefs their faith and confidence in God, who, they were perfuaded, would grant them a frefh fupply, the following day.
And the throwing away the fuperfluous manna was no fign of
contempt; any more than the burning what was left of the
pafchal lamb; but rather an evidence of a fincere truft and confidence in God.

XLIII. The *third* duty was, to referve none of the manna
for the morrow, ver. 19. Not that every perfon was obliged
to confume their meafure daily, and force it upon their loathing
ftomach beyond their appetite : for this, as I have juft hinted,
was inconfiftent with the holinefs, wifdom, and goodnefs of
God. It was enough, if nothing was referved for the ufe of
the following day. What remained might either be burnt in
the fire, or buried in the earth, or given to the cattle, or deftroyed fome other way. But God, by this method, was pleafed to try their obedience, Exod. xvi. 4. and to exercife their
diligence every day, and teach them contentment, and to inculcate faith and truft upon them, that depending alone on his
providence, they might wholly commit to him the care for the
morrow, Mat. vi. 25, 31.

XLIV. *Fourthly*, The day before the fabbath they were to
gather a double quantity, ver. 7. And were allowed to lay
up whatever was left of that till the next day, ver. 25. which
neither ftunk, as what was referved on other days, nor had any
worm therein, ver. 26. By this God intended, that on the
fabbath, they fhould defift from every work, that regards the
care of this animal life, devote themfelves to him alone. And
in faCt he fhewed, that he would add other things to thofe
that feek his kingdom and righteoufnefs; and that it would
prove no detriment to any, if laying afide the care of the body,
they at ftated times laid themfelves out for God : as alfo, that
during the fix days of this life, we are to gather thofe things
which may be of fervice on the fabbath; for, on the feventh
day, that is, after this life, there will be no longer time for
working : " Whatfoever thy hand findeth to do, do it with thy
might ;

might ; for there is no work nor device, nor knowledge, nor wifdom in the grave, whither thou goeft," Ecclef. ix. 10. We are far from thinking, that this here was the firft inftitution of the fabbath, but rather that it was a folemn renovation of what was inftituted from the beginning of the world, but had been interrupted by the bondage in Egypt, and a confirmation of it by the miracle of the manna. For Mofes, ver. 3. fpeaks of the fabbath, as a thing formerly known by the Ifraelites, " this is that which Jehovah hath faid, to-morrow is the reft of the holy fabbath unto Jehovah, &c." We are not ignorant of what the great Selden, *de jure nat.* and *Gent. &c. lib.* 3. *c.* 9. *feq.* has largely, and learnedly indeed, oppofed this ; but it is not of that weight, as to fway with us.

XLV. *Fifthly,* and *laftly,* God commanded an homer of manna to be laid up in a golden urn or pot, for a perpetual memorial thereof, and placed before his face through all the generations of Ifrael. Aaron did this accordingly ; namely, at the due time, when the tabernacle, and ark were reared up. For thefe things are related here; by an evident prolepfis or anticipation, on occafion of this hiftory, ver. 33. though as is very plain, it was not done till afterwards. God, indeed, would not have the memory of fo great a miracle die away from among the Ifraelites : and therefore he not only took care to have thefe prodigies recorded ; but the remains of the miracle, great beyond all exception, and adapted to ftrike every one with amazement, to furvive. Neverthelefs, to prevent their being made an occafion of fuperftition or idolatry, wifely ordered them to be laid up in the moft holy place, and removed from the ufe of the common people.

XLVI. We muft here, by the way, remove an apparent contradiction. Mofes fays, Exod. xvi. 34. that a pot with manna, agreeably to the divine command, was by Aaron laid up *before the teftimony* to be kept. But the teftimony is either the ark, fo called, becaufe the teftimonial tables of the covenant were laid up in it, or the tables themfelves that were in the ark : but Paul writes, Heb. ix. 4. " in which (the ark) was the golden pot, that had manna, and Aaron's rod that budded, and the tables of the covenant :" where he places the pot with the manna in the ark, as well as the tables of the covenant. This difficulty is fo much the greater, if we compare 1 Kings viii. 9. and 2 Chron. v. 10. where it is exprefsly faid, that there was nothing in the ark, but the two tables of the law. Many things have been ingenioufly devifed by the learned, to take off this apparent contradiction. I own, I am beft pleafed with the obfervation of Drufius on Exod. xvi. 34. that the particle *in* with the Hebrews,

rews, and thofe that adopt their way of fpeaking, fometimes
denotes, *at, near, by*. To prove this he quotes Joſh. x. 11. and
Judges xviii. 12. Another learned author has very properly
added Joſh. v. 13. 1 Kings xvii. 3. Jer. xiii. 5. Col. iii. 1. And
therefore, *in which*, here denotes, *at* or *near the ark*. Yet Druſius
himſelf ſtarts a difficulty, which he owns he is not able to remove. " Every thing would anſwer well," ſays, he, " unleſs
there followed, *the tables of the covenant*: for thefe were within
the ark. But that the prepofition *in* ſhould fignify two different things in the fame place, is not very probable: take care
therefore, how you believe this." But we are not ſo ſoon to loſe
heart. We have at leaſt found this, that *in* fometimes denotes
ſuch a latitude of place, that it even comprehends thofe things
which are *near* and *by*. Moreover the ark was ſo framed, that
fome things might be placed on the fides of it without, as appears in the caſe of the volume of the law written by Moſes,
which was placed " in the fide of the ark of the covenant of the
Lord," Deut. xxxi. 26. All the things therefore mentioned by
Paul were *in the ark*, that is, *within the compaſs of the ark*, though
fome of them were within it more than others. Nor could Paul
ſpeak leſs properly thus, than we do, when, for inſtance, we ſay,
*in* the human body there are ſkin, and fleſh, and bones and bowels:
where *in* is uſed in the fame ſenſe, and yet with fome latitude.

XLVII. There are three *ſins* of the Iſraelites recorded with reſpect to the manna. 1ſt, That feveral of them, contrary to the
expreſs command of God, referved fome of it for the morrow,
Exod. xvi. 20. With ſuch inſolence does the wiſdom of the fleſh
ſet itſelf in direct oppofition to God, though, by his aſtoniſh-
ing goodneſs, he renders himſelf amiable, and at the fame time
venerable. And this obſtinacy of corrupt nature, is not to be
ſubdued by any miracles. But what was referved, began to
ſwarm with worms, and was putrified. To teach us, that
whatever is unjuſtly and covetouſly referved, contrary to the
command of God, ſtinks before God and men; and hence
worms ariſe, that is, various kinds of evils, eſpecially the
worm of conſcience: whereas, on the contrary, what was referved againſt the future ſabbath, proved permanent and incorruptible, Mat. vi. 20. 1. Tim. vi. 19. 2dly, That they
went forth on the very ſabbath to ſeek for it: however then
they found nothing, ver. 27. God juſtly fruſtrates the defires of
thoſe, and renders their labours abortive, who undertake any
thing contrary to his command. Nor have ſuch any reaſon to
expect the divine bleſſing on their labours, who, on the day
of the Lord's reſt, are employed in things that regard their
own ſubſiſtence, while they omit the worſhip of God, Iſa. lviii.

13, 14. 3dly, That at laſt they loathed and diſdained the manna, though it was the ſweeteſt and moſt wholeſome of all food, eſpecially in compariſon of the cucumbers, the melons, the leeks, the onions, and the garlick, Num. xi. 5, 6. Thus men uſually prefer the carnal refuſe of this world, to the treaſures of heaven, the huſks of the earth, to the dainties of angels. And that nothing on this earth, is ſo delightful, but that one time or other it begets a loathing: even the moſt excellent gifts of God, natural as well as ſpiritual, on account of this perverſe-neſs of our minds through cuſtom, loſe their value in our eſteem.

XLVIII. Now let us conſider the *myſtery* of the manna; Paul teacheth us, that this food was ſacramental, 1 Cor. x. 3. where he calls it *ſpiritual meat:* but it was ſo, not in its own nature, for it was appointed for the ſupport of the animal life, but in ſignification, wherein it anſwers to our myſtical ſupper. Anguſtin on Pſal. lxxvii. 1. ſays, " it was ſpiritual, that is, it ſignified ſomething ſpiritual." And Chriſt declares, John. vi. 32. himſelf was that true bread, which came down from heaven and was prefigured by the manna. The Jews however blind, promiſe to themſelves a new manna by the Meſſiah: For thus in " Midras Cohelet, fol. 86. col. 4. the firſt redeemer cauſed the manna to deſcend, ſo alſo the latter redeemer will make the manna to deſcend: as it is written, and there ſhall be an handful of corn in the earth," Pſ. lxxii. 16. Though their expectations were really carnal and corrupt, yet they are the remains of ancient and ſpiritual inſtruction. So likewiſe in " Midras. Canticl, fol. 16. c. 4. " The laſt redeemer ſhall be revealed to them. 'And whither will he lead them? ſome ſay, to the wilderneſs of Judah; others, to the wilderneſs of Sihon and Og, and he will cauſe the manna to deſcend to them." But it is to be obſerved, that Chriſt frequently fed the multitude in the deſerts of Judea, and in the wilderneſs of Og, with the food of his word, which is more excellent than any manna: and when there was occaſion for it, ſtayed the hunger of the body with bread, which he multiplied no leſs miraculouſly, than the manna formerly was. See other teſtimonies of the Jews in Viega on Rev. ii. 17. But according to the method preſcribed, let us come to particulars.

XLIX. Manna denotes that food, which was *appointed, prepar-ed* by God, and given to the Iſraelites for their *portion,* in order to the ſupport of life. So Chriſt is *the gift of God,* John iv. 10. *That excellent gift forcordained* by God, 1 Pet. i. 20. and by his unſpeakable goodneſs beſtowed on the true Iſrael, for *their portion,* Pet. x. 16. *by which they ſhould live:* thus Jeſus himſelf declares, John vi. 51. " I am the living bread, which came down from heaven: if any man eat of this bread, he ſhall live

for

for ever."——The manna was given to the Ifraelites, when they were leaft concerned about the bleffings of God, and put a greater value on the good things of Egypt, and had again tempted God. Chrift came into the world, when it was moft corrupted, and offered his fpiritual bleffings, at a time, when the very beft could fcarce afcend above earthly and carnal things. ——Ifrael did not know the manna, when it was firft given, though promifed by Mofes. Though Chrift was fo often promifed by Mofes and all the holy prophets, and defcribed to the life, yet when he came into the world, the world knew him not, John i. 10.

L. Though the origin of the manna was from heaven, yet the vapours or exhalations, from which it was congealed together, were raifed from the earth by the efficacy of the fun. Chrift feveral times repeats it, that he came down from heaven, to give life to the world, John vi. He, who is the " dayfpring from on high," Luke i. 78. is alfo the " fruit of the earth," Ifa. iv. 2.——We have already obferved, that angels were employed about the defcending manna. A great multitude of the heavenly hoft, fung the birth-day fong, when Chrift firft came into the world, Luke ii. 13.——Mofes, indeed, could not give the manna, yet he promifed it, and explained the nature of it. So neither was he the author of true falvation, but teftified of Chrift, and taught that the life of the foul confifts in communion with him, John v. 46.

LI. The manna was, in its form and figure, fmall and minute, promifing nothing great at firft fight: thus alfo Chrift, when he was feen only with the eyes of flefh, had neither form no comelinefs, that we fhould defire him, Ifa. liii. 2.——Yet the white colour of the manna, and ufually that of pearls too, reprefented the moft excellent purity of the Lord Jefus, and the glory of the divine majefty *fhining* forth in the affumed form of a fervant.——The tafte of the manna, that was fo very fweet, like honey, and the moft excellent oil, fignifies the unfpeakable delights of that grace, we obtain by Chrift, whofe fweetnefs none underftand but they who tafte it, Pfal. xxxiv. 8.——In order to be a more proper food for Ifrael, it was ground in mills, or pounded with peftles, or baked in pans, Numb. xi. 8. Chrift was alfo prepared by various fufferings, that he might be moft fweet and wholefome food to our foul.

LII. The manna was rained down in the wildernefs: and Chrift came into the world, and to the people of Ifrael, when, like a wildernefs, it was overgrown with thiftles, and thorns, and moft barren of good fruit: and by his coming " comfor all the wafte places of Zion, and made her wildernefs like E

and her defart like the garden of Jehovah," Ifa. li. 3.——It
was then, that the Ifraelites obtained the manna, when all that
they had brought out of Egypt, was fpent, and they faw, they
muft inevitably perifh, by famine, unlefs they were relieved by
the unexpected favour of heaven. Chrift beftows his grace
only on thofe, who fenfible of their want, and rejecting every
worldly comfort, choofe to owe their falvation to him alone,
Luke i. 53. " he filled the hungry with good things, and fent
the rich empty away.——Nor can any one hope for the confolations of divine grace, unlefs they firft quit the Egypt of this
world, and the prifon of fin, and paffing through the Red Sea
of forrowful. repentance, he gives himfelf up to be led and directed by the Holy Spirit, in the way to the heavenly Canaan,
Ifa. xxxii. 16, 17.

LIII. The manna came down every day, and when ever the
morning dawned, prefented itfelf frefh to the Ifraelites. Thus alfo
the grace and tender mercies of the Lord are new every morning, Lam. iii. 23.——Yet this bread was in fuch manner given
for fix days, as none of it was to be feen on the feventh. This
feems to fignify, that Chrift would in his appointed time appear among the Ifraelites, and converfe daily with them; but
afterwards would neither be feen, nor fought for, any where
on earth, nor be imagined, to be either in this or in the other
place. But becaufe that day was the feventh of the week, this
fet forth, he fhould ceafe to be feen by men on the feventh;
but on the firft day of the week, when he returned from the
grave, he would prefent himfelf to the view of his people almoft as early as the fun.——When the Ifraelites were come
into Canaan, the manna ceafed; every thing which regards
the ftate of the church, wandering in the wildernefs of this
world, confequently every healing grace, and every thing,
which flows to us from Chrift, as mediator, and fuppofes any
defect, fhall ceafe after the laft day, when God himfelf fhall be
all in all to his church, when introduced into the heavenly
country, 1 Cor. xv. 28.

LIV. The manna was not beftowed on the Ifraelites, as the
effect of their fowing or culture, or of any human induftry:
but by the gratuitous gift of the divine goodnefs and bounty
alone: the only thing required of them, was to receive, to
gather and make ufe of that gift of God. Thus in like manner
the life and falvation, we have in Chrift the Lord, " is not of
him that willeth, nor of him that runneth, but of God that
fheweth mercy," Rom. ix. 16. And his grace is " as a dew
from Jehovah, as the fhowers upon the grafs, that tarrieth not
for man, nor waiteth for the fons of men," Mic. v. 7. It is
                                                        however

however our duty, by faith to receive, and apply to ourfelves the offered grace. And this was what our Saviour meant, when he faid, John ix. 27. " labour not for the meat which perifheth but for that meat which endureth unto everlafting life, which the Son of man fhall give unto you."——And this, indeed, was to be done early in the morning, not letting flip the opportunity, Ifa. lv. 6. " Seek ye the Lord, while he is near," Pfal. lxiii. 1. " O God, thou art my God, early will I feek thee."——The Ifraelites were to go without the camp, in in order to have the manna. Whofoever labours to find Chrift, muft not indulge too much the eafe of the flefh. When the fpoufe foughther beloved in her bed, fhe found him not, Canticl. iii. 1. but when fhe had gone a little further fhe found him, verfe 4.

LV. Though God gave the manna in a certain ftinted meafure, yet in a quantity fufficient for thofe of the largeft appetite ; Chrift deals out a portion of his grace to each, in fuch a manner, as nothing may be wanting to their falvation, 2 Cor. xii. 9. His grace, however is equally fet before all the elect, that each may take of it to his full fatisfaction, Cant. v. 9. If they open their mouths wide, they fhall be filled with the goodnefs of the Lord, Pfal. lxxxi. 10. Pfal. xxxvi. 8, 9.—— Our efteem and longing for the divine grace can indeed never be to excefs ; nor are we forbid to ftrive after more : let each account it faid to himfelf, 1 Cor. xii. 13. " covet earneftly the beft gifts." But yet every one ought to be contented with the moft free and wife difpenfation of our Father, humbly confeff: ing ourfelves unworthy even of the leaft. But if any, by the bleffing of God, is found to have gathered more than others, his duty is to lay out his abundance for the common benefit, and fupply the wants of others from the plenty of his gifts.

LVI. The manna, that was kept to the following day, became tainted, and ceafed any longer to be either the ufual, much lefs the facramental bread. Thus alfo the eucharistical bread, the antitype of the manna, after the time is over, when it is diftributed to be eaten, lofes the virtue of a facrament ; and if it be kept contrary to the command of God, inftead of being a fpiritual food, will be found tainted with the maggots of a bafe fuperftition.——A double quantity was gathered the day before the fabbath, for the ufe of that day of reft : on the fame day of the week, the labour of Chrift's foul being redoubled, fuch an abundance of grace was purchafed for the elect, even enough to fatiate, and make them happy through an eternal fabbath.——Nor are we to apprehend, the fpiritual gifts, laid up for that day, can be tainted by any corruption——In a word,

word, the keeping the manna in a golden pot, and the laying
it up in the tabernacle, before Jehovah, and the teftimony, fet
forth, that he who came down from heaven, to be the bread
of life to finful man, fhould again be taken up into heaven,
and continue in the fanctuary, not made with hands, and in
a ftate of uninterrupted life before God; whence alfo the communion with Chrift in glory is called " the hidden manna,"
Rev. ii. 17.——However, we are above all things, to be on
our guard, leaft, with the ungrateful Ifraelites, we loath the
incomparable delights of the heavenly grace, and prefer the
hufks of this world before them, and fo incur the jufteft vengeance of a defpifed deity.

LVII. But for as much as *the favour of meat is nothing, if
there be no drink,* as Jofephus introduces Mofes fpeaking to
God; and becaufe the fuperabundant fulnefs, which is in
Chrift, was to be fhadowed forth to the ancient people, as
well as to us, the divine goodnefs indulged the murmuring
Ifraelites likewife with drink, which was as miraculous as their
meat. For, the people being parched with thirft, and finding
no water, either for themfelves or children, much lefs their
cattle in the parched wildernefs, Mofes at God's command, ftriking with his rod, the rock, which was in Horeb, on whofe fum-
mit the glorious majefty of the divine prefence was feen, opened large veins of water, Exod. xvii. 2—6. This miracle is
celebrated in many places of fcripture, Pfal. lxxviii. 15, 16. " he
clave the rock in the wildernefs, and gave them drink, as out
of the great depths : he brought ftreams alfo out of the rock,
and caufed waters to run down like rivers." Some imagine
the rock itfelf was turned to ftreams of water, from Pfal. cxiv,
8. where the Vulgate tranflates, *qui convertit petram in ftagna
aquarum, and rupem in fontes aquarum,* which turned the rock
into a ftanding water, the flint into a fountain of waters; the
Septuagint τὰ τείψαίλος. But this is a poetical hyperbole, as if
we fhould fay, heaven itfelf was diffolved into fhowers. Nothing is more ridiculous, than to bring this in fupport of the
monfter of tranfubftantiation. But whether God firft
miraculoufly produced the water in that place, or whether
when Mofes fmote the rock with his rod, he fuddenly fet open
the veins of water, which had been there before, but had been
fhut up till then, is not for us to determine, fince the fcripture is filent. What the Jews feign, that the rod of Mofes
was made of adamant, and hence penetrated the rock by the
ftroke; and that therefore Mofes is faid not to have ftruck,
*upon the rock,* but, *in the rock,* ver. 6. is trifling to the higheft
degree.

LVIII.

LVIII. As there is no great difficulty in this historical account, we hasten to the consideration of the mystery set forth 1 Cor. x. 4. " and did all drink the same spiritual drink." Spiritual, not surely in its own nature, but in its signification, as we have intimated concerning the meat. " For they drank of the spiritual rock that followed them," that is, the water of the rock, which followed them in a plentiful stream in the wilderness. " And that rock was Christ," that is, as " Tertullian, de Patientia," says well, " signified Christ :" with whom Augustin agrees, Quæst. 57. " in Leviticum, the rock was Christ, not in substance, but signification." Let us take a survey of the similitude.

LIX. It is certain, Christ is often called a rock in scripture ; on account of his eternal duration, Isa. xxvi. 4. and impregnable strength, Ps. xxxi. 2. and, which is the consequence of that, a most safe habitation, Ps. lxxi. 3. Yet I imagine these respects do not come under our present consideration. Christ is here represented by a rock only, as that gave water to quench the thirst of the Israelites.

LX. The true similitude is this. 1st, This rock hath its name from a *parched dry waste* (for this is the meaning of Horeb in Hebrew,) and seemed to promise nothing less than what it produced, namely, streams, for giving water to such a number of people with their cattle. Is not Christ also " as a root out of a dry ground," Isa. liii. 2. And is it not something above a prodigy, that he, who complained of thirst on the cross, should call out to others, " if any man thirst let him come unto me and drink. He that believeth on me, as the scripture hath said, out of his belly shall flow rivers of living waters." John vi. 37, 38. 2dly, The rock did not produce water till it was smitten. Thus also " it became God to make the captain of our salvation perfect through sufferings," Heb. ii. 10. When his side was pierced with the spear, immediately there issued out blood and water, John xix. 34. And by this means he became " a fountain opened to the house of David, and to the inhabitants of Jerusalem for sin, and uncleanness, Zech. xiii. 1. 2dly, Nor was it lawful to smite the rock with any other instrument than the rod of the Lawgiver: to intimate, that Christ was to undergo the same sufferings and the same curse threatened by the law to the sinner man, Gal. iii. 13. 4thly, The smiting of the rock was performed in the sight of the elders of the murmuring people. At the loud clamour of an enraged multitude, and at the desire of the elders, many of them also standing by Christ when he was nailed to the cross, Mat. xxvii. 41. 5thly, The majesty of the supreme Being displayed itself on the top of the rock. When Christ suffered, did he not even

at

at that time, fo vail himfelf as if he was void of divine glory?
But they who were moft unwilling to own it, were obliged to
confefs it, Mat. xxvii. 54. 6thly, Such a quantity of water
flowed from the rock, that was fufficient not only to quench the
thirft of the Ifraelites, but alfo to follow them in ftreams, whitherfoever they travelled in the wildernefs, Pfal. lxxviii. 15,
20. Pfal. cv. 41. Thus alfo the abundance of grace, that is
in Chrift, makes " our cup to overflow, and goodnefs and mercy to follow us all the days of our life," Pfal. xxiii. 5, 6.

LXI. What we have recorded, Numb. xx. 8. Is different
from this hiftory, and is likewife myftical. There Mofes is
commanded, indeed not to fmite the rock with his rod, but
only to fpeak unto the rock, before the eyes of the Ifraelites,
in order to its producing water. By which it feems was
fignified, that Chrift ought to fuffer but once, and that his one
offering was fufficient for perfecting believers, Heb. ix. 27,
28. Heb. x. 14. The efficacy of which was to be difpenfed to
the elect by the preaching of the gofpel. But Mofes, contrary
to the will of the precept, though according to the will of the
divine decree, in fmiting the rock twice, was a type of thofe,
who wickedly indeed, but by the determinate counfel of God,
perfecute over again, and evil entreat Chrift, after once fuffering on the crofs, in his myftical body, Acts ix. 4. Col. i. 26.
As out of the rock, which was fmitten twice, there iffued out
much water, and the congregation drank, Num. xx. 11. fo in
like manner, even the afflictions of believers have turned out
to the advantage of the church, Phil. i. 12. the blood of the
martyrs, like a fructifying rain, has watered the paridife of
God; and the fparks, flying every way from their funeral piles
have far and near kindled a new light of faith, and new flames
of love: fo that the church never experienced a greater abundance of divine confolations, than when fhe was forced to endûre
the heavieft ftrokes of perfecution. Yet as Mofes himfelf,
who was fo faithful, fo dear to God, was for this very thing
excluded the land of Canaan, Num. xx. 11. fo none of thefe
perfecutors fhall go unpunifhed for this their rafh prefumption,
Pfal. cv. 14. 2 Theff. i. 6.

LXII. There now remains the facrament of the *brazen ferpent,* whofe hiftory recorded, Numb. xxi. 6.—Bochart has
diftinctly explained, Hierozoic. p. 2. lib. 3. c. 13. The fum of
which is this. The Ifraelites, for murmuring againft God and
againft Mofes, and fpeaking with contempt of the heavenly
manna, incurred the heavy difpleafure of the deity. And
therefore ferpents were fent among them, to bite the people,
and immediately cut off many by an infectiou: calamity. The

Scripture

scripture call thefe ferpents שרפים *Seraphim*; which name they
have in common with the moft exalted angels, and is derived from *burning*; but are fo called becaufe they fend a
flame out of their mouth, and burn by their venomous breath.
The Greeks call fome ferpents, from their heat πρηςῆρἀς and καυ-
σωνας. But whether feraph here denotes a water-ferpent, or an
amphibious ferpent, which is Bochart's opinion, or any other
fpecies of ferpents, is neither fo very certain, nor much our
concern to know. It is more profitable to confider how the
divine mercy, importuned by the complaints of the people, and
the confeffion of their fin, and the prayers of Mofes, afforded a
prefent remedy for fo great an evil. At the direction of God
a *brazen ferpent* was framed by Mofes, and put upon a pole;
that whoever looked upon it when it was thus erected, might
find a moft infallible cure for the mortal bites of the ferpents:
which alfo the event plainly proved. Three things are here
diftinctly to be obferved. (1.) The mifery of the people. (2.)
God's favour and goodnefs. (3.) The duty required of man,
in order to his partaking of that goodnefs.

LXIII. In the mifery of the people, we are to confider both
the fin and the punifhment of it. It was a fin, to throw
contempt upon the manna, and to murmur againft God and
againft Mofes. The depraved corruption of nature fcarce any
where more plainly fhews itfelf, than in the people of Ifrael;
who though loaded with fo many benefits by God, fo often
chaftifed with paternal rods, yet inceffantly returned to their
natural difpofition. Nor do they rife up againft Mofes alone,
by whofe means they had efcaped fo many dangers, but againft
God himfelf who was prefent among them, by fuch extraordinary figns of his majefty; and with a frantic wantonnefs
lothe the manna, even the heavenly manna, which they had
lately received with fo much eagernefs. Does not this plainly
argue the unconquerable depravity of our nature, and the incredible abufe of the divine beneficence in man, when left to
himfelf? And as we are all of the fame frame, we may behold
a fpecimen of our own perverfenefs in the Ifraelites.

LXIV. The punifhment, confequent on the fin, was the
bites of fiery ferpents; by which it is not improperly imagined, are fhadowed for the fuggeftions of the devil, when he
tempts to difpair, and which Paul calls *the fiery darts of Satan*,
Eph. vi. 16. and which fpread their poifon through every part.
For the devils are truly feraphim; who, as in their firft
creation, they fhone fair with the flames of divine love, fo after
their fin, became horrid and fcorching ferpents. As themfelves are fcorched with the fire of divine vengeance, fo they

burn with rage againſt God and his people. And indeed, they
are juſtly given up to the vexations of Satan, who contemptu-
ouſly rejeċt the word of the gòſpel, and the grace of God in
Chriſt, which is ſweeter than any manna; or blaſpheme againſt
God himſelf, as Hymeneus and Alexander, 1 Tim. i. 20.

LXV. But as thoſe Iſraelites who found the bites of the
ſerpents mortal, not being careful to obtain a cure, are an
emblem of the impenitent, who, deſpiſe the grace of God, and
ſo die in their ſins : ſo they who had recourſe to Moſes, con-
feſſing their ſins, and imploring the grace of God, plainly
ſignify thoſe, whom a ſenſe of ſin, and dread of divine judgment, excite to wiſer reſolutions; ſuch as thoſe, who were
pricked in their heart, and ſaid to Peter and the other apoſtles,
" Men and brethren what ſhall we do?" Aċts. ii. 37. and the
jailor, Aċts xvi. 29, 30. But for their ſake, God commanded
Moſes to put a brazen ſerpent on a pole, and promiſed, that
as many as were bitten, ſhould, by looking to it, be cured.
Indeed, I make no manner of doubt, but this ſerpent was a
repreſentation of Chriſt ; for he himſelf aſſerts, John. iii. 14.
" as Moſes lifted up the ſerpent in the wildernefs, even ſo
muſt the Son of man be lifted up." This type repreſents the
antitype ſeveral ways.

LXVI. Firſt, as to the *form*. That the ſerpent was a type
of the devil, not of Chriſt, is aſſerted by a learned author without any probable reaſon. Though the ſerpent, which deſtroyed the Iſraelites by their venomous bites, were a figure of the
devil, yet all circumſtances loudly declare the brazen ſerpent,
which was made at God's command, and ordained to cure the
bites of the other ſerpents, was a ſacrament of Chriſt. Nor
is it more improper to repreſent Chriſt by the figure of a ſerpent,
than, what the learned author ſo often inculcates, by that of
a wanton goat. The ſimilitude conſiſts in the following things.
1ſt, That Chriſt, though himſelf free from all ſin, came " in
the likeneſs of ſinful fleſh," Rom. viii. 3. 2dly, That by a voluntary covenant-engagment, he ſubſtituted himſelf in the room
of thoſe, who by nature, like all others, are a " generation of
vipers," Mat. iii. 7. 3dly, That by virtue of that engagement,
by bearing their ſins, he was made *ſin and the curſe*, 2 Cor. v. 21.
Gal. iii. 13. And ſo had truly the figure of a ſerpent, without
its poiſon.

LXVII. *Secondly*, as to the *matter* of it, whereby in different
reſpeċts, were repreſented both the vileneſs of the human nature,
the excellence of the divine, and the efficacy of the goſpel, as
the learned have obſerved. 1ſt, The ſerpent was not of gold,
but of braſs, which is a nearer metal, to hold forth Chriſt to

us, as one " in whom there is no form, nor comelinefs, no beauty, that we fhould defire him," Ifa. liii. 2. 2dly, To fignify the divine power of Chrift by the firmnefs and durable-nefs of brafs. Whence Job vi. 12. " is my ftrength the ftrength of ftones? Or is my flefh of brafs?" And in the Poet, *a monument* is faid to be *more lafting than brafs*. 3dly, As among metals brafs is the moft founding. Whence Paul, 1 Cor. xiii. 1. " I am become as a found brafs. Thus Chrift crucified feems to be rightly fet forth by brafs, as alfo the preaching of the crofs, " whofe found went into all the earth," Rom. x. 18.

LXVIII. *Thirdly*, as to the *lifting up*. This lifting up of the ferpent on a pole, prefigured the lifting up of Chrift, not his glorious exaltation in heaven, but his ignominious lifting up on the crofs, John iii. 14. As John himfelf explains that phrafe, John xii. 32, 33. For, according to the Syriac and the lan-guage of the Targum, *to lift up*, fignifies *to hang up on a tree*. Both actions are denoted by the fame term נשא. And as Bochart has learnedly obferved, that manner of fpeaking feems to have taken its rife from the decree of king Darius; at leaft it may be confirmed by that Ezra vi. 11. " whofoever fhall alter this word, let timber be pulled down from his houfe, and being fet up, let him be hanged *(put to death)* thereon: fet up, that is hanged up. But holocaufts, or whole burnt-offerings, called in Hebrew נשוה, that is, *elevations*, becaufe they were carried upwards, fignified, that Chrift, when offering himfelf for fin, fhould be lifted upon the crofs. Nor is it for nothing, that God would have the ferpent lifted up by Mofes. Becaufe it was in confequence of the curfe, thundered out by the law, given by Mofes, that Chrift was nailed to the crofs.

LXIX. *Fourthly*, With refpect to the *benefit*: as from the fer-pent the Ifraelites obtained the cure of their mortal bites; fo " in the wings *of Chrift* there is healing," Mal. iv. 2. " he heal-eth all our difeafes," Pfal. ciii. 3. Wherefore as the Jews, de-pending on fuch a prefent help, little dreaded the bites and ftings of the other ferpents; fo the believer, who relies upon Chrift, and makes nothing of the affaults of devils, cries out with full affurance, " O death, where is thy fting?" 1 Cor. xv. 55.

LXX. In order to partake in fo great a benefit, 'God re-quired nothing of the Ifraelites, but to look to the brazen ferpent; juft fo a bare look to Chrift, lifted up on the crofs, perfectly cures the wounds given by the devil; namely, a look of faith by which Mofes faw him, who is invifible, Heb. xi. 27. Thus Chrift himfelf explains it, John iii. 14, 15. " As Mofes lifted up the ferpent in the wildernefs, even fo muft the

R r 2                                             Son

Son of man be lifted up: that whofoever believeth in him, fhould not perifh, but have eternal life." If therefore any a-mong the Ifraelites were blind, or voluntarily turned away their eyes, there remained no hope of falvation for them : fo neither at this day for unbelievers, or for " thofe that rebel againft the light," Job xxiv. 13. or for thofe, " whofe minds the god of this world hath blinded, leaft the light of the glorious gofpel of Chrift, fhould fhine unto them," 2 Cor. iv. 4. Yet as even a v eak fight might be faving; fo a faith ftill in a ftate of weak-nefs, if it be genuine and fincere, refcues us from death : and as whoever was once bit and cured by the fight of the ferpent, if again bit, he was to have recourfe to the fame remedy : fo if after our reftoration, we fall again into fin, the fame faith fuccours, as before.

---

## CHAP. XI.

### Of the Bleſſings of the Old Teſtament.

I. AS the Old Teftament is nothing, but the covenant of grace, as it was difpenfed before Chrift came in the flefh, it is neceffary, that all the bleffings or good things, which were promifed by the covenant of grace, as fuch, have like-wife a place in the Old Teftament. But the benefits of the covenant of grace are eternal falvation, and whatever has a neceffary connection therewith; fuch as, regeneration, voca-tion by the word and Spirit of grace, faith, juftification, fpirit-ual peace, adoption, and, in a word, all the particulars ex-plained in the preceding book. Though moft of thefe are much more eminent under the New Teftament, yet all of them as to their fubftance, were conferred even under the Old, as this is evident from the nature of the thing, and from what we have proved before. We fhall only treat of the good things peculiar to the Old Teftament, efpecially under the Mofaic difpenfation.

II. And they are five. I. The election of the Ifraelites for a peculiar people. II. The inheritance of the land of Canaan. III. The familiar demonftration and inhabitation of the divine majefty. IV. The fhadowing forth of divine myfteries, and daily fealing them by a religion of ceremonies. V. An almoft uninterrupted fucceffion of infpired prophets.

III. It was certainly a great benefit, that God *fhould choofe*
the

the people of Ifrael, above all other nations of the world, to have communion with himfelf in a moft ftedfaft covenant. God himfelf declares this in thefe words, Deut. vii. 6. " for thou art a holy people unto Jehovah thy God, Jehovah thy God hath chofen thee to be a fpecial people unto himfelf, above all people that are upon the face of the earth." In confequence of this election, it was. 1ft, That Ifrael was called, " the firft-born fon of God," Exod. iv. 22. That is, above all other people, whofe fouls the fame God had made, and to whom he gives life and breath and all things; a fingular people, his only beloved, Lord of all the reft, having a double portion of the bleffing, an inheritance, not only earthly, but alfo fpiritual. 2dly, That they fhould be the peculiar property of God, his treafure, *segulla* and as it were, his royal riches, which he boafts of in the world, and glories in *as his Segullah*, concerning the emphafis of which word, fee what we have faid, Book 3. chap. xii. §. 7. and chap. xiii. §. 19. 3dly, That they again might glory in God, as in their portion. For, when God took them for a people to himfelf, he, at the fame time, gave them a right to call him their God, and to have him for their portion: as thefe things are joined together, Deut. xxvi. 17. 18. " thou haft avouched Jehovah this day to be thy God; and Jehovah hath avouched thee this day to be his peculiar people," Jer. x. 16. " The portion of Jacob is the former of all things: and Ifrael is the rod of his inheritance. 4thly, That they fhould have a right to expect the Meffiah, from the midft of them, as one of their brethren, Deut. xviii. 15, 18.

IV. In thefe things certainly, great was the " advantage of the Jew, and much the profit of circumcifion, much I fay every way," Rom. iii. 1, 2. Hence the apoftle, Rom. ix. 4, 5. in ftrong terms amplifies that *advantage* of the Jews; " who are Ifraelites, to whom pertaineth the adoption, and the glory, and the covenants, and the giving of the law, and the fervice of God and the promifes: whofe are the fathers, and of whom as concerning the flefh Chrift came." Yet none of thefe things, nay not all of them together, if we only confider the external confederation, was fufficient to them for falvation: for " they are not all Ifrael, which are of Ifrael: neither becaufe they are the feed of Abraham, are they all children," Rom. ix. 6, 7. Very many of them, notwithftanding they were the children of the kingdom, were caft out, Mat. viii. 12. Yet in this election of the whole body of the people to the communion of a very clofe but yet external covenant, there was a certain type of thofe, who were actually chofen to grace and glory: and the godly among the Ifraelites, befides thefe

thefe outward prerogatives, enjoyed the faving favour of God, and the privilege of the myftical covenant, in and by them.

V. The *Second* benefit or privilege of the Old Teftament was the *land of Canaan*. This God had promifed to Abraham and his feed, Gen. xii. 7. Gen. xiii. 15. and Gen. xv. 7. nay, and affigned it to them by oath, Gen. xxvi. 3, 4. Exod. xxxiii. 1. Ezek. xx. 6. This promife, confirmed by oath, God calls a *covenant*, διαθηκη, *a teftament*, that is, the laft and irrevocable difpofal of his will, Gen. xv. 18. " in that fame day Jehovah made a covenant with Abraham, faying, unto thy feed have I given this land." And becaufe, in confequence of that teftament, the feed of Abraham was to poffefs that land, it is therefore called their inheritance, Lam. v. 2. Heb. xi. 8.

VI. But we are by no means to underftand this, as if that typical inheritance made up the whole inheritance of the Old Teftament, or that we are to give fuch a confined definition of the Old Teftament, as if it was only the will of giving the land of Canaan. Much lefs are we to fay, that they who deny this, either admit no Old Teftament at all, or confound it with the New. For, the Old Teftament, as I have feveral times repeated, is nothing but the teftament of grace, as propofed under the vail of types, which were abrogated. But heaven and falvation, and God himfelf are the inheritance of the children of God, by the teftament or covenant of grace: and as that teftament is invariable, the fubftance of the inheritance cannot be one thing under the Old, and another under the New economy of the fame Teftament. The difference of the economies confifts in this, that the fame inheritance is held forth different ways: in the New Teftament clearly and without any vail; in the Old, wrapt up in many types and earthly pledges; among which, after the covenant was made with Abraham, the typical inheritance of the land of Canaan was the moft eminent. In the Old Teftament it was conjoined with bondage; in the New with liberty; to which the inheritance of the Gentiles is likewife added.

VII. That this inheritance was typical, both reafon declares, and the fcripture attefts. For, as the whole habitable world cannot be the happinefs of the foul, and is fubject to vanity, by reafon of fin, there is no country, confidered in itfelf, of fuch value, as to deferve to be called the inheritance of the people of God. And certainly, God's covenant-people have fomething more to expect from him, than what even the wicked may poffefs. Nor is there fo vaft a difference between Syria Egypt and Canaan, if we confider only the fertility and pleafantnefs of countries, as that the poffeffion of the Ifraelites, unlefs

lefs fomething higher was implied, fhould be fo much commended, as to be the * envy of all other nations. In fine, if, their happinefs confifted in the fields which they poffeffed, what became of thofe pious perfons, who, at the rifk of this life, and this earthly inheritance, willingly laid down their lives for the love of their God? and what was the reafon, why Mofes juft on the confines of death, expreffed fo great a defire after, that land, at leaft to fee it with his eyes, Deut. iii. 25. but becaufe he eagerly wanted fome way or other, to tafte that pledge of heaven which he was debarred from entering into.

VIII. But fcripture alfo very plainly declares the fame thing. When the ungrateful Ifraelites had, by ther murmurings, provoked God, he fware in his wrath, " as truly as I live, they fhall not fee the land, which I fware unto their fathers," Num. xiv. 21, 23. It is thus expreffed Pfal. xcv. 11. " unto whom I fware in my wrath, that they fhould not enter into my reft." Which Paul, Heb. iv. 1.—11. refers to the Meffiah, and to the fpiritual and heavenly reft, purchafed by Chrift: intimiting, that the quiet poffeffion of the land of Canaan, into which Jefus, or Jofhua the fon of Nun, introduced the children of thofe rebels, was a type of the fpiritual reft, purchafed for the elect by Jefus the Son of God, and of Mary.

IX. The analogy or fimilitude confifts in the following particulars. 1ft, The land of Canaan was eminent for its fituation, pleafantnefs, fertility, and for the excellent fruits of the earth, above very many other countries of the world; whence it is fo often called " a goodly land, a land flowing with milk and honey," a phrafe ufed even by poets as well Greek as Latin; *the pleafant land*, Pfal. cvi. 24. Zech. vii. 14. and in a word, *the glory of all lands*, Ezek. xx. 15: where the inhabitants " were made to fuck honey out of the rock, and oil out of the flinty rock, and butter of kine, and the pure blood of the grape," Deut. xxxii. 13, 14. It therefore reprefented the delightful pleafantnefs and abundant plenty of the fpiritual bleffings in the kingdom of Chrift, both of grace and of glory: concerning which Jeremiah prophefied, chap. xxxi. 12. " therefore they fhall come and fing in the height of Zion, and fhall flow together to the goodnefs of Jehovah, for wheat, and for wine, and for oil, and for the young of the flock, and of the herd; and their foul fhall be as a watered garden, and they fhall not forrow any more at all:" compare Joel iii. 18.

X. 2dly, The land of Canaan was, in a peculiar manner, *Jehovah's*

The author's words are *tam invidiofe praedicanda fit* which could not, I conceive, be rendered, but by a paraphrafis.

*Jehovah's land,* Hofea ix. 3. where himfelf intended to dwell, Pfal. lxxxiii. 12. Whence it is called "the place where Jehovah had made for himfelf to dwell in," Exod. xv. 17. " and his holy habitation," ver. 13. But it is called fo, not only becaufe God was to have a temple in that land, and to difplay fome peculiar fymbols of his prefence but alfo becaufe in that land, he was to fend his Son to them, and to anoint him in the midft of them, both king and Lord by pouring out his Holy Spirit. The Ifraelites therefore in their land, which in a peculiar manner was the land of God, had a pledge of the revelation of the Meffiah in the midft of them. That השׁכינה, inhabitation of God in Canaan was a fymbol of what John defcribes, Rev. xxi. 3. "behold the tabernacle of God is with men, and he will dwell (tabernacle) with them." And in the laft place, Jerufalem,which *was the throne of glory* in the land of Canaan, Jer. iii. 17. was a pledge of heaven, which is *the habitation of the holinefs and glory of God,* Ifa. lxiii. 15.

XI. 3dly, The land of Canaan was given to Ifrael in virtue of the teftament of grace, not for any merit or worth of theirs, but by the mere favour of God, Deut. vii. 7, 8. " not becaufe ye were more in number than any people——but becaufe Jehovah loved you, and becaufe he would keep the oath, which he had fwore unto your fathers, hath Jehovah brought you out with a mighty hand;" compare Deut. iv. 37, 38, Ezek. xvi. 60. and Ezek. xxxvi. 32. Thus alfo the inheritance of heaven comes to believers from the moft free grace of God alone, and the moft free teftament of God the Father and of Chrift, Luke xii. 32. Eph. ii. 8. But yet Ifrael was to travail through a large and great wildernefs, and to conflict with the Canaanites, in various and fevere battles, before they could enter upon the poffeffion of the promifed land. They alfo, to whom a full right to heaven is freely given, through the grace of Chrift, are to walk in that narrow way, befet with briars and thorns, and to fight valiantly againft the enemies of their falvation, and take the kingdom of heaven by violence.

XII. Laftly, though Mofes indeed, brought Ifrael out of Egypt, yet he could not bring them into the promifed land : that office was referved for Jofhua. And certainly when the law is fubfervient to the covenant of grace it tends to drive the elect out of themfelves, by making them acknowledge their vilenefs and mifery : neverthelefs it is by Jefus only, that we are introduced into a ftate of grace. Mofes is to begin the work and prepare the foul, and lead the people round through the wildernefs : but it is the office of Jefus to put the laft hand to the work, to say *it is finished*, and procure true rest to the souls of his people, Mat. xi. 28.

XIII. The *third* blessing of the Old Testament, is the familiar and clear *demonstration* or display *of the divine majesty*: such as was made in the appearances of angels, when they declared the will of God; nay, and of God himself, when he presented himself to the view of the patriarchs and prophets under a visible appearance. But that glorious epiphany or manifestation of God before the assembly of the whole people, when he came to give his law, and to establish his covenant, is of all others the most remarkable. This prerogative of Israel was indeed so great, that no people on earth ever enjoyed any thing like it, Deut. iv. 32, 33. " For ask now of the days that are past, which were before thee, since the day that God created man upon the earth, and ask from the one side of heaven unto the other, whether has been any such thing, as this great thing is, or hath been heard like it? Did ever people hear the voice of God speaking out of the midst of the fire, as thou hast heard, and live?" There were likewise the conspicuous symbols of the divine presence in the pillar of cloud and fire, in the sacred and heavenly fire, in the cloud of the sanctuary, and many other things of a similar nature: wherefore God is said, " to have had his fire in Zion and his furnace in Jerusalem," Isa. xxxi. 9. Which visible symbols of the divine familiarity gradually ceased upon the manifestation of Christ in the flesh, of which they were appointed to be types and figures.

XIV. The *fourth* blessing of the Old Testament consisted in the *ceremonies* and in the daily use of them. I own, that, in a certain respect, the ceremonies were a grievous yoke, and belonged to the faults or defects of that testament: but there was likewise a remarkable representation of Christ in them, and of the grace that was to be obtained by him. And because God was pleased in those times to set his mysteries before them in riddles, parables and figures; it was the extraordinary happiness of Israel, that they had continually before their eyes these pictures of the divine goodness, and of a Saviour to come, while other nations were left to themselves. And the rather, as the elect were instructed by the patriarchs, and the prophets, and by those, who had been taught by them, in their mystical signification, according to the measure of those times. And in them they had not only a prefiguration, but also a confirming seal of the coming of the Messiah, to whom they all led as by the hand, and without whom they had been a ludicrous farce, and unworthy of God, 1 Pet. i. 10——12.

XV. And for this reason it is, that the scripture so often

mentions this thing, as a great blessing granted to the Israelites. Pfal. cxlvii. 19, 20. "He shewed his word unto Jacob, his statutes and his judgments unto Israel: he hath not dealt so with any nation," Isa. xlii. 21. " Jehovah is well pleased for his righteousness' sake," that is, for his truth and goodness, *he will magnify* (him by) the law *and make it* (him) *honourable*: Hof. viii. 12. *I have written to him the great things of my law.* Which is not only, nay I may venture to say, not principally, to be understood of the moral, or even the forensick or judicial law; but chiefly, of the doctrine of grace, which was prefigured by the ceremonial law. For, the principles of the moral law, implanted in man at his creation, still remain in the conscience of men, though no new revelation had been superadded: and for the safety of bodies politic, many things have been happily devised by wife men. But as to the mysteries of the ceremonial law, these were the peculiar privilege of the people of God; and, on account of them, the Israelites looked on themselves as having the pre-eminence above all other nations.

XVI. For the same reason, the godly assisted at those ceremonies with so much delight and chearfulness of soul, and on the contrary accounted it the greatest part of their unhappiness, if at any time they were banished from their country, and forced to live at a distance from these holy things for it was their continual prayer, that they might be allowed to live in the house of God for ever : See Pfal. xxiii. 6. Pfal. xxvii. 4. Pfal. xlii. 2, 5. Pfal. lxxxiv. 2, 3. Pfal. lxxxix. 15. As without all doubt, they learned from these ceremonies, their uncleanness and guilt, which tended to the saving humiliation of their soul; so in them also they beheld the expiation of guilt and the sanctification from sin, the absolution or purging of the conscience. True that was only typical by the ceremonies, but it was true and spiritual through him, who was prefigured by them.

XVII. Which things being so, those persons seem too much to depreciate those salutary institutions of God, who scarcely ever consider them, but as an unsupportable burden, and a handwriting contrary to those who observed them, and as the penalty of breach of covenant; and insist, that what God declares Ezek. xx. 25. is to be applied to them, namely, that he gave Israel *statutes that were not good*, and judgmts whereby they should not live. But the celebrated Dr John a Marck, who was formerly my intimate colleague, has vindicated this passage in such a manner, as entirely to supersede any defence of mine. We acknowledge, that there was something in the ceremonies, which was both grievous, and testified their imperfection, and that the expiation of sin was not yet perfected; but of these things we shall speak in their place. But at the same time, we insist, that

they

they had a reference to the gospel, and were a picture of Christ and his benefits, and seals of grace: neither are we to think, that they were effects of his wrath in such a manner against Israel, as if they were not given as tokens of a singular favour to that people. The Jews themselves really were, and at this day are still sensible of this; for though they acknowledge, they cannot find out the reason for these ceremonies, yet they affirm, that a more secret wisdom is contained in them, than they can perceive. To this purpose Abarbanel in Legem. Fol. 197. col. 2. writes concerning them: " Lo! the principal intention in them, is to be as a book of sublime wisdom and divine doctrine, which students in the law may contemplate, till they perfect their souls by those apprehensions and notions."

XVIII. The *fifth* and last blessing of the Old Testament is an almost uninterrupted *succession of inspired men*, by whom the the church in those days instructed in all their doubts were without any hazard of being deceived. For, in the first ages, the patriarchs might be consulted, to whom God immediately revealed himself, and who in a state of such longevity, were generally many at a time, or at least were almost contemporary with one another. After them succeeded Moses. He was followed by a long succession of prophets, even to the time of the Babylonish captivity, if we except some very few and short intervals, such as are mentioned, 1 Sam. iii. 1. and 2 Chron. xv. 3. Under the Babylonish captivity flourished Ezekiel and Daniel: after this last came Haggai, Zachariah and Malachi, not to say any thing now of Nehemiah and Ezra. And after the Holy Spirit ceased to dictate things to be written for the canon of the church of Israel, yet even to the coming of Christ, he ceased not to move, in an extraordinary manner, the minds of some by his divine inspiration, as is evident in Simeon, in Zachariah the father of John the Baptist, and in Anna the prophetess. But under the New Testament, after the canon of Scripture was completed by the apostolic writings, those prophetic enthusiasms or impulses gradually expired.

---

## CHAP. XII.

*Of the Imperfections falsely ascribed to the Old Testament.*

I. THAT the Old Testament required no deficency to be supplied, appears even from this, because otherwise a

place

place would not have been fought for a fecond : as the apoftle, Heb. viii 7. proves to a demonftration. Having therefore treated of the bleffings and privileges of that teftament; it is proper, that we now confider its *imperfections* and defects. Not that we would detract any thing from the divine grace, as it was difplayed in the times of old, (becaufe the ancient fathers both acknowleged and actually experienced, that it was fuffi-cient for their falvation) but that we may fet a higher value on the infinite riches of the divine bounty, which were referved for the more aufpicious age of the New Teftament.

II. But in handling this, two prudential precautions are to be premifed. 1ft, That, in order to overvalue our own con-dition, we do not too much undervalue that of the ancients. 2dly, That, by duly acknowledging our own privileges, lefs than they deferve, we may be found unthankfully to undervalue the grace of God. And becaufe fome have erred in both thefe extremes, we propofe to manage this fubject in the following method. In this chapter we fhall confute what fome perfons, who in other refpects are learned and orthodox, feem to have advanced with too little caution againft the Old Teftament ; and then fhew from fcripture, in what things it was really de-fective.

III. We here pafs over unregarded the herefy of the Socinians, who affert, with the utmoft effrontery, that there was no pro-mife of eternal life in the Old Teftament ; that Jefus Chrift was the firft and only preacher of that important truth : a blaf-phemy we have already confuted. At prefent our bufinefs is with brethren, whom we efteem in the Lord ; only we muft always give the preference to the facred truth. It does not become us nor any Chriftian, to multiply difputes without caufe and to wreft things, well or tolerably faid, to a worfe meaning than they will bear, and when we have wrefted them, invidi-oufly to expofe them : a manner of procedure this not to be ufed with enemies, much lefs with brethren. It is, however, incumbent on all, to endeavour to fpeak with the utmoft cau-tion, and perfpicuity they are able ; nor fhould any one take it amifs ; if things, which are fpoken improperly and harfhly, and lefs confiftently with the truth, are modeftly, calmly, and without any party zeal, taken notice of and corrected : efpecial-ly if they have efcaped from perfons of character in the church ; and are urged by fome with a warmth not to be commended, as if they excelled the common doctrine of the reformed churches by the commendation of a purer and more fublime knowledge : fo if any perfon that does not affent to them in all

all respects, is scarce accounted a learned and unprejudiced divine.

IV. In the first place, I imagine, that these following words of a celebrated interpreter have justly given offence to learned men; " the scope of these words is to shew, that though very great temporal benefits were bestowed on the Israelites, yet before the last times, none that were *true and permanent: nor was salvation itself actually* discovered to them," Coccei. Ult. Mos. p. 886.

V. Who that reads or hears these words, would not be led by their very sound to imagine even this, that though the Israelites really enjoyed temporal privileges, such as possession of the land of Canaan, a peaceable government, a flourishing kingdom, prosperity as subjects, long life, and the like, yet they had no benefits, that were true and permanent: by which one can scarce forbear thinking, that they had no communion with the Messiah, nor part in his peculiar blessings, as reconciliation with God, peace of conscience, reformation after the image of the divine purity, foretastes of the joys of heaven, and a happy removal of the soul from this to an immortal life ? For, these, if any, are deservedly and usually called true and permanent benefits, and salvation itself. Whoever therefore affirms, that very great temporal privileges, and, in the same breath denies, that such as were true and permanent were bestowed on, and salvation itself disclosed to the Israelites, speaks in such a manner as to suggest to the mind of the reader, that the spiritual blessings of the soul, and eternal life were neither bestowed on, nor discovered to them.

VI. And it is also scarce possible for the reader not to be confirmed in that suspicion, if in another part he reads, that the only delight the Israelites had, was that they could extend their meditations to the felicity of the latter times, which yet they were not to see with their own eyes. But the same author's preface to the Psalms inculcates this in a set, premeditated discourse, not far from the begining. " This, indeed, was their only solace; for, while they were singing most of the Psalms, they were, in the type of David, either singing before hand the afflictions and exaltation of Christ, or reaching forward to the latter times ; and deploring their present forlorn case, were endeavouring to change it into the joy of the future time, nay, assuming the disposition, the joy, the zeal, and sharing in the combats and victories of those who were to see what themselves did not, to hear what themselves did not hear. *This, I say, was their only comfort. For, neither what they saw could yield them any delight ; because they were shadows : nor what*
they

*they heard; because it was only, partly a promise, partly an accusa-*
*tion of sin and guilt, with which man is born, but was not then*
*abolished and blotted out ; nor what they possessed; because they were*
*to leave them, or because the wicked enjoyed them as well as they:*
*in fine, because they were no real blessings, capable to satisfy the*
*soul.*" Who may not gather from this, that, in the Pſalms of
David, the preſent bleſſings of ſaving grace were neither foretold, commended or celebrated, and therefore the Iſraelites did
not poſſeſs them, though not only the hopes of theſe bleſſings,
but alſo the actual poſſeſſion of them, have been in all ages, the
ſubject and cauſe of unſpeakable joy. For, if David, in his
pſalms, can celebrate even ſuch ſpiritual bleſſings, which are
connected with eternal ſalvation as himſelf and other believers
enjoyed even at that time : with what deſign can it be ſaid,
that their only ſolace and comfort conſiſted in meditating on
the joy of the time to come, and that they poſſeſſed bleſſings,
which were neither real, nor ſufficient to ſatisfy the ſoul,?
Who, on reading theſe things could imagine he was peruſing
the writings of a reformed doctor ?

VII. But I would not have you to believe, that this very
learned author, though he writes in this ſtyle, is gone over to
the Socinians, whom, in almoſt all his writings, he has ſtrenu-
ouſly oppoſed, and happily confuted. He repeats it a thou-
ſand times over, and makes it appear, by cogent arguments
againſt thoſe moſt peſtilent heretics, that the promiſe of the
ſpiritual and heavenly inheritance was made to the fathers of
the Old Teſtament, and the poſſeſſion of it granted to them in
conſequence of the teſtament of grace. And in the very place
we firſt quoted, §. 885. he writes : that "Jehovah was the father of that people ; for he purchaſed and made them, and beſtowed all good things upon them, which is to be underſtood
not only in a figurative ſenſe, or with reſpect to any external
favour ; but with reſpect to the benefit of redemption, the
new creation, and the donation of all things neceſſary for life
and godlineſs, by which he is in truth manifeſted to be the father of that people, with reſpect to his elect children, who
were at all times contained in that people, as in a ſeminary,
but leſs frequently in the great multitude of the Iſraelites of
that age." So far well : I could wiſh, he had ſtopped here.

VIII. But theſe two aſſertions are ſo different, that they
ſeem to be even contradictory. For, as the bleſſing of redemption, the new creation, and the donation of all things neceſſary for life and godlineſs; and in fine, to have God not in figure, but in truth, for their father, are indiſputably true and permanent bleſſings, and are even ſalvation itſelf. Whoever aſ-

ſerts

forts, that thefe things were beftowed on, and difcovered to
the Ifraelites, and yet denies, that true and permanent bleffings had been conferred upon, and difcovered to them, feems
to involve himfelf in a manifeft contradiction.

IX. What then? Did memory, did judgment, did foundnefs of mind fail this very learned author, when he advanced
things fo contradictory? But his acknowledged learning forbids us to fufpect any fuch thing. Let us then declare the
matter as it is. By true and permanent benefits, which, he
fays, were not beftowed on the fathers of the Old Teftament,
he means the bleffings peculiar to the New, as the truth is oppofed to the type, and what is permanent to the fhadow, that
was to evanifh. And falvation with him denotes complete falvation. He has found an interpreter and apologift in a divine
of very great name, who, with great confidence, tells us, that
this affertion is, for the moft part in fcripture terms; which
might have been better underftood by divines, if they had tak-
en as much pains to read and meditate on the writings of God
as of men: and he endeavours to fhew, that fome of the things
peculiar to the New Teftament, as fuch, are fometimes held
forth by the name of falvation, and of true and permanent benefits. For this purpofe he quotes, Heb. ii. 3. where *falvation* is faid, " at the firft to have begun to be fpoken by the
Lord:" that is, the work of falvation, which Chrift now began
to perform: or even that clear and effectual doctrine of the
gofpel, which calls us to falvation. He further obferves, that
thofe benefits are fometimes called *true*, which are oppofed to
thofe which were *typical*, as John i. 17. " the law was given
by Mofes, but grace and *truth* came by Jefus Chrift:" and as
the blotting out the hand-writing, which was againft us, and
that glorious degree of adoption, mentioned, Gal. iv. 5. are
faid to be true benefits; he afferts, that they are juftly called
*permanent*, in contradiftinction to the covenant of grace, as it
was a covenant with the Ifraelites, which was neither faultlefs,
nor permanent, Heb. viii. 7, 9. From all which he concludes
that is to fpeak agreeable with the fcriptures, to fay, that true
and permanent benefits, and falvation itfelf were not beftowed
on, and difcovered to Ifrael.

X. Thefe things require a particular confideration. It is my
real judgment and perfuafion, that thefe learned men would
have acted a far more prudent and generous part, if fometimes
for the fake of truth, they had abandoned thofe, whom they
have fet up as heads of their party; confeffing both that they
were men, and that fometimes their thoughts and difcourfes
were lefs accurate; and not firft to excufe every thing, however

ever uncautiously fpoken, with great confidence, and then to
defend it as moft genuine, and moft exactly agreeable to fcripture language, though but with very indifferent fuccefs, and at
the expence of the reputation of their brethren.

XI. But let us confider the conftant tenor of the facred writings. Thefe call the fpiritual bleffings of the foul, τό ἀληθινόν
*the true*, Luke xvi. 11. in oppofition to the unrighteous mam-
mon, or the falfe riches of this world: and the grace granted
to the elect, as fuch, τὴν ἀληθῆ χάριν τῆ θεῦ " the true grace of
God, wherein they ftand," 1 Pet. v. 12. Whether we underftand this of the doctrine of grace, or of that faving grace itfelf, which by that doctrine is offered to, and conferred on the
elect, which ver. 10. was called *the eternal glory of God*, it is
very evident, that true grace is oppofed to any falfe perfuafion
whatever concerning falvation. They are alfo exprefsly called
*permanent* bleffings, Heb. x. 34. " knowing in yourfelves, that
ye have in heaven a better and an *enduring* fubftance," which
is not oppofed to types and fhadows, but to the good things of
this world, which are fading, and fubject to fpoiling or ra-
pine. Ὑπαρξις μίνουσα, *enduring fubftance*, anfwers to the Hebrew words חון and יש, which fignify, *a true folid and permanent
fubftance*. But this what the fupreme wifdom has, from the
beginning, promifed to, and beftowed on thofe who obferve
her, Prov. ii. 7. *he layeth up found wifdom* (fubftance) *for the
righteous*, and Prov. viii. 21. *to caufe thofe that love me, to inherit
fubftance*. Our Lord calls thefe very benefits " treafures in heaven,
where neither moth nor ruft doth corrupt, and where thieves
do not break through and fteal," Mat. vi. 20. Now the believing
Ifraelites were undoubtedly admitted to the poffeffion of thefe. The
learned author himfelf writes, Jadagnt. Natur. Sabbat. §. 4. that
" holy perfons, who believed the promife and expected falvation had, the ornament of a meek a quiet fpirit. Which no one
doubts, are permanent. In a word what does *falvation itfelf* more
commonly fignify, than that happinefs of the foul, which is begun here upon earth, and will be perfected in heaven, and is the
end of our faith? Of which, 1 Pet. i. 9. " receiving the end
of your faith, even the falvation of your fouls." The falvation
of the foul is its deliverance from the condemning and dom-
ineering power of fin, and its delighting in God as the fountain
of happinefs. And this is the end of faith, not only under
the New, but alfo that which obtained under the Old Teftament. Which was, indeed, difcovered to Jacob, and by him
to his children, when he faid, " I have waited for thy falvation,
O Jehovah," Gen. xix. 18. As therefore fpiritual bleffings are
called in fcripture true, permanent, and falvation itfelf; and
the

the brethren dare not refuse that these were granted and discovered to the ancient Ifraelites: muſt we not acknowledge, that whoever, fays, that true and permanent benefits, and falvation itſelf were not granted and diſcovered to the Ifraelites, does not ſpeak according to ſcripture?

XII. Moreover ſhould we allow, that ſome benefits were peculiar to the New Teſtament, which may be eminently called true and permanent, and falvation itſelf; yet it does not follow, that he ſpeaks truly and adviſedly, according to the rules of logic and divinity, who without reſtriction, denies that true and permanent bleſſings were granted to Iſrael; ſince, beſides thoſe benefits peculiar to the New Teſtament, there are others alſo which are true, permanent and faving. An univerſal negative propoſition does not exclude ſome one, but every ſpecies without exception. It is one thing to fay, that Iſrael had not ſome degree or meaſure of true and permanent benefits; another, that they had not the bleſſings themſelves. He who would aſſert the former, which is true, ſhould not uſe words, that ſignify the latter, which is abſolutely falſe.

XIII. But let us take a more diſtinct view, how well the brethren maintain their ground by ſcripture. 1ſt, We allow, that the Apoſtle, Heb. ii. 3. by falvation underſtands that great happineſs, whoſe cauſe was then preſent, and the goſpel in its perfect ſtate, wherein the falvation, now begun to be impetrated, and ſoon to be fully ſo is declared: and it is certain, falvation in that ſenſe was not before the manifeſtation of Chriſt; nor did the Ifraelites enjoy it. But he, that would illuſtrate this, ſhould diſtinguſh between this falvation, already impetrated, or obtained, and falvation about to be impetrated; or between falvation, and the promiſe of falvation: and not, as our author does, between falvation and temporal benefits. For certainly eternal falvation was given and manifeſted to Iſrael, though the cauſe of falvation, as it now appears, and the work of falvation, as already begun, could not be preached to them. Becauſe, what Chriſt had promiſed and engaged was at that time ſufficient to procure falvation, to be manifeſted and beſtowed.

XIV. 2dly, None will deny, that true benefits are ſometimes oppoſed to typical: but this obſervation is altogether foreign to the caſe in hand; unleſs the brethren mean, that the Ifraelites enjoyed only typical good things, but were deſtitute of thoſe true or ſpiritual bleſſings, which were ſignified by the typical. What we juſt quoted from the preface to the Pſalms, and which I own, I do not ſufficiently underſtand, ſeems to tend to this. But let theſe things paſs. Let us go on with what is perspicuous. Moses indeed, who was a servant, could not bestow those true blessings. Yet Christ, who was the same yesterday and to day, bestowed on believers even under the Mosaic economy true benefits, in and with the typical. And when they deny, that true benefits were bestowed on Israel, I cannot think, they will reckon remission of sins, and redemption, and a new creation, &c, among the number of those, which were typical; and they own that these were bestowed on Israel. To what purpose then is the inculcating here a distinction between true and typical benefits? But, say they, the blotting out the hand-writing, and that glorious degree of adoption are true benefits. Are they so? And is not also remission itself, the hand-writing not being yet blotted out, and adoption itself, though not in that degree, to be reckoned among the true benefits? Did the types of the Israelites only prefigure that measure of grace, peculiar to the New Testament; not saving grace itself, which is common to both dispensations? Were their sacraments signs only of this grace, which is freely bestowed on us, and not also of that, of which they themselves were made partakers? Let the learned authors tell me I pray, whether the new creation, redemption, remission of sins, adoption, friendship with God, and the salvation of the soul, both in heaven and on earth, and the like spiritual blessings, which the Israelites enjoyed, belong to the law, and are given by Moses, or to the truth and grace, which came by Christ? If they affirm the latter, as I imagine they will, I again beg of them to explain, what the passage quoted from John makes to the purpose: as from that it is clear, that true benefits, as opposed to typical, were bestowed even upon Israel: which yet the words, now under examination, deny.

XV. 3dly, The main point is, that the economy of the Old Testament was not permanent and stable, like the economy of the New. In the former there is *the removing of those things that are shaken*, that, in the latter, "those things which cannot be shaken, may remain," Heb. xii. 27. But it is wrong to infer from this, that under a mutable economy, which was, in due time, to be changed, there were no permanent blessings either bestowed or made known. Because the bestowing and manifesting permanent benefits proceed not from those circumstances, which are mutable, but from the very covenant of grace, which is God's eternal testament. Then again granting, there is some permanent benefit under the New Testament, which was not under the Old, I cannot therefore indeterminately affirm, that permanent blessings were not bestowed on Israel. I shall give a palpable instance. The apostle says even to believers under the

the fear of death in liberty and joy.   For, in circumcifion the
the New Teftament, while they fojourned on this earth, Heb.
xiii. 14. " here have we no continuing city."   The celebrated
interpreter fays well on this place; " it is peculiar to Chriftians,
and thofe who join themfelves to Chrift, that they have not
here a city.   They are without a city in the world.   Some
may fay, the apoftle denies not that they have a city, but they
have no abiding one : nay, he denies, that we have a city here,
becaufe no city is abiding."   Can I therefore be allowed to affert, that no permanent benefits are beftowed on believers of
the New Teftament ?  I cannot think it.   I conclude : It had
been much better, the brethren had frankly owned, that the
learned author, while he was writing thefe things, betrayed
human frailty, and fpoke uncautioufly, than, by far fetched
pretences, to palliate things, which the reformed churches will
never acknowledge as their doctrine.

XVI. *Secondly*, The excellence of the Old Teftament is too
much leffened by afferting, that the *circumcifion of the heart*,
mentioned, Deut. xxx. 6. was a bleffing peculiar to the New
Teftament.   It is worth while to hear, how the learned author
explains himfelf.   Firft, he defires us to obferve, that this
verfe treats of the time of the Meffiah, the foregoing figns of
whom are explained in the preceding verfes : and therefore
he enumerates circumcifion of the heart, mentioned here among
the bleffings of the New Teftament, de foed. §. 352.   Confequently he fays, " that God hence promifed a kind of circumcifion of the heart, which he would not give till that time,"
Sum. Theol. c. 53. §. 7.   But what is that circumcifion of the
heart here promifed ?  Let us hear the learned author himfelf, when profeffedly commenting on this place.   " By circumcifion of the heart we are here to underftand, whatever
anfwers to circumcifion, as a figure, and is contained in God's
covenant, except thofe things, that do not belong to this life,"
Ultim. Mof. §. 334.   And more clearly ftill : " to fum up the
whole briefly, the circumcifion of the heart here promifed, ver.
6. is regeneration by the fpirit of adoption.   Above all it fignifies regeneration, or fanctification by the fpirit of faith and
the love of God.   Secondly, it denotes confolation in hope of
eternal life, by the expiation of Chrift."   Ibid. §. 336, 337,
338.   From thefe quotations, if duly connected, arifes this
argument: The circumcifion of the heart promifed, Deut. xxx.
6. is a benefit of the New Teftament, which God did not beftow till then: but regeneration by the fpirit of adoption, or
fanctification by the fpirit of faith and of the love of God, and
confolation in hope of eternal life by the expiation of Chrift,
is the circumcifion of the heart there promifed :   therefore fuch

regeneration

regeneration or fanctification and confolation in hope of eternal
life is a benefit of the New Teftament, which God did not
beftow before that time.    This conclufion neceffarily follows
from the premifes, when placed in due order.    But the premifes
are the very words of the learned author.

XVII. And yet he does not admit the conclufion ; but protefts againft it.    " And the fathers had both ; for, they could
not, without the Spirit of God 1 Cor. xii. 3. and the creation
of a clean heart, Pfal. li. io. and the circumcifion of the heart
call Chrift Lord, as David does, Pfal. cx. 1.    And they had the
hope and joy of Salvation," Gen. xlix. 19. Pfal. li. 12. Pfal. xvii.
15. Pfal. xlix. 15. Ibid. §. 339.    If any can reconcile thefe things;
I own, I cannot.    There is only one way of getting clear; namely, by making a diftinction in regeneration, fanctification, and
confolation in hope of eternal life ; as that there is a certain
regeneration by the fpirit of adoption ; another from fomething
elfe, than from that Spirit ; a certain fanctification by the Spirit
of faith and love of God ; another not : a certain confolation in
the hope of eternal life by the expiation of Chrift ; another
from fome other way.    The former of thefe are indeed peculiar
to the New Teftament ; and the latter belong to the Old.
But thefe very learned perfons muft excufe me, if I confidently
affirm, I never learned from fcripture of any regeneration, but
what is from the fpirit of adoption, any fanctification, but
what is from the fpirit of faith and love : any hope of eternal
life, but what is by the expiation of Chrift, either to be made,
or already made.

XVIII. What does he then intend, when he denies, that the
fathers had circumcifion of heart ? I know not whether, in
what I am to fay, I fhall exprefs the whole of his meaning ;
but I had rather err on this fide, in not faying the whole, than in
charging the author with what either he has not faid, or I have
not fufficiently underftood.    " It appears," fays he, " that here a
fpiritual grace is fignified, in fome meafure common to thofe
under both Teftaments, but in its fulnefs peculiar to thofe under
the New: and that this fometimes is promifed to be fuperadded
to what they had received, peculiar to the New Teftament,"
ibid. §. 335.    They had therefore regeneration, fanctification
and confolation, but in fome meafure only.    But what is there
to be fuperadded to what they had received ? That muft be
fome third thing, even that which the circumcifion of the heart
denotes ; namely, " the removing the vail from the eyes, and
the yoke from the confcience, in order to ferve God without
taking away the flefhy fubftance doubtlefs fignifies freedom
from the yoke of fuch a law," ibid. §. 340.

XIX.

XIX. But we diſtinctly offer the following conſiderations againſt ſuch intricate notions. 1ſt, Thus the circumciſion of the heart is a bleſſing of the covenant of grace as ſuch, and equally belongs to believers of both Teſtaments. Which we make appear thus. The foreſkin of the heart always ſignifies in ſcripture that impurity and depravation, which is naturally inherent in the ſoul, and is increaſed by repeated evil actions: but the circumciſion of the heart is nothing but the taking away that foreſkin, that is, that depravation; which is done by regeneration and ſanctification. This Moſes declares; Deut. x. 16. " circumciſe therefore the foreſkin of your heart, and be no more ſtiff-necked." And Paul, in like manner, Col. ii. 11. deſcribes the circumciſion of the heart, which is done without hands, to be *the putting off the body of the ſins of the fleſh*. But that this was the privilege of believers in all ages, appears from this, becauſe without it none can be *a Jew, whoſe praiſe is of God*, Rom. ii. 28, 29. But none will deny, that, in conſequence of the covenant of grace, there were always ſuch. And as circumciſion of the heart, is this very regeneration and ſanctification, without which none can ſee God, we muſt of neceſſity ſay, that it is the privilege of all thoſe that were ſaved at any time. A greater or leſs degree of ſanctification alters not the ſpecies. Nor do I imagine any be- liever at this time will, even as to the degrees of ſanctification, claim to himſelf a ſuperiority above David, or Moſes, or Abraham. Who will aſcribe the circumciſion of the heart, to himſelf, and refuſe it to thoſe heroes, who were alſo partakers of the ſame grace with them, though not in an equal degree.

XX. 2dly, Beſides, to underſtand by circumciſion of the heart, the removing the vail and yoke, or which is the ſame, the ab- rogation of the ceremonies, is contrary to all ſound divinity and reaſon. For, 1ſt, Let but one ſingle teſtimony of ſcripture be produced, where the Holy Spirit thus explains it. 2dly, We are, on the contrary, taught, that circumciſion was, as it were, the entrance to the obſervance of that law, in which it was a yoke, Gal. v. 3. How then could it ſignify to the Iſ- raelites on their receiving it, the abrogation of that yoke? 3dly, Circumciſion itſelf was a great part of the yoke, Acts xv. 5. compared with verſe 10. Beſides, what is more abſurd, than that the receiving the yoke ſhould ſignify the removal of it ? What ſacramental analogy is there here ? 4thly, As there is a relation between circumciſion and uncircumciſion, if circumci- ſion be the abrogation of the ceremonies, it neceſſarily follows, that the ceremonies themſelves are the foreſkin, or uncircum- ciſion of the heart, than which what can be more contrary to

scripture

fcripture language ? 5thly, If it be objected, that the ceremonial law is called *a carnal commandment*, Heb. vii. 16. therefore its abrogation was fitly prefigured by cutting away a fmall part of the flefh. I fhall invert the argument, and conclude; therefore it hath its confirmation in that act, which, if any thing, fhould be accounted among the carnal, as it was performed in the flefh ; wherefore it is also called *the covenant of God in the flefh* of the defcendants of *Abraham*, Gen. xvii. 13. For, the apoftle calls that commandment carnal, which, as to the external rites, is performed not in the fpirit or mind, but in the members of the body. Otherwife it might, with equal reafon, be faid, that the killing and burning the facrifices prefigured the abrogation of the carnal ceremonies : which is unworthy divines. There was, indeed, that in circumcifion, as also in the other ceremonies, which might difcover imperfection, and give hope of a more joyful time and prefignify, that when that time fhould come ; the ceremonies were to be abrogated ; yet the thing fignified was not the abrogation of the fame.

XXI. 3dly, And though fometimes circumcifion of the heart was the fame thing as taking away the vail and yoke; yet it is not promifed in that fenfe, Deut. xxx. 6. For, God himfelf explains it otherwife in the following words, which runs thus : " and Jehovah thy God will circumcife thine heart, and the heart of thy feed, to love Jehovah thy God with all thine heart, and with all thy foul, that thou mayeft live." That circumcifion, therefore, is meant, whofe immediate effect is the fincere love of God, and the more remote life, or falvation. Now what is this but regeneration, or fanctification, without which there can neither be the love of God, nor life. But both may be, where the vail and yoke of ceremonies are not yet removed. The Jewifh doctors also agree, that here fanctification is meant; though they give it too great an extent, and think that a perfect fanctification is here promifed. We fhall not fcruple to tranfcribe a few things out of Mofes Gerundenfis. " Their heart will defire nothing, but what, in every refpect, is virtuous. And this is the circumcifion, mentioned here. For concupifcence and appetite are the forefkin of the heart : but to circumcife the heart is to fet it free from that appetite and concupifcence."

XXII. 4thly, If we grant, that fomething is here promifed, which was to be performed to the elect Ifraelites in the time of the Meffiah : yet this by no means proves, that this benefit was peculiar to that time, and was not beftowed on their anceftors before. I fhall not go far to fhew the weaknefs of that confequence. In ver. 8. God promifed converfion to the Ifraelites

of

of that time, that they might hearken to the voice of Jehovah and do all his commandments. Yet fuch a converfion is no peculiar benefit of the New Teftament: becaufe in almoft the fame words, the Lord afcribes to the Jews in the Babylonifh captivity, verfe 2. Therefore we conclude, that they by no means fpeak according to fcripture, who deny that circumcifion of the heart, in whatever fenfe performed, had place under the Old Teftament.

XXIII. *Thirdly*, In the fame bafe manner; they make the *writing the law on the heart*, a bleffing peculiar to the New Teftament: becaufe Heb. viii. 10. it is faid from Jer. xxxi. 34. " for this is the covenant, that I will make with the houfe of Ifrael after thofe days, faith the Lord ; I will put my laws into their mind, and write them in their hearts :" that is, fays our author in Jer. xxxi. §. 61. " I will caufe them to receive my law, delight therein, and not forget it." If thefe words be taken as they lie, it follows, that the ancient believers, who lived before the times of the New Teftament, did not receive the law of God, nor delight in it but forgot it. But that thefe things are moft eminently falfe, appears from the example of David alone : who profeffes, that *he received* the law, when he fays, Pfal. cxix. 11. " thy word have I hid in my heart :" and adds ver. 16. I will *delight* myfelf in thy ftatutes, I will not *forget* thy word." How then is this a bleffing peculiar to the New Teftament, in which David claims an intereft in fo many words.

XXIV. But there is fomething elfe implied. Here, fays the celebrated interpreter, the law of the love of God is fpoken of. But that commandment " thou fhalt love the Lord thy God," Deut. vi. could not, under the Old Teftament, have its full efficacy on the hearts of believers : becaufe *where there is fear* (which they *who differed nothing from fervants, could not be without* Gal iv. 1.) *there is no perfect love*, 1 John iv. 18. And when " the love of God is fhed abroad in the heart by the Holy Ghoft," Rom. v. 5, and the love of God is not beftowed with fadnefs, as formerly, but with the *exceeding joy of fons*, it is excellently, and as it were, peculiarly faid, that *the law of God is written in the heart*. All this we may find in *Sum. de foed.* §. 352.

XXV. But I do not meet with thefe things in the facred writings; for they declare that even the ancient believers *loved* God, Pfal. xviii. 1. and Pfal. cxvi. 1. And that *as their Father*, Ifa. lxiii. 16. and with the *exceeding joy* of fons, Pfal. xliii. 4. and *without any fear*, that did become the children of God," Pfal. xlvi. 2, and Pfal. xxxiii. 3. nay, that they had a joyful fenfe of the love of God, *fhed abroad* in their hearts, Pfal. iv. 7. and hear God, " faying to their fouls, I am thy falvation," Pfal. xxxv. 3.

word,

In a word, that " they delighted themfelves in God's commandments, which they loved," Pfal. cxix. 47. What can now remain as a requifite towards writing the law on the heart?

XXVI. But yet you will fay, fomething is here promifed, to be obained by virtue of the New Covenant, which the old could not give, in the place of which the new was fubftituted on account of its imperfections. I anfwer: the apoftle does not here oppofe the covenant of grace, as it is difpenfed after the coming of Chrift, to the fame covenant of grace, as it was difpenfed before: but oppofes the covenant of grace, as in its full efficacy under the New Teftament, to the national covenant made with the Ifraelites at mount Sinai; and as a fpiritual covenant to a typical. In which covenant the people promifed obedience to God; and God promifed the people, that, if they performed that obedience, he would accept and reward it; but did not promife, to give them a heart to obey: as may be feen in their firft engaging in covenant, Exod. xix. 5, 6, 8. and in the folemn confirmation of it, Exod. xxiv. 7, 8. where there is no promife made of a new heart. And therefore, in confequence of this covenant, the law was not written on the heart of the people of Ifrael. And hence it was, that they broke that covenant by their apoftafy, and made it of no effect: And that God refufed to be called their God, and to acknowledge them for his people; and that in contempt he called them the people of Mofes, rather than his own, Exod. xxxii. 7. Here a better covenant is oppofed to that Ifraelitifh covenant, which is not formally the covenant of grace, but is only confidered with refpect to typical or fhadowy pomp, the effect of which is the writing the law on the heart, and communion with God, as the fountain of falvation. Moreover, that covenant is referred to the days of the Meffiah, not that it was only then to exift in thofe effects of it; but that at that time it would be exceeding glorious, and produce effects very confpicuous. However, the elect among Ifrael, even in the ancient times, befides their engagements by the Sinaitic covenant, were joined to God by the covenant of grace, which he had folemnly renewed with Aabraham. And from that covenant they had every thing, that the writing the law on the heart comprizes; and God himfelf for their God; that is, the fountain of falvation. As the covenant of grace, under which the ancients were, is not to be confounded with, fo neither is it to be feparated from, the Sinaitic covenant: neither are we to think, that believers were without all thofe things, which were not promifed by the Sinaitic covenant, and which the typical covenant, *becaufe of its weaknefs and unprofitablenefs,* could not beftow; as they were

likewife;

likewife, partakers of the Abrahamic covenant, which was a pure covenant of grace: and hence were derived the fpiritual and faving benefits of the Ifraelites.

XXVII. *Fourthly*, The godly, who are zealous for the truth, are not without cauſe offended, when they read in expreſs terms, that " juſtification is promiſed in ſcripture, as a bleſſing not of the ancient, but of the latter times," Sum. Theol. c. 69. § 3. that " remiſſion is promiſed as a gift of the New Teſtament," de foed. § 353. That " before Chriſt came, *there was no remiſſion*," Indag. nat. Sabbat. § 3. And in a word, that " no ſin was properly forgiven under the Old Teſtament," Sum. Theol. c. 96. § 26.

XXVIII. But he who ſpeaks ſo, underſtands by remiſſion of ſins, and by juſtification, ſomething more than the will to remit the puniſhment of ſin, and to beſtow eternal life for the ſake of the Mediator, received by faith. He means by theſe terms, " That then the will to puniſh ſin is excluded, by appointing a ſacrifice for ſin; and the declaration and teſtimony included; that ſin is blotted out and expiated:" as he explains himſelf in Animad. v. ad. Quæſt. 83. Quæſt. 68. This he has expreſſed more clearly, Sum. Theol. c. 51. § 9. *As to that juſtification which is* the diſcharge and perfecting of the conſcience, *or* the conſolation ariſing on account of the cauſe of righteouſneſs being now manifeſted, *they had not that formerly.*——He has accurately and briefly explained the whole of his meaning in Comment. ad. Col. 2. § 110. " In ſum, the difference of remiſſion according to the times, is thus: (1.) There was a remiſſion of ſins, and indeed a confeſſion of as ſin not yet expiated, and of righteouſneſs not as yet brought in, but without bondage and a yoke; even before the law: previous to which ſin was not imputed. (2.) There was a remiſſion of ſins with bondage, a yoke and ordinances, which exacted a hand-writing contrary to them, both evident and plain; and that under the law. (3.) There is a remiſſion of ſins, with a declaration of righteouſneſs being brought in, and of the death of Chriſt, for the doing away of ſin, even on account of the blotting out the hand-writing, and that under the New Teſtament.

XXIX. Againſt all this I offer the following conſiderations. As the ſcripture aſſerts, in expreſs terms, that the ancient fathers had remiſſion of ſins and juſtification, it is neither laudable nor prudent to deny it. For in what ſenſe ſoever you do it, it looks at leaſt like an attempt, to gainſay God, and correct his language. Which ought to be very far from every one, that loves and reveres God. Beſides, the ſcripture is expreſs; as concerning remiſſion of ſins, Pſal. cxxx. 4. " but *there is for-*

*giveness with thee,"* Exod. xxxiv. 8. "forgiving iniquity and tranfgreffion and fin;" fo concerning juftification, James ii. 21.
*Abraham our father was juftified,* and Rom. iv. 2, 3. As God
has declared, that thefe had remiffion and juftification, to what
purpofe then this is denied? You will alledge, you have done fo
in a different fenfe: but let us now confider whether in a right
and a good one.

XXX. By remiffion of fins and juftification, you underftand
abfolution, on account of the payment being actually made,
together with an entire difcharge from the hand-writing; fuch,
as certainly did not exift under the Old Teftament.  But I do
not remember, that any has proved, that the term *juftification,*
is ufed in that fenfe any where in fcripture, to diftinguifh it
from that abfolution which the ancients enjoyed.  For what is
faid, Acts xiii. 39. " by him all that believe are juftified from
all things, from which ye could not be juftified by the law of
Mofes," is not to the purpofe.  There it is fhewn, we have
the truth in the faving grace of Chrift, of which they had only
the fhadow in the external ceremonies of the law of Mofes.
There is no oppofition made in that text between the Old and
New Teftament only between internal communion with Chrift
and the external ceremonies.  But it is beyond all controverfy,
that believers, even under the Old Teftament, were partakers
thereof.  We have the term ἄφεσις, *remiffion,* once in that fenfe,
Heb. x. 18. but once only, that I know of.  In other refpects
ἄφεσις is frequently afferted of the ancient fathers, as we fhall
prefently fhew.  Seeing therefore the fcripture *frequently* declares, that the ancient fathers enjoyed remiffion of fins; and
either *once,* or but *rarely* afcribes remiffion with any annexed
limitation to the New Teftament, contradiftinguifhed from the
Old; it does not appear confiftent with Chriftian prudence, *fo
often* to deny a *remiffion* under the Old.  It had been better, in
order to prevent offence, to fay plainly and diftinctly, that fuch
a *mode* or manner of remiffion did not obtain under the Old, as
does now under the New Teftament.  Nor can any plead in
excufe fuch fcripture expreffions, which fays, that the Old
Teftament had not benefits in fuch abundance, as John vii. 39.
for thefe expreffions are not fo common.  And whoever in his
difcourfes attempts to render fcripture more intelligible to the
lefs experienced, ought not to frame his expreffions, by what
is both more rare and obfcure, but by the ordinary tenor of
fcripture, in order to throw a light on the more obfcure paffages
and phrafes.

XXXI. In fine, we cannot approve his faying, that the hand-
writing was not exacted of the fathers before the law of Mofes.

' For,

For facrifices, and circumcifion, which " is not of Mofes but
of the fathers," John vii. 22. belong to the ordinances, and
were types of Chrift to come, and implied a confeffion of guilt,
which was not then expiated, but are abolifhed by the crofs
of Chrift. And if they made no part of the hand-writing, is
there any reafon, why they may not be obferved under the
New Teftament, at leaft in the manner, in which they were
obferved before Mofes? The brethren make the ftate of the
Ifraelitifh church too fervile, beyond the other periods, both
the preceding and the following. But thefe do not properly
concern this controverfy.

XXXII. Many have alfo been offended, that Pfalms xxxii.
li. ciii. and the like which exactly defcribe remiffion of fins and
the juftification of a finner, fhould be thought to contain a
prophecy concerning the New Teftament times, as if the pfalmift on that occafion, " delighted himfelf in the anticipation
of the joys of the New Teftament times," *Sum. Theol. c. 69. §.
24.* and frequently elfewhere, efpecially in his commentaries
on thefe pfalms. Thefe things feem very difagreeable, nor are
they thought poffible to proceed but from one, who denies that
the fathers had remiffion of fin, together with that holy fecurity of foul, which delights itfelf in God. Yet it is not to
be denied, that the brethren elfewhere loudly proteft, that they
afcribe to the ancient fathers that remiffion of fins, which begets a full affurance of hope concerning happinefs and a confolation, and a glorying even in death. And charity, which
thinketh no evil, obligeth us to believe, that they fpeak thus
from the heart. However I look upon that method of interpretation to be very indecent, whereby things of a doctrinal
nature, which have no refpect to the different economy of
times, are rafhly transformed into prophecies concerning the
New Teftament. And I find nothing in thofe pfalms, at leaft
fo far as they declare the grace of God in the remiffion of fins,
which may not be applied to David, and to believers, his cotemporaries. Nor does any thing occur in the New Teftament,
which authorizes believers of the laft times to appropriate thefe
things to themfelves beyond others. Let us confider each of
them.

XXXIII. There is nothing in Pfal. xxxii. that favours of
prophecy. The title fhews, it is * *a doctrinal ode*, containing
the doctrine concerning the true happinefs of a finner, as common to every age. And declares, that this confifts in remiffion
of fins. Moreover, by his own example, he fhews to whom
that happinefs belongs, and after what manner it may be obtained

* *A Pfalm of David of Mafchil, that is giving inftruction.*

tained.  This he propoſes, ver. 5. for the imitation of others,
and preſſes it, ver. 8. and the following in very ſtrong terms.
Who, but one blinded with prejudice, can find a propheſy in
all this? And certainly, when David pronounces the perſon bleſſed, "unto whom Jehovah imputeth not iniquity," &c.  I would
fain know, whether he includes himſelf in that bleſſedneſs.  If
he does, it is no prophecy of the New Teſtament times, which
is what I contend for.  But if he excludes himſelf from that
happineſs, he alſo excludes himſelf from the benefit of that
juſtification, which is obtained by faith; but Paul brings in
this happineſs of David, Rom. iv. 6. to prove the doctrine
of juſtification by faith, and ſhews that Abraham was made
partaker of it; but this I imagine none of the brethren will ſay.
I would alſo fain know, what perſon ſpeaks, ver. 3, 4.  Is
there here any kind of proſopopoeia repreſenting to us a believer of the New Teſtament? But what proof is there for ſuch
a fiction? What demonſtration have we for it? Or does David
himſelf ſpeak? Certainly, the title of the pſalm leads us to this:
and there is nothing in theſe words, which are not true concerning David; and which he does not elſewhere affirm of
himſelf; ſee Pſal. vi. 2, 3.  But if the prophet affirms of himſelf what is there ſpoken of the grief and anxiety of a ſoul not
yet ſenſible of God's being reconciled, he certainly alſo ſpeaks
of himſelf, ver. 5. "and thou forgaveſt the iniquity of my ſin:"
for, theſe words cannot be ſeparated from the foregoing.
I entreat the pious reader to compare this commentary, by which
ſuch a plain pſalm is turned to I know not what kind of drama,
where, under the maſk of David, quite different perſons lie
concealed; with the clear and ſavoury commentary of Calvin,
and if I am not miſtaken, he will evidently ſee the maſk fall off.

XXXIV. Of the ſame nature is, Pſal. li.  The inſcription
and occaſion of it there mentioned, prove, that it is ſo evidently
applicable to David, that it is ſuperfluous to add a ſingle word.
The learned author himſelf, in his commentaries, applies many
things to David.  And on the title of the pſalm he expreſsly
ſays, "it is a prayer of David to God, after his converſation
with the prophet Nathan."  And on ver. 1. " all are bound to
have recourſe to grace, and lay hold on that, and conſequently,
with David, to apply to themſelves the grace of God."  Why
then does he elſewhere wreſt theſe things to the New Teſtament
times? Is it becauſe ver. 7. he ſays, "ſprinkle me with hyſ-
ſop;" by which ceremony the atoning ſacrifice of Chriſt was
repreſented? But is not that very expreſſion more applicable
to a believer under the Old, than under the New Teſtament?
How could he more effectually expreſs the activity of the ancient

cient faith, which takes a distant prospect, of a Saviour to
come through a thick cloud of ceremonies? " The man of
God knew," says Musculus, " that the expiation of sin confists not in ceremonial actions; but is rather by the grace and
Spirit of God in Christ to come." Or, is it because ver. 18. he
speaks of the sacrifices of righteousness, which were to be offered after the rebuilding of Jerusalem, or of the sacrifice of Christ,
whereby he made the fullest satisfaction to the justice of God?
But what can be inferred from this? Could not believers of the
Old Testament sing praises for the benefits bestowed on them,
and, at the same time, make mention of the future satisfaction of Christ, in virtue of which they obtained those blessings?
And then why may we not, with Bucer and Musculus, understand by these sacrifices, those spiritual sacrifices, of which Peter speaks, 1 Pet. ii. 5. and which are abundantly offered to
God, when he does good to Zion, &c. that is, enriches his
church with his spiritual grace, as well under the Old, as under the New Testament? Unless, with Calvin, Mollerus, Pif-
eator, the Dutch commentators, and others, we had rather explain it of the legal sacrifices themselves, but offered in a proper manner according to the divine prescription, and by faith:
which is still farther confirmed from the sentiment of Cocceius.

XXXV. The hundred and third Psalm, contains nothing
which regards only the New Testament times. And the ver.
19th and 22d, are to no purpose produced, as if they treated
concerning the kingdom of liberty and grace; which was to extend through all the world. For, it is not certain, that these
words are to be referred to the kingdom of heaven under the
New Testament. There is nothing in them which may not be
applied to the kingdom of God's power or providence. " It is
plain," says Musculus, " these things are not spoken concerning
the kingdom of grace but of the kingdom of God's power, authority and dominion." But was it not likewise true under the Old
Testament; that " Jehovah hath prepared his throne in the heavens; and that his kingdom ruleth over all?" Was the state
of the New Testament times represented to Micaiah, when he
saw Jehovah sitting on his throne, and all the host of heaven
standing by him? 1 Kings xxii. 19. Did Nebuchadnezzar also
prophecy of the New Testament times, when he called God
*king of heaven*, and ascribed to him an " everlasting kingdom
over all the inhabitants of the earth?" Dan. iv. 36, 37. Can
it be said under the New Testament alone, " bless the Lord all
his works?" But the Psalmist, Psal. cxlvii. even under the Old
Testament, united every thing in heaven, and in earth to that
duty. I omit other passages, least, in a thing so plain, I should
be

be charged with a too superstitious exactness. However, I will not deny, that those things, which are spoken concerning the kingdom of God's power, which extends itself over the whole earth, and concerning his eminent majesty over all creatures, do illustriously shine forth in the kingdom of liberty and grace, as Mollerus has likewise observed. But yet there is no reason, to turn all this into a mere prophecy concerning the time to come. Well says Amyraldus in his preface to this psalm: " there is nothing here, which can be properly typical, or which, by any mystical interpretation, can be referred to the fulness of time. But should we grant, that the prophet, filled with the abundance of divine grace, was, from the sense thereof, moved to sing, towards the close of the psalm, concerning the kingdom of liberty and grace; does it therefore follow, that what he had before sung of the bounty of God towards himself and of the pardon of all his sins, was not applicable to himself, but only to believers under the New Testament.

XXXVI. What has also perplexed some, is that laboured distinction, and so often inculcated, of πάρεσις, *passing by*, and ἄφεσις, *pardon*, which is usually pretended to be of extraordinary use in divinity. But they generally explain it thus: that πάρεσις denotes a *passing-over*, a *passing by*, a *concealing*, whence it comes that God does not punish sins, nor has a purpose of exacting them of the sinner; nevertheless he does not declare, that satisfaction has been made, but on the contrary reserves to himself a power to call the sinner before him, that is, to remind him, that the debt is not yet cancelled, and to exact of himself the hand-writing, by which he may own, as by the subscription of his own hand, that guilt is not yet abolished and expiated. This the scripture would call παρεῖναι, *to pass by*, to which answers חרש, *to be silent*, Psal. l. 21. and Esther vii. 4. They distinguish this *passing* by two ways. 1st, Before the law of Moses, when God was altogether silent, and sin not *imputed*, by exacting the hand-writing. 2dly, After the law, when God called the sinner before him, and demanded the hand-writing. But by ἄφεσις, properly so called, they understand that pardon of sin, by which God declares, that Christ has made satisfaction to his justice, and pronounces the meritorious cause of the right to life to be now actually in being, affirms sin to be blotted out, tears the hand-writing, and finally gives a discharge; as if he should say, *I have received, I will not give in pledge*. All this we find in *da foed.* §. 339. *Sum. Theol. c.* 51. §. 11. *Animadvers. ad Quaest.* 83 *Quaest.* 68. *Ad Rom.* 3. §. 72. *More Nevo, p.* 65. &c.

XXXVII. On this I observe, that in the main there can be
no

no controverſy, if it be allowed, that the guilt of ſin did not lie upon believers, in ſuch a manner, that they, on ſuppoſition of Chriſt's ſuretiſhip, ſhould be forced to bear the puniſhment of it in their own perſon. So far, indeed, they were obliged to remember. 1ſt, That according to *the law, they* are debtors 2dly, Though on account of the covenant-engagement of the Meſſiah, they are abſolved from the penalty, yet as that engagement was not yet actually fulfilled, ſo far their guilt was not yet expiated; but that it continues to lie on him, who was ſtill *their ſurety, from whom* it will demand ſufferings and death; and as they themſelves, *by* the decree of election, are *one* myſtical body *with the ſurety,* ſo far *it lies upon them ;* to give ſatisfaction, not in their own perſon, but by the ſurety. Juſt as the catechiſm ſpeaks : *we are to make payment by another.* If ſo, as I apprehend, this is what the brethren mean, none will diſſent from them. But then their boaſting of the extraordinary uſefulneſs of their diſtinction will appear groundleſs : ſince they ſay nothing, but what all orthodox divines either have ſaid, or would ſay.

XXXVIII. Moreover that diſtinction cannot be proved, from the terms πάρεσις and ἄφεσις. For, it is certain, that ἄφεσις is aſcribed to believers before the actual expiation of ſin, Lev. v. 10. και ἀφεθήσεται αὐτῷ, *and it ſhall be forgiven him,* and ſo in other places. And leaſt any ſhould cavil, that this is meant of a typical forgiveneſs (which yet was a ſymbol of the true, and to which the auguſt term, ἄφεσις, ſeems leſs applicable than to that real forgiveneſs the ancients enjoyed) I add from Pſal. lxxxv. 2. ἀφῆκας τας ἀνομίας τῷ λαῷ συ, *thou haſt forgiven the iniquity of thy people.* I deny not, that this pſalm was to be ſung by the Iſraelites, when they were to be converted to Chriſt the Lord ; but I think it cannot be proved, that it was not ſung by believers, when they returned from the Babyloniſh captivity, with an application to their condition at that time. To omit other conſiderations, it is beyond all exception, that Chriſt, before his ſatisfaction, beſtowed his ἄφεσις, *forgiveneſs,* on ſome Mat. ix. 2. ἀφέωνται σοι αι ἁμαρτίαι σου, *thy ſins be forgiven thee.* In like manner, Luke vii. 47.

XXXIX. But we have not yet ſeen it proved that πάρεσις ſignifies *paſſing by, concealing, ſilence.* Budæus, indeed, in comment. Ling. Græc. p. 286. ſhews, that παρεῖναι is ſometimes *to paſs over ;* but that is in a quite different ſenſe, for he quotes a paſſage from Zenophon, Lib. 4. Hellen. ὑπὲρ αὐτῷ μηδένα παρεῖναι εἰς ἀκρόπολιν, *commanded him not to paſs* or *ſend over any into the citadel.* Moreover, he ſays, that παρεῖναι, is to indulge, to promiſe, *to forgive* ; and Heſychius ſpeaks to the ſame purpoſe.

Παρίημι

Παρίημι is συγχωρῶ, *yield*, ἀφίημι, *remit*; and he explains πάρεσις by ἄφεσις, *remiffion*, συγχώρησις, *conceffion*, *pardon*, ſo far are theſe words from being diftinguiſhed, that the one may be explained by the other. I am aware, that a certain author ſays, that "the authority of Hefychius does not move him, becauſe he had before his eyes this paſſage of Paul, and explained it from the ſubject matter itſelf, on which Paul is ſpeaking." Mor. Nebo. p. 29. But neither do I imagine, the celebrated perſon would have us to be moved by his own authority. Hefychius is no contemptible author. Let us hear the judgment of *Dan. Heinſius, Ariſtarch. Sac. p. 9. Edit. 8vo. In Hefychius* "is contained not only the learning of all Greece, but alſo of the eaſt, p. 14. A Grammarian of ſurpriſing and profound learning, p. 18. A Grammarian, who is an abyſs of the ancient erudition, p. 11. 6. Hefychius is no mean author, whoſe gloſſes are certainly for the moſt part, adapted to explain the Greek authors, and eſpecially the Septuagint." And if Hefychius had this paſſage of Paul before his eyes, and explained it from the ſubject matter, and from his acquaintance with a language, which was his mother tongue, certainly he has not explained it amiſs.

XL. The learned author, indeed ſays, that πάρεσις anſwers to חֲרִישׁ *to be ſilent*; but does not prove it. He quotes Efth. vii. 4. but πάρεσις is not there, in the copies I have. That of Walton and the London in 8vo, A. 1653 have πάρεσιν. However that I may not conceal any thing, I have been made to underſtand, that it is in another copy. But ſuppoſe it was in them all, what is it to the purpoſe? For, *I had been ſilent*, does not there ſignify, I had paſſed over that injury unpuniſhed, but I had in ſilence ſubmitted myſelf to that indignity, nor troubled the king with any petition of mine. By which our πάρεσις gains nothing. And then alſo when God Pſal. l. 21. ſays to the wicked "theſe things haſt thou done, and I kept ſilent," which the *Septuagint* tranſlate ταῦτα ἐποίησας καὶ ἐσίγησα; there is no ſuch thing intended by that term, like that πάρεσις *remiffion*, which Paul deſcribes and the brethren inſiſt upon. For, that is the abſolution of believers from the penalty, on account of Chriſt's ſuretiſhip. But this ſilence is the deferring the puniſhment of the wicked in order to compenſate its ſlowneſs by its ſeverity: things widely different. I cannot conceive with what judgment the celebrated author quote, theſe things here, in which thoughs even the word, πάρεσις, was to be found, yet certainly, not the thing itſelf, which he would have ſignified by that term.

XLI. The learned author ſhould have alſo more fully explained, *in what manner God kept ſilence* in former times. For, *he did not keep ſilence with reſpect to ſin,* when he demanded the

hand-

hand-writing of the finner, and charged him with guilt not yet expiated, which according to this famous author, was done by the law of Mofes, but as I think, by the firft inftitution of facrifices; and if thefe were types of Chrift's facrifice, as doubtlefs they were, they at the fame time fignified, that the true expiatory facrifice was not yet offered. *Neither did* God *keep filence* as to *pardon*, but proclaimed the teftament of grace, whereby he affured believers, that, on account of the Meffiah's covenant-engagement, he would never require them to pay a ranfom for their own fins. What is then that important filence, on account of which that act of God towards the ancients may be called πάρεσις?

XLII. We conclude, that the diftinction of πάρεσις and ἄφεσις, fo much commended, is not of that importance, as, on that account, to fet on fire the academical chair, the pulpits and the prefs now, for fo many years paft, and the giddy vulgar rent into factions thereby. Since it cannot be denied, that the remiffion, which the fathers enjoyed, may, from the practice of the Greek language, be called, and was actually called by Greek authors ἄφεσις: and no paffage can be produced, where it is called πάρεσις, in the fenfe now forced upon us.

XLIII. But the illuftration given by the excellent James Altingius, merits our regard; who Heptad. 2. Differt. 2. §. 92. Seq. fpeaks almoft to the following purpofe: Three things are required to a full and perfect ἄφεσις, *forgivenefs*, namely, *the taking away, the transferring* and the *expiating* of fin. *The taking away of fin* is that act, whereby the guilt is removed from the offender, that though he has finned, yet he is not under the obligation to punifhment. This is pointed out by the term, נשא, when it fignifies *to remove* and *take away*, Exod. xxxiv. 7. Pfal. xcix. 8. Pfal. xxxii. 5. Pfal. lxxxv. 2. Pfal. xxv. 18. *The transferring of fin* is that act, whereby the guilt, which is removed from the offender, is transferred to the furety, that he may be obliged to anfwer for it; as was done in the cafe of a facrifice, by the impofition of hands, which then bore and carried the guilt. This, he thinks, was pointed out by the word העביר, *he caufed to pafs, he transferred:* 2 Sam. xii. 13. when David faid, *I have finned* or I am guilty *againft the Lord:* Nathan anfwers, Jehovah *alfo hath put away (caufed to pafs) thy fin, thy fin,* guilt *thou fhalt not die.* And the angel, the Lord, Zech. iii. 4. fays: behold, " I have caufed thine iniquity to pafs from thee." Which words afcribe this transferring to God, as the creditor, and to Chrift, as the *furety.* But it is alfo what the *debtor* may claim; whence David prays for it, 2 Sam. xxiv. 10. " and now I befeech thee, O Lord, take away" (caufe to pafs) *the iniquity*

*of*

*of thy servant.* And Solomon, Eccl. xi. 10. because we muſt give an account of all our actions to God, as the laſt judgment enjoins us to *put away* (cauſe to paſs) *evil from thy fleſh.* Which cannot otherwiſe be done, (as the evil done can on no account be undone) than by transferring or tranſporting ſin. And he imagines, that this transferring is what the apoſtle calls παρεσις *remiſſion. The expiation of ſin* is that act, by which, the guilt, removed from the offender, and transferred to the ſurety, is expiated by him who bears all the puniſhment, to which the ſinner was bound, ſo that divine juſtice ſhall have nothing more to demand, much leſs to inflict. This is expreſſed by the word כפר *to expiate, to cover* with the blood of payment, that the writing of ſin may be cancelled, and no longer appear. This laſt act is at length followed by a complete ἀφεσις *remiſſion,* which abſolutely diſcharges from every demand, either upon the debtor, or the ſurety ; ſo that after this, there is no further any occaſion for a ſacrifice for ſin, Heb. x. 18. all remembrance of it being entirely effaced, ver. 3. compared with ver. 17. Having thus explained theſe things, the very learned author proceeds as follows. Under the Old Teſtament, believers were without this laſt degree of *expiation,* becauſe the time appointed was not yet come, and conſequently the ἀφεσις *forgiveneſs,* which follows upon it. Their ſins were not expiated, and the handwriting remained in its full force uncancelled, as alſo the remembrance of tranſgreſſion was often repeated, &c. All which were at length aboliſhed by the death, croſs, and the blood of Chriſt's croſs. But yet theſe believers were not without the two former degrees, of taking away and transferring ; which are elegantly joined together by Job, chap. vii. 20, 21. " I have ſinned, what ſhall I do unto thee, O thou preſerver of men ? Why haſt thou ſet me as a mark againſt thee, ſo that I am a burden to myſelf ? and why doſt thou not pardon (take away) my tranſgreſſion, and take away (cauſe to paſs) mine iniquity ?" Take away from me the guilt, under the weight of which I ſhall otherwiſe faint and ſink ; and transfer it to another, who is able to bear it ; namely, the ſurety ; ſeeing by all means ſatisfaction muſt be made. The very learned author proſecutes this ſubject at further length, at which none will repent their having peruſed. And indeed I always looked upon the ſubject thus explained to be true and found doctrine, which I likewiſe publicly teſtified. My only ſcruple was, whether this clear and explicit doctrine relating to the transferring of ſin to the ſcore of the Meſſiah, could agree with the ſimplicity of the Old Teſtament, and was generally thus known to the ancient believers ; and likewiſe whether it could be ſolidly

proved

proved by the word רעמן. Should any think me too fcrupulous
in hefitating about this, I am not now inclined obftinately to
contradict him; but have I, on that account, deferved fo un-
kind a treatment at the hands of the learned author, as may be
feen Heptos 3. Differt. 4. §. 27, and Heptos 4. Differt. 3. §. 14?
I am indeed, forry, that fuch refentment dwells in heavenly
breafts, however I think, that I muft take care leaft either the
paffions of others, or my own, fhould at any time cloud my
mind in the difcernment of truth. Sacred candour! defcend
and gently glide into our foul, that, with the greateft cheerfulnefs, we may receive what is well faid, even from thofe who
are difpleafed with us: and with equal readinefs difclaim
what we ourfelves may have lefs accurately advanced.

XLIV. *Fifthly*, We dare not deny that *adoption*, in a certain
refpect and in fome degree of eminence, may be accounted a
bleffing of the New Teftament ; fo far, namely, as it imports
that condition, not whereby believers are diftinguifhed from the
children of the devil and of wrath, and conftituted heirs of divine grace and glory, (which is a dignity common to all believers
in all ages) but whereby believers of the New Teftament are
preferred to children, who differ not much from fervants. In
which fenfe the apoftle afcribes adoption eminently to the fulnefs of time, Gal. iv. 4——7. Where Calvin, comments thus
on ver. 5. " For even the fathers under the Old Teftament
were affured of their adoption: but did not then fo fully enjoy
their privilege. Here therefore adoption is taken, juft as redemption, Rom. viii. 23. for poffeffion itfelf. For, as at the
laft day, we fhall enjoy the fruit of our redemption ; fo now
we enjoy the fruit of adoption, of which the holy fathers
before the coming of Chrift, were not partakers." And on
verfe 7. " wherefore thou art no more a fervant but a fon: that is,
in the Chriftian church there is no longer any ftate of fervitude,
but the condition of fons. He again therefore fpeaks of the
difference between the Old and New Teftament. Even the
ancients were the fons of God, and heirs through Chrift : but
we in a quite different manner; becaufe we have Chrift prefent,
and therefore enjoy his benefits." Confult what we have more
largely explained Book 3. Chap. 10. And if I miftake not,
this is the very meaning of the brethren, in commenting on
Gal. iv. §. 56. " Let it only be obferved, that adoption is not
faid to be fo peculiar to the New Teftament, as if the Old was
entirely deftitute of it. For the apoftle prefuppofes, that even
thofe, that were in bondage under the elements of the world,
were heirs."

XLV. But what is faid elfewhere, *de foed.* §. 352. is very

harfh;

harfh : " though the faints under the Old Teftament received the fanctifying Spirit, yet he did not work in them that affection, which was either worthy of God as a father, or of them as children ; but there was in them a fpirit of bondage to fear. On the contrary, they who are under the New Teftament, do, immediately upon believing, receive the promife of the Holy Spirit," Gal. iii. 14. that is, the Spirit of fons, which was promifed, and whofe it is to cry, Abba, Father, Rom. viii. 15.

XLVI. On which I obferve, 1ft, It is fuppofed without proof, that the fpirit of bondage was peculiar to the Old Teftament. For even under the New, thofe effects of the Spirit are obfervable, which are to be referred to fear and to bondage. Even at this day, it engenders terror in the elect, becaufe they look upon themfelves to be in very bad condition, while they live in fin, nor can poffibly be otherwife, till by a true faith they are reconciled to God, Luke xv. 17. Moreover, by this terror it drives them to lay hold on the fortrefs of falvation in Chrift, 2 Cor. v. 11. By the fame terror alfo it reftrains them from fin, and extinguifhes the defire of finning in them. In fine, it very often redoubles this terror, racking their confcience with anguifh and pain, and leading them in a way, juft by the brink of hell, in which rarely with joy and exultation, generally with a kind of anxiety of a trembling heart, yet in fincerity, they can ferve God. Juft as at this day thofe, whofe office it is familiarly to enquire into their ftate, find believers very often affected. It cannot be denied, that in all thefe there is fear; nay, that there is fomething, which proceeds from bondage, and is, in fome meafure, different from that ingenious performance of duty, which only arifes from the cheerfulnefs of a heart actuated by love. Why then may not the fpirit who works thefe things even under the New Teftament, be called the fpirit of bondage to fear. .

XLVII. 2dly, It is alfo falfely afferted, that thofe affections, which the fpirit of bondage formerly wrought in the faints, were unworthy of God, as a father, and of the faints as children. For as thofe affections were holy, and the effects of the fanctifying Spirit, whom God beftows upon none but his own children, nay, as they were moft certain figns of their adoption, and of their right to the inheritance, is to entertain unworthy thoughts of God their Father, and of his children, to account them unworthy of both. True indeed it is, that in thofe affections of the faints, there was a kind of relation, like that of fervants to a mafter ; yet that by no means deftroyed, but only in fome meafure modified, the relation of fons to a father; as

even

even at this day God is held forth to us under both thefe relations.

XLVIII. 3dly, The fanctifying fpirit, abfolutely as fanctifying, which was in the ancient believers, ought to be diftinguifhed from the fpirit of bondage, as it precifely begets fear. Though therefore the affections, produced by the fpirit of bondage, as fuch were inconfiftent with the moft free condition of fons of God; yet the effects of the fanctifying fpirit, in all the elect, are a fincere love to God, and obedience arifing from that love, with a complacency and delight in his commandments; now can there be any reafon, why thefe may not be declared highly worthy of the faints, as fons of God?

XLIX. 4thly, It is contrary to all reafon to fay, that the ancients had not the fpirit of fons, whereby they cried Abba Father. For this fpirit is not fo contrary to the fpirit of bondage, as if it was not poffible for both to refide together. The contrary to which we have proved already, Book 3. chap. xi. §. 9. As this fpirit therefore, is always operative fuitable to its condition; fo it wrought thofe affections even in the believers of the Old Teftament, which were worthy of God, as a Father, and likewife taught them to cry, *my Father*, Job xxxiv. 36. Ifa. xliii. 16.

L. *Sixthly*, It is not confiftent with that divine grace, which was beftowed even on the ancients, to deny, that they had *peace of confcience*. On which head we find written, on Heb. x. §. 15. as follows: " Confcience cannot be eafy, before a man is expiated by a facrifice, (with and by which we ought to approach unto God) and knows, that in confidence of that facrifice he approaches to God. For it is by this, that the confcience is at laft calmed and perfected. And till then a man muft of neceffity have a confcience, both accufing him before God, and feparating from all communion with him."

LI. And yet the fame perfon, who fpeaks thus, openly protefts, that he by no means deprives the ancient believers of their affurance of hope, and the joy of a confcience, that gloried in God. For, he thus fpeaks elfewhere, on Pfal. li. §. 15. " This is the wifdom of God, that he fuffers not finful man to perifh ——and for that purpofe, he gives the finner a teftimony of his righteoufnefs, and the affurance of the hope concerning eternal happinefs: fo as with an uninterrupted joy to bear all croffes and afflictions, and glorify God, and give him thanks, in life and in death.——This wifdom of God, as Nathan had notified to him (David) by the word, fo God had fealed it to him in his very inmoft foul."

LII. Thefe indeed, are things very difficult, if at all poffible

to be reconciled. For, where there is a confcience of fin, accufing man before God and feparating from all coummunion
with him, how, in that cafe, can there be a teftimony of righteoufnefs given the finner by God? Again, where there is the
affurance of hope concerning eternal happinefs and an uninterrupted joy, what can there be wanting in that cafe to a calmed and perfected confcience? But let us explain, what we are
to determine concerning the former affertion.

LIII. 1ft, The fcripture no where fays, that the ancient believers had not peace of confcience; but on the contrary, that,
from an affurance of the favour of God towards them, they
flept fecure, Pfal. iii. 5. that, with full affurance of faith, they
gloried in their prefent grace, Pfal. iv. 3. and with the fame
affurance of hope expected future glory, Pfal. xvii. 15. 2dly,
Nor does it any where fay, that believers under the Old Teftament had the confcience of fin, accufing them before God, and
feparating from all communion with him. But on the contrary
that confcience bore them witnefs, that fin was forgiven, Pfal.
xxxii. 5. and Pfal. ciii. 3, 10, 12. And how could fin accufe
them before God, and feparate from his communion feeing it
was charged to the furety, and was to be exacted of him?
3dly, The fame fcripture teftifies, that believers under the Old
Teftament acted, what the redeemed act, and gloried and rejoiced in God, Pfal. cxvi. 7, 8. " Return into thy reft, O my
foul, for Jehovah hath dealt bountifully with thee. Thou haft
delivered my foul from death, mine eyes from tears and my
feet from falling.

LIV. Heb. x. 1. is here mifapplied: for, the apoftle does
not there deny, that the ancient believers had a confcience perfected: only denies, that there was perfection from the law,
which had but the fhadow of good things to come: denies,
that the facrifices, which were offered year by year continually,
could make the comers thereunto perfect, that is, as Pareus
fays well, *fanctify and fave them*. But what the law could not,
the grace of the furety, of which they were partakers, both
could and actually did effect. 5thly, The confcience of fin of
which ver. 2. is not of fin as accufing before God, and excluding from all communion with him (for, the furetifhip of
Chrift apprehended by faith, was a bar to fin's effecting that,)
but it is a confcience of fins, as not yet *actually* expiated, and
which were not to be expiated by the facrifices of beafts. Thefe
were therefore repeated, that believers might teftify, that they
only ufed them as fymbols, which God appointed, but did not
expect to obtain remiffion but from the furetifhip and future
facrifice of the Meffiah.

LV.

LV. 6thly, Believers under the Old Teftament had not, indeed, that calm or peace of confcience, which arifes from the ranfom being fully paid by the furety, nor fuch a difcharge, as by the refurrection of Chrift from the dead. Yet they had in Chrift's furetifhip engagent, truly and fully what was fufficient to calm the confcience, for by that they might be affured, all their fins were blotted out of their account, and laid to the charge of Chrift, who had alfo taken them upon himfelf, and made himfelf a debtor to undergo the punifhment of them: and indeed, in fuch a manner, that they fhould never afterwards be charged to believers, nor God ever *have any will to punifh their fins in their own perfons*, as the learned author fpeaks, Sum. Theol. c. 35. And why were not thefe things fufficient to produce a like compofure of mind, nay and a tranquillity almoft equal to that, which arifes from the ranfom actually paid? For believers are as much exempted from all obligation to perfonal fatisfaction, whether the ranfom was to be paid, or was actually paid by the furety.

LVI. *Seventhly*, It feems likewife to tend to undervalue the Old Teftament church, that it is faid to have been, in an efpecial manner fubject to the *dominion of angels*. Concerning this, he fays on Heb. 2. §. 39. " The former world, that is, the people of the land of Canaan was fubject to angels, being fubject to the word fpoken by angels, and to the difpofitions and appointments of angels, as well the heavenly, as thofe that fat in Mofes' feat, and who, in like manner, are called Gods. For the heavenly angels, who affifted at the promulgation of the law, were the avengers or defenders thereof, as they were the guardians of the authority of the elders." Here then they prefent us with two forts of angels; the heavenly, who are fpirits; the earthly, who are men fitting in the feat of Mofes. The people of Canaan is faid to be fubject to both: to the heavenly. 1ft, as the law was publifhed by them. 2dly, As they were conftituted the avengers or defenders of the law. 3dly, As the guardians of the authority of the elders. To the earthly; as the people was obliged to apply to them, to feek the teftimony and the law, and to obey them, juft as if God himfelf in perfon had publifhed his commands with an audible voice. And on account of this dominion, both the earthly and the heavenly angels were called Gods.

LVII. I anfwer, the fource of this error is a mifinterpretation of what the apoftle fays, Heb. ii. 5. Where indeed, it is denied, that this habitable world is put in fubjection unto angels; but this is no ways afferted of the former. And from the denial of the one, the affirmation of the other cannot be
concluded.

concluded. The apostle's whole discourse is with a view, to
gain the greatest authority to the doctrine of Christ. For this
purpose he had in the foregoing chapter, described in magnificent encomiums the excellence of his person; he then established the great pre-eminence of the gospel above the law.
And now he urges, that Christ was to be obeyed, because the
Father had given him the government of the whole world,
which is an honour not at all conferred on angels. He speaks
of the world to come, not in contradistinction 'to the past, as
if angels exercised dominion in that, as Christ does in this :
but because, it is a part of Christ's exaltation, to be appointed
Lord of that world by God, a world far more excellent than
the past. This then is the apostle's reasoning. We are, with
the greatest reverence, to attend to the word of Christ, because
he is appointed Lord of the whole world; and indeed, especially at that time, wherein the state of all things, and particularly of the church is the most perfect : but no angel had
ever such an honour conferred upon him. How do you torture the word, when you extort the subjection of the ancient
church unto angels from this text.

LVIII. 2dly, The law published by angels, was the decalogue; which we are bound to own as the rule of our obedience, equally with the Israelites. Are we then also on that
account subjected to angels ? 3dly, The part which the angels
acted, in promulgating the law, was purely ministerial, and
therefore implies no dominion : John was not therefore subject
to an angel, because the apocalyps was sent and signified to him
by an angel, Rev. i. 1. 4thly, I cannot see, how it can be proved,
that the avenging the law was enjoined upon angels under the
Old Testament by any special command, which is revoked under the New. And the brethren themselves will not deny,
that the words, Psal. xxxv. 5, 6. belong even to the times of the
New Testament and to the enemies of Christ. The punishment
of rebels, the chastisement of the miscarriages of the righteous,
the defence of those under unjust oppression, argue indeed, the
ministry not, the empire of angels. And what peculiar has the
Old Testament in this respect to which the New cannot show
the like ? For, here also the apostle, 1 Cor. xi. 10. 1 Tim. v.
21. urges the observance of decency in the church because of
the presence of the angles. But it is worth while to hear
Cocceius himself, commenting to this purpose on John i. 52.
" Moreover, that angels were present with the Christian church,
appears from the preservation, enlargement and purging of the
Christian church, and from the astonishing protection of those,
that came out of Babylon." And a little after: " As he subjects
                                                            our

our members to our will, and infpires us with a good will; fo
he alfo makes his will known to his angels, and fanctifies their
will, and if there be any thing that regards the good of man,
he inclines them to it.   Thus while he reigns in the church, he
reigns in the angels, and the fame fpirit is in the angels, which
is in the church: as in the vifion of Ezekiel, the fame fpirit was
in the wheels, which was in the living creatures," Ezek. i. 20.
Let us add what he fays *in Difput. ad.* Mat. xxiv. Thef. xxxviii.
" The angels affift the preaching of the gofpel, no lefs than
they were folicitous, that the law fhould be obferved for the
determined time."    5thly, I know not on what ground it is fo
confidently afferted, that angels were formerly, in a peculiar
manner, guardians of the authority of the elders; unlefs perhaps on that general one, that God ufually employed them, to
keep up the order he had eftablifhed upon earth; but they
ceafe not to do this under the New Teftament.   6thly, They
are called *gods*, becaufe of the excellency of their nature and
office, and of the image of God in that refpect; not becaufe
of any empire they had over the people of God of which they
are now deprived: for, Paul, in his time called them " thrones,
dominions, principalities and powers," Col. i. 16.

LIX.  7thly, It is fcarce needful to mention any thing about
men fitting in the feat of Mofes, who are called earthly angels.
For who will deny, that in the commonwealth of Ifrael, which
was a royal priefthood, God appointed a magiftracy that was
both civil and ecclefiaftical with proper authority, in order to fee
to the due obfervance of his law? And I fhall eafily grant, that
this magiftracy received authority, to deal fomewhat more feverely with the church, while fhe was an infant-heir, under
tutors and guardians, than can now well fuit with an advanced
age, and days of greater liberty.  But I do not fee, who can
prove, that the apoftle, in the quoted paffage to the Hebrews,
treats of them under the name of angels : efpecially as in the
whole of this difcourfe he conftantly means by angels, thofe
miniftring fpirits whom God commands to be ready to ferve
his beloved people, Heb. i. 14.   And then even the New Teftament church hath its angels, of which in the Revelatior.
Shall we alfo affirm, that therefore it is fubject to angels? 8thly,
and laftly, The name *gods*, is common to any civil magiftrate,
who difpenfes juftice in the Gods' name, even in pecuniary
caufes; as appears from Exod. xxi. 6. and Exod. xxii. 28.
Deut. xix. 7.   That notion therefore, about the church of the
Old Teftament being in a peculiar manner fubject to angels,
falls to the ground.

LX.  8thly, It alfo deferves our enquiry, whether we are to

reckon the continual *fear* of temporal *death*, to which believers
of that time, were all their life fubject among the defects of
the Old Teftament? Concerning this fear the brethren argue
to this purpofe. They diftinguifh between a good and an evil
fear of death. This laft is attended with a horror, and hatred
of the holinefs of God proceeding from an evil confcience, in
every unregenerate finner, who knows and reflects, that God
is judge: the former again is twofold: either common or peculiar in the faints under the Old Teftament: common in all
thofe that account this life and freedom from mifery, to be an
extraordinary gift of God, and which may be profitable both
to themfelves and others. This fear is not unbecoming the
pious, nor renders them miferable. That which in an efpecial
manner belonged to the Ifraelites, the inhabitants of the land
of Canaan, arofe from caufes which were peculiar to them:
namely, 1ft, From an affection for the land of Canaan, which
was given them with a promife of long life therein, as a pledge
of the heavenly inheritance. And therefore it was neceffary,
that believers fhould defire to enjoy that pledge. 2dly, From a
defire and hope of feeing, in due time, the Saviour in that land.
3dly, From the bondage to the elements of the world, to which
they were tied down by that law, that, if on fet purpofe they
neglected it, they became as tranfgreffors of the law, obnoxious
to temporal and eternal punifhments; but, if through infirmity
or thoughtleffnefs, they acted againft the ordinances, they had
reafon to apprehend immediate death to be inflicted upon them
by the hand of God: terrible examples of which were fometimes fet before their eyes. This fear was good, proceeding
from the love of a good confcience and of the grace of God;
and made them, with diligence and care, perform the fervice
of the ceremonies: for the godly had this all their life long.
But they were delivered from it by the death of Chrift. And
this Paul is thought to have declared, Heb. ii. 15. This is the
fum of what is almoft every where repeated, and more fumma-
rily explained, *Animad. v. ad Quæft. de V. and N. T. Quæft.* 31.

LXI. For my own part: I will not difown, that there was
fomething in the rigour of the Mofaic polity, that had a tendency to make them afraid of fome dreadful death, Heb. x. 28.
" He that defpifed Mofes's law, died without mercy, under
two or three witneffes." God himfelf commanded, that fuch
as thefe fhould be punifhed with death, Lev. xxiv. 16. Numb.
xv. 34. and fometimes made examples of thofe, who had not
very carefully obferved fome circumftantials, by a death altogether extraordinary, Lev. x. 2. 1 Sam. vi. 20. 2 Sam. vi. 7—9.
This, efpecially if it was juft before them, or had lately happened,

pened, could not but strike a terror, and excite the righteous to take diligent heed, lest they should split on that rock. But it is not probable, that they, who walked in a good conscience before God, and knew they had to do with a most merciful Father, were tormented all their life, with the continual dread of death: for examples of such rigour were rare; but instances of paternal indulgence common and conspicuous before their eyes.

LXII. True it is, long life in the land of Canaan was a pledge of eternal life in heaven; and it was necessary to love this pledge, as it pleased God to grant the enjoyment of it. But I cannot conceive, how the taking away of the external and perishing pledge, was to be so much dreaded, when they were to obtain, an eternal good in its room, of which they had only an earnest in the pledge; since the godly were assured of receiving the heavenly inheritance, immediately upon, and even by death. For the exchange of the typical for the true and heavenly inheritance is not to be dreaded, but rather to be desired and longed for.

LXIII. Pious persons under the Old Testament, who deprecated an untimely death, are not said to have done so from any fond love to the earthly pledge, but from a desire of glorifying God among the living, Psal. vi. 4, 5. Isa. xxxviii. 18, 19. This exercise of piety made the Psalmist's life agreeable and truly worthy of the name of life, Psal. xviii. 17. And then they were public persons, who were fond of longer lease of life, not so much out of a regard to themselves, as to the kingdom and church, whose advantages they watched over. However, it is not to be doubted, but all the saints, whenever they considered themselves separately, and compared the imperfections of this life with the perfections of the future, desired to be dissolved, and be with God in glory. For this was then to them, as it is now to us, far better.

LXIV. The people of Israel in general, had hopes of seeing Christ in their own land; but this was not the case of every individual. Nor was it lawful for those, who lived in Canaan many ages before the coming of the Messiah, to expect such a long term of life, as to see Christ's day; nor be struck with horror at the thoughts of a death, that perhaps might cut off all those hopes. Those who were actuated by a higher spirit, had more exalted apprehensions than the vulgar, longed indeed to see those things which the disciples of Christ saw, Mat. xiii. 17. searched diligently what, or what manner of time, the prophetic spirit, which foretold those things should happen, 1 Pet. i. 11. But I know not from whence the brethren could have

learned,

learned, that every one in particular, whom they make fubject
to the fear of death, or that the generality of believers without
diftinction, expected perhaps, in their time the coming of
Chrift, and hence arofe their horror of death.   Peter fpeaks the
contrary, ver. 12. " that it was revealed unto them, that not
unto themfelves, but unto us they did minifter thofe things."
Can the brethren then mention fo much as a fingle inftance of
any, who, on that account, is faid to have been afraid of death?

LXV.  Thefe hypothefes are groundlefsly built on the faying
of Paul, Heb. ii. 15. where the fruit of Chrift's death is faid to
be the " delivering them, who through fear of death were all
their life-time fubject to bondage."   For, 1ft, What reafon can
perfuade, nay admit, that the fruit of that death, for undergoing which it was neceffary Chrift fhould become man, fhould
be reftrained to the Jews alone, the inhabitants of Canaan?
For the benefits of Chrift's death belongs to all the elect from
the beginning to the end of the world, and the apoftle is here
treating of all thofe, that are fanctified by Chrift, whom Chrift
calls his brethren, and the children given him by the Father.

LXVI.  2dly, It is without proof inferred, that thofe here
defcribed are confidered as believers already; fince it is more
fuitable to imagine, that the moft miferable ftate of the elect is
here delineated while they were themfelves out of Chrift.   For,
during all that time they muft needs be tormented in a fearful
manner with the dread of death, whenever they think of God
as a judge : and unlefs the death of Chrift had intervened, that
dread would continue upon them all their life long.

LXVII. 3dly, We are here by bondage under no neceffity to
underftand bondage to the elements of the world; for as the
apoftle a little before had faid, that the devil is deftroyed by
the death of Chrift, what is more natural than to explain, what
he now fpeaks of bondage, concerning that wretched condition
of men, when under the tyranny of the devil ?   And furely it is
a much greater bleffing to be delivered from the bondage of
the devil, than from that to the elements of the world; and as
both is a fruit of Chrift's death, why fhall we reftrict the a-
poftle's meaning to the leaft, and exclude the greateft ?   Befides
there is no fuch difference between the fear of death, and the
bondage of the devil, as to make it improbable for them to be
joined together in the fame difcourfe : for the one is cherifhed
by the other : the bondage of the devil begets the fear of death:
and the fear of death in an unfanctified confcience, heightens
the hatred of God, and confequently the bondage of fin and
the devil.

LXVIII. 4thly, The term death is moft unreafonably reftricted

stricted to temporal death. The apostle argues in this manner:
It was necessary for Christ to become man, because he was to
die.  He was to die.  (1.) That, by his death, he might destroy the devil, who had the power of death.  (2.) That he
might deliver his people from death itself, and from the fear of
it.  What can be more plain, than that the whole of that death
is here meant, over which the devil has power, both temporal
and eternal, especially the last.  The fear of temporal death,
as the brethren describe it, was good and holy in itself, only
somewhat troublesome and uneasy : and can it be thought probable, that the apostles, when speaking of the effect of Christ's
death, should explain in very magnificent terms the freedom
from a thing, good and holy in itself, because it produced
some uneasiness, and omit the deliverance from that which
comprehends all evils and miseries ? And yet so form his discourse, as if he seemed to have spoke rather of that which is
the greatest, than of that which is the least evil, and what he
alone intended ?

LXIX.  5thly, and lastly, I could also wish it was explained,
what is that universality of saints, denoted by the term, ὅσοι,
which Christ delivered from the fear of losing the pledge by
death.  Were the saints, who died before Christ, of this number ?  That does not appear ; for they are supposed to be
troubled by the fear of death all their life time.  And yet, if
I mistake not, they were delivered from this, when once they
died.  What then did the death of Christ profit them in this
respect ?  Are we then to understand those saints, who lived at
the time of Christ's death ?  The brethren seem to intend this,
when they say : " as many as bore bondage with that disposition, were delivered by Christ when he died ;" Ad. Heb. 2. §. 89.
But who are those ?  Not believers of the Gentiles, who had
no country given them for a pledge.  It must then be the Jews.
But it could not be all of them.  For, many of them lived out
of the land, in a voluntary exile, without enjoying that pledge.
How greatly then is this fruit of Christ's death limited ?  Let
us suppose it was they, who, after the death of Christ, received
Christ by faith in the land of Canaan, that constituted this universality.  But how were these delivered from the fear of losing the pledge ?  Was it because, after Christ's death, the land
ceased to be a pledge, and was shortly to be given up to the
Gentiles to a total destruction ?  Is this the meaning of the
brethren ?  How flat and mean !  Well says the celebrated interpreter on Zech. ix. §. 23.  " They voluntarily renounced the
inheritance of the land of Canaan, and exchanged it in order
to partake of the heavenly Jerusalem, and the inheritance of the

world." But neither will this remove all the difficulty; for, Paul speaks of those who, *all their life-time* were subject to the fear of death, which the brethren themselves, at other times, urge; but they, whom we suppose to be delivered by Christ, cease not to live, when delivered from the fear of death. I beg of these learned persons, again and again to consider, in what intricate perplexity they entangle themselves, while, without any just ground, they quit the trodden, plain road.

LXX. *Ninthly*, It is most of all grievous, and tends to stir up the resentment of the meekest person, that *believers* under the Old Testament are often, and that at great length, said " to have been *under wrath and the curse*." And indeed, this assertion is shocking to tender ears, and unusual in the reformed churches. The brethren took occasion to speak thus from Gal. iii. 10. " as many as are of the works of the law are under the curse." Which passage they think is to be explained, as if it was there said; whoever are subject to the ceremonial law, bear testimony, that the curse is not yet removed by Christ, nor the blessing yet actually obtained. For, though they are free from the curse belonging to the wicked, and partakers of the blessing of the sons of God, yet, by the use of the ceremonies, they openly avow, that the meritorious cause of the blessing was not yet come. But let us hear their own words. In Comm: ad Gal. 3. §. 104. " The ancient interpreters have here departed a little from the meaning of the apostle, not adverting, how believers and the saints of the Old Testament could be said to be under the curse, for they think, it necessarily follows, that it is not possible for him who is under the curse, to be saved—In this they are mistaken. For, according to the apostle, *to be under the curse*, signifies here not to be without the covenant of grace, but to undergo something on account of the curse, which was not yet blotted out by the payment of the price: either for the sake of the hand-writing against themselves on account of sin, and of the curse annexed thereto, and so far the sake of God, who neither did, nor was to punish their sins, as if he was to pardon them; and who had promised life to believers; that he might be sanctified by declaring his righteousness, which he was to manifest in Christ.

LXXI. But though this explication sufficiently provides for the salvation of the fathers; yet I think it harsh, and very far from *the scope of the apostle*, and the *language of scripture*. The *scope of the apostle* is to refute the opinion of the false apostles, by which they disturbed the quiet of the churches of Galatia, as if faith in Christ alone was not sufficient to justification, but that the Gentiles were bound to observe the Mosaic ceremonies, as a part of that righteoufnefs and holinefs commanded by the law. For, certainly, the Jews were, and ftill are, at this day, tainted with the herefy, that the ceremonies contribute to juftification. The apoftle briefly fets the truth in oppofition to that falfe notion, Gal. ii. 16. which he confirms by feveral arguments. After many others he makes ufe of this. For as that fanction, by which the curfe is threatened againft tranfgreffors, is annexed to all God's laws; and as there is none, who ought not to confefs, that they have one time or other tranfgreffed fome one law of God; fo far then can any hope for life from any obfervance of any law, that, on the contrary, " as many as are of the works of the law," that is, who take part with thofe, who would be juftified by works, *are under the curfe*, Gal. iii. 10. This inference is folid and clear, and in Paul's ufual manner.  See him arguing the fame way, Rom. iii. 19, 20.

LXXII. But many things prove, that nothing is meant by the curfe, but the curfe of the covenant of works, which excludes man from communion with God, and is oppofed to the bleffing of the covenant of grace.  1ft, He does not fpeak of that curfe, which hangs over the godly, becaufe and in fo far, as by obfervation of the ceremonial law, they fubfcribe a handwriting againft themfelves, but that, which hangs over the proud tranfgreffors of the law. For the apoftle does not fay, that the godly of old confeffed, that they were under the curfe, becaufe they obferved the ceremonial law; but thofe who are of works; jufticiary or felf-righteous workers, who endeavour to eftablifh their own righteoufnefs; thefe are they who are under the curfe, becaufe they have not obferved the law as prefcribed.

LXXIII. 2dly, Paul means here the fame curfe that Mofes did; from whom he quotes a paffage for eftablifhing his doctrine, Deut. xxvii. 26. But fince that Mofaic formula, which undoubtedly contained the fanction of the covenant of works, fpeaks of that curfe, which all finners naturally are under, becaufe they continue not in all things commanded by the law, and which is oppofed to the favour and faving grace of God. Had the apoftle meant another curfe, he would have trifled, and not argued, but this is far from his character.

LXXIV. 3dly, He fpeaks here of that curfe, from which Chrift has delivered his people. But he delivered them, not only from the hand-writing, declaring the ranfom not yet paid, but from all guilt and condemnation, from all that curfe, which we deferved on account of fin. It is a bad practice which the celebrated Cocceius every where juftly condemns in the Socinians,

ians, fo to wreft the divine words of fcripture, as to put a low and mean fenfe upon them. And is not this done, when that divine fentence, " Chrift hath redeemed us from the curfe of the law," is brought fo low : he freed us from the yoke of the ceremonies. This, certainly, is among the very leaft of the bleffings, which acrue to believers from the redemption of Chrift.

LXXV. 4thly, Moreover the curfe, we are delivered from, is of the fame kind with that, which Chrift underwent for us : he therefore underwent it for us, as an expiatory facrifice in our ftead, becaufe it lay upon us on account of fin. But Chrift was made a curfe for us, not as he obferved the ceremonial law, but as he bore the wrath, the fury the indignation of God a-gainft our fins. He complained, that he was forfaken of his Father, grappled hand to hand with dreadful horrors and an-guifh of foul, and with the infernal powers themfelves. In a word, he endured all the curfe, that the law threatened againft finners, he was not only *accurfed* but even a *curfe ;* which was fhewn by crucifixion, as the fymbol.

LXXVI. In the laft place, I do not imagine, that either of thefe can be proved from any paffage of fcripture: either, that thofe who can be called true and fpiritual fons of Abraham, *who are of the works of the law :* or, that thofe, who, in faith and a good confcience, obferve the precepts of the ceremonial law, can, on that very account be faid to be *under the curfe.* I find Rom. iv. 16. is quoted as a proof of the former : " to the end the promife might be fure to all the feed, not to that only which is of the law, but to that alfo which is of the faith of Ab-raham, who is the father of us all." But the cafe is very dif-ferent : for, 1ft, That expreffion *to be of the law,* and that, *to be of the works of the law:* are not in all refpects the fame; for, thofe may fimply be faid *to be of the law, to whom pertained the giving of the law,* Rom. ix. 4. that is, the Jewifh nation, to whom the law of God was delivered, and who, in confequence of that giving of the law, and of the covenant founded thereon, became what they are, a people peculiar to God. But feeing works, in the bufinefs of juftification, which was the difpute among the Galatians, are always fet in direct oppofition to faith, thofe who are of the works of the law, cannot be of juftifying faith. If you object, that the law is in like manner oppofed to faith ; I anfwer, the law has a twofold *relation :* a *legal,* ftrictly fo cal-led, as it contains the condition of juftification, by a perfonal and proper obedience ; and an *evangelical,* as, by its types and fhadows, it leads to Chrift. Whoever, according to the for-mer relation, are of the law, are not heirs, Rom. iv. 14. but

whoever

whoever were of the law, so as to discover in it the gracious promises of the gospel, belonged to that seed of Abraham, to which the promise was declared.   And, according to this different relation of the law, the apostle in a different sense says, that some are of the law ; some who, because they want to be of the law, are not heirs; namely those, who reckon their works as a condition of righteousness with God, either for purification or satisfaction; and some again who are of the law, and yet are heirs; namely those, who suffer themselves to be led by the law, as a schoolmaster, to Christ.   But works contradistinguished from faith, can have no other than an opposite relation in justification.

LXXVII.   To this purpose I formerly wrote with the generality of interpreters, and even Cocceius himself ; who so explains the words of Paul, that he divides into two classes all that seed, to which he maintains the promise was made sure ; one of which classes is said to be *of the law ;* the other, *of the faith of Abraham :* the one, *of the Israelites,* to whom pertained *the giving of the law ;* the other of the Gentile believers, who without circumcision, but only in imitation of his faith, become the seed of Abraham.   But I afterwards met with the discourses of James Atingius, who observes that the Greek of Paul, παντὶ τῷ σπέρματι, ὀ τῷ ἐκ τῷ νόμου μόνον ἀλλὰ καὶ τῷ ἐκ πίστεως Ἀβραάμ, is not necessarily to be translated, " to all the seed, not to that only which is of the law, but to that also which is of the faith of Abraham ;" so as to apply the restrictive particle only to the seed ; but is more properly translated, " to all the seed, not to that which is of the law only, &c."   So that the restrictive particle should be joined to the law, not to the seed.   And he thinks this verse is to be compared with verse 13. " the father of circumcision to them who are not of the circumcision only, but also walk in the steps, &c."   That the meaning is, that those are the seed of Abraham, to whom the promise can belong, not who, by circumcision only, or any other carnal precept, in which they vainly glory, may in some measure resemble Abraham ; but who resemble him in faith.   Thus both members belong to the Jews, and those are excluded from partaking in the blessing, who are only of the law, verse 14.   Those only being admitted who are of the faith of Abraham.   But those descendants of Abraham, who received the covenant proposed to them by God, as a covenant of works, and circumcision as the sacrament of such a covenant, are of the law, and indeed only of the law. These things are at large and with accuracy deduced by the very learned author.   But if this interpretation holds, the brethren are fo far from finding any fupport in the paffage, that rather every thing is againft them.

LXXVIII. For the proof of the latter, it is alledged, that the time of the Old Teftament is called the time of *wrath* and *fiverity*, Ifa. x. 25. Dan. viii. 19. and that Mofes, the minifter who gave the law, is called " the minifter of death and condemnation," 2 Cor iii. 7, 9. and that " the law worketh wrath," Rom. iv. 15. that is, impofeth fomething, which proceeded from fin and guilt, and fo from wrath. But thefe things are not to the purpofe. For, 1ft, There is nothing there concerning a curfe or execration, which conftantly in fcripture denotes the deplorable condition of the wicked, efpecially if any one is faid to be under it. 2dly, Ifaiah and Daniel fpeak not of the time of the Old Teftament in oppofition to that of the New ; but reprefent that period of time, in which God more feverely punifhed the fins of his people : which he likewife does fometimes under the New. 3dly, Mofes is called *the minifter of death and condemnation*, becaufe his miniftry, for the moft part, tended to terrify the finner, and convince him of his fin and curfe. 4thly, In the fame fenfe *the law* is faid *to work wrath*; which is not to be underftood of the ceremonial law alone, but alfo, and indeed, chiefly of the moral law, which, by its moft accurate precepts, difcovers fin, and, by the dreadful comminations of divine wrath againft finners, raifes in the foul a fenfe of wrath. But thefe things are no proof that believers of the Old Teftament were under the curfe,

---

## CHAP. XIII.

### *Of the real defects of the Old Teftament.*

I. HOWEVER the Old Teftament had really fome peculiar defects, on account of which *it is found fault with*, Heb. viii. 7, 8.; and becaufe of thefe, it was to make room for the New. When we fay this, we do no injury to the divine wifdom, as if it was inconfiftent with that, to make the firft covenant with his people, fuch as would afterwards want correction. For as God, in the firft creation of the world, began with things, that were more rude, and by degrees, as it were firft roughhewed them, then polifhed and exactly fquared them, till they attained to that beauty, in which he acquiefced : fo, in like manner in the formation of his church, he would

have

have the beginnings to be more unpolished, which, in the regular course of things, were to arise, in process of time, to a more beautiful symmetry and proportion, till he should put the the last hand to them, at the consummation of the world. And if it was not unworthy of God, to have made something imperfect in the kingdom of grace, which shall be brought to absolute perfection in the kingdom of glory: neither is it unworthy of him, to have granted something more sparingly under the Old Testament, which he could most liberally vouchsafe under the New. Nay, by this very thing he displayed his manifold wisdom, in that he distinguished the diversity of times by proper and suitable marks or signs. Paul represented the Jews, as resembling children; Christians, grown men. What irregularity is there in God's thus ordering matters, that he should confine the former to the rudiments, as being more suitable to their measure of age, and train up the latter in a more hardy, and as it were manly discipline.

II. But let us particularly rehearse in order the things, in which the Old Testament was defective. The *first* is, that the fathers under the Old Testament had not the *cause of salvation present*, much less *completed*. They had the figure of Christ in various appearances, as preludes of his future incarnation, in the pillar of cloud and fire, in the tabernacle, the temple, in the pictures of the ceremonies, the riddles of the prophecies: but they had not the privilege of beholding him present among them. The prophets of those times, " prophesied of the grace that should come unto us." " And unto them was revealed, that not unto themselves, but unto us they did minister the things, which are now reported unto us concerning the sufferings of Christ, and the glory that should follow, 1 Pet. i. 10, 11, 12.

III. And as the cause of salvation did not then appear, namely, God manifested in the flesh, neither did *righteousness*, or that on account of which we are justified. Because *the captain of their salvation*, was not yet made " perfect through sufferings," Heb. ii. 10. that in which the expiation of our sins consists, did not then exist, and consequently, " everlasting righteousness was not yet brought in," Dan. ix. 24. For as the ransom was not yet paid, the debts were not actually cancelled, *that day* had not yet shined, on which God " removed the iniquity of the earth," Zech. iii. 9. The fathers, indeed, had a true and a sufficient remission of sins; yet had not that, for which sins are justly, and in a manner worthy of God, remitted ; namely, the satisfaction and expiation of Christ. Pareus says well, ad Heb. viii.

18. " the expiatory offering was not yet made, in which the remission of sins, wherewith they were favoured, was founded."

IV. In this respect it is no absurdity to say, that the sins of believers *remained*, and still *existed*, till they were cancelled by Christ's satisfaction. For, they existed in the accounts of the surety, who was to answer for them : nor were they blotted out, till after the payment was made. We are not to think, they so lay upon believers, as that they went to heaven loaded with the guilt of them; than which nothing can be more absurd; nor are we to maintain, that they were entirely cancelled out of the book of God's accounts: for, in that case, Christ's satisfying for them had been superfluous. But they remained as debts upon the surety, which he was to pay. And therefore God, who had already before hand, remitted very many sins, exacted them of Christ at the time appointed, Isa. liii. 7. " to declare his righteousness for the remission of sins that are past," Rom. iii. 25. Pareus again l. c. " In the mean time therefore, sins even remitted without true expiation, remained till they were at length expiated by the death of the mediator: which expiation being made, both their sins and ours were at last *truly abolished* in the judgment of God. Calvin uses the same way of speaking, Instit. Lib. 2. c. vii. §. 17. " For which reason the apostle writes, that the remission of the sins which *remained* under the Old Testament, was at length accomplished by the intervention of Christ's death." This then was the first defect of the Old Testament, that it had not the cause of salvation completed, and consequently not a true expiation of sins.

V. The *second* defect was the *obscurity* of the old economy. This follows from the preceding. What can there be at most but twilight before the rising of the sun ? The Lord therefore dispensed the light of his word to them in such a manner, that they could only view it still at a distance and obscurely. Peter has elegantly represented this, by comparing the prophetic language " unto a lamp that shineth in a dark place," 2 Pet. i. 19. When he calls it a lamp, he intimates the absence of the sun ; and when he speaks of a dark place, he represents the condition of the ancients, which, amidst the darkness, had the glimmering small light of a burning taper, and no more than a taper, which is used only in the night time, not in the full day. To this purpose also is the saying of Christ, Mat. xi. 13. that " the law and the prophets were until John. From that time the kingdom of God was preached." What did the law and the prophets discover to those who lived in their days ? Certainly nothing but a taste of that wisdom, which was afterwards to be clearly displayed, by foretelling it as shining at a distance.

Whenever

Whenever Chrift can be pointed out with a finger, the kingdom of God is difclofed.

VI. There was certainly in the ceremonies, an inftituton concerning Chrift's perfon, offices, and 'benefits. And therefore it was a diftinguifhing favour, that God fhould honour Ifrael alone, above all other people, with that kind of inftruction, as we have formerly intimated. But, as the ceremonial rites were vaftly increafed, and the repetition of the promifes of grace was in the mean time more fparing and uncommon; the very great number of rites was like a vail, by which the naked fimplicity of the ancient promife was very much clouded. And the event fhewed, that the greateft part of the Ifraelites cleaved to the ceremonies themfelves, fought for juftification and expiation of fin in them, and did not penetrate into the fpiritual myfteries, which were hid under the vail, with the eyes of the underftanding and of faith. This, indeed was their own fault; but that method of teaching was not fo well adapted and effectual for the correcting of it. This is alfo reprefented by the type of Mofes, who "put a vail over his face, that the children of Ifrael could not ftedfaftly look to the end of that which is now abolifhed as ufelefs," 2 Cor. iii. 13. There the apoftle by way of allegory propofes the perfon of Mofes, to reprefent the economy of the Old Teftament. It had indeed the light of the promifes of grace, as the face of Mofes had an extraordinary glory, ver. 7. But while Mofes fpoke with the Ifraelites, he covered his glory with the vail of the ceremonies, which he had introduced; the end of which, indeed, was Chrift and his grace; but Ifrael being intent on the contemplation of thefe, fatisfied themfelves in them, and forgot to look to that, to which had they turned their mind, as became them, they would have been led by the ceremonies themfelves. And this is " that vail, which, in the reading of the Old Teftament, not being taken away, ftill remaineth on Ifrael, ver. 14.

VII. To the fame purpofe, was the vail of the tabernacle and temple, which kept the Ifraelites from entering and beholding the facred things. Thefe two vails may be thus compared together. By the vail of the temple they were reminded of fomething, which they were not yet fuffered to behold, becaufe fomething ftood in the way; namely, guilt, which was removed in the flefh of Chrift, Heb. x. 19. and that the way to the heavenly fanctuary was not yet fet open to them, Heb. ix. 8. By the vail over the face of Mofes, they were put in mind, that the eyes of their underftandings were weaker, than that they could bear the naked declaration of the truth. For if it

was

was thus at that time with Chrift's apoftles, John xvi. 12. how much more with ancient Ifrael?

VIII. It is remarkable, that the Lord Jefus himfelf, in the days of his flefh, fuited his doctrine to that more obfcure difpenfation; and laid before the promifcuous multitude, the myfteries of the kingdom of heaven, fcarce in any other manner than under the vail of parables, the meaning of which was to be rather gueffed at, than thoroughly underftood. And himfelf gives this reafon for it, Mat. xiii. 10, 11. when his difciples afked him, " Why fpeakeft thou unto them in parables?" He anfwered, " Becaufe it is given unto you to know the myfteries of the kingdom of heaven, but to them it is not given." And ver. 13. " Therefore fpeak I to them in parables, becaufe they feeing, fee not; and hearing, they hear not, neither do they underftand." But as the time of his confummation was drawing nearer, he more clearly, and without further circumlocution, propofed the truths of falvation, John xvi. 25. which the difciples themfelves obferved, ver. 29.

IX. The *third* defect was the great *rigour* and unrelenting feverity of that economy, on account of the threatenings of the law, which fo often occur, and of the promifes of grace, which are more feldom and more obfcurely repeated. To this purpofe is what we have, Heb. xii. 18. that believers are not now come to the mount that might not be touched, and that burned with fire, unto blacknefs, and darknefs, and tempeft, where nothing was to be heard or feen, but what was apt to ftrike the mind with dread and terror, fo that Mofes himfelf quaked and feared: where the terrible voice founded in their ears, which all of them intreated, they might not hear any more, to all which he oppofes the mild fweetnefs of mount Zion, and of the heavenly Jerufalem. Neither was that rigour and terror without reafon; for it was fcarce poffible, by any other means, to conquer the forwardnefs of the Ifraelites, whom Mofes and the prophets fo often reproached as a ftiff-necked generation, and a people whofe heart was like an adamant.

X. The *fourth* defect of the Old Teftament was, the *bondage under the elements of the world*, of which Paul fpeaks, Gal. iv. 3, 9. By the *elements of the world*, he underftands the ceremonies of the old economy; which he calls ϛοιχεια *elements*, becaufe of their rudenefs and imperfection; by a twofold metaphor; the one borrowed from nature, the other from art. Nature hath her elements, that is, bodies more fimple and rude, from whofe various combination and mixture others more perfect are generated. And the rudiments of art, or the firft more eafy precepts, fuited to the capacities of children,

· are

are ufually called elements, Paul himfelf ufing this term in that fenfe, Heb. v. 12. *the firſt principles* (elements) *of the oracles of God.* He adds, the elements of the *world*, either because they were earthly, borrowed from the world, and from thofe things which even worldly men have in common with the pious, and which contain not in themfelves, the bleffings and privileges of the inheritance : or because God being willing to inftruct the world, that is, the inhabitants of the world, began, from thefe flender principles, having firſt fet up a lower form or fchool, as it were in one corner of the world only. The *Iſraelites were in bondage* to thefe elements. For God had alfo given thefe elements with a fevere commination, leaft they fhould be either neglected, or ufed any other way, than he had prefcribed : and they had princes and elders, with fufficient authority, and fitting in Mofes's feat, to keep and conftrain them to the obfervance of the rites. In fine, the obfervance itfelf had an air of fervility inconfiftent with the full liberty of fons.

XI. But let us take a more particular view of what was hard and unpleafant in this bondage. 1ſt, There was, in that vaft multitude of rites, which were enjoined upon Ifrael under fuch a fevere threatening, a grievous *burden*, and a *yoke* hard to be borne, Acts xv. 10. which the apoftle calls the *yoke of bondage*, Gal. v. 1. Circumcifion, which was, as it were, the firſt undertaking of the yoke, caufed fuch pain, that even adults were heavily afflicted with it, Gen. xxxiv. 25. The number of the other ceremonies exceedingly fatigued the people, and involved them in difficulties. They were not allowed to light a fire on the Sabbath; nor to fow on the feventh year. All their males were obliged thrice a year to go up to Jerufalem. The paying the firſt-fruits and tithes was to be fcrupuloufly obferved. They were put to great expence in all kinds of facrifices. Moreover there were fo many wafhings, diftinctions of meats, legal pollutions from the touch of a dead body, and of any unclean thing whatever, and pollution in fleep. And all thefe things wherewith they were harraffed, were but " weak and beggarly elements," Gal. iv. 9. which could not " make the comers thereunto perfect," Heb. x. 1. and in the obfervation of which, of themfelves, there was no holinefs, nor the image of God, nor *a reafonable fervice*, Rom. xii. 1. However their myftical fignification, and the relation they bore to the Meffiah and his grace, made believers cheerfully undertake, and joyfully bear, that yoke, grievous in itfelf, and beggarly and ufelefs feparately from Chriſt.

XII. 2dly, There was alfo, in that bondage, *the reproach of childhood*; for it was wholly pedagogical, or adapted to children,

Gal.

Gal. iv. 2. which confifted of little, minute precepts and ordinances, fuch as are prefcribed to young children, *touch not, tafte not, handle not*, Col. ii. 21. On which place Theophylact fays elegantly, " fee alfo how he tacitly upbraids them, faying, *ye are fubject to ordinances*, ver. 20. You fit as children, fays he, as juft beginning their elements, who require what they ought to do to be faid before and prefcribed to them."

XIII. 3dly, There was alfo *the middle wall of partition*, not only feparating them from all other nations, and depriving them of the joy, which, in other refpects, would refult from the Gentiles being taken into communion with God, but alfo, in fome meafure, fecluding themfelves from familiar accefs to God, Eph. ii. 14, 15. The apoftle feems to allude to the double wall, or enclofure of the temple. The Jews, who were clean, met for worfhip within the outermoft of thefe, which had a fence or breaft-work, on which fmall pillars were ranged at equal diftances, infcribed with Greek and Latin characters, to fignify, that no ftranger was allowed, under pain of death, to pafs over that breaft-work, and break into the inner enclofure. In like manner, there was in the inner inclofure, another breaft-work like the former, whereby the people were excluded from entering into the temple, and the porch of the priefts, who were there employed in facred fervices; which Lud. Capellus has obferved on this paffage from Jofephus. See what *Conft. l'empereur* has *ad titul Middoth, c. 2. §. 3.* and *Selden de jure Natur. Lib. 3. c. 6.* With both thofe walls or breaft-works the apoftle ingenioufly compares the ceremonies, which feparated the Gentiles from the Jews (on which account they refembled the breaft-work of the firft enclofure) and the Jews themfelves, in fome meafure, from God, and familiar accefs to him. For they themfelves were commanded to ftand at a diftance, while God kept himfelf, as it were, concealed in the inner fanctuary, and to treat with him, about the expiation of fins, only by the intervention of a prieft. And in this refpect the ceremonies are compared with the latter enclofure.

XIV. 4thly, Befides this, the apoftle calls the law of commandments, contained in ordinances, *enmity*, becaufe, in a certain refpect, they were a fymbol of the enmity both between God and man, and between Ifrael and the Gentiles. For the ceremonies, in their *legal confideration*, were figns of that hatred, wherewith God, from the righteoufnefs of his nature, purfues finful man: becaufe our guilt was typified by thefe, and man behoved to be expiated and purged by thofe rites, before he could be allowed, with hope of pardon, to have accefs to God. They alfo begat a mutual hatred and contempt between Jews and Gentiles. The

Jews

Jews being proud of the ceremonies of God's inftitution, defpifed the Gentiles, who were enflaved to human, or even diabolical fuperftitions. The heathen, on the other hand, looked
upon many of the Jewifh ceremonies, as is plain from Tacitus
and others, as hateful, ridiculous, and abfurd. And hence
arofe a mutual and national hatred and enmity : by no means
commanded, far be it, but yet, as it were rivetted by that law
of difcriminating rites. And this alienation of mind was at
fuch a height that the godly themfelves judged it a crime in a
Jew to come near, or approach to a ftranger, Acts x. 28.

XV. 5thly and laftly, There was a *hand-writing* in the religion of ceremonies ἰσισωιλίον, " contrary (in part) to thofe who
loved and obferved them," Col. ii. 14. On which Calvin particularly has learnedly difcourfed, as well in other places, as in
his *Inftitutions, Lib.* 3. *c.* 7. §. 17. In his commentary on Col.
ii. 14. he declares, that no one had given him any fatisfaction
in explaining this matter. " But I truft," fays he, " I have
reached the genuine meaning, if it be only granted me as a
truth, what Auguftine has fomewhere very truly written ; nay
which he deduced from the plain words of the apoftle, that, in
the Jewifh ceremonies, there was rather a confeffion, than an
expiation of fins ; for, what elfe did they by their facrifices,
than confefs their being confcious to themfelves, that they were
worthy of death, who in their own ftead fubftituted defpicable
animals ? What, by their purifications, but to teftify their uncleannefs ? So, upon this, they renewed the hand-writing of
their guilt and impurity. Yet in that declaration there was no
manner of payment. Juftly therefore does the apoftle call
them hand-writings, contrary to thofe who loved and obferved
them ; fince, by them they openly declared their own condemnation and uncleannefs."

XVI. But this, on no account is to be fo underftood, as if believers were bound, in part by the exacting of this hand-writing, to fatisfy divine juftice in their own perfon ; for that would
be contrary to the promife of grace, which was founded on the
irrevocable furetifhip of Chrift, and accepted by the Father,
whofe infeparable fruit is the difcharge of the principal debtor.
But by this hand-writing they acknowledged two things, 1ft,
That they were unclean, and deferved utter deftruction, if confidered in themfelves, and could not efcape deftruction, unlefs
fatisfaction was made to divine juftice. 2dly, That this fatisfaction was not yet accomplifhed ; nor the true expiation, in
virtue of which they were to be juftified, yet performed ; thus
far that hand-writing was *contrary* to them. But becaufe, as I
have often obferved, the ceremonies had, befides a legal, alfo

an evangelical confideration, believers were, at the fame time, confirmed, by the ufe of them, in the faith of the Meffiah, who was to come and fatisfy for them.   And thus the hand-writing was only *in part contrary* to them, ἐναντίον   For, though it fhewed, that fatisfaction was not yet made, a circumftance which was againft them, yet it affured them, that fatisfaction was never to be demanded of them, but was certainly to be performed by the furety; which certainly was very much for them.

XVII. The *fifth* thing, in which the Old Teftament was in-ferior to the New, was a fpirit fuited to that fervile economy; which Paul, in his epiftle to the Romans, chap. viii. 15. calls the *fpirit of bondage*.   " For ye have not received the fpirit of bondage again to fear.   Where the particle *again*, denotes a diftinction, by which the prefent condition of the Chriftian church is contradiftinguifhed from the preceding condition of the church of Ifrael, as interpreters generally obferve.   But they do not by this explain the full force of that particle.   I take it in this light.   The Romans, having now become be-lievers, were united into one body with believing Ifrael, Eph. iii. 6.   For in Chrift there is a gathering together of all in one, Eph. i. 10.   *He made both one*, Eph. ii. 14. and would have be-lievers both of the Jews and of the Gentiles *be accounted one feed*, Gal. iii. 16.   And therefore what was formerly granted to Ifrael, was accounted to have been alfo granted to them.   And if the Gentiles, after the liberty of a more joyful teftament was proclaimed, fhould put on the ancient fetters of the Ifraelites, they were faid to return to bondage;   " how turn ye (back) *again* to the weak and beggarly elements, whereunto ye defire, πάλιν ἄνωθεν, *returning back to the former*, to be in bondage ?" As Paul chides the Galatians, chap. iv. 9.   In this fenfe there-fore it might alfo be faid to the Romans.   You who are now believers, living under the New Teftament, have not received *again* the fpirit of bondage, or the fpirit of bondage *again to fear*; fuch as believers of the Old Teftament had, with whom you have been incorporated, and fuch confequently as you had in and with them.

XVIII. Moreover that fpirit of bondage, as we now confider it, is the good Spirit of God, working in thofe, that belonged to the Old Teftament, in a manner fuitable to that fervile eco-nomy.   It is plain, that under the Old Teftament, the things which regarded the law and its terrors, were very often and clear-ly inculcated upon them, and confirmed by extraordinary prodi-gies, and by fearful judgments, ftriking the eyes of all; but the other things, which belong to the gofpel, and were adapted to

beget

beget filial boldnefs and alacrity, were propofed more fparing of God externally propofed, and to render them internally effectual, fuited himfelf to that difpenfation, and *commonly* rather wrought terror by the law, which daily founded in their ears, than cheerfulnefs by the doctrine of grace, which was more fparingly and more obfcurely preached unto them.

XIX. Befides, as it is a great degree of bondage, to fatigue one's felf in carefully keeping the law of a carnal commandment; the Spirit, who made them undergo with complacency and in faith this bondage, deferves in a peculiar manner to be called the fpirit of bondage. But, its operations in believers were thefe following. 1ft, He taught them, that it was juft in itfelf, good for them, and glorious to God, fuitable to the economy of his covenant, willingly to fubmit to the bondage of the elements of the world, which God commanded them. 2dly, He ftirred them up to dive into the myftery of that bondage, and not to cleave to the outfide of the ceremonies. 3dly, He inclined the wills of believers, to be thus willingly and faithfully in bondage, and, in the mean time, to long for the liberty of a happier period.

XX. This Spirit which wrought thefe things in them, was indeed, an eminent gift of God, fuitable to that age; yet a much inferior gift, than is the Spirit of pure grace and liberty, which declares, that the yoke is broken, the hand-writing torn, and excites to a reafonable fervice, which alone it enjoins to perform with joy and chearfulnefs.

XXI. We would again have it remembered, that we fpeak not thefe things, as if we thought, that the Spirit of God was only a fpirit of bondage in the believers under the Old Teftament, or as if he wrought nothing, that may be called fervile in its meafure, in believers of the New Teftament, againft which we argued with care in the laft chapter. Neither do we imagine, that all the operations of the fpirit of bondage, are to be confined to thofe we juft recited; becaufe thefe alone made, for our prefent purpofe. What we mean, is, that the operations of the Spirit of God, under the Old Teftament, compared with the operations of the fame Spirit under the New, favoured *commonly* fomewhat more of bondage than what can be fuitable to the full liberty of the fons of God; in a word, were accommodated to that condition, in which the infant heir differed not much from a fervant. We willingly conclude this point in Calvin's words; to which we heartily fubfcribe, Inftit. lib. 2. c. 11. § 9. " But the whole comes to this, that the Old Teftament ftruck horror and dread into the confciences of men; but, by the benefit of the New, thefe

are

are fet at liberty, and made to rejoice. That the former bound the confciences to the yoke of bondage : which, by the bounty of the latter were fet at liberty. But, if the cafe of the holy fathers of the people of Ifrael be objected, who were evidently partakers of the fame fpirit of faith with us; it follows, they were partakers of the fame liberty and joy : we anfwer, that neither was from the law. And then, we deny, they were fo endowed with the fpirit of liberty and fecurity, as not to experience, in fome meafure, both a dread and a bondage from the law." See what follows.

XXII. *Sixthly*, There was alfo, under the Old Teftament *a more fcanty meafure* of the gifts of *grace ;* both with refpect to * *extent* and *degree.* That the extent of thefe was very much confined, appears from thefe. 1ft, Becaufe God communicated himfelf to the nation of Ifrael alone, who yielded themfelves to him, as *his portion, and the lot of his inheritance :* Deut. xxxii. 9. and in the mean time fuffered other nations as if they had no concern or intercourfe with him, *to walk in their own ways ;* Acts xiv. 16. fo that as they were " aliens from the commonwealth of Ifrael," they were alfo " ftrangers from the covenants of promife, having no hope, and without God in the world," Eph. ii. 12. " Darknefs covered the earth, and grofs darknefs the people ;" while Jehovah did arife, and fhine upon Ifrael alone, Ifa. lx. 2. 2dly, In that one nation of Ifrael, very few were partakers of faving grace ; 1 Cor. x. 5. *with many of them God was not well pleafed:* and therefore Mofes faid to the whole people, with a reference to the generality of them, Deut. xxix. 4. " Jehovah hath not given you a heart to perceive, and eyes to fee, and ears to hear :" for they who were favoured with that grace, compared with the reft, were inconfiderable.

XXIII. If we confider the *degree,* the meafure of the grace was *commonly* fmall. 1ft, With refpect to the knowledge of fpiritual myfteries. For it was proper, fince the Sun of righteoufnefs was not yet rifen, that there fhould be neither that clearnefs of revelation, nor that quicknefs of underftanding. And therefore Paul expreffes this flendernefs of conception, by the term *childhood.* Inftances of grofs ftupidity are all along obvious in the very difciples of our Lord, Ifa. xlii. 19. " Who is blind, but my fervant ? Or deaf, as my meffenger that I fent ? Who is fo blind as he that is perfect, and blind as Jehovah's fervant ?" 2dly, With refpect to the abundance of fpiritual confolations. This is a neceffary confequence from what we have

---

* The author's words are *tam quoad extenfionem, tam quoad intenfionem.* Literally both as to *extenfion* and *intention.*

have faid before, concerning the condition and manner of that economy, and the operations of the Spirit, who fuited himself to that difpenfation. 3dly, With refpect to holinefs: and this alfo depends on the preceding two. For, where there is a fmaller degree of fpiritual light, a lefs abundance of the love of God fhed abroad in the heart, a lefs meafure of familiarity and friendfhip with God, it is reafonable to believe, that there was alfo a fmaller degree of holinefs.

XXIV. However, we by no means fpeak thus, as if we would reprefent the ordinary believers of the New Teftament, either as preferable, or even as on a level with thofe ancient heroes. For how few in the Chriftian church are found comparable to Abraham in excellence of faith? In light of knowledge to the prophets, who, even at this day, enlighten the whole univerfe? In abundance of confolations, and eminence of holinefs, to David, who was both a man according to God's heart, and fo often chanted forth thofe moft delightful odes, with a foul exulting in God? For the queftion here is not, What meafure of grace the Lord beftowed on a few; but, What ordinary difpenfation he obferved towards the whole body of the people? It is proper to compare church to church, prophets to apoftles, ancient heroes to martyrs of the New Teftament, and ordinary believers to their like.

XXV. It will not be from the purpofe, to explain, on this occafion, that faying of our Lord, Mat. xi. 11. "Verily, I fay unto you, among them that are born of women, there hath not rifen a greater than John the Baptift: notwithftanding, he that is leaft in the kingdom of heaven, is greater than. Little regard is to be had to thofe, who, with fome of the ancients, underftand by the kingdom of heaven, the ftate of the church triumphant; and tell us, that this is the meaning of Chrift's words: the leaft of the bleffed in heaven is greater, that is, more happy, perfect, excellent and glorious, than John, who was ftill in a ftate of mortality, and a traveller. For who can be ignorant, that the ftate of the heavenly country is far more excellent than that of travellers on the earth? This being fo evident in itfelf, there was no occafion for our Lord to fpeak it with fuch folemnity, as if he afferted fomething extraordinary.

XXVI. They come nearer to our Lord's meaning, who, by the leaft in the kingdom of heaven, think is intended the leaft minifter in the Chriftian church, who is entrufted to preach the gofpel in its perfect ftate. He is compared to John, not in refpect of knowledge, holinefs, and gifts of the like nature; but in refpect of his miniftry, as John himfelf was compared to his predeceffors the prophets. For John was greater

than

than all of them, becaufe he was the immediate harbinger and brideman of the Meſſiah; and pointed him out with the finger as prefent, or come. Again, any preacher of the gofpel is greater than John in that refpect, who declares, Chriſt not only born, but alfo dead and rifen, and afcended to heaven, and as fitting at the right hand of God, and as having happily erected the kingdom of liberty. The comparifon therefore is not fo much of perfons in their abfolute qualities, as of their miniſtry. The miniſtry of Mofes, and the other prophets, may not improperly be compared to the night, diftinguiſhed by many prophecies concerning Chriſt, as to many interlucent conſtellations. The miniſtry of John to the dawn; when the fun not being yet rifen, yet drawing towards the horizon, the heavens brighten with fome light: but the gofpel to the day, when, the fun being rifen, fills all things with the brighteſt and pureſt light.

XXVII. It may, however, feem ftrange, that the Lord Jefus, who, in the whole of his difcourfe, fpeaks fo many excellent things concerning John, ſhould prefently, when one could have leaſt expected it, reprefent him as lefs than the leaſt of his difciples. And, therefore, fome of the ancients think, there is a comparifon rather made betweeń John and Chriſt, who calls himfelf the leaſt in the kingdom of heaven; either becaufe he was really fo, in the opinion of men; or rather, becaufe he was younger than he, and poſterior to him in the miniſtry. In which fenfe, James the fon of Alpheus, was called the lefs; Mark xv. 40. that is, the younger, in refpect of James, the fon of Zebedee, who is called the elder. What Chriſt then intended was, that though John was truly far greater than all the other prophets, yet he was not that great prophet, not the Meſſiah, which fome, but falfely imagined; Luke iii. 15. but, that himfelf, though inferior to John in age, and poſterior to him in preaching the kingdom of heaven, yet very far excelled him in dignity. And thus, this faying of Chriſt would very well agree with the teſtimony of John concerning himfelf and Chriſt; John i. 15. " He that cometh after me, is preferred before me; for he was before me. To this fame purpofe, almoſt, Epiphanius adverfus gnoſticos, Chryfoſtom, Theophylact, Euthymius, Clarius, Zegerus, Salmero, Janfenius, and others, from whofe opinion, I own, I am not * averfe.

XXVIII. Seventhly, All thefe things, joined together, excited an ardent defire in the ancient church, and a kind of hunger and

* The generality of our Engliſh commentators incline to the fenfe given in the laſt fection.

and *thirst* after a better condition, which God had promised with the coming of the Messiah. For as most of all the things hitherto bestowed upon them, were evidences of their imperfection, and in the mean time, better things were pointed out to them at a distance, they could not, without throwing contempt on the grace of God, but desire these things. Whatever the mercy of God had thus far bestowed on them, especially when more precious promises were added, tended rather to raise than quench their thirst. Even Abraham, to whom God so familiarly revealed himself, *rejoiced to see Christ's day:* John viii. 56. The whole church cried out, " Oh that thou wouldst rend the heavens, that thou wouldst come down!" Isa. lxiv. 1. " O that thou wert as my brother, that sucked the breasts of my mother!" Cant. viii. 1. That is, O that thou wast made partaker of flesh and blood, that thou wouldst shew thyself familiarly in the midst of our congregation, in the communion of the same worship! We cannot have a better interpreter of this their desire, than our Lord himself, Mat. xiii. 17. " Verily, I say unto you, many prophets and righteous men have desired to see those things which ye see, and have not seen them; and to hear those things which ye hear, and have not heard them." The ancient fathers certainly enjoyed the grace of God with a quiet and joyful heart, knowing, that it was sufficient for their salvation; they glorified God, and gave him thanks on that account: yet, as a better condition was made known as at a distance, they reached out also in desire after it. " These all died in faith," and therefore calmly and happily; yet, " not having received the promises, but seen them afar off, and were persuaded of them, and embraced them," Heb. xi. 13.

XXXIX. I dare not, for this purpose, wrest Deut. xxix. 19. למען ספות הרוה את הצמאה, *to add the drunken,* or, *the watered, to the thirsty:* as if a twofold state of the church was imitated here; that of *thirst,* under the Old; and of *watering,* under the New Testament: and *to add the watered to the thirsty,* was to reduce the church, when satisfied with the exhibition of the promise, to the order and rank of the thirsting church; to load the believers of the New Testament with the ancient ceremonies: and from another signification of the word ספה, *to destroy the satiated with the thirsty:* to endeavour the destruction of those in covenant with God, first, while they expect the salvation of God; and then, when they have received the gospel of salvation. To these interpretations, we have a third to this purpose, that *the full shall destroy the thirsty;* that is, that those who falsely think themselves full, shall, at the time expected, oppress

press those that are thirsty; and afterwards harrass those that are filled. And these things are so joined, as, taken together, to complete the full meaning of the words. See Ult. Mosis, §. 121—138. and Lexicon ad vocem. But I think, that as these things are altogether new; so they are remote from the meaning of Moses, for the following reasons.

XXX. 1ft, Because in these words, Moses describes the language of an idolater, whose heart is turned away from the Lord God, to go after the worship of the gods of the Gentiles, and who, having renounced all fear of God, slights the solemn engagements of the covenant, and notwithstanding this, promises peace to himself, ver. 16, 28. such as were those of whom Jer. xliv. 17. But surely such an idolater as this, can give himself no trouble to force New Testament believers, who are free, to submit to the yoke of the Mosaic bondage, which he himself has shaken off, and has in abhorrence. 2dly, The person whom Moses here represents, is one of abandoned impiety, which he himself does not so much as conceal, and an avowed despiser of God and religion: but they, whom the celebrated interpreter imagines to be here pointed out, put on a great appearance of sanctity, and, in all their actions, made religion a pretence; as is well known from the gospel-history. 3dly, If *the thirsty* signifies the church of the Old Testament, and *the watered,* the church of the New; *to add the watered to the thirsty,* can only signify, *to add the New Testament church, to that of the Old, and join both together:* which the scripture declares was done by Christ, Eph. ii. 13. and Eph. iii. 6. But it is one thing *to add the satiated to the thirsty;* another *to reduce the satiated to the condition of the thirsty.* The obstinate zealots for the ceremonies are no where said to have joined to themselves the free Christians; but rather to have separated them from themselves, and expelled them the synagogues, Isa. lxv. 5. and Isa. lxvi. 5. 4thly, As there can be only one literal sense, it is asserted, contrary to all rules of right interpretation, that the word נספה, can, in the very same proposition, be taken for, partly, *to destroy,* or *consume;* partly, *to join* and *unite;* and the participle רוה, partly, for עם. *with;* partly, for the sign of the accusative. It is one thing, under the general signification of one word, to comprize more things pertaining to the same signification, which often takes place in explaining scripture: another, to ascribe to the same word, at the same time, different, or opposite significations; which is contrary to all reason. If נספה signifies here *to join,* it cannot signify *to destroy.* If רוה signifies *with,* it cannot be the sign of the accusative. 5thly, What is more absurd, than, after having established at large,

that

that the *full* signifies the church of the New Testament, to understand by the *thirsty*, that which is *oppressed with the ceremonies;* and immediately to undo all this, and turn the words to this meaning, *that the full shall destroy the thirsty;* that is, the Jews, who are zealous for the discarded ceremonies, who seem to themselves be to full, shall persecute those, that pant after Christ. What is it to put white for black, if this is not? Can any thing more absurd be devised, than that one word should signify, at the same time, the Christian church, which suffers persecution, and the congregation of the malignant Jews, who persecute her? And yet learned men fondly please themselves with such inventions.

XXXI. What then, you will say, is the genuine meaning of the words of Moses? I really think, it is plain and obvious. When any person commits, with pleasure, the crime he has conceived in his mind, he is said, proverbially, " to drink iniquity as water," Job xv. 16. When a person ruminates on impious projects in his mind, he is as one that thirsteth after evil. But when he executes his premeditated designs, he surfeits himself with diabolical delights, and becomes, as it were, satiated, or drunk. Finely says the celebrated Cocceius, on Zech. ix. §. 14. · " Outrageous, savage men are said to thirst after blood, and, while they shed it with pleasure, are said, to drink it, Rev. xvi. 6. What any one is delighted with, is said to be his meat, and he is said to drink it as water, John iv. 34. Job xv. 16. and Job xxxiv. 7. To add, therefore, the drunken, or the satiated, to the thirsty, is, not only to burn with an eager desire to commit wickedness, but also to accomplish it by abominable actions, and to follow after it, till his mind, which is bent upon evil, is fully satisfied. This the despisers of the deity do, who secure in their crimes, call the proud happy, and give way in all things to their unbridled lusts. And these are they whom Moses here describes. Should these things give less satisfaction, I recommend above others, the discourses of the very learned *Lud. de Dieu,* who is large on this passage.

XXXII. They also seem to be as far from the meaning of Zechariah, who think, that he compares the condition of the fathers of the Old Testament, " to the pit wherein is no water," Zech. ix. 11. For, 1st, Those very fathers sung, Psal. xxiii. 2. " he maketh me to lie down in green pastures, he leadeth me beside the still waters." Which is quite different from the pit, wherein is no water. 2dly, We admit, as a most certain rule of interpretation, which the brethren usually insist upon, that the words, unless any thing should hinder, are to be taken in their full import. But the emphasis is far greater, if, by the

pit without water, we underſtand the condition of an unregenerate ſinner; who, while in himſelf, he is without Chriſt,
is whòlly deſtitute of all thoſe things, which can yield him conſolation, and quench his thirſt after happineſs. And there is
no reaſon, why we may not thus explain it. For, the prophet
ſpeaks concerning what is impetrated by the blood of Chriſt,
which is the blood of the covenant, or New Teſtament, and
ſhed, not only to remove the yoke of ceremonies, but eſpecially
to abòliſh the bondage of ſin. Why ſhall we confine what is
ſpoken, to that which is the leſs, ſince the words may not only
bear, but alſo perſuade, nay almoſt conſtrain us, to interpret
them of what is greater? 3dly, The prophet here comforts the
mourners in Zion, and promiſes them deliverance from that evil,
with which they were moſt of all oppreſſed, and for which
they expected a remedy from the Meſſiah, who was to come.
But that evil was not the bondage of ceremonies, which yielded little or no comfort; but rather the abyſs of ſpiritual miſery,
into which ſin had plunged them. The yoke of which, under
the devil, who exacts it of them, is infinitely more grievous,
than that yoke of ceremonies, that God laid upon them. 4thly,
Though the ceremonies, conſidered in themſelves, and ſeparate
from Chriſt, could not yield ſo much as a drop of comfort:
yet the fathers were not, on that account, in a pit, wherein is
no water. For, what they could not draw from the ceremonies,
they drank out of the ſtreams of divine grace, flowing from
Chriſt, an everlaſting fountain, to whom they looked by their
faith. We therefore dare not ſay, the ancient condition of the
fathers, was a pit, wherein is no water: though, with ſcripture
we maintain, that they had a thirſt after better things; never-
theleſs they were not deſtitute of the waters of ſaving grace,
for their neceſſary conſolation.

---

## CHAP. XIV.

### Of the Abrogation of the Old Teſtament.

I. IT now remains, we ſpeak of the *abrogation* of the Old
Teſtament, or of thoſe things which were formely ſuper-
added to the covenant of grace, as ſhadows, types, and ſymbols
of the Meſſiah to come. For the more exact proſecution of
this ſubject, we ſhall proceed in the following order. I. Shew
that the ancient ceremonies were of ſuch a nature, that, in a
way

way confiftent with the honour of God, *they might be abrogated.*
II. Prove, that they were really and actually *to be abrogated.*
III. Make it appear, that they *ought*, one time · or other *to be*
*abrogated ;* and that it was not poffible the cafe fhould be otherwife.   IV. Explain the *progreft* itfelf and the *various degrees* of
their abrogation.

II. To begin with the *firft*.   The foundation of the moral
laws, whofe perpetuity and unchangeablenefs is an unqueftionable truth, is of a quite different nature, from that of the ceremonial inftitutions, as appears from the following confiderations.
1ft, Becaufe the former are founded on the natural and immutable holinefs of God, which cannot but be the exemplar to rational.
creatures; and therefore cannot be abolifhed, without abolifhing
the image of God: but the latter are founded on the free and arbitrary will of the lawgiver.   And therefore only good, becaufe commanded; and confequently, according to the different nature of
times, may be either prefcribed, or otherwife prefcribed, or not at
all prefcribed.   This diftinction was not unknown to the Jewifh
doctors; and hence was framed that of Maimonides, in præfat.
Abhot. c. 6. fol. 23. col. 3. into *intellectual precepts*, whofe
equity was felf-evident to the human underftanding; and into
thofe " apprehended by the hearing of the law," whofe entire
ground is refolved into the faculty of hearing, which receives
them from the mouth of God.   Concerning the former, the wife .
men have faid that " if they were not written it was juft they
fhould:" concerning the latter Maimonides affirms, that " if the
law had not been declared, thofe things, which are contrary to
them, would not have, on any account, been evil.

III. 2dly, Becaufe God himfelf frequently, on many accounts
prefers the moral to the ceremonial precepts ; and as the fame
Maimonides, More Nevoc. P. 3. c. 32. has wifely obferved, God
very often, by the prophets, rebukes men for their too great
fondnefs and exceffive diligence in bringing offerings inculcating upon them, that they are not intended principally, and for
themfelves, and that himfelf has no need of them.   Thus
Samuel fpeaks, 1 Sam. xv. 22.   " Has the Lord as great delight
in burnt-offerings and facrifices, as in obeying the voice of the
Lord ?" In like manner, Ifa. i. 11.   " To what purpofe is the
multitude of your facrifices unto me ? faith the Lord.   And
Jer. vii. 22. " for I fpake not unto your fathers, nor commanded them in the day, that I brought them out of the land of
Egypt, concerning burnt-offerings or facrifices: but this thing
commanded I them, faying, obey my voice, and I will be your
God, and ye fhall be my people."   On this place Maimonides
obferves.   It feems ftrange, how Jeremiah fhould introduce

God

God fpeaking in this manner, fince the greateft part of the precepts is taken up about facrifices and burnt-offerings: but he
anfwers, the fcope of thefe words is thus. The firft intention
certainly is, that ye cleave to me, and not ferve another, that
I may be your God, and you my people. But this precept
concerning offerings and my houfe, is given you to the end,
you might learn it hence for your advantage. The parallel
places are many, Pfal. l. 9——11. Jer. vi. 2. Hof. vi. 6. Am.
v. 22. If God, therefore, when thefe precepts were ftill in
full force, rebukes men for their too great attachment to them,
we fpeak nothing unworthy of God, when we affirm, that, for
very weighty reafons, it was poffible, he fhould entirely abrogate them.

IV. 3dly, We add, that the church, without any prejudice
to religion, was, for many ages, deftitute of the greateft part
of the ceremonies; as the Jews themfelves reckon two thoufand
years before the giving of the law. Why then could fhe not,
without detriment to religion, afterwards want the fame ceremonies; in the practice of which, there was no intrinfic
holinefs, nor any part of the image of God? This at leaft is
evident, that they are not of the effence of religion, and that
it was entirely in God's power to have made them either fewer
or more in number, with even a ftricter obligation; or again
entirely to abolifh them.

V. Nor ought this to ftand in the way as any prejudice;
that it was indeed convenient, that God fhould fometimes inftitute new ceremonies, to render religion more neat, graceful,
and pompous; but not fo proper to abrogate what he had once
inftituted; becaufe both the inftitution of rites, which are
afterwards wifely abrogated, and the abrogation of rites, which
were wifely inftituted, equally argue fome defect of wifdom.
But we are to have quite different conceptions of thofe things.
God, indeed, in this matter has difplayed his manifold, and
even his unchangeable wifdom, which is ever moft confiftent
with itfelf, in fuiting himfelf to every age of his church: a
more plain and eafy kind of worfhip became her firft and
moft tender infancy: but a ftricter and pedagogical difcipline
was better fuited to her more advanced childhood, but yet childhood very unruly and headftrong. And adult and manly age
required an ingenuous and decent liberty. Our heavenly
Father therefore does nothing inconfiftent with his wifdom,
when he removes the pedagogue, whom yet he had wifely
given his fon during his nonage; and treats him, when he is
now grown up, in a more free and generous manner.

VI.

VI. Moreover, as the ceremonies were not inftituted for themfelves, but for fomething elfe, as we have juft had Maimonides confeffing, the fame wifdom, wherewith they were inftituted, requires, that when the reafon of the inftitution ceafes, they fhould ceafe alfo. But when the Meffiah is once manifefted, we fhall in its proper place make it appear, by invincible arguments, that thofe reafons ceafed, for which the ceremonies were inftituted. I am only now fhewing, that the ceremonies *may* be abrogated without any, even the leaft blemifh on the wifdom and unchangeablenefs of God.

VII. But let us now proceed to the *fecond* head; namely, that God really *intended* they fhould ceafe in their appointed time. This is evident from the following arguments : *Firft*, The very inftitution of the ceremonies leads us to this: for, fince they were given to one people, with a limitation to their particular ftate, country, city, and temple, the legiflator never intended, that they fhould be binding on *all* whom he favours with faving communion with himfelf, *and at all times and in all places.* But this was really the cafe. And the Jews have always boafted in this, that the body of the Mofaic law was only given to their nation, " even the inheritance of the congregation of Jacob," Deut. xxxiii. 4. And God confined it *to their generations,* Gen. xvii. 7. Lev. vii. 36. and Lev xxiv. 3. But as thefe generations are now confounded, and the Levites, by no certain marks, can be diftinguifhed from the other tribes, or the defcendants of Aaron from the other Levites ; it follows, that the law ceafes, which was confined to the diftinction of generations, which almoft all depended on the tribe of Levi, and the family of the priefts. God alfo appointed a certain country for the obfervation of the ceremonies, Deut. vi. 14. Deut. iv. 1. and Deut. xi. 31, 32. a certain city and houfe, Deut. xii. 5, 13, 14, 16. Since therefore the prophets all along foretold, that the church fhould afterwards be enlarged, by having many nations added to it; who as they belong not to the generations of Ifrael, fo neither could they inhabit the fame country with them, nor meet in the fame city, much lefs houfe ; it is evident, that the lawgiver never intended, that his people fhould, at that time, be bound to the practice of the ceremonies. For, as we fhall more fully prove in the fequel, the condition of the Ifraelites could not then be different from the other nations, fince all were to be united in one body with Ifrael.

VIII. This argument will have further ftrength when we fhall have obferved, that the reafons of moft of the ceremonies were altogether peculiar, and taken from the fpecial confideration

eration of thofe times, and of the countries bordering on that of the defcendants of Abraham, from whofe errors and worfhip, God would have his own people to keep at the greateft diftance. Abraham, the patriarch of the nation of Ifrael, came forth from among the Zabians. God therefore generally fo framed his ceremonies, as to be directly oppofite to the rites of the Zabians. Maimonides has frequently infifted upon this, and acknowledges, that he came to know the reafon of many laws, from the alone knowledge of the faith, rites, and worfhip of the Zabians. For inftance, thefe idolaters offered only leavened bread; made choice of fweet things for their offerings, which they ufed to anoint with honey, but made ufe of falt. God therefore prohibited to offer either leavened bread or honey, but exprefsly commanded, that falt fhould be ufed in all facrifices, Lev. ii. 13. Again, when thefe worfhippers of the fun, were to pray, they turned themfelves to the eaft: and hence the holy of holies was placed in the weft. Again, the Zabians did eat blood, though they looked upon it as a moft impure thing; for they imagined it was the food of devils, and by eating it, one might attain to fome familiarity with them: God therefore, under a fevere threatening, prohibited the eating of blood, Lev. xvii. 10. Nor did God prefcribe rites, contrary to the Zabians alone, but alfo to the other heighbouring nations. The Egyptians worfhipped the fign of the ram, and therefore were forbid to kill fheep. But in the facrifices of the Ifraelites no beafts were more acceptable, and more frequent than fheep. Plutarch affures us, that rabbits and hares, on account of their fwiftnefs and the perfection of their natural fenfes, were facred to the Egyptians. But God would have his people to account all thefe unclean and profane. The worfhippers of Baal-peor adored their idol by uncovering their nakednefs: and hence the priefts of God are commanded to make to themfelves breeches to cover their nakednefs, Exod. xxviii. 42. with many other things to the fame purpofe, which Maimonides has collected in More p. 3. c. 45, 46. and after his example Hottinger in Hift. Oriental. lib. 1. c. 8. and Selden de Jure nat. &c. Lib. 2. c. 7. And we now quote them, to make it appear, that thefe and the like commandments were given to one nation only, for reafons peculiar to them, and appropriated to thofe times, without affecting other nations in fuch a manner, or having now that weight as formerly, the madnefs of the ancient fuperftitions being now long fince abolifhed.

IX. *Secondly*, We argue from the prophecies, by which the abrogation of the ceremonies is very clearly foretold; but thefe are either more general, or more fpecial. In general, Mofes

himfelf

himfelf has prophefied concerning this thing, Deut. xviii. 15, 18. Where God, and Mofes in God's name, promife to Ifrael a prophet from among their brethren, like unto Mofes himfelf: into whofe mouth, God fays, he would put his words, and threatens to take vengeance on the perfon, who fhould not hearken to the words of that prophet.

X. For underftanding that place, and the force of our argument taken from it, we muft obferve the following things. 1ft, Mofes forbids Ifrael to have any communion with foothfayers and diviners, holding forth himfelf and recommending the law given by his miniftry, which contained every thing neceffary to be known for that time. And leaft they fhould pretend, that upon his removal, fomething more would be granted them in this matter, he intimates, that his law would be fufficient till God fhould raife up another prophet, like unto himfelf, to whofe words they were afterwards to give diligent attention. 2dly, That prophet was to be like unto Mofes: but it is without all difpute, that there was never any in Ifrael equal to him, except this, of whom we are now fpeaking, Deut. xxxiv. 10. Moreover that likenefs and equality was not to confift in fome minute circumftances, or fuch qualities, as the following prophets had in common with Mofes; but principally in the authority and exercife of the prophetical office. As Mofes by the authority of God had polifhed the more grofs worfhip of the ancients, and reduced it to a more perfect form; fo himfelf was to change that carnal worfhip of Mofes into another more fpiritual. 3dly, God promifes, that he would put his words into the mouth of that prophet, not only in that fenfe in which all the true prophets fpoke the words of God, as his faithful minifters: but thofe words, which God had referved to be fpoken by himfelf in the laft days, and which none but God can fpeak, fee John iii. 35. Hence it follows, that prophet was not to be a bare interpreter of the law of Mofes, but the true Lord of the law, and to fpeak thofe words of God, which were not hitherto fpoken in that manner. 4thly, That prophet can be none but the Meffiah, whofe prophecy, according to Abarbanel in Prophet. fol. 27. col. 1, was in the higheft pitch of prophetic degrees; and who, according to the faying of the Rabbins, which he fubjoins, " is more exalted than Abraham, higher than Mofes, and more fublime than the miniftering angels," compare Acts iii. 22. 5thly, The fcripture all along infifts upon it, fee Ifa. xlii. 4. and the Hebrew doctors do not deny it, that the Meffiah was to bring in a new form of doctrine. See Ifa. xlii. 4. Jonathan thus paraphrafes on Ifa. xii. 3. " and you fhall receive a new doctrine with

with joy from the chosen from among the just." Kimchi
gives a remarkable reason why the paraphrast called this doctrine *new;* " because really that doctrine will be new: and then
they shall learn the knowledge of the Lord in such a manner,
as none ever learned before that time." 6thly, God commands
them to hearken to that prophet, and to subdue and captivate
every thought, which exalts itself against him. Baal Hatturim
has observed, that ver. 15 contains ten words, to set forth, that
" he is to be obeyed equally with the decalogue." Though this
observation be a specimen of Jewish fancy, yet the thing is certain : for, the words of that prophet are as much the words of
God as the decalogue. 7thly, God threatens to take vengeance
on every one who should disobey him. The stubborn and rebellious Jews have experienced this; for they obstinately contend-
ed for the discarded ceremonies of Moses against Jesus and his
disciples. All this tended to recommend to Israel another prophet, who was to institute a new form of worship, just as
Moses had done before.

XI. Let us now take a view of the principal exceptions of
the Jews. 1st, This promise contains God's gracious answer
to the prayers of the Israelites at Horeb, when they entreated,
that God would speak to them by a mediator, least perhaps the
glory of his majesty should overwhelm them. But it is certain
that at Horeb they did not ask for a prophet, to substitute another law, when that of Moses was abrogated. Thus Lipmannus Sepher Nitzachon, No. 137. 2dly, By the prophet is here
understood the whole order of prophets in every age, and who
may be said to be like unto Moses in point of authority and
faithfulness, as they declared the words of the living God, as
Moses had done: and the Israelites had such a number of them
that they had no occasion, in doubtful cases, to consult sooth-
sayers or diviners. *The same author.* 3dly, If any one is pointed out in particular, he was either Joshuah, of whom it is said,
Deut. xxxiv. 9. " and the children of Israel hearkened unto
him," as seems to be the opinion of Aben Ezra and Bechai;
or Jeremiah, because the words, להם אקים נביא, *I will raise up a*
*prophet to them,* are by the Gematria, equal in number to these
ירמיה זה *this is* Jeremiah, according to Baal Hatturim. And
Aberbanel de præfat. ad Perenniam, least he should be thought
he had nothing to say, runs the parallel between Moses and
Jeremiah, in fourteen particulars. 4thly, Our Jesus cannot
be here intended, because, neither according to us, nor according to the Jews, was he like unto Moses. Not according to
us, because we believe him to be God: but Moses was a mere
man; not according to the Jews, who firmly maintain, that
there

there never afterwards was a prophet equal to Mofes. But it is abfurd, a lefs fhould abrogate the ordinances of a greater, Lipmannus. 5thly, The fame author likewife fays, that our explication contradicts the words of Chrift, who protefted, that he came not to deftroy the law, Mat. v. 17.

XII. To the *firft* of thefe we anfwer. 1ft, God, indeed, by this prophecy, anfwers the petition of the Ifraelites; for though they did not did not directly pray for the abrogation of the Mofaic manner of worfhip; yet that was no reafon, why God might not promife a prophet, who was to do and teach, what they had not once thought of in their petition. For God frequently hears the prayers of his people, fo as to grant them more than they had either afked or thought of. The Ifraelites had prayed, that for the future God would fpeak to them by a mediator: he promifes that he would not only do this, but alfo, * by giving the character inftead of the proper name, he promifes them a certain prophet equal to Mofes, who would perform as great, nay greater things for the true Ifrael. We are to confider well, what was tranfacted, when the Ifraelites prefented this their petition to God: they certainly expected, after hearing the decalogue, that God would publifh more laws, and ftatutes, which they were as yet ignorant of, and in a word, give them a model of a new and complete formulary of religion, Deut. v. 33. They prayed, that thefe might be declared to them, not as the decalogue was, by an awful an immediate manifeftation of the divine majefty, but by the intervening miniftry of Mofes. God complies with their requeft, ver. 37. but does not ftop there: for he promifes to deal with them in a like manner, when a like cafe fhould fall out. As in forming the old economy he made ufe of the miniftry of Mofes; fo at the time, when the new fhould fucceed the old, and be much more glorious than the former, he promifes to make ufe of an interpreter, who fhould vail the awful majefty of the deity, and deal with them in a way of grace and mercy. As God therefore conftituted Mofes a mediator, when he was refolved, in the place of the ancient plain way of religion, to inftitute a more burdenfome kind of worfhip; fo when he promifes another prophet, equal to Mofes, he intimates that by him he would do fomething, like what he had done by Mofes, in reforming the Mofaic economy: which remarkable goodnefs of God Mofes here inculates.

XIII. To the *fecond* I anfwer. That indeed for ordinary, Ifriel was not without prophets, whom they might more pioufly

Vol. II.      3 C      and

* This I apprehend, is the fenfe of the author, whofe words are, αττωρμαρμαζος pollicetur.

and fafely confult, than either foothfayers or diviners, or the like impoftors: neverthelefs this was not abfolutely perpetual, 1 Sam. iii. 1. 2 Chron. xv. 3. But there is nothing faid here of a mutual fucceffion of prophets; but concerning fome prophet eminently fo called, and diftinguifhed by his character; fince it is allowed, that in the whole feries of prophets, none came up to Mofes. But it is unpleafant minutely to purfue feigned refemblances of a perfon, who puts not a due value on the greatnefs of God's promife; or which is ftill worfe, knowingly depreciates it. But I would have the mutual coherence of the context well obferved, which reprefents the matter thus. Mofes diffuades the people from giving ear to aftrologers and diviners by this argument, becaufe God was to raife up a prophet, equal to himfolf, to whom they were to hearken in all things. But you will fay, that was not to be till after many ages. What then? They had a written law, which was abundantly fufficient for them, till the time of that prophet. This, upon any doubt arifing, was to be confulted, Ifa. viii. 19, 20. For ordinary they were to have prophets, to interpret that law, who were familiar with God. And when the common prophets ceafed, and the period of the law was drawing towards its final conclufion, that great prophet was to arife, at whofe mouth they were to enquire, and in whofe ordinances they were to acquiefce. What probable reafon then could make them have recourfe to aftrologers or diviners?

XIV. I anfwer to the *third*. The facred text evidently fhews, that the prophet here pointed out is not Jofhuah, Deut. xxxiv. 9, 10. for, after he had told, that Jofhuah fucceeded upon the death of Mofes, it is immediately and exprefsly fubjoined. " and there arofe not a prophet fince in Ifrael, like unto (as) Mofes:" as if God would purpofely take care, that none fhould imagine Jofhuah to be the prophet, he had promifed te give them, Deut. 18. What is added, " and the children of Ifrael hearkened unto him, can not confirm fuch a confiderable point without farther proof. Aberbanel being to prove, that Jeremiah is here meant, contends for it by an argument of a quite contrary nature, and makes the fimilitude to confift in this, that as his countrymen oppofed and refifted Mofes, fo they alfo did Jeremiah. But both is abfurd. It was the common lot of all the prophets, to be fometimes liftened to, but more frequently to be rejected; to have fometimes pious hearers, who trembled at the words of the living God; fometimes profane defpifers and fcoffers, who made a jeft of them. You will no where find a more perfect fulfilment of this word than in the Lord Jefus himfelf, of whom the Father proclaimed from heaven, *hear ye him*, Mat. xvii. 5.

XV.

XV. Much lefs are we to explain thefe things of Jeremiah, to whom the things that have been faid before are no more applicable, than to any other of the prophets. For, 1ft, The Cabbaliftical Gematria, which is the entertainment only of idle minds, has perhaps now and then, fomething ingenious, but nothing folid. We may juftly fay of it, what, in a fimilar cafe Aben Ezra fays on Ifa. vii. 6. *this is vanity*. For, the mafter of the Cabala exprefsly contradicts himfelf : fince he had a little before declared, that the prophet here promifed would open all the fifty gates of intelligence, becaufe the 15th verfe begins and ends with the letter *mun*, which is the numeral character of fifty. But to fay this of Jeremiah is altogether contrary to the hypothefis : for, in that cafe, he would be preferred to Mofes, to whom as they foolifhly talk, forty-nine gates of intelligence were fet open. The fimilitudes affigned by Abarbanel, are trifling : for, either they are common to Jeremiah with the other prophets, or only taken from external circumftances, or even fome of them falfe. And then among the prophets there were others, whom he himfelf greatly prefers to Jeremiah. In his preface to Ifaiah, he at large contends, that he is the next to Mofes in the excellence of the prophetic qualifications : nay he even prefers Ezekiel in many refpects to Jeremiah. It is therefore aftonifhing, he fhould felect him from the reft of the prophets rather than fome other.

XVI. To the *fourth* I anfwer. This prophecy is on all accounts to be applied to the Lord Jefus, who was like to Mofes in the exact knowledge of divine things, in familiarity with God, in miracles ; in fine, in every pre-eminence, by which Mofes excelled the other prophets. He was of their brethren, who fpoke fuch words ; as God had referved to be declared in the laft times ; to whom the Father bore teftimony from heaven, with an exprefs charge to hear him in all things. Nor is it any objection, that we affirm him to be greater than Mofes. For, he who is greater, has every thing that is in the lefs, and thus far is like and equal unto the lefs. Befides Mofes did not intend an abfolute equality between himfelf and that prophet, who was promifed to be given them ; but that at leaft he was not to be lefs than himfelf. But the greater he is, the ftronger is the argument, and the ftricter reftraint is put upon idle curiofity. The general affertion, that a prophet did not arife like unto Mofes, is improperly objected : for, what is faid of the time paft, is not to be underftood in prejudice of the future ; and it is felf-evident, that faying puts no bar to the excellence of that prophet, whom Mofes himfelf affirms, was in all refpects to be equal to himfelf. It is alfo improperly urged, that

the

the lefs cannot abrogate the ordinances of the greater; for, befides, that the doctrine of the prophets has not its authority from
them, but from God, Chrift was fo much greater than Mofes,
by how much the Son is greater than the fervant, and the build-
er than the houfe, Heb. iii. 3, 5, 6.

XVII. I anfwer to the *fifth*. 1ft, When Chrift fays, he came
not to deftroy the law and the prophets, he principally means
the moral law, for, this is what he there explains, vindicates
and inculcates; and he fubjoins to the fum of it, which he elfewhere publifhes, " on thefe two commandments hang all the
law and the prophets," Mat. xxii. 30. Whence we learn,
what our Lord means by the law and the prophets. 2dly,
Καταλύσαι τὸν νόμον, does not fignify to abrogate the law, when it
had performed its part, but to overturn, and deftroy it, loofen
its frame, either by perverting its true meaning, or abolifhing
its fcope, or in fine, by falfifying and rendering 'it ineffectual.
In which fenfe our Lord fays, John x. 35. *the fcripture cannot
be broken.* That is, what the fcripture fays cannot but be
true. Briefly, to deftroy the law, and the prophets, is to
contradict them, either in doctrine or practice. And it is
certain, our Lord came not in this manner to deftroy the
law and the prophets, not even the ceremonial; fince, on the
contrary, he accomplifhed, in the moft exact manner, whatever the law commanded, moft faithfully explained its
genuine fenfe, and moft exactly fulfilled whatever either the
ceremonies prefignified, or the prophets predicted. 3dly, That
abrogation of the ceremonies, which we fay was made by
Chrift, is their glorious confummation and accomplifhment, all
their fignification being fulfilled; not an ignominious deftruction, which our Lord juftly difclaims.

XVIII. The prophecy of Jeremiah concerning the abrogation
of the Old Teftament, Jer. xxxi. 31—34. is no lefs remarkable
than illuftrious. Where obferve, 1ft, That by the old covenant,
is meant, that which God made with the Ifraelites on their departure out of Egypt, the tenure of which Mofes has fully fet
forth, Exod. xxiv. 3. and following verfes. Thus Mofes rehearfed
not only the decalogue, but alfo many judicial and ceremonial
precepts, which are declared in chap. xx. and the following, at
the command of God to the people, and ftipulated obedience
from the people. Which ftipulation being performed, he proceeded to the folemnity of the covenant, and on the day following, erected an altar, reprefenting Chrift, and twelve pillars,
which reprefented the twelve tribes of Ifrael. And then, as
God's ambaffador, he read out of a book, in their hearing, all
thofe precepts, moral, judicial, and ceremonial. The people
anfwered, that they would perform all that was read before
them.

them. Then Mofes fprinkled both the altar of the Lord, and the twelve pillars of the people, with the blood of the facrifices. This blood he called the blood of the covenant. Where we are to obferve, that all the folemnities of that covenant were entirely ceremonial; the altar, the facrifices, the blood, the fprinkling. And therefore that covenant itfelf which confifted in rites, was ceremonial too, Heb. ix. 1.—For, though thefe were only the accidents of the covenant, or at leaft appendages thereto; yet, becaufe they were the inftruments of its adminiftration, they are called the covenant: And therefore, in fum, the folemn manner of ratifying this covenant, confifting in ceremonies and facrifices, is, in this placec alled the old covenant.

XIX. 2dly, To that old covenant is contradiftinguifhed the new, which can be no other, but God's agreement with Ifrael, without the vail of ceremonies; in which there can be nothing typical or fhadowy, but all things real and fubftantial; the facrifice not brutal, but rational; the blood, not of beafts, but of the Meffiah; the fprinkling, not of an altar of earth on one hand, and of pillars reprefenting the people on the other; but of heavenly things, which are reprefented by earthly, on the one, and of the confciences on the other hand. As the apoftle fets the one over againft the other, Heb. ix. and x.

XX. 3dly, The old covenant is here found fault with, accufed, and charged with defects: not only becaufe the new is promifed, for which there would have been no place, had nothing been deficient in the former, Heb. viii. 7. but alfo becaufe the former is faid to have been made void by Ifrael. It had not, therefore, at leaft, as old and fhadowy, and as explained by Mofes in the faid place, the promife of fanctifying grace. It had the decalogue engraven on tables of ftone, the reft of the laws written down in a book: but in the whole folemnity of the covenant, there is not the leaft mention of writing the law on the heart. The old covenant was, therefore, of fuch a nature, as to leave room for a new and a better.

XXI. 4thly, The new covenant, that was promifed to fucceed the old, has the following fuperior privileges. 1ft, It fhall be fure and ftable, becaufe it was not to be external but fpiritual; engraven not on tables of ftone, but on the flefhly tables of the heart. 2dly, Clearly propofed, and made known, by a more plentiful unction of theSpirit, fo that there would be no neceffity for one to be taught by another, 1 John. ii. 27. as formerly; when the myfteries of falvation were exhibited to be gueffed at, rather than contemplated. 3dly, It fhall have a true expiation and remiffion of fins, which the old economy, as legal, excluded, and as typical, could not give. Whence it appears,
that

that the new covenant, which is here promifed, confifts in mere promifes of an *irrevocable* grace, is held forth to us without the vail of ceremonies, and has the reality of thofe things of which the types were only the fhadows.

XXII. 5thly, From thefe things, moreover, it is now eafy to conclude, that the new covenant was not promifed to ftand, to-gether with the old, and be fuperadded, to fupply its defects; but to come in the place of the former, when that, as obfcure and typical, fhould be entirely removed; as is plain from thofe words. " Not according to the covenant, that I made with their fathers, &c. In that he faith a new covenant, *he hath made* the firft *old:* now, that which decayeth and waxeth old is ready to vanifh away," Heb. viii. 13.

XXIII. The exceptions of the Jews againft this ftrong argument, are very weak. 1ft, That the eftablifhment, and not the renewal of that covenant, is here promifed: thus Kimchi. 2dly, That it does not neceffarily follow, from the mention of the new covenant, that the Lord will give a new law, only renew the former on their hearts. For whatfoever was not fufficiently manifeft at firft, when afterwards more fully declared, is faid in fcripture to be new. Thus Samuel fays to Saul, 1 Sam. xi. 14. " Come and let us go to Gilgal, and renew the kingdom there." Where it is plain, there was no new kingdom given, but only the old confirmed: Thus Menaffe Ben Ifrael, Quæft. 7. in Levit.

XXIV. I anfwer *to the firft.* 1ft, That it is begging the queftion. 2dly, A direct contradiction of God's word. God fays, I will make a new covenant, not like the former, which was made void: man ventures to anfwer, it is not an eftablifhment of a new, but a repetition of the old; and fo far the new covenant confirmed the old; yet at the fame time this was its abrogation; becaufe the prefence of the truth, and of the body, is the removal of the figure, and the fhadow. But thefe things the Jew did not underftand.

XXV. *To the other.* We fay, That here is no promife of a new law; becaufe none can be better and more perfect than that of the ten commandments: however, we have a promife of a new covenant, not a covenant of works, or of the law, but of grace, promifing to write the fame law on the heart, which before was written on ftone. 2dly, That the renewal of the covenant does not confift only in a clearer repetition of the law, or infcription on the heart. For, the new covenant is oppofed to the old, and fubftituted in its place, and completes it, fo as likewife to put an end to it, as we have juft now fhewn. 3dly, That the two cafes are not parallel; for, Sam-

uel

uel fays not to Saul, let us go to Gilgal, and I will give thee a new kingdom, unlike to the former; as God fpeaks here to Ifrael. Thefe are things very different, I will renew with thee the covenant which I made; and I will make a new covenant, not like unto the former.

XXVI. Let us now defcend to *particulars* : Where the firft thing, that offers, is the prophecy concerning the removal of the *ark of the covenant*, not only out of the world, but alfo out of the memory and heart of believers, expreffed Jer. iii. 16, 17. in the following words : "And it fhall come to pafs, when ye be multiplied and increafed in the land; in thofe days, faith Jehovah, they fhall fay no more, the ark of the covenant of Jehovah; neither fhall it come to mind, neither fhall they remember it, neither fhall they vifit it, neither fhall that be done any more : at that time they fhall call Jerufalem the throne of Jehovah, and all the nations fhall be gathered into it."

XXVII. On this prophecy we obferve. 1ft, That the ark of the Lord was the centre and compendium of all the ceremonies. It was the holieft of all facred places, to which they looked in all their ceremonial worfhip, and before which they were alfo to adore, 2 Sam. vi. 2. and to facrifice; the throne of God, erecting a prieftly kingdom : in fine, it was the principal fymbol of the whole typical covenant : whence it is alfo called *the ark of the covenant*, both here and in many other places; becaufe in it, at leaft in its fide, was kept the book of the covenant, Deut. xxxi. 26, 27. and "the ark of the teftimony," Exod. xxvi. 33. or alfo *the teftimony* itfelf, Lev. xvi. 13. becaufe it teftified concerning the covenant of God with Ifrael, of which it was a pledge. 2dly, That the entire removal of the ark is here foretold, not only out of the world, but alfo from the memory, love and defire of believers, all opinion of typical holinefs, which formerly the ark was eminently poffeffed of, being erafed out of the minds of God's people. To this purpofe is that repetition, by way of climax or gradation, "they fhall fay no more, neither fhall it come to mind, neither fhall they remember it, neither fhall they vifit it, or feek it, neither fhall that be done any more." They fhall not make a new one, when the old fhall be loft, or have it in any efteem. Poor Aberbanel looks on this repetition with a kind of aftonifhment. 3dly, That it is not here foretold in the form of a threatening of mifery, fuch as was the lofs of the ark, while the ceremonies were in force; but as a promife of the moft happy times, in which the church fhall have that in reality, which formerly fhe had typically in the ark; and while fhe enjoys the fubftance will bear the lofs of the fhadow, not only with equanimity

and

and compofure of mind, but alfo with gladnefs of heart.  4thly,
It is added, that all Jerufalem, and not the cover of the ark only,
as formerly, fhould be the throne of glory.  " For, all Jerufalem fhall obtain a degree of the ark in holinefs and glory,"
fays Aberbanel.  That is, God will manifeft himfelf, by much
more glorious indications of his grace, in the whole church of
believing Jews, and converted Gentiles united together into one
holy city, than he did formerly within the enclofure of the fanctuary: words which overturn the typical holinefs of places.
5thly, That all thofe benefits accompany the coming of the
Meffiah, whofe diftinguifhing characters are the multiplying
and the increafing of the people in the land, fee Deut. xxx. 5.
even above their anceftors, after having fubdued and incorporated Edom with themfelves; the giving of paftors according to God's heart, who as Kimchi interprets, are " the rulers
of Ifrael, who fhall be the attendants on the king Meffiah."
We call thefe the apoftles of the Lamb, and their faithful af-
fiftants and fucceffors, and in fine, the gathering together the
Gentiles into the church who could neither be burdened with
ceremonies, as we fhall prefently fhew; nor, while the religion
of ceremonies continued, live peaceably in the fame holy city
with the Jews without them.  The fum of the whole comes to
this, that when the Meffiah fhould difcover thofe things, which
were fignified by the ark and the other ceremonies, he would
then abolifh all the holinefs of the ark and the like types, as
well in reality, as out of the minds of believers.

XXVIII. It is excepted, 1ft, that the ark which was wanting in the fecond temple, is to be reftored by God under the
Meffiah.  Thus Sephar Afkat Rochel refuted by Hulfius on
the tenth fign of the Meffiah's coming.  2dly, That the meaning
of this prophecy is, that, during thefe profperous circumftances,
Ifrael would have no reafon to fear the envy of the other nations,
for they fhould not make war, fo as to be obliged to go out,
and take the ark of the covenant with them, as they ufually did,
in the days of Eli, and as often as war happened to break out,
And therefore, there was no prediction of the removal of the
ark fimply, but in fome refpect, namely, as to its fpecial ufe in
time of war.  Thus Jonathan, Kimchi, and Menaffe, Quæft.
2 in Levit. and others.  3dly, That the abrogation of the ceremonies cannot be inferred from the abfence of the ark, fince
it is without controverfy, that thefe remained in force, though
the ark has been wanting ever fince the Babylonifh captivity.
4thly, That the ten commandments, formerly enclofed in the
ark, are even at this day accounted and regarded by all as eternal, Menaffe, ibid.

XXXIX.

XXIX. I answer *to the first*, that it is a mere Jewish tradition, without any foundation in scripture, and directly contrary to this prophecy of Jeremiah.

XXX. *To the second*, 1st, That it is supposed without proof, that the principal use of the ark was in time of war. They took it with them to the field of battle in the time of Eli, but with bad success, being found " to have in vain put their confidence in the ark," Joseph. Antiq. Lib. 5. c. 11. 2dly, That, after the dedication of the temple, and the solemn introduction of the ark into it, it was never any more moved from its place, and carried out to the field of battle, 1 Kings viii. 8. 2 Chron. v. 9. Therefore the temple is called, " the resting place of Jehovah, and of the ark of his strength," 2 Chron. vi. 41. and " an house of rest for the ark of the covenant of Jehovah," 1 Chron. xxviii. 2. so that the Levites were relieved from the burden of carrying it, 2 Chron. xxxv. 3. What new thing then could Jeremiah foretel here, should he prophecy, that in the time of the Messiah, the ark was not to be carried out to battle, as all knew, that was prohibited so many ages before ? 3dly, That reiterated repetition of phrases plainly indicates an entire removal of the ark : And justly said Abarbanel of this exposition. " All these things are foreign to the purpose, there is not a single word in the text concerning war, and the other things of which they speak, and therefore I cannot be satisfied with this explication."

XXXI. *To the third :* the absence of the ark in the second temple, which was to be honoured with the presence of him, who was prefigured by it, did even then signify the future abrogation of the types in due time. 2dly, We do not argue from the bare absence of the ark, but from its being foretold, that it was neither to be in the world, nor so much as have a place in the mind, love and desire of believers: and this was promised as a great blessing, as a token and evidence of the liberty purchased by the Messiah : which was not the case before the coming of the Messiah, when the memory of the ark was still dear to the godly among them. 3dly, We likewise argue from this ; namely, that the holiness and glory of the ark may be said to be imparted to all * Jerusalem, inhabited by Jews as well as Gentiles, in the sense we have just explained. Whence the abrogation of that typical holiness, which the ark formerly had above all, is most evidently concluded.

XXXII. *To the fourth :* 1st, The laws of the covenant, of which the ark was the symbol, were not only the ten commandments,

---

* i. e. To the whole church made up of Jews or Gentiles.

ments, but all the laws of Moses. Accordingly the book which
contained them was placed in the side of the ark. That symbol therefore of the covenant being thus abolished, both the
covenant itself and the laws, fo far as they comprifed the *conditions* of that *covenant*, are abrogated. 2dly, The cafe of the laws
of the decalogue; is different from the reft: for, they were
engraven on tables of ftone, and laid up in the ark, to
reprefent, that they were to be the perpetual rule of holinefs, and continually to be kept in the heart both of the Meffiah and of his myftical body; while the others were only written on paper or parchment, and placed in the fide of the ark.
Their abrogation therefore would be ill concluded from the removal of the typical ark: feeing their being engraven on ftone,
and kept in the ark fignified their indelible infcription on, and
continual prefervation in the hearts of believers.

XXXIII. David prophefied concerning the abrogation of the
*priefthood*, Pfal. cx. 4. " The Lord hath fworn and will notrepent; thou art a prieft for ever after the order of Melchifedec." From which place the apoftle long ago argued thus,
Heb. vii. 11—13. " If therefore perfection were by the Levitical priefthood, (for under it the people received the law),
what further need was there, that another prieft fhould rife
after the order of Melchifedec, and not be called after the order of Aaron? For, the priefthood being changed, there is
made of neceffity a change alfo of the law: for he of whom
thefe things are fpoken, pertaineth to another tribe, of which
no man gave attendance at the altar." The following obfervations will fhew, that this reafoning is folid and conclufive.

XXXIV. 1ft, The infcription proves, that the author of this
pfalm was David, *a pfalm of David*, which is no where found
in the titles of pfalms compofed by another. 2dly, The perfon,
to whom both the kingdom and priefthood are promifed, is not
David himfelf, but the Lord of David as appears from the connection of ver. 4. with ver. 1. 3dly, The Lord of David is not
Abraham, but the Meffiah. Becaufe the things afferted and
declared in this pfalm, as the fitting at God's right hand, the
fending the rod of his ftrength out of Zion, the making all his
enemies his footftool, his eternal priefthood, &c. do not agree
to the former, but to the latter. 4thly, All are agreed, that
the Meffiah is not of the tribe of Levi, to which by the law of
Mofes, the priefthood was limited; but of Judah, and of the
family of David. But by the Mofaic law, that family was not
allowed to exercife the priefthood, 2 Chron. xxvi. 18. 5thly,
A priefthood, even an eternal priefthood is promifed to the
Meffiah, and that by an oath, fee Zech. vi. 13. Which cannot

not be, while the Mosaic law concerning the priesthood remains in force. 6thly, That priesthood is of another order than that of Aaron, namely, of Melchisedec: which cannot subsist at the time with the Levitical both for other reasons, which it is not to the purpose now to unfold, and especially on account of the diversity of descent. 7thly, If the Aaronical priesthood had been perfect, and could have perfected the consciences, there neither had been, nor ought there to be a place for this change. But the weakness and unprofitableness thereof made way for an amendment. 8thly, With the change of the priesthood is conjoined the change of the law. Because the priesthood is not only a great part, but also the foundation of all the ceremonies.

XXXV. The Jewish interpreters wonderfully perplex themselves in darkening this illustrious passage: but it is not worth our while to discuss all their misinterpretations here; they are both so many and so impertinent. We shall only run over such exceptions, as are more plausible, and directly contrary to what we maintain. It is therefore objected, 1st, That this is not a psalm of David's, but composed by some inspired singer in commendation, and on the account of David: and that the inscription is no objection ל sometimes, even in the inscription of psalms, is the sign of the dative case, and signifies the same thing, as for, as Psal. lxxii. 1. to, for, or concerning Solomon: nay, that we have the same inscription prefixed to some psalms, of which he does not seem to be the author, as Psal. xx. and xxi. where the singer prays for the preservation of the king; under which name it is not very likely, that David should pray for himself. 2dly, That therefore the singer means David by his lord; whom he calls not Adonia, a sacred name; but Adoni, a human and common appellation. 3dly, That the term אדני Cohen does not here signify a priest, but a king and prince, as 2 Sam. viii. 18. where the sons of David are called כהנים, that is princes of the court; and 2 Sam. xx. 26. where Ira the Jairite is called a prince of David. Accordingly even the Chaldee has translated it, "thou art constituted a prince." 4thly, That "because thou art the king of righteousness," as if the meaning was, thou shalt be a prince for ever, shalt reign by a long succession of descendants, not as Saul, whose goverment was execrable, and of short continuance, "because of righteousness, for thou art a righteous king," as the Chaldee paraphrases. If this be a true explication, nothing is here said about the change of the priesthood.

XXXVI. I answer to the first. 1st, If you say, that this is

not

not a pfalm of David, you cannot prove him to be the author
of any pfalm, that has the fame infcription. 2dly, The ancients all acknowledge, that it is David's. If it had not been fo,
Chrift would not have afferted it as a thing of undoubted truth,
Mat. xxii. 45. and the Pharifees might eafily have eluded that
argument, by which they were conftrained to hold their peace.
The Chaldee alfo has it, *hymn by the hand of David.* 3dly,
We allow, that the letter ל is fometimes the fign of the dative;
but we deny, that here, or elfewhere, when the title runs לדוד
מזמור, ל fignifies the fame with בעבור, nor, by any other defcription, are thofe pfalms diftinguifhed, which we all believe to be
David's, in confequence of that infcription. 5thly, The inftances mentioned, do not prove any thing to the contrary :
for in, Pfal. lxxii. we read not, מזמור לשלמה a pfalm for Solomon,
but לשלמה abfolutely, for Solomon, and then there is no reafon,
why it may not be a pfalm of Solomon's, which he received,
as it were, from David's mouth; fince he likewife wrote feveral proverbs from the mouth of his mother, Prov. xxxi. 1.
And there is as little reafon, why Pfams xx. and xxi. may not
be accounted David's. For, as God had appointed him to the
office of a prophet, he juftly alfo dictated to the people thofe
forms of prayer, with which they were to intercede for their
king. And that he might fing this in one fpirit with them, it
is not without reafon, that he fpeaks of himfelf as king in the
third perfon. And thus he might properly name himfelf; but
he could not call himfelf, *his Lord*, whether finging by himfelf or with others. Befides the appellation king, even in thofe
pfalms, may look further and be applied to the Meffiah. For,
how could the church in after times, by finging, pray for David
and his pofterity, when they were extinct? And in what fenfe
fhould fhe fing thefe things of an earthly king, when there was
no fuch king in Ifrael?

XXXVII. To the *fecond* we reply. 1ft, It is affirmed without proof, that thefe things were foretold, concerning David,
when David fpeaks them concerning his Lord. 2dly, David's
Lord is the Meffiah; for David was his fervant. He fits at
God's right hand, having the next degree of honour to God;
all the other things, which are declared in the pfalm, emphatically belong to him. 3dly, As he could be called Adonai by
David on account of the excellence of the divine effence; fo
he is alfo juftly called Adoni on account of the eminence of
his power and dominion. 6thly, The more ancient Jews themfelves explained this pfalm of the Meffiah, from whom we have
                                                    teftimonies

teſtimonies in Munſterus on this pſalm and in Cocceius on Heb. vii. §. 12.

XXXVIII. To the *third* we ſay. 1ſt, Though the term *Cohen* may ſometimes denote a political dignity, yet royal majeſty is never expreſſed by that word. *Cohen*, as Aben Ezra has well obſerved, ſignifies a *miniſter*, who is next to the king. But there is a king, who has power over conſcience, and God only is ſuch a king: and there is a king, who has power over the body, and ſuch are the ſupreme rulers of this world. Therefore there is a twofold *Cohen*, namely, with reſpect either to God, or to kings. With reſpect to God, ſuch are called *Cohanim*, who were over the people in performing divine ſervice, becauſe they appear to be next to God. With reſpect to kings, theſe are *Cohanim*, who are next to them. In that ſenſe, *Ira* the *Iairite* is called David's *Cohen*, and David's ſons *Cohanim*. That is, as it is explained, 1 Chron. xi. 15. *captains*, or *principal men next to the king*. And if we may believe the Jews, becauſe Abſalom was not admitted to partake of this dignity, he therefore took occaſion to form his unnatural conſpiracy. But in none of theſe ſenſes could David be called *Cohen*: not in the former, becauſe the prieſthood was confined to the deſcendants of Aaron alone: nor in the latter, for thus he himſelf had his *Cohanim*. But the Meſſiah is in ſuch a manner a king, as, at the ſame time to be prieſt: juſt like Melchiſedec, who diſtinctly diſcharged both offices, for the Holy Spirit directs us to this.

XXXIX. To the *fourth* we anſwer, that there is a miſtake, through the miſinterpretation of the words. For, 1ſt, Melchizedec is always in the ſacred writings a proper name. The Hebrews ſhould appellatively call, *king of righteouſneſs*. 2dly, The word never ſignifies *becauſe*, but when it is placed, as here, *according to the order* or *manner*, Eccl. iii. 18. and Eccl. viii. 2. if *w* follows in Hebrew, or *וו* in Chaldee, it ſignifies *with that intention*, or *deſign* as Eccl. vii. 14. Dan. ii. 30. and Dan. iv. 14. Seeing then neither the one nor the other ſignify what the Jews would have, our argument remains in its full force.

XL. And indeed, the event has confirmed this prophecy: for about the time, when our true Melchiſedec began his prieſtly office, the Levitical had loſt its dignity, till it was at laſt entirely aboliſhed, without any hopes of a reſtoration, all the diſtinction of tribes being confounded. And the Jews themſelves have taken notice of this, whoſe opinion we have in the Miſna, tit. Sota, c. 9. " From the death of Rabbi Iſmael, the ſon of Phabi, the ſplendor of the prieſthood has ceaſed." But this man was made high-prieſt by Valerius Gratus, preſi-
dent

dent of Judea under Tiberius Cæsar. About that time, this most sacred office was tossed about and sported with, like a ball, and any of the most profligate; as he favoured and made presents to the Roman president, grasped at it by the foulest ambition and the basest arts. And matters at length came to such a pitch of profaneness and wickedness, that the high-priests were not only chosen by lot, but even the high-priest hood fell by lot to one Phannias; who not only was a " worthless high-priest, but also, through his gross ignorance, incapable to distinguish what was the nature of the high-priesthood," Josep. de Bel. Jud. Lib. 4. c. 12. Yet from the utmost contempt and derision they constrained this man, whom they forced even against his will from the country, and brought him on the stage like a kind of actor, and clothed in the sacred vestments to act the part of high-priest, who like a child had prompters always at hand to remind him how to behave, and maintain his character. Which *impiety*, as Josephus justly calls it, sufficiently shews, that God no longer regarded that office; after the true priest according to the order of Melchisedec had once appeared.

XLI. From the priesthood let us proceed to the *sacrifices* Daniel speaks of the ceasing of these, chap. ix. last verse, " and he shall confirm the covenant with many for one week: and in the midst of the week, he shall cause the sacrifice and the oblation to ceaſe."

XLII. We are here to observe, 1st, That the prophet speaks concerning the times of the Messiah, who, ver. 25. is called *the Messiah the prince*, by way of eminence, and with respect to his character and office: compare, Isa. lv. 4. His office was to " finiſh (restrain) the transgression, and make an end of (seal) sins, and to make reconciliation for (expiate) iniquity, and to bring in everlasting righteousness," ver. 24. These are the offices and benefits of the true Messiah alone.

XLIII. 2dly, That the abolishing of the sacrifice and oblation is foretold, to be done by the Messiah: for he, *who confirmed the covenant with many*, whom Paul calls, *the surety of a better covenant*, Heb. vii. 22. even he shall cause the sacrifices to cease. But whatever the Messiah does is undoubtedly right: since at least he is a prophet, and faithful in the house of God.

XLIV. 3dly, That this abolishing was both just, and actually took place. It was just, by reason of the introduction of a new covenant, which was confirmed, not by sacrifice and the blood of brute beasts; but by the offering of the Messiah himself, that lamb without blemish, whose blood is the blood of the New Testament, shed in order to procure, or obtain, true remission, for many. Accordingly the future abolishing

ing of the sacrifices was foretold to be in the midst of that week, in which the Messiah was to be cut off, when he was to " make his soul an offering for sin," Isa. liii. 10. His sacrifice put an end to typical sacrifices. And the abrogation of the sacrifices is joined with the confirmation of the new covenant; for, that being sealed by the sacrifice of Christ, and preached by the apostles, and confirmed by the effusion of the Holy Ghost, and by very many miracles; the sacrifices of beasts, which constituted a great part of the old covenant, immediately lost all their efficacy and dignity, and so were justly abrogated. It actually took place not long after, on the destruction of the city and temple; for, all the sacrifices ceased upon that. Josephus relates, that Titus answered the priests, who begged for their lives, after the burning of the temple; that " that was destroyed, on account of which he would have justly saved them; but that it was proper for the priests to perish with the temple." And what Chrysostom relates, Orat. 3. contra Judæos, agrees with this, that the Jews should have said to Julian, when he exhorted them to sacrifice in the ancient manner: " if you would see us sacrifice, restore our city, rebuild our temple, and we will sacrifice even now as before." As the profane emperor, from the hatred he bore to Christianity, attempted this, and furnished the expence out of the public treasury, God prevented it by his almighty hand thereby shewing, that he had no pleasure in new sacrifices. Not only our own writers have this history, but also Ammianus Marcellinus, Lib. 23. among the Gentiles, and Zemach David, P. 2. p. 36. among the Jews. Both these kinds of the abrogation of sacrifices may be ascribed to the Messiah. He had a right to do it, as a priest, who had offered a better sacrifice; and as a king, who appoints religious ceremonies for his church. He actually did it, as the asserter of his own majesty and grace, which the rebellious Jews trampled under foot; for which end, he made use of Titus and his armies, as his ministers.

XLV. 4thly, That the removal of sacrifices and offerings infers the abrogation of the whole ceremonial worship. Not only because sacrifices constitute a principal part of the ceremonies, and we may say the same of things of a like nature; but also because the whole external worship is sometimes expressed by the name *sacrifice*, as Hof. vi. 6. *for I desired mercy and not sacrifice:* which the Septuagint here translate by ἔλεος, as also Matthew, chap. 12. 7. signifies ἔλεον (a word very plainly derived from the Hebrew or the Chaldee, or *a diligent love of God*. But ἔλεος is that internal purity and holiness of heart, which comprehends all those virtues, or graces, wherein the image of God consists.

And

And therefore in order to a juſt oppoſition, will ſignify the whole external and ceremonial worſhip. Which Kimchi himſelf ſeems to have obſerved, who explains ſacrifice by " the worſhip of the Lord in the houſe of his ſanctuary." The interpretations, which the blind and fooliſh Jews give of this prophecy of Daniel, are ſo foreign to the words of the text, to the deſignation of the time, and to the hiſtory of the events, that they confute and overthrow themſelves. Whoever deſires to ſee them exploded, may conſult *Conſt. l'Empereur* on Daniel, and the celebrated Cocceius, Hornbeck and Hulſius, in their writings againſt the Jews.

XLVI. The Spirit which ſpoke by the prophets, not thinking it ſufficient the ceaſing of the ceremonies, foretold alſo, that, in the days of the Meſſiah, ſuch rites ſhould be inſtituted, as are entirely repugnant to the ancient inſtitutions: that he would take for himſelf prieſts and Levites out of all nations without diſtinction, Iſa. lxvi. 20, 21. That in all places incenſe and a pure offering ſhould be offered to his name, Mal. i. 11. that there ſhould be an altar, acceptable to himſelf in the midſt of the land of Egypt, Iſa. xix. 19. that on the bells of the horſes ſhould be engraven, *holineſs to Jehovah*; which was formerly engraven only on the golden plate faſtened to the mitre of the high-prieſt; and God has graciouſly promiſed, that all the pots in Jeruſalem, and in all Judea, ſhould be holineſs unto him, Zech xiv. 20, 21. Theſe things cannot be reconciled with the ancient privileges of the prieſts and Levites, and with the earthly ſanctuary, and the prerogatives of the land of Canaan, and with the ſpecial holineſs of the pontifical pomp. God intimates, that he would be worſhipped in the uſe of other ſacred ordinances, which ſhould not be confined to any forms of the ancient ceremonies, but be duly performed in ſpirit and in truth, by every believer, in all places whatever.

XLVII. Let us now come to the *third* thing propoſed, and ſhew, that the ceremonies *ought* to be abrogated in the time of the Meſſiah, and that it was not poſſible, the caſe ſhould be otherwiſe. This may be ſhewn two ways: Firſt, if we conſider the *material*, or matter of the ceremonies, as they are acts of the obedience, preſcribed by the law of ordinances: ſecondly their formal, or eſſence, as they were types and ſhadows: but in neither of theſe ways can they have place in the kingdom of the Meſſiah. I make the firſt of theſe appear thus.

XLVIII. It is evident from the prophecies, that a great multitude of the Gentiles would be called by the Meſſiah to communion with God and Iſrael. That God would allure Japheth to dwell in the tents of Shem, Gen. ix. 27. that in the

the feed of Abraham, all nations of the earth fhould be bleffed, Gen. xxii. 18. that unto the Meffiah fhould the obedience of the people be, Gen. xlix. 10. that the Egyptians and Babylonians fhould be mentioned among thofe, who know Jehovah; and that it fhould be faid of the Philiftine, the Tyrian, and the E-thiopian, they were born in Zion, Pfal. lxxxvii. 4. And that all nations fhould flow to the mountain of the houfe of Jehovah, Ifa. ii. 2. and that Ifrael fhould be the third of Egypt and Af-fyria; and that the Lord fhall fay, bleffed be my people the Egyytians, and the work of my hands, the Affyrians, and Ifrael mine inheritance, Ifa. xix. 24, 25. and numberlefs other paffages, which frequently occur in fcripture to the fame purpofe.

XLIX. Moreover, Ifaiah declares, that both Ifrael and the converted Gentiles fhould obey the fame laws, and be bound together by the fame religious ties, chap. xliii. 4. " and the ifles fhall wait for his (the Meffiah's) laws." Again, Ifa. ii. 3. " and many people fhall go and fay, come ye and let us go up to the mountain of the Lord, to the houfe of the God of Jacob, and he will teach us of his ways, and we will walk in his paths: for out of Zion fhall go forth the law, and the word of Jehovah from Jerufalem." And he adds, no ftranger who hath joined himfelf to Jehovah, fhall fay, Jehovah hath utterly feparated me from his people: but on the contrary, even unto the eunuchs fhall be given, in the houfe of God and within his walls, a place, and a name better than that of fons and of daughters, Ifa. lvi. 3, 5. that is, that the converted Gentiles fhould, in matters of reli-gion, be on an equal footing with the Ifraelites. To this pur-pofe is that of Zeph. iii. 9, 10. " for then will I turn to the people a pure language, that they may all call upon the name of Jehovah, to ferve him with one confent: from beyond the rivers of Ethiopia, my fuppliants, even the daughters of my dif-perfed fhall bring mine offering:" and Zech. xiv. 9. " and Je-hovah fhall be king over all the earth: in that day fhall there be one Jehovah, and his name one:" one fhall be the worfhip, and one the veneration of the one God. The Jews themfelves alfo frequently declare, that, in the time of the Meffiah, many nations fhall be converted to the God of Ifrael, and that then they fhall walk *in the doctrine of that law*, as the Chaldee fpeaks on Ifa. ii. 3. and *fhall embrace one common law with the Ifraelites*, as Menaffe fpeaks, *de Refur. Lib.* 2. *c.* 3. and fo fhall incorporate into one people with Ifrael, and be partakers of the fame privi-leges, as being profelytes of righteoufnefs.

L. Whenever this fhall come to pafs, it is plain, that the an-cient ceremonies cannot poffibly be obferved by all the fubjects of the Meffiah. For how is it poffible, the paying of vows and

tythes, the prefenting the firft-born, the obfervation of the paffover, pentecoft and feaft of tabernacles, which were confined to
the place, which God had chofen, fhould be binding on thofe,
who are to be at a great diftance from Judea ? And how can
men, who dwell in the utmoft parts of the earth, come to
Jerufalem, to offer facrifice for every fin, and every pollution,
in order to avoid the curfe ? How could women, newly delivered, undertake fo long a journey, and prefent themfelves in
the place chofen by God, to perform the offerings commanded ?
Where could fo many beafts, fo many priefts, fo many altars be
found, fufficient for all the facrifices ? What extent of country,
much lefs town, could be large enough to hold fuch numbers ?
Menaffe, if I rightly remember, idly talks, that then the gates
of Jerufalem fhould be extended to Damafcus; but had he extended them, which he might with equal eafe, beyond the *Porta
Cafpia,* or pafs of Teflis, he would have more commodioufly
provided for fo prodigious a conflux of people, flocking from all
parts to the facrifices. Put the cafe of the leprofy, and of a
houfe infected with that plague, of which Lev. xiii. muft the
priefts make incurfions to the Scythians, the Sarmatians and the
Indians; to the Britons feparated from the reft of the world,
and to the outmoft Thule, to form a judgment of the fcab or
fcall ? To omit many other confiderations, which might with
equal propriety be urged; and which Eufebius among the ancients, *Demonftr. Evangel. Lib.* 1. and among the moderns, *Spa-
hemius, Dubior Evang. P.* 3. *Dub.* 112. have fully and learnedly
done.

LI. You may poffibly alledge, that God will grant a kind of
difpenfation of, and relax thefe impoffible laws. But where is
there any promife to that purpofe ? Have not thefe laws been
made by the fame authority with the others ? is not their duration in like manner extended *for ever,* which in other refpects
is fo much objected to us ? Do not thefe, and the like laws,
conftitute the principal part of the ceremonial ? And if the confcience can be fet free from the obligation of thefe, why not
alfo from that to the others, which are of the fame nature ?

LII. Shall they not ceafe to bind, becaufe the obfervation of
them is impoffible, any more than we teach, that the moral law
is binding, though we allow the perfect performance thereof
to be a thing impoffible ? But who does not fee a very wide
difference here ? That the moral law cannot now be perfectly
performed, is a thing accidental, owing to our corruption. That
thefe other laws cannot be obferved under the kingdom of the
Meffiah, arifes from the nature of the laws themfelves, without
any default of man. And thus we have demonftrated, that the

ceremonies,

ceremonies, in fo far as they are acts of the obedience, prefcribed by the old law, cannot be obferved in the univerfal church, gathered together from among Jews and Gentiles, under the king Meffiah.

LIII. This will be more manifeft, if we, moreover, confider the *formal* of the ceremonies : thus there was a yoke in them, that muft be broken off; a pedagoguy, and an accufation of childhood, which cannot take place in a more advanced age. There was a partition-wall to be broken down, when, on removing all diftinction of nations, the Meffiah is to be all in all; an enmity, to be abolifhed at the time, in which the Meffiah is to publifh to the Gentiles, that they fhould have peace both with Ifrael and with God. There was, in fine, a hand-writing, bearing teftimony concerning guilt not yet expiated, and payment not yet made. This, when all things are fulfilled by the Meffiah, is to be taken out of the way, left any inftitution of God fhould be found to teftify againft the truth and Son of God. Such are either ignorant of, or overturn all the fignification of the ceremonies and their true efficacy, who bind the obligation of them on the confciences, after the Meffiah had perfected all things.

LIV. There now remains the *fourth* head, namely, to explain the progrefs and the various degrees of this abrogation, which we digeft in the following order : 1ft, When Chrift came and was manifefted to Ifrael, the ceremonies loft much of their fplendor, as when the fun in the heavens extinguifheth the ftars. Neverthelefs they were binding, while Chrift was not yet made perfect by fufferings, but yet their abrogation was drawing near : " Jefus faith unto her, Woman, believe me, the hour cometh, when ye fhall neither in this mountain, nor yet at Jerufalem worfhip the Father. But the hour cometh, and now is, when the true worfhippers fhall worfhip the Father in fpirit and in truth," John iv. 21, 23. To this purpofe is that proclamation, which John feveral times publifhed, that the kingdom of heaven is at hand. 2dly, They were abrogated in point of right by the death of Chrift; for, all their typical prefignification being fulfilled in Chrift, and the blood of the New Teftament being fhed, and the guilt expiated, which they were appointed to be a charge of, with what right could ceremonies lately difcarded claim any longer to keep their former ftation ? Hence Chrift is faid, " to have taken the hand-writing out of the way, nailing it to his crofs," Col. ii. 14. and to " have abolifhed in his flefh *(on his flefh being broken by death)* the law of commandments, contained in ordinances," Eph. ii. 15. Certainfy the flefh of Chrift was the vail; and while that was ftill entire, a new and living way was not opened to the heavenly fanctuary, Heb. x.

20.

20. For, while Chrift was not yet made perfect by fufferings, the ceremonies which required that perfection or confummation, were in full force. But whenever the utmoft farthing was paid by the death of Chrift, the vail and enclofure of the ceremonies being taken down, there was a free accefs to God; which was fignified and confirmed by the rending the vail of the temple upon the death of Chrift. 3dly, God declared, confirmed, and fealed this abrogation by the refurrection of Chrift from the dead, and his afcenfion into heaven, and the plentiful effufion of the Holy Spirit. For the hand-writing was then difcharged. He, who hitherto was in bondage to the elements of the world, equally with the other worfhippers of God, was placed with his people in heavenly places, where no fuch bondage takes place; and the fpirit was given, as the feal of a more delightful difpenfation of the covenant. 4thly, But this liberty was for fometime not fufficiently known, even to the apoftles themfelves, till Peter was inftructed therein by a heavenly vifion, Acts x. 11. 5thly, Then, by a folemn decree of a fynod of the apoftles, under the prefidence of the Holy Spirit, it was ordained, that a yoke was not to be put on the neck of the difciples, befides thofe few things neceffary for that time; namely, *to abftain from meats offered to idols, and from blood, and from things ftrangled;* to which was fubjoined, though of a different kind, *fornication,* Acts xv. 10, 28, 29. 6thly, Afterwards Paul preached freedom from thefe things alfo, excepting fornication, that being contrary to the moral law, 1 Cor. viii. 4, 8. and 1 Cor. x. 25—29. 7thly, Yet becaufe the Jews, who were converted to Chrift, having been accuftomed to the ceremonies, were with very great difficulty drawn from them, the apoftles and other believers with them, that they might not offend the weak, according to the rules of Chriftian charity and prudence, freely ufed thofe ceremonies, not with any opinion of holinefs; but in order not to wound tender confciences, accommodating themfelves to all, to gain fome to Chrift, fee Acts xxi. 22.— 8thly, But after that the church feemed now to be fufficiently inftructed in her liberty, and the fondnefs for the ceremonies was no longer a degree of weaknefs but of obftinacy, Paul would not give place by fubjection, no not for an hour, and fharply rebuked Peter, whofe conduct was rather too remifs, Gal. ii. 5, 14. and exhorted every one in particular, to ftand faft in the liberty wherewith Chrift had made us (him) free, and not to be entangled again with the yoke of bondage, nor to make Chrift of no effect to themfelves, Gal. v. 1, 2. 9thly, and laftly, All the ceremonies were actually taken away at the deftruction of

Jerufalem

Jerufalem and the temple, and buried as it were in their ruins, never to be revived any more.  See what we have faid con-cerning circumcifion, chap. viii. §. 21, &c.

---

## CHAP. XV.

### *Of the Benefits of the New Teſtament.*

I. **A**S the darknefs of the night is only difpelled by the beams of the rifing morn, fo the Old Teſtament was abrogat-ed only by the introduction of the New.  But at what time this firſt began to take place, by what degrees it advanced, by what intervals of time it was confirmed and completed, we have ex-plained in the third chapter of the foregoing book.  We are now, in the firſt place, to treat of the *benefits* of the New Teſta-ment: then of the *facraments :* the othe particulars are obvious, from what we have fpoken concerning the covenant of grace fimply confidered, and by comparing with them, what we have more largely treated of concerning the Old Teſtament.

II. We rehearfe the benefits of the New Teſtament in the following order.  I. The firſt is the exhibition of the Meffiah made perfect.  II. The gofpel * under another name or defignation.  III. The calling of the Gentiles.  IV. A more abundant and delightful meafure of the Spirit.  V. A greater and better liberty.  VI. The reftoration of Ifrael.  VII. The revival of the whole church, as from the dead.

III. The *firſt* fpring of our glorying, and the fum of our felicity beyond thofe that expected the confolation of Ifrael, is, that " Chriſt Jefus came into the world," 1 Tim. i. 15.  He who was promifed from the beginning, fhadowed forth by fo many types, fo ardently longed for, and for fo many ages ex-pected, came forth in the fulnefs of time, in that place, from that tribe and family, in that manner from a virgin, and appear-ed in the flefh, juſt as the holy prophets had long before-pro-phefied he fhould come.  " Through the tender mercy of our God, whereby the day-fpring from on high hath vifited us," Luke i. 78.  " we have found him, of whom Mofes in the law, and the prophets did write, Jefus of Nazareth the fon of Jofeph," John i. 45.  This, as the angel told the fhepherds of

* The author's words are, Evangelium ανευαγγελιαν, which I know not how to render otherwife to make it intelligible to the Englifh reader.

of Bethlehem, was matter of great joy, and not only Mary and
Zacharias and Simeon, but alfo the whole choir of the heavenly angels celebrated this in their fongs : fee Zech. ix. 9.

IV. And the Meffiah was not only exhibited, but alfo " made
perfect through fufferings," Heb. ii. 10. and thus being " made
perfect, he became the author of eternal falvation unto all,"
Heb. v. 9. For, in the fufferings and death of Chrift, there
is a true expiation, a cancelling, a blotting out of our fins, a
bringing in of everlafting righteoufnefs, a tearing and removing
of the hand-writing, nay, there is an eternal redemption.

V. But this was not all ; for *he was alfo received up into glory*,
and being placed in the throne of his majefty, he brought the
kingdom of heaven to us, having removed every thing, by
which the fpiritual and myftical government of God over the
confcience, which is the government of liberty, was formerly
obfcured. While David in fpirit had this kingdom of the Meffiah before him, as in a figure, he joyfully fung, " Jehovah
reigneth, let the earth rejoice, let the multitude of ifles be glad,"
Pfal. xcvii. 1. " Jehovah reigneth, let the people tremble,"
Pfal. xcix. 1. This is that kingdom of heaven, which the Baptift fo often proclaimed was at hand ; and concerning which
our Lord declared, that there were fome of his hearers, " which
fhould not tafte death, till they faw the Son of man coming
in his kingdom," Mat. xvi. 28. It cannot but be moft delightful to all, that love the Lord Jefus, " to fee him crowned with
glory and honour, who was made a little lower than the angels,
for the fuffering of death," Heb. ii. 9. This great benefit the
apoftle has fet forth in thefe important words, 1 Tim iii. 6.
" God made manifeft in the flefh, juftified in the fpirit, feen of
angels, preached unto the Gentiles, believed on in the world,
received up into glory." And our Saviour himfelf has taught
us, that a great part of our happinefs confifts in the enjoyment
of this bleffing, Mat. xiii. 16, 17.

VI. The *fecond* benefit is the gofpel of the kingdom, " which
God had promifed afore by his prophets in the holy fcriptures,"
Rom. i. 2. Namely, the gofpel as completed, " which, at
the firft, began to be fpoken by the Lord, and was confirmed
unto us by them that heard him," Heb. ii. 3. For, this " myftery was kept fecret fince the world began : but now is made
manifeft, and, by the fcriptures of the prophets, according to
the commandment of the everlafting God, made known to all
nations for the obedience of faith ;" Rom. xvi. 25, 26. Not
that they had no gofpel before : for, even unto the ancients
was the gofpel *formerly preached*, Heb. iv. 2. But that this

proclamation

proclamation of future grace was προευαγγελισμὸς *the gospel preach-ed before,* Gal. iii. 8. And the preaching of the present grace is eminently the gospel now. Hence it is mentioned as an argument of the presence of the Messiah, that the " poor have the gospel preached to them," Mat. xi. 5.

VII. Moreover, the gospel of the New Testament has the following excellencies above the Old. 1ft, That it sets forth Christ as come, and declares that all those things are fulfilled, which were formerly foretold, to come to pass long after, 1 Cor. ii. 7—10. 2dly, That it declares in clear terms, every thing relating to the common salvation, without the covering of figures, or the labyrinths of dark sayings, 2 Cor. iii. 14. 3dly, That it now allures the hearts of believers with the sweetest, and most abundant consolations, and without that severity, which according to the old legal dispensation, mixed the words of grace with so much rigour, whence it is called " the ministration of righteousness," 2 Cor. iii. 9. and " the word of reconciliation," 2 Cor. v. 18. " The mouth of our beloved is most sweet," Cant. v. 16. And Isaiah prophesied concerning his servants, chap. lii. 7. " how beautiful upon the mountains are the feet of him, that bringeth good tidings !" *&c.* Add Isa. xl. 1.—and Isa. lxi. 1.—and Isa. lxvi. 10—12. 4thly, That it dwells now more abundantly in us, and is preached more fully and frequently, and with a greater demonstration of the Spirit, and a deeper insinuation or sinking into the conscience, Rom. x. 8.

VIII. The *third* benefit is the calling of the Gentiles by the gospel, which followed upon the Messiah's being made perfect : according to the promise, Psal. ii. 8. " Ask of me, and I shall give thee the heathen for thine inheritance, and the uttermost parts of the earth for thy possession :" likewise Isa. xlix. 6. Luke ii. 40. Paul, as in other places, so especially Eph. ii. and iii. has, in a magnificent manner, set forth the perfections of God, as being illustriously displayed in this admirable work, and, above all, the unsearchable riches of the patience, goodness, and manifold wisdom of God in Christ. " And, indeed, who can but stand amazed at such a surprising thing, (we may justly exclaim with Eusebius) to see those, who, from the beginning, paid divine honour and worship to stocks and stones and devils, to ravenous beasts feeding on human flesh, and to venomous reptiles, to fire and to earth, to the very inanimate elements of the universe; to see, I say, such calling on the most high God, the Creator of heaven and earth, the very Lord of the prophets, the God of Abraham and his ancestors, after the coming of our Saviour ?" Pray, read what follows; as it is too long to be

here

here tranfcribed. This very circumftance affures us, that the Lord Jefus is the true and only Meffiah, by whofe word, Spirit, and miniftry, fo aftonifhing a work was accomplifhed, the like, or equal to it was never feen or heard, were we to go back to the remoteft antiquity.

IX. But we are to obferve, 1ft, That thefe things were accomplifhed by the apoftles of Chrift, and their fellow labourers, who were not remarkable, either for any excellence of worldly wifdom, or furnifhed with any charms of Greek and Roman eloquence, or fupported by any human affiftance; but by the naked demonftration of an admirable and almoft incredible truth to the confcience, while the gates of hell raged, the lords and dreaded tyrants of the world oppofed, and the fchools of conceited philofophers clamoured: that the glory of God and his Chrift might fhine forth with the greater luftre and brightnefs, the meaner and lefs adapted for the work, were the inftruments he ufed, 1 Cor. ii. 4, 5.

X. 2dly, That the kingdom of Chrift was fet up among the Gentiles with an aftonifhing quicknefs. For, " as the lightning that lightneth out of the one part under heaven, fhineth unto the other part under heaven, fo fhall alfo the Son of man be in his day," Luke xvii. 24. Ifaiah had foretold this with a kind of aftonifhment, chap. lxvi. 7, 8. " Before fhe travailed fhe brought forth; before her pain came fhe was delivered of a man-child. Who hath heard fuch a thing? Who hath feen fuch things? Shall the earth be made to bring forth in one day, or fhall a nation be born at once? For, as foon as Zion travailed, fhe brought forth her children.

XI. 3dly, That this calling extended very far, Rom. x. 18. " Their found went into all the earth, and their words into the ends of the world:" Col. i. 6, 24. Mark xvi. 20. " Tertullian adverfus Judæos fays, c. 7. In what other perfon befides have all the Gentiles believed but in Chrift, who is now come? On whom elfe have the Parthians believed, the Medes, Elamites, the inhabitants of Mefopotamia, Armenia, Phrygia, Egypt, that part of Africa beyond Cyrene; the Romans, the Jews then in Jerufalem, and other nations; and at this day, the various tribes of Getulians, many parts of Mefopotamia, Spain in all its extent, the different nations of Gaul, and the parts of Britain unacceffible to the Roman arms, made fubjeft to Chrift; the Sarmatians, Dacians, Germans and Scythians, many nations yet undifcovered, many provinces and iflands unknown to you, and which we cannot enumerate? among which the name of Chrift, as now come, prevails." In a like ftrain has Jerome celebrated this abundance of heavenly grace, in *Epitaphio Nepotiani ad Heliodorum, fiodorum*, and *in Epiſt. ad Lætam*, and in general, the other fathers, exulting in ſo great a happineſs of the New Teſtament. Yet we are not to think, that there was no corner of the world, where the name of Chriſt was not preached: nor to believe, that the apoſtles failed over to America, and to countries then unknown to the reſt of the world: theſe univerſal expreſſions only intimate, that the goſpel of Chriſt was extenſively propagated, without any diſtinction of countries or people, on each ſide of the ſun's courſe. See the expreſſions Rom. i. 8. Luke ii. 5.

XII. 4thly, The goſpel did not reach to the Gentiles, till after it was rejected and deſpiſed by the Jews. "Through their fall ſalvation came to the Gentiles. The fall of them was the riches of the world," Rom. xi. 11, 12. We have an expoſition of this paſſage, Acts. xiii. 46, 47. where Paul and Barnabas ſpeak thus. "It was neceſſary, that the word of God ſhould firſt have been ſpoken to you (the Jews); but ſeeing ye put it from you, and judge yourſelves unworthy of everlaſting life, lo, we turn to the Gentiles: for, ſo hath the Lord commanded us," &c. We may add Acts. xviii. 6:

XIII. 5thly, However the polity of the Jews was not overturned, before the kingdom of the Meſſiah was made illuſtrious among the Gentiles, Mat. xxiv. 14. "And this goſpel of the kingdom ſhall be preached in all the world, for a witneſs unto all nations, and then ſhall the end come," namely, of Jeruſalem and the temple: which was very wiſely ſo ordered: for byt his means. 1ſt, the The ungrateful Jews had not the leaſt ſhadow of excuſe left: for what excuſe could they have for continuing in their hardneſs, who had ſeen his power in a very ſhort ſpace of time, ſhining like lightning through the whole world? This is Chryſoſtom's obſervation, Serm. 76 *in Mattheum*. 2dly, By the preaching of the goſpel, he would have all the world know the crimes of the Jews, the guilt they had contracted by the paricide of Chriſt, and their obſtinate and invincible malice, in ſtubbornly rejecting all offers of mercy, before he would execute ſo terrible a vengeance on a people, who were under ſo many obligations to him: that all nations might be obliged to adore his juſtice with trembling. 3dly, He would not caſt off his ancient people by an ultimate deſtruction, before he had gathered, from among the Gentiles, another people for himſelf. Nor make the material temple an Anthema, till he had built a ſpiritual temple of lively ſtones. For, it was never intended, that Chriſt ſhould be a king without a kingdom.

XIV. The *fourth* benefit is a more abundant and delightful meaſure of the Spirit, frequently foretold by the prophets, to

be fent together with, and poured out on the church by Chriſt.
To this purpofe, if I miſtake not, is Zech. ix. 12. *even to day
מגיד משנה* * *another declarer do I render unto thee. That day is*
meant, on which the king of Zion had, by the blood of the
covenant, ſet at liberty, thoſe who were bound in Zion, and
was delivered from death. At that time *a declarer, diſcoverer,
or ſhewer forth,* is promiſed, the participle being uſed as a noun:
and he is indeed *another diſcoverer.* The firſt is the Son of
God, and who is the other, but the Holy Spirit ? who is alſo
a *diſcoverer,* as he teaches the elect, and brings all things to
their remembrance, John xiv. 26. *the next to Chriſt* or *another
comforter,* ver. 16. Him God promiſes *to give,* that is, in place
of the Son, after he was gone to the Father, John xvi. 7. To
this likewiſe I apply, what the Meſſiah ſays, Iſa. xlviii. 16.
אדני יהוה שלחני ורוחו, which is very properly tranſlated, *the Lord
God hath ſent me and his Spirit.* Add the like promiſes Iſa.
xliv. 2, 3. and Iſa. xxxv. 7. and Joel ii. 28. The fulfillment
of which is in Chriſt, who *baptizeth* his people *with the Holy
Ghoſt and with fire,* Mat. iii. 11. compare John vii. 38, 39. of
which paſſages we have ſpoken elſewhere.

XV. The effects of this Spirit, are ; 1ſt, A more clear and
diſtinct knowledge of the myſteries of faith, Iſa. xi. 9. and
Iſa. liv. 13. Jer. xxxi. 34. 1 John ii. 27. 2dly, A more
generous, a more ſublime, and cheerful degree of holineſs, Iſa.
xxxiii. 24. and Iſa. xxxv. 9. and Iſa. lx. 21, 22. Zech. x. 5.
and Zech. xii. 8. 3dly, A more delightful conſolation, Iſa.
xl. 1, 2. and Iſa. lx. 1, 2. and Iſa. lv. 11. and Iſa. lxvi. 12.
13, 14. John xiv. 16. Acts ix. 31. Eph. i. 13. 2 Cor. i. 22,
4thly, A filial boldneſs, which is now the greater, as adoption
itſelf, and its effects are more conſpicuous, Gal. iv. 6. 5thly,
The extraordinary and altogether miraculous gifts, which were
plentifully beſtowed at the beginning of the goſpel, not only
on the apoſtles, but alſo often on other miniſters, nay, on
common believers, and even virgins, Mark xvi. 16—18. Acts
x. 45, 46. and Acts xix. 6. and Acts xxi. 8. 1 Cor. xii. 7—11.
But in what manner the New Teſtament is to be compared
with the Old, we have frequently ſhewn already.

XVI. The *fifth* benefit is *Chriſtian liberty,* which Paul, the
moſt diligent interpreter of, and warmeſt advocate for, uſually
ſo conſiders, that he makes it generally to conſiſt in a freedom from that bondage, which the Jews were under ; and
he

* Our verſion renders, *will I render double unto thee.* Double, ſays a modern com-
mentator, ſignifies any thing large, ſufficient, plentiful, Iſa. xl. 2. and lxi. 7. particularly the Spirit and his grace. See Gill. in Loc. our author here follows
Cocceius.

he rarely treats of it, unlefs when he compares Chriftians with Jews, and fets the Old difpenfation in oppofition to the New. Yet divines have prudently. obferved from Paul himfelf, that Chriftian liberty may be confidered, either as *common* to believers in every age; or as a fpecial immunity of the children of God, who live under the New Teftament difpenfation.

XVII. This common liberty confifts in a manumiffion or freedom, 1ft, From the tyranny of the *devil*, whofe deftruction was promifed, as early as in paradife, Col. i. 13. 2dly, From *the reigning and condemning power* of fin, Rom. vi. 14. Rom. viii. 1. 3dly, From the rigour of *the law*, fo far as it is contradiftinguifhed from grace, Rom. vi. 14. For, thus far it is to the finner *the law of fin and death*, oppofite *to the law of the Spirit and of life in Chrift Jefus*, Rom. viii. 2. Moreover this rigour confifts, (1.) In the fevere demand it makes of obedience without a promife of fanctifying grace. (2.) In requiring a moft perfect holinefs, to be performed by man himfelf, as the condition of eternal life. (3.) In threatening the curfe, for the leaft deviation. For, fo far the law belongs to the covenant of works, which in regard to all believers, is abrogated, by the introduction of the covenant of grace. 4thly, In a freedom from an accurfed *death*, both of *body* and *foul*. For, though the *body* of believers is *dead becaufe of fin*, Rom. viii. 10. yet death has loft its fting, 1 Cor. xv. 55. and is become the period of fin and mifery, and the paffage to eternal life, John v. 24. And thus far believers are freed from that death, with which God threatened finful man, as a punifhment properly fo called, and the effect of his dreadful difpleafure, John viii. 51, 52. Nor is the *formal* nature of punifhment only removed from the death of believers; but whatever belongs to the remains of death, will at laft be deftroyed by a glorious refurrection, 1 Cor. xv. 54. As therefore liberty with refpect to fin, as to its right, is adjudged to believers in juftification, and as to its power, performed gradually and by fome certain fteps; the fame alfo is the cafe with refpect to corporal death; the curfe and penalty of which fo to fpeak, are removed, as foon as the perfon is ingrafted into Chrift by faith, who is the fountain of life, but at the laft day, all its power will be fwallowed up in victory. 5thly, From *human empire*, or conftraint, with refpect to divine worfhip, and the actions of religion, as fuch: For God alone has dominion over the confcience, James iv. 12. Nor is it lawful for the fons of God, who know themfelves to be bought with a price, to become the fervants of men, 1 Cor. vii. 23. Mat. xv. 9. Col. ii. 18, 22, 23. Though

formerly

formerly the Scribes and Pharifees fat in Mofes' chair, yet
God never gave them a power, to load the confcience with
new inftitutions, beyond and befides the law of God, to which
all were equally bound, Deut. iv. 2. and Deut. xii. 34. All
the authority of the doctors of the law tended to keep the people to the obfervance of the law of Mofes; Chrift juftly rebuked them, when they went beyond that. Whatever man has devifed from h's own invention, in matters of religion, has ever been
difpleafing to God.  6thly, From the obligations to things *indifferent*, which are neither good nor bad in themfelves, and which
God has neither commanded, nor forbidden.  When the knowledge and fenfe of this liberty is wanting, the confcience in
that cafe, is difquieted, and fuperftition has neither meafure
nor end, Rom. xiv. 5, 14, 23. The *poffeffion* however, is to
be diftinguifhed from the *ufe*; the *right* from the *exercife* of it,
the former ought ever to remain inviolable to the confcience,
the latter to be circumfcribed by the rules of prudence and
charity, to avoid giving offence to weak brethren, 1 Cor. vi.
12. and 2 Cor. x. 13. Rom. xiv. 19.

XVIII. The liberty, we have thus defcribed, abfolutely belongs to the benefits of the covenant of grace: and fhould not
be reckoned among thofe, which are peculiar to the New Teftament.  Unlefs fo far, as it is more clearly explained, more
frequently infifted upon, more effectually and abundantly applied by the Spirit of Chrift, and infinuated into the confcience
for the greater confolation and joy, and finally demonftrated
by more glorious effects.  And, as I imagine, none will queftion, that the rigour of the old economy greatly obfcured the
fenfe and joy of that liberty, which believers in other refpects
enjoyed.  At leaft none will deny, that the liberty, as to things,
in their own nature indifferent, was greatly diminifhed by the
inftitutions of Mofes.

XIX. That liberty, therefore, which is peculiar to the New
Teftament is, 1ft, A difcharge from *the bondage of the elements
of the world*, or of the ancient ceremonies, from whofe religious
obligation, as of things neceffary, the confciences of men were
firft fet free, Acts xv. 10. though their arbitrary ufe continued
for fome time, and might with prudence be advifed, Acts xxi.
24.  Afterwards their ufe was entirely forbid, fo that now we
are to abftain from them altogether, Gal. iii. 25. Gal. iv. 5,
26. and Gal. v. 1.  For, from being in force, they firft lofe their
vigour, of neceffity become arbitrary: afterwards from being
dead they become hurtful and deadly; and from being arbitrary become unlawful, never to be revived, after the full promulgation of the gofpel, and the deftruction of the temple of
Jeru-

Jerufalem, which was the feat of the ceremonies. 2dly, Liberty with refpect to many *things indifferent in their own nature,* the ufe of, or abftinence from which was formerly enjoined the Ifraelites, Tit. i. 15. Col. ii. 20, 21. 1 Cor. x. 25. 3dly, Immunity from the *forenfic or judicial laws of the Ifraelites ;* not as they were of univerfal, but as of particular right or obligation made for the Jews as fuch, diftinguifhing them from other nations, adapted to the genius of the people and country, and fubfervient, for the greateft part, to the Levitical priefthood, with which almoft the whole polity was interwoven. 4thly, There is a clearer and more perfect promulgation, knowledge and practice of Chriftian liberty, in all its parts and degrees.

XX. *fixthly,* We may reckon among the benefits of the New Teftament the reftoration of the Ifraelites, who were formerly rejected, and the bringing them back to the communion of God in Chrift. Paul has unfolded this myftery to the Gentiles, Rom. xi. 25—27. " For I would not brethren, that ye fhould be ignorant of this myftery (left ye fhould be wife in your own conceits) that blindnefs in part is happened to Ifrael, until the fulnefs of the Gentiles be come in. And fo all Ifrael fhall be faved : as it is written, there fhall come out of Sion the deliverer, and fhall turn away ungodlinefs from Jacob. For this is my covenant unto them, when I fhall take away their fins."

XXI. On this place obferve, 1ft, That the apoftle here explains fome *myftery ;* that is, a fecret thing, not known but by revelation, and taken notice of by few, and happening beyond the expectation and judgment of reafon; in fine, the whole method and manner of executing which, lies in a great meafure concealed : fee 1 Cor. ii. 7. and 1 Cor. xv. 51. and Eph. iii. 3. 2dly, That it is the intereft of the Gentiles to be acquainted with this myftery, to prevent their entertaining higher thoughts concerning themfelves, and lower concerning the Ifraelites : we are therefore to take care, to enquire diligently, and with attention, into what the prophets have foretold concerning this matter, 3dly, The apoftle here fpeaks of the people of Ifrael, not figuratively but properly fo called; who were at this time blind, obdurate, ftupid, and hardened, of which ver. 7. Ifaiah foretold this judgment of God againft Ifrael at large, chap. vi. 9, 10. compared with Act. xxviii. 26. Ifa. xxix. 10, 11. To this alfo feems applicable, *that whirlwind of the Lord, that fury, and continuing whirlwind, which fhall abide on the head of the wicked,* of which Jer. xxx. 23. In fhort, this is that forlorn condition of the blinded nation of Jews, which taking its rife in the apoftles' time, continues to this our day. 4thly, That this blindnefs is *in part* happened to Ifrael. The whole

whole nation, from its first origin even to the end of the world, is considered as one whole; a certain part of which are those, who either have, or now do, or hereafter shall live in the days of the wrath and indignation of God: *blindness has seized that part only.* 5thly, That blindness is to continue upon them no longer, *than till the fulness of the Gentiles be come in;* that is, till the gospel is preached among all nations of the world whatever. Which indeed, began to be done by the apostles and their fellow-labourers; but could not be done perfectly, both on account of the extent of the world, and the shortness of human life, and likewise because many nations (as all the American) were at that time unknown. This therefore still remains to be done successively; God in his admirable providence paving the way for his word. The offer of grace was first made to the Israelites. When they refused it, it was sent to the Gentiles; but when the fulness of them shall be brought in, it will be again given to the Israelites; " that the last may be first, and the first last," Luke xiii. 30. see Luke xxi. 24. 6thly, That when the fulness of the Gentiles is brought in, *all Israel shall be saved:* that is, as our Dutch commentators well observe, not a few, but a very great number, and in a manner the whole Jewish nation, in a full body. Peter Martyr has judiciously explained the fulness of the Gentiles, and the whole body of Israel in the following words: " But we are to understand a limited fulness, and a fixed or determined collection: which is therefore called fulness, because there will be an exact and a very great number of believers; so that the church shall be publicly owned, and had in great esteem among the Gentiles, just as all Israel is to be taken for a great number of Jews, among whom Christ should be publicly acknowledged: not that some, as well of the Gentiles as Jews shall not be lost.

XXII. From what we have said before, it appears, that they depart from the apostle's meaning, who, by *all Israel,* understand the *mystical Israel,* or the people of God, consisting both of Jews and Gentiles, without admitting the conversion of the whole Jewish nation to Christ, in the sense we have mentioned. Notwithstanding this may be confirmed by the following arguments. 1st, The apostle speaks of that Israel, to whom he ascribes his own pedigree, ver. 1. whom he calls his flesh, that is, his kindred, ver. 14. and the natural branches, ver. 21. whom he constantly distinguishes from the Gentiles; to whom he testifies, blindness is happened.' All this is applicable to Israel properly so called. 2dly, He lays before us a mystery; but it was no mystery, that a very few Jews were converted to Christ together with the Gentiles; for we have daily instances

of

of that. 3dly, He reminds the Gentiles, not to exult over, or despise the Jews, from this argument, that, as they themselves were now taken in among the people of God, so, in like manner, the Jews were in due time to be taken in again. But if the apostle meant, that the body of the Jewish nation was to continue in their hardness; and but a few of them to be saved, who joined to the Gentiles, should form a mystical Israel, the whole of that discourse would be more adapted to the commendation of the Gentiles, than of the Israelites; and encourage rather than repress the pride of the Gentiles. 4thly, As the fall and diminishing of Israel, ver. 12. and their casting away, ver. 15. are to be understood; so likewise the receiving and saving them; for here the rules of a just opposition must be observed. But the fall, diminishing, and casting away of Israel are to be understood of the generality of the Jewish nation; therefore the receiving and saving of Israel in like manner.

XXIII. From which it is evident, that Grotius trifles, when he is positive, that this prophecy was fulfilled, at that time, when the idols and military ensigns of the Romans were openly seen in the temple; because, that then many, who had embraced Christianity, together with those, who had been Christians before, were exempted from the following calamities. To which was added, the conversion of many Jews, upon the destruction of the city and temple, since now the truth of Christ's predictions appeared in a much clearer light and the galling yoke of personal bondage had broke the obstinacy of many, as Vespatian and Titus put no bar in the way for proving this he quotes a passage from Justin, *adversus Tryphonem*. But such absurd imaginations are contrary to the light of all history. For, during the siege the whole of the Jewish nation, which was all over plunged in their guilt and perfidy, were made to suffer the just punishment of their sins. Which is very far from that salvation, which Paul here assures us of. If any joined the Christians at that time, their number was so inconsiderable, compared with the rest, as that it is ridiculous to give them the name of *all* Israel. Justin says nothing, but that " some of them being daily instructed in the name of Christ, had quitted the way of error:" which differs very much from *all Israel*. We may add, that by that fancy of Grotius, the times of casting away and receiving are entirely confounded. For never was the breaking off; and cutting away the natural branches more palpably seen, according to the Baptist's prophecy, Mat. iii. 10. than at the time, that Grotius imagines they were grafted in.

XXIV. In fine, the prophetic testimony, alledged by the
apostle

apostle from Isa. lxi. 20. confirms our explanation: where the Hebrew words properly denote; *the Redeemer shall come to Zion;* or according to the Septuagint, *ἥξει Σιὼν, on account of Zion, and unto them that turn from defection in Jacob.* Paul, generally following the Septuagint, has rendered the words somewhat differently, but to the same purpose and meaning.

XXV. Observe. 1st, That the apostle here very justly explains Zion and Jacob of the Jews; for, these are the natural sons of Jacob, natives, citizens of Zion; the others are only naturalized, that name therefore primarily and of itself agrees to them. And then also he speaks of those, with whom the covenant was made; as it is said in the text ver. 21. *this is my covenant with them;* but that testament and covenant belong to Israel: " whose are the covenants and promises," Rom. ix. 4. see Lev. xxvi. 44, 45. Moreover, Zion and Jacob denote not some few of Israel, but the whole body of that notion, as Gen. xlix. 7. For in Zion all the tribes had a right, Psal. cxxii. 4.

XXVI. 2dly, The *Goel* is promised to Zion, that is, the Kinsman-Redeemer, who can justly say, these are mine, and that in right of consanguinity, for I am the nearest kinsman, True it is, Christ may be called the *Goel* and near kinsman of all nations, on account of his being of the same human nature with them, which he assumed: yet he is chiefly and first of all the *Goel* of Israel, because of them are the fathers, of whom as concerning the flesh Christ came, Rom. ix. 5. And therefore, perhaps, the apostle said, the Redeemer shall come *out of Zion:* for as the relation, which is expressed by the term *Goel,* could not be set forth by the Greek, *ῥυόμενος* he was willing, by this means, to make up the imperfection of the Greek language, by intimating, that the Redeemer was in such a manner to come to Zion, as at the same time, with respect to his human nature, to come out of Zion. The advent of the deliverer supposes also such a time, in which other Lords, besides Jehovah, were to rule over Zion, Isa. xxvi. 13. from whose illegal dominion he was, with a stretched out arm, to set free and deliver his people.

XXVII. 3dly, The work of this Redeemer will be " to turn away iniquity from Jacob." In the Hebrew it runs, " He shall come to those that return from defection." The meaning is the the same: he will impart his grace and salvation to those, who, by a true faith and repentance, shall return unto God. And as they cannot give this repentance to themselves, the Redeemer will bestow it upon them, see Acts v. 31. Not only the Greeks have thus rendered the words of the prophet, but also

to

to the law." And to this purpose is what follows in Isaiah, chap. lix. 21. concerning giving the Spirit of God in Israel, and the putting his word in their mouth. The sum of the whole is, that, by the efficacy of the Redeemer, the Jews are in due time to be converted from their rebellion and transgressions.

XXVIII. 4thly, As this not yet accomplished, as to the whole body of the Israelites, and yet the scripture must be fulfilled, the apostle has justly inferred, that in the last times, it will be perfectly fulfilled. For, seeing the foundation thereof is God's covenant with Israel, and this a firm covenant, stable, immutable, and suspended on no ambiguous condition (for what condition could that covenent admit, which allots both remission of sins and repentance to Israel? it is not possible but that every thing shall happen exactly, according to the promise and prediction. *And this is my covenant with them saith God.* But concerning this covenant he speaks as follows, Isa. liv. 10. " For the mountains shall depart, and the hills be removed, but my kindness shall not depart from thee, neither shall the covenant of my peace be removed saith Jehovah that hath mercy on thee." And again Jer. xxxiii. 25, 26. " Thus saith Jehovah, if my covenant be not with day and night, and if I have not appointed the ordinances of heaven and earth: then I will cast away the seed of Jacob, and David my servant." Add Psal. cv. 8, 9. and Deut. iv. 31. All this being addressed to the whole body of the nation, it must of necessity be fulfilled at the appointed time.

XXIX. 5thly, But because some perhaps might think, that those horrid crimes, of which the Israelites had been guilty, might hinder that blessing of God from coming to them: the apostle adds a testimony whereby God promises to take away their sins; which cannot but be accompanied with repentance and faith in the Messiah, and the communication of his grace. True, indeed, it is, we have not those words in Isa. liv. But yet they are in Isa. xxvii. 9. where the Greek version has the very words οταν αφιλωμαι τας αμαρτιας αυτων. It is not unusual with the apostle to collect several testimonies into one, and to explain the words of one passage by those of another. And indeed this observation was of great importance: for, if any thing should seem to stand in the way of the restoration of the Jews, it was their extreme impiety. Wherefore there are frequent promises concerning the expiation of the crimes they had committed, as Deut. xxxii. 43. Jer. xxxiii. 8. and Jer. l. 20.

XXX. Some perhaps may say, are there not clearer expressions in proof of this matter in the prophets? Why then does the apostle pitch upon these, the force and cogency of which does not at firft fight appear ? I anfwer, there are fuch, which we fhall prefently produce : but here the fupreme and admirable wifdom of the Holy Spirit fhines forth, partly, becaufe by felecting thefe, he would bring us to confider entire prophecies, which as it were, he points out to us, and of fuch a nature, as to give full conviction of this matter. Partly, that by arguing from prophecies lefs evident, he might conftrain us to give credit to fuch as are more clear and exprefs. For, who will take upon him to wreft to a different meaning fuch evident teftimonies, as by the very found of their words lead to this fenfe, when he obferves, that Paul draws his reafons from fuch as feemed much more remote from the purpofe ?

XXXI. Should any one defire clearer teftimonies, we offer the following to his confideration : from Mofes, Lev. xxvi. 41—45. Deut. iv. 30, 31. Deut. xxx. 1—6. and Deut. xxxii. 43. From the Pfalms, Pfal. cii. 14—18. and Pfal. lxxxv. 9, 10. From Ifaiah, Ifa. xi. 11, 12. Ifa. xix. 24, 25. Ifa. xlix. 14, &c. Ifa. lxii. throughout. From Jeremiah, Jer. iii. 18, &c. Jer. xxxi. 1. and from ver. 31. to the end. Jer. xxxii. 37, &c. Jer. xxxiii. 24—26. From Ezekiel, Ezek. xxxvi. 24. to the end. Ezek. xxxvii. throughout, efpecially from ver. 15. Ezek. xxxix. 25. to the end. Add Hof. iii. 5. All thefe promifes are more fublime, than that the time can be affigned, in which they can be fuppofed to have been as yet fulfilled. From the New Teftament, add Mat. xxiii. 29. Luke xxi. 24. 2 Cor. iii. 16. The reader may pleafe to fee what we have faid on this head in a particular book concerning the ten tribes of Ifrael, from chap. ix. to the end ; where he will find moft of thofe prophecies carefully, and at greater length explained.

XXXII. As from all this it is evident, we are to expect the general converfion of the Ifraelites in time to come, not indeed of every individual,/but of the whole body of the nation, and of the twelve tribes. We choofe not to multiply minute queftions, either out of curiofity, or incredulity, concerning the time, place, manner, means, and the like circumftances of this myftery, which God has referved in his own power. Let us maintain the thing itfelf, and leave the manner of it to God. We fhall then beft of all underftand thofe obfcure prophecies which defcribes it, when we fhall be able to compare the event with them. Our Calvin, as his manner is, fpeaks with prudence and gravity. " When ever the longer delay is apt to throw us into defpair, let us recollect the name myftery, by which Paul clearly puts us in mind, that this converfion is not to be in the ordinary or ufual manner ; and therefore they act amifs, who attempt to meafure it by their own private fentiments.

ments. For, what more perverfe, than to account incredible
what falls not in with our opinion? Being therefore called a
myftery, becaufe incomprehenfible, until the time of its revelation. Moreover, it is revealed to us, as it was to the Romans,
that our faith, acquiefcing in the word, may fupport our expectation, until the effect itfelf be made manifeft," We fhall
conclude thefe things with the wifh and words of Maimoinides
at the end of his *More Nevochim.* "But may the great and
good God himfelf purify all Ifrael, according to his promife;
then the eyes of the blind will be opened. The people fitting
in darknefs have feen a great light: to thofe who fat in the
fhadow of death, the light is arifen."

XXXIII. *Laftly,* To this reftoration of Ifrael fhall be joined
the riches of the whole church, and as it were, life from the
dead, Rom. xi. 12. "Now if the fall of them be the riches of the
world, and the diminifhing of them the riches of the Gentiles;
how much more their fulnefs?" and ver. 15. "For if the cafting
away of them be the reconciling of the world; what fhall the
receiving of them be, but life from the dead?" The apoftle intimates, that much greater and more extenfive benefits fhall
redound to the Chriftian church from the fulnefs and reftoration of the Jews, than did to the Gentiles, from their fall and
diminution; greater, I fay, *intenfively,* or with refpect to degrees,
and larger with refpect to *extent.*

XXXIV. As to *intenfenefs* or degrees, it is fuppofed, that,
about the time of the converfion of the Jews, the Gentile world
will be like a *dead perfon,* in a manner almoft as Chrift defcribes
the church of Sardis, Rev. iii. 1, 2. namely, both that light of
faving knowledge, and that fervent piety, and that lively and
vigorous fimplicity of ancient Chriftianity, will, in a courfe of
years, be very much impaired. Many nations, who had formerly embraced the gofpel with much zeal, afterwards almoft
to be extinguifhed by the venom of Mahometanifm, Popery,
Libertinifm and Atheifm, would verify this prophecy: but upon
the reftoration of the Jews, thefe will fuddenly arife, as out of
the grave: a new light will fhine upon them, a new zeal be
kindled up; the life of Chrift be again manifefted in his myftical body, more lively, perhaps, and vigorous than ever.
Then, doubtlefs, many fcripture-prophecies will after their accomplifhment, be better underftood, and fuch as now appear
dark riddles, fhall then be found to contain a moft diftinct defcription of facts many candles joined together give a greater
light; a new fire laid near another, gives a greater heat. And
fuch will the acceffion of the Jews be to the church of the
Gentiles.

XXXV.

XXXV. And not only fo, but alfo many nations, among whom the name of Chrift had·long before been forgotten, fhall be feen to flock again to the ftandard of falvation then erected. For there is a certain fulnefs of the Gentiles, to be gathered together by the fucceffive preaching of the gofpel, which goes before the reftoration of Ifrael, of which ver. 25. and another richnefs of the Gentiles, that comes after the recovery of Ifrael. For, while the gofpel, for many ages, was publifhed now to this, then to that nation, others, gradually departed from Chrift : but when the fulnefs of the Jews is come, it is altogether probable, that thefe nations will in great numbers, return to Chrift. An almoft innumerable multitude of Jews refide in Afia, and Africa, among the Perfians, Turks, Indians, Chinefe, Japanefe, and Tartars. When therefore, by the almighty hand of God, thefe fhall be brought to the communion of the Meffiah, their love to him will be the more ardent, as their hatred againft him had been formerly more bitter. And is it not more than probable, that the nations, among whom they live, being excited by their example and admonitions fhall come into the fellowfhip of the fame faith? Certainly the words of the apoftle lead us to this.

XXXVI. Agreeably to which James has faid, Acts xv. 15—17. " And to this agree the words of the prophets; as it is written, after this I will return, and will build again the tabernacle of David, which is fallen down, and I will build again the ruins thereof, and I will fet it up : that the refidue of men might feek after the Lord, and all the Gentiles upon whom my name is called, faith the Lord, who doth all thefe things." The reparation of the fallen tabernacle of David fignifies the reftoration of true and fpiritual worfhip, among the Ifeaelites. And when that fhall come to pafs, the reft of mankind, who never gave up their names to Chrift, and the nations, upon whom his name was formerly called, but who, by their thoughtleffnefs, loft the benefit of the gofpel, will then with emulation feek the Lord.

XXXVII. And what is more evident than that prophecy in Ifaiah ? the prophet, chap. lix. 20, 21. having foretold the reftoration of Ifrael, according to the apoftles commentary, immediately, chap. lx. 1. exclaims, " Arife, fhine, for thy light is come, and the glory of Jehovah is rifen upon thee : ver. 3. and the Gentiles fhall come to thy light, and kings to the brightnefs of thy rifing," &c. Moreover, the riches of the church at that time are defcribed ver. 17. " for brafs I will bring gold, and for iron I will bring filver, and for wood, brafs, and for ftones iron ;" the moft magnificent words to the fame purpofe, follow

theſe,

thefe. From the confideration of which Peter Martyr has faid; " that, indeed, according to almoft all the prophets, efpecially Ifaiah, the happinefs of the church will be great: which it has not yet attained to, but it is probable that it will then (on the converfion of the Jews) attain to it." We have not indeed, the leaft doubt, that there are many prophecies both in the Old and New Teftament to this purpofe the full meaning of which we ardently pray the fupreme Being may teach his people by the event, the only undoubted interpreter of prophecies. It is however our duty to be modeft on the head, and not rafhly intrude into the fecrets of providence, nor boldly abufe, what we are neither allowed to know, nor fuffered to fearch into.

## C H A P.  XVI.

### Of Baptifm.

I. THE ordinary *facraments* of the New Teftament are only two; *baptifm* and the *Lord's Supper*. Thefe are fignalized by the exprefs inftitution of our king. Thefe were made ufe of by our Lord himfelf, to fet us an example, and by this ufe they were confecrated to the elect. Thefe are recommended to the Corinthians, as excellent privileges of the New Teftament church, and two like them, but of an extroardinary nature, were granted to Ifrael in the wildernefs, 1 Cor. x. 1—4. Thefe are held forth by the apoftle, 1 Cor. xii. 13. as facred feals of the union and communion of believers, both with Chrift, and with one another; and if there were any more of the kind, the apoftle, according to his ufual accuracy and diligence, would not have paffed them over in filence. Thefe in fhort, are fufficient to fignify and feal the fulnefs of grace we have in Chrift. For as two things are requifite to complete our happinefs: firft, our being abfolved from our fins, and wafhed from our pollution; that we may be regenerated by the communication of the Spirit of Chrift to a new life of grace: and then nourifhed in that life of grace, that is, fuftained, ftrengthened and increafed therein, until we be promoted to the life of glory: both thefe are fufficiently confirmed to us by thefe two facraments. Our firft ingrafting into Chrift, and our regeneration by his Spirit, are fet forth by baptifm; and the nourifhment of our fpiritual life by the holy fupper.

II. Concerning both thefe facraments of the New Teftament we are to obferve, that fomething correfponding to them, but only

only of ecclefiaftical ufe, not of divine inftitution, was practifed
by the ancient Ifraelites.   And herein the Lord Jefus difcovers
his exceeding great wifdom and goodnefs, that he would not
difcompofe the weak minds of his people, by too much inno-
vation, but retained the ancient rites, eftablifhed them by his
own authority, and rendered them more illuftrious, by their
fignifying the moft noble and myftical things which depended
wholly on his own inftitution.

III. And with refpect to *baptifm*, of which we are firft to
fpeak ; it appears, that there was a twofold baptifm in ufe
among the Jews; the one of which they called *the baptifm of
uncleannefs* or of *Luftration*, whereby legal uncleannefs was
wafhed away ; the other, *the baptifm of Profelytifm or initiation*,
whereby thofe of the Gentiles, who were converted to Judaifm,
were initiated into the church of Ifrael.   Omitting the former,
which is not fo material to the prefent fubject, we fhall mention
a few things concerning the latter.

IV. When a Gentile was received into the Ifraelitifh covenant, and, as the Jews fpeak, became a Profelyte of righteoufnefs, three ceremonies of initiation were ufed, without which
even the Ifraelites themfelves, according to their received notion
could not enter into that covenant ; to wit, *circumcifion, baptifm*,
and *facrifice*.   And the Jewifh mafters have fixed it as a law,
that this baptifm is fo neceffary, that without it, as much as without circumcifion, there can be no profelytifm ; but this along
with facrifice is all the initiation, that is neceffary in the cafe
of a female profelyte.

V. The manner of baptifm among the Ifraelites was this.
1ft, They examined the profelyte, who.was to be initiated, with
refpect to the fincerity of his converfion to Judaifm : whether
he defired to make a profeffion thereof, from the hopes of
riches or honours in a flourifhing republic ; or from fear ; or
from an affection for an Ifraelitefs: or any other fuch like motive
that was not good.   And after he declared, that his motive
was the alone regard he had for God, and an unfeigned love
to the divine law, they inftructed him in the feveral articles
thereof; as concerning the unity of God, the abominable nature
of idolatry, the reward of obedience, and concerning the future
world, and other heads of their divinity.   Which after he folemnly profeffed to receive without the leaft exception, he was
directly circumcifed.   2dly, After the wound of circumcifion
was perfectly healed, he was led to baptifm ; which was not
performed, but in the prefence of Triumvirs or three men,
who were the difciples of the wife לית בשים *who could exercife
judgments*, that is, Ifraelites of the pureft blood.   It was their
bufinefs

bufinefs not only to take care, that every thing was duly performed, and to teftify concerning this due performance, ˜ac-
cording to the practice of their anceftors : but further to inftruct the perfon to be baptized, and already placed in the
water, concerning fome more, and fome lefs, important precepts of the law.   Such Triumvirs are generally in Scripture
called Elohim.   Chrift in like manner declares, that, in the
baptifm of the New Teftament, the Elohim are prefent, Mat.
xxviii. 19. who are called the three witneffes in heaven, 1 John
v. 7.   3dly, It was unlawful to adminifter baptifm but in a
natural *current* or *collection of waters* ; as a river, lake, fountain:
becaufe according to them, none could be duly baptifed in
water fetched from any place, and received in artificial recep-
tacles.   4thly, The entire body was to be plunged at once,
for if but the tip of a finger was undipt, fuch a perfon was
accounted to remain ftill in his uncleannefs.   Yet it was not
neceffary, that the perfon to be baptized fhould put off all his
clothes, provided they were fuch, as the water could eafily
penetrate.   5thly, But we are efpecially to obferve, that even
little children were baptized, generally at the fame time with
their parents.   For thus it is faid in *Talmud. Babylon. Tit. Erub.*
fol. 11. c. 1.   " They baptize the little young profelyte in confequence of the mind of the Sanhedrim."

VI. The effect of this initiation was, 1ft, That the perfon
fo baptized, " being taken out from among the body of the
Gentiles," was accounted *a fon of the covenant*, who was permitted " to come and have a fafe retreat, under the wings of the
Divine Majefty."   2dly, He was looked upon as one that was
new born.   Hence that common faying in the Talmud ; " when
ever one becomes a profelyte, he is accounted an infant newly
born."   For, they fuppofe, that fome new foul, inftead of his
Gentile foul, is fent down, from fome palace in heaven, into the
body of the profelyte, after he is once come under the wings
of the Divine Majefty, and honoured with his k˙fs.   Affertions
which either have no meaning, or enigmatically fignify regeneration by the Spirit of God.   3dly, The confequence of this
regeneration was a new kindred ; fo that he was not to look
upon his former relatives (as brothers, fifters, parents, children)
as belonging to him ; nay, after this regeneration, he was to
have no more any heathen kindred, or ftand related to thofe
born in the time of Gentilifm ; juft as, by the imperial law,
all fervile relation ceafed upon manumiffion.   Hence Tacitus
fays, Hift. Lib. 5. " nor do they entertain any notion more than
that of making no account of their parents, children, brethren."
With which may be compared Luke xiv.26.

VII.

VII. They make the firſt practice of this baptiſm to be very ancient. Some aſcribe it to the patriarch Jacob, when he received into his family and domeſtic church the Shechemite. young women and other Gentiles, who reſided with him ; becauſe it is ſaid, Gen. xxxv. 2. " then Jacob ſaid unto his houſe-hold, and to all that were with him, put away the ſtrange gods that are among you, and be clean, and change your garments." Where Aben Ezra explains the words *be clean*, by the *waſhing of the body*. Others derive the firſt teſtimony, or practice of this baptiſm, from what is ſaid to Moſes, Exod. xix. 10. " Go unto the people and ſanctify them to day and to mor-row; and let them waſh their clothes." And again, ver. 14. " and he ſanctified the people, and they waſhed their clothes." Thus they would have the waſhing of the perſons to be inclu-ded in, or ſet forth by, the waſhing of their clothes. But theſe things are uncertain. They would have ſpoken more to the purpoſe, had they obſerved with Paul, that the " Iſraelites were baptiſed unto Moſes in the cloud and in the ſea, 1 Cor. x. 1, 2. of which we have formerly ſpoken at large. It is more pro-bable, what they ſay elſewhere, that, in the time of David and Solomon, when the republic of Iſrael was in its moſt flouriſhing ſtate, a great number of proſelytes were initiated by baptiſm. Whoever would know more of this baptiſm, and learn the teſ-timonies of the Jews themſelves, may conſult *Selden, de jure Nat. & Gen. Lib.* 2. c.2 and 4. as alſo, *de Succeſſionibus ad leges Hebræor. c.* 26. And again *de Synedriis Lib.* 1. c. 2. and *Light-foot.* on Mat. iii. 6. Alſo *Altingu diſſertat. de proſelytis*, Theſ. xxvii. ſeq.

VIII. But whatever be the caſe as to the antiquity of that rite, no divine inſtitution can be aſſigned for it prior to John, the harbinger of Chriſt, who was ſent by God to baptize. For, this was expreſsly given him in charge, " the word of the Lord came unto John," Luke iii. 2. John i. 33. From this, however, it appears, whence it came, that. the Scribes and Phariſees are never ſaid to have found fault with John for his baptiſm, but that they only aſked him, by what, and whoſe au-thority, he baptized ? John i. 25. hence alſo it was, that ſuch numbers of people flocked to his baptiſm : for, he was celebrat-ed both for his piety and doctrine ; nor did he uſe a new rite ; he taught, that the kingdom of heaven, which was ardently longed for and expected by all at that time, was at hand ; ex-horted every one that came to him, to ſuffer himſelf to be initiated therein, as it was now at the door; by taking upon him his baptiſm, and by a profeſſion of repentance. From that time baptiſm was of divine inſtitution among the Jews.

IX.

IX. But it was not yet a facrament of the New Teſtament: for, as the whole of John's miniſtry was, as it were, ſomething intermediate between both Teſtaments, and tended to prepare the way for the Lord, the author and herald of the New Teſtament; ſo, in like manner, his baptiſm initiated the penitent and believing into the kingdom of heaven: which indeed, was near, but not yet actually come, Mark i. 2—8. Hence *Tertullian, adverſus Marcionem, Lib.* 4. *c.* 33. calls "John the boundary ſet between the Old and New, at which Judaiſm ſhould terminate, and from which Chriſtianity ſhould begin." *Nazianzenus* alſo, *Orat.* 39. *quæ eſt in Sancta lumina,* calls him the "middle perſon between the Old and New Teſtaments." Yet his miniſtry belonged rather to the New, than to the Old Teſtament: as a forerunner is rightly judged to be of, and with that king, whom he precedes. Whence the baptiſm of John is by the author of *Queſt ad Orthodoxos,* which we have in Juſtin Martyr's works, Queſt. 37. called the *proem* or introduction *to the goſpel of grace.* To which that baptiſm came neareſt, *which* John adminiſtered unto the faith of the Meſſiah, now preſent, and manifeſting himſelf to Iſrael, John i. 29, 31.

X. I take the firſt baptiſm of the New Teſtament to have been that, which was adminiſtered by Chriſt's diſciples, at the command of their maſter, for a confeſſion of the preſence of the Meſſiah, John iii. 22. Yet at that time it was confined, for the moſt part to the Jews. But it was made a ſacrament of the univerſal church, after the New Teſtament was ſealed by Chriſt's blood, and confirmed by his reſurrection, to be preached all over the world by the apoſtles, who were very ſoon to be baptized with the Holy Ghoſt, Mat. xxviii. 19.

XI. John's baptiſm differed from that adminiſtered by Chriſt's diſciples, not in eſſence, but in circumſtances only. For, 1ſt, Both were from heaven, and grounded on God's command: which we are ſure of with reſpect to Chriſt's baptiſm, and as to John's appears from John i. 33. Luke vii. 30. Mat. xxi. 25. 2dly, In both there was a dipping in water, Mat. iii. 11. Acts viii. 36. 3dly, Both adminiſtered into the faith and confeſſion of Chriſt, Acts xix. 4, 5. 4thly, Both were a ſign and ſeal of the remiſſion of ſins, Mat. iii. 6. Luke iii. 3. Acts ii. 38. 5thly, In the participation of both, there was an obligation to repentance on the perſon: ſee the laſt text. Neverthelefs they differ. 1ſt, In that John's baptiſm was indeed from God, but not from Chriſt, as the incarnate Mediator, acting as the king of his church. 2dly, In that, as we have ſaid, it was rather a preparation for, than a ſacrament of the New Teſtament. Baſil in his treatiſe, *quomodo baptizetur aliquis baptiſmate, quod eſt in*

*Evadgelio Domini noſtri Jeſu Chriſti.* How a perſon is baptized with the baptiſm, which is in the goſpel of our Lord Jeſus Chriſt, diſtinguiſhing between John's and Chriſt's baptiſm, ingeniouſly writes, *the baptiſm of the former was introductory,* or initiatory ; *that of the latter perfective.* 3dly, In that God communicated therein a more ſparing meaſure of the Spirit ; whereas in the beginning of the goſpel, the gift of tongues and prophecy, which in ſcripture comes under the appellation *ſpirit,* was conferred on very many, who were baptized with Chriſt's baptiſm.

XII. But we are principally to treat concerning this baptiſm, which has Chriſt for its author. For the fuller underſtanding of which we are diſtinctly to explain. I. The external *ſign.* II. The ſpiritual *thing ſignified.* In the *ſign* we are to diſtinguiſh between the *element* and the *ceremony,* or ſacred rite employed about the element. The *element* here to be uſed, is true, plain, natural *water :* ſuch as John baptized with, Mat. iii. 6, 16. John iii. 23. the apoſtles and others, as Acts viii. 28. and Acts x. 40. Accordingly Eph. v. 26. it is called *the waſhing of water.* The ſacred rite conſiſts. I. In the application of the water to the body of the perſon to be baptized. II. In pronouncing a certain form of words.

XIII. Concerning the former it is queried, whether baptiſm may be duly adminiſtered by *immerſion* only, or alſo by *effuſion* of the water out of a veſſel, or by *aſperſion* or ſprinkling ? To which we anſwer in the following poſitions. 1ſt, It is certain, that both John and the diſciples of Chriſt, ordinarily uſed dipping : whoſe example was followed by the ancient church: as Voſſius, *Diſput. 1. de baptiſmo, Theſ. 6.* and Hoornbeck *de baptiſmo Veterume, Sect. 4.* have ſhewn from many teſtimonies both of the Greeks and Latins. 2dly, It cannot be denied but the native ſignification of the words, βάπτειν and βαπτίζειν is to *plunge* or *dip :* ſo as to be altogether ſomething more than ἐπιπολάζειν, *to float on the ſurface ;* but leſs than δύνειν, *to go to the bottom* and periſh : as Voſſius remarks, *Theſ. 1. ibid.* However, I have obſerved, that the term κατάδυσις, *going to the bottom,* is frequently uſed by the ancients in the matter of baptiſm Athanaſius, Queſt. 94. τὸ καταδῦσαι τὸ παιδίον ἐν τῇ κολυμβήθρᾳ, &c. *the going down or dipping of the child in the bath.* And Sozomen, Lib. 6. c. 26. has charged Eunomius with a hereſy, for teaching, that " the ſacrament of baptiſm ought to be performed by once dipping." Similar examples are every where to be met with. Salmaſius, in his obſervations on Sulpitius Severus, de Vita Martini, c. 15. has made the following obſervation, βάπτειν, *from which* βαπτίζειν, " ſignifies immerſion, not aſperſion : nor did the ancients baptize any but by dipping, either once or thrice : except clinicks, or perſons confined

fined to a sick bed, because these were baptised in a manner they could bear; not in an entire font, as they who put their head under water, but their body was sprinkled all over." Cypr. 4. Epist. 7. " Thus when Novatus in his sickness, received baptism, he was but sprinkled all over, Euseb. 6. Hist. c. 43. Nor are we to conceal. 3dly, That there is a greater copiousness of signification, and a fuller similitude between the sign and the thing signified in immersion: as we shall shew, when 'we come to that point. 4thly, Nay, that immersion may be performed in cold countries, without any great danger of health and life, appears from the example of the Russians, who plunge the children that are to be baptized three times all over: not believing, that baptism can be duly performed any other way; and never use lukewarm water, but for persons infirm. As the Muscovite writers relate at large, in *Georgius Fenlavius Annotationes ad Enchiridion Christophori Angeli de Statu hodiernorum Græcorum, p.* 470, *Seq.* 5thly, But that if cold water should be thought more inconvenient or dangerous, it may be warmed: which the said Christophorus Angelus testifies, c. 24. is done among the Greeks. " The Greeks," says he, " keep in their churches a kind of large vessels called baptisteries, that is, vessels so large, as are sufficient to admit the infant to be plunged all over therein." When therefore any child is to be dipt in this font, " the relations of the infant first of all warm the water with some odoriferous herbs." And if the water was in like manner, warmed in our climate, there would seem to be no such great hazard in the dipping of persons to be baptized.

XIV. 6thly, But then we are not to imagine, that immersion is so necessary to baptism, as that it cannot be duly performed by pouring water all over, or by aspersion; for, both the method of pouring, and that of aspersion are not without arguments for them. 1st, Though we find the apostles dipped, it does not follow they always observed this method. It is more probable, the three thousand, who were baptized in one day, Acts ii. 41. had the water poured or sprinkled on them, rather than that they were dipt. For it is not likely, that men, who were so much employed in preaching, as the apostles were, could have leisure for so tedious an immersion of so many thousands. Nor is it probable, that Cronelius, Lydia and the Jailor, who were baptized in private houses, with their families, had baptisteries at hand, in which they could be plunged all over. Instances of pouring the water over persons are brought from antiquity by Vossius *Disput.* 1. *de Baptis. Th.* 9. Which Joshuah Arndius, without mentioning Vossius, has inserted in the same order in his *Lexicon Antiquitat. Ecclefiaft. p. 66.* 2dly, Though βαπτιζω properly fignifies to plunge or dip, yet it is alfo more generally ufed for any wafhing; as Luke xi. 38. Well therefore fays Dominicus a Soto, *Diftinct. 3. Quoft. un. Art. 7.* " In baptifm there is fomething effential, as the wafhing," according to Eph. v. 26. where the apoftle calls baptifm the wafhing of water: " fomething accidental, namely, the wafhing in this or the other manner." 3dly, The thing fignified by baptifm is explained both in the Old and New Teftament by the terms of pouring water over, and of afperfion. Concerning pouring water over, fee Ifa. xliv. 3. concerning afperfion, Ifa. lii. 15. Ezek. xxxvi. 25. Heb. xii. 24. 1 Pet. i. 2. I deny not, that, in thefe quotations, there is an allufion to the Levitical fprinklings; yet from them it appears, that the application of the blood and fpirit of Chrift, which believers of the New Teftament enjoy, is properly fhadowed forth by the rite of afperfion. To this the apoftle leads us in exprefs terms, Heb. ix. 13. 14. " for if the blood of bulls and of goats, and the afhes of an heifer, *fprinkling* the unclean, fanctifieth to the purifying of the flefh, how much more fhall the blood of Chrift purge your confcience from dead works?" 4thly, We add, that the whole nature of the New Teftament, which is wholly made up of mildnefs and liberty, frees the tender age of infants to be baptized, efpecially in northerly climates, from the neceffity of being ftripped naked and plunged all over. Though that poffibly might be done without hazard of life, yet not without fome other inconvenience. 5thly, Others add that in ancient times, in which candour and fimplicity flourifhed more, the perfons to be baptized were, without any indecency, ftripped naked: yet afterwards, as the lewdnefs of others, fo of thofe, on whom it was incumbent to adminifter baptifm increafed, experience clearly teftifying it to the whole world, this could no longer be done with decency: and therefore, for five centuries back, that cuftom has been gradually difcontinued almoft all over the weft. See Voffius in the place already quoted. Who has this from *Jofephus Vicecomes, de ritibus Baptifmi, Lib. 4. c. 10, 15.* To whom however Gifbert Voetius, a divine of immortal memory, oppofes his learned confiderations, *Polit. Eccles. T. p. 690,* proving, by no contemptible arguments againft Vicecomes and Voffius, that perfons to be baptized, quite naked, did not obtain in the ancient church. But though this act of ftripping fhould be more referved and modeft, than is ufually reprefented by painters; yet on account of the depravity of men, the rite of effufion or afperfion feems to be fafer, for which no fuch naked expofure of the body is requifite. From all which we conclude, that the Latins

were

were very unkindly, and therefore without reason, called by some Greeks in the council of Florence, Abaptists, because they did not go into the water and were plunged. See the history of that council, Sect. 9. c. 9.

XV. Whether immersion or aspersion be done once or thrice, I take not to be material : as we have no precept of our Lord concerning this.. Yet the trine immersion was more usual among the ancients : who also therein placed some mystery. For thereby they would have it to signify. 1st, A confession of the adorable Trinity, in whose name baptism was submitted to, 2dly, " The death and resurrection of Christ after three days," as Athanasius speaks, Quest. 94. 3dly, Ambrose adds a third reason but of less weight, *Lib.* 2. *de Sacram. c.* 7. " Thou hast plunged for the third time, that the third confession might wipe away the manifold failures of thy former life." But afterwards in Spain, while the Arians numbered the immersions, in order to divide the divinity, Leander, bishop of Seville, consulted Gregory II. bishop of Rome, about the question concerning the trine, or single immersion; who answered, that though the church of Rome dipt thrice, yet the church of Spain would rather be content with a single immersion : and it was decreed in the fourth council of Toledo in the year 633, that it should be so; where Canon 5, or according to another edition, Canon 6, both is accounted right, and both irreprovable in the holy church of God. Yet * one religious ceremony of a single sacrament is preferable; that every one may see the unity of the Godhead, and the trinity of persons therein. The unity, when we dip once; the trinity, while we baptize in the name of the Father, the Son and the Holy Ghost.: See Vossius *Disput.* 2. *de baptis.* And Forbes, *Lib.* 10. c. 5. §. 48. *Seq.*

XVI. Indeed, it is not proper to administer baptism without some words, by which the mystery of it may be briefly explained : according to that well known saying of Augustin, " take away the word, and what is the water but water only?" Yet we are far from thinking, that Christ prescribed a form of words, which all were to make use of at all times, and in all places. Christ, indeed, commanded to baptize in the name of the Father, Son and Holy Ghost, but not precisely to say, I baptize thee in the name of the Father, &c. The apostles are said " to have baptized in the name of Jesus," Acts ii. 38. and Acts viii. 16. Acts xix. 5. and yet it does not follow, that they used this form, *I baptize thee in the name of Jesus.* But

as

* This I apprehend, is the sense of the author, whose words are, *simpli tamen mysterium sacramenti praefertur.*

as baptifm ought, by all means, to be performed in the name
of the facred Trinity, to whofe obedience and worfhip we are
confecrated by the wafhing of water, it alfo feems neceffary,
in the adminiftration of it, to make either an explicit, or at
leaft an implicit mention of the Trinity. Nor is it to be
doubted, but he maintains fome mifchievous error, who refufes to follow a cuftom received by all the Chriftian world,
and probably derived from apoftolic example. But I dare not
abfolutely condemn the baptifm adminiftered and received in the
name of Chrift, without any mention of the Father and Holy
Spirit, both becaufe the baptifm of the Apoftles is defcribed in
thofe words by Luke, and becaufe, as Bafil has ingenioufly
obferved, *de Spiritu Sancto*; " to name Chrift is to confefs the
the whole Trinity; for this fets forth both God who anoints,
the Son who is anointed, and the unction, even the Holy
Ghoft." We have fomething like this in Amboofe, *de Spir.
Sancto, Lib.* 1. *c.* 3. quoted alfo by Peter Lombard, *Sentent.
Lib. 4. Diftinct.* 3. where he treats of the form of baptifm.
Neither is it an improper obfervation, that there is fome difference in the cafe of baptized perfons, who from Judaifm,
and of thofe who from Gentilifm embraced Chriftianity: for,
is it proper, that the Gentiles, who are converted from idols
to the true God; to that God, I fay, who, by the diftinction
of the three perfons in one effence, is difcriminated from thofe
that are not God's, fhould be baptized into the exprefs confeffion of the Trinity: but as the God of the ancient Ifraelites
and of the Chriftians is one and the fame, the profeffing the
Lord Jefus feems to have been fufficient in the baptifm of
the Ifraelites. And it is poffibly for this reafon, enjoined
Mat. xxviii. that the Gentiles fhould be baptized in the name
of the Father, Son and Holy Ghoft; but the Jews either fuch
by birth, or formerly become fuch by profeffing the Jewifh religion, are faid to be baptized in the name of Jefus.

XVII. Peter, 1 Epift. iii. 21. gives us to know, that baptifm
is a kind of type or figure, which fignifies to commemorate
and teach fomething more heavenly and fublime. And therefore having explained what is external and fenfible, we are now
to treat of the *Spiritual thing fignified*; which may be confidered
either *generally*, or *particularly*.

XVIII. The thing fignified by baptifm *in general* is the *reception into the covenant* of grace, as adminiftered under the *New
Teftament*. As circumcifion was the fign and feal of the Old
Teftament, Gen. xvii. 11. fo baptifm, which fucceeds circumcifion, Col. ii. 11. is the fign of the new covenant, and as Bafil
fpeaks, *the inviolable feal* thereof. Moreover that reception into
the

the covenant of grace imports two things. 1ft, Communion with Chrift, and his myftical body, and confequently a participation of all his benefits. 2dly, An engagement to incumbent duty. Both are fignified and fealed by baptifm. In refpect of the former, we are faid " to be baptized into one body," 1 Cor. xii. 13. and " faved by baptifm," Tit. iii. 5. 1 Pet. iii. 21. With refpect to the latter, baptifm is called ἐπερώτημα ἀγαθῆς ἐπερώτημα εἰς Θεόν, " the anfwer of a good confcience towards God," 1 Pet. iii. 21.

XIX. A paffage certainly that merits an accurate explication. Therefore we fhall firft fhew what is *a good confcience:* then what *ἐπερώτημα anfwer,* imports: laftly, to what the words εἰς Θεόν *towards God,* are to be referred, whether to ἐπερώτημα, *anfwer* or to *a good confcience.* A confcience is good in a twofold refpect: 1ft, *Sincerely good,* when it faithfully, in God's name, lays before a man what is to be done, and what to be avoided, and continually excites him to the careful practice of holinefs. 2dly, *Chearfully good,* when it makes him joyful, by giving him the teftimony of a fincere holinefs. And therefore to have a good confcience, as our apoftle fpeaks. ver. 16. is to live according to the dictates of the mind in fuch a manner, that you may be affured that you do well and pleafe God. This Paul calls ἀπρόσκοπον συνείδησιν, " a confcience void of offence," Acts xxiv. 16.

XX. The word ἐπερώτημα (which we tranflate *anfwer,*) is varioufly explained by the learned. Oecumenius explains it by ἀῤῥαβών, ἐνέχυρον, and ἀπόδειξις *earneft, pledge,* and *demonftration.* Which the celebrated Cocceius has adopted, who generally infifts, that ἐπερώτημα denotes an argument, a ground of afking God as a father; and a fign and feal, which we may ufe with boldnefs, and when we draw near to God may beg his faving graces without fear. But this explication does not feem to agree with the origin of the word: and I doubt, whether any example of fuch a fignification can be produced from any approved author. Voffius, in my opinion, obferves much better, that ἐπερώτημα does not fimply fignify an interrogation, but that which is anfwered to another interrogation. For, the perfons to be baptized afk of God, whether he will be their God: and God, on the other hand, afkes and reftipulates, whether they themfelves will maintain a good confcience towards him. Grotius's annotations here are very learned: he obferves, that ἐπερώτημα is a law term, and generally ufed in Theophilus, and the other Greek interpreters of the Roman law for a *ftipulation:* as alfo in the Gloffary, ἐπερωτῶ, *I ftipulate.* But adds, that, by a metonomy, as is often the cafe in the law, an *anfwer,* or *promife* is comprehended under the name *ftipulation.* Hence in

-the

the same Glossary, ἐπεροτῶμαι, *I promise, I engage.* If Beza had attended to this, possibly he would not have said, that it was harsh to translate ἀπεκρίαν *to answer*, as Erasmus has done.

XXI. But which of these significations, whether that of stipulating, or of promising, should here take place, depends very much on the construing the words *towards God.* Which may either be so connected, as that *a good conscience* may be said to be *towards God*, that is before God, or respecting him in all its actions; as Acts xxiv. 16. or so, that ἐπερότημα may be said to be *towards God.* If the former, it seems more agreeable to translate ἐπερότημα, *stipulation*, as Beza has learnedly done. For, it is God who stipulates with, or requires of the Christian, that he maintain a good conscience towards him. But should the latter be more agreeable, and the conscience itself, or the Christian, considered as ἐπερότων giving an answer to God concerning a good conscience; it is plain, *answer* or *promise* is the more proper signification. And both so beautifully agree with the apostle's design, that I can scarce tell which to prefer.

XXII. For, there are these two things in baptism, God *stipulates*, or requires a good conscience *towards* himself; and the conscience "answers and promises to God," that it will endeavour to be so; or which seems more plain, man engages to keep a good conscience. Formerly the Bishop, or some other person in his name, interrogated thus, or which is the same thing, stipulated, Ἀποτάσση τῳ Σατανᾶ *dost thou renounce the devil?* The person to be baptised made answer, 'Ἀποτάσσομαι, *I do renounce.* Again being asked *dost thou consent to Christ?* He answered, *I do consent: Tertullian de Baptismo* calls this *the engagement of salvation.* And *de resurrectione carnis* says, " the soul is established not by washing, but by the answer." Cyprian called it the " interrogation of baptism," Epist. 76 and 80. To the very same purpose are the words of Peter: for, it is probable, that if not the very same, yet at least a similar form of asking and engaging, and of the same import, was used in the susception of baptism, even from the days of the apostles. And though there had been no express form of this; yet baptism, being the first entering into covenant, virtually contains such a stipulation and engagement.

XXIII. But we are likewise more particularly to explain; first, what may be signified by the *water* in baptism; and then what by the *rites*, commonly used about the water. And the *water* certainly denotes both the *blood* and *Spirit* of Christ. It is plain, such effects, are in the sacred writings ascribed to these, as to the mystical water, that signify and seal the communication of them by baptism: namely, to the *blood*, as the
*impetrating*

*impetrating caufe;* to the *Spirit* as the *applying caufe,* Paul, Heb. xii. 24. and Peter 1 Epift. i: 2. fpeak of the blood of Chrift, with which we are fprinkled. But the Spirit is exprefsly reprefented by the term water, Ifa. xliv. 3. Ezek. xxxvi. 25—27.

XXIV. The analogy or fignification of this facrament principally confifts in thefe three things. 1ft, Water is of all things moft proper, either from the nitre, with which it is replete, or from fome other quality, to wafh away the filth of the body. But the blood of Chrift wafhes the foul from all the pollution of fin, 1. John i. 7. becaufe by his fufferings he certainly merited, that we fhould be prefented pure before God, Eph. v. 25, 26. And the Spirit of Chrift, who applies the merits of his blood, actually cleanfes us, 1 Cor. vi. 11. 2dly, Water alfo has a power to drown and to fuffocate: the fame efficacy is exerted by the blood and Spirit of Chrift, for the mortification of the old man; of which we fhall hear more prefently, and, on this account, Gregory Nazianzen called baptifm the *deluge of fin.* With which Ambrofe agrees *de Initiandis, c.* 3; " the water is that in which the flefh is drowned, in order to wafh away all fin." 3dly, Water is the *principle* of very many *living things,* and in their creation the Spirit brooded on the waters, Gen. i. 3. The earth fcarce produces any living thing, either of the vegetable or reptile kind, unlefs impregnated with water, Pfal. lxv. 10. The very generation of the human fœtus is faid to be from water, Ifa. xlviii. 1. Pfal. lxviii. 27. Thus in like manner, the blood and Spirit of Chrift, as the myftical water, are the principles of our regeneration and new creation, John iii. 5. And as that is fignified by the water of baptifm, fo baptifm itfelf is called, Tit. iii. 5. " the wafhing of regeneration, and renewing of the Holy Ghoft."

XXV. With refpect to the ceremonies in the adminiftration, we are diftinctly to take notice : I. Of the immerfion into the water, and the wafhing, that is the confequence of it. II. The continuing under the water. 3dly, The emerfion out of the water. Thefe rites referred either to the *remembrance* of thofe things, which Chrift underwent, or fignify the *benefits,* which Chrift beftows upon us, or put us in mind of our duty.

XXVI. Firft therefore, the *immerfion* into the water, reprefents to us that tremendous *abyfs of divine juftice,* in which Chrift was plunged for a time, in fome meafure, in confequence of his undertaking for our fins : as he complained under the type of David, Pfal. lxix. 2. " I fink in deep mire, where there is no ftanding : I am come into deep waters, where the floods overflow me." But *more particularly,* an immerfion of this kind deprives us of the benefit of the light, and the other enjoyments

of this world ; fo it is a very fit reprefentation of the *death* of
Chrift. *The continuing* how fhort, foever, *under the water*, reprefents his *burial*, and the loweft degree of humiliation, when
he was thought to be wholly cut off, while in the grave, that
was both fealed and guarded. *The emerfion, or coming out of
the water*, gives us fome refemblance of his *refurreftion*, or victory, obtained in his death over death, which he vanquifhed
within its inmoft receffes, even the grave : all thefe particulars
the apoftle intimates, Rom. vi. 3, 4.

XXVII. Moveover, baptifm alfo fignifies thofe *benefits*, which
believers obtain in Chrift: and thefe are either *prefent* or *future*.
Among the *prefent*, the principal is, fellowfhip in the death, burial, and refurreftion of Chrift; and the confequence of it, viz. the
mortification and burying of our old man, and the raifing of the
new, by the efficacy of the blood and Spirit of Chrift. For,
the *immerfion* into the water, reprefents the *death of the old man*,
even in fuch a manner, that it can neither ftand in judgment
to our condemnation, nor exercife dominion over our bodies,
that we fhould ferve it in the lufts thereof. In the former ref-
peft, the death of the old man appertains to juftification ; in
the latter, to fanftification. The *continuing* under the water,
reprefents the *burying* of the body of fin, whereby all hopes of
a revival are cut off ; fo that after this, it is neither able to
condemn, nor rule over the eleft. For, as in burying, the
dead body, which is covered over with earth, is removed from
the fight of men, and fo weighed down by the earth thrown
upon it, that, fhould we fuppofe fome life to have remained
in the buried perfon, to be beftowed upon him anew by a miracle, yet it cannot fail to be ftifled by the load of earth lying
upon it, nor recover to any degree of permanence. In the
fame manner, when in baptifm the perfon funk under the water, is for fome time detained therein ; this fignifies and feals
to us, that our fins are removed from the view of the divine
juftice, never to be imputed to our condemnation : or as Micah
fpeaks, chap. vii. 19. " He will fubdue our iniquities, and caft
all our fins into the depth of the fea." likewife that the power of
fin is fo depreffed and weakened, that it can no longer drive
us at its pleafure, or hinder our falvation, or be able to refume
the power, which it has once loft, in order to bring us again
under its dominion. The *emerfion* out of the water is a fymbol
of the revival of the new man, after our fins are now funk, to
a fpiritual life by the refurreftion of Chrift. And this alfo
the apoftle declares, Rom. vi. 3—6. and Col. ii. 11, 12. where
he intimates, that our baptifm is fuch a memorial of the things
that happened to Chrift, as at the fame time to feal our communion

munion with him in all these things, and our union as it were into one plant.

XXVIII. But *future blessings* are also signified by baptism. For as in baptism, after we are immersed in the water, we directly come out of it in safety; so in like manner, it shall be, that though we may be pressed with afflictions in this life, yet we shall not be overwhelmed by them, but being at last delivered from them, shall be translated into everlasting joys. That calamities in scripture are compared to waters, appears from many passages, as Psal. xviii. 4. Psal. xxxii. 6. Psal. xlii. 7. Psal. cxliv. 7. And afflictions are sometimes called by the name of baptism, Mat. xx. 22. Mark x. 32. Luke xii. 30. Therefore the coming out of the water, or the wiping off the water signifies, that we shall happily surmount all the difficulties of this life. See 1 Pet. iii. 20, 21. " Wherein *(in the ark of Noah)* few, that is eight souls were saved by water. The like figure whereunto even baptism, doth also now save us." And as the Israelites when they entered the Red Sea, under great apprehensions of danger, were, upon the Egyptians being drowned, amazed, that at length they came safe to land; so in like manner, believers having surmounted all the miseries of this life, and standing on the sea of glass, shall sing *the song of the Lamb*, Rev. xv. 3. saying, " he brought me up also out of an horrible pit, out of the miry clay, and set my feet upon a rock, and established my goings," Psal. xl. 2.

XXIX. Moreover, as in baptism are set forth the death, burial and resurrection of Christ: but his resurrection is a pledge of our glorious resurrection: we may learn from our baptism, that after being buried, as it were in the water, we directly rise out of it, so at the last day, we shall be raised out of our graves, to eternal life. Hence Theodoret says of baptism. " It is an earnest of good things to come, a type of the future resurrection, a communion in the sufferings, and a participation of the resurrection of our Lord:" Agreeably to the words of Christ, Mark xvi. 16. " He that believeth and is baptized, shall be saved."

XXX. From what we have said, it appears, that the rite of immersion into the water, upon which emersion follows, as was generally the practice among the ancients, has some significancy and analogy to represent both the effect and the cause of that effect: yet we are not to imagine, that all analogy is destroyed by the practice of aspersion, or pouring on the water. For, the pouring out, or aspersion of the water, answers to the immersion into it, and perhaps it would be better, if it was so copious, as to run over the whole face, and as it were cover it: by which

means

which fet before us an extraordinary pattern, to the likenefs of which we fhould be conformed. For as Chrift, when he fuffered death, was deprived of the enjoyment of the light, and of the function of his fenfes, and of all the other operations of life, and thus was broke off from all commerce with the world, that he might have nothing farther to do with it. In like manner, it behoveth us, if we would have any true union with Chrift, to ceafe from all thofe works, to which we were formerly addicted, and to renounce the world, almoft as if we were dead. And as Chrift, when he arofe, commenced a new kind of life, quite different from that natural life, which he enjoyed in this world before his death; fo it becomes us, if we would have any communion with him in his refurrection, to rife to a new life, and altogether different from that life, which was corrupted and ftained with fin, to which we were given before our calling; as thofe things are urged by the apoftle, Rom. vi. 3—6.

XXXVI. As to ourfelves, we are reminded in baptifm; that, being once wafhed, we do not again pollute ourfelves with the filth of fins; nor being baptized into Chrift, we do not again mix with, or immerfe ourfelves in the world: leaft " it fhould happen unto us according to the true proverb, the dog is turned to his own vomit again: and the fow, that was wafhed, to her wallowing in the mire," 2 Pet. ii. 22.

XXXVII. Befides, feeing " by one Spirit we are all baptized into one body," 1 Cor. xii. 13. we are alfo reminded, as members of one body, to love one another, and keep up brotherly concord; being careful to maintain the unity of the Spirit in the bond of peace: For, there is one baptifm, Eph. iv. 3, 5. In a word, as baptifm is the feal of God's covenant, by the fufception thereof, we bind ourfelves to that holinefs of life, which becomes God's covenant-people.

. XXXVIII. To all thefe things very great weight is added, in that baptifm it is adminiftered in the name of the Father, Son, and Holy Ghoft. For thereby God the Father promifes to thofe, who are truely baptized, that with refpect to them, he will fuffer nothing to be wanting, which they can reafonably expect from a moft affectionate father: God the Son, in like manner promifes, to execute in their behalf all the offices of a moft perfect Saviour: the Holy Ghoft likewife appoints for them both, fanctification, confolation, indwelling and perptual confervation. And they, who are thus baptized, not only profefs their faith in the myftery of a Trinity, which we have treated of more fully elfewhere; but alfo bind themfelves to filial obedience to . God the Father: give up themfelves to Chrift, as a Prophet, to be his difciples as a King to ferve him; and as a Prieft, for

the

the expiation of their sins. In fine, they bind themselves to the Holy Spirit, not to grieve him, but reverently to obey all his inspirations and motions.

XXXIX. What we have thus far said concerning the signification of baptism, we have borrowed for the most part from Voffius's Disputations, which we have already often commended; as I likewise observe others have done before me. Things also similar to these, and sometimes almost in the very same words, I find in Gomarus Thesis. But which of these learned men first led the way to such very accurate and solid conceptions, I cannot now say. The other usual disputes about baptism, have been fully discussed by our writers, and are generally to be met with in their *Loci communes*, and unnecessary to be repeated here. Should any be desirous to know the rites of the ancient church about baptism, they may consult *Josephi Vicecomitis Observationes Ecclesiasticus de Antiquis baptismi ritibus :* and among our writers, *Voffius* and *Voetius's Polit. Eccl. p.* 1. *Lib.* 2. *Tr.* 2. *Forbesius, Lib.* 10. *and Hoornbeck in Disput. de baptismo Veterum. Georgius Fehlavius ad cap.* 24. *Christophori Angeli de Statu hodiernorum Graecorum,* has collected from different authors, the ceremonies used by the Greeks and Muscovites in baptism.

XL. There is one thing that, I think, ought not to be omitted here, seeing it is of very great moment to our consolation : namely, that baptism is, by the will of God, to be administered not only to adult believers, but also to their children. The grounds for this, and those beyond all exceptions, are to be met with in scripture : so that there is no necessity, with the Papists, who shamefully prevaricate in a good cause, to have recourse in this matter to unwritten tradition.

XLI. We readily acknowledge, that there is no express and special command of God, or of Christ, concerning infant-baptism : yet there are general commands, from which this special command is deduced by evident consequence. For to begin with what is most general; God declared to Abraham, that it was his constant and unchangeable will, that the sign of the covenant should not be denied to those in covenant with him, when he said, Gen. xvii. 13. " And my covenant shall be in your flesh for an everlasting covenant." By these words, he commands the sign of his covenant to be in the flesh of all the posterity of Abraham, with which he had enterd into a covenant of grace. From this general injunction, he infers, ver. 14. the necessity of circumcision, because he then gave it as a sign of the covenant. When therefore upon the change of the economy, he substituted, in the place of circumcision, another

sign

fign of the covenant, in confequence of that general command, all thofe in covenant are bound to take upon them the new fign. Moreover believers under the New Teftament belong to the fpiritual pofterity of Abraham, and are, if we confider its fubftance, partakers of the fame gracious covenant, Rom. iv. 16, 17. not adults only, but alfo their children, as we fhall prefently fhew. Whence it follows, that the fign of the covenant in their body, is not to be denied to the young children of believers, any more than to believers themfelves.

XLII. There is another command of Chrift, Mat. xxviii. 19. *Go ye therefore, and, μαθητευσατε, difciple all nations, baptizing them, &c.* There Chrift commands difciples to be gathered into his fchool, and fealed, as perfons in covenant with him, with the feal of baptifm. But it is evident, when parents become the difciples of Chrift, their children are alfo accounted in the number of difciples. Juft as among the Jews, together with the profelyte parents, their young children were initiated in the Jewifh rites. It was not therefore neceffary, that Chrift fhould exprefsly mention the baptifm of infants. For, as it was a re-cieved cuftom among the Jews, that, together with the parents, who gave up their names to the God of Ifrael, their young children fhould be baptifed (as we have fhewn above,) the apoftles being fent to baptife the nations, and accuftomed to the rites of their own country, could not but think, that toge-ther with the parents, who made a profeffion of the faith of Chrift, they ought to baptize their infants, unlefs Chrift had repealed the received cuftom by a contrary command. Which as we no where read he did, we are abfolutely to conclude, that what we have now explained was our Lord's intention.

XLIII. Peter fupplies us with another argument, Acts ii. 38, 39, " Be baptifed every one of you in the name of Jefus Chrift, for the remiffion of fins, and ye fhall receive the gift of the Holy Ghoft. For the promife is unto you, and to your children," &c. Where the apoftle argues thus: they to whom the promife of grace was made, are to be baptifed, we fubmit, but the promife of grace was made not only to parents, but al-fo to their children: it therefore follows, that not only parents, but alfo their children are to be baptifed. Both propofitions are the apoftle Peter's. Now the whole difficulty confifts in this; who are we here to underftand by the children, who partake of the promife of grace: whether adults only actually called, who are capable of making a profeffion of their faith; or alfo young children and infants? The Orthodox juftly affirm the laft: not only becaufe mention fimply is made of children, without diftinction of age; but alfo becaufe God exprefsly

prefsly promifed to Abraham, to be the God of his feed, which he applies to an infant eight days old, Gen. xvii. 7, 12. We add as that Chrift permitted *little children* to come to him, laid his hands upon them, and declared that of fuch was the kingdom of heaven, Mat. xvi. 13—15. But whom Matthew calls *παιδια*, *little children*, Luke, chap. xviii. 15. calls *βρεφη, infants ;* which word, according to Euftathius properly fignifies *a new born child at the breaft.* Hence alfo Peter fays, *ως αρτιγεννητα βρεφη*, *as new-born babes*, 1 Pet. ii. 2. And here it appears we are, by all means, to keep to the propriety of the terms, both in the noun *βρεφος*, and the verb *προσφερω*; when it is faid, *προσεφερον δε αυτω τα βρεφη, and they brought unto him alfo infants*, they appear to have been carried in arms. It is therefore evident, that to infants are alfo made the promifes of grace and falvation.

XLIV. Let the fourth argument ftand thus : It is unjuftifiable to exclude from baptifm, thofe who are made partakers of the Holy Spirit: for, thus Peter, Acts x. 47. "Can any man forbid water, that thefe fhould not be baptifed, which have received the Holy Ghoft, as well as we?" True, indeed it is, that the Holy Spirit difcovered himfelf in thofe, of whom Peter there fpeaks, by fome extraordinary gifts, which of themfelves were not faving : yet the principal argument for the right to baptifm cannot be drawn from hence. The apoftle therefore confiders thofe extraordinary gifts, as the effects of the fanctifying Spirit, beftowed on all the elect ; and as fpecial indications of the divine bounty towards them: whereby the truth of the gofpel was fealed in them, and the fincerity of their faith adorned : compare Gal. iii. 2. and thence, as from the thing fignified, he argues to the participation of the fign. We moreover fubfume : even the children of believers have received the Holy Spirit : for otherwife they could neither be *holy*, which yet Paul declares them to be, 1 Cor. vii. 14: nor *be Chrift's*, to whom none belongs, who has not his Spirit, Rom. viii. 9. nor fee the kingdom of heaven, to which none is admitted, but he who is born of water and of the Spirit, John iii. 5. Whence it follows, that water cannot be forbid, that infants fhould not be baptifed.

XLV. Fifthly, They who belong to the church of God, have a right to baptifm. The reafon is, becaufe baptifm is the fign of affociation with, and feal of initiation into the church, Acts ii. 41. "they were baptifed; and the fame day there were added, *namely to the church*, about three thoufand fouls." And then it is reprefented as the privilege of the whole church, that fhe is "cleanfed by Chrift with the wafhing of water, by the word," Eph. v. 26. But that infants belong to the church, appears from this, that when God commanded his church to be gathered together, he did not fuffer their " little ones, and thofe that fucked the breafts to be abfent," Deut. xxix. 10, 11. Joel ii. 16. and protefts that " they were born unto him," Ezek. xvi. 20.

XVI. Sixthly, We argue from this, that baptifm has fucceeded in the room of circumcifion. The apoftle declares this, Col. ii. 11, 12. where he proves the abrogation of the ceremonial law, and efpecially of circumcifion with refpect to believers of the New Teftament, from this confideration, that the fpiritual thing formerly fignified and fealed by circumcifion, is now fignified and fealed by baptifm; intimating, that what circumcifion was to the Old Teftament-church, the fame now is baptifm to the New, and indeed in a far more eminent and perfect manner, becaufe baptifm is an introduction at once into the liberty and grace of the New Teftament, whereas circumcifion contained the profeffion of a bondage and yoke. But it is evident, that circumcifion was adminiftered to infants; it therefore follows, that we are to have the fame fentiment concerning baptifm. And indeed nothing can be advanced againft the baptifm of infants, which may not equally militate againft their circumcifion.

XLVII. Here certainly appears the extraordinary love of our God, in that as foon as we are born, and juft as we come from our mother, he hath commanded us to be folemnly brought from her bofom, as it were into his own arms, that he fhould beftow upon us, in the very cradle, the tokens of our dignity and future kingdom; that he fhould put that fong in our mouth, " thou didft make me hope, when I was upon my mother's breaft : I was caft upon thee from the womb: thou art my God from my mother's belly," Pfal xxii. 9, 10. that, in a word, he fhould join us to himfelf in the moft folemn covenant from our moft tender years : the remembrance of which, as it is glorious and full of confolation to us, fo in like manner it tends to promote Chriftian virtues, and the ftricteft holinefs, through the whole courfe of our lives.

XLVIII. Nothing ought to be dearer to us than to keep facred and inviolable that covenant of our youth, that firft and moft folemn engagement, that was made to God in our name. Nor is it any objection, that we were firft bound in that covenant without our knowledge. For, no adult perfon, when he is informed of the excellency of that holy facrament, which was beftowed in infancy, can be offended, that, according to the will of God, he was devoted fo early by his pious parents to the fupreme being; unlefs, at the fame time, he is refolved

to

to renounce entirely the name of a Christian, and all his hopes
of eternal salvation.

XLIX. It cannot also fail to be very delightful to godly
parents, to present to God and his Christ, their dearest
pledges just began to enjoy the light, and consecrated in
the water of the mystical font, or as Dionysius the Pseudare-
opagite elegantly expressed it, *in the divine symbols of a divine
birth*, and recommended to the grace of God by the prayer of
the whole church. Let this be the first care of their piety.
*Gregory Nazianzen, Orat.* 40. *in sanctum baptisma*, speaks as
follows: " hast thou a child? give not time to vice to gain upon him : let him be sanctified from a child, and consecrated to
the Spirit from his tender years." And certainly, if no other
benefit accrued from infant-baptism, every prudent person will
own it to be very great, that it lays the most inviolable necessity
on parents, carefully to train up their children, which they
have so early devoted to God, in the mysteries of the Christian
religion, and the practice of true piety, both by instruction,
admonition and good example. *They incur the guilt of an impious robber or thief*, as Bucer has gravely observed, *de Regno
Christi, Lib.* 2. *c.* 9. " who are not at the greatest pains to
bring up and form those they have consecrated by baptism, to
the Lord Christ, to the obedience of Christ. For, by this neglect, as much as in them lies, they again rob God of the children they gave up to him, betray and enslave them to the devil."
See what we have more fully written on *Infant-baptism* in a particular dissertation.

L. And therefore it was a very laudable practice of the
Bohemian brethren, who were wont to present their children
at about twelve years old, in the church to the pastor, in order
to make a public profession of their faith, and to shew, whether
the parents had done their duty in instructing them, to which
they had bound themselves at the baptism of their children, as
Lasitius relates, *de Moribus & institutis Fratrum Bohemorum*, *c.*
12. §. 28, 29. Which, with the solemnity they usually performed this, is related at large, *in Ratione disciplinæ Ordin. Trat.
Bohem.* p. 46 *Calvin. Instit. Lib.* 4. *c.* 19. §. 4. has hinted that
a like practice obtained in the ancient church, and that from
hence, in latter times, arose the imaginary sacrament of Confirmation. And *Durel, in Vindiciis Ecclesiæ Anglicanæ*, observes, that the like custom is still retained in the church of Eng-
land.

## CHAP. XVII.

### *Of the Lord's Supper.*

I. THE other facrament of the New Teftament is the *holy supper of the Lord;* which the Lord Jefus inftituted immediately after his laft paffover, becaufeit was to fucceed the paffover, from which he transferred alfo to this moft of the rites and phrafes, ufed by the ancient Jews in their paffover. 'As this has long ago been obferved by the learned, fo it will appear from the brief explication, we are now to give of this facred fymbol.

II. This facrament is called ΔΕΠΝΟΝ the *fupper,* 1 Cor. xi. 20. not becaufe its celebration is neceffarily confined to the evening or night. For, though in the ancient church this was frequently done ; yet that was owing not fo much to the relïgion of Chriftians, as to the cruelty of perfecutors, who by their tyranny, obliged believers to meet altogether privately, and in the night time: but becaufe the Lord inftituted this feaft after the paffover, which was to be flain between the two evenings, and eaten in the night. It was likewife inftituted in the " very night in which he was betrayed," 1 Cor. xi. 23. and which was the laft before his death; hence this moft facred feaft was conftantly called the *Supper.* Befides moft fumptuous entertainments among the ancients, efpecially in the Jewifh nation, at leaft their nuptial feafts were generally in the evening : as appears from the parable of the ten virgins, Mat. xxv. And therefore it was proper, that that feaft, which reprefents the unfpeakable dainties of heaven, and is an earneft of the " marriage-fupper of the Lamb," Rev. xix. 9. fhould be held forth to us under the name and emblem of a fupper. Nor is it for nothing, that Paul obferves, that Chrift gave the fupper to the church, in that night *in which he was betrayed.* For, befides that, we have in this an illuftrious difplay of Chrift's infinite love to men, in that he fhould vouchfafe to have fuch an anxious concern for us, efpecially at that time, when his mind was otherwife fo much taken up, and diftreffed with the horror of his approaching fufferings: but what, above all, ought to make it facred to us, and very highly valuable, is, that it was inftituted by our Lord, juft as he was preparing himfelf to die.

III. Again, it is called ΚΥΡΙΑΚΟΝ δειπνον the *Lord's Supper,* 1 Cor. xi. 20. both becaufe the Lord was the author of it, and becaufe the whole of it agrees to the Lord, and to the remembrance

membrance of him ; fo that the Lord himfelf, in the right ufe of it, is exhibited to believers : and laftly, becaufe it ought to be celebrated by us, according to the will and prefcription of the Lord.

. IV. But the Lord's Supper, to pafs on from the name to the thing, is the facrament of education, or nourifhment, in the New Teftament church, wherein by the fymbols of bread broken, and wine poured out, the dreadful fufferings of Chrift are reprefented to believers; and the promifes of the New Teftament and enlivening communion with Chrift, made perfect by fufferings, both in grace and glory are fignified and fealed unto them.

' V. For the illuftration of this defcription, it will be ufeful we firft diftinctly confider the external *figns* ; then the *thing fignified* by them. The *figns* are either the * *fymbols* themfelves, or certain *actions* about the fymbols. The *fymbol* is twofold, *bread* and *wine* ; and both of them are joined together, to fignify the fuperabundant fulnefs we have in Chrift. Here we are to adore the divine providence, which hath given to his church things fo fimple and eafily obtained, as pledges of things heavenly : and feveral reafons may be affigned. 1ft, That this facrament might, in all places, even to the end of the world, be in perpetual ufe among the faithful, it was fuitable fuch fymbols fhould be inftituted, as might, in all places and at all times, be ready at hand for the church's ufe. 2dly, It is more confiftent with the fpiritual economy of the New Teftament, to be led by fome plain and ordinary fymbol, which fhould neither detain the eye nor the mind, prefently to behold, meditate on, receive the thing fignified, than to be fo dazzled by fome illuftrious and miraculous fign, like what was granted to the Ifraelites in the wildernefs, as to be made to give lefs attention to the myftical fignification. 3dly, And then, the danger of fuperftition, which can fcarcely be altogether avoided in the cafe of bread and wine, would have been far greater in that of a more illuftrious fign. 4thly, Nor is it from the purpofe, that Chrift has not again given us the flefh of flain animals, nor bloody meals, fuch as the fathers formerly eat in their facred feafts ; but has furnifhed out his table with plain bread and wine. For Chrift's blood, by which all our debts are cancelled, and the fire of divine wrath is quenched, being once fhed, it became a crime any longer to fhed any blood in the facred rites of Chriftians.

VI.

* Thefe are frequently called with us, the Sacramental elements and the Sacramental actions.

VI. Common and ordinary *bread* is to be made ufe of, as Chrift ufed that which lay before him, Mat. xxvi. 26. But it was an old fubject of debate between the Greek and Latin churches, whether it ought to be leavened or unleavened, both of them appealing to the example of our Lord. The Latins infift that Chrift ufed unleavened bread, becaufe immediately after the pafchal feaft he inftituted the fupper; at which time it was altogether unlawful for any leaven to be feen among the Ifraelites. The Greeks, on the other hand, contend, that Chrift eat the pafchal lamb, the day before the Jews celebrated their paffover; from which they infer, that the days of unleavened bread were not yet come, when our Lord celebrated the firft fupper, and therefore it is moft probable, that our Lord ufed leavened bread, which, before the days of unleavened bread came, was moft commonly made ufe of. And indeed, as to Chrift's example, we make no manner of doubt, but the Latins have the better of the Greeks in this argument. For, whether our Lord celebrated the paffover on the fame, or on a different day from the other Jews : what was the day of the paffover to him, was alfo to him the day of unleavened bread : which the Evangelifts exprefsly affirm, Mat. xxvi. 17. Mark xiv. 12. Luke xxii. 7. Nor is it fo certain, that Chrift celebrated the paffover before the Jews, as Gerard Voffius imagines with the Greeks. The difputes of the celebrated John Cloppenburg and Lud. Capellus have already laid before the learned world, what probably may be faid on both fides of the queftion. Nay, the oppofite opinion feems to be much better founded, as Bochart, whom we have already fo often quoted, has made out by cogent aruments, who feems to have taken off all the difficulty of this queftion, *Hierozoic. Lib.* 2. *c.* 1. However, we agree not with the Latins, who would have the example of Chrift, in fo flender a circumftance, to retain the force of a perpetual law. For as this is no part of the effence of the facrament, fo the ufe of either fort of bread at this facred feaft, as occafion fhall offer, is indifferent and arbitrary; fince Chrift, without any decifion of this queftion on either fide, ufed that bread which was then at hand. Wherefore it is a matter both of aftonifhment and grief, that the Greek and Latin churches fhould have difputed, with fo much eagernefs and warmth, now for above five hundred years about fuch a trifling matter. Du Plefis de Eucharistia, Lib. 2. c. 5. may be confulted on this fubject.

VII. But we can by no means approve of the fmall round things, made of meal, commonly called *hofts* or *wafers*, fuch as now the Romifh church is pleafed to make ufe of. 1ft, Becaufe they are moft difagreeable to the inftitution and practice
.of

of Chrift. For it is very probable, that Chrift ufed fuch an unleavened cake, as the mafter of the family, in whofe houfe he kept the paffover, laid before him, according to the cuftom of the Jews. But thefe cakes were fomething large, in order to be diftributed in pieces among the guefts at the table ; they were alfo thin and broad, but yet of a moderate thicknefs like our fweet and round cakes, that they might be adapted for the nourifhment of the body. As to their matter, form, and pre-paration, fee Buxtorf's Synagoga Judaica, c. 12. 2dly, Be-caufe in that cafe, there is either no analogy, or an obfcure one, between the fign and thing fignified. Neither is there that ferviceablenefs for fupporting life, nor that nourifhing quality, nor fweetnefs of flavour in thofe wafers, as in common bread : by which both the ferviceablenefs, and nourifhing efficacy and grateful fweetnefs of the grace of Chrift are reprefented. 3dly, Becaufe they were unknown in the church for near a thoufand years. Voffius in his *Thefis de S. cœnæ Dominicæ Symbolis,* has laid open their origin from Honorius Auguftodunenfis. His words are thefe. " It is faid, that formerly the priefts received from every houfe or family, a quantity of meal, which cuftom at this day the Greeks ftill obferve, and of that made the Lord's bread, which they offered for the people, and after confecra-tion, diftributed among them. But after the church really in-creafed in numbers, but abated in holinefs : it was decreed, on account of the carnal, that fuch as could fhould communicate every Lord's day, or every third Lord's day, or on the high feftivals, or thrice a year. And becaufe the people did not communicate, there was no occafion to make fo large a cake, it was decreed to make it in the form of a penny." This is the true reafon, why the hoft has the form of a penny : but afterwards men of fubtlety fought, as is ufual in fuch cafes, for a myftery, where there was none : whence he immediately fubjoins ; " and that the people, inftead of offering meal fhould offer a penny, as an acquittance for receiving the Lord." Du-randus in Rationali, Lib. 4. c. 14. has words alfo to the fame purpofe. " It is prepared in the form of a penny, both becaufe the bread of life was betrayed for pennies, and becaufe a penny was given as wages to the labourers in the vineyard." Thefe are foolifh conceits, and foreign to the auguft myftery of the holy fupper.

VIII. The other fymbol is *wine :* which the evangelifts call Ἰσσημα τὸς ἀμπίλυ, *the fruit of the vine,* in conformity to the Heb-rew phrafeology, Mat. xxvi. 29. Mark xiv. 25. Luke xxii. 18. But it does not certainly appear, whether it was red or white. The Jews ordered the beft and moft generous wine to be purchafed

chafed for celebrating the paffover. But in that country the red was generally accounted fuch, Prov. xxiii. 31. Ifa. xxvii. 3. Hence in the Jerufalem Talmud, Tractat. de Sabbato, fol. 11. " it is commanded, that red wine be ufed for that purpofe." But if it appeared, that the white was better than the red, the preference was given to that. It is therefore probable, and only probable, that Chrift ufed red wine. And it feems we fhould not altogether overlook the fimilitude there is between the blood of the grape, by which name red wine is chiefly intended, and the blood of Chrift.

IX. And with no greater certainty can we determine, whether Chrift ufed pure neat wines, or wine mixt with water. Thofe fpeak too freely, who affirm, that it was the cuftom of that country, in order to moderate the ftrength of their wine to mix it with water, that all might drink of it. For that this was left to the difcretion of the Jews, as a matter of indifferency, on the very folemnity of the paffover, appears from Sepher Mitzvoth Haggadol, fol. 118. col. 1. " The meafure of the cup is a quart of wine either new or old; either neat or diluted." On the other hand, the argument of thofe is alfo weak, who contend, that Chrift ufed pure wine, becaufe it is called the *fruit of the vine:* but the vine produces wine not water. We have fhewn above, that Chrift fpeaks after the manner of his country. But the Jews called the wine, even that mixed with water, in their folemn bleffings over it, *the fruit of the vine,* having regard to the greater and better part of it. Thus the Jewifh mafters exprefsly write in Talmud. Babylon. Tit. Berachot, fol. 50. col. 2. " They pronounce not the bleffing on the wine, in which no water is mixed, faying, Bleffed be he, who created the fruit of the vine-tree, but bleffed be he, who created the fruit of the tree."

X. Nothing therefore can here with any certainty, be affirmed concerning Chrift's practice. Yet it has been the prevailing cuftom of the ancients, as well the weftern as eaftern church, if we except the Armenian, to mix the wine with the water; becaufe, after the fupper, they kept their *Agpæa,* or love-feafts, with the fame wine, not choofing to give any handle to the Gentiles, as if they ufed pure wine to excefs. They add a threefold myftery in this, in framing which they have given too much fcope to their own fancy. 1ft, That by the wine and water might be held forth the blood and water, which flowed from the pierced fide of Chrift. 2dly, That by that mixture the union of the two natures in Chrift might be reprefented. 3dly, That fince, in the Revelation of St John, the people are called water, the union of the fame faithful people with Chrift,

the

the head is exhibited by that mixture. And as it is the way of human nature, to be fond of its own fancies, the Greeks put not only water, but also boiling water into the wine, and least it should, on any account, cool before they receive it, they do not pour it in till after the elevation: to signify, say they, that, from the side of our Lord on the cross, flowed hot blood and water, as quickening things from a quickening body; or even (adds Cabasilas in Expolit. Liturg. c. 37.) " to sanctify the descent of the Holy Spirit upon the church, who is otherwise compared to fire." Nor did the rashness of their determining, and allegorizing stop here. In the synod of Tribur, under the emperor Arnulphus, in the year 895, or according to others, 899, it was provided, that " none should perform the holy mysteries, without mixing wine and water; but that two parts should be wine: because the majesty of the blood of Christ is greater than the weakness of the people.

XI. Our judgment is this: It does not appear, whether Christ mixed the wine, or drank it pure. Yet we grant the former to be probable; because it was a more frequent practice among the Jews, on account of the generousness of their wines: hence, in the rubric of the festivals, when they speak of the wine, they always use the phrase, *they mix him a cup*. There are also those, who forbid pronouncing a blessing over the cup, before the wine is mixed with water. It is probable, Christ did what seemed to be most suitable to the rules of sobriety. However, we imagine it cannot thence be proved, that Christ would prescribe any thing by this his example, especially to those people whose wines are not so generous, as to require mixing in common use. For every thing, that Christ did, according to the custom of his nation, and on occasion of the passover, does not belong to the essence of the sacrament nor has a mystical signification, nor in all its circumstances obtains the force of a perpetual law. The allegorical interpretations of the ancients appear somewhat insipid, and without any foundation in the sacred writings. Nor is the practice of the ancient church to be too much insisted upon in this case: for, as the thing is indifferent, the modern church has the same right that the ancient had. In such things, the liberty, which Christ hath left his people, ought to remain inviolable; who are to look on nothing as binding and necessary, but his word only. Nay, after the rite of mixing began to be accounted necessary, it was prudently done in the reformed churches, for the preservation of liberty, to prefer pure wine. Just as if ever the necessity of pure wine should begin to be established, it would be, perhaps, better to return to the practice of mixing it. Certainly those

plainly

plainly shew, that they put a greater value on their own imaginations, than on the very inftitution of Chrift, who have thought it fuperfluous to ufe wine in the holy fupper, which by the command and prefcription of our Lord, is a neceffary part : but on the contrary, have judged water neceffary, which is of human appointment, as if we were loft to our own liberty by the divine inftitution.

XII. But as it is poffible, nay, frequently happens, that, in fome countries, neither bread nor wine are ufed, as in America, and other parts of the world, where, inftead of bread, they have a food prepared of pulfe, or herbs, or of the fruits or even the barks of trees ; and inftead of wine, their drink is made of honey, or fugar, or other aromatics, or even the juice of the cocoa-tree. It is juftly queried whether, in thofe countries, they are wholly to abftain from the Lord's fupper, or whether, inftead of bread and wine, it may be lawful to ufe that food in the fupper, which anfwers the purpofes of bread and wine, and is adapted for ftrengthening the body and cheering the heart. Indeed we think, that no rafh innovations fhould be made in the ufe of the facraments : but then neceffity has no law. And it feems very hard, fhould any one take upon him to order, that the natives and the foreigners in thofe fpacious countries of the world, fhould be deprived of the Lord's fupper, and their Chriftianity maimed without the facramental food. Efpecially, as the principal thing in the analogy is retained, when that food and drink is made ufe of, by which the body may be properly nourifhed, and the heart made glad. Thus much for the *fymbols* or elements.

XIII. Let us now confider the *actions* with refpect to the fymbols. And they are either thofe of *Chrift*, to be performed, after his example, by his *minifters* ; or of the *difciples*, to be imitated by the *guefts* or communicants. The *actions* of *Chrift* are either *words* or *deeds*, and both thefe again either about the *bread*, or about the *wine*.

XIV. With refpect to *bread*, there are four things mentioned, which Chrift did. 1ft, He *took* the bread ; namely, into his hand. For, it was provided, by an exprefs canon of the Jewifh law, that the mafter was not to pronounce the bleffing, till he took the bread into his hand, that all might fee, over what he pronounced the bleffing.

XV. 2dly, *He bleffed it*. This action is in the Evangelifts called ευλογια, *bleffing*, Mat. xxvi. 26. Mark xiv. 22. at other times ευχαριτια, *giving of thanks*, Luke xxii. 19. It is a fine faying of the Jews, mentioned by Buxtorf on this occafion : "a man is forbid to enjoy any thing in this world without a bleffing."

blessing." But the usual form of blessing pronounced over the bread, was this: " Blessed be thou, O Lord our God, king of the world, who producest bread out of the earth." Yet it is more probable, Christ used a peculiar form, and one adapted to the present case, whereby he consecrated the bread to be a sacred symbol of his body. For, as in other respects, Christ sanctified, by blessing and giving of thanks, bread and other food for natural use, Mat. xiv. 19. Luke ix. 16. so, by this blessing and giving of thanks, he dedicated the bread, as he did afterwards also the wine, set them apart from their natural use, to be sacraments of his body and blood.

XVI. 3dly, *He broke* the bread. And this also after the manner of the Jews. For thus, the *Talmud. tit. Berachot, fol. 39. col. 22. he* (the master of the family) *blesses, and afterwards breaks.* This the apostles also carefully observed: hence, 1 Cor. x. 16. the *bread, which we break.* And therefore this is a mystical rite, and, as it were, essential to the holy supper; at least so necessary to the purity and completeness of it, that this whole feast is therefore called *the breaking of bread,* Acts ii. 42. and Acts xx. 7. Nor do they sufficiently clear themselves of a violation of the Lord's institution, who, keeping their bread (if it may deserve that name) whole, maintain, that they have fulfilled its purport, because with them the lump is divided into many small wafers. For that breaking of the lump is culinary, not mystical, being performed in the kitchen, not in the church, and done before the sacrament, not at the administration of it. It is to no purpose objected, that breaking among the Jews is sometimes equivalent to distributing, as Isa. lviii. 7, " deal *(break)* thy bread to the hungry," and Sam. iv. 4. " The young children ask bread, and no man breaketh unto them." For, to break is there a *metalepsis* taken for that distribution, which is made after the breaking. But that none should feign any such *metalepsis* in the words of the supper, these two actions of Christ are distinctly mentioned, *he broke, and he gave.*

XVII. 4thly, The bread broken *he gave to the disciples,* Mat. xxvi. 26. And this also was according to the ancient custom of the Jews, of whom there is an express canon on this head in Maimonides: " Breaking it, he sets a piece before each, and the other (to whom it is given) takes it up in his hand: nor is it allowed to put it into the hand of the eater, unless he is mourning." If therefore it was not a Jewish custom to put the piece broken off into the hand of the eater, but to lay it before him, that he might take it up with his own hand: how much less probable is it, that Christ put that morsel into the

mouths

mouths of his difciples? They who, at this day, obferve that
cuftom, depart both from the practice of Chrift and from the
purer antiquity: For, believers were formerly wont " to reach
out their hands to take the facred food," as Dionyfius Alexandrinus fpeaks in *Eufebius, Lib.* 7. *c.* 8. But the other cuftom of
putting the bread into the mouth feems to have begun about
the year 600; andwas owing to nothing but a fuperftitious veneration for the figns, which at length degenerated into *Artolatry*
or bread worfhip. See Voffius *de S. Cæn. Symbol. Difput.* 3. §.
4, 5.

XVIII. Thefe then are the *actions* of Chrift about the bread.
Let us now confider his *words.* And they are twofold; either.
*preceptive* or *explicatory.* The preceptive either fimply enjoin
fome acts, or at the fame time point out the end of thofe acts.
The former are contained in thefe words: *Take,* namely, that
which is broken, and fet before you on the table. *Eat :* exactly
as in the pafchal folemnity: *whoever is hungry, let him come
eat of this bread of affliction.* The latter, in which the end is fet
forth, are thefe: *Do this in remembrance of me.* To do, does not
here fignify, to make the body of Chrift, or to facrifice, as in
Virgil, *cum faciam vitula,* as fome ridiculoufly contend for: but
is to be referred, partly to what our Lord did; the like to which
was to be done by the apoftles in the difcharge of their office;
partly to what he commanded the difciples, as communicants,
to do; and regards both the difpenfing and the receiving. And
this command ought to be compared with that concerning the
paffover, Exod. xii. 24. " And ye fhall obferve this thing for
an ordinance to thee and to thy fons for ever." Moreover,
what he recommends concerning the remembrance of himfelf,
is alfo borrowed from the pafchal ceremonies. For, the whole
paffover was celebrated *for a memorial* of their miraculous deliverance out of Egypt, Exod. xii. 14. And almoft every circumftance, even what the later Jews added to the divine inftitution,
had their peculiar *memorial.* But how the fupper is a memorial
of our Lord, fhall be afterwards confidered.

XIX. The *explicatory* words, in which the myftery of the facrament is explained, are thefe: *This is my body,* Mat. xxvi. 26.
Mark xiv. 22. *which is given for you,* Luke xxii. 19. and *broken
for you,* 1 Cor. xi. 24. And thefe things are alfo borrowed
from the Jewifh antiquities and the pafchal phrafes. For, when
the Ifraelites did eat their pafchal bread, they were wont to
fay : " this is that bread of affliction, which your fathers did
eat in the land of Egypt." And what feems to come nearer
the purpofe, they called the roafted lamb, which was ferved
up in the pafchal fupper, *the body of the paffover.* But no one
underftood,

underſtood, or even could underſtand it otherwiſe, but that
the bread, which they yearly eat on the feſtival day, was a
ſymbol and memorial of that bread, which their anceſtors were
formerly fed with in Egypt. In the ſame ſenſe therefore, the
bread of the holy ſupper is called the body of Chriſt. Hitherto
they had ſlain and eat the body of the paſchal lamb, which was
a type of the body of Chriſt, afterwards to be delivered up to
death for them: at preſent, Chriſt, inſtead of the paſchal lamb,
gave them bread, for a ſymbol of his body : in the partaking
of which holy bread, they were to have for the future, not a
kind of type of things to come, or a memorial of a typical deliverance but the body of Chriſt, Col. ii. 14. the very ſubſtance, as
it were of things already done, and of a ſolid and eternal deliverance. It is therefore evident, that they have wandered a great
diſtance from the ſcope of our Lord's words, who would infer
from them a change of the ſubſtance of the bread into the body
of Chriſt: becauſe as this is moſt contrary to all reaſon; ſo alſo
to the nature of ſacraments and ſacramental language. Thus
much concerning the actions and words of Chriſt, with reſpect
to the bread.

XX. Now follows what he both *did* and *ſaid* with reſpect to
the *cup*. There are three things Chriſt did with reſpect to this :
1ſt, *He took* the cup, as the maſter of the family uſually did a-
mong the Jews, *taking it in both his hands*, before he pronounced
the bleſſing over it.

XXI. 2dly, *He gave thanks* : ſeparately over the cup. For,
though bleſſing the bread conſecrates all other kinds of food
and liquors without any further conſecration; yet according to
the doctors of the Jewiſh law, that does not ſerve for the wine;
but a *peculiar bleſſing* is appointed for it *on account of its ſingular
excellency*. The ordinary form of bleſſing was thus: " Bleſſed
be thou, O Lord our God, king of the world, who createſt
the fruit of the vine." But we are here to maintain, what we
aſſerted concerning bleſſing the bread, that it is conſiſtent with
truth, that Chriſt, at this time, made uſe of a peculiar form
of conſecration. On account of this bleſſing, Paul calls it the
*cup of bleſſing*, 1 Cor. x. 16. probably in imitation of that cup,
which the Jews called the *cup of bleſſing the table*, or of thankſ-
giving, with which the feaſt was cloſed. And this cup Chriſt
alſo took *after ſupper*, 1 Cor. xi. 25.

XXII. 3dly, *He gave* it to them; namely, his diſciples. For,
it was the cuſtom of the Jews, that all the gueſts, after the
maſter of the family had taſted it, ſhould drink ſome of it.
Hence it is probable, that Chriſt after bleſſing, firſt drank of
the cup; which thoſe words ſeem to intimate, which we have

in

in Mat. xxvi. 29. " I will not drink henceforth of this fruit of the vine," &c. then diftribúted it among his difciples.

XXIII. We might here enquire, why nothing is faid of pouring out the wine, which, in other refpects, anfwers to breaking the bread. But Buxtorf *in Exercitat. de prima cæna ritibus & forma,* by which I gratefully own I have profited very much on this fubject, learnedly affigns the reafon of that, namely, that the Jews, in their ordinary entertainments, obferved no peculiar rite about pouring out the wine. This was done promifcuoufly by a fervant, or any other perfon, as occafion offered. But in the feaft of the paffover, they order that, if by any means it can be done, the mafter of the family do not pour it out himfelf, but endeavour to get it done by another; becaufe every thing, at this feaft ought to be done with an air of magnificence, to denote their liberty from Egyptian bondage, to which they were reftored. And therefore it is very probable, that neither our Lord himfelf, nor his apoftles, but fome fervant attending at the feaft, belonging to the family of him, who gave the furnifhed room to Chrift, poured out the wine at the command of our Lord. Whence it appears that our churches alfo in this refpect come neareft to antiquity, in which the elders or deacons perform that office.

XXIV. Chrift's *words* with refpect to the *cup*, correfpond with thofe he had fpoken about the bread, and they are, firft, fimply *preceptive*, " drink ye all of it," Mat. xxvi. 27. where that univerfal particle has its peculiar emphafis: then he fhews the *end*, " This do ye, as oft as ye drink it, in remembrance of me," 1 Cor. xi. 25. all which is clear from what was aforefaid. The *explicatory* words are; " this is my blood of the New Teftament, which is fhed for many for the remiffion of fins," Mat. xxvi. 28. That is, the wine, contained in this cup, is the fymbol of blood, not the typical blood, as was that of the pafchal lamb, but of my blood; by which is ratified, not that fame Old Teftament, which the blood of the lamb, they had now eaten, did ratify and confirm; but a New and a better Teftament, which brings not a typical, but a real remiffion; conjoined, not with the rigorous demands of the hand-writing, but with the giving a difcharge in virtue of my blood, very foon to be fhed, not to a few among the Ifraelites, but to very many nations all over the world. Thus much concerning the *actions of Chrift* about the fymbols.

XXV. Next follow the *actions of the difciples*, and confequently of the other guefts. And thefe according to Chrift's appointment, are three: firft, *to receive* both the bread and the cup: but each feparately: for fo Chrift diftributed them: in

this

this manner he commanded his people to take them: thus the body of Chrift, as broken for us; his blood as poured out of his body, are more diftinctly reprefented: and in fine, as a complete entertainment requires both meat and drink, fo this moft complete fpiritual repaft, which we have in Chrift, is thus moft excellently reprefented. And therefore we cannot fo well approve of that cuftom, which prevailed in Cyprian's time, to give a piece of bread dipt in wine, to infants and the fick: which was the practice in fome places, about the year of Chrift 340, in the public and ordinary celebration of the facrament. The fame judgment we are to pafs on the cuftom of the Greeks, who crumble the confecrated bread into the wine, and take it out with a fpoon.

XXVI. The other action of the guefts is to *eat* the bread taken; for this is the immediate end of its being diftributed and taken. Whence it follows, that thofe deftroy the end of the facrament, who take the bread or *hoft*, as they call it, that they may keep it honourably in a *pyx* or box. This is altogether contrary both to the inftitution of Chrift, and the cuftom of the ancient church. For, Chrift has exprefsly commanded, they fhould directly eat. And indeed, as the ancient Chriftians under heathen emperors, by reafon of the danger of perfecution, could not at all times have priefts, eat part publicly and part they carried home: yet they, by no means kept it in a religious manner, in order to adore, but to eat it on the next occafion. To this purpofe is the decree of the council of Saragofa, which was held in the year 381, Canon 3. " If any perfon is convinced, that he has not ufed the received grace of the Eucharift, let him be Anathema for ever." For that purpofe alfo, the Eucharift was publicly kept by the prieft, to be carried out of the ordinary courfe, to the fick, not to be adored but eaten. But in the earlieft times, as the facrament was celebrated every day, it was to no purpofe to lay by the Eucharift; but, when the fupper was publicly adminiftered, it might be fent by the hands of the deacon to the fick, or to thofe who were abfent on fome other account. Which Juftin, Apolog. Secunda, mentions, was often done in his time. But what was left of the fupper, or not made ufe of, was either thrown into the fire, or given to the fchool-boys to eat; as Voffius has proved from the fecond council of Mafcon, from Hefychius and Evagrius Scholafticus, Difput. 3. de S. cœnæ Domin. Symbol. §. 8.

XXVII. The third action of the guefts is, *to drink* the confecrated wine out of the cup. It is remarkable, that our Lord faid concerning the cup, not only " take this, and divide it
among

among yo.. felves," Luke xxii. 17. but likewife added a mark
of univerfality, " drink ye *all* of it," Mat. xxvi. 27. And
we are told how they complied with this command, Mark xiv.
24. " and they *all* drank of it." As if the Lord Jefus purpofely intended to obviate the facrilegious boldnefs of thofe men,
who deprive the Laicks, as they call the common people, of the
confecrated cup. It is an infipid exception, that the *all* ought
to be reftricted to the apoftles, to whom our Lord is there only
fpeaking. For the apoftles, in that cafe, reprefented the whole
church. And unlefs the papifts will own this, whence will
they ever prove, that the eating of *the bread* belongs to the laity
or common people: efpecially, as no univerfal particle is added
to that command. We add the authority of the apoftle Paul,
who diffuades the whole church of Corinth by this topic from
the worfhip of idols: becaufe, fays he, " ye cannot drink the
cup of the Lord and the cup of devils," 1 Cor. x. 21. and again
writing to the whole church, " as often as ye eat this bread
and drink this cup, ye do fhew the Lord's death, &c." Where
he all along joins the eating of the bread and the drinking of
the cup, as actions to be alike performed by the fame perfons,
1 Cor. xi. 26—29.

XXVIII. But who are they on whom it is incumbent to obferve thefe duties according to Chrift's command. Paul has
briefly refolved this, 1 Cor. xi. 28, 29. " Let a man examine
himfelf, and fo let him eat of that bread, and drink of that
cup: for he that eateth and drinketh unworthily, eateth and
drinketh damnation to himfelf, not difcerning the Lord's body."
In which words he fhews: 1ft, That no perfon fhould approach the table of the Lord, but he who, having a knowledge
of the facred myfteries, can difcern the Lord's body, and, in
fome meafure at leaft, underftands the analogy between the
facred fymbols and the thing fignified by them, and on that
occafion can fhew the Lord's death. 2dly, That there is alfo
required in the communicant that experience of the ways of
God about the elect, as to be able to examine himfelf; whether
befides the external profeffion of faith, he hath alfo the genuine
marks of the Holy Spirit dwelling in him, or which is the fame
thing, of a fincere and internal Chriftianity: fuch as the forrow
of a penitent heart which is after a godly manner; a lively
faith refting on Chrift, as the alone atthor of life: in fine, an
unfeigned love towards God and his neighbour, joined with an
effectual purpofe of reformation of life. Whoever, upon a previous examination, finds thefe things in himfelf, is not to account himfelf, as an unacceptable gueft to the Lord.

XXIX. Thefe things were carefully obferved in the ancient
church,

church, while zeal was fervent, and difcipline in its vigour.
How diligent they were in inftructing the Catechumens; with
what circumfpection they acted in admitting them to the holy
sacrament, cannot be unknown to thofe, who have but juft
looked into the writings of the fathers. And that none but the
worthy might come to the communion, the deacon called
out with a loud voice to all, before the adminiftration, *Sancta
fanctis, holy things to the holy:* and the prieft, *Surfum corda, to
heaven with your hearts.* To which words the faithful anfwered
*habemus ad Dominum, we have raifed them to the Lord.* In Clem-
ent alfo, *Conftit. Lib.* 2. *c.* 61. the deacon duly, at the beginning
of the communion, fays to the people, " Let none have a grudge
againft another, none be in a ftate of hypocrify." And the
cuftom of the Greeks, at his day, differs not from this; among
whom they, who are to communicate, turn themfelves to every
fide of the church, and on bended knees addrefs thofe around
them; " Forgive us brethren, we have finned both in word and
deed." To which they who were prefent anfwered in this
manner, " Brethren, God will forgive us." Moreover juft
when the communicant was to partake of the facred feaft, he
addreffes himfelf to Chrift in thefe words; " I will not kifs
thee as Judas did, but, after the example of the thief, I confefs
to thee: Lord remember me, when thou comeft into thy kingdom." Thefe things we have in *Chriftopborus Angelus de Statu
hodiernorum Græcorum, c.* 23.

XXX. We may eafily gather from what we have quoted from
Paul, what to think of the communion of infants. It appears
to have been a cuftom in the ancient church, to put the fymbols of the holy fupper into the mouths of infants juft after
baptifm. A practice ftill obferved by the Orientals. I will
here fubjoin the words of Metrophanes Critopulus, Hiero-
monachus, confeff. *c.* 9. " But even infants themfelves are
" partakers, beginning immediately upon their baptifm, and
" afterwards as often as the parents will. And if any one
" fhould blame us for the communion of infants, we can
" eafily ftop his mouth. For, if he be an Anabaptift, we ufe
" this faying againft him: " Suffer little children, and for-
" bid them not to come unto me," Mat. xix. 15. Alfo that
" other: " except ye eat the flefh of the Son of man, and
" drink his blood, ye have no life in you," John vi. 53. But
" the prophetefs Anna makes very much for us, who dedicated
" Samuel from his early infancy to God; who alfo requires
" the firft-born of the Jews to be given up to him, from their
" very birth, though not yet endowed with a competent mea-
" fure of underftanding. But if our adverfary be no Anabaptift
" we will alfo ufe the very fame arguments againft him, which
" he ufes for infants againft the Anabaptifts; that as they ought

" to be baptifed, 'fo alfo to be made partakers of the Lord's
" fupper. And thus with the help of God we have got the
" better of our argument." Thus far Metrophanes.

XXXI. But we are of a`quite different opinion. For,`
all the words of our Lord's command, [with refpect to this fa-
crament] are fo expreffed, that they cannot belong to infants,
who can neither receive the bread, nor eat it, unlefs it be
chewed for them or foaked. For, " babes are fed with milk,
and not with meat," 1 Cor. iii. 2. Heb. v. 12. Infants cannot
examine themfelves, nor difcern the Lord's body, nor fhew his
death, all which we have juft heard, the apoftle requires of
communicants.

XXXII. The arguments of Metrophanes are very eafily refuted. For, 1ft, It does not follow, becaufe our Lord was
willing, that young children fhould come to him, and declared,
that theirs was the kingdom of heaven, that they are to partake
of the fupper. Chrift is there fpeaking of fpiritual and myftical
communion with himfelf, which does not imply any facramental communion whatever; but that only, of which the
fubjects he is fpeaking of, are capable. 2dly, The nature of
baptifm and of the fupper is different. Baptifm is the facrament of regeneration and ingrafting in the church: in the adminiftration of which, the perfon to be baptized is merely paf-
five: to the receiving of that, the fcripture does not fo univerfally require felf-examination, and the fhewing the Lord's
death. And therefore it may be properly applied to young
children. But the fupper is the facrament of nutrition, by
means of a folid food: to the partaking whereof, the communicants are required to perform certain actions both by
the body and the foul: of which infants are incapable, and
therefore it belongs to thofe, who are come to the years of
difcretion, and not to little children. 3dly, Our Lord, John
vi. 53. is not treating of a facramental, but of a fpiritual and
myftical eating by faith, For, neither was the Euchariift then
inftituted or known: nor will any one readily urge fuch an
abfolute neceffity for the Euchariift, as that without it none can
be faved; which yet our Lord afferts of that eating of his flefh.
4thly, The example of the prophetefs Anna who confecrated
Samuel a little child to God, is not at all to the purpofe. For
nothing can be concluded from that, but that it is a part of the
duty of parents, to give up their children, as early as poffible,
to the obedience and fervice of God. 5thly, And what they
pretend concerning the dedication of the firft-born of the Jews
to God, is ftill more impertinent. For, that dedication of the
firft-born, previous to the fetting apart the tribe of Levi, fhewed that they were God's, and to be employed in his fervice:
in them the other children were accounted to be confecrated

and

and even the whole family; and in a word, they were types of Chrift, in whom, as the firft-born among many brethren, all the families of the earth are bleffed.    All which has nothing to do with the participation of the Euchariſt. .

XXXIII. In the ancient church, the communion of the Lord's ſupper was far more frequently celebrated than it is at this day. It is the advice of Baſil to Cæſaria Patricia, Epiſt. 289.  " Certainly, to communicate every day, and to partake of the holy body and blood of Chriſt, is a good and uſeful practice." Thus alſo Auguſtin relates in his former epiſtle to Januarius, that ſome *communicated every day*. And to this ſenſe ſome people wreſted the *daily bread*, mentioned in the Lord's prayer: as Fortunatus; but the aſking our daily bread, ſeems to inſinuate, that we ſhould every day, if poſſible, reverently take the communion of his body." Afterwards the church increaſing in numbers, but abating in zeal, the clergy communicated daily with their prieſt, while the people thought they had done their duty, if they communicated every Lord's day.    But neither did they ſtop here: for, the people knowing no meaſure to their neglect, it was decreed in ſeveral Synods, that whoever did not communicate every third Lord's day at leaſt, ſhould be cut off from the church.    At laſt matters came to that paſs, that the people ſcarce communicated on any other days, than the moſt ſolemn feſtivals; eſpecially on the Eaſter holy-days.  Compare what we have already quoted, ſect. 7. from *Honorius Auguſtodunenſis*.  This neglect of the common-people was frequently reprimanded with ſeverity by the holy men of God.    But that cuſtom, which enjoins the communicating once a year, was ſo diſpleaſing to Calvin, that he did not ſcruple to call it a *moſt certain device of the devil*; and thinks, we are by all means ſo to order matters, " as that no meeting of the church be without the word, prayers and partaking of the ſupper :" gathering from Acts ii. 42. that ſuch was the practice of the apoſtolical church; where Luke ſays, that " the faithful continued ſtedfaſtly in the apoſtles doctrine, and fellowſhip, and in breaking of bread, and in prayers."    He at leaſt imagines, the ſupper may be moſt decently adminiſtered, if each week at leaſt it be ſet before the church.  See *Inſtitut. Lib.* 4. *c.* 17. §. 43—47.  Alas ! what a departure is there at this day, from the ſanctity and zeal of the ancients ! yet as our Lord has determined nothing as to the time, and in general only recommended frequent communion, by that word, *as oft*, 1 Cor. xi. 25, 26. a certain medium, eſpecially amidſt ſuch a corruption of manners, ſhould ſeem to be obſerved; leaſt, either by the too frequent uſe, this ſacred food ſhould be diſeſteemed, or we ſhould ſlight or neglect that auguſt table of the Lord.

3 M 2                              XXXVI.

XXXIV. Let us now come to the *myftical fignification* of the supper, and introduce the beloved fpoufe of Chrift into the inner bed-chamber, where fhe may delight herfelf, not with any outward appearance or figure, but exult and melt away in the moft defirable embraces of her hufband, and in the pleafures of the pureft love: and forgetting the world, forgetting herfelf, but full of Chrift, fhe may diffolve away in reciprocal returns of mutual fondnefs. For this purpofe the holy fupper is to be confidered. I. As a *fign, teaching* us by the inftitution of Chrift. II. As a *feal, ratifying* the promifes of the New Teftament. III. As a *ftipulation*, or folemn engagement, binding on us every duty of piety and love.

XXXV. If we confider the fupper as a *fign*, given us for inftruction ; it exhibits a *remembrance* of Chrift, and a lively reprefentation of moft of Φριχτῶν τῆς ἐνσβιιας ἡμῶν μυσηρίων *the awful myfteries of our religion*, as the Greek fathers often fpeak. The *bread* fignifies the *body* of Chrift. For, as *bread ftrengtheneth man's heart*, Pfal. civ. 15. fo the flefh of Chrift, and the fpiritual bleffings and graces, purchafed for us by Chrift, when he was incarnate, are the food of our foul, fupporting and ftrengthening it in the fpiritual life, into the hope of life eternal. "I am the living bread, which came down from heaven. If any man eat of this bread, he fhall live for ever : and the bread that I will give, is my flefh, which I will give for the life of the world," John vi. 51. Again, as corn, from which bread is prepared, is ground to meal, kneaded to dough, and baked in the oven, before it can be agreeable and wholefome food for man; fo in like manner, the Captain of our falvation was made perfect through various fufferings, Heb. ii. 10. and fcorched both in the fire of the divine wrath kindled againft our fins, and in the flames of his own love.

XXXVI. The *wine* fignifies the *blood* of Chrift. For, as wine allays the thirft, revives the animal fpirits, cheers the heart, Pfal. civ. 15. Prov. xxxi. 6, 7. and makes the maids cheerful (eloquent) Zech. ix. 17. fo in like manner, the grace purchafed by the blood of Chrift, allays the thirft of our foul, abundantly fatisfying all our holy longings, John iv. 14. to a kind of a holy and myftical ebriety, Pfal. xxxvi. 8. Cant. v. 1. it fupports and fuftains the foul, when fick of love, Cant. ii. 5. and "puts gladnefs into the heart, more than in the time that the corn and wine of worldly men are increafed," Pfal. iv. 7. in fine, "caufes the lips of thofe that are afleep to fpeak," Cant. vii. 9. and to become eloquent in the praifes of God and of his Chrift. And hence it is, that the Lord compares the participation of his grace to a "feaft of fat things, a feaft of wines on the lees, of fat things full of marrow, of wines on the lees well refined," Ifa. xxv. 6. And we muft not omit, that as

w i n e

wine is fqueezed with much force from the grapes, when trodden in the wine-prefs; fo in like manner the Lord Jefus *was ftraitened*, Luke xii. 50. and oppreffed with much anguiſh, that the blood might flow to us from his bleffed body, and his fpiritual grace with his blood.

XXXVII. When the difpenfer of the myfteries of God, *takes* the bread and the cup of bleffing into his hands, before the eyes of the faithful, that feems to intimate, that Chrift was thus conftituted and taken to be Mediator, and *fet forth* to believers, " to be a propitiation through faith in his blood," Rom. iii. 25. The *bleffing* and *thankfgiving* pronounced over the bread and wine, teach us, that Chrift is that bleffed feed of Abraham, " in whom God hath bleffed us with all fpiritual bleffings in heavenly places," Eph. i. 3. and the greateft gift of divine bounty, for which to all eternity we fhall not be able to render fuitable thanks : nor are we to fet about this facred feaft, otherwife than by devout prayers, and a grateful acknowledgement of that infinite mercy, which the Lord vouchfafes to us, who are fo unworthy. The *breaking* of the bread reprefents the breaking of Chrift's body, efpecially that by death ; for, the foul is the band, by which all the parts of the body are preferved united. But on its departure, the carcafe is nothing but a heap of dufty particles, which are foon to be feparated upon its putrefaction. Which would alfo have been the cafe with the dead body of Chrift, had not a fpeedy refurrection prevented that holy One of the Lord from feeing corruption. The *pouring out* of the wine reprefents the fhedding of Chrift's blood, that efpecially, which was done on the crofs, for the confirmation of the New Teftament. And thus in the holy fupper, there is a commemoration of the death of Chrift, not in words only, but alfo by thofe myftical rites. The *diftribution* of thefe facred pledges is a figure or emblem of that gratuitous offer, by which the Lord Jefus, with all his faving benefits, is prefented to the elect, with the moft alluring invitations to accept of him : nor offered only, but actually reached out, and freely given to believers for their eternal falvation. In the preaching of the gofpel, there is alfo a certain, but a more general offer of Chrift made to all, who ferioufly long after his grace. But in the diftribution of the facrament, a much more particular offer and communication of fpiritual grace is given to every believing communicant.

XXXVIII. But when believers *receive* the bread and wine, they declare by that action, that they receive by a true faith Chrift himfelf, and all he is, that they may have a right to become the fons of God, John i. 12. But the *eating* the bread and *drinking* the wine fignify fomething more. And *firft*, they

really

really fet forth the devote and lively employment of the foul,
engaged in holy meditations on Chrift, who is all its defire that
it may derive from him every thing, it knows to be needful for
its fpiritual life.  For, what feeding is to the body, that meditation is to the foul : whereby, from the things, the thoughts
are employed about, it fucks a fuitable aliment, as the body is
nourifhed by eating.  *Again*, thefe actions alfo fignify that intimate union, which fubfifts between Chrift and believers : as
meat and drink, when put into the mouth, are not only received into the ftomach, but alfo converted into the very fubftance of the perfon.  This union the fcripture calls an abode,
John xiv. 23. *a joining*, 1 Cor. vi. 17. *the fame body*, Eph. iii. 6.
*Laftly*, They reprefent that fweeteft delight, which the hungry
and thirfty foul enjoys from the fruition of Chrift and his grace :
not only believing, but feeing and tafting, that the Lord is good,
Pfal. xxxiv. 9. 1 Pet. ii. 3.  And as all are partakers of *one*
bread and of *one* wine, this is a figure of that amicable unity,
whereby they, who partake of the fame facred feaft, are united together, as domeftics of the fame Lord : " for we being
many are one bread and one body : for we are all partakers of
that one bread, 1 Cor. x. 17.

XXXIX. But in the holy fupper, we have fomething more
than an inftructing fign.  It is likewife a *feal ratifying* to us the
promifes and grace of God.  And *firft* it really feals all the
promifes of the *covenant of grace*, which was formerly fealed to
believers by the paffover, and all thofe other facrifical feafts,
to which they were admitted.  *Again*, more efpecially, the
promifes of the *New Teftament*, better than thofe of the Old,
which the fathers were obliged to be fatisfied with.  And in
this refpect the fupper of the Chriftians greatly excels the paffover.  " This is my blood of the New Teftament, which is
fhed for many for the remiffion of fins, Mat. xxvi. 28. in order to a real and not a typical expiation of fin, blotting out
the hand-writing, quenching our thirft, and enjoying a fulnefs
of delight in a perfect liberty.  *In fine*, it moft efpecially feals
fome *faving bleffings*, both of *this life* and of *that to come*.

XL. The bleffings of *this life*, which are fealed to us by the
fupper, are principally three.  1ft, Intimate union and communion with Chrift, as made perfect by fufferings.  Had it
pleafed our Lord, to give to his difciples a piece cut off from his
body for them to eat, or fome drops of his blood to drink; even
that of itfelf would not be fufficient to falvation, nor have accomplifhed a faving communion with Chrift, which is not a
carnal, but a fpiritual thing : yet the difciples would thereby
have had a very effectual fign of the myftical union.  But now
he fubftitutes bread in place of his body, wine in place of his
blood,

blood, when he fays *this is my body ; this is my blood :* and bids
us be no lefs affured, by that pledge, of his myftical communion, than if we took his very body and blood into our hands
and mouth. 2dly, The confervation, and nourifhment, the
ftrength and increafe of fpiritual life, which flow from communion with Chrift. As by the ufe of bread and wine, he who
communicates, experiences his bodily ftrength renewed; fo at
the fame time it is intimated to the believing foul, that he fhall
not want that grace of Chrift, which " giveth power to the
faint, and to them that have no might increafeth ftrength," Ifa.
xl. 27. 3dly, A fatisfying fulnefs of every defirable good,
which neither the world could beftow upon any, nor the beggarly elements of the world, feparated from Chrift, furnifh the
ancient Jews with : while the Lord Jefus, prefenting thefe
fymbols, calls out to believers ; " Ho ! every one that thirfteth,
come ye to the waters, and he that hath no money ; come ye,
buy and eat : yea come, buy wine and milk without money and
without price. Wherefore do ye fpend money for that which
is not bread ? and your labour for that which fatisfieth not ?
hearken diligently unto me, and eat ye that which is good, and
let your foul delight itfelf in fatnefs, Ifa. lv. 1, 2.

XLI. The bleffing of the *life to come,* an earneft of which
Chrift gives us in the fupper, is that moft abundant fatisfactory
fulnefs of glory, both in foul and body, which the Pfalmift has
defcribed, Pfal. xvi. 11. and Pfal. xvii. 15. and which is frequently reprefented under the fimilitude of a marriage-feaft.

XLII. Laft of all, with refpect to us, the holy fupper is a
kind of *folemn engagement,* ftrongly binding us to every duty of
piety and love, both to Chrift and to our neighbour. It binds
us to Chrift in feveral refpects. 1. In general, on receiving
this earneft of the covenant of grace, in which Chrift joins himfelf to us in a marriage-covenant, we, by that very thing, promife
and openly declare and avow, by an oath, that we fhall fulfil every duty of a chafte faithful and loving fpoufe towards
him. Every one of the communicants, by this public and
folemn feaft, which is appointed for confirming this myftical marriage, makes an open profeffion of that before God,
angels and the whole church. Whoever partakes of the
bread broken, and wine poured out, fays to Chrift, if not
in plain words, and an explicit meditation on the thing, yet in
the implicit meaning of his act ; as " I defire, Lord, to be a
" partaker of thy body broken, and blood fhed for my falvation,
" fo I declare, that I deferve to have my body, no lefs than
" this bread, broken or torn in pieces, to have my blood, no
" lefs than this wine, poured out, if, in the renewal of this
" covenant, I fhall, with an evil and perfidious heart, break
" my word to thee." 2dly, Befides, as in the communion of
the

really
engag
it ma
...s sp
tation
are...
...oup
...im
...ne
...ceit
...ta
Jo
L
a
...u
P
b

the holy supper, the greatest, and an almost ... of the love of the Lord Jesus, towards us, is ... before our eyes, but exhibited to our taste ... is proper, that the flames of our love towards him ... ticipation of that feast, kindled up, and the love ... all other love ... kept inviolate, and become the love ... moving thoughts. In the same breath, that the ... ing forth the love of her beloved to be better than ... infinitely preferring the kisses of his mouth to all ... the most desirable in other respects; the also ... 2, 3. " therefore do the virgins love him." ... supper is especially instituted in remembrance of our L ... in commemoration of his death, believers, in the use ... bound to have always fresh in their memory the L ... and the dreadful sufferings he underwent, which are ... solid foundation of our hope, and the only matter of ... solation; and to esteem Christ crucified, as " a bundle ... lying all night betwixt our breasts," Cantic. i. 13. ... lastly, As a greater mark of familiarity, our Lord ... mutual supper, " I will sup with him and he with me," ... iii. 20. It is therefore proper, that they, who are enter ... by our Lord, with so magnificent a feast, should be care ... give him a becoming entertainment in return: invite him to ... into his garden, and eat his pleasant fruits," Cantic. iv. 16. ... give him to " drink of spiced wine, and of the juice of ... pomegranate," Cantic. viii. 2. That is, they should give ... delight by the sincere practice of internal Christianity; ... which neither spices, nor the honey-comb, nor milk, nor w ... can be sweeter to him.

XLIII. To conclude, by the use of the supper we are al ... bound to the practice of brotherly concord, and the sincere ... love towards our brethren and sisters, partakers with us of the ... same table: that in the hearing, and with the applaud of angels, ... may be sung in the church of God, with one mouth and one ... heart, " behold! how good and how pleasant it is, for brethren ... to dwell together in unity," Pf. cxxxiii. 1. Thus the apostolic ... church both set us an example for our imitation; " and they ... continuing daily with one accord in the temple and breaking ... bread from house to house, did eat their meat with gladness ... and singleness of heart," Acts ii. 46. To this purpose was the ... holy kiss, by which they, on all occasions, kept up a mutual ... peace; of which frequent mention is made in scripture, and ... of which, especially in these rites of the supper, the innocent ... use was for some time continued among Christians. God ... grant we may in such a manner solemnize this mystical supper on ... earth, that we may eternally feast with Christ in heaven. Amen,

FINIS.

the greateſt, ...
the Lord Jeſus, ...
but exhibit ...
the flames of ...
feſt, kindled ...
inviolate, ...

In the ſame ...
of her beloved ...
the kiſſes of ...
other reſpects ...
the virtues ...
uted in ...
death, ...
th in the ...
he ...
, and the ...
crucifi...
Cr...
...
...
that the ...
a ...
...
from ...
, and d...
That is, the ...
internal ...
communi...

of the ...
concern, ...
partaken ...
th the ...
th ...
faction ...
. Thus ...
...
...
...
...
...
...
...
...
...

the holy fupper, the greateft, and an almoft incredible inftance of the love of the Lord Jefus, towards us, is held forth not only before our eyes, but exhibited to our tafte ; in like manner it is proper, that the flames of our love towards him, be, in the participation of that feaft, kindled up, and the love of him beyond all other loves kept inviolate, and become the object of our admiring thoughts. In the fame breath, that the fpoufe was fetting forth the love of her beloved to be better than wine ; and infinitely preferring the kiffes of his mouth to all other things, the moft defirable in other refpects ; fhe alfo adds, Cant. i. 2, 3. " therefore do the virigins love him." 3dly, As the holy fupper is efpecially inftituted in remembrance of our Lord, and in commemoration of his death, believers, in the ufe of it, are bound to have always frefh in their memory the Lord Chrift, and the dreadful fufferings he underwent, which are the moft folid foundation of our hope, and the only matter of our confolation; and to efteem Chrift crucified, as " a bundle of myrrh lying all night betwixt our breafts," Canticl. i. 13. 4thly and laftly, As a greater mark of familiarity, our Lord defires a mutual fupper, " I will fup with him and he with me," Rev. iii. 20. It is therefore proper, that they, who are entertained by our Lord, with fo magnificent a feaft, fhould be careful to give him a becoming entertainment in return: invite him to "come into his garden, and eat his pleafant fruits," Canticl. iv. 16. and give him to " drink of fpiced wine, and of the juice of their pomegranate," Canticl. viii. 2. That is, they fhould give him delight by the fincere practice of internal Chriftianity ; than which neither fpices, nor the honey-comb, nor milk, nor wine, can be fweeter to him.

XLIII. To conclude, by the ufe of the fupper we are alfo bound to the practice of brotherly concord, and the fincereft love towards our brethren and fifters, partakers with us of the fame table: that in the hearing, and with the applaud of angels, may be fung in the church of God, with one mouth and one heart, " behold! how good and how pleafant it is, for brethren to dwell together in unity," Pf. cxxxiii. 1. Thus the apoftolic church both fet us an example for our imitation ; " and they continuing daily with one accord in the temple and breaking bread from houfe to houfe, did eat their meat with gladnefs and finglenefs of heart," Acts ii. 46. To this purpofe was the holy kifs, by which they, on all occafions, kept up a mutual peace ; of which frequent mention is made in fcripture, and of which, efpecially in thefe rites of the fupper, the innocent ufe was for fome time continued among Chriftians. God grant we may in fuch a manner folemnize this myftical fupper on earth, that we may eternally feaft with Chrift in heaven. Amen,

*F I N I S.*